Cases in International Business Strategy

Werner Ketelhöhn and Jan Kubes

With special contributions by:
James C. Ellert, George Taucher and Dominique Turpin

BUTTERWORTH
HEINEMANN

Butterworth-Heinemann Ltd
Linacre House, Jordan Hill, Oxford OX2 8DP

 A member of the Reed Elsevier plc group

OXFORD LONDON BOSTON
MUNICH NEW DELHI SINGAPORE SYDNEY
TOKYO TORONTO WELLINGTON

First published 1995
Reprinted 1995

British Library Cataloguing in Publication Data
Ketelhöhn, Werner
    Cases in International Business
    Strategy. – (Contemporary Business Series)
    I. Title II. Kubes, Jan III. Series
    658.4012

ISBN 0 7506 1949 X

Composition by Genesis Typesetting, Laser Quay, Rochester, Kent
Printed and bound in Great Britain by Bath Press, Avon

Contents

Preface

Business strategy is dependent upon the forward-looking beliefs and values of management and more specifically, by the belief that the future can be determined by executive decision-making. Strategists firmly believe that the future can be shaped.

In practice, however, the first obstacles to strategic choice are the fatalistic beliefs and values found in some management teams. Team members may place undue emphasis on assumptions such as: everything is preordained; forecasting is usually inaccurate; of course, our formula is the right one; with this method we will outsmart our competitors; to succeed all we need do is imitate the market leaders, etc.

If such attitudes predominate, the future of the company will be determined more by external forces than by the decisions of the management team. To exercise a positive influence on the company's future, the management team must develop its own sense of direction – its own strategic intent.

To develop this sense of direction, a model for the understanding of the economic activity in the industry at hand must be used. Here we would recommend, besides the ideas gained from discussing the cases in this book, those ideas that make the most sense to *you*. Complicated explanations of business are of no use to strategic decision-makers, and, in practice, would be substituted by those concepts, ideas and simple models that proved to be the most helpful.

We do not recommend using impractical concepts, or models from elasto-mechanics, Boolean algebra or even militaristic metaphors or myths with mysterious connections with the Japanese and Germans. Our recommendation is simple: use only the business ideology that helps you to understand what is going on in your economy, industry and business; that business ideology which helps you to set your own strategic direction and influences your strategic decision-making.

If your current business ideology fails you in a particular situation, don't take refuge in some mystical Far Eastern philosophy or military tradition. Seek help in the business frameworks explained in Dr Ketelhöhn's book *International Business Strategy*; they have a good track record in understanding business with the purpose of problem-solving.

We're not arguing that ideas, models and experiences in other human activities are of no use in creating appropriate analogies for business. We believe that our duty as students is to get out there and learn how real business people understand their businesses, and then – based on their constructs – try to make some generalizations that can be used in other businesses. This, we propose, you can do with the cases presented in this volume.

This book is based upon the value of learning from real businesses. Many of the cases were derived from our personal observations – Benetton, NWZ, SEMCO and other companies – yet some other cases were written by colleagues, both in Europe and abroad. This approach to learning from reality contributed to the creation of other cases both in Europe and Central America. In this regard we would like to thank the many people who contributed in one way or another to the documentation of the many cases

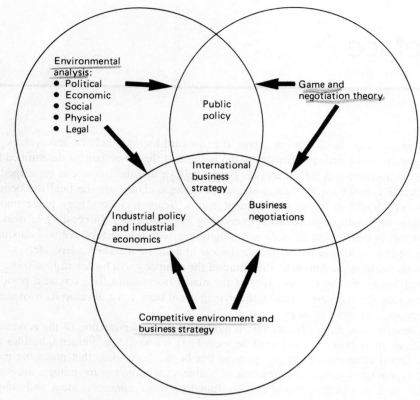

One view of international business strategy

included in this volume. The list is long and it starts with researchers and staff way back in 1979–1982 at INCAE, Nicaragua; and ends with researchers and staff in 1993 at IMD, Switzerland. The business world has seen many changes during this period – events nobody could have dreamed of back in 1979. Thanks to everyone that contributed, and our apologies for not mentioning all the names that we forgot in the currents of time and space. You may be satisfied to know that your work provides today's managers with situations that help develop their business acumen in international business strategy.

These cases help illustrate that the beliefs, values and attitudes about the future and the superstitions about successful foreign competitors – generally the Japanese and Germans – are at the centre of developed and underdeveloped[1] minds. Whereas the former strongly believe in controlling the future and consider it in terms of business ideologies; the latter either seek refuge in fate or worse still, use meta-economic models and reasoning to cover up for their lack of understanding of business and management. In essence, there are no developed or underdeveloped countries; there are only people with beliefs, values and attitudes that are developed or underdeveloped.

We have found that an underdeveloped, fatalistic attitude exists where people believe that only fools work, and that workers are, and always will be, exploited by the ruling

---

[1] This is a relative concept; people are developed or underdeveloped depending on to whom they are being compared.

classes. A belief that the future is somehow preordained. Obviously, such attitudes are useless for strategic thinking.

 The figure on page viii illustrates the three groups of disciplines in which our conception of international business strategy has its roots. The circle on the left groups the disciplines providing conceptual frameworks that help practising managers to understand the country environment in which their business units operate. We discovered the need to understand environmental forces while living through several years of Central American social revolt. From this experience we offer cases in which the frameworks that proved useful for understanding a business environment can be applied.

 The circle on the right groups the theoretical foundations with which the allocation of resources in a society can be examined. We researched in detail case studies on business negotiations – point observations of reality. Finally, the third circle at the bottom of the graph groups concepts and frameworks useful for understanding the competitive environment.

 We have been engaged in research and business strategy consultancy since 1974, in Latin America, USA and in Western and Eastern Europe, and have gained numerous insights on how to understand an industry. In our view, international business strategy is the overlap of the three circles, and we present in this book some of the best cases ever written to build experience in these fields.

 We would like to acknowledge the contributions of many students of the management problem, whose ideas can be discussed with these cases. Without those thinkers these cases would not have been written. We realize that their ideas may have influenced the conception of the cases, and that by giving credit to one author, or none, we may fail to acknowledge someone's contribution. For this we apologize in advance and ask for understanding. We are especially grateful to Barbara Robins who had the patience to put all these cases into book form and for providing ideas that improved the quality of the material. Only Barbara knows what it means to deal with us.

 We apologize to our female readers for the use of male gender in some cases and introductions of the book. We made this choice – when needed – for reasons of style, and advise them to read *She* whenever it says *He*.

Werner Ketelhöhn and Jan Kubes

Introduction

Cases In International Business Strategy draws its justification from the fact that case books on international business seldom present *case studies* illustrating the impact of events, trends and environmental pressures occurring in foreign markets on the strategic posture of business units. The purpose of this book is to provide a set of case studies from which ideas and organizing frameworks can be discussed for thinking about the strategic posture of business units operating in international markets. It is hoped that the discussion of these cases will help practising managers, strategy consultants and business schools' professors in the solution of international strategy problems.

The cases contained in this book have been selected with the purpose of illustrating situations that can be analyzed with the frameworks presented in Professor Werner Ketelhöhn's book *International Business Strategy* (Butterworth-Heinemann, 1993). Thus, the cases contained in Chapter 1 of this book illustrate the frameworks explained in Chapter 1 of *International Business Strategy*; the same holds true for each succesive chapter in both books.

The key message in *International Business Strategy* is that there is no such thing as a purely deliberate – nor randomly generated – strategic posture[1] in corporations engaged in global competition: a business unit's strategic posture results from adapting corporate strategic postures to a market's environmental pressures. In short, global corporate strategic postures are sensitive to market-specific environmental events, human resources, leadership style and subsidiary culture.

Since no one knows enough to work out every detail of a strategic posture in a market in advance, nor how to correctly forecast all environmental pressures, business unit managers must constantly adjust the strategic posture of their firm to the pressures of the environment in which they operate. Business unit managers must construct a strategic posture that incorporates all market-specific demands and pressures while maintaining those key elements of the corporate, strategic posture that characterize their firm. This process of strategic adaptation is essentially a synthetic proposition: the business unit manager identifies key events, trends and pressures in his environment and examines their impact on the strategic posture and operations of his company.

At some point in an international manager's career he or she has to live, work and successfully lead a business unit within a foreign environment, where economics, politics and other events interact with the strategic posture and operations of the firm. Therefore, this book not only offers cases with which to discuss a unified framework for the country manager's job, but also complements case publications in other management functions, particularly those dealing with managing subsidiaries in foreign markets.

---

[1] The strategic posture of a corporation is composed of its shared vision, specific objectives, strategic decisions and business policies.

These cases are expected to have a considerable impact on management thinking about the way a corporation's strategy is crafted, adapted and implemented in foreign markets. They illustrate the need for coherence in the incorporation of environmental happenings to the strategic posture of a firm; they explicitly deal with issues which have so far escaped unified academic consideration.

Because the cases illustrate real-life strategic issues, and document field experiences, their discussion is of interest to both non-academic and academic audiences as classified by the following three major target groups:

1 General managers and country managers involved in one way or another with strategic investments
2 Business school professors and consultants interested in international strategy
3 Undergraduate and graduate students of international business.

We believe that our duty as students of management is to get out there and learn how practising business-people understand their businesses, and then – based on their constructs – try to make some generalizations that can be used in other businesses. This book provides the opportunity to learn from real businesses.

Strategic thinking demands a proactive attitude and a deeply-held conviction that the future is built with managerial decisions based on appropriate business ideologies and not with mysterious meta-economic myths.

Part One
Competitive and Cooperative Business Strategy

1 The enterprise system
  Case 1.1 The European newspaper industry in 1988
  Case 1.2 Competing in the European packaging industry in 1990

These cases were selected for discussion of the following concepts: the business web; business nodes; strategic decision-making; vision: a strategic intent; the enterprise system; and the value added chain

2 Generic strategies
  2.1 Ecco: Swiss temporary employment industry

This case was selected for discussion of the following concepts: distinctive and core competence; core technology; integration strategies, the business system: a company's value activities; sourcing; processing; delivery and support activities; and key success factors

Part One
Competitive and Cooperative Business Strategy

1 The enterprise system

2 Teamwork in industry

Introduction

Overview

In this part we present cases for discussing our framework for the understanding of management and business strategy. This framework or business ideology combines Michael Porter's ideas with those originating in systems analysis, which have been developed by academics and consultants. We have found this model very useful when trying to understand an industry.

An ideology is a set of interrelated beliefs,[1] values[2] and attitudes[3] that form the basis upon which we construct our frameworks and models to pass judgements, generate alternatives, make choices and express preferences. An ideology provides us with the means to understand the world: it provides our 'weltanschauung'.

What we propose is a 'geschaeftsanschauung' – business perpective – that is consistent in explaining most events in the business world, no matter what industry we examine. For business strategy we present a robust ideology, capable of explaining an industry in a way that is consistent with the understanding of other industries.

All frameworks are created to simplify complexity in a way that helps the thinking processes of decision-makers. The goal is to understand reality, and then to shape it. Useful models have three properties: first, they increase our understanding of complexity; second, they are used for proactive decision-making; and third, they produce simple, feasible, acceptable and implementable decisions.

We believe that our business ideology is able to incorporate the changes occurring in technological, physical, political, economical and social environments into the analysis. Our ideology is dynamic, it changes to explain new events in the environment, and does so in a way consistent with all previous explanations of similar phenomena.

Consider the Benetton's rags-to-riches story which provides fantastic opportunities to learn about strategy and management. Over the past thirty years, self-made billionaire Luciano Benetton has created, without formal education or business degrees, the world's best example of a successful network company. By the mid-1970s, when Benetton's agent-retail concept was already fully developed, Luciano, his brothers and sister, still lacked formal training in finance and business strategy, let alone in agency and network theory. However, they created a network of entrepreneurs

---

[1]Beliefs are the basic relationships that we assume exist between two things. e.g. work produces prosperity and freedom as opposed to work is God's curse on mankind. Our belief and value systems determine our understanding of ourselves and our surrounding world.

[2]Values are concerned with what is right or wrong, with what should and should not be done, e.g. people should work as opposed to people should avoid work.

[3]Attitudes are assumptions based on our beliefs and values, e.g. people in the southern hemisphere will never reach Japanese productivity, as opposed to people's productivity depends on their beliefs, values and attitudes.

in ignorance of the many game-theoretic lucubrations discussed by outstanding mathematicians. This success demonstrates that there are no right or wrong business ideologies; rather, we would argue that managers should use the ideas that help them the most in understanding their businesses.

The strategy concept

Our concept of strategy is dynamic. Dynamic, because it evolves as the environmental conditions evolve. According to Aldo Palmeri, chief strategist of the Benetton family for ten years, 'the nature of a network organization changes in different environments: what works well in Italy may not do so in Japan, and vice versa; that is why we must adapt our organization to the local conditions and culture.' Thus the concept of strategy must be adaptable to different cultures and industries.

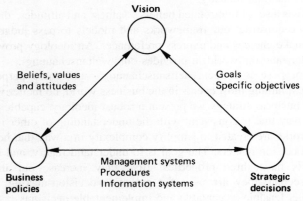

Strategic posture

Our concept of strategy is really 'a strategic management process' which adapts the corporation's basic posture to the different environments in which it is present. These processes can be summarized within the **strategic posture** presented in Figure A, which is defined as the set of management processes that specify the following components:

1 A vision for the business.
2 Its specific objectives.
3 The corresponding strategic decisions.
4 The business policies that ensure that the myriad of small daily decisions are complementary.

The **vision** of the business is defined for an environment by its socioeconomic mission in that society, in terms of the needs of consumers and other interest groups,[4] in that country or in its country of origin.

---

[4] An interest group is an individual or group of individuals who influence, directly or indirectly, the behaviour of an organisation.

For instance, IBM's vision to emphasize systems integration in the 1990s originated in an earlier outlook for the computer industry. Based on this vision, top managers set in motion a series of organisational changes designed to create the organization capable of competing in the solution business of the 1990s.

Choosing a vision is like choosing the destination for a journey. The point on a map results from past visions, present environmental conditions and scenarios of possible futures. The vision results from a complex blend of people's desires, company capabilities and environmental opportunities.

The vision generates a set of clear and achievable specific objectives, the mission, which guides **strategic decision-making**.[4] These are important investment decisions taken to accomplish strategic objectives. Strategic decisions make use of considerable corporate resources, have long-term consequences and are extremely difficult to reverse. Strategic investments put the business one step closer to fulfilling its mission in the market place.

The vision is also dynamic and flexible because it evolves over the years as it is adapted for changing environmental conditions; thus it is fair to say that the mission of a business is fulfilled each time a set of specific objectives is achieved, but that the vision of the business is an ever escaping goal.

Finally, **business policies** are the set of formal and informal rules which guide the thousands of small decisions taken by corporate executives managing a wide variety of issues. These policies guide daily operative decisions so that they are consistent with the overall strategic direction of the business; they can be used to concentrate operative decision-making on a chosen strategy. Business policies coordinate operative decision-making by providing a guide that produces complementary decisions in the different parts of the corporation.

Nestlé, for example, modified its strategic posture in baby foods in the 1980s because of intense pressure originating from radical groups in developed countries. Motivated by this pressure, Nestlé's specific commercialization policies for baby food in developing countries were modified.

Clearly, since the strategic posture is dynamic: it changes through time and environments, it is very important to understand the processes that generate its different components. By controlling these processes one controls the shape of the future strategic posture. For instance, a shared vision, an institutional vision, of the business and its goals, guides the diverse business activities of the long line through space and time of executives, employees and projects.

The development of a shared vision is not based on large analyses nor does it require star consultants. A shared vision evolves over time by accumulating experience on technologies, industries and markets, in which, and with which, the company competes. This shared vision emerges from the interactions of executives, employees and workers; and from the processes set in motion by management and pressure groups.

Our concept of strategy comprises of processes that generate strategic postures in the various countries in which a corporation competes.

About the cases

Part One of *Cases In International Business Strategy* presents case studies that lend themselves to discussion of useful frameworks for understanding Competitive and

Cooperative Business Strategy. Before we present the cases in this section, we would like to recognize the contributions of Professor Michael Oliff to the packaging industry note, and research associates James Henderson, Mark Brazas and Amy W. Webster to different cases. Some basic research was performed by our students Graham Wickenden, Graeme Chipp, Nina Linander, Jayne Buxton, Kasimir Nordenswan, Juergen Fisher, Marion Grimmer, Nicholas Obelensky, Dejan Tadic and Ernst Urschitz during their MBA consulting projects. Undoubtedly, we are indebted to many staff members at IMD for their enthusiastic support during the different phases of our research.

Answers to the question, 'How do we add value in this business unit?' are found in two steps. First, we investigate the systemic question of how the different businesses participating in this industry are linked. Our cases lead us to understand the structure and dynamics in the industry as well as the alternative coordination mechanism found in the management of the flows of people, information, goods and money. The **enterprise system** can be used with these cases to understand the links between raw material suppliers, intermediate businesses and the final consumer. An industry's definition depends on the businesses included in the enterprise system, clearly a personal decision. The enterprise system is industry-related: it defines the industry and describes how the different businesses are linked.

Similarly, we can use these cases to investigate integration strategies followed by successful competitors in different industries, as well as the activities they chose to perform themselves in their search for profits. This defines the **business system** used by the different competitors. Understanding their business system permits us to also understand the way these companies have chosen to add value – their *value adding activities*; the technology used in these activities – the *technological chain*; and the cost incurred with these activities – their *cost structure*. The business system is company-specific, and can be used in these cases to describe how specific competitors have chosen to deliver their products/services to the final consumer.

To compete in today's demanding environment, companies must make sure that the business system that they choose to manage can deliver the desired goods/services with the high perceived quality and low delivered cost of world class competitors. This can be achieved if the whole system is coordinated. But coordination really means strategic management. Therefore, the cases can also be used to understand how companies make sure they choose the right integration strategy in the enterprise system; and the way to do that is to recognize and adopt – over time – those generic strategies that yield the most profitable system in the long run.

In this sense, vertical integration decisions are at the centre of a company's strategy: they not only determine the shape of its activity chain but they also determine the long-run overall efficiency of the business system that the company adopted and the coordination mechanisms required to manage the company's strategic posture.

The process of strategic analysis – illustrated with these cases – is straightforward. It begins by understanding the possible integration strategies as well as the possible sourcing, processing, delivery and support activities in an industry. That is, it identifies the generic ways of competing within the industry and the corresponding key success factors (KSFs).

A company that chooses to compete with one set of generic strategies must be well able to identify the KSFs. By matching the strengths of the company with the KSFs of each generic strategy we can determine which of the many strategies may be followed by the company. Clearly, for each different set of strategies, there may be some KSFs in which the company is weak. Strategic investment projects are conceived to increase company capabilities in key success factors that are needed when we follow a chosen generic strategy.

In summary, to understand the strategy of a company, consulting teams start with a set of hypotheses about the generic strategies in the industry and the key success factors for each strategy. Then they check their understanding of the industry by comparing their hypotheses with documented facts. Once they are satisfied with their understanding of the industry, they compare the company's capabilities with the KSFs of the generic strategies. By identifying the strategy that best fits the company's capabilities, consultants are able to select and recommend investment projects necessary to build strengths in those KSFs in which the company is weak. The cases presented here can be used to illustrate how to perform strategic analysis.

1

The enterprise system

Case 1.1 The European newspaper industry in 1988

This case was prepared by Research Associate Amy W. Webster, under the supervision of Professor Werner Ketelhöhn, as a basis for class discussion rather than to illustrate either effective or ineffective handling of a business situation.

We are witnessing the rejuvenation of the newspaper industry. It is getting its costs into line, updating its products, adding value to those products and trying to make money!
(Publishing and Printing Analyst, Phillips & Drew 1988)

In 1988, there was no such thing as a European newspaper industry;[1] there were, however, many national newspaper industries in Western Europe. International newspapers like the *Financial Times*, *Le Monde* or the *Frankfurter Allgemeine* – offshoots of strong national publications – were read worldwide by an elite readership, but these cross-border or cosmopolitan publications primarily served the increasing number of travellers and expatriates from a particular country or culture. In fact, most European newspapers rarely crossed borders as their first and foremost function was to provide local news to local readers.

Indeed, political and cultural traditions, consumer habits and competitive environments varied greatly from one country to another. More particularly, reading habits differed. Political affiliation remained important in some countries, while in others the press was independent from party politics. Another example of differences Europe-wide was the sensational press, which was extremely popular in

[1] This case study focuses solely on the press industry in Western Europe.

some countries (West Germany, the UK) yet was unknown in other parts of Europe (Spain).

Nevertheless, European newspaper publishers were facing similar challenges. Since the 1960s, technological developments had precipitated radical changes in the newspaper production process. Publishers all over Europe had experienced painful and costly labour struggles when the new phototypesetting printing process was introduced, as a smaller labour force was required. After being set back by newer electronic media and by union power, most newspapers had managed to recover profitability. But new challenges lay ahead. Press experts agreed that information technology was likely to affect the newspaper business and the competitive game in the following decades.

The product

In 1988, newspapers provided readers with printed information, i.e. news, articles, stories, features, pictures and advertising. It was a perishable product of low unitary value as it was produced and consumed within 24 hours:

> ... a product which is developed from trees at a very high cost, passed through an even costlier production process, distributed around the country in a variety of ways and then used and disposed of in a matter of minutes![2]

Newspapers varied in format – from tabloid to broadsheet – as well as in content – from popular scandals (*Bild Zeitung*) to highly intellectual subjects (*Le Monde*). The fact that newspapers were readily available, were portable, easily scanned, folded, or clipped, and covered a variety of news items, made them a unique means of information transmission in a cost-effective package. There were various classifications: daily, weekly or Sunday; morning or evening; general news or specialized; partisan, sensational or élite; community/suburban or metropolitan/urban; local, national or international.

During the early 1980s, the image of the written press had suffered in many European countries and newspapers had lost some credibility. The fact that they had been considered the most reliable source of news for a long time was no longer taken for granted. In France, for example, audio-visual media was increasingly considered more reliable than the written press. By 1988, however, many trends indicated a renewed confidence in the future of newspapers, with an increased focus on the product itself and on ways to improve it.

The business system

Components of the Business Chain (see Exhibit 1.1)

Raw material

The newspaper publishing industry was supplied with ink[3] and newsprint (a cheap paper made chiefly from groundwood pulp and used mostly for newspapers). Newsprint essentially came from Scandinavia and Canada, which respectively

---

[2] Mr. Eddie Shah, Chairman of the Newspaper Group Limited, at the Newspaper Industry Conference, London, April 1988.

[3] Ink for the new offset printing process was mostly oil-based, which was impractical as it would rub off. However, ink producers were trying to develop a low-rub-off resin-based offset ink.

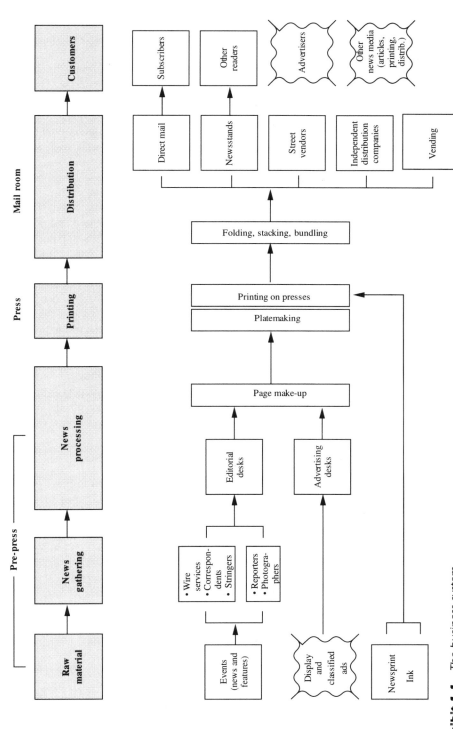

Exhibit 1.1 *The business system*

accounted for 24% and 62% of world exports in 1987. Both items had jumped in terms of price during the last decade.[4]

News gathering

News came from various sources. Wire services (Agence France Presse, Deutsche Presse Agentur) transmitted national and international news by teletype to all newspapers. In addition, many papers had foreign correspondents and stringers, namely reporters working occasionally for publications or news agencies on individual stories. Nevertheless, most published material was generated by the paper's own staff of reporters and photographers who covered local news.

News processing

Articles, illustrations and advertisements were collected, selected, edited and prepared for publication under the supervision of the editor-in-chief. In 1988, desktop publishing was changing the face of the industry. Computers were used for both editorial and administrative tasks: electronic editing, typesetting, composing, management control, as well as control of printing and distribution. Editorial information was introduced 'on-line': text was entered into the computer and then transmitted directly from computer to plate.

News technologies also allowed the development of completely electronic pre-press systems, including the integration of text and graphics in both black and white and colour (electronic page make-up[5]). Pictures could not yet be dealt with by the computer, but it was expected that by the 1990s editorial contributions would be completely computerized. Direct input from journalists moved newspapers from being production-driven (with union dominance) to editorial-driven. As a result, the industry was becoming increasingly market-led.

Printing

During the 1980s, most European newspaper publishers had invested in news printing plants with modern technological equipment. Offset[6] printing and photopolymer plates had replaced the older Gutenberg letterpress process, where hot metal was poured into moulds for each page to be printed. The advantages of offset printing were manifold: better reproduction, possible use of thinner paper, and more reliable colour. In addition, new presses brought higher running speeds and lower waste. Photographic typesetting was cheaper, less labour-intensive[7] and simpler. Journalists and advertising staff alike were keying their material into new, flexible and increasingly cheaper direct-entry systems. Only the smallest newspapers were still using traditional composing rooms, which had become a feature of the past. Those that wanted to avoid heavy capital investment and possible industrial disputes relied on contract printing.

---

[4] Newsprint price in the UK had increased by 6.25% between 1987 and 1988, to £425 per ton of 48.8 gsm (grams per square metre) quality newsprint.

[5] The average cost of a page make-up system in the UK in 1988 was £400,000.

[6] In 1988, offset presses were the most widely used. Flexographic printing, using water-based non-rub-off ink, was also becoming increasingly popular.

[7] In the USA, Philadelphia newspapers reduced production hours per page by 11.5% in 1987.

Distribution

After newspapers were printed, folded and stacked, they would be sent to a mailroom to be bundled and shipped by various means of transport. They were then delivered to newsstands and distributors. In many countries, postal services imposing prohibitive prices were the only means of delivering papers to subscribers. Distribution was handled through retail outlets (such as newsstands or street vendors), independent distribution companies, home delivery systems or direct mail. Vending machines were sometimes used in cities.

The newspaper business was a service industry, which meant the papers had to be delivered at the reader's convenience even if it meant altering press schedules. Regularity and punctuality were paramount. Circulation increased when governments subsidized the distribution of newspapers in sparsely settled areas (e.g., in Sweden, 5% of the industry costs were supported by the government). In many southern countries, circulation suffered from a poor distribution system. Distribution was one reason why local newspapers were often more successful than national or international ones. Local papers were close to their readers and usually handled delivery themselves or through well established distributors. Larger papers often depended on and paid high prices for these local distribution networks.

Distribution wholesalers tended to be powerful and not service-minded. Consequently, they were the source of many problems and often the vulnerable part of the business chain. Many publishers were trying, as a result, to review their distribution strategies.

Customers

Unlike most other products, newspaper publishers sold two components: information to readers and advertising space to advertisers. Competition for circulation and advertising was an interactive process, as one source of revenue generally increased when the other did. As a result, newspaper publishers strove to meet both readers' and advertisers' requirements. Tough competition sometimes caused wars over advertising rates and cover price.

1 *Readers* Newspapers competed for readership on the basis of price, delivery service, editorial quality and perceived value, improved design and use of colour, content, etc. In France, many specialists believed that the price escalation in recent years had caused an overall decline in the daily press. The sales price of a daily newspaper was considered more decisive than for weeklies or magazines. At FF4.50 ($0.80) a copy, French newspapers were twice as expensive as dailies in Germany (see Exhibit 1.2). In the UK, the cover price of most quality broadsheets had also increased in 1988 by about 10–15%. Most European governments fixed a limited price range for newspapers. Some even fixed a minimum selling price as a protective measure for newspaper publishers (i.e. Portugal and Greece).

Another major concern in European press industries was the uncertainty of the future tax treatment of printed material within the European Community. In most countries, publishers were all pressuring to maintain the VAT[8] (Value Added Tax)

---

[8] At 10%, Ireland had the highest VAT rate on newspaper cover prices in Europe.

Country	Local Price		Price in US$ at August 1988 rate
Austria	SCH	7	0.50
France	FF	4.50	0.80
Greece	GRD	50	0.30
Italy	LIT	900	0.60
Netherlands	HFL	1.10	0.50
Portugal	ESC	50	0.30
United Kingdom	£	0.30	0.50
USA	US$	0.30	0.30
West Germany	DM	0.70	0.40

Source: *The Press in Europe*, Publicación de la Asociación de Editores de Diarios Españoles, Madrid, 1987.

Exhibit 1.2 *Newspaper prices in Europe in 1987 (average for high-quality daily)*

zero rating of newspapers in order to avoid another cover price escalation and an ensuing decline in circulation.

Efficient promotion of newspapers often helped increase circulation. Discount policies, advertising campaigns, direct mail pieces, one-month free subscriptions or special incentives such as linking new subscriptions to a gift, were various ways used by newspaper publishers to promote their products. Many other instruments were available; in France recent increases in national circulation for dailies such as *Le Figaro* were attributed to new weekend supplements and weekday special interest sections. Serious efforts were made to offer added value to the reader with extra sections, magazines, supplements, etc.

By the 1980s, most newspaper publishers realized that one of the key factors for success was to accurately identify target customers. Editorial content and newspaper format had to be designed for particular customer groups. In Germany, regional editions tried to satisfy the needs of target customer groups. In Spain, local newspapers were the most successful in their particular local areas. In addition, publishers had to adapt to changing consumer tastes; readers wanted more entertainment as well as shorter and more concise articles.

In 1988, newspapers were constantly competing for ways to reinvent the newspaper concept and to restructure the business game as quickly as possible. Some objectives were lower unit prices, cooperation and efficiency in the distribution system, or improved design. In France, for example, most major newspapers (*Le Figaro*, *Le Monde*) had been recently restructured and had launched a new look, or were in the process of doing so (*Libération*).

2 *Readership* Readership in Europe had not kept pace with the demographic explosion of the past decades. All over Europe, the younger generation read less; most countries were trying to cultivate newspaper readership at an early stage through Newspaper in Education (NIE) programmes. In addition, some papers were trying to be youth-oriented, while others published special junior pages or weekly supplements aimed at the 15 to 24-year-old age group.

Country	Number of newspapers				Total Circulation (000s)				Circulation per 1000 inhabitants			
	1970	1975	1979	1984	1970	1975	1979	1984	1970	1975	1979	1984
Austria	33	30	26	29	–	2,405	–	2,735	–	320	–	365
Belgium	49	30	26	26	–	2,340	2,242	2,209	–	239	228	223
Denmark	58	49	49	47	1,790	1,723	1,876	1,837	363	341	367	359
Finland	67	60	62	67	–	2,100	2,289	2,599	–	446	480	535
France	106	92	90	101	12,067	10,615	10,619	11,598	238	201	199	212
FRG	1,093	375	380	359**	19,701	22,702	25,016	21,362	–	367	408	350
Greece	110	106	116	107	705	921	–	981	80	102	–	–
Ireland	7	7	7	7	686	693	771	663	232	216	229	186
Italy	73	78	75	70	7,700	6,469	5,308	5,477	144	116	94	96
Netherlands	169	–	80	84	4,100	–	4,553	4,474	315	–	323	310
Norway	81	80	83	82	1,487	1,657	1,859	2,071	384	414	457	501
Portugal	33	30	22	25	743	612	493	495	86	65	50	49
Spain	116	115	105	102	3,450	3,491	–	3,053	102	98	–	80
Sweden	114	112	114	99	4,324	4,413	4,378	4,340	538	539	529	521
Switzerland	117	–	88	90	2,318	–	2,501	2,494	370	–	395	392
UK	–	111	120	108	–	24,127	25,221	23,206	–	431	–	414
Japan				125				57,380				562
Soviet Union				724				116,096				422
USA				1,687				63,263				268
Canada				112				5,544				220

* 'Daily' is defined as a paper published at least 4 times per week.

** 1982 data.

Note: For France, the data shown in the 1975, 1979 and 1984 columns refer to 1976, 1978 and 1983 respectively. For the Federal Republic of Germany, the number of dailies in 1970 includes regional editions. For 1975 and 1979, the data include non-daily newspapers issued 2 to 4 times a week. For Greece, 1984 data refer to 1983 and the circulation figure refers to 22 dailies only. For Portugal, the 1984 circulation figure refers to 17 dailies only. For the UK, the 1979 circulation figure refers to 117 dailies only.

Source: UNESCO Statistical Yearbook 1986.

Exhibit 1.3 *Newspaper circulation by country*

Readership in Europe varied significantly. In 1984, Scandinavian and Germanic countries, along with the UK, were way ahead of their Latin counterparts, where an average of only 10% of the population read newspapers (see Exhibit 1.3). Consumption of newsprint followed the same lines; it was three times as high in Northern as in Southern Europe.

Factors affecting circulation included literacy, income, education and population homogeneity. In Scandinavian countries, advanced educational systems, even distribution of income and effective distribution systems were all reasons for high readership. Circulation had also grown with the greater choice of newspapers available to readers.

3 *Advertisers* Newspapers were the fastest advertising medium and, in most countries, still the major one (see Exhibit 1.4). Often closely identified with their communities, newspapers were able to reach a target market quickly. Advertisers tended to choose a paper on the basis of its circulation number, readership and reputation. Generally, two-thirds of the advertising space in a newspaper was devoted to local advertisements (See Exhibit 1.5 for a list of advertising rates in Europe).

Advertisements had become the first source of revenue for most newspapers and were therefore critical to newspaper economics. Growth in newspaper advertising revenue had exceeded that of the general economy in the 1980s (15% growth in the UK from 1985 to 1986). In total annual advertising revenues, most European newspapers still led over all other media, including television. Overall, the public still considered advertisements in newspapers more reliable than in any other medium.

Advertising revenue came from both ads and inserts. Classified advertisements were the most profitable and fastest growing. They dealt mostly with automobiles, real-estate and jobs, and were very sensitive to economic factors. In the field of display advertisement, retail ads were placed by local firms, such as department stores, grocery chains or discount stores. Finally, national and international ads, also closely related to the state of the economy, were the slowest growing and most cyclical. Retail, national and classified ads usually represented about one-third of advertising space each.

	France	FRG	Belgium	UK	Italy	Netherlands	USA
Press	31.0	67.0	60.2	63.5	50.5	56.8	35.2
Television	11.5	9.6	8.6	29.7	36.4	5.5	21.5
Outside advertising	10.0	3.1	12.5	4.0	5.9	4.9	1.1
Radio	6.0	3.8	0.1	2.2	5.9	1.2	7.0
Movies	1.5	0.8	1.2	0.6	1.3	0.4	
Total large media	60.0	84.3	82.6	100	100	68.8	64.8
Direct advertising	40.0	11.4	17.4			31.2	15.5
directories		4.3					19.7
Total	100	100	100	100	100	100	100

Source: Presse actualité, hors série, 1985, p. 78.

Exhibit 1.4 *Percentage advertising media market shares in 1985*

Type of newspaper (periodicity)	Circulation (000)	Type of publication	Full page B&W US$
USA			
The Wall Street Journal	2,082	National Business	80,381
U.S.A. Today	1,329	National	20,698
The New York Times	911	National Quality	29,329
The Washington Post	788	National Quality	25,780
Europe			
Austria			
Neue Kronen Zeitung	857	National	8,841
Belgium			
De Standaard	315	National	9,474
Le Soir	224	National	9,322
Denmark			
Ekstra-Bladet	267	National	2,225
B.T.	233	National	2,878
Politiken	154	National	3,335
Politiken (Sun)	226	National	5,385
Berlingske Tidende	121	National	3,691
Berlingske Tidende (Sun)	198	National	5,956
Jyllands Posten	109	National	2,901
Jyllands Posten (Sun)	219	National	5,802
Finland			
Helsingin Sanomat	420	National	8,606
Helsingin Sanomat (Sun)	491	National	
France			
Ouest France	721	Regional	25,715
France Soir	418	National	13,982
Le Monde	385	National	8,501
Le Figaro	361	National	14,541
Libération	101	National	2,908
Le Quotidien de Paris	78	National	2,740
Germany			
Bild	5,565	National	85,452
Bild am Sonntag (Sun)	2,448	National	16,668
Süddeutsche Zeitung	345	National Quality	11,088
Die Welt am Sonntag (Sun)	330	National Quality	13,069
Frankfurter Allgemeine	320	National	12,274
Nordwest-Zeitung	302	West Friesland	11,395
Die Welt	202	National Quality	9,479
Greece			
Ethnos	190	National	4,603
Ireland			
The Sunday Press	311	National	11,390
Irish Independent	175	National	9,450

Exhibit 1.5 *Advertising rates (continued overleaf)*

Type of newspaper (periodicity)	Circulation (000)	Type of publication	Full page B&W US$
Italy			
Corriere della Sera	475	National	22,622
La Stampa	397	National	20,210
La Repubblica	289	National	13,272
Luxembourg			
Luxemburger Wort	78	National	2,250
Norway			
A. Magasinet (supp)	258	National	1,963
VG. Verdens Gang	257	National	4,000
Aftenposten	231	National	8,460
Spain			
El. Pais	353	National	3,078
La Vanguardia	196	National	1,833
Sweden			
Expressen	548	National	4,230
Dagens Nyheter	466	National	9,047
Switzerland			
Blick	364	National	5,525
Tages Anzeiger	260	Zürich	3,200
Neue Zürcher Zeitung	131	National	4,160
24 Heures	93	Vaud District	2,222
La Suisse	65	French Switzerland	2,129
United Kingdom			
The Sun	4,187	National Popular	26,608
Daily Mirror	3,365	National Popular	26,130
Daily Telegraph	1,260	National Quality	26,871
The Guardian	473	National Quality	17,160
The Times	381	National Quality	13,395
Financial Times	216	Business	19,219

Exhibit 1.5   *Continued*

Newspaper cost structure

Raw material usually represented 10–30% of total operating expenses. Labour was the highest cost item (40–60% of operating expenses). Wages were increasing, but manpower had been reduced due to automation, so labour costs had remained relatively stable.

The cost structure of a newspaper can be best illustrated with one specific example. The following statistics are only representative of élite newspapers, however, which have an important editorial staff with many foreign correspondents. In 1987, the most prestigious French newspaper, *Le Monde*, recorded the following breakdown of its total costs: paper 12.7%, editorial staff 15.5%, administrative overhead 11.3%, production 28.2% and distribution 32.4%.[9]

In Spain, raw material accounted for, on average, 25% of the total costs, labour 41% and transport 5%. In Finland, the same numbers were 20%, 53% and 16% respectively. Average labour costs for Austria were: production 43%, editorial 22%, distribution 20% and administration 15%. For Spain: production 40%, editorial 26%, distribution 13% and administration 21%.

Newspaper revenues in 1988 were, on average, distributed as follows:

	Germany	Austria	Spain	Finland	Luxembourg
Ads	64.6%	56%	45%	75%	65%
Sales	35.6%	42%	50%	25%	35%
Other		2%	5%		

See Exhibit 1.6 for a table of revenues and costs of a few selected European dailies.

	UK national	West Germany regional	France regional	Sweden average	USA big newspapers
Revenues	100%	100%	100%	100%	100%
Circulation	56	31	61	35	19
Display advertising	34	41	29	52	54
Classified advertising	10	28	10	–	23
Other	–	–	–	13	4
Costs	100%	100%	100%	100%	100%
Paper	35	13	23	12	35
Production	50	65	62	71	42
Distribution	15	22	15	17	23

Source: Advertising will drive up demand, *Pulp & Paper International*, June 1987, p. 46.

Exhibit 1.6 *Revenues and costs for newspapers in June 1987*

Technological changes

In the 1980s, sometimes after a long battle, most newspaper companies had signed agreements with their unions, enabling them to introduce new technologies, which increased productivity and reduced costs. For a long time, typographers' and printers' unions had been a barrier to technological change, and the issues of automation had led to many long, expensive strikes. For example, the revolution which took place in the

[9] Distribution costs include postage for subscriptions, commissions to street vendors' newsstands and distributors, as well as transportation costs.

London district of Wapping[10] illustrates how the industrial relations environment was normalized in the British press industry.

After the agreements, most editing rooms were computerized, mostly with personal computers and systems, pagemaker software and laser printers, thus eliminating typography, layout and proofreading costs. Many small regional newspaper publishers shed up to one-third of their composing room workforce. Press manning levels dropped while the number of employees in the administration, news and advertising departments often increased, together with the number of mechanics, engineers and technical support people.[11] In many cases this reduction of personnel had not resulted in the traumatic social reaction that had been expected and the transition had been smooth. Adequate solutions were found in collective bargaining, such as anticipated retirement, special treatment for the unemployed, special compensations or retraining of personnel. Nevertheless, periodical negotiations with unions still played an important role.

After the general conversion to new printing technologies, newspaper publishers began investing in many other aspects of the business. Improved colour quality came with the new offset printing presses and colour scanners. The trend toward using colour was expected to accelerate as advertisers put on pressure to improve a publication's quality for their own ads. In the USA, colour was the cornerstone of the newspaper industry's new look – both in photography and as an accent device. It was effective in attracting advertisers and street sales, but it had to be of good quality and used judiciously as colour could repel readers.

Other technological improvements included stuffing or inserting equipment, which could allow national dailies to regionalize or zone their editions with varying sections, or to publish pre-printed inserts. Inserting technology, widely used in Germany and the USA, could provide newspapers with major benefits such as lower press investment by producing pre-printed sections, better equipment utilization, unlimited pagination, greater publishing flexibility, and the possibility to publish higher quality colour advertising leaflets.[12] Overall, inserting increased revenue opportunities from distributing advertising supplements.

Some newspaper publishers, in an effort to save on distribution costs and improve timeliness, were pursuing another technological novelty, namely using satellite technology and home-based microcomputers to transmit facsimiles to faraway printing sites or even to readers' homes![13] The customer could then watch the news on his screen or print a hard copy.

Competition with other media

In the age of electronic media, newspapers could no longer provide the major news exclusively; they had lost that role to television. As a result, newspapermen were

---

[10] In January 1986, Rupert Murdoch of News Corporation moved his printing operations from Fleet Street to Wapping, where modern equipment had been secretly installed. The stormy dispute which ensued between newspaper publishers and print unions broke the union dominance of the British press industry. It allowed numerous investment decisions to take place and Fleet Street finally caught up with the rest of the Western world in the way newspapers were produced.

[11] In 1988, the proportion of electronics relative to mechanical components in new presses was ever increasing, more particularly in press control which coordinated all specified press functions on a programmed basis.

[12] Advertisers were finding that leaflets were an attractive alternative to mail pieces.

[13] The *International Herald Tribune* in 1988 was printed at 10 different sites around the world. The *IHT* only needed 10,000 sold copies to make local printing pay.

Country	Population (millions) 1983	GNP per capita (US$) 1982	Daily papers circulation Total (000s)	Daily papers circulation Per 1000	TV broadcasting per 1000	Radio broadcasting per 1000	Ad spends per capita 1981 (US$)
Austria	7.6	9,880	2,656	320	306	475	83
Belgium	9.9	10,760	2,204	224	304	507	54
Denmark	5.1	12,470	1,821	356	366	384	129
Finland	4.8	10,870	2,484	515	348	346	178
France	54.6	11,680	10,332	191	313	326	83
FRG	61.5	12,460	25,103	408	354	392	89
Greece	9.9	4,290	1,184	102	174	352	13
Ireland	3.5	5,150	771	229	181	196	42
Italy	56.3	6,840	4,632	82	238	247	60
Netherlands	14.4	10,930	4,610	322	305	318	127
Norway	4.1	14,280	1,986	483	315	320	167
Portugal	9.9	2,450	493	50	149	160	6
Spain	38.4	5,430	2,978	79	256	274	35
Sweden	8.3	14,040	4,363	524	387	383	131
Switzerland	6.5	17,010	2,465	381	278	370	196
UK	56.0	9,660	23,472	421	331	986	106
Japan	119.2	10,080	68,142	575	255	696	95
Soviet Union	272.0	3,890	134,515		295	511	
USA	234.2	13,160	62,415	269	646	2,133	266
Canada	24.9	11,320	5,570	226	460	758	146

Note: For radio and television broadcasting per 1000 inhabitants, the data are based on either the number of licences issued or sets declared, on the estimated number of receivers in use, or on estimates.

Source: Media Consumption Worldwide: Key Data in *The World Media Today* 1985, p. 27–30. Sources stated are: L'Expansion; UNESCO Statistical Yearbook; Atlaseco (France) 1980, 1982; Europa Yearbook (UK) 1981.

Exhibit 1.7 *Media consumption per 1000 inhabitants*

becoming analysts of international and national issues and reporters of regional news. In many countries, TV was blamed for the drop in readership.[14] In 1988, France counted 375 TV sets per 1000 inhabitants, which was representative of most Western European countries (see Exhibit 1.7). According to a recent survey in France, many of the irregular readers considered radio and television as sufficient information media. The others claimed a lack of time or interest.

The environment for press industries in Europe was increasingly competitive. In the UK, magazines intruded more than television on newspaper circulation. France was leader in magazine consumption and magazines dominated the French written press, directly grabbing market share from newspapers.

In addition to cutting circulation, competing news media lured substantial advertising revenues away from newspapers. In competing with television, newspapers had to provide advertisers with the exact number and response level of their readers. Television broadcasting had handled this requirement more successfully and precisely than newspapers. Advertisers were demanding more dynamic data. However, industry observers predicted that, as the number of television outlets increased, newspapers would become a stronger advertising vehicle, because covering a market in a fragmented broadcast media would become increasingly difficult.

Competition between newspapers for advertising revenue was exacerbated by the recent growth of TV and radio advertising. In France, daily newspapers held 26% of the advertising market in 1986 compared with 32% in 1974. In Austria and Italy, the written press had lost its leadership position in the advertising media to television. In Austria as well as in Germany, large scale ad campaigns in the printed media were launched to improve the image of press advertising. In the UK, television was the fastest growing advertising medium; it accounted for 32% of advertising expenditure in 1986 compared to 26.6% in 1977. However, the emergence of new channels, high advertising production costs and prohibitive pricing of advertising space temporarily slowed down the process. In Germany, a similar growth was also inhibited by legislation and delays in installing cable networks and satellite technology for the recently launched private TV channels.

Industry trends

The state of the industry in 1988

In most European countries, the number of newspapers had notably decreased since the 1970s (see Exhibit 1.3). In Western Germany, for example, the great number of papers relative to the size of the population had encouraged publishing regional editions of the same paper, which had brought the total number of papers down. Many other newspapers in Western Europe had merged and many had gone out of business due to overwhelming competition and rising costs.

In addition, the amount of capital needed to start a new paper was high in relation to profit level (see Exhibit 1.8 for appropriate investment costs in the UK). The difficulty of finding new customer segments and the market franchise of

[14] As a result of new technology, deregulation and huge capital investments in most European countries, some 35 international channels would be broadcasting to around 125 million potential European viewers in the 1990s.

Pre-press

Direct input	£2.5 million (based on average 300 terminal system)
Colour system	£0.75–£1 million
Fax system	£1 million (based on 2–3 printing sites)
Platemaking	£1 million (based on 2–3 printing sites)
Total	**£5.5 million**

Presses	£3–£5 million each
Mailroom	£0.75–£2 million per line
Buildings and M&E	£25–£50 million

Note on the cost of a press line in the UK in 1988

Assuming each press line starts at the pre-press and finishes at the delivery window, including the cost of press foundations and services, the total spent can be between £10 and £12 million per press line (a lot of money to recover if you are only using the press for say 5–6 hours per 24).

Obviously if the press can be used for, say, 15–18 hours daily, the investment payback in theory is three times faster. There is also less risk of the equipment becoming redundant technology before you have paid for it!

Source: The Newspaper Industry, A Perspective of the Next 5 Years, Financial Times Conference, London, April 1988.

Exhibit 1.8   *Investment costs – approximate breakdown in the UK in 1988*

existing papers were additional barriers. Often the only solution for entering the industry was acquisition. In addition, increasing internationalization of the owner-ship of newspapers and other printed material was changing the broader picture of the industry.

In countries with relatively low purchasing power or low readership (Portugal, Greece, Italy), press activities were heavily regulated. They also often received circulation subsidies, such as paid postal freight, and subsidies for technological conversion. Since 1986 in Italy, deregulation had enabled newspapers to compete in a free market; subsidies were being slowly eliminated, and prices and points of sale were freely determined.

Historically, newspapers had generated impressive revenues and profits. In the late 1970s, the energy crisis and rising newsprint costs, together with the economic recession, had caused a circulation and advertising slump. In an attempt to combat rising costs, some papers decided to integrate their operations vertically by acquiring newsprint manufacturing and printing technologies. In the Netherlands in 1988, the before-tax profit of a newspaper publisher averaged 10%. The success of *Le Figaro* in France had even attracted foreign investors. French experts were predicting the appearance of a new generation of press entrepreneurs.[15]

[15] In the US in 1986, high prices had been paid for newspaper companies, reaching 8.5 times the company's annual revenues.

Diversification

Many European newspaper companies in the 1980s were striving, with the large-scale development of the electronic media, to become multi-media communications enterprises rather than mere newspaper publishers. In most countries, prohibitive broadcasting legislation relating to cross-media ownership was being dismantled. In an effort to guard against potential competitors who might enter those fields if they were left unattended, many publishers decided to enter other information-related businesses. This entrepreneurial sprit led them to invest in cable television, videotex, audiotex, interactive data retrieval services and other computer-based information systems, radio stations, TV networks, satellite and other high-tech means of delivering information, free sheets,[16] sales offer sheets,[17] magazines, books, etc. Most media-related expansion opportunities had more or less been explored.[18]

More particularly, newspaper publishers were looking for ways to combine the advantages of printing with those of electronic transmission, namely immediate worldwide transmission of a large variety of constantly updated information, which could be selected as needed. In addition, newspaper archives and databases could be made available to future users. In other words, the trend was moving toward a new concept, the tailor-made newspaper.

The major obstacle to smooth cooperation between newspapers and electronic media, however, was the high costs. There was also the difficulty journalists and reporters had getting acquainted with the broadcasting world, which they believed placed more value on the presentation of information than on its content. This difference in approach could also explain the limited cooperation between the written press and television.

Radio stations

Cooperation between newspapers and radio increased with the recent deregulation of radio in many European countries (Switzerland, France, Germany), which gave rise to a variety of local radio stations. Indeed, in Belgium and France, most dailies held direct or indirect participation in private local radio stations. No financial benefits could be anticipated in the short run, but such cooperation was considered by many as a real challenge, as well as an opportunity to counter potential competition for customers and advertisers.

Cable newspapers

In the Netherlands in 1983, national authorities granted permission to use local cable networks for transmitting information and launching a cable 'newspaper', including text and colour photographs. Cable newspapers were limited, however, to viewers subscribing to cable networks. In 1986, there were 30 such operations in the Netherlands.

---

[16] Free sheets are weekly newspapers delivered free to households and depend solely on advertising revenue. They often have more than 75% ad content. Free sheets were a major growth area in the UK in 1988, especially within the regional press. They remain the major single factor in resurgence of weekly titles.

[17] Sales offer sheets contain private ads, free of charge to advertisers, and can be purchased by consumers from newspaper dealers. They prove to be a threat to the classified ads business done by dailies.

[18] In the US, for example, one-third of all recent mergers and acquisitions took place in the information sector.

Videotex

This system offered a wide range of services, from the latest news update to electronic messaging systems. It was transmitted on a terminal linked to a telephone line, whether a TV set (in this case, known as the 'Teletext' – usually less sophisticated and less interactive than videotext), a personal computer or a special terminal, all equipped with special modems. Prohibitive pricing in most countries prevented its development; it was a failure in the USA but encountered some success in Europe. Many tried to imitate the French 'Minitel', but with much less success. The potential success of visually transmitted information was inevitably limited because reading from a screen was a tedious operation.

Concentration

In 1988, many newspaper publishers in the USA were selling their peripheral activities to concentrate time and resources on their core business, namely newspaper publishing. Some reasons for this trend were the slowdown of the economy and the realization that these endeavours had turned out to be less profitable and more troublesome than anticipated. In addition, some of these activities were not such threatening competitors. The same trend was likely to hit Europe sooner or later.

Nevertheless, newspaper publishers were looking ahead and preparing for future communication needs. Most were planning to participate in the inevitable information evolution more than they had during the 1980s. According to one industry expert, the role of the press could even increase in the future:

> Consumers will increasingly need a single, reliable source that will serve as the starting point in the quest for information. Newspapers will remain a more efficient, more secure, more convenient way to store information and to share it.

Case 1.2 Competing in the European packaging industry in 1990

This case was prepared by James Henderson, Research Associate, under the supervision of Professor Jan Kubes, as a basis of class discussion rather than to illustrate either effective or ineffective handling of a management situation. This case is based on previous work done by Research Associate Mark Brazas and Professor Michael Oliff.

Driven by general economic growth, the estimated $67 billion European packaging industry was projected to grow at a modest 3% per year. But, what was the packaging industry? Was it defined by materials – plastics, metals, paper/board or glass? Was it defined by the products – boxes, cartons, cases, bottles, jars, tubs, canisters, tubes, drums, bags, sachets or pouches? Was it defined by end-user markets – food, beverage, health and beauty, or industrial? Or was it defined by a combination of all three, materials, products and end-user markets? Where were the growth opportunities? (*This note will look at the materials used in the packaging industry, focusing primarily on Western Europe.*)

Despite the lack of statistical data, analysts agreed that plastics were enjoying much faster growth rates than the other materials – metal, paper and glass. Yet, within each material category, packaging companies were facing several issues:

- *Plastics*:
    - Environmental problems
    - Rapid changes in material technologies
    - Rapid changes in processing technologies
    - High degree of fragmentation
- *Metal*:
    - High degree of dependence on fluctuation of raw material prices
    - Changes in processing technologies
    - High industry concentration
    - Low growth prospects
- *Glass*:
    - Very low growth prospects
    - Changes in process technologies
    - High industry concentration

- *Paper*:
  - Low growth prospects
  - Changes in process technologies
  - Fluctuations of raw material prices
  - Highly fragmented (in some sectors)

Given these issues for each material, packaging companies faced a complex task of deciding how to compete in the industry.

Packaging industry overview

Materials/products

Packages were made in many shapes and forms: boxes, trays, cartons, cases, bottles, jars, tubs, canisters, tubes, bags, sachets, etc. However, each packaging product provided the same basic functions:

- protection from spoilage
- improvement in logistics and handling
- marketing appeal.

Each type of packaging material – glass, plastic, metal and paper – had its own packaging properties that protected food or beverages from spoiling (Exhibit 1.9). At the same time, packages that were designed properly could be easily handled. For example, the Tetrabrik, a square aseptic carton for liquid products, was extremely

---

Paper and paperboard
No barriers without coatings, etc.
Good stiffness
Low density
Absorbent
Not brittle, but not so high in strength as
   metal
Creasable
Light weight
Tears easily

Plastics
Wide range of barrier properties
Low density
Flexible (creasable)
Low stiffness (usually)
Transparent
Can react with foods
Tensile and tear strength variable
Light weight

Metal
Perfect barrier if sealed
Rigid (flexible in foil format)
High density
Can react with foods
Good tensile strength
Needs joints and closures to form packs
Moderate (aluminium) to heavy (tin) weight

Glass
Perfect barrier
High density
Rigid
Brittle
Transparent
Inert
Brittle
Heavy weight
Needs separate closure

Exhibit 1.9 *Technical description of each packaging material*

Form	Plastics	Metal	Paper	Board	Glass	Foil
Boxes/trays	×	×	-	×	-	-
Cartons	×	-	-	×	-	-
Cases/pallets	×	×	-	×	-	-
Bottles	×	-	-	-	×	-
Jars	×	-	-	-	×	-
Tubs	×	-	-	×	-	-
Canisters	×	×	-	×	×	-
Tubes	×	-	-	×	×	-
Drums/kegs	×	×	-	×	×	-
Labels	×	-	×	-	-	×
Bags	×	-	×	-	-	×
Sachets	×	-	×	-	-	×
Pouches	×	-	×	-	-	×

Source: Frost and Sullivan, London 1989.

Exhibit 1.10 *Packaging applications by material*

simple to pack and ship. A package could also help sell a product by appealing to end users visually and/or with convenience features. By providing qualities desired by distributors – ease of handling, or attractive display, for example – packages could also help win retail listings or prime shelf space for a product.

Only certain packages – rigid (bottles), semi-rigid (tubes) or flexible (pouches) – could be produced from each material according to its properties. For example, glass could only be used for bottles and jars (with a closure) but not for cartons. Yet there was significant overlapping and, subsequently, a great deal of cross-material competition. For example, beer came in glass bottles, aluminium cans, and plastic PET bottles (Exhibit 1.10).

The usage of packaging materials had shown definite shifts over the years. On the whole, glass, metals and wood had lost out to paper and plastics. Often the reason for the substitution was the performance/cost ratio. As new materials such as plastics or composites provided better performance, through their superior properties and ease of

Type	1986e	%	1987e	1988e	1989e	%	1986–1989 Growth p.a.
Metal	12,866	23	13,069	12,397	13,659	21	2.0
Glass	6,334	11	6,205	6,557	6,564	10	1.5
Plastics	14,007	25	15,239	16,712	17,310	27	7.5
Paper/board	22,962	41	23,817	24,984	27,110	42	5.5
Total	56,169	100	58,330	60,650	64,643	100	4.5

Source: Economist Intelligence Unit, 1991, and case writer's estimates.

Exhibit 1.11 *European packaging output by materials and value, 1986–1989 (millions of $)*

Type	1988e	Forecast 5 Year Growth p.a.
Glass	13.6	2.0
Plastics	6.0	7.5
Aluminium	0.4	
Tinplate	3.6	
Total metal	4.0	1.0
Paper	2.0	
Corrugated board	11.2	
Folding cartons	3.2	
Total paper board	16.4	3.0%

Source: Frost and Sullivan, 1989, and case writer's estimates.

Exhibit 1.12 *European packaging output by materials and volume (millions of tonnes)*

converting, all for less cost than the traditional materials, fillers tended to start substituting. For example, in the US, tinplate oil drums had been virtually wiped out by plastic oil drums (Exhibits 1.11 and 1.12)

Value added

When a customer purchased a package, what part of the value of that package would go to the retailer, wholesaler, filler, the converter and, finally, the raw material supplier? On average, for any package that was retailed, the retailer/distributor would receive 30–35% of the value added, the processor/filler would receive 40–45%, the converter/packager, 10–15%, and the raw material supplier 10–15% (Exhibit 1.13). These values would change depending on the packaging shape and the packaging material used.

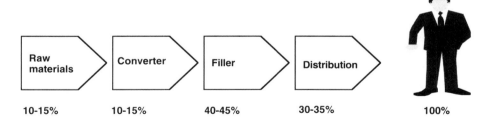

Exhibit 1.13 *Value added to package*

Materials/markets

Almost all consumer and industrial products used some form of packaging. About 45% of packaging was used for the food segment, 23% for beverages, 9% for the health and beauty markets, and 23% for industrial markets. (The following section describes the

Material	Food	Beverage	Health/beauty	Industrial
Plastics	8,655	2,250	1,731	4,673
Paper	14,097	4,067	1,898	7,049
Metal	4,644	5,053	1,775	2,185
Glass	1,969	3,938	656	0
Total	29,365	15,308	6,060	13,907

Source: Case writer's estimates and industry interviews

Exhibit 1.14 *Estimated material/market sizes in value, 1989*

primary segments for packaging companies. For more specific information on the size of each material/market segment, refer to Exhibit 1.14. For the growth in various market segments, refer to Exhibit 1.15.)

Material	1988	1992	Growth
	(in millions of units)		*per annum*
Plastics			
Blown bottles			
Processed foods	1,439.7	1,459.2	0.3
Drinks	9,874.9	10,771.6	2.2
Health/beauty	3,141.3	3,635.7	3.6
Other non-foods	4,262.4	4,625.3	1.4
Plastic containers			
Processed foods	28,580.8	32,387.4	3.2
Drinks	24.7	26.0	1.3
Fresh foods	16,457.1	18,823.8	3.4
Health/beauty	3,931.2	4,634.5	4.2
Other non-foods	341.7	565.3	13.9
Flexible (plastic only)			
Processed foods	28,107.3	30,911.0	2.4
Fresh foods	10,408.5	11,466.1	2.4
Health/beauty	62.9	55.4	−3.1
Other non-foods	115.7	136.2	4.0
Paper/board			
Aseptic cartons			
Processed foods	1,311.0	1,556.8	4.4
Drinks	22,158.1	23.394.1	1.4
Folding cartons			
Processed foods	15,909.5	17,906.2	3.0
Fresh foods	5.0	10.7	21.0
Other health/beauty	5,314.9	6,054.3	3.3
Non-foods (tobacco)	18,944.5	18,923.3	0.0

Exhibit 1.15 *Projected growth rates for each packaging material for each market segment*

Material	1988	1992	Growth
	(in millions of units)		*per annum*
Board-based packaging			
Processed foods	7,292.3	7,819.3	3.0
Drinks	117.2	132.9	3.1
Fresh foods	430.5	424.3	−0.4
Health/beauty	0.3	0.4	7.5
Other non-foods	481.0	464.5	−1.0
Flexible packaging			
Processed food	39,097.3	39,987.7	0.6
Fresh foods	418.6	393.9	−1.5
Non-foods	1,581.5	1,798.8	3.3
Metal			
Open top cans			
Processed foods	12,420.0	12,831.0	0.8
Drinks	15,066.0	17,618.0	4.0
Non-foods (pet foods)	4,958.0	5,604.0	3.1
General line containers			
Processed foods	1,437.0	1,565.0	−2.2
Drinks	80.0	90.0	2.8
Health/beauty	1,402.0	1,182.0	−3.9
Other non-foods	761.0	656.0	−3.4
Aluminium foil trays			
Processed foods	127.0	133.0	1.2
Non-foods (pet foods)	681.0	924.0	8.0
Glass			
Glass bottles/flasks			
Processed foods	10,111.0	10,988.0	2.1
Drinks	78,105.0	80,848.0	0.9
Health/beauty	1,148.0	1,140.0	−0.2

Source: Marketpower, 1988

Exhibit 1.15 *Continued*

Food and beverage segments

Packaging expenses for food and beverage companies represented 2–20% of their total sales, depending on the product. Typically, the less that packaging was an important part of the total product, the more the converter could reap gains. On average, packaging was an estimated 10% of the total cost of the food product. For example, Nestlé, the largest food processor in the world, spent SF 4.4 billion for packaging on SF 46 billion in sales in 1990.

Food and beverage companies had four key packaging needs: protection to meet health standards and prolong shelf life; presentation to attract the shopper and sell the product; low cost to improve the product's price competitiveness and appeal to retail distributors, including handling ease (to lower handling cost); and shape (to maximize the number of product units that would fit on a retailer's shelf).

Food and beverage manufacturers could gain leverage over their packaging suppliers through their absolute size and through their level of integration.

Industry concentration was generally higher for highly processed foods like instant products, canned and frozen foods, breakfast cereals, potato products, margarine and beverages. Meat, milk, flour, fruit and vegetables required minimal processing, and these segments tended to be highly fragmented. Converters of meat trays enjoyed relatively high profit margins because of the fragmentation and therefore low bargaining power of the meat packing industry (mainly butchers). On the whole, the top ten food manufacturers accounted for 40% of the total food retail sales in Europe.

Some manufacturers had integrated backwards into packaging, most often when low initial investments were required. For example, Cadbury Schweppes had its own PET bottle blow-moulding facility next to its bottling plant. Unilever had gone even further: it had bought 4P, a major plastics converter (which it subsequently divested in 1991.)

Health and beauty segments

Packaging was about 10–20% of the fillers' total sales. For beauty products (cosmetics, lotions, etc.) product appearance was by far the most important purchase criterion. In pharmaceuticals, however, more generic plastic or glass containers were used as a low-cost option.

The health and beauty industries were both highly concentrated, with the top 10 companies (such as L'Oréal, Procter and Gamble, Estée Lauder and Ciba Geigy) accounting for more than 50% of the market share.

Integration of packaging varied in the health and beauty industries. Most often, packages were bought from the package makers and then filled in-house. Alternatively, the manufacturers subcontracted the filling and packaging to a specialist. For example, for aerosols, which had a complex technology requiring heavy capital investments, the manufacturing of the aerosol can and the filling took place in the same plant.

Industrial segments

Industrial packaging covered a whole range of industries such as paints, lubricants, chemicals, construction equipment, household cleaning products, bulk food items, and tobacco. The majority of these markets were looking, first, for inexpensive packaging materials to improve the product's price competitiveness and, secondly, for packaging that would ease logistics and handling. Most of the packaging materials were plastics and paper, although tinplate maintained its share in some niches. Packaging accounted for 4–10% of the manufacturer's total sales.

Secondary and tertiary markets

Packaging companies often disregarded markets beyond their primary concern, i.e., the immediate purchasers of their products. However, retailers and end users were increasingly having more say in packaging matters.

Retailers looked for packages that improved their logistics (simplified handling, longer shelf life, and minimized breakage) and boosted their image (high-quality graphics and environmentally friendly).

Packaging companies were beginning to feel the upstream effects of retail actions. The segment had become more concentrated. For example, the market share of the top 10 buying organizations was 81% in Germany, 66% in the UK and 62% in France. As a result, they demanded lower prices from the manufacturers who, in turn, looked to packaging as a potential cost saver.

About 20–30% of all retail food products in Europe were 'own label'. Thus, many food retailers were also setting up their own packaging design departments and starting to negotiate directly with the converters. For example, Marks and Spencer, a leader in private label branding, had six packaging technologists who researched new packaging designs.

Finally, retailers were in the forefront of the environmental campaign. Many chains had already banned certain materials from their stores. For example, Migros, the giant Swiss food chain, prohibited the use of polystyrene for meat trays.

End users were interested in a package's final function and its marketing appeal. Tetrabriks were found to be an excellent package for handling, but they also had received criticism from consumers because the contents tended to spill after being opened. Buyers did exert a powerful yet indirect influence on the packaging industry by expressing preferences for certain types of products. For example, in the food industry, overall demand grew at a modest 1–2% per year, but the demand for convenience and snack foods was growing rapidly.

Business activities in the packaging industry

In the following sections, a description is given of the business activities required to get the packaging product to market: research and development, raw material supply, manufacturing/converting, marketing and finally distribution. For each material, plastics, paper, metal and glass, the steps were the same but their relative importance was different.

Plastics

The plastics category of the packaging industry comprised several different elements: research and development, production of plastic pellets, extrusion of the pellets, conversion (into flexible, semi-rigid, or rigid packages), printing and, finally, filling.

Research and development for the converter (packaging company) typically consisted of developing improved printing quality and developing new package types through its close association with package machinery manufacturers. At this time, demand was strong to use environmentally friendly materials such as water-based inks, and processes such as the inclusion of regenerated waste in the extrusion process. Typically, a converter would spend 1% of sales on research and development efforts. Plastics manufacturers, more heavily involved in research and development, were most interested in developing plastics with improved properties such as premium polypropylene containers capable of high temperature sterilization. Research and development in plastics companies tended to range around 7% of their sales.

Raw material supply for the converters consisted of either the plastic granules (or films, if extruded). These supplies accounted for approximately 40–60% of the converter's final sale. Most of the supply came from large multinational chemical companies (such as BP Chemicals, Shell, Exxon, Hoechst, etc.), where packaging accounted for an estimated 29% of their total plastics sales. Industry concentration for each plastic type (polypropylene, polystyrene, polyethylene, and the others) was quite high (Exhibit 1.16). Because capacity expansion was incremental, the plastics industry was faced with a cycle of oversupply, then undersupply – 5–6 years in length. Often plastic suppliers integrated forward into extrusion to ease the capacity problems associated in such a high volume commodity business. Once extruded, the plastic companies had two markets to serve: the end-user market and the converter for further processing. Plastic film could be sold to end-user markets as 'cling film' or 'stretch film' for meat packing or for everyday household use. Otherwise, the film (in various thicknesses) was supplied to the converters directly.

The **manufacturing** of plastic packaging consisted of two separate procedures: primary processing (extrusion of the polymer granules into sheet film) and secondary processing (printing, and converting). Many of the smaller converting companies did not have extrusion facilities and therefore bought film on the open market. Converter companies would then take the plastic film (of various thicknesses and types) and produce either rigid or flexible packaging. Rigid packaging (such as PET bottles or yoghurt tubs) went through such processes as thermoforming, blow-moulding or injection moulding where a final shape was created before being sent to the filler. Flexible packaging (such as pouches, wrappers, sacks, etc.) were printed, and then often crimped or laminated before being sent to the filler. During the filling process, the shape of the package would be created. Out of the total production costs (approximately 30–45% of sales), printing required the largest amount with 45%;

Tinplate	Aluminium	Plastic resins	Pulp
Thyssen	Pechiney*	BASF*	Iggesund
Krupp	Alusuisse*	Atochem*	Enso Gutzeid
British Steel	Alcoa	ICI*	Stora
Usinor	Alcan*	Dow Chemical*	Finnboard
Basse Indre*	Reynolds*	Himont*	Feldmuhle *
Hoogovens*	Others	Hoechst*	Saffa
Otto Wolf		Solvay*	Mayr Meinhof *
Rasselstein	*Integrated forward	BP Chemicals*	Bowater *
Hoesch	into cans and/or	Enichem	ASSI*
	aerosols	DSM	International Paper *
*Integrated forward		Orkem	SCA*
into can making		Exxon*	Cellulose du Pin*
		W.R. Grace*	
		Neste*	*Integrated forward into
		Courtaulds*	corrugated/carton board
		Shell*	
		Mobil*	
		*Integrated forward into film and sheet extrusion	

Exhibit 1.16 *Major raw material suppliers to the packaging industry. General characteristics of each: concentrated, capital intensive and regionally focused*

finishing used 30% and extrusion 20%. Converting was not capital intensive. For example, start-up investments could be as low as $500,000 for a used blow-moulding machine. As a result, many industry players were involved (in France, over 350 companies existed for flexible packaging alone).

Marketing and distribution usually accounted for 5–7% of the converter's sales. These companies tried to provide rapid and complete responses to customer inquiries about prices, design, and delivery times. Typically, the salesforce would be organized by region. Success often depended on the converter's exclusivity with their customers. Plastic converters had to be located fairly close to their customers to provide the maximum service levels (design, pre-press and platemaking).

Paper/board

The paper category of the packaging industry consisted of the following elements: pulp processing, paper and board processing, and further conversion (coating, corrugation, box manufacturing, paper bags, sacks, etc.)

Research and development ranged from developing new grades of paper, more efficient and environmentally friendly processes for both paper and board manufacturing, different coatings for specialty papers, improved printing quality, and, finally, development of new packaging products. Some of the new packaging products in recent years were: the bag-in-box systems for fruit juices and wine, and various forms of aseptic packaging. Research and development costs were usually low – at less than 1% of sales.

Raw material supply consisted of the pulp which was either made from logs unsuitable for other uses or from sawmill waste. Two processes were used to convert hardwoods and softwoods into the different grades of pulp: a mechanical and chemical process. Packaging products usually consisted of the following raw materials:

Category	Chemical	Mechanical	Wastepaper
Cartonboards	medium	high	high
Casemaking	low	medium	high
Wrapping materials	high	low	medium
Cost	highest	medium	lowest

Pulp was sold as a commodity which meant that prices were determined by overall demand, wood supplies, and pulp production capacity. Over-capacity was a cyclical problem due to the incremental character of capacity expansions. Approximately 80% of the world's pulp companies had integrated forward into paper or board manufacturing to try to escape from the fluctuation of world pulp prices and to regulate demand. Often these companies tried to focus on a few downstream products (that relied on the type of pulp that they produced) to reap gains from economies of scale. Typically, raw materials were around 40% of the paper and board manufacturers' costs. (They were less for pulp made from waste.) The pulp and paper industry was highly concentrated: the top 9 players accounted for 95% of the business (Exhibit 1.16).

The *paper and board manufacturing process* was over 1,000 years old. Pulp (which could either be virgin pulp or pulp from waste) was dispersed in water, spread in a uniform layer according to its thickness, and then dried. This process, with the help of modern technology, was performed continuously, with paper travelling at 1500 metres per minute. Capacity utilization was a major concern for the paper and board manufacturers. Break-even volumes ranged from around 80–90% capacity utilization. Total manufacturing costs for a paper and board manufacturer were approximately 42% of its sales. For further processing, paper as a raw material accounted for up to 50% of the converter's sales.

Further processing could consist of coating (for higher quality products) and converting. Some of the conversion processes comprised making corrugated board, carton board, folding cartons and packaging paper. Many of the larger paper and board manufacturers had integrated forward into converting operations. Yet, most of the converting industry remained highly fragmented. For folding cartons alone, a total of 2100 companies were involved with the top 60 companies controlling 45% of the market. (In contrast, only 5–6 companies in Europe were involved in converting machinery manufacturing.) In aseptic cartons, however, the segment was dominated by three players: Tetra Pak, Elopak and PKL. Further processing (depending on the amount) accounted for approximately 20–30% of the converter's total sales.

Marketing and distribution of paper-based packaging depended on the package type. For commodity packaging such as unprinted corrugated board, large plants were constructed to maximize on economies of scale. When printing was required for higher value added items, then smaller, more service-oriented plants were located closer to the customer. Marketing and distribution accounted for 5–7% of the converter's total sales.

Metal

The metal category of the packaging industry consisted of several different elements. First, two metals – aluminium and tinplate – were used in the production of metal packaging materials. Secondly, the packages manufactured – such as aerosols, three- and two-piece cans, aluminium foil, collapsible tubes, drums and metal trays – used vastly different process technologies. However, in general the activities in manufacturing metal packaging comprised raw material supply (tin forging, aluminium smelting), printing and conversion (manufacture of cans, aerosols, etc.) before the filling process.

Research and development in metal packaging consisted of process improvements in the raw material supply, light-weighting, new package developments and print quality improvements. Continuous efforts in reducing the thickness of tinplate and aluminium cans took place as did the amount of tin used in tinplate. The two-piece can, as opposed to the traditional three-piece can, was a significant product breakthrough in the early 1970s. In 1990, American National Can (part of Pechiney) had introduced a new fluted two-piece can that both saved on material costs and gave the product a certain differentiation. Metal packaging manufacturers usually spent approximately 3% of their total sales on research and development.

Raw material supply consisted of tinplate, tin-free steel and aluminium. Tin was produced from a low carbon mild steel which was electrochemically coated with tin. The tinplate was then processed further to achieve the extra protective properties for its downstream packages. Approximately 95% of tinplate went into packaging products.

Aluminium, more expensive but less dense, was derived from bauxite, a mineral containing aluminium oxide. Through an electrolytic process, aluminium ingots were hot-rolled into coils. The coils were then cut and sold to the can manufacturers. Approximately 10% of aluminium was used in packaging products. Often aluminium manufacturers – such as Pechiney, Alcoa, Alcan and Alusuisse – integrated forward into can and foil production (Exhibit 1.16). For a can manufacturer, raw materials accounted for an estimated 50% of the cost. For an aerosol manufacturer, the raw materials accounted for even more.

There were several different **manufacturing processes** for metal packages, depending on the final product. General line containers, two-piece cans, aerosols, and collapsible tubes all required different manufacturing processes. For cans, the manufacturing process represented approximately 30% of the packager's sales. For aerosols, it was approximately 20% of total sales. A minimum investment in metal can manufacturing was around $35 million. As a result, each major country was served by two or three can and aerosol manufacturers.

Printing could take place before or after the package was produced. For cans, as an example, printing could be on paper labels, on plastic labels, or on the metal itself, depending on the market positioning of the package. Less expensive cans often used paper labels (and more recently plastic labels), whereas the printing would be directly on the metal on more up-market cans.

Distribution of metal packages such as cans and aerosols was extremely important, as the distance served would be included in the cost of the packaging. Decisions regarding plant location and plant size were continually made to optimize the transportation costs and economies of scale trade-off. The optimum radius for a can manufacturer was 300–500 km. Marketing and distribution costs accounted for approximately 6% of a metal packaging manufacturer's sales.

Glass

The manufacture of glass bottles, flasks and jars was a continuous process, starting with the supply of raw materials – sand, potash and lime.

Research and development efforts in glass production focused mainly on light-weighting and process improvement (increasing the production speed). One of the greater improvements in glass production occurred in 1968, when the West German glass manufacturer, Heye, developed a process which reduced the weight of a bottle by 30–40%. Often glass manufacturers tried to boost their sales through new glass designs such as black glass or enamel printing. Research and development for a glass producer were less than 1% of sales.

The **raw materials** in glass were silica (60%) and alkali (20%). Silica was found in many forms such as sand, quartz and flint; alkali was typically in potash or soda ash. Many other minerals (20%) were added, depending on the finished product (different metal oxides for colour, magnesium for clarity, etc.) Often pieces of broken glass or cullet were mixed in as well. The **manufacturing process** consisted of melting the mixture into a molten state so that the glass could be shaped into the various products (bottles, jars or flasks). The raw materials, abundant in supply, accounted for approximately 17% of the glass manufacturer's sales, whereas the production process accounted for 57% of sales. The European glass manufacturing industry was highly concentrated, with the top seven companies accounting for approximately 70% of the total production.

Marketing and distribution of glass bottles were large-cost items for the glass manufacturers, at approximately 26% of sales. Glass bottles could either be positioned as mainstream products or as a high value added item. For example, printed glass bottles were often positioned in up-market segments whereas glass bottles with paper labels were more mainstream. With respect to distribution, manufacturers – like those in the metal packaging industry – constantly had to consider the trade-off between economies of scale and transportation costs.

Issues in the packaging industry

Both the diversified and focused packaging companies had to confront issues such as the environment, and the recent spate of mergers and acquisitions.

The environment

Packaging was seen largely as an invisible industry whose products were taken for granted. Yet, with the growing environmental debate in Europe, a new awareness of the industry was taking place. European governments, buoyed by consumer pressure, were busily introducing legislation to curb the amount of packaging materials and to promote its recovery and re-use. For example, the German government had taken bold steps by forcing the industry into recycling 64% (or more) of all packaging materials by the year 1995. The European Commission directives on packaging waste were less severe, but the message was the same: packaging companies had to respond quickly.

For some of the materials – such as paper and glass – the waste recovery and recycling processes were already firmly established. However, with stricter legislation coming on stream, more recycling plants would have to be constructed. Metals and plastics would have a more difficult time. But the producers of coextruded plastics and laminates (where recovery was extremely costly and difficult) would be the most affected. Tetra Pak, for example, recovered its used Tetrabriks, but recycled them for different markets (Exhibit 1.17).

Material	Europe 1990	Germany's recycling targets for household waste 1993	1995
Glass	37%	42%	72%
Tinplate	20%	26%	72%
Aluminium	6%	18%	72%
Paper/board	50%	18%	64%
Plastics	neg.	9%	64%

Source: Case writer's estimates and Duales System Deutschland, 1991.

Exhibit 1.17 *Europe's recycling of each material, 1990 and Germany's targets for 1993 and 1995*

Mergers and acquisitions

The packaging industry in Europe was flooded by mergers and acquisitions because of the European Single Market starting in 1993. In a low growth market, leading companies were trying to gain an edge on market share by acquiring other companies. Some of them were trying to diversify into other packaging materials, whereas others were focusing on their core material. For example, Pechiney, the French aluminium group, a relatively unimportant player in 1987, became the largest packaging company in the world by acquiring American National Can in 1988. The company continued its acquisitions of packaging companies by purchasing Techpack International, the world's largest plastic packager for the cosmetics industry. The merger between the French company, Carnaud, and the British company, Metal Box, created the largest European packaging concern and the third largest packager in the world.

Type of package	Company name	Market share (%)	
Metal cans	CMB	35	22
	Continental Can/VIAG	7	24
	Pechiney	10 Food	39 Beverage
	Crown	1	3
	LMG	3	–
	PLM	–	9
Aerosols	CMB	40	
	Crown	29	
Glass bottles/jars	St. Gobain	22	
	BSN	9	
	Rockware	6	
	United Glass	5	
	Gerresheimer/VIAG	5	
	PLM	5	
	Vetropack	3	
Corrugated board	SCA	9	
	Jefferson Smurfit	6	
	International Paper	5	
	St. Gobain	5	
	ASSI	5	
	Buhrmann-Tetterode	4	
	Stone Container	3	
	PWA/VIAG	3	
Aseptic cartons	Tetra Pak	60	
	Elopak	20	
	PKL	10	
Folding cartons	Many		
Plastic packaging	Many		

Exhibit 1.18 *Market shares in European packaging, 1989*

Competitors in the European packaging industry

Overall, the packaging industry was highly fragmented, with the top nine firms holding 22% of the total market. However, higher degrees of concentration were found in segments based on geography, materials and/or products. (Exhibits 1.18 and 1.19).

In the following sections, major competitors will be described according to background, packaging materials used, packaging products manufactured, markets served, geography covered, level of integration and, finally, apparent strategy. Comparative financial data can be found in Exhibit 1.20.

Pechiney

Pechiney was the third largest aluminium producer in the world. During the 1980s, it was rumoured that the president was interested in acquiring a large packaging operation to provide a secure market for its cyclical primary product, aluminium. Although its packaging subsidiary, Cébal, had made several small acquisitions, it was in 1988 after acquiring American National Can, the leading low-cost producer of food and beverage cans, that Pechiney vaulted into the top spot in packaging worldwide. In 1990, the company continued its acquisition spree by purchasing Techpack International, a maker of high quality plastic packaging for the cosmetics industry. By 1990, packaging accounted for approximately 39% of Pechiney's total sales. (The rest of the group consisted of aluminium, engineered products, and other industrial activities.)

With all its packaging acquisitions, Pechiney could boast that it used all packaging materials (primarily aluminium and plastics), produced a variety of products (both commodity and up-market) mainly for the food, beverage, health and beauty markets, and marketed them around the world:

Percentage of 1990 packaging sales

Materials		Markets		Geography	
Aluminium	69	Food	35	Europe	28
Glass	10	Beverages	55	N.A.	70
Plastics	19	Health/beauty	10	Other	2
Tin	< 1				
Paper	< 1				

Source: Annual Reports and case writer's estimates.

Pechiney's apparent strategy seemed to be one of geographic and material diversification and profit improvement. After the acquisition of Techpack International, it was not clear which direction the company would pursue – specialty plastics or high volume aluminium packaging.

Country	Metal	Glass	Plastics	Paper/board
West Germany	Schmalbach (Continental)	Gerresheimer (VIAG)	*Thermoformed containers*	*Cases*
	Zuchner (CMB)	Oberland (St. Gobain)	Polarcup	Europa Carton
	PLM/Ball (PLM)	Heye Glasfabriken	Uniplast	Sieger
	Gerro/Reynolds (PLM)	Neinburger	Etimex (BP)	Assi
	ANC (Pechiney)	PLM	4P (Unilever)	Holfelder
				Zewawall (VIAG)
	C4 = 90%	**C4 = 78%**	**C4 = 50%**	**C4 = 33%**
			Containers	*Folding cartons*
			Alpha	Copaco
			Raku (PLM)	4P (Unilever)
			Kautex (VIAG)	Edelmann
			Kutenholz	Europa Carton
			C4 = 55%	**C4 + 36%**
			Flexible	*Liquid*
			Fragmented	Tetra Pak
				PKL
				Elopak
				C4 = 100%

Exhibit 1.19 Leading packaging suppliers in Western Europe in all types of packaging (in order of size) (continued overleaf)

Country	Metal	Glass	Plastics	Paperboard
France	*Cans* CMB Cébal (Pechiney) Ferembal Massilly Safet **C4 = 80%** *Aerosols* Boxal (Alusuisse) Cébal (Pechiney) CMB **C4 = 90%** *Flexible aluminium* Cébal (Pechiney) VAW (VIAG) Morin (Alusuisse) **C4 = 30%**	Saint Gobain BSN Pochet Corning **C2 = 85%**	*Plastics* Monoplast BSN CMB Cope Allman Cébal (Pechiney) Van Leer Nord Est Lin Pac Allibert **C4 = 9%**	*Corrugated* SOCAR (St. Gobain) OTOR Giepac Rochette **C4 = 47%** *Cartonboard* Cascades Beghin Say (Feldmeuhle) International Paper **C4 = 100%** *Folding cartons* **Highly fragmented** *Liquid* Tetra Pak PKL **C4 + 100%**

UK

Cans
ANC (Pechiney)
Continental
Crown
Metal Box (CMB)
Lawson Mardon

C4 = 90%

Aerosols
Metal Box (CMB)
Crown Cork

C4 = 80%

Flexible aluminium
Alcan
Alusuisse

United Glass
Rockware Glass
Redfearn (PLM)
Beatson Clarkson

C4 = 94%

Courtaulds
Borden
BXL (BP)
Fibrenyle (LMG)
CMB
Rockware
Smith Bros (LMG)

Redfern (PLM)
Reedpack
Bowater

Fragmented

Corrugated board
Reedpack
D.S. Smith
UK Corrugated
Lin Pac

C4 = 60%

Cartonboard
Lawson Mardon
Reedpack
Waddington
Thames Board

C4 = 40%

Folding cartons
250 manufacturers

Paper sacks
DRG
Lin Pac
Bowater

C4 = 20%

Source: C4 = Combined market share of the top four companies in the segment. *Euromonitor 1989, Keynote 1988,* and casewriter's estimates.

Exhibit 1.19 *Continued*

Sales	1989	1990
Pechiney (France)	5,812	5,397
CMB (France)	3,875	4,439
Tetra Pak (Sweden)	3,732	4,376
VIAG (Germany)	1,863	3,795
St. Gobain (France)	2,431	2,508
SCA (Sweden)	858	1,264
BSN (France)	1,010	1,068
PLM (Sweden)	997	949
Lawson Mardon (Canada)	760	870

Note: Average exchange rates used against the US dollar: FF/USD = 5.5; DM/USD = 1.61; Can$/USD = 1.155; SKR/USD = 6.17; SFr/USD = 1.42

Pechiney (in million of FF)		
Total sales	88,472	76,869
Group income	4,221	5,638
R&D (Group)/sales	1%	1%
Packaging sales	31,968	29,686
Operating results	2,370	2,285
Total packaging assets	17,714	17,273
Capital expenditures	755	1,802
Employees	25,800	25,366

CMB (in millions of FF)		
Sales	21,316	24,415
Operating profit	2,084	2,333
of which steel	114	289
Financial charges	553	726
Profit before tax	1,531	1,607
Tax and extraordinary items	399	579
Net income	1,132	1,028
Total assets	25,530	26,810
Capital expenditures	1,768	1,803
Employees	36,616	33,948

Tetra Pak (in millions of Skr)		
Sales (estimates)	23,000	27,000
Net income (estimates)	n/a	4,000
Employees	n/a	11,000

VIAG (in millions of DM) (excluding CCE)		
Total sales	10,434	19,423
Net income	265	336
Aluminium segment (VAW)		
Sales	5,689	5,778
Employees	17,880	18,152
Glass Segment (Gerresheimer)		
Sales	987	1,193
Employees	5,065	5,708

Exhibit 1.20 *Financial data on the competitors (in millions of US$)*

Sales	1989	1990
St. Gobain (in millions of FF)		
Group sales	66,093	69,076
Group net income	4,311	3,359
Research and development	2%	2%
Glass container division		
Sales	9,198	9,821
Operating income	1,403	1,581
Net income	656	730
Capital expenditure	1,179	867
Employees	13,217	12,917
Paper-Wood Division		
Sales	9,710	9,236
of which packaging	43%	43%
Operating Income	995	789
Net income	382	244
Capital expenditures	540	1,060
Employees	10,482	10,060
SCA (in millions of SKr)		
Total sales	24,853	31,122
Net income	1,734	1,506
Packaging sales	5,292	7,799
Operating profit	573	585
Capital expenditures	416	632
Assets	n/a	15,625
Employees	4,064	9,236
BSN (in millions of FF)		
Total sales	48,669	52,897
Net income	2,698	3,091
Research and development	0.6%	0.7%
Packaging sales	5,557	5,877
Operating income	620	720
Capital expenditures	550	517
Employees	7,264	7,488
PLM (in millions of Skr)		
Sales	6,152	5,856
Operating results	771	835
Depreciation	336	330
Financial expenses	125	121
Earnings before tax	310	384
Tax and extraordinary items	42	191
Net income	268	193
Capital expenditures	2,403	1,583
Total assets	4,886	4,485
Employees	7,954	6,342

Exhibit 1.20 *Continued*

Sales	1989	1990
Lawson Mardon (in millions of C$)		
Total sales	989	1,134
Net income	68	78
Employees	7,500	7,800
Packaging sales	878	1,005
Net income	61	71

Exhibit 1.20 *Continued*

CMB

CMB was Europe's largest and the world's third largest packaging company. It was created from the merger of the packaging interests of the Metal Box Group with Groupe Carnaud in March 1989. The merger leveraged the partner companies' geographic strengths: MB Group was active in the UK, Italy, Spain, and Greece, while Carnaud's main markets were France, West Germany, Belgium, Portugal and Turkey.

CMB had an unusual organization structure – shaped like an inverted pyramid. In this structure, the customer stood at the top of the hierarchy; directly below were CMB's 85 local business units which were clustered into material and geographical groups. At the bottom – the tip of the triangle – were group management and the shareholders. With the recent departure of its innovative CEO, Jean-Marie Descarpenteries, this organizational structure was, however, likely to disappear.

CMB used all packaging materials except glass in a variety of different products such as cans, aerosols, cartons, closures, and so on. The majority of the company's sales were in the food and beverage industry in Europe:

Percentage of 1990 sales

Materials		*Products*		*Markets*		*Geography*	
Metal	70	Beverage cans	10	Food	53	France	26
Plastics	20	Food cans	53	Beverage	15	UK	30
Composites	5	Aerosols	4	Health/beauty	10	Italy	9
Other	5	Metal Closures	5	Industrial	20	Spain	8
		Plastic tubes	8			Germany	8
		Flexible				Benelux	5
		General line	20			Greece	2
		Folding cartons				Africa/Middle East	5
						N.A.	4
						Asia	4

Source: Annual Report.

Carnaud, which had originated as a steel producer, continued its tinplate production operations until it was sold off in 1991. Since then, the company had no longer been vertically integrated and had concentrated solely on packaging.

The company's apparent strategy was to attain a 10% market share of the European packaging market. It mainly used two materials – metal and plastics, but would probably move into a third one – paper/board even more heavily.

Tetra Pak

Tetra Pak, the fourth largest European packaging company, had originated in Sweden when it was founded by Ruben Rausing in 1951. Still in family hands, Tetra Pak had not diversified into other packaging materials as other European packaging companies had done.

Unlike other packaging companies Tetra Pak produced only one type of product for one market. It laminated paper, aluminium and plastics together to produce its aseptic material before manufacturing cartons ('briks', and tetrahedrons) of less than 1 litre in size. The company concentrated solely on the beverage and liquid food markets on a global scale:

Percentage of 1990 sales

Geography	
Europe	54
N.A.	12
Africa	5
Asia	26
Oceania	3

Tetra Pak was also unique in its approach to packaging. Unlike many of its competitors, the company was fully integrated into manufacturing the packaging material, transporting it, developing the filling and packaging machinery, as well as operating the filling plants. Its latest move, the acquisition of Alfa Laval – a world leader in the manufacture of dairy and food processing equipment, suggested that Tetra Pak was ready to expand beyond the liquid food and beverage packaging markets.

VIAG

VIAG was a conglomerate with interests not only in packaging but also in energy, aluminium and chemicals. Originally the majority shareholding of the company had been held by the German government; then in May 1988 it was privatized. Since that time, the company had made a number of acquisitions, many of which were in the packaging industry. By 1991, VIAG had majority or minority stakes directly or indirectly in the following companies:

- VAW: the largest German aluminium manufacturer vertically integrated into flexible packaging (of which 13% of sales was for packaging)
- PWA: a large pulp and paper company vertically integrated into corrugated board manufacturing in Germany
- Gerresheimer Glass: a major German manufacturer of glass containers
- Gloeckner and Co.: which had a number of packaging interests in plastics
- Continental Can Europe (CCE): the conglomerate's most recent acquisition, a leading European manufacturer of cans for both food and beverages (a valuable source of supply for VAW's aluminium).

As a result of these acquisitions, approximately 30% of VIAG's total sales were in packaging. The industrial holding group could boast it used all packaging materials, for virtually all types of packaging products in a variety of markets, mainly in Germany:

Percentage of 1990 packaging sales

Materials		Geography	
Metal	50	Germany	69
Plastics	25	Europe	30
Paper	11	Other	1
Glass	14		

Source: Annual Report and case writer's estimates.

VIAG's apparent strategy was to get ready for the single European market. Based on its past record, the company's acquisition drive was probably not finished. More acquisitions in the paper industry could be an option to even out the materials balance. The company had yet to integrate its packaging interests into one division despite the fact that packaging accounted for about 27% of its sales.

St. Gobain

St. Gobain was a world leader in materials engineering, mainly in the area of ceramics and glass. In 1990, the company was the leading European player in flat glass production, insulation, industrial ceramics, fibre reinforcements, glass containers, and iron pipes. The company also had interests in building materials, paper and paper packaging. The organization of the group was largely decentralized by activity sector and by geographical area. No one sector dominated; packaging – including glass containers and paper packaging – accounted for 17% of total sales.

St. Gobain dominated the European market for glass packaging for both food and for health and beauty products, whereas it focused mainly on France with its paper packaging. In paper packaging, the company was integrated backwards into pulp production from both virgin fibre and waste paper. The company, at one time, had diversified into plastic packaging, only to divest its interests in 1986 and 1987. Since the divestment, the company had recentred its focus on glass packaging by acquiring minority or majority stakes in several other firms: Oberland Glass in Germany, Vetri in Italy, Vicasa in Spain and Vidraria do Mondego in Portugal.

The majority of the products produced were bottles (for the wine and mineral water industries), flasks (for the health and beauty sector) and jars (for food). Paper packaging consisted of paper sacks (for industrial use and for shopping bags) and corrugated cases (for a wide range of uses:)

Percentage of 1990 packaging sales

Materials		Products		Markets		Geography	
Glass	74	*Paper*:		*Paper*:		*Paper*:	
Paper	26	Paper sacks	25	Various	27	France	88
Plastics (divested)		Corr. board	75	*Glass*:		Europe	12
		Glass:		Food	13	*Glass*:	
		Bottles	56	Health/beauty	18	France	54
		Flasks	32	Beverage	42	Europe	35
		Jars	17			Other	11
		Other	5			*Combined*:	
						France	63
						Europe	29
						Other	8

Source: Annual Report and case writer's estimates.

St. Gobain's apparent strategy was to maintain its leadership position in glass manufacturing, possibly by searching for more acquisition targets (such as in the UK or Eastern Europe). Through its Paper–Wood Division, St. Gobain was cautiously moving forward by expanding internally and acquiring externally. The likelihood of diversifying into another material was very small.

SCA/Reedpack

Within two decades, Svenska Cellulosa Aktiebolaget (SCA) had transformed itself from a pulp producer for the Swedish market to a major European forest products group with downstream operations in graphic paper, hygiene, healthcare and packaging. In 1990, it acquired Reedpack of the UK, a major producer of corrugated board, printed cartons, and plastic containers. SCA subsequently sold off its printed cartons and plastics divisions, but held onto the corrugated board. With the Reedpack acquisition, the company became a leader in corrugated board in Europe with 9% market share (ahead of Jefferson Smurfit and St. Gobain).

Packaging accounted for 24% of total sales and 19% of its operating profits. The division relied heavily on its internal sales of raw materials. The level of integration (reliance on internal raw materials) had increased from 31% in 1989 to 48% in 1990. The division defined its market as transport packaging (which consisted mainly of food and other products). Sales were spread evenly throughout Europe:

Percentage of 1990 packaging sales

Materials		Products	Markets	Geography	
Paper	100	Corrugated board	Various	Benelux	20
				France	14
				Italy	17
				Sweden	15
				UK	19
				Denmark	15

Source: Annual Report and case writer's estimates.

Vertical integration was one of the cornerstones of SCA's corporate strategy. Downstream products such as hygiene, packaging and graphic paper all relied on its upstream operations in forest and timber, pulp production, energy and waste paper. In the packaging division, the company was likely to continue its focus on corrugated board, looking for potential acquisition targets in Germany and Spain.

BSN

BSN was formed in 1966 by the merger of two French glass manufacturers, Boussois (flat glass) and Souchon Neuvesel (containers). Although originally a packaging company, BSN redirected its focus in the early 1970s towards the food industry. By 1990, BSN claimed to be the world's leading supplier of dairy products and mineral water, the second largest brewer and pasta manufacturer in Europe, the third largest biscuits and champagne manufacturer, while maintaining a leading position in the European packaging industry. The group was organized into six divisions: dairy products, groceries, biscuits, beer, champagne, and mineral water and containers. Packaging accounted for 11.5% of sales in 1990, down from 17.5% in 1984.

Approximately 20% of BSN's packaging output was directly used for BSN's products (mainly beer, mineral water and champagne), but this figure had been declining over the years. BSN used glass, plastics and metal as its packaging materials for bottles, flasks, plastic containers and closures. Its markets were mainly beverage, food, and health and beauty care for France and the rest of Europe:

Percentage of 1990 packaging sales

Materials		Products		Markets		Geography	
Glass	86	Bottles	76	Beverages	75	France	53
Plastics	10	Flasks	9	Health/beauty	9	Europe	46
Metal	4	Plastic cont.	9	Food	16	Other	1
		Others (closures)	6				

Source: Annual Report and case writer's estimates.

BSN's apparent strategy for its packaging division seemed to be to maintain the existing operations. The focus of the company was still on food operations rather than packaging.

PLM

Since 1960, PLM had transformed itself from a medium-sized packaging company serving the Swedish market to a major European diversified packaging player. PLM manufactured metal, glass and plastic containers in 13 plants spread across Sweden, Denmark, the Netherlands, the UK, Germany and, most recently, France.

In 1986, PLM management replaced its geographic divisions with four product/service divisions: beverage cans, food cans, glass and plastics. The company used two main materials: metal (both tinplate and aluminium) and glass. It also had interests in plastics, yet this division had performed consistently poorly with respect to the others. As a result, the company had divested a few of its plastics companies, thus reducing its share of sales from 17% in 1988 to just 7% in 1990. The company focused mainly on the beverage market throughout Europe. It served such customers as Coca-Cola, Pepsi-Cola, Cadbury-Schweppes, Heineken and Carlsberg:

Percentage of 1990 sales

Materials		Products		Markets		Geography	
Metal	54	Beverage cans	38	Beverage	75	*Beverage Cans*:	
Glass	39	Food cans	15	Food	21	Europe	
Plastics	7	Bottles	32	Health/beauty	4	*Glass*:	
		Flasks	3			Europe	
		Jars	5			*Food Cans*:	
		Plastic cont.	7			Scandinavia	
						Plastics:	
						Scandinavia	
						Combined:	
						Scandin.	51
						Holland	9
						UK	12
						Germany	29

Source: Annual Report and case writer's estimates.

The company's apparent strategy, as laid out in the annual report, was to focus squarely on becoming the European leader in beverage packaging (using all three materials). PLM would continue to search the continent for acquisition targets that would contribute to this goal or would set up greenfield plants where necessary. It had already constructed an aluminium beverage can plant in Southern France to serve the Mediterranean markets.

Lawson Mardon Group

The Lawson Mardon Group was formed in 1985 when BAT Industries, the British food/tobacco conglomerate, sold its packaging division, Mardon International, to its

Canadian subsidiary, Lawson and Jones. The renamed company, Lawson Mardon, was organized into five divisions based partly on product and partly on geography: Flexible Packaging Europe, Rigid Plastics and Metals Worldwide, Folding Cartons Europe, Packaging North America and Graphics North America. Approximately 88% of its sales were in packaging, the rest in printing.

The majority of Lawson Mardon's sales were in Europe. The group specialized mainly in niche segments, using plastics, metals and paper for the production of flexible packaging, folding cartons (mainly for cigarettes), labels, food cans, plastic containers and decorated tin boxes. The main markets served were food, beverages, tobacco and health/beauty care. Lawson Mardon was considered one of the more innovative companies, especially in flexible packaging where it was in the forefront of controlled atmosphere packaging, PVC shrink sleeves and bag-in-box technologies:

Percentage of 1990 packaging sales

Materials		Products		Geography	
Metal	10	Flexible	40	Europe	85
Plastics	14	Cartons	39	N.A.	15
Paper	39	Plastic bottles	14		
Composites	40	Metal cans Metal containers }	10		

Source: Annual Report and case writer's estimates.

The company's apparent strategy was to continue focusing on high value added packaging, using state-of-the-art technologies in printing and converting equipment. Flexible packaging was likely to become its core material as that was by far its fastest growing area.

2

Generic strategies

Case 2.1 Ecco: Swiss temporary employment industry

This case was prepared by Professor Z. Jan Kubes as a basis for class discussion rather than to illustrate either effective or ineffective handling of an administrative situation. Background material comes from industry sources and the work of Juergen Fischer, Marion Grimmer, Nicholas Obolensky, Dejan Tadic, Ernst Urschitz, IMEDE MBA participants 1988.

The Swiss temporary employment industry in 1987: overview

Definition

In 1987, the Swiss temporary employment industry included both temporary placement of a worker and, to a much lesser extent, stable or permanent placement. In temporary placement, the worker was paid by the employment agency and, in effect, remained an employee of the agency. The client was charged 100%, the worker was paid 73% and the agency kept 27%, which included about 8% operating profit. The permanent placement of a worker, where the worker became a full-time employee of the client served, constituted a much lower proportion of a typical company's turnover than temporary placement did. (Exhibit 2.2 shows that on average the five largest players had only 14% of their sales in permanent placement.) Permanent placement was undertaken due to the natural synergies and because it was highly profitable (about 50% profit before interest and taxes to sales).

Size

The total turnover for Swiss temporary employment in 1987 was estimated to be SFr700 million, a dramatic growth from

SFr325 million in 1983. The importance of temporary work in the total employment market was small, however, with only about 1% of the working population being temporary workers. In 1987, the Swiss labour market had dried up. Despite the small amount of temporary work, a recent survey suggested that there was potential for further growth, as 18% of the workers surveyed said that they might be temporary workers at some time; 6% had already been temporary workers.

Segments

The four main segments served by the industry were Construction, Industry, Commerce and Service. (Exhibit 2.1 shows the evolution of the turnover in each segment.) Although Industry was the largest, its growth had recently been slowing. Meanwhile, growth in the Service segment had been dramatic.

	1983	1984	1985	1986	1987
Industry	87	121	172	199	204
Service	60	75	102	123	166
Construction	58	64	79	88	100
Commerce	30	35	39	45	50

Exhibit 2.1 *Evolution of industry sales by segment, SVUTA members (million SFr)*

Competitors

SVUTA was the official organization representing the companies in the Swiss temporary employment industry. It had strict rules of competition designed as much to maintain peace among its members as to keep the unions representing the full-time work force happy. The rules of competition made aggressive competition illegal; for example, SVUTA members were not allowed to advertise holiday pay bonuses for their temporary workers. In 1987, SVUTA accounted for some SFr520 million of the industry's total of SFr700 million. However, it only accounted for 44 companies out of

	Adia	Manpower	Ideal	Ecco	Bis
Turnover	178	173	59	42.9	35
Temporary sales	165	130	48	40.9	30
Permanent sales	13	43	11	2	5
% temp sales	93%	75%	81%	95%	86%
No. of agencies	43	34	18	7	8
Hrs sold (million)	6.5	5.5	1.8	1.41	1.25
Full-time workforce equivalent	3870	3273	1070	839	744
Growth 1987	16%	11%	34%	5%	22%

Exhibit 2.2 *Details of some main Swiss competitors, 1987*

an estimated 344. (A more detailed look at SVUTA competitors follows later). The barriers to entering the industry were low (only SFr25,000), with 15 temporary workers (temps) a year per counsellor to break even. While many 'one-man show' businesses entered the market, many of these also left due to an inability to manage the receivables (60 days of sales industrial average), failure to keep up high service levels for their clients and to build a loyal temp base.

Future outlook

The industry was facing an uncertain future. The SVUTA rules of competition were becoming fragile in an increasingly competitive environment. (Manpower, for example, was willing to pay a SFr3000 fine for advertising additional benefits for its temps). Meanwhile, future demographic trends were not likely to improve the already dried-up market. The industry was also susceptible to GNP fluctuation, with a 1% decrease depressing the industry turnover by 10%, as seen in the 1981–82 downturn (an upturn in GNP would have a similar effect in increasing the industry turnover). New legislation proposed in Switzerland threatened the future flexibility of the industry by increasing the notice time to be given to workers from two days to one month. However, it was hoped that this would not apply to SVUTA members.

The business system: temporary workers, agencies, clients

Temporary workers

The average temporary worker in Switzerland in 1987 was under 25 years old, worked 15 weeks a year and signed up with three temporary employment agencies. 57% were male. 48% took on temp work as a transition either between two jobs, military service or travel. Only 19% did temp work because of the freedom and flexibility it afforded. A *first-round temp* would look for fast placement, good pay and the agency's image. He was also fickle and typically would sign up with three temporary employment companies. On the other hand, a *regular temp* valued the personal relationship with the agency's counsellor, effective administration of the agency (in terms of correct pay, etc.) and the quality of the job offered. The regular temp was more loyal and tended to stick with one agency and one counsellor. As outlined above, Swiss temps were a scarce resource but, surprisingly, competing to attract them was not as compelling as, for example, in England or France. This was partly due to the Swiss market not being as mature as the rest of Europe and the fact that, although changing, some stigma was still attached to the concept of temporary work.

Agencies

Agencies accounted for 27% of the value added as follows: temporary selection and testing 2%; staff training 1%; matching temps to client 3%; administration 7%; marketing 6%; profit before interest and taxes to sales 8%. The three key functions were human resource management, marketing and administration.

Human resource management (HRM) was a key to success. Staff not giving personal service could damage an agency's image and thus cause it to lose business. HRM in the Swiss industry in terms of incentive schemes for temps and internal staff, as well as training, was weak by European standards. Only Manpower offered tangible extra perks to its temps and spent more than the average 1% on staff training. The general lack of motivating schemes in the industry explained the high degree of staff turnover; for example, one of the leading companies had a 100% turnover per year in its counsellor staff. Average staff turnover in the industry was around 45% a year. This turnover was not due to movement within the industry or to employees setting up their own businesses. Unless the employee was actually fired, it was forbidden to join the competition or set up a business within two years after leaving a company. Such a high turnover directly affected any personal relationship a client could have with an agency. Even compensation schemes played a central part. For example, some companies that did not manage their staff tended to 'oversell', providing temps who did not meet their clients' needs. The poor HRM of the major companies enabled small players to participate, attracting business by offering more personal, cheerful and caring service.

Marketing was another key activity for an agency. Marketing targeted at temps, clients and internal staff ranged from direct ads and image ads to gifts and public relations events. Yet, there were still some misconceptions in the Swiss market: 53% of the population thought that temp work was for manual labour only; 79% thought that a temp salary would be lower than the permanent counterpart (on the contrary!); 34% thought the agencies were a 'rip-off'. The agency's location was becoming a more important marketing tool with the increasing changes in the Swiss conservative attitude to temp work, and competitors were beginning to look for 'shop-front' locations. In England and France, for example, the location was considered as vital as in the 'fast-food' business.

Administration between front office operations and back office accounting was important. Orders could be lost due to poor invoicing and temps lost because of mistakes in pay. The level of sophistication (with the possible exception of Manpower) was relatively low, and most administrative tasks were done manually with little if any computerisation.

Financial size of the agencies differed. In 1987, the average amount of turnover for SVUTA members per agency per year was around SFr2.1 million. Non-members of SVUTA averaged SFr0.5 million, while larger players like Adia and Manpower averaged SFr3.8 million.

Clients

Two-thirds of the clients in 1987 were companies with over 50 employees. They valued the quality of the temp worker placed and the speed of response more than anything else. However, the personal service provided by the agency was also an order-winning criterion. Price was less important, although it also played a part. Reasons for ordering a temp were: flexibility, seasonal requirements, sudden increase of business, illness and holiday substitutes. Further, there was an increasing tendency to test possible future permanent employees using the 'try and hire' system. With this scheme, the worker was placed as a temp for three months and, if all went well, would then move into the job full time.

Companies found 60% of their temps directly, either through friends and families of employees or by hiring former employees for a short time. Clients normally had a list of three agencies they would use. If the client could not find a temp independently, the preferred company would be contacted first. Then, if the first company could not fill the order, the other two were called.

The competitors and typical company evolution

Svuta

As shown above, SVUTA, the official Swiss temporary employment organization, consisted of the largest 44 companies. In 1987 these companies generated a turnover of SFr520 million (temporary sales only), but five agencies alone accounted for SFr414 million. (Statistics for these five are given in Exhibit 2.3.)

The major five

The five major competitors, listed by size of turnover, were: Adia, Manpower, Ideal, Ecco and BIS. Each had a different mix of segments served (see Exhibit 2.3); Ecco was not available.

	Service	*Commerce*	*Constr.*	*Industry*
Adia	28	10	12	50
Manpower	30	11	19	40
Ideal	30	7	33	29
Bis	50	10	20	20
SVUTA average	31	9	19	39

Exhibit 2.3 *1987 Segments served (% of total temp sales)*

- *Adia* was following an aggressive acquisition policy and, in 1987, had recently overtaken Manpower as Number 1. The newly acquired companies, although strongly and centrally controlled, maintained their own original names. This gave Adia the advantage of being able to offer high quality service as a major player while closing offices in a downturn with no damage to its name. Adia had strong central controls. Sometimes Adia lost sales due to an over aggressive staff that was being paid on a commission basis. Adia was the only player to cover the whole of Switzerland, including Ticino (the Italian area).
- *Manpower* was traditionally the market leader, with probably the strongest market awareness. Manpower agencies were centrally controlled and used computerized cheques, which led to a perception that the service was not as personal as some of its competitors. Its clients also had to deal with more than one counsellor when a variety of skills were being considered. On the other hand, Manpower was very efficient and respected. They were also advanced in offering training to temps.
- *Ideal* was the newest large player, recently overtaking ECCO as Number 3. Previously, according to SVUTA, the agency had been accused of market share stealing using unfair methods. In 1987, such tactics were no longer evident, However, the company still had an aggressive marketing policy, and it was positioned well with a grasshopper logo and a sporty image. Its growth over the last five years was impressive, having the highest growth of the top five companies in 1987. It used modern, open plan, visible locations with small staffs.

- *Ecco* was originally set up by ECCO France (Number 1 in France in 1987). The majority of shares then passed to a Swiss shareholder, who ran the company in a centralised, patriarchal and rather secretive manner. Under this leadership, the company became an efficient but small 'cash machine'. In 1987, ECCO France bought the company back and appointed a new managing director who was to ensure 'growth with profits'.
- *Bis* was a lead competitor in France. In Switzerland, the company was positioned with a differentiated strategy, i.e., providing highly skilled temps such as computer workers with Bis Informatique. As of 1987, it was still unclear which way Bis would move – a specialised niche player or a more general competitor.

Company evolution

The evolution of a typical temporary employment company had four stages. In the first stage, the company would serve a specialized niche in a small area. As it grew, it would begin to serve more segments in the area, thus reaching the second stage. It would move into the third stage as it began serving all segments on a wider geographic basis. Finally, the company would become a national player with full coverage and segments served. In this last stage, the company could choose either a highly centralized approach (as used by Adia and Manpower) or be a decentralized company (as found elsewhere in Europe). With either system, it was important that all the management systems, HRM and marketing policies be consistent throughout the organization. The main danger in growing companies was losing the attributes of a smaller company (such as personalized service), thus becoming vulnerable to loss of market share to smaller players.

Part Two
International Business Strategy

Introduction

3 What do we mean by cooperative advantage?
Case 3.1 Turning the tables: Virando à propia mesa
Case 3.2 *Nordwest Zeitung*

These cases were selected for discussion of the following concepts: outsmarting versus out-managing the competition; usefulness of military metaphors; and subcontracting decisions

4 Effective organization
Case 4.1 Aldo Palmeri: Taking charge (A)
Case 4.2 Aldo Palmeri: Taking charge (B)
Case 4.3 Aldo Palmeri: Managing growth (C)

These cases were selected for discussion of the following concepts: network organizations; a different organization; creating a network organization; and concentrating on a strategy

5 The missing link in the solutions business: managing flows through business systems
Case 5.1 Compaq Computer Corporation

This case was selected for discussion of the following concepts: corporate strengths in the marketing of solutions; three major pitfalls in the solution business; and five distinctive competencies to cultivate

6 Global corporate strategies
Case 6.1 Nestlé-Rowntree (A)
Case 6.2 Nestlé-Rowntree (B)
Case 6.3 Edizione Holding SpA (A)
Case 6.4 Edizione Holding SpA (B)
Case 6.5 Edizione Holding SpA (C)
Case 6.6 Jeanneau 1986

These cases were selected for discussion of the following concepts: diversification strategies; distinctive competencies in the diversified corporation; identifying core competencies; building core competencies; and the global business group of the year 2000

Introduction

Overview

In this section we introduce cases for discussing alternative ways of doing business on a global scale. The cases deal mainly with interesting ways of getting organized for global competition.

In their study of corporations doing business around the world Bartlett and Ghosal[1] found that the most important factor influencing the strategic posture of a corporation was the generic way in which they *organized* for worldwide market dominance. Their generic organizational strategies were characterized by typical structures, management systems and corporate cultures.

They classified nine corporations into three groups of similar organizational forms. First, the classical form, which they named *multinational organizations* who decentralized their assets and capabilities to facilitate their subsidiaries' adaptation to specific market conditions. As a result, resources were dispersed and most responsibilities delegated to country managers. Philips, Unilever and ITT were their examples of multinationals which functioned as loose *federations* of country businesses.

Second, the Japanese model, which they named the *global corporation*, was comprised of companies like Matsushita, NEC and Kao, who are characterized by their investments in centralized global-scale factories geared to manufacture standard products under a centralized worldwide market strategy.

Third, the *international corporation*, a group of corporations like General Electric, Procter & Gamble and Ericsson, whose organizational strategy managed to transfer and adapt the core company's know-how to foreign markets. The core maintained influence over the subsidiaries, but to a lesser extent than the global corporation, whereas the subsidiaries were able to adapt products and policies coming from the core, but less than in the case of a multinational corporation.

Bartlett and Ghosal proposed that it was the *transnational corporation* that was able simultaneously to develop global efficiency, adapt to market needs and learn from all markets. The transitional corporation is capable of learning in all the markets in which it is present and of exploiting this knowledge in other markets, by adapting it to the local country conditions, while achieving cost efficiencies on a global scale.

In summary, multinational corporations evolved from trying to adapt themselves to local market conditions; the global corporation evolved from the need to achieve worldwide cost efficiency; and the international corporation was best equipped for transferring knowledge from the centre to its markets.

---

[1] Bartlett, Christopher and Ghosal, Sumantra, *Managing Across Borders: The Transnational Solution*, Harvard Business School Press, 1989.

About the cases

In Part Two of *Cases In International Business Strategy* we take an additional step to those taken by the above-mentioned students of management, as we present cases that can be used to discuss some of the hidden assumptions in 'strategic speak', as well as propose new organizational forms for corporations engaged in selling solutions to customer problems.

We present case studies useful for discussing frameworks for understanding International Business Strategy. Before we present them, we would like to recognize the contributions of Professor Raph Boscheck to the Compaq case; Professors James C. Ellert and J. Peter Killing for their prize-winning Nestlé-Rowntree series; and research associates Michael Birchard, Juliet Burdet Taylor, James Henderson, Robert Howard, Dana G. Hyde, Barbara Robins and Amy W. Webster to different cases. Undoubtedly, we are indebted to many staff members at IMD for their enthusiastic support during the different phases of our research.

The essential forces affecting the corporation and their organizational forms can be discussed with the cases in this section. We found that an internally negotiated strategy allows a company's management and workforce to concentrate on the value-adding activities in their organization, while avoiding unnecessary overhead costs and diluted energy in political fights. As at SEMCO, employees in companies following internally negotiated strategies concentrate on adding value.

An externally negotiated strategy allows a company to concentrate on its distinctive competence while benefiting from efficiencies in other firms which, in turn, concentrate on their distinctive competencies. The specialization choice is based on a complicated blend of motivation, participation, information and technology. Benetton is able to invest in big warehouses and telecommunication technology while its subcontractors do so in labour-intensive activities; the NWZ is able to concentrate on national news editing, printing, and advertising while the local partners concentrate on what they do best, local news editing and newspaper distribution; and IMS' machinists are able to concentrate on improving their skill base and manufacturing processes while management gets the space to pursue a bigger client base.

Building a negotiated strategy is based on Kupia Kumi[2] – the attitude of letting others prosper while we prosper. In fact, successful growth in cooperative networks can only be achieved if all members of the partnership can grow and prosper simultaneously. The reason for this is that the core company has chosen not to compete with them, but rather to concentrate its efforts on specific and complementary economic activities: managing the flows of people, information, goods and money.

The network organization also seems to be an effective answer to the question of how to inject entrepreneurialism into mammoth corporations. We have seen how Lithonia and General Electric are in the process of creating external networks and internally negotiated strategies respectively. We believe that after careful study of a company's industrial environment, some type of network partnership can be developed in its industry – as illustrated by discussing the Compaq case. The advice we offer is: go out and look for potential partnerships that have not yet been created.

For instance, marketing solutions to customer problems does not provide a fundamental answer to competing against low-cost hardware manufacturers. Adding

---

[2] 'Kupia Kumi', a Nicaraguan Misquito Indian expression for 'eat and let all eat'.

new service layers to the core hardware product brings high margins. However, the high-risk nature of the business, and the new market in which the corporation gets involved, changes the basis for profitability. We can't pretend that the exploitation of this additional value added costs nothing. In fact, if exploited to perfection, not one cent of the additional profits generated should go to the hardware vendors; they should all belong to the partners of the service organizations. Thus, if a corporation wants a share of these additional profits, without degenerating into a simple distribution channel of value-adding service subcontractors, a new form of industrial organization needs to be created: the Hammock Organization.

Thus, to remain competitive in the marketing of solutions in the 1990s, a corporation needs to implement a dual market strategy: first, exploit the top of the pyramid by offering solutions that really add value; and, second, face the lowest-cost hardware competitor with low-cost, high-quality, commodity hardware, and compete with them in exploiting the price umbrella created by proprietary top-of-the-range models.

Moreover, the Nestlé-Rowntree cases show that corporate competitiveness is gained by cultivating core businesses. Strategies management must identify which core competencies and supporting technologies are to be cultivated. Corporate management should then spend time nourishing, building, and protecting the people that carry the corporation's distinctive competencies. Furthermore, these people should be placed in core businesses so that synergy can take place, protected from organizational politics.

3

What do we mean by cooperative advantage?

Case 3.1 Turning the tables: Virando à propia mesa

This case was written by Research Associate Barbara Robins, under the supervision of Professor Werner Ketelhöhn, as a basis for class discussion rather than to illustrate either effective or ineffective handling of a business situation.

'This is an experiment in socialism that people must learn from!' wrote an ardent defender of the Brazilian left. 'No!' answered a senator in Brazil's most right-wing magazine. 'This is an example of capitalism at work!' They were discussing SEMCO's management practices in Brazil.

SEMCO, a diversified machinery manufacturing company, had been led by Ricardo Semler (Exhibit 3.1) since 1980 when he was 20 years old. Between 1980 and 1989, SEMCO had grown in size many times over in Brazil, despite some of the harshest economic conditions anywhere (Exhibit 3.2). Semler confirmed that the leap in SEMCO's sales from $4 million in 1980 to $50 million in 1989 (Exhibit 3.3) had brought it from 56th to 4th in the competitive field of mechanical equipment manufacturing, thus attracting the interest of major local and foreign companies. Ricardo Semler became a local celebrity. He explained:

> Representatives from dozens of companies walk through SEMCO's assortment of structures twice a month. The waiting list for a tour is seven months. No one comes to see what we make, though we are quite proud of pumps that can empty oil tankers in a night, dishwashers that clean 20,000 saucers per hour, and mixers that blend everything from rocket fuel to bubble gum. But what people want to see is how we work.

Personal data
Semler was born in June 16, 1959, in São Paulo, Brazil.

Academic background
He was educated in both Brazil and the United States. In 1982, he graduated in law at São Paulo University. Twice turned down from Harvard's AMP for being too young, he was admitted in 1987 and attended the 13-week executive programme at the Harvard Business School.

Semler and SEMCO
Semler started to work at SEMCO during his summer vacations at age 16. He assumed the business direction of the company in 1980 at age 20, and became President of the company at age 22.

Professional activities
Director-President of SEMCO S.A.
Collaborator of Folha de São Paulo (Brazilian newspaper)
  Vice-President of the Federation of Industries of Brazil
  Board member of SOS Atlantic Forest (Brazilian environmental defence organization)
  Author of *Virando à Propia Mesa: Turning the Tables* – a management book which was on Brazil's best-seller list for more than a year.

Other activities
As a teenager, Semler led a Brazilian rock band.

Exhibit 3.1   *Ricardo Semler*

Semler implemented a participatory management style which was developed from three fundamental values: democracy, profit sharing, and information. In Semler's words:

> Our workers have a voice in hiring, firing and promoting their bosses. Some of our managers get to set their own salaries, naming any figure they want, with no catches. And they get it. For big decisions, such as relocating a factory or buying another company, every employee gets a vote – and management abides by the outcome. It sounds, well, too democratic for a corporation, but it works.

What set SEMCO apart from other businesses was the sheer extent to which Semler claimed to apply his participatory management practices in a Latin culture where an authoritarian, patriarchal style was the norm.

Brazilian background

Brazil was comparable in size to the United States, with two-thirds of its land mass covered by the Amazon Rain Forest (Exhibit 3.4). In 1989, a majority of the 147 million Brazilians lived within a few kilometres of the Atlantic coastline, with equatorial beaches stretching for hundreds of miles and the land gently rising to form cool highlands. The North East interior, the only large lowland area and home to 40 million people, was an exhausted land which had experienced cycles of flood and drought since the early 19th century. By contrast, the lush, expansive farming land in the South and South East was the nation's most prosperous region, and often described as the 'tropical Europe'.

65

	1980	1981	1982	1983	1984	1985*	1986	1987	1988	*1989
Current GNP per capita (US$)	2,060	2,030	2,050	1,820	1,700	1,630	1,780	1,910	2,040	2,400
Billions of current Brazilian Cruzados										
GNP	1.20E-2	0.024	0.048	0.110	0.364	1.000	3.000	11.000	83	1,228
GDP at market prices	1.24E-2	0.025	0.051	0.117	0.386	1.000	4.000	12.000	86	1,266
GDP at factor cost	1.12E-2	0.022	0.045	0.105	0.352	1.000	3.000	10.000	78	1,154
Agriculture	1.23E-3	0.002	0.004	0.012	0.040	0.145	0.364	1.000	8	99
Industry	4.90E-3	0.010	0.021	0.046	0.161	0.570	1.000	5.000	34	495
Manufacturing	3.75E-3	0.007	0.016	0.035	0.119	0.425	1.000	3.000	24	342
Services, etc.	5.05E-3	0.010	0.021	0.048	0.151	0.543	1.000	5.000	36	561
Manufacturing Activity (Index 1987 = 100)										
Employment	106.9	92.1	90.9	82.8	87.6	95.5	106.2	100.0	98.1	—
Real earnings per empl.	90.7	103.2	111.6	102.8	95.3	98.7	102.5	100.0	98.6	—
Real output per empl.	80.8	83.8	78.7	91.2	93.3	91.8	91.9	100.0	94.0	—
Monetary holdings (Millions of current Brazilian Cruzados)										
Money supply, broadly defined	2.900	6.300	13.1	36.3	127.0	467.9	—	—	—	—
Money	1.300	2.400	4.0	8.0	24.4	106.1	456.5	1,439.9	—	—
Quasi-Money	1.600	3.900	9.2	28.3	102.6	361.7	—	—	—	—
Government deficit (Billions of current Brazilian Cruzados)										
(−) or Surplus	−3.00E-4	−0.001	−0.001	−0.005	−0.019	−0.154	−0.488	−1.400	−13.200	−204.400
Current revenue	2.80E-3	0.006	0.013	0.030	0.030	0.091	0.363	0.829	4.000	37.100
Current expenditure	2.30E-3	0.005	0.010	0.024	0.078	0.349	1.000	3.000	28.000	506.100
Current budget balance	5.00E-4	0.001	0.003	0.006	0.012	0.014	−0.171	1.000	9.000	633.800
Capital receipts	—	0.000	0.000	0.001	0.001	0.005	0.000	0.027	0.221	31.000
Capital payments	8.00E-4	0.002	0.004	0.012	0.032	0.173	0.317	2.400	22.500	869.100

Foreign trade (Millions of current US dollars)

	1980	1981	1982	1983	1984	1985	*1986	1987	1988	*1989
Value of exports	20,132	23,929	20,173	21,898	26,976	25,594	22,382	26,229	33,759	34,290
Nonfuel primary exp.	12,005	12,650	10,758	11,828	13,705	12,506	10,772	12,079	14,863	14,703
Fuels	358	1,178	1,444	1,158	1,824	1,624	699	946	894	850
Manufactures	7,770	9,465	7,971	8,911	11,447	11,464	10,911	13,203	18,003	18,736
Value of imports	24,949	24,073	21,061	16,784	15,208	14,329	15,555	16,578	16,054	19,173
Non-fuel primary prod.	4,010	3,197	2,646	2,043	2,168	2,116	3,502	2,585	2,136	3,850
Fuels	10,749	12,159	11,276	9,381	8,036	6,766	4,165	5,397	4,836	4,317
Manufactures	10,190	8,716	7,140	5,360	5,005	5,447	7,887	8,595	9,082	11,006

Source: World Tables 1991 – The World Bank.

	1980	1981	1982	1983	1984	1985	*1986	1987	1988	*1989
Exchange rate (NCz/US$)	65.50	127.80	252.67	984.00	3,184	10.49	14.90	72.25	765.3	11.36

Balance of payments (Millions of current US dollars)

	1980	1981	1982	1983	1984	1985	*1986	1987	1988	*1989
Export of goods and services	23,275	26,923	23,469	24,341	30,205	29,309	25,131	28,730	36,823	38,817
Imports of goods and services	36,250	38,873	39,773	31,286	30,334	29,737	30,522	30,250	32,758	38,036
Private current transfers net workers' remittances	127	189	–10	106	161	139	89	113	107	226
Curr. A/C bal. before off. transf.	–12,848	–11,761	–16,314	–6,839	32	–289	–5,302	–1,407	4,172	1,007
Transf. curr. A/C bal. after off.	–12,806	–11,751	–16,312	–6,837	42	–273	–5,304	–1,450	4,159	1,025
Transf. long-term capital, net	6,207	11,647	8,011	7,744	8,080	1,105	–265	–995	451	–3,025
Direct investment	1,544	2,313	2,534	1,137	1,556	1,267	177	1,087	2,794	744
Long-term loans	4,623	8,721	8,005	4,617	5,392	514	135	–847	2,243	–1,992
Other long-term cap.	40	613	–2,528	1,754	1,132	–676	–577	–1,235	–4,586	–1,777
Other capital, net	2,839	657	1,466	–1,493	–3,244	–958	1,941	4,085	–2,972	2,602
Change in reserves	3,706	–553	6,835	586	–4,878	126	3,628	–1,640	–1,638	–602

Exhibit 3.2 *Economic indicators for Brazil (continued overleaf)*

	1980	1981	1982	1983	1984	1985*	1986	1987	1988	*1989
(Billions of US dollars outstanding at end of year)										
External debt total	70.98	80.93	92.90	98.27	105.25	105.97	113.55	123.67	115.67	111.31
Long-term debt	57.43	65.56	75.37	83.91	94.13	96.35	103.87	110.01	104.75	92.73
Short-term debt	13.55	15.37	17.53	14.36	11.13	9.61	9.68	13.66	10.92	18.58
Memo items (Millions of US dollars)										
International reserves excluding gold	5,769.3	6,603.5	3,927.9	4,355.1	11,507.9	10,604.6	5,803.0	6,299.2	6,971.8	7,535.4
Gold holdings at market prices	1,105.9	876.1	69.4	206.4	452.9	1,013.4	950.7	1,177.8	1,118.3	1,193.4

(−)   data not available.

e.g. (2.63E-2)   data with insignificant digits, using units appropriate for the latest year.

*1986   Feb. 1986 the cruzeiro was replaced by the cruzado (Cz) at a rate of 1000:1.

*1989   Jan. 1989 the cruzado was replaced by the new cruzado (Ncz) at a rate of 1000:1.

Source: World Tables 1991 – The World Bank; *International Financial Statistics Yearbook, 1991 – IMF.*

Exhibit 3.2 *Continued*

Year	% of last year	Revenue (thousands)
84	74	US$ 5,797
85	89	US$ 10,972
86	5	US$ 11,527
87	63	US$ 18,825

Source: SEMCO – Cesde Pesquisa e Desenvolvimiento Gerencial, Brazil and the School of Business Administration, The University of Western Ontario, Canada 1989

Exhibit 3.3   *SEMCO: financial information*

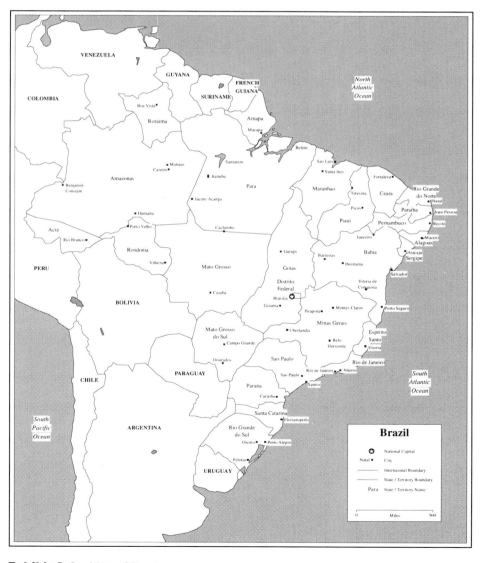

Exhibit 3.4   *Map of Brazil*

	1980	1981	1982	1983	1984	1985	1986	1987	1988	1989
Population (millions)	121	124	127	130	133	136	139	141	144	147
Total fertility rate	4.0	3.9	3.8	3.8	3.7	3.6	3.6	3.5	3.4	3.3
Infant mortality rate	74.2	72.6	71.0	69.4	67.8	66.2	64.6	63.0	61.2	59.3
Life expectancy rate	62.8	63.1	63.4	63.7	64.0	64.3	64.6	64.9	65.3	65.7
Urban population %	66.2	67.2	68.1	69.1	70.0	71.0	71.8	72.6	73.3	74.1
Food production per capita (1987 = 100)	93.3	92.1	95.9	92.7	93.0	99.8	92.5	100.0	103.1	106.3
Labour force fem. %	26.9	27.0	27.0	27.1	27.1	27.2	27.2	27.3	27.3	27.4
Primary sch. enroll. ratio	99.0	–	–	103.1	103.1	101.0	103.0	101.0	104.0	105.0
Secondary sch. enroll. ratio	34.0	–	–	35.0	35.0	36.0	37.0	37.0	38.0	39.0
Illiterate pop. %	–	–	–	–	–	22.2	–	–	–	–

Source: World Tables 1991 – The World Bank.

Exhibit 3.5 *Social indicators for Brazil*

The Brazilian people evolved from waves of migration from Europe and Africa; the Europeans came to find a better world and the Africans were brought as slaves. In 1989 most Brazilians were of mixed race and almost 75% of the population was urban. São Paulo, with a population of 17 million, was described as 'the engine which drives Brazil' because of its prosperous manufacturing sector and incredible wealth. Rio was still one of the world's most glamorous cities, especially during its elaborate carnival time. Brasilia, the capital city, was planned as the first 'interior' city for 600,000 government workers. It was built in a thousand days and inaugurated in 1960 – it has since become a metropolis which supports over 2 million people, many of whom live in suburban shanty towns. However, some of the fastest growing cities were in the Amazon; for example, Vilhena, in the state of Rondônian, doubled its population to one million in the four years prior to 1986.

By 1989, the top 20% of Brazil's population earned more than 65% of the national income; the bottom 20% earned less than 3%. The education budget was split, with 60% being used to provide places, free of charge, to Brazil's 1.5 million university students; the remaining 40% was spent on basic education for 30 million Brazilian children. Over a fifth of the population was estimated to be illiterate, the infant mortality rate was 60 per 1000 births, and life expectancy was 65.7 years (Exhibit 3.5).

Political and economic background

The 1964 military coup heralded a military dictatorship that endured for 20 years. The dictatorship's first objective was to combat inflation, which was showing an annual average increase of over 50%. The measures imposed included the curbing of public sector spending, a severe squeeze on wages, and steps designed to increase exports by allowing market forces freer play. In addition, the government introduced a 'monetary correction' system to help remove some of the uncertainties of inflation. The system, which was a form of indexing, allowed the price of everything – wages, goods, taxes, social security payments, corporate assets, working capital, etc. – to be adjusted in line with inflation on a monthly basis. From 1965–1974, virtually no spread existed between the monetary correction and the annual average inflation rate. Furthermore, in 1968 the government introduced a system of mini devaluations, sometimes called the 'crawling peg system',[1] to reduce the uncertainties of future price movements and the de-stablizing impact of currency realignments (Exhibit 3.6).

For the first decade of military dictatorship, Brazil experienced economic expansion, swift industrialization and a 10% average annual growth of real GDP. Brazilians became masters at living with and profiting from their country's chronic inflation. During the second decade, Brazil's balance-of-payments became the central problem. For example, Brazil's oil import bill jumped 300% as a result of the 1974 oil crisis, which not only increased the current-account deficit, but also accelerated Brazil's borrowing on the international money markets. From 1975–1984, service payments on foreign debt swelled at an average annual rate of 25%.[2]

---

[1] The 'crawling peg system' adjusted the rate of the cruzeiro to specific currencies at frequent intervals.

[2] The annual average increase on service payments was calculated in US dollars.

	1980	1981	1982	1983	1984	1985	*1986	1987	1988	*1989
Inflation (%)	110.2	109.9	99.7	211.0	223.8	225.5	—	366.0	933.6	1,765
Monetary correction (%)	50.8	95.6	97.8	156.6	215.3	227.5	—	331.6	816.1	1,310
Devaluation (%)	54.4	95.1	97.7	289.4	227.5	236.1	—	383.5	947.1	1,401

*1986 Feb. 1986 the cruzeiro was replaced by the cruzado (Cz) at a rate of 1000:1.
*1989 Jan. 1989 the cruzado was replaced by the new cruzado (Ncz) at a rate of 1000:1.
(–) data not available

Source: Brazil in Figures 1990, The Bank of Boston.

Exhibit 3.6 Financial variables (% annual increase)

By the early 1980s, the country's financial situation had worsened. The government had been borrowing more just to meet debt repayments and interest charges, and spending more to make itself less unpopular as democracy approached. The annual inflation increase had grown from 20% in the early 1970s to over 100% in 1980. In the early 1980s, the spread between inflation and the monetary correction system was averaging 16%. In 1982, creditors held back on increased lending and bankers cut their net financing to Brazil by half. Over the next two years, Brazil tried to pay interest out of its own pocket by increasing exports and cutting imports. In 1984, Brazil had a foreign debt of a hundred billion dollars, a sum so large that the nation's trade surplus could barely pay the interest.

In 1984, military rule ended when the armed forces cleared the way for the indirect election of opposition candidate Tancredo Neves. On the eve of his Presidential inauguration, Neves was rushed to hospital with a burst appendix; he died a few weeks later. The vice president, José Sarney, somewhat reluctantly took over. He did little to counter inflation and lost control of the congress, which resulted in unsuccessful government policies and implementation problems. Inflation continued to rise: in 1987 the annual inflation increase was 366%; in 1988 it was 933.6%. In the same year, the government introduced a daily indexing rate.

In 1989, Brazil held the first direct and free elections in 29 years. Voters elected the centre-right candidate, Fernando Collor de Mello.

SEMCO – company background

SEMCO was founded in 1953 by Antonio Semler, who had immigrated from Austria to Brazil and started producing oil–water separators for São Paulo's vegetable oil industry, as well as marine pumps and shafts for the shipyards. During the 1970s, the company's strategy was to market high-quality products using up-to-date technology. In the late 1970s, the Brazilian shipbuilding industry started to decline as a result of the oil crisis, high inflation and an international recession.

In 1980, Ricardo Semler, Antonio Semler's son, assumed the business direction of SEMCO; he became the President of the company in 1982. In 1980, the company employed 100 people and 90% of its sales were concentrated in hydraulic pumps for the shipbuilding industry. Semler reported that SEMCO was close to financial disaster and that it was clear to most managers and board members that the company had to professionalize and diversify. In May 1980, more than 30% of the staff were fired, including the general manager, board members, the production, sales and financial managers.

The next two years, 1981–1982, were difficult for the company. A large amount of energy was spent in efforts to secure loans from banks, searching for contracts, and fighting off rumours that the company was going under.

Acquisitions

Starting in 1980, SEMCO sought licences to manufacture other companies' products in Brazil; by 1982, seven licence agreements had been signed. For example, agreements with companies such as Philadelphia Gear, Ross, Stall, Fluidrive, Bofl & Kirch, Gemco, and Sandvik, provided the company with an opportunity to extend the present product lines and to develop new ones. As a result, the marine division, once the entire company, was down to 60% of total sales.

In 1983, SEMCO acquired Flakt, ASEA's air-conditioning factory in Brazil; Flakt was a world leader in air conditioning and refrigeration for specialized applications such as oil platforms. In the same year, the company acquired Baltimore Air Coil Ltd, a subsidiary of the Merck Group, and Brazil's biggest installer of air conditioners and refrigeration systems. In 1984 SEMCO acquired Hobart Ltd, a traditional Brazilian company which manufactured industrial washing machines, food processors and cold-meat cutters. In 1987, SEMCO made its fourth acquisition – the equipment division of Sandvik. SEMCO also entered into joint-venture arrangements: SEMCO-VICARS, for example, made equipment for producing biscuits.

Semler explained that the acquisition phase 'cost millions of dollars in expenditures and millions more in losses over the next two to three years. All this growth was financed by banks at interest rates that were generally 30% above the rate of inflation, which ranged from 40% to 900% annually. There was no long-term money in Brazil at that time, so all those loans had maximum terms of 90 days.' Semler stated, 'We didn't get one cent in government financing or from incentive agencies either, and we never paid out a dime in graft or bribes.'

Semler introduces change

Semler firmly believed that the traditional 'pyramid' business structure emphasized power, promoted insecurity, distorted communication, and made it difficult for the strategist and those executing that strategy to work in the same direction. Furthermore, he was convinced that the biggest obstacle for implementing a participative management style was created by the managers themselves. With this in mind, he set out to professionalize and diversify the company, and to find a structure with no one between the people who 'do things' and the people who 'sell'. He recalled:

One of my first acts when I took over at SEMCO was to throw out all the policy and procedure manuals. Who needs all those rules? At SEMCO we stay away from rigid formulas and try to keep our minds open and our thinking flexible. Nothing is more difficult to use than common sense.

I started trying things out bit by bit. First I asked: if we let people decide what time they'll come to work, will they still come? They did; so I asked: if they set their own salaries, will they ask for too much? They did not. Then I said, if I get rid of office boys and secretaries, people will stop filing things which don't need to be filed, and they did. The point is, we started treating people like adults and they respected that.

In my view, organizations are meant to create situations and opportunities for people to be satisfied and to benefit the community and the country through results. My mission in SEMCO is to help install a philosophy and a process that encourages and requires people at all levels to participate in the operation and growth of the business. My views are not based on any theory, they are just a natural way to do things.

I think not having a business degree has helped me. In many respects, the business world and some business schools in particular, promote organizational behaviour keened on self defence and protection, both from the owners and employees, rather than in promoting results and innovations.

New management style brought conflict[3]

Semler brought a strong commitment to a participative style of management (Exhibit 3.7). Initially, owners and managers met together once a month to talk about philosophy, style and participative processes. Operational issues were not discussed at all. Strong conflicts arose during the transition. Semler remembered:

> Conflicts helped convert some, others left the company. There were even some attempts to sabotage the participative process. Several Directors and Managers were asked to leave the company and SEMCO provided relocation pay. Some Directors wanted to have separate Director/Manager meetings. When they asked my views I said, 'No, let's do it right!'

1   To transmit to clients, employees, suppliers and all those who have any contact with us the certainty that we are a serious, reliable company having as our constant concern the respect for the regulations that affect our activities and the ethics of our business.

2   To always keep in mind that the profit at long range is more important than taking advantage of opportunities at short range.

3   To manufacture and market goods which are of differentiated quality and recognized reliability at fair and competitive prices.

4   To give the best attendance and attention to the client so as to make him feel sure that we are always sensitive to his needs and that we fulfil commitments undertaken, putting our responsibility ahead of profit.

5   To be a professional company, creating an atmosphere of sincerity, justice and informality, without prejudices and favouritism, where people feel they have recognition, and where everybody participates and is openly proud to work.

6   To stimulate the individual action of the employees in the fulfilment of their duties by the use of their own knowledge and creativeness, with as much freedom as possible so that their performance may be measured mainly by the results and the company may be able to maintain itself ahead of others through innovation.

7   To urge a high degree of participation, contribution and questioning by all concerning everything that involves the company's activities, avoiding to the utmost decisions passed from the top to the bottom.

8   To develop a style of relationship with clients, employees, suppliers, unions and the community at large, where open-mindedness, truth, and sincerity in communication and dialogue are above momentary interests.

9   To always maintain safe and healthy working surroundings for the employees and externally to take steps for the protection of the environment through control of its industrial processes.

10   To recognize that there will always be room for improvement, keeping in mind that these principles require a lot of determination on our part so as to make them reflect the company's conduct.

Source: SEMCO–Cesde Pesquisa e Desenvolvimiento Gerencial, Brazil and the School of Business Administration, The University of Western Ontario, Canada 1989.

Exhibit 3.7   *SEMCO's management principles*

[3]Employee quotes in this section are from SEMCO – Cesde Pesquisa e Desenvolvimiento Gerencial, Brazil, and the School of Business Administration, The University of Western Ontario, Canada 1989.

I remember that when we started encouraging people to increase their participation in the development of operating budgets, hours and hours were spent in some units without agreement. Managers complained about the amount of time wasted. Nevertheless, I continued to urge them to believe in the consensus philosophy.

At SEMCO's new naval equipment plant – the location of which was chosen by the workforce, two former union militants, Demerval Matos and Oseas Santos, confirmed the slow start. 'We had worked under the whip, so we started off being extremely suspicious, but then contacts with management became more collegial,' said Santos.

According to Ricardo Ciliento, the plant manager, participation revolutionized productivity and results despite the voting out of time-clocks and quality control policing. 'We just don't have quality control any more,' said Ciliento, who had worked under the old system. 'It simply isn't needed. But, the new approach is actually a lot more work for me. It was easy just to put a notice on a board, now I have to explain *why* we are doing things and have to change my mind if people don't agree. However, satisfaction comes from results.'

A circular organization

After a lot of trial and error, an organization based on a circle with four concentric job classifications was created. Groups of associates (workers and employees) were led by coordinators (supervisors) who reported to partners (plant managers). Partners, in turn, reported to counsellors (business unit managers) who reported to the CEO. Therefore, the traditional command structure was replaced by a set of negotiated relations between associates, coordinators, partners and counsellors.

Furthermore, in November 1984, Semler replaced the traditional divisions of production, marketing and finance with three new divisions: Capital Goods, Durable Goods and Refrigeration Systems. These three Divisions were further organized into nine Strategic Business Units (SBUs). (Exhibit 3.8). The SBU concept essentially allowed each manager to run his own company while operating within the general policies of the corporation. Each SBU manager was evaluated and rewarded in accordance with the results achieved in his unit. SBU Managers reported to Arno Witte, the Vice-President of Operations.

At the same time, a small Corporate Support Group was set up to include Human Resources under the direction of Clovis Bojikian, and Modernization and Development under the direction of Joao Vendramin Neto.

This organizational form facilitated employment growth from 100 to 800 over a ten-year period. Semler elaborated:

One of the first questions I am asked is, what do the bosses at SEMCO think of all this? Well, we don't have all that many bosses anymore. As workers began to wield more and more power over their jobs and have more influence in the company, the need for bosses diminished. We went from eight management layers to three in just a few years. We've reduced the corporate staff, which provides legal, accounting and marketing expertise to the business units, to just 14. We no longer have data processing, training or personnel departments. We just didn't need them anymore.

To ensure that value-added activities were protected, the following principles were observed. First, the after-tax profit-sharing programme (Exhibit 3.9) sustained workers'

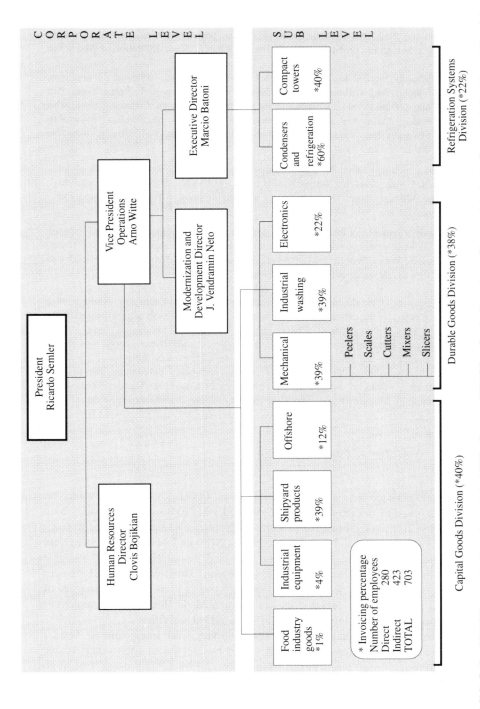

Exhibit 3.8 SEMCO organization chart, July 1987. [Source: SEMCO – Cesde Pesquisa e Desenvolvimiento Gerancial, Brazil, and the School of Business Administration, The University of Western Ontario, Canada, 1989]

Profit-sharing for employees and workers was negotiated at SEMCO in 1987. At the time, less than a handful of Brazil's 1.3 million companies had profit-sharing plans. Many of these were profits handed down by the owners: they decided how much would be distributed each year, and who would get what. SEMCO, instead, spent 18 months bargaining with the Metalworkers Union to achieve a democratic profit-sharing system that it had no legal obligation to give in the first place.

Eventually, the union agreed to 23% of SEMCO's corporate profits after taxes, and after subtraction of dividends and working capital needs; this was equivalent to 1–5 months of extra pay for an average worker. It was distributed twice a year to three worker representatives who were elected to manage the money, and to lead worker assemblies who decided how to spend it. SEMCO's workers understood that, if there were no profits, there would likewise be no profit-sharing. According to Semler:

> Sharing profits increases profits. We want more profits, so we want everyone to think about making a profit. I understand that sharing profits is the result of sharing power, information and knowledge. We cannot motivate people only by a having good working climate. Instead of giving higher salaries, why not share the company's profits with its employees?

In January 1988, a protocol of intentions for a profit-sharing programme was signed between SEMCO, its employees represented by their Plant Commission, the Unions, and DIEESE (Inter-Union Studies and Statistics Department) in the presence of representatives from the Ministry of Labour. The profits would be distributed as follows:

1   A profit-sharing fund would be created at each company unit. Each unit would have a commission elected by the entire staff which would be charged with the administration of the fund.
2   At the end of each semester, after the results had been determined, the enterprise would give each unit a cheque for the amount estimated as the profits from that unit.
3   The criteria for distributing the profits (per person, per salary percentage, per time of employment, etc.) would be defined by the employees at a meeting. The decisions would always be made by a majority – that is, 50% plus one of the employees in the unit.

Source: The company.

Exhibit 3.9   *Profit-sharing program – SEMCOPAR*

motivation levels. Twice a year, 23% of after-tax profits[4] from each SBU's income statement was given to the employees, who decided what to do with the money by a simple majority. To help facilitate the process, all employees attended classes to learn how to read balance sheets and income statements. Second, business units were kept small (150 people) so that close personal ties and familiarity existed amongst employees. Semler was convinced that keeping the units small was a crucial element in the success of the company. Third, the familiar syndrome of having managers of managers and supervisors of supervisors was eliminated. In this way, all employees from counsellors on down contributed to the value-added activities.

Besides changing the relationship between workers and management, Semler changed the way the departments at SEMCO did business with each other. If one department preferred not to buy services from another SEMCO unit, it was free to go outside the company and buy from another company.

---

[4] 23% of SEMCO's corporate profits – after taxes and the subtraction of dividends and working capital needs.

Plant commissions[5]

To provide an additional communication channel between labour and management within SEMCO, the first of several plant commissions was introduced in June 1985. The objective of the Plant Commission was to establish a harmonious working atmosphere, and to improve and maintain good relationships between the employees and the management. Its major responsibility was to represent the basic needs of the employees to management. By late 1986, each Strategic Business Unit had a commission comprised of three factory and one office representative elected by all members of the unit. Each commission member's term in office was 18 months. According to Ozeas dos Santos, a factory representative on the Industrial Products Unit plant commission, it operated as follows:

> Managers as well as employees can raise issues for us to deal with. In the beginning, we were quite nervous. We did not know what we would really do. Now we are more relaxed and feel equal. It has been a learning experience for us; first of all learning how to work as a group. Secondly, we have learned a lot of new business skills. We think as well that management has learned a lot from us. We were able to reduce the working hours from 48 hours per week to 43 – a first for Brazil. We try hard to resolve issues before serious conflicts develop and, if we can't work out the agreements with the unit's management, we go straight to the corporate group. Not everything works. We have had some strikes already. But, we have also enjoyed the experience.

Manufacturing

The elimination of rigid thought and hierarchical structure influenced how products were manufactured at SEMCO because employees had control of activity-based decisions. For example, workers and engineers designed a new layout for the shop floor in order to increase flexibility and productivity. Semler described the set-up:

> We call the set-up our manufacturing cell layout. Rather than ten lathes in a row, as in an assembly line, we'll have a lathe, a drill and a welding machine, all clumped together so that small teams of workers can turn out an entire product, from start to finish. Our workers know how to operate more than one machine and can often set them up and maintain them. They even drive forklift trucks around the floor to keep their clusters supplied with raw materials.

Each cell was self-contained, so that the products, and the problems, were segregated from each other. Employees within each cell coordinated themselves; for example, they set their own hours,[6] production quotas, and deadlines. In the past, cells have worked all night or on weekends to meet their own deadlines. Semler explained:

> Once, our dishwasher plant could not reach its goal because they did not have enough parts. The workers sent a delegation to talk to the workers at the parts manufacturer, and came back with the parts they needed. In several instances, SEMCO employees have actually worked temporarily at a supplier's factory to ensure that their colleagues back home would have the materials they needed.

---

[5] Employee quotes in this section are from SEMCO – Cesde Pesquisa e Desenvolvimiento Gerencial, Brazil, and the School of Business Administration, The University of Western Ontario, Canada, 1989.
[6] Employees introduced factory-floor flexitime.

Performance evaluations

Semler introduced a subordinate evaluation programme in which each subordinate evaluated his immediate supervisor anonymously. The programme was designed to keep supervision to a minimum but, at the same time, make accountability as meaningful as possible. The objective was to provide feedback from subordinates to supervisors that could be used in making changes in style, attitude and behaviour, and to improve performance.

Twice a year, each subordinate filled out a multiple-choice questionnaire (Exhibit 3.10) and sent it to the Corporate Human Resources group who posted the results on a bulletin board, and sent each supervisor a copy of his or her evaluations. An evaluation meeting with supervisors and subordinates was held to identify necessary changes and to establish the individual and group commitment needed to improve the relationship and achieve better results. The Human Resources group was responsible for giving support to those who needed help with an analysis of their evaluations.

02: The individual being evaluated reacts to criticism:

   a. badly, refusing to acknowledge the author of the criticism

   b. badly, doesn't recognize any criticism

   c. reasonably well

   d. well, accepts the criticism

15: The evaluated staff member is:

   a. a weak leader who is unable to motivate the team

   b. a weak leader, but would be able to motivate the team

   c. a strong leader who is unable to motivate the team

   d. a strong leader who is able to motivate the team

51: How does the evaluated staff member accept opinions that differ from his?

   a. does not accept

   b. generally does not accept

   c. sometimes accepts, sometimes does not

   d. always accepts well

Source: SEMCO–Cesde Pesquisa e Desenvolvimiento Gerencial, Brazil and the School of Business Administration, The University of Western Ontario, Canada, 1989.

Exhibit 3.10 *Sample items from the Subordinate Evaluation Form (three items from a 55-item questionnaire)*

This evaluation programme allowed, in theory, senior staff to be voted out of office – including Semler himself – if these managers should be found wanting by their immediate subordinates. When asked if workers could *really* fire their bosses, Semler replied, 'Well, anyone who consistently receives bad grades usually leaves or is dismissed. I made it clear that I wanted to be graded, too, and would leave whenever there was a downward trend.' On the other hand, Semler believed that 'when the people who work with an employee say he is good, that means he's good.'

Managers at SEMCO

At SEMCO, managers had no secretaries; they answered their own phones, made their own copies, and sent their own faxes. There was no dress code: some wore suits and ties; others wore jeans and sneakers. Offices were separated only by tropical plants and, through the greenery, everyone could see everyone else. Semler elaborated:

> At SEMCO, we don't segregate white-collar people. We encourage them to mix with their blue-collar colleagues. We don't have an executive dining room. Everyone eats in the same cafeteria. We eliminated separate bathrooms and rest areas for workers and employees. Moreover, there aren't any places in our parking lot reserved for V.I.P.s – it's first come, first served, even me, even on rainy days.

Managers at SEMCO were required to set, and then justify, their own salaries based on market data and personal performance, the latter to be regularly evaluated by their immediate subordinates. They could name any sum they wanted, although they did get reviewed annually to see if they were worth what they thought. Semler believed that if managers were embarrassed by their salaries, it meant they were not earning them. He explained:

> At first, people tended to underestimate their value, not knowing what would happen if they proposed too high a number, and they hoped that the company would make up the difference – which it did not. Eventually, they adjusted their estimates and I must say that, after several years, their numbers are almost exactly what our numbers would be. One day, we hope that everyone at SEMCO will be able to determine his own wages. For now, we're proceeding slowly, a dozen people at a time, mostly because top management is scared of having to deal with hundreds of self-set salaries before the mentality is truly a part of our corporate culture.

Regarding travel expenses, Semler claimed that managers could spend whatever they thought they should, just as if they were taking a trip with their own money. 'If we can't trust people to decide where to sit in a plane, or how many stars their hotel should have, we shouldn't be sending them abroad to do business in our name. We won't humiliate 99% of our people because of the 1% who may be dishonest,' said Semler. 'And, we don't need to worry about everyone starting to fly first class either,' he argued, 'because everyone has a direct stake in our company's success.'

At SEMCO, people were hired and promoted only when they had been interviewed and accepted by all their future subordinates. Profit-sharing provided an incentive for the employees to pick the best, not merely the most likeable boss. Safeguards were built in to protect SEMCO's unique corporate culture. For example, when vacancies occurred, staff members who could meet 70% of the job description were preferred over outsiders who met 90%. In this way, SEMCO emphasized internal promotion. 'I think that more than half of the outsiders are not hired,' said Semler.

Anything is possible at SEMCO

Semler's basic message is simple: anything is possible at SEMCO; the standard policy is *no policy*:

> I look at it this way: either you choose centralized management or a participatory system. With the former, the CEO surely can't be out of touch for nine weeks at a clip, as I was when I traced Marco Polo's route through Asia. But, my role is really that of a catalyst – I try to create an environment where things happen.

Semler's story is that SEMCO – a moribund company in 1980 – grew ninefold in a decade, despite the worst recession and inflation in Brazilian history. Productivity increased sevenfold. Profits rose sixfold. SEMCO has had the lowest number of strike days of any company in Brazil: nine days in eight years. The company has had periods of up to 14 months in which not a single worker has left and there is a backlog of more than 2000 job applications from people who say they would take any job just for the chance to work there.

It was a surge in output that helped the company survive its early mistakes with acquisitions, a fierce recession, and borrowing that at one time represented 11 months of sales when real interest rates were 41% above Brazil's notorious inflation.

SEMCO received the President's Award as Company of the Year in 1990. These accomplishments, Ricardo Semler argued, were the fruits of his participative management techniques.

Case 3.2 Nordwest Zeitung

This case was written by Research Associate Amy W. Webster, under the supervision of Professor Werner Ketelhöhn, as a basis for class discussion rather than to illustrate either effective or ineffective handling of an administrative situation

'We have to find a new market where we can grow,' exclaimed Reinhard Köser, General Manager of Oldenburg's newspaper *Nordwest-Zeitung*, one morning in May 1988. He was having a heated discussion with his top management team: Advertising Manager Peter Bremer and Circulation Managers Erich Hellmann and Hans-Peter Thiele. In 1987, 84.4% of the population in the Oldenburg region read a newspaper belonging to the *NWZ* partnership. Such a high penetration could hardly be improved and the geographical scope of the paper was limited. Köser wanted to safeguard his paper's future profitability and net income through some form of expansion.

History of the paper

The *Nordwest-Zeitung* had been founded in Oldenburg in 1946 by Reinhard Köser's grandfather, Fritz Bock. Oldenburg was situated in the north-western German state of Lower Saxony. From the start, the newspaper was conceived as a regional paper. Given the unstable post-war political and economic situation in Germany, the paper's first years were difficult. Through sound management, local know-how and excellent contacts with the community, the *Nordwest-Zeitung (NWZ)* became, over the years, the leading newspaper in the north-western part of Lower Saxony.

From the start, *NWZ* had adopted a zoning strategy;[1] it published seven different editions, one for each main locality served by the newspaper (Exhibits 3.11 and 3.12).

[1] Zoning was the process of publishing different editions of a newspaper with the news and/or advertising content directed at specific geographic areas.

Exhibit 3.11 *'One paper – seven editions'*

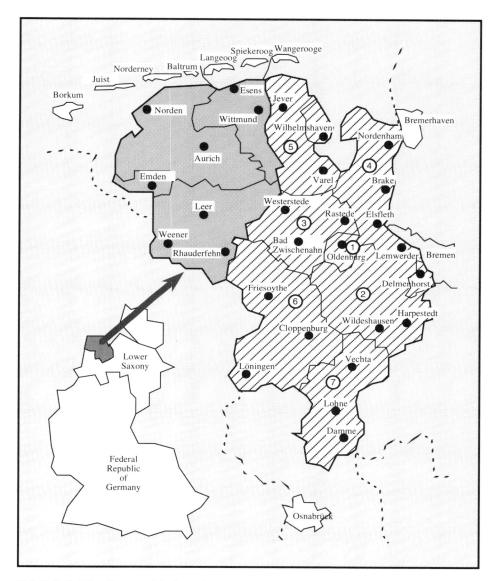

Exhibit 3.12 *Geographical markets of NWZ*

'In this respect, there are many similarities with the US newspaper industry,' commented Köser. 'We try to follow the readers' needs and provide what they want most, which is local news. Broader news is provided by the other media, but newspapers are the leaders in local news. In order to be successful in this country, a newspaper has to be local.'

The zoning strategy was organized according to a practical format (four sections, with one that varied in each edition), making the seven editions easier to manage. 'We firmly believe in following the needs of the readers before those of our advertising customers. Let's not forget that our customers are also our readers!'

Sold issues	1977	1978	1979	1980	1981	1982	1983	1984	1985	1986	1987
1 Oldenburger Nachricht	40,122	41,170	41,601	42,265	42,826	43,088	43,144	43,310	43,834	44,171	44,409
2 Oldenburger Kreiszeitung	12,794	13,297	13,698	13,997	14,257	14,426	14,540	14,796	14,948	15,170	15,293
3 Ammerländer Nachricht	21,223	21,700	22,321	23,064	23,398	23,621	23,924	24,348	24,598	24,885	25,096
4 Wesermarsch Zeitung	15,992	16,407	16,586	16,921	17,078	17,221	17,168	17,327	17,468	17,423	17,599
5 Kreiszeitung Friesland	12,338	12,594	12,822	13,187	13,225	13,303	13,498	13,632	13,729	13,940	14,149
6–7 Der Münsterländer	5,115	5,309	5,518	5,719	5,904	5,939	6,041	6,257	6,521	6,593	6,799
NWZ total	107,584	110,477	112,546	115,153	116,688	117,598	118,315	119,670	121,098	122,182	123,345

Exhibit 3.13 Development of circulation 1977–1987

The positive development of the newspaper's circulation (Exhibit 3.13) was accompanied by major building extensions around the headquarters of *NWZ* in Oldenburg. In addition, a new printing house WE-Druck GmbH & Co. KG, located in Etzhorn, six kilometres from company headquarters, was founded in January 1981. It was headed by Production Manager Peter Bachmann.

In 1988, the operation was still owned by family members, namely the founder's two daughters. Reinhard Köser, the grandson, had joined the company in 1967 at age 30. Before joining the family business, Köser had worked for the German Savings Banks Association in Bonn, where he had managed its magazine and paper for five years. He had also worked for a newspaper in Saarbrücken.

The *NWZ* newspaper was independent and liberal. The information was neutral, although editorial opinions varied. Within this framework, editors were free to write what they pleased, as long as it was in accordance with the Federal Republic's Constitution. The newspaper was based on democratic principles, truth and righteousness, and on the desire to contribute to a serious and reliable German press.[2]

A partnership

As early as 1950, *NWZ* established a cooperation with one other newspaper in the coastal region of Ostfriesland, the '*Ostfriesen-Zeitung*', in both editing and advertising.[3] This type of cooperation became useful throughout the Federal Republic.

When Köser joined in 1967, the newspaper market in Lower Saxony[4] had been fragmented. On the one hand, newspapers in the three harbour cities of Bremen, Bremerhaven and Wilhelmshaven were cooperating on the basis of common interests. On the other hand, Cloppenburg was in a partnership with Münster, to the south. In addition, other Ostfriesland papers had a small association bureau for the allocation of national advertising. Köser's first task was to unite these various groups. He had envisioned a solid single regional cooperation to strengthen the *NWZ*'s competitive position.

This vision gradually became reality after two long years of intense negotiations with the various newspaper publishers. The partnership was formally established in October 1969 among 12 members.[5] Several smaller papers joined in the following years, in particular newspapers from Ostfriesland, which embarked in an editorial cooperation with *NWZ*. Where the editorial activities of the *NWZ* and its new partners overlapped, the *NWZ* closed down two of its editorial bureaus. By 1988, only two newspapers in that region[6] were not part of the partnership: *Oldenburgische Volkszeitung* and *Kreiszeitung Wesermarsch*, an edition of *Nordsee-Zeitung* in Bremerhaven, with about 23,000 and 8000 daily copies sold respectively. Altogether, the 12 partners sold more than 308,000 daily copies.

The *Nordwest-Zeitung* had been published six times a week since 1949. It was divided into four sections (Exhibit 3.14). Three non-local sections were the same in all

---

[2] See Annex 1 for a background note on the German newspaper industry.

[3] This newspaper had belonged to Mr Bock's publishing group. He had to sell it in 1950 in order to buy out his partner. The contract with the publishers called for an advertising and editorial cooperation.

[4] See Annex 2 for the population figures of the main cities and districts.

[5] See Annex 3 for a list of the 12 members and their circulation figures.

[6] The *NWZ* 'region' covers the seven areas of the map in Exhibit 3.12.

Exhibit 3.14 The four sections of the NWZ

seven editions: Section 1 (international); Section 2 (regional); and Section 4 (entertainment). Section 3, the local section, containing local news for the local community, would vary.

For *NWZ*, the editorial cooperation consisted in selling these non-local sections of the paper to the partners. The small papers thus only developed their own local section, which they were best at, but printed the whole paper themselves. Several combinations of *NWZ* sections and sections produced by local newspapers had been established as a response to market demand.

Cooperation in allocating advertising, on the other hand, prevented aggressive competition in this field. As the leading newspaper in the region, NWZ monitored the allocation of advertisements – national, job, or real estate – among the 12 members of the partnership. *NWZ* received the ads directly from the agencies and other customers, because they refused to deal with small individual newspapers. *NWZ* then allocated these ads among the partners, thus serving as a wholesaler of newspaper space. Advertisers used a price list to choose the combination of publications where they wanted to advertise. Smaller papers thus secured advertising revenues which they would not have received otherwise, while *NWZ* generated extra income through a 10–11% commission for this service. The smaller papers were able to save costs as administrative processes were greatly facilitated. Most of them registered a growth in advertising revenues of 50% after they entered the partnership. In 1988, this growth averaged about 5% a year.

The product

Like most general newspapers around the world, *NWZ* covered the traditional areas of politics, economics, sports, feature stories and local news. Regular supplements concentrating on the region, youth, or television programs were provided. Local news, however, was given utmost priority and resources. An editorial bureau in the town of Oldenburg worked closely with the provincial bureau and the 12 external offices spread around the region, where more than half of the 70 editors were kept busy. In addition, three in-house photographers and hundreds of freelancers all contributed to an average of 40 local pages daily. Local news was combined with regional news to give the readers the most at both levels. Another much sought-after feature was the extensive family advertisements (obituaries, marriages, births, baptisms, etc.), which often covered five pages.

The paper's layout was the same every day, except for the daily specials: sports on Mondays, television magazine on Wednesdays, food advertisements on Thursdays and entertainment on Saturdays. The paper was not published on Sundays.

The layout was a result of both the reader's need for local news and the need for a simple production pattern. It was introduced in 1983, when the new printing plant at Etzhorn became operational. The new design was developed with the help of a US expert in newspaper design, Rolf Rehe from Indianapolis. 'Our paper is perceived as modern,' Köser said, 'particularly by the younger generation. It has also attracted editors from the competition. We used to have a traditional layout, almost old-fashioned (Exhibit 3.15), which was confusing[7] to the reader. But all newspapers were

---

[7] For example, important pages such as the TV guide were found in different places in the newspaper from one day to another. Also, 'reader-friendly' block layouts were not used then.

Exhibit 3.15   *The newspaper's layout in 1983*

like that at the time! We were one of the first German newspapers to change our layout to a clear readable pattern.' The objective of the new design (Exhibit 3.16) was to allow the reader to have a quicker overview of the paper and to stimulate his interest. It was based on three principles: clarity, liveliness and legibility. Top management assumed it generated an increase in circulation for all seven editions, because survey results indicated that 82% of *NWZ* readers found that the newspaper's quality had improved.

The seven editions were published under the same name *Nordwest-Zeitung*, with a second local name, following the motto 'Seven editions – one paper'. *NWZ* was considered a regional paper, or rather a set of seven local papers. Each edition was

Exhibit 3.16 *The newspaper's layout in 1988*

easily recognizable, as the most important local story was always found on the front page. The name was well established within the region as well as beyond, although the readership was essentially local. About one-third of the 123,345 daily copies were distributed in the town of Oldenburg. A 1985 market survey revealed that each copy of the *NWZ* was read by three readers on average; 95% read at home, while 54% looked at the paper two or more times a day.

The local sections of two editions shared many common features. The six provincial editions also included, on the last page of the local section, news from the city of Oldenburg, the capital of the district. In addition, special care was taken to provide readers living near borderlines with special news from neighbouring localities.

Operational features

Cost control

Cost control was, in Reinhard Köser's opinion, one of the basic responsibilities of a newspaper publisher. (Exhibit 3.17). On one side, unions were pressuring for higher wages and a 35-hour week, while on the other, most newspaper publishers were investing in new printing technologies. New technological input would inevitably mean less manpower in the longer run.

Revenues	(DM)	Expenses	(DM)
Advertising	33.84	Production	21.36
Inserts	4.66	Editorial	9.21
Circulation	20.79	Advertising	7.07
		Circulation	8.76
		Administration and profit	12.89
Total	59.29	Total	59.29

Exhibit 3.17 *Average monthly revenues and expenses per copy of the NWZ in 1987 (without other activities)*

In 1983, the company began using budgets for cost control. Budgets for the following year were established on the basis of a projection for circulation and advertising. Discussions on ways to increase profits took place. Monthly statements and quarterly balance sheets helped management in cost control. Five years later, the system proved successful: in 1988, costs were increasing at a slower pace (less than 3%) than revenues (more than 6%). The technical staff was decreasing because retiring staff were not being replaced.

Personnel management

Personnel management at the *NWZ* was based on retirement planning in order to avoid laying off any employees in the short run. In 1988, the company employed 563 employees, including 89 blue-collar workers and part-time or short-term employees. When the printing technology changed from letterpress to offset at the *NWZ*, a 4-week programme was put together to train the technical staff on the new machinery. The change was not as dramatic as it had been in other European countries. In the 1970s, there had been strikes almost every three to four years whenever agreements with the unions were renegotiated. The last strike at the NWZ had been in 1984 and had continued for four weeks. The current union agreement was valid until 1989.

When the new printing plant was built in Etzhorn, capacity was increased by 40%. Additional employees were hired only to work on the new printing contracts. The company had warned them that their jobs depended on these contracts and were not guaranteed. In the other departments, the number of employees was kept stable.

Editorial

With desktop publishing, the *NWZ* editorial staff received news around-the-clock directly on their computer screens from the various German and foreign news agencies.[8] About 100 photographs came in daily from around the world on the teletype system. In addition, bureau journalists and correspondents[9] regularly sent in stories by telephone, telefax or photocopier. All this information was gathered and selected by the editorial department. Chosen articles, stories and photographs were then prepared for publication. Only 10–15% of the material received from the news agencies was published.

Advertising

National advertisements[10] came in their final form from the various agencies. Local ads, however, were prepared in-house. Computerizing part of the composition process was a great step forward. Classified ads were directly entered from the telephone to the screen. Rates and exact costs were immediately communicated to the customer. At the *NWZ*, advertisements served two purposes: to inform the readers on market supplies and to secure the newspaper's economic independence. The paper published about 300,000 ads each year.

Technological competence

After lengthy preparations, the electronic age was introduced at the *NWZ* in 1971. Mr Heinz Rütten was in charge of data processing, which began in the administrative and technical departments before being extended to the editorial functions in 1980. It was not until later that photocomposition replaced typesetting. The new printing factory, the building of which began in 1981, was ready for operation in 1983. Offset printing then began at the *NWZ*.

In 1987, the electronic processing of advertising was introduced. Laser developers were used for computer graphics and maps. Articles and classified advertisements were composed directly on the screen, stored on a diskette and sent directly to the partners or to the printing house. The company still lacked the on-screen full page make-up technology, which in 1988 was not yet satisfactory. Full-page composition was one of the few activities which had not gone through a revolutionary change. Composers still created the page layout manually. Once the page was ready, a negative was made by a reproduction camera. All the negatives were then transported to the plant in Etzhorn, where plates were made for printing.

---

[8] Deutsche Presse-Agentur, Associated Press, Sportinformationsdienst (sports agency), Vereinigte Wirtschaftsdienste (economics service), etc.

[9] The *NWZ* had correspondents in New York, Washington, Moscow, Paris, London, Rome and Brussels.

[10] National advertising represented about 10% of total advertising revenues.

Technical progress also had a great impact on editorial activities. In 1988, *NWZ* had 220 terminals for data processing, including those in the commercial department. Many different computer programs were developed for the various tasks involved in newspaper publishing. A databank with the capacity to store 10,000 newspaper pages became operational. Word processing, along with the ability to permanently control the length of an article and store the editorial content on electronic databanks, simplified the various tasks. Portable computers and direct electronic communication were additional features of the technological progress. Moreover, *NWZ* had set up archives to complement the data captured on microfilm. About 15,000 texts and 25,000 pictures were archived every year.

Colour printing had begun 20 years earlier with the letterpress, but had been of low quality. Starting in 1983, it was used systematically with the new offset machines, which together could print up to 70,000 newspapers of 64 pages per hour, in black and white as well as in colour. The first production of regular colour printing took place in 1984.

Income strategy

Nordwest-Zeitung relied on various sources of income. Besides advertising and circulation revenues, more than 15% of the income came from other sources (Exhibit 3.18). One of these sources was the partnership; each member paid 10–11% of the advertisement revenue to the *NWZ* for the service.

Revenues		Expenses	
Circulation (including distribution revenue)	30	Printing	20
Advertising	50	Personnel	43
Printing	10	Other (including profit)	32
Other (including income from partnership)	5		
Total	95	Total	95

Approximate balance sheet of the NWZ group 1987 (in DM millions)

Assets		Liabilities	
Fixed assets	33	Capital stock	48
Accounts receivable	8	Retained earnings	6
Liquid assets	33	Debt (incl. taxes)	9
Other	14	Reserves (pension dues and taxes)	16
		Other	9
Total	88	Total	88

Remark: The *Nordwest-Zeitung* did not publish their accounts. As a result, figures were obtained for only broad categories of income and expenses, or assets and liabilities. We were told, however, that profits (before tax) were higher than 12% of total revenues.

Exhibit 3.18 *Approximate profit and loss accounts of the NWZ Group for 1987 (in DM millions)*

Another source of revenue was the printing of other publications. After its new offset press was installed in 1983, *NWZ* managed to use part of its printing capacity for subcontracts. These publications were not direct competitors of *NWZ*. They included free sheets, various weeklies and Sunday papers for the Oldenburg, Bremen and Osnabrück regions. The printing operations were a profitable business. Because of German tax regulations, printing on Saturdays was 20% more expensive than on other days. As a result, most printing houses did not print Sunday papers. *NWZ* was able to do so, however, by charging higher prices for it. With the volume of printing the company handled on Saturdays (500,000 copies), the printing machines ran for 10 hours non-stop. This operation generated DM10 million of annual revenues, about 10% of total income.

The last source of revenue was distribution. Besides handling its own distribution, *NWZ* had taken on the local distribution of national publications such as *Frankfurter Allgemeine* and *Die Welt*. National papers needed local distributors to deliver their newspapers early in the morning when the readers wanted them. The only alternative – postal services – was unattractive and inefficient. For distributing national papers, *NWZ* charged 20% of the final subscription price.[11] Although it generated little revenue, this additional load was easy to handle because of the computerized administration of distribution.

Competition

In Northwest Lower Saxony and Bremen, four major competitive newspapers controlled the region's four major cities:

Newspaper	City	1987 Circulation
Bremer Tageszeitungen	Bremen	212,713
Neue Osnabrücker Zeitung	Osnabrück	165,950
Nordwest-Zeitung	Oldenburg	123,345
Nordsee Zeitung	Bremerhaven	59,849

In addition, there were many smaller papers with circulation figures of 5,000–30,000 daily copies. According to Mr Köser, the respective market shares were as follows. With only one small competitor, the Osnabrück paper's market share was 75%. In Bremen and Bremerhaven, each paper fully controlled the entire city. Market shares largely depended on how the markets were defined. 'Our paper holds about 60% of the *NWZ* market,' Köser estimated.

Other competitors in the region included the national boulevard paper *Bild Zeitung*, which only sold 29,000 daily copies locally. This was considered low for a popular

---

[11] Distribution costs for a newspaper publisher generally represented 10–15% of total costs. In 1988, the monthly subscription price of *Frankfurter Allgemeine* was DM33.20, of *Die Welt* DM29.70 and of *NWZ* DM22.40.

nationwide paper. Boulevard papers generally had a difficult time in Lower Saxony. They were most successful in larger metropolitan markets. Finally, *Frankfurter Allgemeine* and *Die Welt* sold about 3000 copies each.

The seven editions of *NWZ* competed locally with some of the papers in the partnership, but it was minimal and not a real threat to either side. Local editors competed on the quality of their local news. Köser was more concerned about another type of competition. 'A real threat would occur if our competitors tried cooperating with our partners. They could potentially disrupt our partnership.' To avoid this happening, management established long-term written agreements with the partners, combined with regular discussions every two to three months. Regular contacts and trust were essential to keep the partnership sturdy and reliable.

There was no fierce direct competition with the three other main newspapers in Bremen, Bremerhaven and Osnabrück. One cooperating partner, however, was in the buffer zone between the Bremen and the *NWZ* territories[12] and had to handle tougher competition than the others. Local papers in Germany generally stayed within their respective local markets, and the rules of the game were rarely changed. It would be difficult, for example, for a Bremen newspaper to gain market share on the *NWZ* market. Readers were loyal and gave clear preference to their local paper. Competition became more difficult, however, where income levels were lower and where population was declining.

Another type of competition had been a major concern at the *NWZ* in early 1985. Classified advertising papers from Hannover had threatened to enter the Oldenburg market and to remove an important source of revenue from the *NWZ*. As a counteractive move, Mr Peter Bremer, Advertising Manager, had started a special and larger classified section in the *NWZ* Tuesday edition, making it particularly attractive by substantially cutting ad prices. The result was an important increase in circulation of the Tuesday paper. In addition, the only competitor to have proceeded with his plan went out of business after six months (see Annex 4 for more details).

Future trends facing NWZ

'One way to ensure growth in a newspaper company, and this applies to other industries as well, is to come up with new ideas for undertakings or new market niches every five to six years. If not, one runs the risk of missing the boat. In our case, we consider that our main business is information, and we realize that it can be gathered, processed, printed, transmitted, or broadcast!' Like many European newspaper publishers, Köser was concerned with the future trends facing *NWZ*. The electronic media, in particular, raised many heated discussions.

In 1987, television in the Federal Republic of Germany was no longer a government monopoly. Two private channels were owned by major media groups. Some newspaper publishers viewed these TV channels[13] as potential customers. Indeed, one possibility was to make local inserts in local television programmes.

---

[12] Refer to map in Exhibit 3.12.
[13] RTL Plus from Luxembourg, and SAT 1 from Mainz.

Another would be to start a joint venture with other leading newspapers for the common production and broadcast of TV programmes. One important difference between newspapers and television, however, was that 80% of TV programmes were entertainment, and only 10% were political interviews and reports, often perceived as dull. In addition, 'Running a television programme is far too costly[14] for a newspaper publisher to consider,' Köser said. 'No profits can be anticipated for many years.' According to state law, only state-wide advertising was allowed on the electronic media in Lower Saxony. In case the law were modified, however, newspaper publishers were already discussing in 1988 the issue of increased competition with the electronic media.

During the 1980s, 45 German newspaper and magazine publishers of Lower Saxony and Bremen had set up a private broadcasting company called FFN (Funk und Fernsehen Nordwest-Deutschland).[15] 'Being part of FFN helps us keep up with the latest developments and ensures us that we will take part in future projects,' Köser observed. 'This business could very well become profitable. We have already become involved in the teletex business, which we do not consider a growth area, but we will keep it just in case. We should, however, remain pragmatic and not waste too much energy on the electronic media.'

'The volume of information is growing daily at a progressive rate. However, the volume of newspapers is not growing, neither is TV broadcasting. The future trend may well be having the possibility to select information of particular interest, to read it on a television screen or print it out. The teletex offers direct access to complete, constantly updated and immediately available information. This could be the business of newspapers too.'[16]

In 1988, the *NWZ* company started another activity when it founded a new daughter company to publish magazines. Its first task was to take over the publication activities of a high quality, local, economic magazine, to be edited and printed by the Oldenburg Chamber of Commerce. After a conflict with its previous partner, the Chamber of Commerce had offered this project to the *NWZ*.

The printing of high quality magazines required not only a different quality and size of paper, but also called for different machinery. The *NWZ* infrastructure, however, could easily take on the circulation and advertising of another publication. 'This new activity will be good business,' Köser commented. 'It will also give us the opportunity to approach a different group of customers. Until now, we have always dealt mainly with retail advertisers. Customers likely to advertise in an economic magazine will be from business and industry, in particular members of the Chamber of Commerce.'

Köser envisaged a positive future for the *Nordwest-Zeitung*. 'I am convinced that newspapers remain the only medium which provides essential orientation in an increasingly complicated lifestyle – what to see, what to do, what others think and do. Newspapers help people solve their problems.'

---

[14] It cost around DM300 million to run a TV programme in Germany in 1988.
[15] The share allocated to each newspaper depended on the circulation figures.
[16] The teletex in Germany had not been successful; there were only 120,000 users in 1988.

Annex 1: Background note on the German newspaper industry

There were 392 general information dailies in the Federal Republic in 1988, 124 with their own editorial staff. The vast majority (371) were regional or local and were sold mostly by subscription. The local press was defined as the 'publications that covered a certain locality, without losing sight of general political news and cultural events.' A regional daily was 'a paper distributed in a certain region and dedicated to news of local and regional interest.' Freedom of the press was one of the fundamental rights guaranteed by the Federal Constitution, and censorship had been abolished. Partisan newspapers had practically vanished from the German scene.

Germans read a lot more than their European neighbours and paid great attention to local and regional news. Between 1950 and 1980, daily circulation increased by 10 million to reach 20.4 million in 1988. Germans were regular and loyal readers. More than 93% of all citizens over 14 years old read newspapers or periodicals (72% were subscribers). Newspapers reached 83.5% of the population; 456 copies were sold per 1000 inhabitants. However, out of 1000 inhabitants, 338 owned a TV set. The definition of a German household was 2.5 persons on average, which meant that TV coverage in Germany neared 100%.

After the war, numerous German newspapers had started operations. In an effort to reduce competition, the industry soon went through a period of concentration. As a result, in 1988, many German towns had only one newspaper. The concentration trend was partly stopped in the 1960s by a Federal law: to protect competition among newspaper publishers, every joint venture and acquisition that could lead to a cartel in the publishing world was examined by public authorities and often prohibited. This did not prevent, however, powerful publishing houses such as the Axel Springer group from controlling 90% of daily prints in West Berlin. In 1988, the Springer Group held 30.1% of the daily newspaper market in the Federal Republic, primarily through ownership of the *Bild Zeitung*, a sensational paper in which text was reduced to a minimum. With a daily circulation of about 5 million copies, it was the only daily which was sold successfully all over the country besides the national papers.

The rise in publishing costs in the 1970s (personnel costs represented about 50% of total costs), along with the increased competition with radio and other media for advertising revenues, had a direct impact on the concentration process. In order to cut costs and ensure survival, economic cooperation plans were started between small and medium-sized publishers, providing for common editing, the joint use of correspondents, unified ad rates, advertising committees and collaboration in printing.

Another characteristic of the German newspaper industry was the spectacular growth of popular dailies sold on the street; in 1950, such papers represented 2.7% of total circulation, and in 1986, 31%. This increase was mostly due to the growth of *Bild Zeitung*, the only paper of national coverage which was sold on the street, although there were 28 separate editions.

Circulation of most German newspapers in the 1980s was at a standstill. This situation could be aggravated by the alarming decline in population being predicted. To gain the readers' loyalty and confidence, newspaper publishers attempted to modernize the production process and emphasize the value of the printed press, distinguishing it from the rest of the media.

Annex 2: Population figures for main cities and districts of the NWZ market

Bremen (city)	521,986
Bremerhaven (city)	131,758
Osnabrück (city)	153,776
1. Oldenburg (city)	139,502
2. Oldenburg district	100,814
3. Ammerland district	93,912
4. Wesermarsch district	89,876
5. Friesland district	94,878
6. Cloppenburg district	112,922
7. Vechta district	102,581
Total all 7 districts	734,485

Note: The numbers 1–7 refer to the areas on the map in Exhibit 3.12.

Annex 3: The 12 members of the partnership

Newspaper	City	Circulation in 1987
1. *Nordwest-Zeitung*	Oldenburg	122,526
2. *Ostfriesen-Zeitung*	Leer	40,762
3. *Wilhelmshavener Zeitung*	Wilhelmshaven	30,083
4. *Anzeiger for Harlingerland*	Wittmund	12,440
5. *General-Anzeiger*	Rhauderfehn	10,068
6. *Jeversches Wochenblatt*	Jever	8,272
7. *Ostfriesischer Kurier*	Norden	14,383
8. *Ostfriesische Nachrichten*	Aurich	12,681
9. *Emder Zeitung*	Emden	9,853
10. *Delmenhorster Kreisblatt*	Delmenhorst	24,070
11. *Münsterländische Tageszeitung*	Cloppenburg	17,467
12. *Zeitung Rheiderland*	Weener	5,776
Total circulation		308,381

Annex 4: Competition for classified advertising

In Germany, the classified advertisement papers were mostly sold through mall retail stores in large cities. Their prices ranged from DM1 to DM2. Classified ads were free of charge, and most of these papers generated their revenues from sales and business ads. Such papers were very popular in West Germany.

In the beginning of 1985, three new classified advertisement papers appeared in Lower Saxony. *Der heiße Draht* (Exhibit 3.19) had started in Hannover and had reached a circulation of 60,000 weekly issues. Hannover newspapers had not considered it a major threat. The result was a sustained growth for the classified ad paper, and a subsequent expansion to Bremen where it sold 10,000 copies.

The classified advertising leader in Bremen, however, was *A bis Z* (Exhibit 3.20) with 20,000 in weekly circulation. Köser believed it was also the only profitable one. It had succeeded in preceding *Der heiße Draht* in Bremen, and had secured itself a large chunk of the market. As a result, Bremen's traditional newspapers had suffered a decline in classified advertising revenues. All three publications were available in retail stores and sold for DM1 to DM1.50.

In 1985, there were rumours that the two publications were contemplating starting an edition in Oldenburg. Köser was concerned about these developments and feared that the new competition would take away market share in classified advertising. *NWZ* charged private customers DM7.52 per line. 'The classified ad papers in Bremen were not considered competitors until we heard about their intention to move in here.'

Mr Bremer, Advertising Manager, decided to counteract such a move at any cost. In late 1985, *NWZ* launched its own weekly classified advertisement section, called *Kleinanzeiger* (Exhibit 3.21). The section was based on different principles: ads would not be free, but the price would be low – DM5 for a maximum of four lines. A special feature including a buy/sell/exchange market with a particular price structure was introduced as a novelty to attract new readers. It was published each Tuesday as a separate section of the *NWZ*.

The success of *Kleinanzeiger* went beyond expectations. The section started with 500 inserts and reached from 2300 to 3000 weekly in 1988 with an average of 12–16 pages. Repeat inserts were rarely necessary. The Tuesday edition of *Nordwest-Zeitung*, which had been the weakest in circulation figures, increased by 3000 copies and became the second strongest daily issue after Saturday. The increase in private ads between 1985 and 1987 was 39.2% in volume. The low price proved to have a positive effect, but Köser admitted to a major loss in advertising revenue. 'The problem was that we experienced a strong increase in the number of classified ads, but a decrease in revenues because of the low dumping prices we had set to be competitive.' The price was increased later in 1988 to DM7 and there was no decline in the number of ads. Revenues were expected to start increasing by the following year.

The Bremen competitors were not playing a major role, simply because no local reader from the Oldenburg region was interested in classified ads from Bremen or any other major city. The Bremen papers lacked the essential local support in Oldenburg. One paper tried to operate in Oldenburg a few weeks after the *Kleinanzeiger* was launched, but closed down after six months.

The *Kleinanzeiger* was initially launched as a strategy against potential competitors, not as a business venture. A second objective was to increase the volume of classified advertisements, which had been low for years. The third objective was to reach a new target group, namely the low and middle income levels. This particular customer

Exhibit 3.19   *Der heiße Draht – a new classified paper appearing in 1985*

Exhibit 3.20 *A bis Z – classified advertising leader in Bremen*

Exhibit 3.21   *NWZ launched a weekly advertisement section in 1985*

segment, not able to afford a newspaper regularly, had until then been neglected. They occasionally would buy a paper just for the classified ads. These ads, when published in a regular newspaper, usually cost DM30–40. Therefore, low-income readers would use only free sheets or public bulletin boards to place ads. The *Kleinanzeiger*'s low rates was one way to attract this particular customer group.

NWZ's success stemmed primarily from the fact that it had pre-empted its competitors. Another strength was that the paper cost only DM1 – less than *A bis Z* or *Der heiße Draht* which sold for DM2, and the same as *Das gelbe Blatt* – and gave quality news at the same time. In addition, *NWZ* provided business and private advertisers with a circulation of almost 125,000, which meant over 350,000 readers daily, along with seven different editions and combinations of the same paper.

The development of *Kleinanzeiger* continued in 1988. Several changes had been introduced when it became clear that readers wanted additional features, more structured and more 'reader-friendly'. In 1987, 47 different features appeared in the classified advertisement section of *NWZ*. That same year, all advertisement-related operations, which had been handled manually until then, were computerized: data capture and processing, along with the billing, were done electronically. *Kleinanzeiger* became the private sales advertising section. It did not hurt the other daily issues, as the majority of real estate and automobile advertisements stayed in the Wednesday and Saturday issues.

4

Effective organization

Case 4.1 Aldo Palmeri: Taking charge (A)

This case was written by Research Associate Juliet Burdet-Taylor, under the supervision of Professor Werner Ketelhöhn, as a basis for class discussion rather than to illustrate either effective or ineffective handling of a business situation.

The biggest knitwear producer in the world

In his job as Economic Consultant to the Italian Ministry of Industry, it was not unusual for Aldo Palmeri to meet important entrepreneurs to discuss questions of business or the economy. A compact, intense man with the power of absolute concentration, Palmeri wasted no time on idle chat. With a degree in law from Rome and a Masters from the London School of Economics, Palmeri entered the Bank of Italy as a manager and was for 10 years the bank's representative to the EEC and OECD. At 34 years old, Palmeri had a wide knowledge of industry, banking and finance, and, not surprisingly, his advice on these subjects was often sought.

At the end of 1981, Palmeri was invited to dinner by Luciano and Gilberto Benetton, who wanted to discuss their company. Benetton, famous for its knitwear and casual trendy clothing, had become a household word in Italy. The faces of the Benetton brothers and sister were rarely absent from the daily press or glossy magazines. At the end of 1981, with 1500 retail outlets and 9 production plants, and sales for 1982 forecast at over $300 million, Benetton was the biggest knitwear producer in the world (Exhibit 4.1).

	1981*	1982
Income statement		
Sales	349.7	309.0
Cost of goods sold	326.5	336.3
Gross profit	75.6	65.4
Expenses	7.9	0.4
Earnings before interest and depreciation	58.8	50.0
Interest expense	11.0	13.2
Depreciation	16.7	14.5
Earnings before tax	30.9	22.2
Tax	14.2	9.7
Earnings	16.7	12.5
Balance Sheet		
Current assets	132.8	163.1
Fixed Assets	37.1	41.7
Intangibles	13.5	9.4
Total assets	183.4	214.2
Current liabilities	84.4	99.0
Long-term liabilities	19.6	42.2
Net worth	79.4	73.0
Total liabilities and net worth	183.4	214.2

*1981 figures for the income statement given covered an 18-month period.

Exhibit 4.1   *Financial statement for Benetton 1981–1982 (in millions of dollars)*

A tiny family business

Palmeri listened to the brothers relating the modest beginnings of the Benetton company, which they had started building up in 1955 with the acquisition of a second-hand knitting machine financed by the sale of an accordion and a bicycle. Luciano had been only ten when the children's father had died, forcing the family to be self-supporting at a very young age. When he reached the age of 15, Luciano started working in a men's clothing shop and, on leaving school, his sister Giuliana found work in a knitwear factory. By the time she was 17, Giuliana was devoting her spare time to designing and knitting her own brightly-coloured sweaters, which were more original than most knitwear found in the stores at the time. Luciano was sure there was a market for these sweaters and, by the time he was 20, he was selling a small collection of Giuliana's work to local shops. He delivered them himself on his bicycle.

Within a year, the Benettons' sales had risen enough to warrant the purchase of a second knitting machine and the hiring of some local help to keep up with demand. From that day on, the Benettons dedicated themselves to the business of making and selling knitwear. In 1965, Luciano and Giuliana formed their own company with the help of their brother Gilberto, who had been with them almost from the start. In the same year, the first factory was opened at Ponzano Veneto, outside the Benetton's home town of Treviso, about 30 km north of Venice.

'I was not afraid of failure at the beginning,' explained Luciano. 'When you start with nothing you don't need to fear failure. I had plenty of time to think about it while I worked at the store. I planned it for years. Now, looking back, I have never asked myself why I decided to go into business. One does not go into business simply to make money.'

By 1968, as soon as they had a big enough collection, the Benettons opened their first shop. In 1978 annual sales were $78 million of which 98% were in Italy. At about this time, the Benettons started making some attempts to enter other European markets. Towards the end of the 1970s, Benetton's foreign sales were approaching 50% of its total business.

Benetton's management

By 1981, the three oldest Benettons shared the running of the company: Luciano was chairman, Giuliana was in charge of design, and Gilberto handled finance. Luciano's childhood friend, Elio Aluffi, who had been with the company from its first days, gradually took over manufacturing (Exhibit 4.2).

Although not a professional manager, Aluffi had learned on the job and, over the years, had gained a wide knowledge of Benetton's business, particularly its plants and production facilities. In 1981, Aluffi, as Manufacturing Director, was in charge of information technology, human resources and production. Over the years, he had recruited an assortment of middle level and functional managers for Benetton, many of whom were local men, some with little professional training. In 1981, 30 or so of these managers were working in the company.

Subcontractors

Luciano introduced many innovations into Benetton in the early years, including a way of alleviating financial stress during the days before the company became sufficiently well known to borrow funds from banks. It was customary in the Treviso area of Italy for a manufacturer such as Benetton to contract out his bit work to a number of small, often family-held, producers or outworkers. Even before the company was officially registered, demand for its products rapidly outgrew Benetton's primitive production capacity. Initially, subcontractors were used for certain manual tasks such as special finishing that could not be done on machines. It was the girls working in the factories who carried out these jobs at night, sometimes with the help of their mothers, who were soon being encouraged by Aluffi to form groups among themselves to meet the increasing demand for this work. After some objections from the unions had been overcome, the idea took root and Luciano, through Aluffi, continued to encourage his employees to become subcontractors and to perform other tasks in the manufacturing process.

Luciano favoured independent contractors with manufacturing experience, and he reinforced their commitment to the business. Apart from adding flexibility to

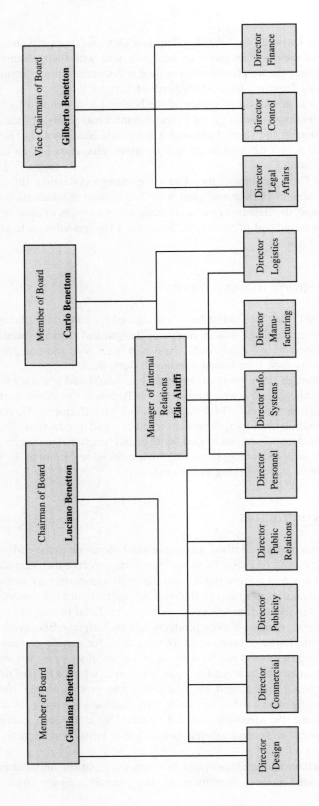

Exhibit 4.2 Benetton organization chart. (Note: This exhibit is a revision of that which appeared in the IMD case Building the Benetton System, GM-437)

manufacturing, the use of small independent producers helped avoid the social contributions that were prevalent in Italy, where companies with more than 15 employees were subject to union and state control, and paid half of workers' salaries in social costs.

Luciano set up ongoing partnership agreements with several of the small manufacturers to whom he was subcontracting work. In exchange for guaranteeing a constant stream of work from Benetton, subcontractors agreed to invest in fixed assets and to work exclusively for the company. By the beginning of the 1980s, Benetton had over 200 subcontractors all working within a 60 kilometre radius of the Ponzano Veneto headquarters. The network was becoming large and somewhat unwieldy, and only Elio Aluffi, who himself owned several external apparel manufacturers, understood all the complexities of the system.

Luciano, a constant source of innovation . . .

Luciano strove constantly to keep manufacturing costs to a minimum by introducing new ideas that he discovered in his travels. When one of his employees suggested purchasing and converting obsolete knitting machines that were being scrapped, Luciano adopted the idea. For only $5,000 each, this manufacturing innovation provided up to 90% of Benetton's initial production at a much lower cost than with more up-to-date machinery.

A major breakthrough for Benetton came in 1972 when it started dyeing *garments* rather than yarn as had previously been done. The whole dyeing process of batches of uncoloured knitwear could be completed in only two hours. Not only did this improvement increase Benetton's inventory turnover for woollen items from 4.5% to 6%, but it also enabled the company to produce colours in accordance with agents' requests. A wool softening technique discovered by Luciano in Scotland, which was added to Benetton's innovative production methods, was considered to be one of the features that helped the company differentiate itself from competition.

Retail strategy

Aldo Palmeri learned about the development of Luciano's early retailing strategy during the 1960s – how the company initially decided to sell its products through specialized knitwear stores rather than department stores or boutiques that sold a diverse range of garments, and how Luciano granted a 10% discount to retailers for cash on delivery.

The late 1960s and early 1970s were devoted to capturing the Italian market. A prototype Benetton store was designed by family friend, Tobia Scarpa, and opened in the mountain village of Belluno. Others followed in Cortina and Padua. This model shop layout was adopted throughout the whole of Italy where, over the next seven or eight years, 200 similar stores were opened.

Agents and retailing

Benetton did not invest in retail outlets. A partnership situation evolved in Italy between Benetton and self-employed agents, who were responsible for locating and setting up stores, usually grouped geographically. The agents, mostly personal friends of the Benettons at the beginning, selected independent small entrepreneurs who were willing to invest in and run Benetton stores. An agent might run a group of stores, usually in one geographical location.

Luciano selected agents personally, in accordance with strict criteria, to ensure that the right choice was made. For Luciano, the ideal person acted as a consumer rather than an agent; he understood Benetton's products, believed in the multi-coloured sweater for what it was in those days, something quite unconventional. Over the years the agents developed their own partnerships with store owners, offering them guidance on merchandising and retailing, display and product selection. If the need arose, an agent had to take over part or all of a store owner's debt. Although the agents were literally Benetton salesmen, they were not direct employees; they were actually independent companies. The agents' incentive was the chance to invest in and take part of the profits from these highly successful and fast growing retail outlets. The agents were paid a 4% commission on the value of all goods shipped from Benetton's factories.

Luciano emphasized that the system they had developed using agents and store owners was not a franchising system, but a totally new concept of retailing peculiar to Benetton. It was the agents who really exported or disseminated Benetton's culture. Even when starting up in other European countries, Benetton used Italian agents. No royalties were paid to the company based on sales results, neither was a fee due to Benetton for the use of its name. Storeowners had to finance their own investment in premises, furniture and displays.

Stores

Benetton dictated merchandising policies that reflected the company's overall image and promotional strategies. The agents were responsible for ensuring that Benetton's homogeneous policies, style and culture were built into every retail outlet.

Stores were to be decorated and laid out according to the standard Benetton design with the green and white logo above the shop window. These shops were generally small and sparsely furnished, and had a central counter for the cash register, and floor to ceiling shelves around the walls with enough space for a third of a year's inventory. The objective was to show the range of Benetton's brightly coloured garments, and ensure that they could be touched and tried on by customers. In-store and window displays, placed closer to the window than is usual in other shops, were standardized. Shopowners were obliged to buy only Benetton clothes, to achieve a minimum acceptable sales level, and follow guidelines for mark-ups and promotions. Return of merchandise was not accepted.

Palmeri learned a lot about the company from the Benettons at their dinner together, but then did not hear from them for several months. One morning, unexpectedly, Gilberto turned up at the Ministry of Industry to speak to Palmeri. 'During this meeting,' Palmeri explained, 'Gilberto Benetton continued to talk about the company and its successes. He gave more details on the internal organization, and on the key managers and their personalities. Gilberto also touched upon the brothers' future strategy, which he hinted included a further thrust into Europe and the USA as well as entry into Japan and other Far Eastern markets. Palmeri's knowledge of Benetton, its history and its future plans was widening. Yet, Gilberto made no reference to another meeting . . . .'

What about joining Benetton?

'What about joining Benetton ... taking over the company and helping us with our growth plans?' It was Gilberto, calling Palmeri on behalf of Luciano about a month after their last meeting. 'Come and talk to us in Ponzano Veneto.'

Aldo Palmeri flew to Ponzano Veneto the following weekend, and discussions with Luciano and Gilberto continued. 'This time, Luciano did all the talking, while Gilberto seemed to be trying to guess his brother's reaction to me.' So far Palmeri had done little more than sit across the table and listen. Luciano expanded on the internal workings of the company, its management and its culture, which he tried hard to convey to Palmeri, returning several times to anecdotes about the early days ....

As coffee was served, Palmeri's thoughts went back over the dinner conversation. 'These people really were strange – two meetings, months without news, then a phone call ... and now, they want me to run their business ... that's trust.'

We want to be everywhere ...

Using a sheet of paper covered with numbers and diagrams, Luciano outlined for Palmeri how he wanted Benetton to develop throughout the decade. 'Look at these numbers over the past few years ... 200 stores in 1975, all in Italy. Today, we have 1500 in Italy and 500 outside. By the end of this year, we'll have as many outside Italy as we have inside. A new Benetton store opens every day ...' Luciano jabbed at a map of the world with his finger ... 'Look here, the US ... we've barely scratched the surface. The potential is huge ... then here, the Far East, Japan, enormous opportunities ... and the rest of the world. Benetton's goal is to be everywhere.'

Luciano described what he thought were two of the key factors of Benetton's success – its unique sales and distribution system, and its decentralized manufacturing system. 'We are working on it all the time. Information. We must have instant feedback from the market to production sites so we can remain flexible, keep ahead of trends and manufacture runs in accordance with customers' most popular colour choices. Then we minimize unsold inventory. We still manufacture almost everything in Italy in seven factories, using about 200 subcontractors. The faster we grow, the more we depend on good information. Elio Aluffi is looking at computerized information systems at the moment. Soon we shall be able to cut 15,000 garments in eight hours. That's with our CAD/CAM ... and we reduce the time between design approval and manufacture, which also cuts down material waste ... We are constantly trying out new techniques.'

Luciano went on to describe his philosophy as far as business relations both inside and outside the company were concerned. 'We work largely on trust. We have very special acquaintances, encounters in which we've had faith, and they have inspired us because this type of work implies a rapport. It is not a traditional rapport made of written documents, concessions, lawyers and so on. It is a rapport of handshakes, of understanding and knowledge on a human level, and also of extreme faith, total faith. Even our agents don't have contracts. We've found many of this kind of person. Let's say that we work only with people whom we like on a human level.'

As he listened to Luciano speaking, Palmeri remembered the many press articles that had appeared on the Benettons and their company. Could this affable, bespectacled guru with the preppy clothes keep control of this business? If Luciano's plans were realized, Benetton was about to launch itself into an almost uncontrollable growth spiral ... To set up 5000 stores all over the world would mean a crazy amount of money. Could the family steer Benetton towards the goals they seemed to have set? He had heard that the management team was rather small-town Italian, with a provincial view of the rest of the world, or even the rest of Italy. Some of them felt uncomfortable going as far as Rome, and few spoke anything but Italian. Most had close ties to Luciano, Giuliana and Gilberto.

As Luciano and Gilberto discussed something between themselves, Palmeri took another cup of coffee and tried to remember the dinner conversation and the two earlier meetings he had had with the brothers. By the sound of it, they could certainly use some strong financial and logistic guidance. When he had asked one or two questions on the labour situation, plant locations and the size of the total work force, neither brother seemed to know the answers, nor did they possess a clear organization chart for the 30 or so managers they had recently hired. Luciano had tried to improvise on a napkin, but admitted that he was not absolutely sure of the answers. When asked about fixed costs and variable costs, the brothers shrugged off the question, hinting that Aluffi took care of things like this ....

As Palmeri replaced his cup on the table. Luciano's voice broke into his thoughts, 'Well, Mr. Palmeri, when can you start?'

INTERNATIONAL

Case 4.2 Aldo Palmeri: Taking charge (B)

This case was written by Research Associate Juliet Burdet-Taylor, under the supervision of Professor Werner Ketelhöhn, as a basis for class discussion rather than to illustrate either effective or ineffective handling of a business situation.

Manage our growth . . .

Aldo Palmeri joined Benetton in January 1983 and within a short time was made Managing Director, sharing the title with long-standing employee, Elio Aluffi. 'Of course he knew just about everything there was to know about Benetton; he had been there from the start. One of his relatives was in charge of personnel, a good reason for me to find someone to take over human resources.'

Benetton in 1983

Palmeri was alarmed at the limited information systems capacity and logistic support, particularly in view of Benetton's accelerating growth (Exhibit 4.3). He took immediate action by contacting a firm of information systems consultants with whom he planned to work on redefining the system.

He was also concerned by the way financial operations were handled and the amount of interest Benetton paid to banks. He immediately set about improving this situation and, as neither a family member nor Elio Aluffi was involved in finance, Palmeri was able to act freely in this area.

'The right men must be selected,' Palmeri told Luciano. 'If you want to go international, the company will need a new flavour, a new culture. Local non-professional people can no longer do the job.' It was obvious to Palmeri that many of the managers, who had been hired locally and who could not be expected to follow Benetton into the next phase of its development, would have to be replaced.

What Palmeri needed was a strong human resources manager to help him recruit new people.

	1981*	1982	1983	1984
Income statement				
Sales	349.7	309.0	370.1	406.4
Cost of goods sold	326.5	336.3	258.9	270.8
Gross profit	75.6	65.4	111.2	135.6
SG & A Expenses	7.9	0.4	73.5	72.0
Earnings before interest and depreciation	58.8	50.0	37.7	63.6
Interest expense	11.0	13.2	19.0	17.4
Depreciation	16.7	14.5	5.3	9.2
Earnings before tax	30.9	22.2	13.4	36.9
Tax	14.2	9.7	5.7	17.5
Earnings after tax	16.7	12.5	7.7	19.4
Minority interest	–	–	1.0	1.7
Earnings	16.7	12.5	8.7	21.1
Balance sheet				
Current assets	132.8	163.1	239.1	239.8
Fixed assets	37.1	41.7	62.1	50.0
Intangibles	13.5	9.4	8.6	6.4
Other Assets	–	–	3.9	3.1
Total assets	183.4	214.2	313.6	299.3
Current liabilities	84.4	99.0	179.0	179.9
Long-term liabilities	19.6	42.2	57.2	40.9
Net worth	79.4	73.0	75.4	78.4
Total liabilities and net worth	183.4	214.2	313.6	299.3

*1981 figures given for the income statement covered an 18-month period.

Exhibit 4.3 *Financial statements for Benetton 1981–1984 (in millions of dollars)*

Giovanni Cantagalli, previously with 3M Corporation, was in charge of organization and human resources for a joint venture between Occidental Petroleum and an Italian state-owned company when he was contacted by Aldo Palmeri. 'I asked him to join us and he came. Together we looked at what needed to be done to organize a successful Italian operation with a good network of sales outlets into the same type of thing but on a European and then a worldwide scale. It was quite a simple problem, not a huge task, but there were two main blocks to progress. One was the level of Benetton's existing management and the other was service to our customers out in the market, service to our agents and our retailers. We needed a very good information system as insufficient information could create blockages in the flow of goods to clients. If Benetton, as supplier, made it difficult for storeowners to run their businesses, these people risked losing their investments.' Within six months of hiring the information system consultants, an improved system was in place.

Finding the right managers

Palmeri explained:

> Finding the right managers was not easy. Not many people want to live in Treviso. Managers mainly come from the northwest of Italy and not many want to leave Milan for a small provincial town with under 100,000 people. We had to play up two main features of the company to attract the talent we wanted. We presented Benetton as a company that would grow fast – 'OK, sure we're small now, but stick with us; we are going to be big. You can be manager of a large company within a few years.' The other attraction we offered was the Benetton trademark, which had benefited from an increase in communication spending and promotional energy. When recruiting, a company with a well-known trademark is far more attractive than one that is unknown.

Less than a year after Palmeri's arrival at Benetton, a new management was in place. Most of the existing management team had been replaced and, by 1984, Aluffi himself had gone. The youngest Benetton, Carlo, was in the process of developing production (Exhibit 4.4).

Growth problems

Benetton continued to consolidate its hold on European markets, with the emphasis on France, W. Germany, Switzerland and the UK. The system of agents that existed in Italy had been maintained when going abroad. Italian agents were selected with whom Benetton management would share major decisions on marketing, retailing, structure, store location, etc. The agents in turn supervised and sometimes owned the retail stores.

In France, where fashion was sophisticated, the agents were demanding a wider range of items from Benetton. The French fashion business had been seriously affected by the recession that struck most of Europe in 1983/84 and people who had previously shopped in boutiques could no longer afford to do so.

By increasing production of the more exclusive items in its collection, the agents felt that Benetton would be able to tap this new segment of more affluent users. However, to really attract this segment, the agents in France felt that Benetton's standard store design needed restructuring. The traditional $40\,m^2$ sweater shop would have to be replaced by larger and more luxurious premises with space for a whole line of coordinated casual wear for the chic French clientele. The Benettons' guidelines for shop size and layout had always been respected. Palmeri wondered how much attention he should pay to these new requests.

The Benetton trademark, promotion and protection

Sitting in his office one afternoon in early 1983, Palmeri leafed through a file containing requests for use of the Benetton trademark. Clearly the name that could become a gold mine for the company was a highly vulnerable asset. The more famous the company became, the more requests for its trademark were received. Aldo Palmeri

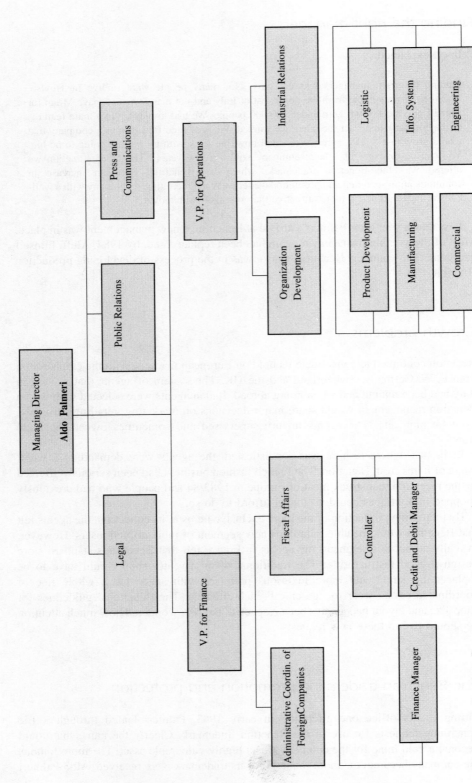

Exhibit 4.4 *New Benetton management structure*

was confronted with demands from all sides and had difficulty knowing what to reply.

Could the Benetton name be used by a war toy manufacturer or for computerized electronic games where points were scored for killing animals or birds? What about the maker of hunting weapons, or teenage games in which sex and violence were the overriding theme? The requests by manufacturers of less controversial products – watches, sun-glasses, perfumes and so on – were not necessarily any easier to answer. However inoffensive a product, or however compatible it may have seemed, answering a manufacturer's demand was difficult, for beyond the simple logistics of the matter lay the question, was it right for Benetton? Or, could it be sold in the Benetton stores? Did it fit? Palmeri was often forced to refuse because such requests had no clear answer.

Palmeri knew it would be tempting to use Benetton's name for a much wider range of products, taking advantage of the company's quality image and goodwill to sustain competitive advantage in other businesses. This was often done and in many cases it worked; some companies granted others the right to use their brand names while they sat back and raked in the royalties . . . a lot of money for not much work. But, an inferior quality extension of the brand name that was given wide exposure could backfire. In the 1970s, when General Mills tried extending the prestigious Lacoste alligator name into a wider variety of clothing to reach new markets, it worked for a while. But when tastes and status symbols changed, sales started dropping sharply. By 1982 the alligator had lost its snob appeal, and the up-market sports association had weakened. Risk of overexposure or undisciplined use of the Benetton name needed serious consideration.

Palmeri knew of other companies that suffered deeply after diluting their valuable image by over-extension of their trademark. The fall of Gucci was partly attributed to its 14,000 products. The extension of a brand name was controversial because, even when successful, there would always be someone who was not satisfied with some detail or someone who had had a bad experience with the name. This could rub off on the way these people perceived the original brand, making it difficult for the manufacturer to win them over and keep them. Clearly, when a brand received wider exposure through extensions, it reached more people, thus increasing the chances that customers would have a bad experience and develop a negative attitude toward the brand.

Palmeri turned the page . . . and the next and many more. They were full of stories about Lacoste, one of Benetton's closest rivals. 'Crocodiles a dollar apiece, Lacoste copies made in Turkey, Thailand, the Philippines. Lacoste's emblem appears on millions of non-Lacoste shirts, hundreds of thousands of crocodiles – or were they alligators – seized in Italy on their way to clothing manufacturers in Morocco, Korea, Hong Kong.' One Hong Kong-based imitator of Lacoste had become so large and successful that it was fighting off its own imitators and had overtaken Lacoste itself in size; 65% of its production was sold anonymously to leading brand name designers in the USA, Europe and Japan.

By the early 1980s, counterfeiting had become a widespread, ever-growing business worth billions. Copies of expensive high quality products – Rolex watches, Gucci and Vuitton bags and an endless array of clothing – were being produced very cheaply and were flooding popular tourist markets under false labels all over the world.

The examples of counterfeiting, illegal copies, and trademark violations continued throughout the thick file. Palmeri read, 'Laura Ashley, the British women's apparel and home furnishing textile company, spent hundreds of thousands of pounds a year bringing lawsuits against counterfeiters and imitators both of its products and its shop design. However, some of those being accused were small Indian or Asian textile printers, who had bought imitation prints from larger imitators and were unaware of their fault. The Swiss watch industry claimed to lose up to a billion Swiss francs a year through counterfeiters, and the French perfume business, 10% of its annual business.'

Palmeri and the Benettons knew the trademark to be an intrinsic part of their company's success and philosophy, and they felt proprietary and protective towards it, yet no official policy existed for its protection or exploitation. As Luciano Benetton set his sights on the world market, one of Palmeri's top priorities was to solve this problem quickly.

Going back to the USA

The USA was the Benettons' next major goal; they planned to expand their hold on the American market considerably in the next few years. An earlier foray in 1980, using Italian agents, had not resulted in any significant penetration. The company had sold both through its usual small specialized shops and by renting space in department stores. Results had been disappointing. With transportation costs at 8% and customs duties at 25% of the US retail price, Benetton could not compete with less expensive goods. By 1983, Benetton had about 66 retail outlets in the USA.

A similar attempt to enter the Japanese market had also proved unsuccessful. Benetton had used the traditional system of shops and Italian agents. There were no tangible obstacles to success, no legal or logistic problems. There were Italian investors ready to open shops; they opened and Benetton supplied the clothes as it did everywhere else. But, it failed . . .

It was the USA that excited Luciano most at the time . . . the sheer volume of the market, the glamour, and the challenges it would present for marketing, production and supply, and distribution. And the challenges of competition. Existing major US competitors were aggressive, big and rich. Successful, long-established players, such as Levi-Strauss with $2.3 billion in sales in 1982, spent over one hundred million dollars on advertising and promotional campaigns each year. Many of these competitors sold through their own wholly-owned stores or boutiques in the shopping malls that were typical in US cities and smaller towns. Others sold their products in large retail stores.

Consolidation of its hold in the US market was a serious challenge for Benetton. Beyond the strong competitive situation, there were questions of product line, whether or not to use agents, and if so, whom? America's preference for synthetic fibres would certainly affect product line selection. The choice of small boutique-style retail outlets or shops inside large department stores or even selling through mail-order catalogues were all options to be considered. Others were the use of flag stores prior to opening standard shops, stores that would be opened in the most prestigious shopping areas in a city, Fifth Avenue or Rodeo Drive. These stores would be Benetton's own investment, intended to draw attention to the brand and the products, and to set the tone for future stores that agents would open in the same town. Other preoccupations when returning to the USA would be the type of advertising campaign, regional or national, the media, promotional effort with storeowners at the point of sale and, of course, a regional segmentation of the country.

On the production and operations level, the question arose as to whether a plant and warehouse should be opened in the USA or simply a warehouse to stock product arriving from Ponzano, or whether the direct distribution of goods from Europe to strategic retail sites in the USA was the best solution. Benetton had recently completed a giant warehouse in Treviso that had cost $30 million.

There were many problems to be solved, but the most important one was – how should Benetton handle the American market?

Case 4.3 Aldo Palmeri: Managing growth (C)

This case was written by Research Associate Juliet Burdet-Taylor, under the supervision of Professor Werner Ketelhöhn, as a basis for class discussion rather than to illustrate either effective or ineffective handling of a business situation.

Victims of our own growth . . .

We are the victims of our own success, so we have to face the consequences and manage the growth we generate.

On a late fall morning in 1985, Aldo Palmeri, Managing Director of Benetton, and Roberto Verdi, a visitor from Milan, sat in Palmeri's office in the magnificently restored 17th century villa that housed Benetton's headquarters at Ponzano in northern Italy. Palmeri had asked Verdi to join Benetton as Director of Information Systems. Palmeri pushed a sheet of paper towards Verdi:

Look at this: the increase in Benetton's stores over the last few years . . . 1917 in 1982, 2296 in 1983, 2644 in 1984 and this year we'll be up around 3200 worldwide. About half of our sales are outside Italy, with almost all manufacturing at home. Two years ago we were selling $370 million (Exhibit 4.3). This year we'll be over $460 million and next year around $700 million, with about 4000 shops. We are not complaining but we are going to have our work cut out keeping up. How do you keep all these shops happy, supply them, bill them and collect their payments? How do you control sales when you don't own the outlet and when you want your storeowners to respect your sales and promotion policies? How do you maintain the balance between a market with a voracious appetite for your products and the resources the company has available to supply this market?

We create demand, we advertise, we promote and so our products are popular. In fact they are so popular that not only does everyone want to buy them, but they want to sell them as well. The stuff is doing so well that everyone wants to open a Benetton store. This is great of course, but production, supply, and capacity have to move very fast. Then as more shops open, the Benetton label gains yet more visibility which, once more, boosts demand and so it goes on . . . .

'It sounds like a real chicken and egg story,' laughed Verdi. 'Well, it is an exciting challenge but as the pace quickens ... accelerates, we need even better professional management, and the quality of our information systems technology must be outstanding,' Palmeri replied.

A tiny family company

The Benetton company had been created when Luciano began selling a small collection of his sister Giuliana's knitwear to local stores. These sweaters were so well received that the brother and sister decided to start a company. In 1965, their business was incorporated as 'Maglificio di Ponzano Veneto dei Fratelli Benetton'. Luciano and Giuliana were joined by their younger brother Gilberto, and in 1966 the family built its first factory in Ponzano near their home town, Treviso. The first independent Benetton shop was opened in Belluno two years later. The number of shops increased as the Benettons concentrated on conquering the domestic market. By 1975, there were 200 Benetton shops selling the company's distinctive knitwear throughout Italy. In 1978, Benetton's sales reached $80 million per year.

The largest knitwear producer in the world

A compact intense man with the power of absolute concentration, Palmeri had joined Benetton in early 1983. The company was already the largest knitwear producer in the world with a fast growing line of trendy coordinated garments. The company was still a tightly held family unit with the four Benettons running and growing the business. Sales for 1983 were $370 million with earnings of $20 million. Luciano, as Chairman of the Board, was most interested in the sales and promotional side of the business. The directors of legal affairs, finance and control reported to Gilberto, Vice Chairman of the Board. Giuliana, a board member, ran everything to do with design, new products and the Benetton collection. Carlo, the youngest member of the family, later became responsible for manufacturing and logistics.

By the beginning of the 1980s, Benetton's exceptionally rapid domestic growth had all but saturated the Italian market. The time had come for the company to consolidate its sales abroad and start operating on a truly global scale. A professional manager was needed to lead the company through the next phase of its development.

Aldo Palmeri

Luciano and Gilberto Benetton recruited Aldo Palmeri themselves from the Italian Ministry of Industry. With degrees in law and economics, as well as a banking background, Palmeri was selected to help the Benettons achieve their ambitious expansion goals, which included substantial consolidation and growth in Europe and eventually the rest of the world.

Palmeri arrived to find what he described as a pure family enterprise without any real managerial structure. 'Economically the company was doing fine,' Palmeri remarked. But, he felt exports were still disproportionately low. Domestic demand had more than doubled in the two years before Palmeri's arrival but insufficient production capacity had caused serious delays in deliveries and, even with the use of subcontractors, only 60% of Benetton's orders had been met in 1981.

After carrying out an initial analysis of the major areas of the Benetton business, Palmeri informed Luciano that he found the company poorly organized and inadequately staffed. He was concerned by the limited information systems capacity and logistic support, and by the way financial operations were being handled. The company's current growth rate and plans for the future demanded immediate reorganization. With the help of a consultant, Palmeri redesigned the information system and, as no family member had financial experience, he rapidly improved Benetton's conditions with its banks.

Recruitment

Before Palmeri joined the company, the Benetton management team comprised mainly locally hired executives, most of whom spoke only Italian. The majority of these managers had been with Benetton for many years. Palmeri wasted no time in recommending a radical change, advising Luciano that no growth goals could be pursued until a new management had been put in place and all the central functions of the company redefined.

Palmeri needed a strong human resources manager to help him recruit new people. Giovanni Cantagalli, previously with the 3M Corporation, was in charge of organization and human resources for a joint venture between Occidental Petroleum and an Italian state-owned company when Aldo Palmeri contacted him. Cantagalli agreed to join Benetton.

Palmeri and Cantagalli started a recruitment campaign that took them up and down the country. Palmeri explained:

> Finding the right managers was not easy. Not many people want to live in Treviso. Good managers come mainly from the northwest of Italy, and are not prepared to leave Milan for a provincial town with less than 100,000 people. We had to play up two main features of the company to attract the talent we wanted. We presented Benetton as a company that would grow fast – 'OK, sure we're small now, but stick with us; we are going to be big. You can be manager of a large company within a few years.' The other attraction we offered was the Benetton trademark, which had benefited from an increase in communication spending and promotional energy. When recruiting, a company with a well-known trademark is far more attractive than one that is unknown.

Within a year of Palmeri's arrival, most of the existing managers had been replaced and a new management structure had been created (Exhibit 4.4).

Palmeri and Cantagalli set themselves the goal of converting Benetton, a successful Italian business with a good network of domestic sales outlets, into a similar operation on a European and, eventually, a worldwide scale. 'It was quite a simple problem, not a huge task,' Palmeri explained. 'We needed a very good information system as insufficient information could create blockages in the flow of goods to clients. If Benetton made it difficult for storeowners to run their businesses, by delaying deliveries, these people risked losing their investments.' Within six months of hiring the information system consultants, installation of an improved system was underway.

The USA and Japan

Luciano Benetton had a weakness for the hype and challenge of the American market, where an initial foray in 1980 had resulted in only limited success. In 1983, there were about 60 Benetton stores in the United States. Differences in retailing techniques and the wide cultural and behavioural gulf between selling in Italy and selling in the USA did not facilitate Benetton's penetration of the American market. Benetton's distinctive European style was not adopted at once by American clients. When selling with the European approach, i.e. using exclusive outlets, the local storeowners had problems understanding the Benetton philosophy. The benefits of putting together coordinated collections of garments to increase sales eluded them. When selling in department stores, sales managers, who did not have the same motivation as Benetton storeowners in Europe, could not give the same level of support. Retailing problems were compounded by the high cost of selling European goods in the USA and by the success of national players. In the ferociously competitive US market where big long-established players like Levi-Strauss spent billions on advertising, Benetton was unable to gain a significant hold. However, Luciano was still convinced that, if properly approached, the American market offered unlimited potential for Benetton. Luciano was also anxious to enter Japan on a grand scale and felt that a strong hold on the US market could help open doors in Japan. An earlier attempt to enter Japan, sending in Italian agents, had resulted in a rebuff for Benetton, once more due to the company's European attitude and inability to grasp the Japanese way of doing business. Palmeri was responsible for the relaunch plans in these two key markets.

The Benetton name

The Benetton trademark was a potential gold mine for the company, but was also highly vulnerable. Constant demands were received from outside companies wanting the right to use the Benetton trademark for a variety of non-apparel products from bed linen to war toys. Before embarking on an intensified world campaign, Palmeri wanted to be sure that Benetton's trademark policies were watertight. There was always the temptation to use the Benetton name more freely for a wider range of goods and so benefit from its extension, collecting large sums of money in royalties with little or no outlay. This had been done successfully by many, but it had also brought some very prestigious suppliers to their knees. The collapse of Gucci, with its 14,000 different products, was a good example of over-extension.

Counterfeiting could have horrendous implications for Benetton, especially when moving into a worldwide market. Lacoste, one of Benetton's major rivals, had a long history of counterfeiting. Stories of Lacoste fakes abounded. 'Imitation Lacoste shirts produced in low-cost developing countries and sold for a fraction of the genuine European version, hundreds of thousands of imitation Lacoste alligator emblems, produced in Southeast Asia, intercepted on their way to Morocco or South Korea where they would be glued onto fake polo shirts.'

Palmeri's theory was that there could be no successful worldwide penetration without a solidly protected brand name. He knew the risks Benetton would run unless proper action were taken. Palmeri felt that the market had to be considered as global and that substantial investment was required to back the brand with the right management and image. Distribution and sales through specialized exclusive retail shops were, he felt, an essential part of a successful brand management effort.

How can production keep up with demand?

Over lunch, Aldo Palmeri continued his explanation of the workings of Benetton. The afternoon was spent visiting the plants and warehouses in the surrounding area. A very modern fully automated plant had been built only 100 yards from the sumptuous villa that housed Benetton's administrative headquarters. As they toured the site, Palmeri stopped in a corner of a factory and yelled at Verdi, 'There'll be 34 million pieces shipped in 1985.'

Cupping his hand behind his ear and leaning towards Palmeri, Verdi shouted something that was lost in the noise of the machinery. 'I said, that's impressive,' Verdi explained as he and Palmeri walked along a calmer corridor. Palmeri smiled at the newcomer:

Yes, it *is* impressive, and it's all going very fast . . . as I said before, the more we make, the more they want, the more they get and the more they sell, so the more we make. Maybe it's more of an egg and chicken problem. Anyway, there are times when it all seems to be going faster than we are. The original little sweater company is now the biggest knitwear producer in the world and makes just about every garment and accessory from head to toe. As I said, next year, we'll probably have 4000 shops to supply and obviously they will all want their stock delivered on time. We are constantly upgrading our plants. With the CAD/CAM system we've just seen, the raw materials are fed into machines programmed to cut 15,000 garments in 8 hours. Very fast, a terrific saving in time, especially between design approval and production and, of course, we minimize waste materials. We can design and manufacture 2000 different garments a year on this software.

When Luciano travels, he comes back with new ideas from all over the world on ways that we can speed up production and delivery. For instance, you may have seen Benetton stores offering basic sweaters in as many as 30 different colours. It's obvious that stocking, let's say, 12 different models in 30 colours, multiplied by the sizes you need, would be out of the question. Luciano solved the problem by treating finished clothes as if they were raw materials. Instead of producing knitwear from different coloured yarns, the garments are knitted in advance from undyed, natural coloured yarn and kept already assembled in batches. Then, when orders are received, the dyeing is done according to the storeowners' colour choices. Shops can wait until just before production to give their colour choices for up to one-third of their stock. This allows them to know the season's favourite colours before committing themselves. We do not accept returned goods. Small batch manufacturing means we can offer a much wider range of colours and gives us the competitive edge we need to lead the market.

Back in Palmeri's office, the men drank coffee and continued their discussion. 'We'll go over and see the new warehouse that has just been finished. It's totally automated and handles 300,000 boxes a year. It's a space-age creation.'

Subcontractors

We don't have intermediary warehouses with our system. Finished goods are shipped directly from the central warehouse to the shops, even for foreign shipments. This means that Benetton bills its clients directly with no middleman wholesalers. Sounds simple enough . . . it is and it isn't. First of all, about three-quarters of our production work is done outside the factories you saw. The factories mainly do the cutting and some dyeing. Sewing, knitting, special finishing and assembly are done outside by independent subcontractors we call 'labs'. Luciano Benetton has helped develop these businesses over the years; some are large, some are small, but most have worked for the company for a long time. Carlo Benetton is responsible for them now. Some are owned or part owned by Benetton. Many were started by Benetton plant workers or factory managers, some of whom remain Benetton employees. Since I have been in the company, the number of plants has dropped from nine to five, and the labs have increased in number. Almost all the knitting is done by labs, which then pass the knitted pieces on to other labs for assembly into jackets or sweaters. There are about 200 labs doing sweaters alone, and 90% of them work exclusively for us.

The subcontractor system gives Benetton the flexibility it needs in manufacturing and supply. We must be first into the market with new styles and, as demands and tastes are cyclical, we must be able to vary output accordingly. Independent subcontractors start up and slow down rapidly and at much lower cost than if we used our own factories for everything. Many of the labs we use have fewer than 15 employees, which means that they are not bound to pay the social charges of 49% of a worker's salary, required by the state. The system of subcontractors lends itself to last minute decisions, fast changes, the possibility of moving garments around between labs. Some labs do part of a process, some all.

There are no written contracts with subcontractors, whose links with Benetton are based on the trust that has grown up between them and the Benetton family over the years. The system seems to work. It was all in place before I joined. When using this type of dispersed manufacturing system, quality is a major concern, of course. Quality specifications are the only thing given in written form. Labs that fall below our quality standards are dropped. The drop-out rate is about ten labs per year. But those which stay remain totally loyal to Benetton, refusing work from other manufacturers. As I said, the problem of ensuring that labs follow Benetton's growth as we increase output is a worry. But all labs are not small family affairs. Some have grown big over the years with Benetton and their owners have made a lot of money. Some of the larger labs subcontract work to the smaller ones. But, many of the subcontractors are still little people with no capital to invest in bigger and faster machines. It's in our interest to ensure that as Benetton grows, they can grow with us.

The labs invest in their own knitting machines but, if a garment is dropped from the line and a machine becomes obsolete, Benetton will probably compensate the subcontractor. Although we do not have a formal policy as far as helping the labs is concerned, we want to make sure that they can lease or purchase the machinery needed to produce for us. Traditionally, the Benetton family has given a hand to subcontractor friends in need of funds for expansion or to those former employees who are taking over facilities previously owned by Benetton to set up their own labs. If Benetton has a sudden overload problem and needs a lab to increase capacity to keep up with the company's growth, Benetton will help out with working capital. In 1983, Benetton started helping labs with liquidity problems by buying back their debt.

Throughput

It's not easy to follow a Benetton garment from its raw material state to the customer. These charts (Exhibits 4.5 and 4.6) give an idea of the throughput of our products from their raw

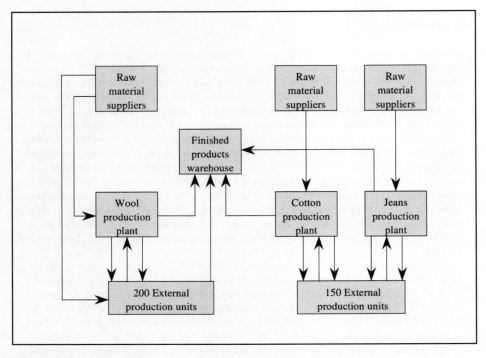

Exhibit 4.5 *Flow of materials. (Source: Benetton Group SpA)*

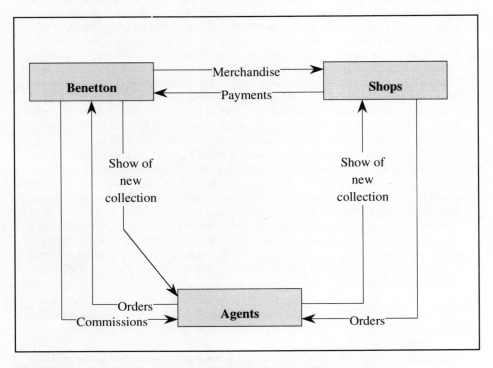

Exhibit 4.6 *Distribution network. (Source: Benetton Group SpA)*

state to the moment they arrive at the shop. The whole procedure is monitored by two computers, one for wool and one for cotton. The suppliers of basic materials, mainly raw wool and pure cotton, deliver to the raw material warehouse here in Ponzano. Then, depending on what it will be used for, the yarns go either to Monzambano or stay in Ponzano. Woven cotton goes straight from the suppliers to one of the cutting plants, Villorba or Cusignana, and then on to the subcontractors for finishing or assembly, then back in garment form to the packaging department of the plant from which it came, or to another plant, depending on its destination. Knitted garments take a more circuitous route and may go through three or four departments at Ponzano and then on to Resana for chemical treatment, before going to a subcontractor for finishing or assembly. It does look complicated at first, doesn't it?

Later in the afternoon as the two men crossed the courtyard, a Maserati pulled out and stopped to let them pass. The driver waved to Palmeri. 'I see your top managers are pretty well paid,' joked Verdi, turning to Palmeri. 'That's a plant manager actually,' replied Palmeri, 'and, of course, he's also a lab owner. The chap over there in the Fiat is a manager. You're right though, subcontractors like Busoni, in the sports car, can make a lot of money on the side. The family does not permit Benetton's professional managers to own labs.' Verdi looked pensive. 'I should think this could cause some problems of motivation inside the company.'

The two men walked back to Palmeri's office through the exquisite gardens along the cloistered stone path that surrounded the estate. 'OK, so that was a very rough outline of how our production is done. The usual final inspection, bagging and tagging operations are done in the plant with computerized boxing, labelling and sealing. Labels in the right languages and prices in the currency of the country of destination are also produced by computer. Goods are transferred to the warehouse for shipping. As I said, the warehouse is quite something. It's just next door at Castrette. I will take you over there later.'

Point of sale – fast market feedback

Fast market feedback is probably one of our key areas of success. We are working towards getting daily feedback from shops on what sells and what does not. Our information systems are being upgraded constantly. The mainframe here is connected to minis in seven major cities in Europe and it works well for now but if we keep on growing at our present rate, it will no longer be cost effective. Our idea at the moment is to run a pilot programme in a limited number of stores, that will give us a continuous flow of point-of-sale feedback. Using a micro-computer linked to a cash register, we should be able to collect data on the day's sales – volume, selling price, type of garment, styles and colours – and relay this to headquarters every evening. The up-to-the-minute findings of this POS audit will be invaluable when we prepare our reassortment and will ensure that Benetton comes out first with new products for the season.

As I explained this morning, our sales growth has been nothing short of volcanic, with eruptions all over the world – Japan, the USA and, of course, everywhere in Europe. We are doing several things right and it seems to be paying off. We are very close to the market, and our feedback and monitoring system enables us to respond faster than our competitors. Traditionally, we have always sold through smallish customized stores that have been specially designed for Benetton's products, and are decorated and fitted out according to our own specifications. However, as we continue to extend our line beyond the original sweater to include a whole collection of coordinates with wool trousers, jeans, blazers and skirts and all the little matching hats, scarves and gloves, storeowners want bigger shops and some need help with the financing.

Retailing: agents – shopowners

Luciano has developed a system whereby Benetton does not invest directly in retailing. Our products are sold by shops that are owned and run by small independent entrepreneurs, who might have invested their savings or even mortgaged their houses to set up a Benetton outlet, or several. Some of these storeowners have become very successful and may own five or six stores. The system has worked well so far and, as I said, some storeowners have made a lot of money. They can earn a gross margin of 45–50% on their sales. Luciano oversees the sales operation and runs it in accordance with a set of rules devised to ensure that Benetton's image and high standards are respected. Storeholders must agree to run their shops in accordance with the very specific conditions which Benetton demands. Annual sales per store must reach a certain level, and a shop may sell only Benetton products. Displays, decoration and promotion must comply with Benetton's norms. It sounds like a franchise but, in fact, it is not. The shops pay no fees to Benetton for the use of its name nor a royalty based on profit. The company gives storeholders no regional exclusivity.

Agents

The storeowners are controlled and advised by agents who have been personally selected by Luciano and who are often old family friends. There are about 30 agents at present and Luciano manages them. Their role is vital as they are responsible for finding and selecting storeowners. They also advise and support their storeowners, teaching them how to manage the Benetton way, and helping ensure that Benetton's image is correctly projected by displays, logos, presentation of garments, etc. The agents' role is crucial to the success of our retail operation. They are selected based on their potential as successful entrepreneurs. They are independent of Benetton, while at the same time protecting the company's interests. They are paid a 4% commission on everything sold by the shops they supervise. By developing this network of self-employed agents, Luciano has succeeded in getting these dynamic, gutsy entrepreneurs into the Benetton sales activity. Their role is key in ensuring the financial success of stores, giving shopowners a helping hand with credit and ensuring that as Benetton grows, its retail outlets grow with it.

Agents act as a bridge between Luciano in marketing, Giuliana in design and, ultimately, the golfer out there on the tee wearing a Benetton cardigan. Agents research and select new areas in which shops will be opened. They counsel shopowners on merchandising and product mix. The agents themselves attend Giuliana's presentations of the collections for the year ahead, making a selection of what they feel their storeowners should sell. Controlling the lines into agents is another logistics challenge. Little by little, we hope each agent will be connected to the Ponzano headquarters through our information system. But as I said, growth is going to make our present system too expensive. Our goal now is to have the agents plus all the data we need from the retail outlets – order-entry, order confirmations, colour instructions and so forth – plus the status of orders inside plants or labs, running through one super network. Maybe we shall hook up a satellite connection and knock out costly long distance phone calls. However, that may take us a year or two.

In the meantime, the selection and treatment of agents in foreign markets, as we continue to strengthen our activities abroad, is a concern. Not long ago, in France where fashion is

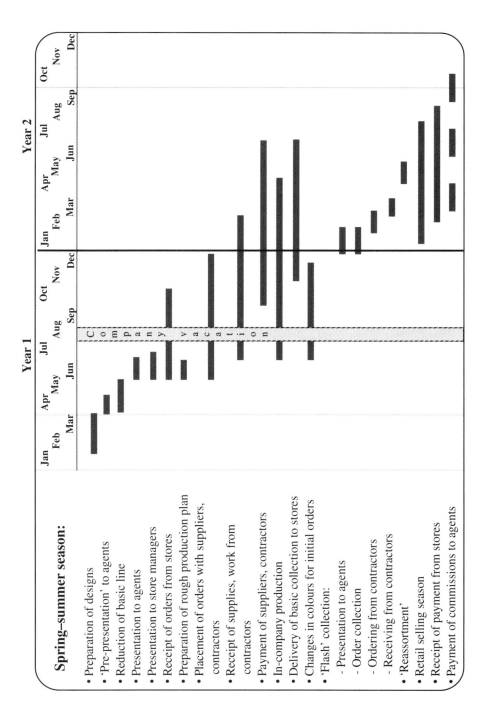

Exhibit 4.7 Operating cycle, Benetton Group. (Source: Benetton Group SpA)

sophisticated, our agents demanded a wider range of items than usual. The French fashion business had been seriously affected by the recession of 1983/84, and people who had previously shopped in boutiques, could no longer afford to do so. The agents felt that Benetton would be able to tap this new segment of more affluent users, by increasing their offering of more elegant clothes to appeal to the chic French clientele. However, this would mean restructuring the standard Benetton store and replacing the old 40 m^2 sweater shop by larger and more luxurious premises. The Benettons' guidelines for shop size and layout had always been respected. This is the type of problem we have to face. How much attention should we pay to these new requests?

The selection of agents for our foreign business can be key to its success or failure. For instance, when the company went into Spain and West Germany, Italian agents were sent to export Benetton's culture and they were successful. The first time Benetton went into Japan, they also used Italian agents. The result was not successful. I have recommended that when returning to Japan, we set up joint ventures with local manufacturers.

Seasons and collections

There are two major selling seasons in the garment business, spring/summer and autumn/winter. This plan (Exhibit 4.7) gives a rough idea of a spring/summer operating cycle from preparation with the designer to the moment the agent has received commission on his shopowner's sales. Agents, product managers and manufacturing managers attend a presentation with Giuliana Benetton in April and make a selection of garments they will recommend to their storeowners. Of the approximately 600 items shown, about one-quarter of these are eliminated. During the summer months, small quantities of the remaining items are manufactured and presented to agents and shopowners. Based on the first 5–10% of orders, production schedules and subcontracts are prepared. After the agents have placed their orders for the basic stock, each order goes into a preliminary production schedule. Storeowners receive 80–90% of their basic collection between November and May.

The 10–20% balance of orders is divided into what we call our 'Flash' and 'Reassortment', which allow shops to adjust their orders placed several months of the selling season. The 'Flash' comprises about 50 items that were not included in the original basic collection and which are based on the style of competitive products. The 'Reassortment' is a collection of 30–50 of our basic pieces, which are expected to be successful in the current season. The idea has two advantages. It gives shops the chance to add to their basic orders placed early in the season, and it also uses Benetton's excess capacity over the summer.

For a winter cycle, production will start between November and January. Half the raw materials are ordered at the same time as the November collection is shown, with completion when firm orders have been received from storeowners in early January. With our growth rate and our reputation for the use of 100% pure wool or pure cotton fabrics, purchasing at optimal price and quality can be extremely difficult unless we have accurate input on timing and quantities.

Production is divided up between in-house work and subcontractors. Deliveries begin at the end of April with payments due from storeholders at 30-, 60- and 90-day intervals, at the end of September, October and November. So from May 1 to the end of September, Benetton, with production completed and deliveries made, has not received payment from its customers.

Benetton pays its raw material suppliers at 90–100 days. Subcontractors are paid at 30 days. Our suppliers can take extended credit, but our subcontractors need fast payments and, as I said, sometimes they need additional financial help to keep up with our demands.

5

The missing link in the solutions business: managing flows through business systems

Case 5.1 Compaq Computer Corporation

This case was prepared by Research Associates James Henderson and Juliet Burdet-Taylor, under the supervision of Professors Werner Ketelhöhn and Ralf Boscheck, as a basis for class discussion rather than to illustrate either effective or ineffective handling of a business situation.

All data in this case was obtained from published sources and third parties. The company was not involved in the development of this case.

In 1981, Joseph 'Rod' Canion left Texas Instruments (TI) after 11 years of doing development work on subsystems and peripherals and two years working on the company's new office microcomputer. Canion, an ardent IBM watcher, had become disillusioned by TI's refusal to acknowledge the significance of IBM's recent entry into the micro-computer market. Canion and two of his engineering colleagues, Bill Murto and Jim Harris, decided to set up a company, which they called Compaq Computer Corpora-tion. With its first product, a portable microcomputer, sales skyrocketed. Compaq, based in Houston, Texas, was to become the fastest growing company in US corporate history. By 1989, Compaq was a $2.9 billion powerhouse with return on sales figures unheard of in the industry. Could it continue its sales and profit growth unchallenged by smaller competitors?

The first PCs

Initially regarded as a toy or a gimmick, the personal computer (PC) was to revolutionize data processing. The PC had grown, in the space of three years, from a microprocessor driven gadget used by hobbyists to a pre-assembled user-friendly microcomputer. Basically a PC was not much more than a box containing the microprocessor and memory chips on a printed circuit board, a power source, disk drives, a keyboard, a TV type screen and additional circuitry.

Apple

The PC was launched into orbit when California computer whiz kids, Steve Jobs and Steve Wozniak, founded their company, Apple Computer, in 1977. The first real PC, Apple II, was simple and economical to assemble. It had a small screen and came in an attractive beige plastic shell with a carrying handle. This product, initially positioned as a home computer, was sold through independent retail computer stores that were serviced by eight regional distribution centres. The price per unit was $1200, with an estimated dealer margin of 30–40%. Apple, unlike other computer companies, invited software programmers to write applications for its new PC. One of these applications, Visicalc – a forerunner to the popular Lotus 123 spreadsheet program, propelled the company into the newly emerging office PC market.

IBM

In 1980, IBM, the largest computer company in the world, with the majority of its revenues coming from mainframes, was forced to react to Apple's precocious launch. In its haste to enter the PC market, IBM broke with its traditional sourcing habits by purchasing components, software support and peripherals from outside. Within 12 months, the company had introduced the IBM PC, which contained Intel's (40% owned by IBM) 8088 microprocessor, Microsoft's MS/DOS operating system (PC/DOS under IBM's logo), Tandon's disk drives, and SCI's electronic circuit boards. Only one element of the PC, the Read-Only Memory Basic Input Output System (ROM BIOS) was copyrighted by IBM. The basic price for the IBM PC was $1600, but an enhanced version with options such as colour graphics, additional memory and a small printer cost up to $4500. Software was written by independent programmers, as well as IBM's own personnel. With the arrival of its PC, IBM changed its policy and appointed independent computer dealers such as Computerland and Sears Roebuck to sell the new product. However, its team of marketing representatives continued to visit clients, thus creating competition with its dealers in the same territories. In order to avoid a two-tier distribution system, the company supplied its dealers directly and assured them an estimated 32% margin.

By the end of 1981, Apple Computer was approaching one billion dollars in annual sales, and IBM was well on the way to sales of $500 million in PCs (Exhibit 5.1).

Compaq – a star is born

Meanwhile, in Houston, Texas, Rod Canion, Bill Murto and Jim Harris each had $1,000 to invest in their new company and in several new product ideas which they submitted to venture capitalist, Ben Rosen. Rosen turned down three or four proposals, but the team's fifth idea – an IBM compatible portable computer – caught the venture

Company	1981	1982	1983	1984	1985	1986	1987	1988	1989
Apple	566	853	1,939	2,679	2,111	1,967	3,190	5,068	6,587
AST Research	0	0	0	0	n/a	n/a	219	703	843
Commodore	159	147	1,437	1,767	1,202	716	1,030	1,731	1,986
Compaq	0	0	175	475	916	1,210	1,695	3,035	4,209
Dell	0	0	0	0	n/a	n/a	207	291	289
Digital	0	27	399	459	580	340	71	59	115
Hewlett Packard	139	72	209	535	692	488	468	754	1,110
IBM	76	631	2,469	6,245	8,659	6,882	7,123	8,032	10,579
Packard Bell	0	0	0	0	n/a	n/a	n/a	255	1,148
Tandy	206	321	606	955	891	654	1,029	875	1,151
Zenith	47	170	117	291	413	629	1,225	2,540	1,969
Other	163	653	3,233	4,036	4,713	6,325	5,438	10,826	11,639
Total American	1,356	2,874	10,584	17,442	20,177	19,211	21,695	34,169	41,625
Total European	102	200	1,356	2,682	3,986	3,581	3,461	4,871	7,117
Epson	0	15	118	150	288	499	543	862	1,478
NEC	92	215	733	956	1,350	1,727	2,017	2,662	4,552
Sony	0	22	32	48	51	56	45	57	209
Toshiba	0	0	85	123	171	279	640	776	2,243
Other Japanese	207	525	1,594	2,844	3,820	4,171	2,542	3,757	4,009
Total Japanese	299	777	2,562	4,121	5,680	6,732	5,787	8,114	12,491
Rest of World	0	0	219	450	868	1,307	1,172	4,549	6,704
Grand total	1,756	3,841	14,722	24,694	30,710	30,830	32,114	51,702	67,936

Source: Dataquest.

Exhibit 5.1 Evolution of PC sales (millions of dollars of retail sales – if sold)

	1982	1983	1984	1985	1986	1987	1988	1989
Sales	–	111,221	329,013	503,880	625,243	1,224,067	2,065,562	2,876,062
Cost of sales	–	80,491	232,197	325,804	360,698	717,336	1,233,283	1,715,243
Gross margin	–	30,730	96,816	178,076	264,545	506,731	832,279	1,160,819
Operating expenses								
R&D costs	1,506	3,731	10,961	15,996	26,594	47,104	74,859	132,474
Marketing and sales	760	11,540	42,065	67,862	95,552	142,774	235,035	332,592
General and admin	2,592	10,798	24,066	42,072	56,491	83,222	162,328	206,129
Unrealized gain on investment in affiliated company		–	–	–	–	(4,468)	(9,683)	(13,691)
Other (income) expense	(258)	(235)	3,330	8,364	9,372	10,034	2,893	18,776
Total operating expenses	4,600	25,834	80,422	134,294	188,009	278,666	465,432	676,280
	(4,600)	4,896	16,394	43,782	76,536	228,065	366,847	484,539
Income tax	–	2,296	3,528	17,187	31,908	92,709	119,296	165,010
Extraordinary items	–	(2,102)	–	–	1,731	911	7,691	13,771
Net income	(4,600)	4,702	12,866	26,595	42,897	136,267	255,242	333,300

Assets							
Current assets							
Cash	51,797	27,499	76,984	57,133	132,276	281,179	161,313
Accounts receivable	27,773	75,680	83,624	116,490	254,596	428,338	530,228
Inventories	25,396	84,732	75,783	81,190	275,988	386,973	559,042
Prepaid expenses	379	1,250	3,291	4,966	17,963	18,152	61,916
Total current assets	105,345	189,161	239,682	259,779	680,823	1,114,642	1,312,499
Property, plant and equipment	12,662	39,130	66,733	101,975	192,271	428,937	705,475
Investment in affiliated company	—	—	—	9,535	18,896	35,731	58,673
Other assets	3,099	2,761	5,583	6,392	9,040	10,687	13,742
Total assets	121,106	231,052	311,998	377,681	901,030	1,589,997	2,090,389
Liabilities and stockholders' equity							
Current liabilities							
Notes payable	—	58,596	15,000	—	—	—	30,000
Accounts payable	24,878	51,078	53,087	64,389	200,323	238,634	253,909
Income tax payable	—	—	9,692	11,961	26,352	23,135	20,100
Other current liabilities	5,534	11,846	21,474	42,487	115,883	218,078	259,439
Total current liabilities	30,412	121,520	99,253	118,837	342,558	479,847	563,448
Long-term debt	—	—	75,000	72,809	148,915	274,930	274,434
Deferred income taxes	—	405	1,137	2,733	10,025	20,666	80,872
Stockholders' equity							
Stockholders' equity	90,592	96,159	97,045	100,842	180,805	340,585	364,366
Retained earnings	102	12,968	39,563	82,460	218,727	473,969	807,269
Total shareholders' equity	90,694	109,127	136,608	183,302	399,532	814,554	1,171,635
Total	121,106	231,052	311,998	377,681	901,030	1,589,997	2,090,389

Source: Annual Reports.

Exhibit 5.2 *Compaq's consolidated Statements of Operations (thousands of dollars)*

capitalist's attention. Impressed by the three men and the blueprint they had sketched on a coffee-house placemat, Sevin Rosen agreed to supply $1.5 million in start-up capital. The Compaq Computer Corporation was founded in a Houston suburb, with Ben Rosen as Chairman, Joseph 'Rod' Canion, President, and Bill Murto and Jim Harris heading up manufacturing and marketing.

Compaq's ambitious launch plan demanded money, space and staff. While Rosen and Canion scoured the country for more venture capital, the developers forged ahead with a prototype of an IBM-compatible portable microcomputer. Canion worked with the advertising agency, Ogilvy & Mather, to develop a launch campaign. Press ads headed, '*The New Compaq Portable Computer: IBM Compatibility to Go*' were ready and approved well before the launch that was planned for November 1982.

The prototype product, a 28 pound compact microcomputer in a carrying case that would fit under an aeroplane seat, was the fruit of a 9 month $1 million development program. The original 3 man team soon grew to 15 programmers, many of whom were ex-TI technicians. Together, they succeeded in reverse engineering and mimicking the IBM ROM BIOS chip, without violating its copyright. Constant tests were made with IBM software until total compatibility was obtained. The rest was merely a question of sourcing subcomponents and assemblies, screens, circuit boards and power supplies, and using Microsoft's DOS operating system and the Intel 8088 microprocessor.

During the summer of 1982, Compaq positioned itself with its dealers. Canion signed up such outlets as Sears Roebuck and Computerland, which were also official IBM distributors. Response to the launch was overwhelming, not only because of the product's superior features, but also due to the huge demand for personal computers. Canion's policy was: reward the dealers generously and don't compete with them. The company offered margins of approximately 36% versus 32% for the IBM PC. As other dealers followed and demand increased, Compaq's business plans and production schedules had to be continually revised.

With $30 million raised through private sources, in 1982–83 Compaq constructed a 114,000 ft^2 manufacturing facility capable of assembling 5000 portables a month, with plans to increase to 10,000. At the time, IBM was producing 20,000 units per month.

After just one year of operation, Compaq had sold 50,000 of its first PCs for a total of $111 million. Net income for this first year was almost $5 million. By December 1984, sales were $330 million and net income $13 million. Hailed by the press as having the fastest growth in sales for any company in its first year of operations, Compaq went public at the end of 1983 at $11.00 per share. Manufacturing capacity tripled from 1983 to 1984. The number of employees increased from 100 in December 1982 to 1318 by December 1984 (Exhibit 5.2).

Microcomputers – industry structure

Cloning

By the time Compaq was ready to sell its first product in January 1983, the microcomputer market was being referred to as the 'PC orgy'. Suddenly all the mystique surrounding computers was dispelled. Anyone could use a PC – it was rapidly becoming a popular hands-on management tool. IBM's open architecture had provoked a frenzied explosion in cloning its PC and, by 1983, over 300 producers were jostling for market share. In this highly competitive environment, there were two principal measures of success for PCs: one was the degree of IBM-compatibility achieved and the other was speed to the market.

The one million PC clones sold in the USA in 1983 were largely the result of the pent-up demand for the IBM PC of which 600,000 units were sold. Demand for the IBM product at the time greatly exceeded the company's ability to supply. Once IBM had stepped up production, launched new upgraded microcomputers (such as the IBM PC XT), and dropped the price on its original version, an estimated 300 clones, particularly the not-fully compatible, were quickly eliminated.

This rapid proliferation of PCs spawned many component and subassembly businesses, challenged established distribution channels, and continued to make demands on a growing body of software writers.

Microprocessor sourcing

The components industry comprised a wide range of technologies and suppliers. Some of these components – such as semiconductors, disk drives, and monitors – required large investments in research and development, and manufacturing. Other components – such as housings, keyboards, printed circuit boards and power supplies – required fewer investments.

Microprocessors were sourced from two US companies, Intel and Motorola, and one Japanese, NEC. These three companies poured large resources into developing the next generation of more powerful microprocessors. Each generation was more expensive to develop and to manufacture. In the early seventies, developing a 4 bit microprocessor cost about $5 million. In the early 1990s, the latest and most powerful 32 bit microprocessor cost $130 million in research and development alone. Similarly, the development and production costs of the memory chips known as DRAMs, Dynamic Random Access Memory, increased with each new generation. A new version was introduced roughly every three years, usually by a different supplier. For instance, Hitachi was the number one supplier of 64 kilobyte chips, introduced in 1979 at a cost of approximately $200 million in development spending. Four years earlier, Mostek, part of the US company, United Technologies, was first in the supply of 16 kilobyte chips.

The proprietary ROM BIOS chip was either reversed engineered by PC suppliers such as Compaq or was sourced from Phoenix Technologies, a US-based chip manufacturer. Semiconductors such as the DRAMs, microprocessors and others were supplied to printed circuit board manufacturers. Often these printed circuit boards were manufactured by the larger PC assemblers whereas smaller PC assemblers purchased them from numerous Japanese, US and Southeast Asian suppliers.

Disk drives were sourced from specialized manufacturers such as Tandon, Seagate, Sony, and Conner Peripherals. Originally, the 5.25-inch floppy disk drive was the standard. However, over time, hard disks and new versions of floppy disks were developed and manufactured. For a typical disk drive manufacturer, research and development costs also ran high – at 8% of sales, with a new disk drive factory costing $20–50 million. Cathode ray tubes used in monitors were usually supplied by large television manufacturers such as Sony, Philips, Panasonic, Samsung and Zenith. These cathode ray tubes would then be sourced by the PC assemblers who would package

Components	Where	Cost
Chassis and casing	Multiple	22
Motherboard**	Taiwan, Japan	48
Controller cards**	Japan, USA	25
Floppy disk drives (5.25)	Japan, USA	25
Keyboard, video screen	Taiwan, Japan	60
Assembly and miscellaneous		35
Total		215

**Note: the motherboard and controller cards were often manufactured in-house by some of the larger PC manufacturers in order to save on costs.

Sources: Computer Strategies, 1990–1999, Technology – Costs – Markets and Business Week.

Exhibit 5.3 *Typical manufacturing costs of a PC XT clone, 1988 ($)*

them into their own specially designed thermoplastic housings. Peripherals such as keyboards, pointing devices, memory expansion boards, modems and printers were either manufactured in-house or sourced from specialized producers. There was no lack of choice for the clone makers (Exhibit 5.3).

Distribution

A whole new distribution pattern emerged with the arrival of the PC. Formerly, the traditional mainframe and minicomputer vendors sold directly to their customers as a part of a total product and service package. IBM, along with other vendors, extended this strategy when selling its PCs to high volume clients. However, the variety of distribution channels increased as PCs were light and easy to carry, and depended on a large range of off-the-shelf software packages. Specialist computer retailers soon accounted for the vast majority of PC sales, followed by department stores, electronic shops, catalogue sales and value added resellers (VARs). VARs were specialized computer systems suppliers usually for a specific industry segment. A typical segment would be hospital administration systems (Exhibit 5.4).

Distribution network	1983	1989 Business PC	1989 Home PC
Mass merchandising	28	6	14
Computer dealers	33	47	59
Office equipment stores	6	5	5
Value added resellers	13	13	3
Direct sales	15	16	0
Mail order	n/a	13	19

Source: Intelligent Electronics and Dataquest.

Exhibit 5.4 *Percentage market shares of PC distribution channels (based in the USA)*

David and Goliath, Compaq and IBM

IBM responded to Compaq's portable microcomputer by bringing out its own Portable PC in February 1984. However, IBM's product was priced higher than Compaq's and dealers' margins were lower. As a consequence, customers who had entered the retail outlets to buy an IBM portable often left with a Compaq instead. IBM removed the portable in question from the dealers only three months after its launch.

Compaq adhered rigorously to the IBM standard as it unveiled its new computers. However, analysts were dubious as to whether the company could sustain its success rate in a market almost saturated with practically identical products, at much lower prices. But Compaq forged ahead, listening carefully to dealer and customer feedback to be sure that its products met their demands.

Product	Compaq introduction	IBM introduction
80386 PC	September 1986	June 1987
Portable 80386 PC	September 1987	May 1989
80386/20 MHz	September 1987	Sept. 1987
80386/25 MHz	June 1988	Sept. 1988
80386SX	June 1988	May 1989
Laptop 80286	October 1988	None yet
80386/33 MHz	May 1989	None yet
Notebook 80286	October 1989	None yet
80486 PC multiprocessor	November 1989	June 1989
Network server	November 1989	None yet
Notebook 80386	October 1990	None yet

Product	Apple introduction
Apple II	June 1977
Apple II Plus	June 1979
Apple III	September 1980
Apple IIe	January 1983
Lisa	January 1983
Apple III Plus	December 1983
Macintosh 128K	January 1984
Apple IIc Portable	April 1984
Macintosh 512k	September 1984
Macintosh Plus	January 1986
Apple IIgs	September 1986
Macintosh SE	March 1987
Macintosh II	March 1987

Source: Adapted from *Business Week* and other articles.

Exhibit 5.5   *Product introduction by Compaq, IBM and Apple*

When Compaq launched its Deskpro 8088 PCs in June 1984, they were not only 2–3 times faster than IBM's PCs, but they had hard disks and tape backups; the price was slightly higher than its IBM rival machines.

IBM strove to hang onto its technological lead by introducing, in August 1984, the PC AT – the first PC to contain Intel's 80286 microprocessor. Only eight months later, Compaq's own product – an Intel 80286 PC called the Deskpro 286 – was on the market. The race intensified.

In December 1985, Compaq had a remarkable stroke of luck when Intel asked the company to put its newest, and more powerful, 80386 microprocessor through a testing programme to ensure total compatibility with software written for its previous versions. Intel and Compaq worked closely together to eliminate any bugs. After nine months of collaboration, Compaq President, Rod Canion, Microsoft's Bill Gates and Lotus' Jim Manzi, announced the Deskpro 386. Canion had convinced Bill Gates and Jim Manzi to design software applications for this new product. The Deskpro 386 was an immediate hit as were Compaq's subsequent offerings, including portables, laptops, notebooks and more desktop computers. Even IBM could not keep up with Compaq's rate of new product introductions (Exhibit 5.5).

Meanwhile Apple

As IBM and Compaq competed for market share, microcomputers proliferated worldwide. In 1986, more than 85% of a total of 47 million PCs were either IBM machines or IBM clones. Meanwhile, Apple continued to turn out its line of Apple IIs, each new model a slight improvement over its predecessor. Apple's early success had been in the home and education markets, where in 1984 it dominated with 60% share. By 1984, the company was selling $1.5 billion worth of computers. However, due to the zany management style of its computer genius founders, internal problems started to erupt.

The rapidly growing business segment ought to have offered a new challenge to Apple. Yet its entry in 1983 with both the Apple III and 'Lisa' was a flop, largely due to its proprietary operating systems and closed architectures. At the same time, in the midst of growing discontent inside the company, Pepsi-Cola's John Sculley was recruited to take over Apple. Meanwhile, Steve Jobs, Apple's original founder, headed up a group of engineers to develop the first of a new line, known as Macintosh or familiarly, 'Mac'. Mac's new user-friendly operating system and superior graphics capabilities had been designed for desktop publishing. The Mac, launched in 1984, did not bring the results Apple expected in the business market, its success limited once more by its closed architecture, and insufficient compatibility in networking. After these three unsuccessful attempts to penetrate the business market, Sculley convinced the board to remove the company's co-founder, Steve Jobs. Sculley then revamped the company, closed plants and laid off over 1000 employees. With a new top management team, Sculley corrected the Mac's deficiencies. He upgraded its memory and opened its architecture to peripheral hardware that would facilitate networking. The Mac's user-friendly operating system was maintained (Exhibits 5.5 and 5.6).

Managing growth at Compaq

By 1984, Compaq was being hailed by the press as the fastest growing company in US history. For Rod Canion, who had never considered himself an entrepreneur, managing

Company	1985	1986	1987	1988	1989
IBM					
Sales per employee	$123.4	$127.0	$139.3	$154.2	$163.6
Profit margin	13.1%	9.3%	9.7%	9.2%	6.0%
ROI	17.6%	12.0%	12.0%	10.4%	6.8%
Cost of goods sold/sales	36.1%	37.8%	38.9%	35.0%	37.4%
R&D/sales	6.9%	7.8%	10.0%	9.9%	10.9%
Capital expenditures/sales	n/a	9.0%	7.9%	9.0%	10.2%
Apple					
Sales per employee	$446.1	$339.4	$475.2	$377.0	$364.0
Profit margin	4.1%	6.9%	8.2%	9.8%	8.6%
ROI	11.1%	16.7%	26.0%	35.4%	29.4%
Cost of goods sold/sales	56.1%	55.3%	46.1%	47.0%	48.6%
R&D/sales	3.8%	4.3%	7.2%	6.7%	8.0%
Capital expenditures/sales	n/a	3.5%	3.2%	3.5%	4.5%
Dell					
Sales per employee				$214.8	$224.5
Profit margin				5.6%	1.5%
ROI				13.2%	5.4%
Cost of goods sold/sales				67.7%	80.3%
R&D/sales				2.8%	5.0%
Capital expenditures/sales				2.6%	4.0%
*Industry average**					
Sales per employee		$126.9	$134.8	$152.4	$168.2
Profit margin		8.9%	9.1%	8.8%	7.1%
ROI		11.9%	12.3%	11.1%	13.6%
Cost of goods sold/sales		39.2%	42.0%	39.4%	51.1%
R&D/sales		7.2%	9.0%	8.7%	9.1%
Capital expenditures/sales		8.3%	7.2%	8.1%	7.3%

*Data from a compilation of 10 US microcomputer manufacturers excluding IBM.

Source: Electronic Business, 1989.

Exhibit 5.6 *Selected financial data on the PC industry: IBM, Apple and Dell*

this type of growth spiral was a true test of survival. In an interview with the *Harvard Business Review*, Canion explained his philosophy:

> I always thought of an entrepreneur as someone who can't work for anybody else and has a burning desire to make his or her own idea known. That just does not fit me or any of our team. And our not being classic entrepreneurs has been a real benefit for Compaq. The typical entrepreneur has the problem of dealing with all the things success brings, things he or she didn't really want in the first place. But because we were really more typical businessmen starting our own company from scratch, when we did grow successful, we had the skills and orientation necessary to manage that growth.

Compaq may have been regarded as nothing out of the ordinary compared to such high fliers as Sun or Apple; at least, no one seemed to criticize its professionalism.

Professional management from the start

Compaq was not afflicted by many of the problems small companies suffered in their early days. In fact, Compaq did not remain small for long, its fabled growth rate moving it up the ranks at a record-making speed. Yet Canion preferred the small company feeling and, in 1983, he is quoted as saying, 'Our culture is designed to keep the characteristics of a small company alive while the company grows.' Cash was not a problem once the initial start-up funds had been found. The company secured access to substantial financial resources until it started to generate operating income. In 1984, Compaq went public. The company installed systems with enough capacity to handle its rapid growth. Finally, right from the beginning, the company hired talented and experienced people from other high technology companies. Of Compaq's 21 top executives, 17 were ex-Texas Instrument managers, of whom some had had as much as 21 years of experience. Ben Rosen's acumen, his confidence in Canion and the team, and the close support he offered from the start made a significant contribution to the company's success.

Organization

By the spring of 1984, some months before the announcement of the new line of desktops, Canion realigned the company into three divisions and established a telecoms subsidiary, a move seen by the industry as a response to the criticism that Compaq would not be able to survive as a one-product company. The three divisions were Portable Computers, Office Computers (including the new about-to-be-launched personal computers) and Advanced Computers (products to be launched in the future). The intention was to maintain the small company concept within the larger company infrastructure. Each division was staffed with its own marketing and engineering personnel.

After less than a year, management realized that the realignment into product divisions had been premature. Marketing overlapped; engineering staff duplicated their efforts and financial resources were too thin to support all four divisions. Canion quickly reorganized the company into its four traditional functional groups: marketing, engineering, sales and manufacturing.

Consensus, continuity, discipline and balance

During its phenomenal growth, Canion was able to maintain a certain culture which he described in a recent interview with the *Harvard Business Review* as embracing consensus, continuity, discipline and balance or, in one word, the 'process'.

Consensus decision-making was a way of life at Compaq. The real benefit of this process, as Rod Canion explained, was the procedure that people applied to obtain the right results. 'You get a lot of facts, you get a lot of people thinking, and the result is that everybody owns the decision when you get through.' Canion relates, 'At Compaq, decisions to proceed or to put a project on hold could be made in a few hours. It takes 200 signatures to get a product out at IBM.'

In 1986, when Compaq was only days away from a merger deal with Tandy Corp., the manufacturer/retailer of low-cost personal computers, this consensus decision-making process worked against Canion. Canion was rumoured to have wanted the alliance, but other executives – such as Michael Swavely, Vice President of North

American Operations – convinced him that Tandy's low-cost image could undermine Compaq's premium brand reputation. The 'process' kept Canion, the president, from pushing his idea through.

To Rod Canion, continuity meant retaining people:

> Most people would point to compensation plans, stock options, and bonuses as the way to keep people. But really, they're just there to prevent people from being stolen. It's not pay or stock or anything else that keeps people. It's whether they're drained or charged emotionally. People stay when they enjoy what they do. People stay when they fit the culture, when they are working in a supportive, helpful environment, and when they get fulfilment from working as part of a winning team.

In this seemingly egalitarian environment with its understated hierarchical structure, there were no assigned parking places, and employees at all levels received perks from soft drinks to stock options. For Canion, finding the facts that would lead to the right answers was key to the discipline of the management decision-making process. Explained Canion:

> Our management process is designed to meet customers' needs, use the latest technology, and – most important – get to the market quickly. To accomplish this in a way that does not burn out our people requires discipline and balance.

Setting directions rather than goals

Compaq was a strong believer in a long-term business strategy, which meant, for example, investing in suppliers or developing dealer networks. Canion did not see himself in the role of driver of the company:

> We set directions rather than goals. We pay more attention to managing the direction we are going in, monitoring progress, and being aware of how we do things, rather than setting a specific goal and then meeting it.

For example, if managers did not meet their numbers, they were not reprimanded for doing a bad job but were simply asked to do better next time.

Market intelligence – keeping in close touch

> One of Compaq's key strengths is the degree to which management stays attuned to customers, markets, and changes in both.

An analyst's report summed up Compaq's understanding of the market: 'Before setting off to develop products, the company ensured there was enough information to "be right the first time", Canion would often say.' Market research would be carried out using focus groups working directly with Fortune 1000 customers or with dealers who suggested improvements to systems. The Dealer Executive Council, composed of owners and managers from a broad cross section of Authorized Dealerships, was a valuable source of ideas for many product features. Apart from one product flop, the company had been right every time.

The 'being right the first time' rule led Compaq to postpone its entry into the laptop computer segment. As early as 1984, Compaq's management discussed the idea of introducing a laptop computer as a logical extension of its portable range. As Compaq engineers started designing a prototype and researching the latest component technologies, marketing assessed the number of potential customers for this type of product. A young market researcher pointed out that dealer and customer response showed that the market was not ready for the product. In spite of Canion's enthusiasm for the laptop, marketing research was able to convince him not to launch at that time. The 'process' worked but the laptop story did not end there. Compaq continued monitoring until a more propitious launch date was selected.

Product development at Compaq

Product development started with the usual creation of core project teams who were advised by internal experts when needed. The typical product development cycle was followed: concept definition, market research, design, testing and, finally, manufacturing. These phases were often performed simultaneously, thus speeding up the product development process:

> In any situation where we're looking for creativity, we begin with the customers' needs.

Canion believed that the company's product successes relied not only on the efficiency of 'the process', but also on defining innovation parameters based on customers' needs. One such parameter was complete compatibility with the IBM PC. Another was offering hard disks for notebook computers. In 1989, most computer vendors that offered notebook computers were unable to supply hard disks. Compaq engineers listened to customer needs and worked closely with suppliers to design the first notebook with a hard disk. The result, the Compaq LTE/286, introduced in October 1989 was a smash hit.

Assurance of supply

As the company was in the forefront of technology and sourced most of its components from outside, Compaq had to ensure that it had not only a reliable source of supply, but also could rely on its suppliers' expertise for new development ideas. Compaq's management paid particular attention to securing quality of supply and on-time delivery.

Right from the beginning, Compaq's suppliers were made 'Certified Vendors'. Essentially, certified vendors supplied components that were defect-free or met stringent quality standards set by Compaq. This arrangement saved Compaq valuable time on inspection and handling. For example, in 1986, as a result of this initiative, Compaq estimated that it saved $2.4 million in inspection costs.

Although Compaq could purchase a significant amount of components from multiple sources, a number of components were purchased through a single source of supply. For example, it sourced all its microprocessors from Intel on a purchase order basis. (However, the company did invest approximately $5 million in a start-up firm, Nextgen, that was in the process of reverse engineering the 80486 chip.) In addition, Compaq made every attempt to place its disk-drive business with Conner Peripherals, a company in which Compaq had a significant financial interest. Compaq's financial interest in Conner was sold to Conner in 1992.

Finally, Compaq, like many other large PC vendors, manufactured its own printed circuit boards. In 1984, it set up its first printed circuit board facility in Houston, and another was added in 1987 in Singapore.

Setting manufacturing priorities: quality and flexibility first

Quality and flexibility took priority over cost in Compaq's assembly operations. Compaq's commitment to quality for its customers began right from the start when the company purchased automated testing equipment to ensure that its own products were fully compatible with IBM machines. From that moment on, the quality ethic penetrated every level of Compaq's business: supplier selection, assemblers' performance and how testing procedures were carried out. Management delegated quality inspection to production line workers, making sure everyone would be responsible for inspecting the previous person's work. If a flaw were found, the whole line would be shut down. Quality results were displayed on wall charts, and zero defect days were frequent. These quality drives paid off and results were reflected in consumer tests. For example, in 1986, the quality of Compaq machines ranked higher than IBM or Apple when measured according to technical specifications.

Flexibility of delivery was an essential priority, according to Rod Canion, in order to fulfil fluctuations in dealer demands:

> The dealers never had the right amount of inventory; they had either too much or too little. They would cut way back on their orders, or they would double their orders. So it was clear that in the PC market, a pipeline arrangement wouldn't work as there just wasn't the stability. The environment forced us to decide that there was real value in being able to switch our production from one model to the next – say from one desktop or portable to another – to capitalize on sales opportunities.
>
> Controlling costs was another priority but not at the expense of quality or flexibility. The company selected its factory personnel carefully and was prepared to pay assembly workers a premium rate in return for higher quality and more efficient teamwork.

Product awareness – it simply works better

From its early days, Compaq's management understood the importance of building a solid reputation. From 1983 onwards, the slogan originally used in its print media, '*It simply works better*' was adopted as the company's credo and advertising platform. Compaq continued to invest heavily in promoting its brand image, through press advertising, direct mail and sometimes television. Extensive media coverage accompanied its lavish new product announcements. As a result, Compaq carved itself a niche as an up-market, reliable, technologically superior supplier.

Dealers as allies

Compaq pledged to sell only through its authorized dealers, whom they regarded as allies. As Michael Swavely, Vice President for North America, explained, 'In our distribution strategy, we don't compete with our dealers; IBM very clearly does. IBM is its own dealers' biggest competitor.'

Compaq invested heavily in nurturing its distribution network by offering more generous margins than competitors selling through the same dealers. The company also provided substantial dealer support through its 'Salespaq' programme, the most comprehensive sales package in the industry when it was introduced in 1985. Manufacturers typically offered computer dealers short-term incentives with limited options. Salespaq was a long-term programme which reimbursed its authorized dealers for expenses incurred in advertising, merchandising, sales incentives and training. By 1986, over 90% of its dealers participated in the programme. In addition to the Salespaq programme, Compaq provided service training, technical hotline support, parts supply and technical information. A field support staff assisted the authorized dealers in resolving customer problems.

Compaq rapidly won its dealers' loyalty. As the Chairman of CompuShop explained, 'Compaq's success isn't due to the latest technology or a lot of razzle dazzle; it's coming out with what the dealers want.'

By 1989, Compaq – up to 3872 from 2000 in 1984 – boasted more authorized dealers than IBM.

Compaq's response to a new IBM challenge

By the time Compaq brought out its Deskpro 386 in September 1986, most analysts agreed that the company was changing from a predominantly PC clone-maker to a manufacturer of microcomputers that supported the industry standard. When IBM – trying to regain its control of the market by creating a new standard – unveiled its new semi-proprietary PS/2 computers in April 1987, it was Compaq that rallied eight other major clone-makers to retaliate.

The PS/2 introduction was another change in direction. Unlike its previous entry in 1981, IBM sourced the majority of its components and subassembled components internally. By designing a proprietary architecture, IBM tried to regain ground lost to the clone manufacturers. The Micro Channel Architecture configuration allowed components of the microcomputer to communicate more easily and to operate simultaneously. Faster data transmission in networking was obtained and multimedia functions could be added. This innovation brought improvements over the original circuit boards for installed base microcomputers while maintaining logical compatibility with available software.

IBM made superlative claims about its MCA and PS/2: 'new computing power, faster desktop processing, increased direct memory access, better graphics, etc.' Some companies followed IBM's tune and accepted the new state of affairs. IBM clone-makers, Olivetti, Tandy and Dell, were willing to pay up to 5% of sales in royalty charges for the rights to the MCA technology.

Compaq engineers succeeded in reverse engineering IBM's Micro Channel Architecture, but Compaq's marketing group concluded, after extensive customer focus groups, that the customer was not interested in a proprietary architecture and was not interested in abandoning its installed base of industry Standard Architecture products and peripherals. Canion described MCA as an unnecessary proprietary alteration intended to lock customers into IBM hardware.

Compaq's president started to talk to other industry participants. His response to IBM's latest manoeuvre was to mobilize eight other computer manufacturers into a consortium to develop an extended industry standard architecture (EISA), a technology compatible with the previous standard set for the PC AT. The consortium comprised major suppliers Hewlett Packard, Wyse Technologies, AST Research, Zenith Data Systems, NEC Information Systems, Epson America, Olivetti and Tandy. However, mobilizing eight major companies to participate in a 'design by committee situation', was a time-consuming task. By the time the Compaq's EISA PCs were ready for shipment in November 1989, two million MCA models were already installed.

The EISA standard was of less significance than the signal given by Canion to the market. Canion knew that in order to sustain Compaq's image as a technological leader, a rapid response to IBM was required. The only way to challenge the MCA launch was this mobilization.

The EISA/MCA war turned out to be a 'storm in a teacup' for standalones. A political shakeout ensued, during which some consortium members opted for the MCA configuration while others remained with EISA. Michael Dell announced that they were offering an MCA-based product, but didn't see 'why anyone would want it.' In the end, Compaq and IBM signed a patent cross-licence agreement in July 1989. By that time, Compaq had already introduced its EISA-based products and had decided not to pursue any MCA-based products.

Rapidly changing microcomputer industry

Products

As the 1980s progressed, data processing reached a dizzying level of complexity and size. Microprocessor and chip development, and their availability at reasonable prices, had given the original boxes huge boosts of power and capacity. PCs continued to turn the computer industry upside down. Powerful microcomputers posed a serious threat to the minicomputer which, in turn, had challenged the mainframe.

Meanwhile, at the other end of the market, laptop and notebook computers – virtually identical in performance to PCs – threatened the standalone microcomputer segment, while the sheer volume of cheaper clones available threatened just about everything in the industry.

Components

The huge PC components industry exploded with new technologies and products. Intel and Motorola were joined by other firms pouring ever-increasing resources into developing new generation microprocessors. Memory chips were increasing in capacity every three years at huge costs to the developers. Industry experts estimated that a new DRAM with capacity of 4 megabytes would cost up to $1 billion to develop and produce. Other firms, including the personal computer assemblers, were designing new applications-specific integrated circuits. Whole printed circuit boards could be reduced onto one chip or a set of chips, thus improving on space and reducing power consumption. Smaller but higher capacity hard and floppy disk drives were developed at higher R & D costs. For example, the once standard 5.25 inch floppy disk was replaced by the new industry standard – the 3.5-inch floppy disk. Monitor suppliers were improving radiation emissions and the graphics quality. At the same time, new screen technologies – such as liquid crystal and gas plasma displays – were being installed in laptops and notebook computers.

Distribution

As the PC grew in power and flexibility, its popularity in the business market increased rapidly, along with an erosion of the larger computer segment. Due to the volumes purchased and the cost per item, companies tended to buy PCs directly through purchasing departments rather than through the IS department. This policy reinforced the strength of the dealers, who responded by maintaining large stocks of PCs and peripherals destined for their clients in advance. By 1989, approximately 82% of personal computer purchases by businesses were through dealers. Dealers preferred to work with large vendors who would assure them high margins and a constant flow of business. Smaller PC vendors, who were shut out by these dealers, were often forced to resort to other distribution strategies. One such company, Dell Computers, successfully circumvented dealer blockades by selling through direct mail and computer superstores.

Dell Computers had been founded in 1984 by a precocious 19-year-old university dropout, Michael Dell, whose sales and distribution strategy enabled him to rise rapidly up through the ranks of various lower-priced challengers to Compaq. By saving on dealers' mark-ups, Dell could offer its powerful PC products through its direct mail and telephone order network at substantially lower prices than those of its competitors. With as many as 2500 calls daily, Dell gained access to and feedback from a healthy chunk of potential users. Dell's deliveries were fast, and the company provided an unusual after-sales service offer – 24 hour toll-free numbers were available even for small technical problems. If a more serious breakdown occurred, Dell had an arrangement with Xerox service staff to investigate at once. From sales of $34 million in 1985, Dell became a serious competitor with an estimated $500 million in sales in 1989 (Exhibit 5.6).

Canion's challenge

'What if we start losing it? What if we get arrogant?' Canion asked in an interview with the *Wall Street Journal* in mid-1989. So far, the soft-spoken president had nothing to worry about as the company raced along, its profitability improving, sales exploding, and a range of products being developed – from small notebooks to the multiprocessor file servers that challenged the powerful minicomputers.

However, as the company grew from a small Houston, Texas, start-up to a sprawling multinational, cracks started to appear. The company had grown so big that it had to rent an amusement park for its annual picnic. Quarterly meetings, that were still being held in the local Baptist church, now required 3–4 shifts. Finally, as more people entered the top management ranks, how many were required to agree to new product decisions in order to maintain the 'consensus management' culture? Would the company become too slow to match the more nimble smaller competitors?

6

Global corporate strategies

Case 6.1 Nestlé-Rowntree (A)

This case was written by Research Associate Dana G. Hyde, under the supervision of Professors James C. Ellert and J. Peter Killing, as a basis for class discussion rather than to illustrate either effective or ineffective handling of a business situation.

Wednesday, April 13, 1988, 10.30 am.

'Our offer to help remains open, Mr Dixon, and I urge you to reconsider our proposals. Please keep in touch.' Mr Helmut Maucher, Managing Director of Nestlé S.A., replaced the receiver and shook his head regretfully as he looked out from his office over Lake Geneva. On receiving the news of Jacobs Suchard's dawn raid on Rowntree plc, Mr. Maucher had called Mr Kenneth Dixon, Rowntree's Chairman, to offer Nestlé's help and renew Nestlé's earlier proposal to purchase a stake in Rowntree.

Rowntree had been an attractive takeover target for some time, and Mr. Maucher and his colleagues had often discussed the possibility of making a bid. However, it was clear that Rowntree would aggressively contest any takeover attempt and, as Nestlé had never engaged in a hostile takeover, Mr Maucher had done nothing more than initiate talks with the British-based confectioner. But as he prepared for the meeting with his Comité du Conseil that afternoon, Mr Maucher worried about Rowntree falling into the hands of one of Nestlé's major competitors.

The chocolate industry

'Confectionery' was conventionally divided into 'chocolate' confectionery and 'sugar' confectionery. 'Chocolate' confectionery included products made with chocolate;

Average currency equivalents, 1983–1988

	1 Swiss Franc equals		1 British Pound equals		1 US Dollar equals	
1983	$0.48	£0.31	SF3.23	$1.55	SF2.08	£0.65
1984	$0.43	£0.32	SF3.13	$1.34	SF2.33	£0.75
1985	$0.41	£0.32	SF3.13	$1.28	SF2.44	£0.78
1986	$0.56	£0.38	SF2.63	$1.47	SF1.79	£0.68
1987	$0.67	£0.41	SF2.44	$1.63	SF1.49	£0.61
1988[1]	$0.71	£0.39	SF2.57	$1.83	SF1.41	£0.55

[1] As at April 1, 1988.

Source: Schweizerische Nationalbank.

'sugar' confectionery included boiled sweets, toffees, chewing gum, and other gums and jellies. Chocolate consumption represented a stable 54% of the total volume of confectionery consumption in the major world markets between 1982 and 1987.

Market

In 1987 the population of the world's eight major markets consumed more than 2.7 million tons of chocolate (the equivalent of over 100 billion Kit Kats), with a retail value of over $19.5 billion (Exhibit 6.1). In volume terms, chocolate consumption in these eight major markets represented 61% of world chocolate consumption in 1987. Average per capita consumption was 4.3 kg per annum, with an annual per capita

	Chocolate consumption (000 tons)[1]	Chocolate expenditure ($US billions)	Population mid-1987 (millions)	Consumption per capita (kg/annum)	Expenditure per capita ($/annum)
US	1,189	5.2	244	4.9	21
UK	455	3.5	57	8.0	61
West Germany	409	3.4	61	6.7	55
France	233	2.8	56	4.2	49
Japan	157	1.9	122	1.3	15
Canada	101	0.5	26	3.9	18
Italy	106	1.8	57	1.8	32
Australia	80	0.6	16	4.9	36
Total	2,730	19.6	639	4.3	31

[1] One metric ton = 1000 kilogrammes.

Sources: United Nations Industrial Statistics Yearbook; World Bank; National Trade Associations; Trade Estimates.

Exhibit 6.1 *Major chocolate confectionery markets: consumption and expenditure per capita, 1987*

	Consumption (000 tons)			Compound average annual growth rate (%)	
	1982 Actual	1987 Actual	1992 Forecast	1982–1987 Actual	1987–1992 Forecasts
USA	1,003	1,189	1,364	3.5	2.8
UK	411	455	469	2.0	0.6
West Germany	401	409	412	0.4	0.1
France	192	233	251	3.9	1.5
Japan	148	157	166	1.2	1.1
Italy	83	106	127	5.0	3.7
Canada	99	101	106	0.4	1.0
Australia	63	80	95	4.9	3.5
8 markets above	2,400	2,730	2,990	2.6	1.8
Rest of world	1,495	1,740	1,990	3.1	2.7
Total	3,895	4,470	4,980	2.8	2.2

Sources: Joint International Statistics Committee of IOCCC; *Euromonitor*; *United Nations Industrial Statistics Yearbook*; IMEDE.

Exhibit 6.2 *Actual and forecasted chocolate consumption in major markets*

expenditure of $31. Between 1982 and 1987, volume growth averaged 2.8% per annum in the eight major markets. Future growth was estimated at 2.2% per annum for the next five years, with some variations across individual markets (Exhibit 6.2).

Product types

Within chocolate confectionery there were three major product types:

- **Blocks:** moulded blocks of chocolate, with or without additional ingredients (Hershey's Chocolate Bar, Nestlé Cailler, Suchard's Toblerone)
- **Countlines:** chocolate-covered products, sold by count rather than weight (Mars' Mars Bar and Snickers, Rowntree's Kit Kat and Smarties)
- **Boxed chocolates:** assortments (Cadbury's Milk Tray, Rowntree's Black Magic) and products such as Rowntree's After Eight.

Product definitions varied widely by country. For the purposes of this case, British product definitions have been used.

A few manufacturers had succeeded in branding **block chocolate**. However, in many markets block chocolate was considered a commodity product. Each manufacturer's range included a standard variety of block chocolate (milk, dark, white, etc.) and additional ingredients (nuts, fruit, etc.) sold in standard sizes (usually 100 g and 200 g). Block chocolate was sold mainly through grocery outlets, where it was displayed by manufacturer's range; all of Nestlé's block chocolate products would be grouped on one section of the store shelf with the other manufacturers' ranges displayed in adjacent sections.

Countlines included a wide range of branded products which were physically distinct from each other in size, shape, weight and composition. Countlines had wider distribution than the other two product types, with a higher proportion sold through non-grocery outlets such as confectioneries, newsagents, and kiosks.

Boxed chocolates were regarded as a 'gift/occasion' purchase with a very seasonal sales pattern. Approximately 80% of sales took place at Christmas and Easter with a high proportion sold through grocery outlets. Steady sales through the remainder of the year were made primarily through non-grocery outlets.

At 7% average annual real growth between 1982 and 1987, countlines was the fastest growing segment of the world chocolate market. Block chocolate sales showed an average annual volume increase of 1% over the same period, while sales of boxed chocolates had declined by an average of 1% per year. By 1987 countlines represented 46% of the world chocolate market by volume, up from 38% in 1982; block chocolate had declined to 30% from 33%, and boxed chocolates to 24% from 29%. In addition to growing demand for countline products, future growth was expected from 'indulgence' products such as chocolate truffles, and from specialist branded chocolate retailing.

Industry structure and performance

In 1987 there were six major producers in the world chocolate industry: Mars, Hershey, Cadbury Schweppes, Jacobs Suchard, Rowntree, and Nestlé. With individual world market shares ranging from 18% (Mars) to 4% (Nestlé), these six companies accounted for 50% of the total world volume of chocolate confectionery. With the exception of Jacobs Suchard and Nestlé, countline production represented the largest proportion of the chocolate confectionery portfolios of the major confectionery producers (Exhibits 6.3–6.6).

The next tier of competitors included Ferrero, George Weston Ltd., Nabisco, and United Biscuits, each of which sold 2% or less of the total world volume of chocolate confectionery. The remainder of the market was supplied by a large number of smaller (largely national) companies.

Turnover	Mars	Hershey	Cadbury	Rowntree	Suchard	Nestlé	Others
Tons (000)	800	400	320	300	220	190	240
World market share	18%	9%	7%	7%	5%	4%	50%
Turnover by product type							
Block	1%	46%	46%	11%	81%	73%	29%
Countline	99%	54%	36%	55%	8%	17%	32%
Boxed	–	–	18%	34%	11%	10%	39%
Total	100%	100%	100%	100%	100%	100%	100%

Sources: International Chocolate Workshop, Vevey, 1988; Trade Estimates; IMEDE.

Exhibit 6.3 *Chocolate product portfolios of major confectionery companies, 1987*

	Total market[1]	Percentage market shares						
		Mars	*Hershey*	*Cadbury*	*Rowntree*	*Suchard*	*Nestlé*	*Others*
North America								
Block	280	–	62	16	2	3	14	3
Countlines	898	53	23	5	2	–	1	16
Boxed	112	–	–	11	17	1	5	66
Total	1,290	37	29	8	3	1	4	18
EEC								
Block	541	1	–	9	4	23	14	49
Countlines	611	49	–	8	19	2	1	21
Boxed	437	–	–	7	14	4	2	73
Total	1,589	19	–	8	12	10	6	45
Rest of world								
Block	521	–	2	10	1	9	4	74
Countlines	544	4	1	4	6	1	3	80
Boxed	526	–	–	3	4	1	1	91
Total	1,591	1	1	6	4	4	3	81
World								
Block	1,342	1	14	11	2	13	10	49
Countlines	2,053	39	10	6	8	1	2	34
Boxed	1,075	–	–	6	9	2	2	81
Total	**4,470**	**18**	**9**	**7**	**7**	**5**	**4**	**50**

[1] In tons (000).

Sources: International Chocolate Workshop, Vevey, 1988; Trade Estimates; IMEDE.

Exhibit 6.4 *Market shares of major competitors by product type and region, 1987*

	Mars	*Suchard*	*Rowntree*	*Ferrero*	*Cadbury*	*Nestlé*	*Others*
United Kingdom	24	2	26	2	30	2	13
Austria	4	73	–	–	–	5	18
Belgium	6	82	2	5	–	3	2
France	11	13	17	6	8	10	35
Italy	1	–	–	4	–	5	60
Netherlands	23	–	13	–	–	–	64
Switzerland	9	17	–	–	–	17	57
W. Germany	22	15	3	6	–	8	36
Total	17%	13%	11%	10%	8%	9%	32%

Source: Henderson Crossthwaite.

Exhibit 6.5 *European chocolate market shares by major competitor, 1988*

	Nestlé	Rowntree	Jacobs Suchard	Cadbury Schweppes	Hershey
Europe	43	61[1]	83[2]	63[3]	–
North America	29	29	17	18	>90
Asia	13				
Oceania	2	4[4]			
Others	3	6	1[5]	19[5]	<10[5]
Total	100	100	101[6]	100	100

[1] United Kingdom and Ireland = 40% of total turnover.
[2] West Germany and France = 58% of total turnover.
[3] United Kingdom = 47% of total turnover.
[4] Includes Asia and Oceania.
[5] Includes Asia, Oceania and others.
[6] Does not add up to 100% due to rounding errors.

Source: Company Accounts.

Exhibit 6.6 *Percentage breakdown of total turnover by region for major confectionery competitors, 1987*

The major industry competitors had healthy rates of profitability. Because Mars was a privately-held US company, it did not publish sales and profit figures. For the other major competitors, trading profit on sales averaged 9.3% over the five-year period ending in 1987; trading profit on assets averaged 16.1% and the rate of return on stockholders' equity averaged 16.1% (Exhibits 6.7–6.12).

	Confectionery turnover as % of turnover[1] (1987)	Trading profit[2] as % of turnover	Trading profit[2] as % of average[3] trading assets[4]	Net income[5] as % of average[3] shareholders' equity
			(Average 1983–1987)	
Hershey Foods	76	14.7	15.8	17.2
Cadbury Schweppes	43	7.5	20.5	17.1
Rowntree	76	8.3	25.5	16.8
Jacobs Suchard	57	5.9	12.3	16.3
Nestlé	8	10.2	14.3	13.1

[1] Turnover = net sales.
[2] Trading profit = operating profit before interest and taxes.
[3] Average of beginning and end-of-year trading assets.
[4] Trading assets equal total assets minus financial assets.
[5] Net income after tax but before extraordinary items.

Source: Company Accounts.

Note: As a measure of relative risk, the 'beta' values for the common stocks of publicly-traded confectionery companies generally clustered around a value of 1.0.

Exhibit 6.7 *Operating and financial performance of major competitors, 1983–1987*

		1984	1985	1986	1987
A. Financial statement data ($ millions)					
1	Turnover (sales)	1,849	1,996	2,170	2,434
2	Gross profit	579	640	716	822
3	Trading profit	223	245	271	294
4	Net income	109	121	133	148
5	Depreciation	45	52	59	71
6	Liquid assets	88	111	28	15
7	Current assets	385	412	393	485
8	Fixed assets	727	785	963	1,160
9	Total assets	1,123	1,197	1,356	1,645
10	Current liabilities	203	195	222	300
11	Long-term liabilities	259	274	406	513
12	Stockholders' equity	661	728	728	832
B. Per share data ($)					
13	Earnings	1.16	1.19	1.42	1.64
14	Dividends	0.41	0.48	0.52	0.58
15	Stock price (average)	11.6	15.0	22.8	29.3
16	Price–earnings (average)	10.0	9.7	16.1	17.9
17	Equity book value	7.0	7.7	8.10	9.20

Source: Company Accounts.

Exhibit 6.8 *Hershey Foods Corp. – selected financial data, 1984–1987.*

		1984	1985	1986	1987
A. Financial statement data (£ millions)					
1	Turnover (sales)	2,016	1,874	1,840	2,031
2	Gross profit	747	683	740	854
3	Trading profit	154	113	140	181
4a	Net income[1]	73	48	76	112
4b	Net income[2]	65	42	102	111
5	Depreciation	56	55	60	63
6	Liquid assets	37	47	177	140
7	Current assets	711	619	723	796
8	Fixed assets	628	594	555	604
9	Total assets	1,338	1,213	1,279	1,400
10	Current liabilities	531	479	537	689
11	Long-term liabilities	288	263	279	234
12	Share capital and reserves	519	471	463	477
B. Per share data (pence)					
13	Earnings[1]	15.7	9.3	14.3	19.1
14	Dividends	5.9	5.9	6.7	8.0
15	Stock price (average)	137	153	170	238
16	Price–earnings[1] (average)	8.7	16.5	11.9	12.5
17	Equity book value	112	92	87	83
18	Employees (000)	35.5	33.8	27.7	27.5

[1]Earnings before Extraordinary Items.
[2]Earnings after Extraordinary Items.
Source: Company Accounts.

Exhibit 6.9 *Cadbury Schweppes plc – selected financial data, 1984–1987*

	1984	1985	1986	1987
A. Financial statement data (SF millions)				
1 Turnover (sales)	5,111	5,382	5,236	6,104
2 Gross profit	1,104	1,156	1,304	1,955
3 Trading profit	244	265	338	471
4 Net income	120	150	191	265
5 Depreciation	84	092	103	128
6 Liquid assets	230	788	1,470	705
7 Current assets	1,390	2,008	2,920	2,206
8 Fixed assets	666	674	832	886
9 Total assets	2,056	2,682	3.752	3,092
10 Current liabilities	796	843	1,417	1,120
11 Long-term liabilities	483	487	885	829
12 Stockholders' equity	777	1,352	1,450	1,143[1]
B. Per share data (SF per bearer share)				
13 Earnings	351	353	414	503
14 Dividends	150	155	160	165
15 Stock price (average)	5,028	6,101	7,324	8,228
16 Price–earnings (average)	14.3	17.3	17.7	16.4
17				
18 Employees (000)	10.6	9.3	10.1	16.1

[1] It is normal accounting practice for Swiss companies to write off 'goodwill' when acquiring businesses. Jacobs Suchard reduced equity by SF1.1 million in 1987 due to write-off of goodwill associated with acquisitions.
Source: Company Accounts.

Exhibit 6.10   *Jacobs Suchard Group – selected financial data, 1984–1987*

	1984	1985	1986	1987
A. Financial statement data (SF millions)				
1 Turnover (sales)	31,141	42,225	38,050	35,241
2 Gross profit	11,301	14,926	13,603	13,616
3 Trading profit	3,206	4,315	3,671	3,651
4 Net profit	1,487	1,750	1,789	1,827
5 Depreciation	1,004	1,331	1,157	1,184
6 Liquid assets	6,168	3,853	5,619	6,961
7 Current assets	16,407	15,236	15,820	16,241
8 Fixed assets	8,067	9,952	9,275	8,902
9 Total assets	24,474	25,188	25,095	25,143
10 Current liabilities	7,651	8,858	8,119	7,547
11 Long-term liabilities	3,834	5,092	4,775	4,939
12 Share capital and reserves	12,989	11,238[1]	12,201	12,657
B. Per share data (SF per bearer share)				
13 Earnings	480	515	526	537
14 Dividends	136	145	145	150
15 Stock price (average)	5,062	7,400	8,600	9,325
16 Price–earnings (average)	10.5	14	16.4	17.4
17				
18 Employees (000)	138	155	162	163

[1] It is normal accounting practice for Swiss companies to write off 'goodwill' when acquiring businesses. Nestlé wrote off SF3.2 million of shareholders' equity on its purchase of Carnation in 1985.
Source: Company Accounts.

Exhibit 6.11   *Nestlé S.A. – selected financial data, 1984–1987*

		1983	1984	1985	1986	1987
A. Income statement data (£ millions)						
1	Turnover (sales)	951.9	1,156.5	1,205.2	1,290.4	1,427.6
2	Gross profit[1]	334.0	417.5	445.8	500.2	590.5
2a	Fixed overhead expenses	265.6	328.3	350.5	400.5	465.8
2b	Other operating income	4.2	4.6	6.0	6.0	5.4
3	Trading profit (2 − 2a + 2b)	72.6	93.8	101.3	105.7	130.1
3a	Interest earned	4.4	3.5	3.8	3.3	6.5
3b	Interest paid	12.2	19.3	22.0	21.7	18.0
4a	Profit after tax	46.5	58.0	60.7	66.2	87.9
4b	Extraordinary items	13.5	11.5	16.5	11.3	0.0
4c	Net profit after tax	32.8	46.5	44.2	54.9	87.9
4d	Preferred dividends	0.1	0.1	0.1	0.1	0.1
5	Depreciation (£m)	28.6	36.2	39.1	43.7	51.0
B. Balance sheet data (£ millions)						
6	Financial assets[2]	25.1	55.7	41.8	69.2	96.7
6a	Debtors (receivables)	144.5	171.1	178.7	208.5	214.9
6b	Stocks (inventories)	160.1	172.9	170.2	176.9	163.5
7	Current assets	329.7	399.7	390.7	454.6	475.1
8	Fixed assets	347.4	408.5	403.1	475.1	463.2
9	Total assets	677.1	808.2	793.8	929.7	938.3
10	Current liabilities	215.9	229.3	242.4	310.2	269.9
11	Long-term liabilities	112.4	186.3	177.0	228.1	259.8
11a	Interest-bearing liabilities	109.6	160.9	144.6	198.2	247.7
12a	Preferred stock	2.7	2.7	2.7	2.7	2.7
12b	Share capital and reserves	346.1	389.9	371.7	388.7	405.9
C. Per share data (pence)						
13	Earnings[3]	31.0	36.1	34.8	35.0	40.8
14	Common dividends	9.8	11.0	12.2	13.6	15.5
15a	Common stock price (high)	258	392	450	545	591
15b	Common stock price (low)	200	210	337	363	367
16	Average price–earnings ratio[4]	7.4	8.4	11.3	13.0	11.7
17	Equity book value (12b/19)	233	243	214	206	189
D. Other data						
18a	Employees, UK (000)	19.7	18.9	17.7	16.4	15.6
18b	Employees, world (000)	31.2	32.4	32.0	32.5	33.1
19	Ordinary shares (000'000)	149.5	160.6	173.9	188.7	215.0
20	Capital expenditures (£million)	59.9	59.9	71.5	76.2	82.5
21	Business acquisitions (£million)	159.6	3.3	34.2	189.9	14.2
22	Asset divestitures (£million)	4.0	3.1	4.5	4.2	5.2

[1] Gross profit equals turnover minus cost of sales.

[2] Cash plus marketable securities.

[3] Earnings per share of common stock equals line 4a minus line 4d.

[4] Average of high and low common stock price divided by earnings per share.

Source: Company Accounts.

Exhibit 6.12   *Rowntree plc – selected financial data, 1983–1987*

In recent years, the major producers had acquired a number of smaller, national chocolate companies. Between 1986 and 1988 Jacobs Suchard acquired six confectioners, including E.J. Brach (the third largest confectioner in the US behind Mars and Hershey), Van Houten (Holland), and Cote d'Or (Belgium). In 1987 Hershey purchased the Canadian confectionery assets of RJR Nabisco. In early 1988 Cadbury acquired Chocolats Poulain, a French chocolatier, and Nestlé was negotiating the purchase of Buitoni, an Italian food group which included the leading chocolatier Perugina.

Business system

Chocolate is made from kernels of fermented and roasted cocoa beans. The kernels are roasted and ground to form a paste which is hardened in moulds to make bitter (baking) chocolate, pressed to reduce the cocoa butter content and then pulverized to make cocoa powder, or mixed with sugar and additional cocoa butter to make sweet (eating) chocolate. Sweet chocolate is the basic semi-finished product used in the manufacture of block, countline, and boxed chocolate products.

Average costs for a representative portfolio of all three product types of sweet chocolate could be broken down as follows:

Raw material	35%
Packaging	10%
Production	20%
Distribution	5%
Marketing/sales	20%
Trading profit	10%
Total	**100%** (of manufacturer's selling price)

For countline products, raw material costs were proportionately lower because a smaller amount of cocoa was used. For boxed chocolates, packaging costs were proportionately higher.

Research and development

Research and development (R&D) generally focused on making a better chocolate and on developing new products, although one executive related, 'there is never really anything brand new in the confectionery market, just different ways of presenting combinations of the same ingredients.'

Raw materials

The major ingredient in chocolate confectionery was cocoa, followed by sugar and milk. Although Jacobs Suchard claimed to benefit from large purchase hedging, some manufacturers purchased cocoa supplies as needed at the spot price quoted on the major cocoa exchanges, while others purchased cocoa a year or two in advance to obtain the 'best price' and to ensure long-term supplies. Between 1977 and 1988, the international cartel of cocoa producers had fallen into disarray; the price of cocoa had fallen by 50% ($US prices), and surplus cocoa stocks continued to accumulate.

Industry practice was for manufacturers to absorb raw material price changes internally to smooth extreme changes in consumer prices. By exception, Mars had taken advantage of declining cocoa prices to stimulate volume demand and gain market share. Mars held the price of its Mars Bar but increased the product weight by 10% in the late 1970's and by another 15% in the early 1980s.

Production

It was difficult to sustain a competitive advantage based on manufacturing process or on product features due to the lack of proprietary technology. However, some manufacturers had developed countline products which were difficult to duplicate (e.g. Rowntree's After Eight and Kit Kat). The major manufacturers tried to be low-cost producers through increased scale economies. Scale economies were more easily achieved in the production of block chocolate and countlines (both relatively capital intensive), and less easily in the production of boxed chocolates (which was more labour intensive). While minimum efficient scale varied by product, most major producers were moving toward fewer and more concentrated production plants, some exclusively dedicated to one or two products.

Distribution

Confectionery products were sold through a wide range of distribution channels. In the UK, for example, wholesalers serving thousands of small 'Confectionery–Tobacco–Newsagent' (CTN) outlets accounted for 50% of total confectionery sales; multiple grocery stores accounted for 30%; department stores and multiple confectionery stores accounted for the remainder.

While distribution patterns and the balance of power between manufacturers and distributors varied across markets, retail concentration was on the increase. Western Europe (in particular the UK, France and West Germany) and Canada were noted for high levels of retail concentration. Manufacturers' trading margins in these countries averaged 8–12%, compared to averages of 14–16% in the USA, where retail concentration was lower.

European multiple retailers tended to stock narrower ranges of competing products than their US counterparts. As one industry executive commented, 'In Europe you pay more of a premium to get shelf space in a store. In addition, many of the (multiple) retailers stock only the leading brand and the Number 2. If you are third, you lose visibility and this damages brand reputation.'

Marketing

Consumers displayed considerable brand loyalty. As one industry executive explained, 'Most people have a "menu" of products they like and know. They will buy a new product perhaps once or twice, but the tendency is to go back to the "old familiars", the popular established brands.' The most popular brands of chocolate were over 50 years old; Mars Bar, for example, was introduced in 1932 and Kit Kat in 1935.

In 1987 the six largest producers spent over $750 million per year on chocolate advertising. In recent years, manufacturers had dramatically increased their overall level of marketing spending, particularly with respect to launching new products. By 1988 one manufacturer estimated that new products, which generally had a much shorter life span than established brands, had to generate at least $25 million in sales over the first two years to cover product development and marketing costs. Manufacturers tended to focus on brand extensions into new product segments and particularly into new geographic markets.

Major competitors

Mars

With the world's best selling chocolate bar, and other famous global brands such as Snickers, M&Ms, Twix, and Milky Way, Mars was the world leader in chocolate confectionery. In 1987 confectionery was estimated to account for $4 billion of Mars' $7 billion total turnover of confectionery, pet food and electronics products.

With 38% market share, Mars dominated the world countline sector, with particular strength in North America and Europe (Exhibit 6.4). In 1987 Mars held the largest share of the European chocolate market and was a close third to Cadbury and Rowntree in the UK (Exhibit 6.5). Like Rowntree and Cadbury, Mars spent approximately £25 million annually on advertising in the UK. In 1987 Mars was one of the top 30 US advertisers ($300 million) and had five of the top ten best-selling chocolate bars in the USA.

The 1986 introduction of Kudos, a chocolate-covered granola bar, was Mars' first new product in over ten years. Since 1986, however, Mars had mounted a major effort to acquire and develop new products, particularly those which would capitalize on the Mars brand name. Recent product launches included a Mars milk drink and Mars ice cream.

Mars' strategy was consistent across all brands: produce high quality, technologically simple products at very high volumes on automated equipment dedicated to the production of either 'layered' (Mars, Snickers) or 'panned' (M&Ms, Maltesers) products; and support the brands with heavy marketing spending and aggressive sales organizations and retailing policies. The company's future strategy focused on building and strengthening Mars' global brands. In 1987, for example, Mars had dropped Treets, a £15 million UK brand, and repositioned Minstrels under the Galaxy label, both in order to strengthen the 1988 launch of M&Ms into the UK market.

Hershey Foods

Founded as a chocolate company in 1893, Hershey was a diversified food group with total turnover of $2.4 billion by 1987. More than 90% of that turnover was in the US (Exhibit 6.6); confectionery accounted for 66% of total turnover and 80% of trading profit. Although Hershey was a quoted company, it could not be taken over easily because 77% of the company's voting stock was owned by a charitable trust.

Hershey's strength was in block chocolate in North America, where it held a 62% market share. With Hershey's Chocolate Bar, Reese's Peanut Butter Cup, and Hershey's Kisses all in the 1987 US 'top ten', Hershey was second to Mars in the US chocolate market. Hershey also produced major Rowntree brands under licence in the USA.

Between 1981 and 1987, Hershey increased its advertising and promotion spending from 8.5% to 11.5% of total turnover to 'consolidate market share'. Hershey's chocolate production was concentrated in Hershey, Pennsylvania, which supplied export markets in Japan, South Korea, and Australia. The company licensed some production in the Far East, Sweden, and Mexico, normally under joint venture agreements.

Hershey's corporate strategy was to reduce exposure to cocoa price volatility by diversifying within the confectionery and snack businesses. The company had expanded into branded sugar confectionery, pasta products, and ice cream restaurants, largely through acquisitions. By 1987 only 45% of Hershey's sales came from products composed of at least 70% chocolate, down from 80% in 1963.

Cadbury Schweppes

Cadbury Schweppes plc was founded in 1969 with the merger of the Cadbury Group plc and Schweppes Ltd. In 1987 confectionery represented 43% of Cadbury's total turnover of £2,031 million.

With 7% of the world chocolate market and brands such as Dairy Milk, Creme Eggs, Crunchie, Flake and Milk Tray, Cadbury was a major world name in chocolate. Cadbury was the market leader in Australia, and three Cadbury brands (Mounds, Almond Joy and Peppermint Patties) were in the US 'top twenty'. However, Cadbury's main business was in the UK where it held 30% of the market and had five of the top ten best-selling chocolate products. In 1986 and 1987, Cadbury had launched nine new UK brands.

During the late 1970s, Cadbury expanded overseas and diversified within and beyond the food sector. However, with the appointment of Mr Dominic Cadbury as Chief Executive in 1983, Cadbury Schweppes embarked on a more focused product and market strategy. Mr Cadbury announced a restructuring of the Group 'to concentrate resources behind (our) leading beverage and confectionery brands in those markets which offer the best opportunities for their development.'

Major divestments were made involving secondary activities in the food and non-food sectors and the assets of some under-performing core businesses. Acquisitions were made to strengthen the mainstream branded product lines and to gain access to new geographic markets. For example, the acquisition of Chocolats Poulain provided Cadbury's first manufacturing facility in Europe. In January 1987, General Cinema Corporation (which controlled the largest US Pepsi bottling operation) announced the acquisition of an 8.5% shareholding in Cadbury Schweppes and, in November 1987, increased that holding to 18.2%. While General Cinema was less than half the size of Cadbury in market capitalization, industry observers speculated that the company was planning a leveraged buyout of Cadbury Schweppes.

Jacobs Suchard

Controlled by the Jacobs family and based in Zürich, the Jacobs Suchard Group was formed in 1982 in a reverse takeover of Interfood (the parent company of the Suchard and Tobler chocolate firms) by Jacobs (a West German coffee company). In 1987 Suchard's principal businesses were still coffee and confectionery, which accounted for 57% and 43% respectively of Suchard's 1987 turnover of SF6.1 billion.

Europe was Suchard's largest market, accounting for 83% of 1987 turnover. However, Jacobs Suchard operated in more than 20 countries, represented by subsidiaries and licensees, and exported its products to over 100 countries. The Group also had substantial operations in the trading of raw materials for coffee and chocolate production.

Jacobs Suchard held 23% of the European block chocolate market. Leading brands included Toblerone, Suchard, Milka and Cote d'Or. Developing and expanding its portfolio of global brands was of primary importance to the Group. As Mr. Klaus Jacobs, the entrepreneurial Chairman of the Board, stated, 'We firmly believe that global brands are the wave of the future.' An increasing number of Jacobs Suchard's brands were marketed globally, under the sponsorship of global brand managers.

Since 1984 Suchard had been concentrating production of individual brands in fewer and larger plants to gain absolute cost leadership. In 1987 European production of chocolate and confectionery took place in 17 plants; Suchard planned to reduce this number to 7 by 1991 as improvements were made in its cross-border distribution system.

Rowntree

Rowntree was founded in York in 1825 by a cocoa and chocolate vendor who sold the business to the Rowntree family in 1862. In 1970 Rowntree merged with John Mackintosh & Sons, Ltd, a British confectioner nearly half the size of Rowntree. In 1988 Rowntree's headquarters were still in York and, with 5500 workers, the company was by far York's largest employer. Many of the traditions of the Rowntree family, including a strong concern for employee and community welfare, had been preserved; many of the current employees' parents and grandparents had also worked for Rowntree.

In 1987 Rowntree was primarily a confectionery company (Exhibit 6.13), with major strengths in the countline and boxed chocolate segments. Rowntree's major market was the UK where, with 26% market share, it was second only to Cadbury. Rowntree's Kit Kat was the best-selling confectionery brand in the UK (where 40 Kit Kats were consumed per second) and number five in both the US and Japan. Kit Kat was part of a portfolio of leading global brands. Many of these brands (Kit Kat, Quality Street, Smarties, Rolo, Aero, Black Magic) were launched in the 1930s; After Eight was introduced in 1962; Yorkie and Lion in 1976. Since 1981 Rowntree had launched seven new brands in the UK, including Novo, a chocolate cereal bar.

Market segment	Turnover (£ millions)	Percentage of total turnover	Trading profit (£ millions)	Percentage of total trading profit	Trading margin (%)
Confectionery	1,088.5	72.6	101.0	77.6	9.3
Snack foods	191.8	13.4	14.5	11.1	7.6
Retailing	97.3	6.8	8.1	6.2	8.3
Grocery (UK)	50.0	3.5	6.5	5.0	13.0
Total	1,427.6	100.0	130.1	100.0	9.1

Source: Company Accounts.

Exhibit 6.13 *Rowntree plc – market segment performance, 1987*

162

Market segment	Turnover (£ millions)	Percentage of total turnover	Trading profit (£ millions)	Percentage of total trading profit	Trading margin (%)
UK and Ireland	566.4	40	61.7	47	10.9
Continental Europe	300.4	21	11.0	8	3.7
North America	416.1	29	41.0	31	9.8
Australasia	57.1	4	4.7	4	8.2
Rest of world	87.6	6	11.7	9	13.4
Total	1,427.6	100	130.1	100	9.1

Source: Company Accounts.

Exhibit 6.14   *Rowntree plc – performance by region, 1987*

In 1987 Rowntree operated 25 factories in nine countries and employed 33,000 people around the world, including close to 16,000 in its eight UK operations. Group turnover was £1.4 billion, with the UK and Ireland accounting for 40% of total turnover (Exhibit 6.14).

Rowntree was headed by Mr Kenneth Dixon, age 58, who had been with Rowntree for 32 years, and was appointed as Chairman and Chief Executive in 1981. In the words of a long-time senior Rowntree executive, 'Mr Dixon fostered a real sense of positive change in the company.'

During the late 1970s, Rowntree's operating performance had shown significant deterioration (Exhibit 6.15). To reverse this trend, Mr. Dixon initiated a long-term programme to improve the efficiency of the UK core business and to diversify into related businesses, principally through the acquisition and development of brand

	1976	1977	1978	1979	1980	1981
	(£ millions unless stated as a percentage)					
Turnover	384.9	469.2	562.7	601.3	629.8	688.0
Trading profit	36.8	46.9	51.7	46.6	44.8	48.0
Net profit[1]	16.9	30.4	34.4	27.2	17.5	29.1
Average[2] assets	194.7	246.8	332.5	396.6	412.5	448.6
Average[2] owner's equity	77.3	120.6	182.3	218.4	231.8	278.9
Trading margin (%)	9.6%	10.0%	9.2%	7.8%	7.1%	7.2%
Trading profit/assets (%)	18.9%	19.0%	15.6%	11.8%	10.9%	10.7%
Turnover/assets	1.8	1.7	1.5	1.5	1.5	1.4
Net profit/equity (%)	21.8%	25.2%	18.9%	12.5%	7.6%	10.3%

[1] Net after-tax profit attributable to ordinary common shares.
[2] Average of beginning and end of year.

Source: Company Accounts.

Exhibit 6.15   *Rowntree plc – operating and financial performance, 1976–1981*

names. Mr Dixon delegated more responsibility to the operating levels of the company, while maintaining a central brand and product strategy.

Branding was the essence of Rowntree's strategy. According to Mr Dixon, 'The fundamental idea which drives Rowntree is branding: the creation of distinct, differentiated, positively identifiable and market-positioned goods. Rowntree seeks to build brands by marketing products and services at competitive prices, positioning them accurately in the markets they serve, and giving them clear identity and character.'

In the 1960s, Rowntree granted Hershey a long-term licence to manufacture and sell Rowntree products in the US. With its expansion into continental Europe underway at the time, Rowntree believed that it lacked the resources to develop an effective marketing presence in both continental Europe and the US. In 1978 the agreement with Hershey was renegotiated, giving Hershey rights in perpetuity to the Kit Kat and Rolo brand names in the US (which would be retained by Hershey in the event of a change in Rowntree ownership). Rowntree was still free to enter the US market with its other brand names. In 1987 royalties from this agreement contributed about £2 million toward Rowntree Group profits.

Between 1982 and 1987, Rowntree invested nearly £400 million to upgrade manufacturing facilities and develop high volume, product-dedicated equipment for several of the company's leading global brands, including Kit Kat, After Eight, and Smarties. Products produced on this equipment had a consistent formulation and were sold all over the world; the Hamburg After Eight plant, for example, shipped to 16 countries.

By 1987 Rowntree's capital investments were beginning to pay off. Over the past five years, the number of UK personnel had been reduced from 19,700 to 15,600, and productivity improvements were running at 9% per annum. Trading margins had nearly recovered to the high level previously achieved in 1977, and Rowntree executives were confident that trading margins would continue to improve due to productivity gains associated with past investments in manufacturing rationalization.

In 1987 Rowntree's £100 million investment in continental Europe was still showing modest financial returns. Rowntree had entered the continental European market in the 1960s, establishing production facilities at Hamburg (West Germany), Elst (Holland), Dijon and Noisiel (France). Although advertising and promotion spending (as a percentage of sales) was double that of the UK, volume growth had not met Rowntree's expectations. The trading margin on the Continental European business had inched up very slowly, from 1.0% in 1985 to 3.7% in 1987 (Exhibit 6.14). As one manager explained: 'Kit Kats go well with a cup of tea, but not with wine and beer!'

Other industry observers concluded that Rowntree's distribution strategy for continental Europe was responsible for the company's relatively poor profit performance there. The conventional entry strategy was to buy directly into local distribution by acquiring popular local brands which already had access to local distribution channels. These distribution outlets were then encouraged to stock the international brands of the new entrant; at the same time, established distribution outlets in other regions or countries were encouraged to stock the newly acquired brand. This was the distribution entry strategy favoured by Cadbury, Suchard and Nestlé.

Rowntree had made no significant entry acquisitions in continental Europe. Instead, the company chose to promote its existing brands heavily to end-consumers in these markets. The objective was to develop consumer loyalty as a way to pressure the large multiple retail outlets into stocking the Rowntree brands. This was an aggressive and expensive entry strategy; and it met with resistance from many retailers. However, by early 1988 Rowntree believed that the long-term brand-building strategy was finally beginning to pay off; Lion Bar had become the second-best selling chocolate bar in France and more After Eights were sold in West Germany than in the UK. 'With brand popularity on the rise, cost-effective distribution access would surely follow.'

Between 1983 and 1987, Rowntree spent nearly £400 million on acquisitions (Exhibit 6.16). The acquired companies expanded the company's presence in some traditional businesses and also provided new activities, particularly in the area of branded retailing of specialist confectionery products. The retail shops acquired by Rowntree were viewed not as outlets for Rowntree brands, but rather as acquisitions of brands in their own right. Because of these acquisitions, a significant stream of Rowntree's profits were being earned in North America. While Rowntree had hedged its foreign exchange risk exposure on the balance sheet, it took a long-term view with respect to foreign exchange risk exposure on the income statement. The resulting transactions exposure concerned some financial analysts.

Company	Location	Primary area of business activity	Year of purchase	Purchase price (£m)
Tom's Foods	USA	Snack foods	1983	138
Laura Secord	Canada	Branded retailing	1983	19
Original Cookie Co.	USA	Branded retailing	1985	32
Hot Sam	USA	Branded retailing	1986	14
Sunmark	USA	Branded confectionery	1986	156
Gales	UK	Honey products	1986	1
Smaller acquisitions	USA, UK, France, Australia	Snack foods, confectionery, branded retailing	1983–87	29
				399

Source: Company Accounts.

Exhibit 6.16   *Rowntree plc – major business acquisitions, 1983–1987*

In a highly competitive US market, Rowntree's snack food acquisitions were not generating trading margins consistent with other company activities (Exhibit 6.13). In January of 1988 Rowntree announced its intention to divest its major snack food businesses to concentrate on confectionery, retailing and UK grocery activities where the potential to develop distinct consumer brands was considered more promising.

Although Rowntree's overall operating performance continued to improve, the company's common share price performance between 1986 and early 1988 was weaker than that achieved by the Financial Times 'All Share' and Food Manufacturing Indexes on the London Stock Exchange (Exhibit 6.17). In early 1988, London's financial

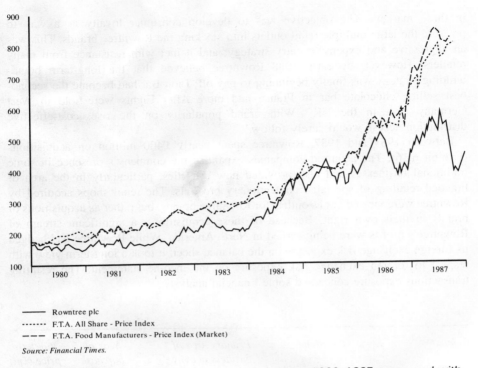

Rowntree plc
········· F.T.A. All Share - Price Index
– – – F.T.A. Food Manufacturers - Price Index (Market)

Source: Financial Times.

Exhibit 6.17 *Rowntree plc share price performance, 1980–1987, compared with the Financial Times Market and Food Manufacturers' Price Indexes on the London Stock Exchange (01/01/80 to 31/12/87, weekly)*

analysts published mixed opinions regarding Rowntree's immediate prospects (Exhibit 6.18). Mr Nightingale, Rowntree's Company Secretary, recalled, 'For years we had been trying to get the value of our brands reflected in our share price, but without much success. As a consequence, there were always takeover rumours.'

Nestlé

The Nestlé Group grew from the 1905 merger of the Anglo-Swiss Condensed Milk Co., a milk processing firm founded in 1866, and Henri Nestlé, a Swiss infant food company founded in 1867 in Vevey. In 1988 the Nestlé headquarters were still in Vevey, and the Group operated 383 factories in 59 countries. In 1988 Nestlé employed 163,000 people, 10,000 in the UK.

Nestlé was the world's largest food company and the world's largest producer of coffee, powdered milk and frozen dinners. In 1987 drinks, dairy products, culinary products, frozen foods and confectionery products accounted for 79% of Nestlé turnover of SF35.2 billion; other food products accounted for 18% and non-food products 3%. Only 2% of the Group's turnover came from sales within Switzerland. The 20 companies acquired between 1983 and 1985 (at a total purchase price of $5 billion) added new brands of coffee, chocolates and fruit juice to Nestlé's line-up of strong world brands such as Nescafé, Stouffer's, Maggi and Findus. In 1985 Nestlé

Name of broker	Date of report	Forecast of 1988 trading profit (£m)	Summary of major comments and recommendations
County Natwest	01/21/88	125	**Sell** – Dollar weakness limits prospects for 1988
BZW	01/25/88	127	Decision to sell snack food business correct but unable to give final verdict until consideration is known
County Natwest	01/26/88	125	Surprise disposals, but good move.
BZW	02/24/88	127	**Buy** – Current rating of shares is not expensive with absence of bid premium
Warburg Securities	03/17/88	128	**Hold** – Core business performed well but reversal in snacks and slowdown in retailing leaves strategy looking threadbare
Hoare Govett	03/17/88	127	Over-valued in short term. Longer term outlook remaining clouded by current divestment/acquisition plans
BZW	03/17/88	129	**Hold** – Lower consideration for disposals than expected would lead to downgrading of forecast. Share price will be susceptible to strengthening of sterling.
County Natwest	03/18/88	125	Good results. Disposal of snack business an excellent move
Kleinwart Grievson	03/18/88	129	**Hold** – Fully valued

Sources: Stock Brokerage Reports.

Exhibit 6.18 *Stockbrokers' comments on Rowntree*

increased its US presence through the $2.9 billion purchase of Carnation and, in early April 1988, was finalizing the $1.3 billion purchase of Buitoni-Perugina.

This series of acquisitions had been spurred by Mr Helmut Maucher, age 60, who joined Nestlé as an apprentice in 1948 and was appointed Managing Director of Nestlé S.A. in 1981. Under Mr Maucher's direction, Nestlé had cut costs and divested less profitable operations, including the $180 million Libby's US canned food business.

Mr Maucher explained Nestlé's approach to acquisitions:

At Nestlé we are not portfolio managers. Acquisitions must fit into our corporate and marketing policy. In other words, they must strengthen our position in individual countries or product groups or enable us to enter new fields where we have not so far been represented. Acquisitions are part of an overall development strategy. That is why we cannot leave acquisition decisions purely to financial considerations. Of course, you must have some figures to evaluate an acquisition; but more important is the feel you have about what you can do with the brands.

Mr Maucher was a strong believer in the importance of a long-term outlook. On his appointment as Managing Director, he banned monthly 25-page reports and quarterly profit and loss statements in favour of a monthly one-page report which highlighted key numbers such as turnover, working capital, and inventories. As Mr Maucher explained, 'With quarterly reports all managers care about is the next three months, and they manage for the next quarter instead of for the next five years.' For this reason, Mr Maucher was reluctant to list Nestlé's shares on any stock exchange which required the disclosure of quarterly reports.

Nestlé entered the chocolate market in 1929 with the purchase of Peter-Cailler-Kohler, a Swiss chocolate group originally founded in 1819. Since 1981, confectionery sales had represented approximately 8% of annual turnover; in 1987 confectionery was Nestlé's fifth largest business. Nestlé's main product strength was in block chocolate, where it held 15% and 14% respectively of the European and American markets (Exhibit 6.4). Nestlé's leading brands included Milkybar in the UK and Crunch in the US. Recent research into the new generation of chocolate and confectionery products had produced 'Yes', a pastry snack product, and 'Sundy', a cereal bar.

As a result of Nestlé's market-oriented organization structure, block chocolate products were generally produced and positioned according to the tastes of local markets. For example, Nestlé's white block chocolate products (often produced in the same plants as coffee and other food products) were made from several recipes and marketed under several brand names. In the UK, Nestlé's white chocolate brand, 'Milkybar', was positioned as a children's chocolate; in the USA it was called 'Alpine White' and was oriented toward the 'female indulgence' market. 'Because block chocolate is a traditional product with traditional tastes,' Mr Maucher explained, 'a local market orientation is particularly important, because this kind of chocolate must taste the way you got it as a child from your grandmother, whether you are French or Italian or German, and so on. This is true for the traditional chocolate products, not so much for the new generation of products such as countlines.'

During the 1970s, Nestlé's confectionery operations had been among the smaller and often relatively less profitable businesses in the company. However, Mr Maucher saw opportunities in the confectionery business: 'The key success factors in confectionery are technology, quality, creativity, and marketing skills, and Nestlé has all of those. If Nestlé cannot be successful at this business, then there is something wrong with Nestlé!'

Nestlé-Rowntree

In the early 1980s, Mr Maucher made confectionery a strategic priority. Nestlé increased investment in research and development and acquired two small US confectionery companies. Nestlé then began to analyse the possibilities for significant expansion in the world confectionery market. 'It would take 25 years to develop a major stake in this industry,' Mr Maucher said, 'so we are looking at acquisitions to accelerate that development.' According to Mr Ramon Masip, Executive Vice President in charge of the European market, 'For some time we had discussed making a "big move" into the confectionery business, and Rowntree has always been the number one choice.'

Synergies and complementarities

'We have always seen Rowntree as a "perfect fit",' Mr. Masip continued, 'because its strengths would complement Nestlé's.' Rowntree's strong position in the growing countlines segment would complement Nestlé's strength in block chocolate. In addition, Rowntree's strong position in the non-grocery outlets such as CTNs would complement Nestlé's strong contacts with the multiple grocery retailers. Rowntree also held a stronger position in the UK and in some markets in continental Europe.

Although Nestlé was interested in Rowntree's recent success in launching new products such as the Lion bar, 'we are much more concerned with the brands that Rowntree already has in the market!' Mr Masip exclaimed. Rowntree's strong, well-established world brands were the key reason for Nestlé's interest. 'There are very, very few companies in the world with such good brands and skills in this particular business,' Mr Masip concluded.

Nestlé believed that, should the opportunity to acquire Rowntree arise, additional operating synergies could be achieved in research and development, administration and the sales force. With the potential acquisition, it was estimated that substantial savings (perhaps 5–15% of Rowntree's fixed overhead expenses) could be realized from combining the operations of the two companies. Most of these savings would come through rationalization of selling effort.

Nestlé did not expect manufacturing synergies from the acquisition. Rowntree had already made the appropriate investments to rationalize its own production, and the scope for cross-product rationalization was minimal given Nestlé's strategy of decentralized multi-product manufacturing facilities located in individual markets.

However, there were possibilities to improve Rowntree's operating profitability in continental Europe by gaining cheaper access to Nestlé's established distribution strength in these markets. Also, the sales growth of Nestlé's chocolate products could be accelerated by gaining access to Rowntree's CTN outlets. Perhaps more important was the potential sales growth acceleration of Rowntree's proven brands in geographic markets where Nestlé had strong distribution presence, but where Rowntree had no market presence – countries like Brazil, Portugal, Switzerland, Sweden, Austria and perhaps 30 more. While more difficult to quantify with precision, this latter opportunity was very appealing given the profit margins of the Rowntree brands.

November 1987

In November of 1987, Mr Maucher and Mr Masip met in Paris with Mr Dixon and Mr Masip's counterpart in Rowntree, Mr Guerin. This meeting had stemmed from quiet discussions between Masip and Guerin regarding possible Nestlé-Rowntree co-operation in continental Europe. For over a year, Mr Maucher wanted to arrange a meeting with Mr Dixon to discuss possible forms of co-operation between Nestlé and Rowntree. In fact, some of Mr Maucher's external financial advisors had advised him to take a position in Rowntree stock, but Mr Maucher had always replied: 'That is not our policy. We do not do anything behind any company's back, and as I have told Mr Dixon, we will not do anything that would be perceived as unfriendly to Rowntree.'

The Paris meeting in November 1987 began with Mr Dixon advising Mr Maucher: 'Nestlé does not appear to be interested in confectionery and Rowntree is prepared to buy Nestlé's confectionery business on a worldwide basis.' Mr Maucher exclaimed: 'We propose just the opposite!' The ensuing discussion explored possibilities for

Takeover bids for public companies in the UK were conducted according to a complex set of formal rules contained in the City Code on Takeovers and Mergers. The City Code was designed to ensure fair and similar treatment for all shareholders of the same class, mainly through responsible, detailed disclosure and the absence of stock price manipulation. The City Code was administered by the Takeover Panel, a self-regulatory body whose members included Bank of England appointees and representatives of participants in the UK securities markets. The Panel was authorized to make rulings and interpretations on novel points arising during the course of a takeover attempt.

The City Code identified consequences associated with the acquisition of certain benchmark percentages of the equity of a takeover target. For example, within 5 days of acquiring 5% of more of the capital of a company, the purchaser was required to inform the target company of its interest; the target company was then required to make an immediate announcement of this fact to the London Stock Exchange.

A purchaser could not acquire 10% or more of the capital of the target within any period of 7 days if these purchases would bring its total interest above 15% of the voting rights in the target company. Between 15% and 30% interest, the purchaser could accumulate shares by tender offer or by a series of share purchases; however, each series of share purchases could not result in the acquisition of more than 10% of the total equity of the target during any 7-day period. Once acquiring an interest totalling 30%, the bidder was obliged to make a general offer for the remaining 70% of the voting capital (at the highest price previously paid by the bidder). After a bidder had obtained 90% ownership of a class of shares, it could compulsorily acquire the outstanding shares from the minority shareholders; similarly, any remaining minority shareholders could require the bidder to purchase their shares at the highest price previously paid by the bidder.

Proposed acquisitions could also be reviewed by the Office of Fair Trading (OFT), a subsection of the Department of Trade and Industry. The OFT had responsibility for deciding whether the competitive implications of the merger warranted investigation. The OFT could refer merger cases to the Mergers and Monopolies Commission (MMC), an independent tribunal which ruled on whether the merger should be blocked in the interests of national competition policy. Referral to the MMC was often prized by managements of takeover targets. Aside from allowing the possibility of a referral decision favouring the target, the referral process gave the takeover target additional time (3–7 months) to mount a more effective takeover defence.

Takeovers of UK public companies were either recommended by the Board of the target company or contested. Action by the Board of a target to frustrate an offer for the target company was prohibited without the approval, in a General Meeting, of the shareholders. Recommended offers in the UK were generally restricted to smaller companies; they were relatively rare for companies with market capitalization in excess of £200 million.

Between 1985 and 1987, takeover bids were initiated for 14 large UK companies, each with individual market capitalizations in excess of £1 billion. Only one of these bids was recommended; the rest were contested. Ultimately, 4 of these bids were successful while 10 failed. For the three successful cash bids, the average share price premium paid was 60%; the individual premiums paid ranged from 40% to 80%.[1]

More recent acquisition activity in France and the UK provided reference points for the value of brand names. During 1987 and 1988, Seagram (a Canadian drinks group) and Grand Metropolitan (a UK drinks and hotel group) waged a fierce takeover battle to acquire Martell (the second largest French cognac house). In February 1988, Seagrams emerged the victor, but only after bidding an estimated 40× the 1987 earnings of Martell. In March 1988, United Biscuits paid a price–earnings multiple of 25× to purchase the frozen and chilled foods division of Hanson Trust. At that time, the average price–earnings ratio for 5 comparable UK food companies was 11.9×.

---

[1] Share price premiums were calculated by comparing final bid offer prices against the share prices of the target companies two months prior to the date of the final offer.

Exhibit 6.19 *The City Code and the UK takeover climate*

cooperation in production, marketing, distribution, or in various geographic markets, in order to optimize the situation for both companies. To facilitate development of a long-term commitment and of further cooperation in the longer term, Mr Maucher suggested purchasing a 10–25% stake in Rowntree.

After a lengthy and amicable discussion, Mr Dixon promised to examine Nestlé's suggestions and take them to the Rowntree Board for consideration. According to Mr Dixon, Rowntree had already considered cooperation with several parties as a basis for market development, particularly in Europe, but 'we felt at Rowntree that we could proceed on our own and would prefer to do so'. After making this reply to Mr Maucher in February 1988, he added: 'Unfortunately, any sort of association with a company of your size can only have one ending and, at this time, we don't feel we need to make that kind of commitment to anyone.' Mr Dixon, responding to Mr Maucher's grave concerns regarding the persistent takeover rumours, admitted: 'This does not mean that we do not recognize there is a risk.'

April 13, 1988

At 8:30 on the morning of Wednesday, April 13, 1988, Rowntree was advised of significant activity in the trading of Rowntree shares. By 9:15 a.m. Jacobs Suchard held 14.9% of Rowntree plc.

While making no contact with Rowntree, Suchard began acquiring Rowntree stock in mid-March. By April 12 Suchard held just under 5% of Rowntree shares. At the start of trading on the London Stock Exchange on April 13, Suchard's intermediary telephoned major institutional holders of Rowntree shares, offering a 30% premium on the opening share price of 477 pence if they sold immediately. The shareholders did not know to whom they were selling but, in less than 45 minutes, Suchard increased its holding to 14.9%, the maximum allowable under the City Code (Exhibit 6.19) for such a transaction. When the news of Suchard's raid reached the markets, Rowntree's share price jumped to over 700 pence.

In what was later described as a 'tactical error' by some City observers, S. G. Warburg issued the following press release for its client, Jacobs Suchard, on the morning of April 13:

> We have acquired a 14.9 per cent investment stake in Rowntree. The stake is a strategic investment in that Rowntree is a company with a great potential based on its excellent global brands. We intend to acquire not more than 25 per cent, at a maximum price of 630p. As you know, we are only permitted to take our holding to 15 per cent today. We hope to buy the remaining 10 per cent, but at no more than the price we are currently offering. This is not a prelude to a full bid and there is no intention of increasing the holding beyond this 25 per cent figure for at least a year although we reserve the right to do so if there is a full bid from a third party in the meantime.

Exercising its interpretative responsibility, the City Takeover Panel swiftly ruled that Warburg's statement prevented Suchard from purchasing any further Rowntree shares for the next 12 months, provided that the Rowntree share price stayed above 630p, unless a bid came in from another party during that time period.

Reaction from the City of London financial community

After years of persistent rumours of a Rowntree takeover, Suchard's move ignited speculation on potential counter-bidders. Hershey was identified by City analysts as a leading candidate; purchasing Rowntree would make it second only to Mars in world confectionery. Other rumoured candidates included Nestlé, Philip Morris, RJR Nabisco, Unilever and United Biscuits.

As external financial advisor to Rowntree, Mr. David Challen, a Director of J. Henry Schroder Wagg, was encouraged by the Takeover Panel's ruling. As he explained, 'The ruling put Jacobs in a box. Provided that Rowntree's share price remained above 630 pence, he could not buy additional shares, or bid again, for at least one year. This would give Rowntree the necessary time to prepare an effective takeover defence.'

Mr. Challen argued that it would be 'madness' for another company, such as Nestlé, to bid now: 'The market would sense an auction and raise the Rowntree stock price above the level of the new bid. Under the UK Takeover Rules, this would place the new bidder in the same box from which they had just released Suchard. The new bidder would be effectively prevented from buying shares, while Suchard could buy shares'. Mr Challen developed a scenario in which Suchard would ultimately emerge with 30% of the shares and be poised to make an offer for the remaining shares. The second bidder would be restricted by the City Code to accumulating 15% of the shares and would always be behind Suchard in share accumulation terms. Thus the second bidder would face a 'mega disadvantage' in gaining effective control.

'On the other hand', noted Mr Challen, 'without bidding, a second interested party could accumulate shares in the market at a relatively low price, leaving Suchard still subject to its self-imposed restrictions. Bidding now could only increase the total acquisition cost to the new bidder.' Mr. Challen concluded that the situation facing Rowntree was not urgent. 'The real challenge for Rowntree is to keep the stock price above 630 pence so that Suchard cannot accumulate more shares.'

Mr Peter St. George, a Director of County Natwest (Nestlé's financial advisor), recalled discussions with Nestlé in the summer of 1987 regarding a possible takeover bid for Rowntree: 'We were in a raging bull market then; paper, not cash, was king. The takeover bid premium required to purchase Rowntree at that time could not be justified on the fundamentals. Besides, any takeover attempt would have been viewed as hostile by Rowntree.'

	1984	1985	1986	1987	1988 (1st quarter annualized)
Inflation[1] (%)					
Switzerland	3.0	1.0	0.8	1.4	3.5
United Kingdom	5.0	6.0	3.4	4.3	1.8
United States	4.3	3.5	2.0	3.6	2.6
Long-term Government Bond yield (%)					
Switzerland	4.7	4.8	4.3	4.1	4.1
United Kingdom	10.7	10.6	9.9	9.5	9.4
United States	12.5	10.6	7.7	8.4	8.4

[1] Based on the Consumer Price Index.

Source: International Money Fund.

Exhibit 6.20 *Selected financial market rates, 1984–1987*

County Natwest had approached Nestlé in early 1988, advising a raid on Rowntree. 'Since the October 1987 crash, the world had changed,' Mr St. George explained. 'Share prices had fallen to reasonable levels where one could justify paying takeover premiums. The market no longer wanted paper; cash was king now, and Nestlé had cash. However, Mr Maucher demurred, stating that hostile raids were not in Nestlé's style.'

'Suchard's raid put Rowntree "in play",' Mr. St. George concluded. 'We contacted Nestlé as soon as we heard the news and encouraged them to make a counter bid for Rowntree. We advised them to act quickly and go into the market with a credible price to test (the fund-raising capability of) Jacobs Suchard. We cautioned Nestlé, however, that a successful bid would require a substantial premium on the current Rowntree share price' (Exhibits 6.19 and 6.20).

Rowntree's reaction

Jacob Suchard's initiative came as a complete surprise to Rowntree and reaction was swift. Mr Dixon stated in a press release that morning:

> Rowntree does not need Jacobs. We regard the acquisition of a stake by Jacobs as wholly unwelcome and believe that the price at which Jacobs acquired its shares is wholly inadequate for obtaining a major stake in the Group. Rowntree has one of the best portfolios of brand names of any confectionery company in the world, far better known than Jacobs' own. We do not believe that it is in the interests of Rowntree, its shareholders, or its employees that a Swiss company with nothing like the breadth of Rowntree's brands should have a share holding in the Group. Jacobs may need Rowntree, but Rowntree does not need Jacobs.

Nestlé's reaction

Suchard's raid also came as a surprise to Nestlé. Mr Maucher's first reaction was to contact Mr Dixon. In his telephone phone call that morning Mr Maucher said: 'I am sorry that what I warned you about has happened. I repeat our offer to help.' He urged Mr Dixon to reconsider Nestlé's earlier proposal to acquire a stake in Rowntree.

Mr Dixon thanked Mr Maucher for his offer of help but replied that he did not expect Suchard to make any further moves in the short term. 'According to the Takeover Panel, Jacobs cannot move for 12 months,' he told Mr Maucher, 'and while I know that Suchard will try to become more involved with Rowntree, we have no intention of having any form of co-operation with Suchard. We fully intend to remain independent. It is our hope and belief that the situation will calm down and that nothing more will come of it.' However, Mr Dixon promised that he and his Board would nonetheless consider Mr Maucher's proposal.

Mr Maucher concluded the discussion by saying, 'Our offer stands, and I hope you will reconsider. However, I fear that, because of Suchard's move, your independence is now an illusion. I must now feel free to act in Nestlé's best interests.'

Case 6.2 Nestlé–Rowntree (B)

This case was written by Research Associate Dana G. Hyde, under the supervision of Professors James C. Ellert and J. Peter Killing, as a basis for class discussion rather than to illustrate either effective or ineffective handling of a business situation.

Nestlé's reaction to Suchard's dawn raid

'I knew one second after hearing the news that, because of Suchard's move, we would have to bid for Rowntree,' Mr Maucher recalled. At the meeting of Nestlé's Comité du Conseil on the afternoon of April 13, the Board decided to do everything possible to acquire an important stake in Rowntree, and to prevent Jacobs Suchard from acquiring an important stake. 'We are still very much against engaging in a hostile bid,' Mr Maucher explained. 'However, our thinking is that, firstly, the company is now on the market, and secondly, strategically speaking, we cannot let Rowntree go to Jacobs Suchard.'

On April 14th, Nestlé purchased its first Rowntree shares. On the weekend following Suchard's dawn raid, at Nestlé's initiative, Messrs. Domeniconi (Nestlé's Executive Vice President, Finance) and St. George (from County NatWest, Nestlé's advisors) met in London with Rowntree's Messrs Nightingale and Bowden (Company Secretary and Finance Director, respectively) and Mr Challen (from Schroder Wagg, Rowntree's advisors). Nestlé proposed a friendly full takeover bid, but Rowntree rejected any idea of a full bid and also declined Nestlé's renewed offer to purchase a stake in Rowntree. Rowntree and its advisors strongly discouraged Nestlé from making any move, particularly a full bid. According to the Takeover Panel's ruling, Suchard could not increase its stake in Rowntree past 15% without making a full bid, unless a full bid were made by another party. Rowntree shares closed April 25 at 755p (pence).

Issued and issuable	Number of shares (000)
Ordinary common shares issued and outstanding (215,024,788)	215,025
Convertible bonds entitle holders to subscribe for 12,169,312 ordinary shares at 567p each during the period to March 2002	12,169
Warrants attached to 7.75% 1989 bonds carry rights to subscribe to 8,858,205 ordinary shares at 330p each in the period to 23 March 2002	8,858
Employee options entitle holders to purchase 7,711,754 ordinary shares at prices varying between 151p and 570p at various dates between 1988 and 1997	7,712
Fully diluted ordinary share capital base	243,764

Source: Company Accounts, 1988.

Exhibit 6.21   *Rowntree ordinary share capital (as of January 2, 1988)*

Nestlé's offer for Rowntree

At 8 am, Tuesday, April 26, Mr Maucher telephoned Rowntree's headquarters in York to inform Mr Dixon: 'This has nothing to do with our desire to maintain a friendly relationship but Nestlé is, very reluctantly, making a bid for Rowntree and, of course, we seek the cooperation of your Board.'

The Nestlé offer was 890p per share in cash, valuing Rowntree at £2.1 billion.[1] In a press release, the company stated: 'Nestlé's considerable resources will accelerate the international growth of Rowntree's brands, and there is an excellent fit between the brands and geographical trading bases of the two companies. Nestlé has had friendly contact with Rowntree in the past and has invited the Board of Rowntree to recommend the offer.'

Mr Maucher commented on the offer to the press:

This proposed merger will create a major confectionery grouping, present in all market segments and better able to exploit new opportunities, particularly in Europe and in the United States. Rowntree will have access to the substantial world-wide commercial, research and development, and financial resources of the Nestlé group. There is an excellent fit between the brands and trading bases of Rowntree and Nestlé. Also, like Rowntree, we are a business which puts great emphasis on people and products. For these reasons, we believe that the merger will benefit both companies and that Nestlé is the best partner for Rowntree. These benefits are reflected in the price we are able to offer Rowntree's shareholders, a price that is substantially higher than that which we believe Rowntree would be able to sustain as an independent business.

'We did not make a bid before because we do not like hostile takeovers,' Mr Maucher told the press conference the afternoon of April 26. 'But we had no other

[1] The valuation at £2.1 billion assumes 215.0 million Rowntree ordinary shares, already issued and outstanding, the conversion of Rowntree convertible bonds into 12.2 million Rowntree ordinary shares, and the exercise of Rowntree warrants into 8.9 million Rowntree ordinary shares. This valuation excludes employee stock options exercisable between 1988 and 1997. See Exhibit 6.21 for further detail on the elements of Rowntree's ordinary share capital base.

choice. We had to move very quickly. We did not want Rowntree in the hands of our primary competitor in Europe. I could nearly say we have been forced into this, for it is no longer a question of if Rowntree will be taken over, but by whom.'

Reaction to Nestlé's bid

Nestlé's bid for Rowntree was the largest ever made by a foreign company for a British firm. When news of the bid reached the Rowntree Annual Meeting held that afternoon in the Joseph Rowntree Theatre in York, the atmosphere became quite emotional as, one after another, shareholders and employees rose to express their support for Rowntree. 'The offer from Nestlé is unwelcome and does not reflect the value of Rowntree's unique collection of international brands,' Mr Dixon told the meeting. 'It is not our intention to lose our independence. We have the best collection of brands in the world, and we are perfectly capable of developing them. We have adequate resources, and we see no advantage in joining together with anyone.' Mr Dixon urged the shareholders to take no action in relation to the offer and received an enthusiastic ovation.

Nestlé's bid released Jacobs Suchard from the Takeover Panel's restriction, and Suchard immediately began to acquire Rowntree shares. On the same day, at the Jacobs Suchard Annual General Meeting in Zurich, Klaus Jacobs stated, 'Ours is a strategic investment, and we will show the London markets shortly how serious we are about Rowntree. A Swiss does not give up so easily.' One analyst remarked, 'Rowntree is a collector's item and is much more important for Suchard's strategy than for Nestlé's. A price of 1000 pence may not put Suchard off.' On April 26, Nestlé increased its stake to 6.6%; Rowntree's share price rose to 934p that day, closing at 925p.

Nestlé's bid triggered what newspaper front pages called the 'Bar Wars', and began an intense period of political and public lobbying by Rowntree and its supporters including Rowntree unions, the City of York, Members of Parliament of all three political parties, and even the Archbishop of York. On April 29, Suchard disclosed that it had acquired another 4.5 million Rowntree shares, at prices between 910p and 925p, to raise its holding to 21.0%. As the share price remained above Nestlé's offer price, Nestlé was unable to increase its stake in Rowntree.

The question of referral

By the end of April, rumours of a 'white knight' appearing to rescue Rowntree had been largely discounted. Pressure from Rowntree's supporters was mounting on the Trade Secretary of Her Majesty's Government to refer the bid to the Mergers and Monopolies Commission (MMC); an enquiry by the MMC would take approximately six months and would effectively cancel all existing bids. At this point, many thought that only a reference to the MMC would keep Rowntree independent.

During the day's trading on May 4, Rowntree's share price fell below 890p (closing at 905p) as fear of a referral to the MMC mounted. Before the beginning of May, the stakes of the two bidders had been built up largely through purchases from individual shareholders. However, worried that the bid would be referred, institutional shareholders sold part of their holdings during the first week of May. This enabled both bidders to increase their stakes; at the close of trading on May 4, Suchard held 25.1%

of Rowntree stock and Nestlé held 7.1%. By May 7, Suchard's stake (29.3%) approached the 30% limit, which (according to the City Code) was the highest possible stake without making a full bid. By May 7, analysts speculated that the 70 institutions that had held approximately 70% of Rowntree's stock had disposed of at least a quarter of their holdings.[2]

Official Custodian for Charities	8.5
Midland Bank Trust Company	2.2
NC Lombard Street Nominees	2.1
Norwich Union	2.1
Bank of Scotland Nominees	2.1
National Coal Board	2.0
Prudential	2.0
Schroders	2.0
British Steel Pension Fund	1.9
Britel Fund Nominees	1.8
National Bank	1.8
Robert Fleming	1.8
Lloyds Bank Branches Nominees	1.8
Pearl Assurance	1.4
Legal and General	1.4
Barings	1.3
Barclays Nominees	1.2
Swiss Bank Corporation	1.2
Rowntree Mackintosh Pensions	1.2
British Gas	1.1
Co-operative Insurance	1.0
	41.9
Other holders between 0.5% and 1.0%	13.3
Other holders of less than 1%	44.7
Directors (including options)	0.1
Total	100.0

[1] The May 1986 Register of Rowntree shareholders was the last accurate table available to Nestlé and its advisors. Since May 1986, there had been considerable trading of Rowntree shares, but the documentation of these ownership share changes had lagged occurrence. As of April 13, 1988 it was estimated that Jacobs Suchard's stake was 14.9%, that the trusts (Official Custodian for Charities) held 8% or 9%, and that no other shareholder group held more than 2.0% to 2.5% of the outstanding Rowntree shares.

Source: County NatWest Limited.

Exhibit 6.22 *Major Rowntree shareholders (as of May 1986[1])*

[2] As outlined in Exhibit 6.22, Rowntree's 215 million ordinary shares were widely held, with the largest block (8.5%) in the hands of a group of British charities, including two Rowntree trusts which together held 7%; no other shareholder held more than 2.2%. Rowntree Board members held a total of approximately 63,000 shares, with options to purchase another 616,000 ordinary shares between May 1988 and March 1988 at exercise prices between 151p and 570p per share (Exhibit 6.23).

	Ordinary shares	Option schemes	Employee share trust	6% preference shares
Dixon	5,913	112,011	1,330	100
Sir Graham Wilkins	1,250	–	–	–
Blackburn	2,184	58,343	1,958	–
Bowden	1,347	65,703	2,204	100
Cook	500	–	–	–
Copley	3,978	65,808	2,353	–
Sir Michael Franklin	500	–	–	–
Guerin	3,406	63,950	–	–
Kaner	6,703	67,437	1,738	–
Mackinlay	12,518	60,828	2,713	–
Nightingale	780	58,739	1,793	–
Sugden	9,829	63,493	–	–
Treasure	500	–	–	–
	616,312	14,089	200	

Source: Rowntree Defence Document, May 26, 1988.

Exhibit 6.23 *Beneficial interests of the Rowntree Directors in the share capital of Rowntree (as of May 26, 1988)*

The possible reference of the bid to the MMC was the most pressing issue facing Nestlé's team at the beginning of May. Mr Frank Edwards, with Nestlé 40 years and since 1986 Managing Director of Nestlé's UK operations, said: 'We had two battles to win, the first with the Government and the second with the shareholders.' Nestlé UK had a policy of maintaining good relations with political and industry contacts and, since announcing the bid, had mounted an intensive campaign seeking support for the bid in the UK, stressing Nestlé's intentions of 'building, not destroying Rowntree'.

This was the theme of Nestlé's campaign for Rowntree, often repeated in the two evenings Messrs Maucher, Edwards, and McClumpha (responsible for Nestlé UK Corporate Affairs) spent in the House of Commons answering questions from MPs of all parties. Nestlé's intentions of building Rowntree were also emphasized in frequent interviews with the press; during this period Mr Maucher gave several hundred interviews, and later wrote an article for the *Times* of London.

During the week of May 9, Rowntree's share price softened, enabling Nestlé to purchase shares. By the close of trading on May 10, Nestlé had increased its stake from 9.5% to 11.6%, with Suchard's share holding at 29.2%; by May 13 Nestlé held 12.6% of Rowntree shares. That week the Lord Mayor of York led a York City Council delegation to Switzerland to meet with Nestlé and Jacobs Suchard, and York's Euro-MP tabled a motion protesting against the bid at the European Parliament in Strasbourg.

Nestlé's formal offer document

On May 16, Nestlé issued its 44-page formal offer document. In the accompanying letter to Rowntree shareholders Mr Maucher wrote: 'We are convinced that a merger of Rowntree's and Nestlé's confectionery businesses is in the best long-term interests of both companies. The confectionery industry is changing and, in our view, Rowntree by itself does not have the resources to compete effectively in increasingly competitive world markets. Rowntree needs a partner of Nestlé's size. Nestlé and Rowntree have highly complementary businesses, and the value of our offer reflects the added potential that Rowntree will have as part of the Nestlé Group.' Mr Maucher concluded: 'Our offer is a most generous one for Rowntree shareholders and, we believe, secures the best long-term prospects for Rowntree's business. We therefore urge you to accept our offer without delay.'

Mr Domeniconi told the press conference that morning: 'We are now in the unfortunately unenviable situation of being seen as unfriendly. We do not seek domination of Rowntree. It is our hope that, even with the present Rowntree management, we could become friendly if we were allowed to.'

'Nestlé has nothing we need,' replied Mr Dixon in a press release, 'not its money, not its research and development, not its marketing, and not its distribution.' By May 16, Rowntree's share price had moved up 21p to 903p.

Rowntree and its supporters continued to fight for the company's independence. Mr Dixon and his colleagues were hounded by the press and often gave as many as six interviews per hour. In addition, Mr Dixon and his team met with politicians at all levels, and made several presentations per day to institutional investors and the financial community. On May 17 a mass rally, organized by the *Yorkshire Evening Post* and sponsored by Rowntree, brought over 1000 employees and supporters to Westminster as part of the 'Hands Off Rowntree' campaign.

The first meeting of the 'Council of the North' since 1641, then held to discuss the invasion of the Scots, was convened to discuss 'the invasion of the Swiss'. MPs continued to lobby the Trade Secretary, and the 'letters to the editor' columns in the national press remained crowded with correspondence urging the Government to refer the bid to the MMC and take action to 'stop the Swiss from stealing our Smarties'. On May 19th, Mr Dixon and two Rowntree Board members travelled to Strasbourg to rally members of the European Parliament.

By May 19, Nestlé's analysis of Rowntree's share Register showed that, without a recommendation of the offer by Rowntree's Board, Nestlé was in a tight spot in terms of achieving the 50% stake needed for control. Suchard's stake was substantial, and the tendency of some of the remaining large shareholders was to follow the advice of the Rowntree Board. All stockholders holding more than 50,000 shares had been contacted at least once by Nestlé representatives and significant shareholders three times. Nestlé's advisors believed that further pestering would be counter-productive. By May 20, Nestlé estimated that small shareholders held no more than 8% of the shareholdings left on Rowntree's Register.

The reference decision

On the morning of Wednesday, May 25, the Trade Secretary, Lord Young, announced that Nestlé's bid would not be referred to the Mergers and Monopolies Commission. Rowntree share prices soared 83p to a record £10 as the market anticipated a counterbid from Suchard. Within minutes of the announcement, Jacobs Suchard issued a press release offering to allow Rowntree to run the combined confectionery businesses of Rowntree and Suchard, in exchange for a 51% stake in Rowntree at 940p per share. The next morning, Jacobs Suchard issued a full bid for Rowntree at 950p per share, valuing the company at £2.3 billion.

On the evening of May 26, Mr Klaus Jacobs flew to London to meet the press and to try to convince Mr Dixon of the merits of joining forces with Suchard. Mr Jacobs, who had reportedly arranged a £1.75 billion loan facility from the three large Swiss banks, rejected suggestions that Suchard had bid in order to force Nestlé to pay more: 'We want Rowntree because we think we are the right partner. If we had known that it was so strategically important for Nestlé to have Rowntree, we would have gone a different route and would have made a full bid right away.' However, Mr Dixon, who refused to meet with Mr. Jacobs that day, replied that he 'had no intention of being taken over by either Swiss company. There is nothing to choose between them. Neither of them has any idea of what our business is worth.'

Rowntree's defence document

In its defence document released on May 26, Rowntree forecasted improved financial results for 1988: increased turnover of 5%, an increase in pre-tax profits of 20%, an increase in earnings per share of 15% (Exhibits 6.24 and 6.25) and a recommended 19% increase in the dividend. The strongly-worded document stated proudly that Rowntree had invested over £900 million in building its long-established, leading international brands during the past ten years. 'Nestlé has bought rather than built brands,' stated the document, which also repeated that, while Rowntree did not need Nestlé, Nestlé desperately needed Rowntree. The document claimed that several of Nestlé's major brands had lost significant market share in the UK in recent years, and concluded: 'Nestlé has clearly recognized Rowntree's strengths. There is no other company available which would offer Nestlé the same opportunities as Rowntree.'

Nestlé was very careful in its public reaction to Rowntree's claims. 'We are convinced we will win,' explained Mr Masip, 'and therefore we don't want to create future problems.' Rowntree's defence document was overshadowed by speculation about Nestlé's reaction and by news of the Suchard bid. Some institutional investors speculated that the final bidding could get as high as £12 per share before one of the Swiss bidders withdrew.

On May 26, Rowntree's share price reached a record high of £10.32 amid City rumours that a third company would enter the battle for Rowntree. In the House of Commons, Mrs Thatcher was presented with a motion signed by 140 MPs (including 60 Conservatives). However, she defended the decision not to intervene in the takeover battle.

On May 27, the Rowntree Board decided that, with over 40% of the company in the hands of Nestlé and Suchard, it was time to open discussions with the two bidders, and Mr Dixon met with Mr Maucher in Frankfurt on May 28. The major topic of discussion was Rowntree's fit into the Nestlé organization if Mr Dixon and his Board colleagues should recommend Nestlé's bid. Mr Dixon proposed the formation of a confectionery unit within Nestlé to be run by Rowntree, telling Mr Maucher, 'Rowntree ought to run the entire confectionery business. We have special skills at confectionery. Confectionery is different from other product groups and, if you hope to compete against the Mars and Hersheys of the world with their strong world brands, then you must be as focused as they are.'

	Actual 1987	Forecast 1988
Turnover	1,235.8	1,295.2
Cost of sales	(662.2)	(674.2)
Gross margin	573.6	621.0
Advertising and promotion	(128.6)	(138.9)
Fixed overheads	(329.4)	(344.2)
Trading profit of continuing businesses	115.6	137.9
Trading profit of snack food businesses[1]	14.5	5.6
Total trading profit	130.1	143.5
Interest	(18.0)	(8.5)
Profit on ordinary activities before tax	112.1	135.0
Taxation	(24.2)	(30.8)
Profit on ordinary activities after taxation	87.9	104.2
Extraordinary items	–	17.5[2]
Retained profit	87.9	121.7
Earnings per share	40.8p	47.0p[3]
Dividends	15.5p	18.5p

[1] 1987 figures for turnover through to trading profit of continuing businesses have been restated to exclude the results of Rowntree Snack Foods Limited, which was sold on 6 April, 1988, and Tom's Foods Inc., the sale of which is expected to be completed by 26 June, 1988.

[2] Extraordinary items in 1988 represent the net profit on the disposals of the Group's snack food businesses.

[3] Earnings per share based on profit after tax but before extraordinary items.

Source: Rowntree Defence Document, 26 May, 1988.

Exhibit 6.24 *Rowntree – profit forecast, 1988 (£million)*

	Turnover		Trading profit	
	Actual 1988	Forecast 1987	Actual 1988	Forecast
Confectionery				
United Kingdom	440.5	470.8	51.2	64.5
Ireland	24.0	24.5	2.1	2.7
Continental Europe	300.4	312.7	11.0	15.3
North America	214.9	213.9	23.1	22.8
Australasia	57.1	61.4	4.7	6.3
Rest of the world	87.6	88.8	11.7	12.5
	1,172.1	103.8	124.1	
Other	111.3	123.1	11.8	13.8
Total	1,235.8	1,295.2	115.6	137.9

Source: Rowntree Defence Document, 26 May, 1988.

Exhibit 6.25 *Rowntree forecast for 1988 (£million). Geographical analysis of turnover and trading profit of continuing businesses*

Mr Maucher responded that, although there was some possibility of leaving Rowntree fairly intact, 'this is not Nestlé's way; we are organized geographically,' and he discouraged Mr Dixon's proposal. 'If there is any question of recommending the bid,' replied Mr Dixon, 'then this proposal must be part of it.' At the close of the

Date		Share price	Date		Share price
April	13	623	May	11	890
	14	710		12	881
	15	708		13	884
	18	737		16	903
	19	739		17	902
	20	729		18	902
	21	717		19	902
	22	717		20	902
	25	755		23	890
	26	925		24	913
	27	928		25	1003
	28	910		26	1032
	29	918		27	1047
May	2	918		30	1047
	3	905		31	1036
	4	903	June	1	1042
	5	902		2	1035
	6	900		3	1035
	9	901		6	1037
	10	902		7	1033
	11	890			

Source: County NatWest Limited.

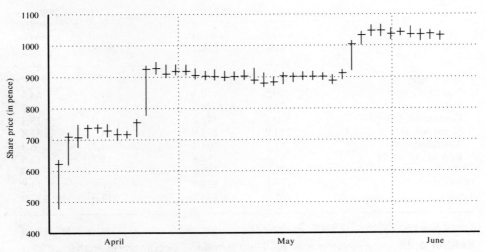

Exhibit 6.26 *Rowntree share price history, April 13–June 7, 1988*

		Rowntree shares in issue (000)	Suchard stake (%)	Nestlé stake (%)
April	13	215,025	14.9	–
	14	215,025	14.9	0.8
	18	215,025	14.9	2.2
	19	215,025	14.9	3.1
	20	215,025	14.9	3.9
	22	215,025	14.9	4.5
	26	215,025	16.1	6.6
	27	215,025	18.8	6.6
	28	216,679	20.7	6.5
May	3	216,735	23.3	6.6
	4	217,854	25.1	7.1
	5	217,917	28.3	7.1
	6	219,115	29.3	7.3
	9	219,683	29.2	9.5
	10	219,683	29.2	11.6
	11	219,683	29.2	12.8
	20	224,128	28.6	13.6
	26	224,241	28.6	13.8
June	7	225,055	28.5	13.7

Note: While there were often minor fluctuations (less than 0.5%) from day to day in the stakes held by each bidder, the major changes are shown above.
Source: County NatWest Limited.

Exhibit 6.27 *Chronology of stakes held by Jacobs Suchard and Nestlé, April 13–June 7, 1988*

meeting Mr Dixon added, 'Of course, the agreed bid price must be a price we can be proud of, a very good price, up towards £12.' However, there was no other price-related discussion. Afterwards Mr Maucher said, 'We made very little progress, but the tone was still friendly. I think we are likely to meet again.'

On June 6, Nestlé extended the deadline for acceptance of its original bid at 890p. On June 7th, Rowntree's share price fell slightly to £10.33 (Exhibits 6.26 and 6.27).

The June 8 meeting

On Wednesday, June 8, at 10 am, Nestlé met with Rowntree at a lesser known London hotel.

The nine executives gathered around a long table, with Messrs Dixon, Nightingale, Bowden, Blackburn (responsible for Rowntree's UK and Ireland operations) and Challen on one side and Messrs Maucher, Domeniconi, Masip, and St. George on the other. Mr Dixon suggested the agenda: introductions, followed by his team's presentation of Rowntree's organization and their vision of how Rowntree would fit into Nestlé should the Board agree to the Nestlé bid, and then Nestlé's counterpart presentations.

Mr Dixon prefaced his presentation by saying, 'We are here to discuss what non-price proposals you have should we agree to recommend the bid, and to tell you how we see Rowntree's fit into Nestlé.' During Rowntree's presentation of its brand and product-oriented organization structure, the tone of the discussion was fairly open and relaxed.

Mr Dixon then began to outline Rowntree's vision of how Rowntree and Nestlé would fit together if Rowntree agreed to the bid. In presenting Rowntree's proposals Mr Dixon said, 'Leaving aside the share price and shareholders' interests for the moment, we have three major concerns: what is best for our business, for our employees, and for our communities.' Rowntree handed Nestlé a list of proposals which included:

- one world confectionery company within Nestlé, based in York;
- which would include all of Rowntree's current business as well as Nestlé's current confectionery business;
- thus, the existing business of Rowntree would be preserved;
- this world confectionery business would be run by Rowntree, with a Rowntree representative on Nestlé's highest Management Board.

Before outlining how his team saw Rowntree's position in Nestlé, Mr Masip explained the Nestlé organization (Exhibit 6.28): 'Nestlé's philosophy is that primary responsibility and authority should lie with the local country managers who know their markets best. So Nestlé is organized geographically, with very strong country organizations reporting to regional managers in Vevey.' Mr Domeniconi added, 'We have very strong managers who are market heads in their particular countries, and all of the power and responsibility lies at that level.'

Outlining Nestlé's proposal for acquiring Rowntree, Mr. Masip emphasized that, like all other Nestlé acquisitions, Rowntree would be absorbed into Nestlé's country organizations: 'Rowntree will be broken up to fit into Nestlé's geographical zone structure.' The Rowntree people fell increasingly silent as they envisioned what would happen to Rowntree if it were acquired by Nestlé. Observing the dismayed faces of the Rowntree people, Mr Maucher whispered to Mr Domeniconi, 'This seems to be a real shock for them. They are thinking, "here is Nestlé as it really is".'

The Rowntree team members appeared completely disheartened by Nestlé's reaction to their proposals, and the discussion became quite strained:

Nightingale: You reject the idea of a central confectionery company, then?
Masip: At Nestlé, the zones are in charge, and there is no question of an operating division separated from Nestlé's traditional structure.
Nightingale: So you will not consider our proposal for a world confectionery business?
Masip: What you are proposing is unacceptable. You are asking us to break with our principles and to change our whole way of operating!
Nightingale: Yes, but you are asking us to recommend the break-up of Rowntree!
Masip: There is *no way* we can adapt our organization structure to your demands!

Mr Maucher, who had spoken relatively little during the meeting, summarized Nestlé's reaction to Rowntree's proposals: 'As Mr Masip has outlined, there will still

Nestlé pursued global expansion through the creation of local operating companies, each with their own local management. This philosophy of market-oriented organization meant that primary responsibility and authority for each market lay with the local operating companies, which had full responsibility for profit and loss as well as for all marketing, manufacturing, financial and administrative functions in their respective markets.

As shown in the following Nestlé organization chart, these local companies were advised by the staff at Vevey headquarters, which supplied Product/Marketing, Finance, Control and Administration, Technical, as well as Research and Development services. This headquarters staff acted in an advisory role only to the local operating companies; for example, if a product director wished to launch a new product in a particular market, he would have to persuade the Market Head in that country to make the necessary investment.

The 75 operating companies within Nestlé reported to five regional 'Zone' managers responsible for Europe; Asia and Australasia; Latin America; North America; and Africa and the Middle East. These Executive Vice Presidents formed part of the Executive Committee of Nestlé S.A.

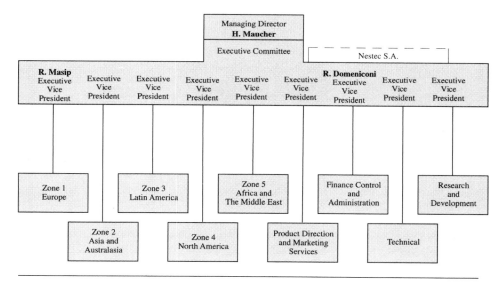

Exhibit 6.28   *Nestlé organization (partial)*

be product coordination through our staff of product directors but, from an operational point of view, Rowntree will benefit from being integrated into our system of regional and country management.'

'It is quite obvious that our proposals are not acceptable to Nestlé,' Mr Nightingale said. Mr Dixon added, 'You are asking us to recommend the dismantling of a great business, the break-up of the Rowntree Group, and this we cannot accept. We cannot recommend Nestlé's offer to our Board on this basis.'

The room fell completely silent. After a long tense pause, Mr Maucher said, 'Would you please excuse us? My colleagues and I must talk.'

'I strongly advise not continuing along these lines,' Mr Masip urged on the way down the hall to another room. 'If they want to recommend the offer on this basis, then we should just go on without them!' 'They are in a very difficult position, though,' Mr Domeniconi said, 'and we have been very tough on them.' 'In fact,' added Mr St. George, 'we may have lost them entirely.' 'Yes,' Mr Masip replied, 'but better to be clear and prevent misunderstandings. We must tell them that it is either our way, or we'll act without the recommendation.' As he followed his colleagues into the room, Mr. Maucher worried about the long faces of the Rowntree people and wondered if Nestlé had gone too far.

Case 6.3 Edizione Holding SpA (A)

This case was written by Research Associate Robert Howard, under the supervision of Professor Werner Ketelhöhn, as a basis for class discussion rather than to illustrate either effective or ineffective handling of a business situation.

When I arrived from The Bank of Italy, in January of 1983, I found a situation typical of most family businesses that have outgrown their entrepreneurial roots. The Benettons had simply hired people without having any clear organization structure in mind; at the start, 20 to 25 people reported directly to me; now only a handful of senior executives dealing with marketing, finance and production do so. (Aldo Palmeri, CEO at Benetton SpA, *International Management*, November 1987)

Meeting the Benettons

In January 1990, Aldo Palmeri, Managing Director of Benetton Group SpA, was looking back on the course he had charted for the company since his arrival in 1983. In his previous job as economic advisor to the Minister of Industry at the Bank of Italy, Aldo had had the opportunity to meet a number of Italy's key entrepreneurs, including Luciano and Gilberto Benetton. After only two meetings, Luciano asked Aldo to oversee Benetton's growth from local sweater manufacturer to international apparel retailer. Aldo accepted and, throughout the 1980s, succeeded in transforming Benetton into a global player. When he began in 1983, over 95% of the company's L200 billion ($250 million)[1] sales were concentrated in Italy; by 1988, the company had achieved L1,475,283 million ($1130 million) in sales, 65% outside the Italian market.

Taking charge

Despite the company's impressive record, Aldo disclosed that these achievements had not been met without growing

[1] L = litre; $ refers to US$ unless otherwise indicated.

pains. Among the first of the changes he implemented was a reorganization of the company's management, to change what was a predominantly local view of the business to an international focus. In his own words:

> When I joined Benetton, the company was doing fine, but the family had sense enough to realize that growth had become a necessity. Exports were stuck at 10%, making expansion into foreign markets a must. But it also meant giving priority to recruiting a staff of top Italian managers.
>
> For the company to become an international company, it was very important to give it a new flavour, a new culture. So we had to abandon the local managers because they were typical local managers, typically provincial. They were not able to understand the problem outside the area and outside the company. Those managers believed that the only company in the world was Benetton.

To replace Benetton's 'local' management, Aldo drew on his extensive network of industry contacts developed over the years in his position at the Bank of Italy. The first person he contacted was Giovanni Cantagalli, former director of human resources at 3M, who also played an active role in restructuring the Italian chemical industry in the early 1980s. Aldo commented on the challenges of recruiting new managers for Benetton in the early 1980s:

> The main problem I had in contacting the managers was that there were many excellent managers for single functions, but there were not so many ready to face the problems of a company like Benetton. Another problem was the location of the company, because most managers live in the north-west area of Italy, the Milano area. It was very difficult to convince managers to move from Milano to Treviso.
>
> And, I remember that I spent a number of weekends with Cantagalli having discussions with managers, convincing them about the opportunity. It was very important to assure people that we were a company with an excellent opportunity for new growth. That's very useful when trying to persuade managers to join the company, because if they believe that in just a few years they will become top managers in a big company, they can be motivated to join that company.

For those who made the move to Treviso, Aldo's promises indeed came true. That is, individuals that came from medium-sized companies found themselves, after a few years, as managers of a very large company with an excellent trademark and an international presence. In addition to Cantagalli, some of these original managers included Carlo Gilardi as Director of Finance, Giulio Penzo as Director of Legal Affairs, Bruno Zuccaro as Director of Information Systems and Guido Venturini as Director of Marketing. By 1986, Aldo Palmeri had filled each of the company's key positions (Exhibit 6.29). Thereafter, in a move to decentralize the organization, Aldo reduced the number of people reporting directly to him. By January 1990, Benetton's internal reporting structure was organized as indicated in Exhibit 6.30.

Along with Benetton's management reorganisation, the company underwent a number of legal changes. In brief, the company bought participations in external companies, transferred subsidiaries within its parent holding companies, and founded new businesses. The company founded in 1965 as Maglificio di Ponzano Veneto dei Fratelli Benetton had grown by 1989 into the international Edizione Holding SpA.

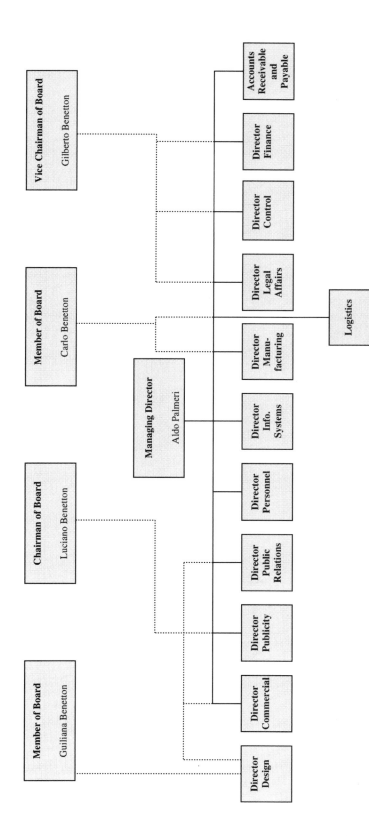

Exhibit 6.29 Top management organization relationships, Benetton Group SpA, 1983–1986. Dotted lines signify informal reporting relationships. (Source: Benetton Group SpA)

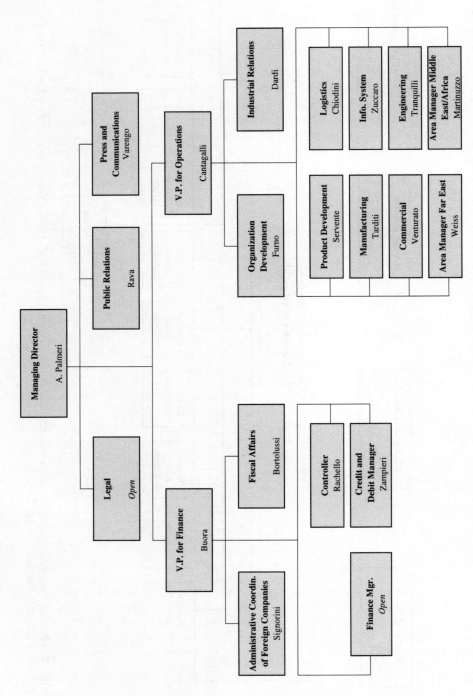

Exhibit 6.30 Top management organization relationships. Benetton Group SpA, from September 1986. (Source: Benetton Group SpA)

Building the lifestyle corporation

INVEP holding, created in 1981 to encompass all the business activities controlled by the family, was folded into the Benetton Group in 1985. In December of 1985, the main business group, Benetton SpA, accounted for about two-thirds of group sales. The group comprised Benetton Lana SpA, Benetton Cotone SpA and Benetton Jeans SpA, its three manufacturing divisions. From the beginning, the group invested in related business activities, such as 70% of Calzaturificio Varese, a leading soft footwear producer acquired in 1981. In 1987, Benetton cosmetic corporation was formed in New York. Sales of its 'Colour' perfumes for women and men reached $23 million in 1988 and were expected to reach $32 million in 1989. The scent was sold through major department stores rather than in Benetton clothing stores.

In the summer of 1988, Benetton acquired 21% of Eliolona, a firm specializing in bed linen. The first collection, scheduled to appear in March 1989, was distributed through specialized Italian boutiques and department stores. In late March of 1989, Edizione, which held 87.5% of Benetton SpA, agreed to purchase 100% of Nordica, the world's leading maker of alpine ski boots; analysts estimated the purchase price at $182 million, Nordica's annual sales. Nordica had a 27% world market share of the ski boot business, with subsidiaries in the USA and Japan. Nordica retained its autonomy and was not integrated into the group in production, distribution or marketing. 'You are not going to start seeing ski boots in Benetton stores,' said Marino Verengo, a Benetton SpA spokesman.

In May 1989, Benetton SpA announced a joint venture to produce eyeglasses with H. J. Heinz Co. of the USA. Called United Optical, the company was jointly owned by Benetton SpA, Anser SpA, an Italian producer of eyeglasses, and Liven SpA, a distributor of glasses owned by Heinz Italia. The glasses were distributed exclusively through opticians in Europe, the USA, as well as in various other countries. Benetton SpA had already licensed Anser, based in northern Italy, to produce Benetton glasses. Alliances had also been formed with Polaroid to produce Benetton sunglasses and with Spring Mills to produce bedding material. 'These small changes are not revolutionary. It's just a series of small things that happen every month, every day,' concluded Luciano Benetton. By 1990, Edizione was organized as shown in Exhibit 6.31.

Franco Furno's views

Up to 1988, we had minor companies within Edizione Holding – mainly shirt makers like Columbia or Altana. Product lines such as accessories or shirts, or perfumes in the USA, were supplied by other companies. Those companies were owned and controlled directly by Edizione Holding, but over the years we moved this participation from Edizione Holding to the Benetton Group. To give another example, we have created a company called Socks and Accessories which is part of the Benetton Group. Other examples are Calzaturificio Di Varese, a shoe maker, Columbia and Altana which are shirt makers, and Benetton Underwear. All of them now form the consolidated data of the Benetton Group.

So, if you look at the growth rate in terms of the number of goods sold within our network of shops, you have to take into account several companies that form the Benetton Group, which is the real public company. Turnover data from 1978–87 give an order of magnitude relative to more recent years. We must keep in mind the above comments when

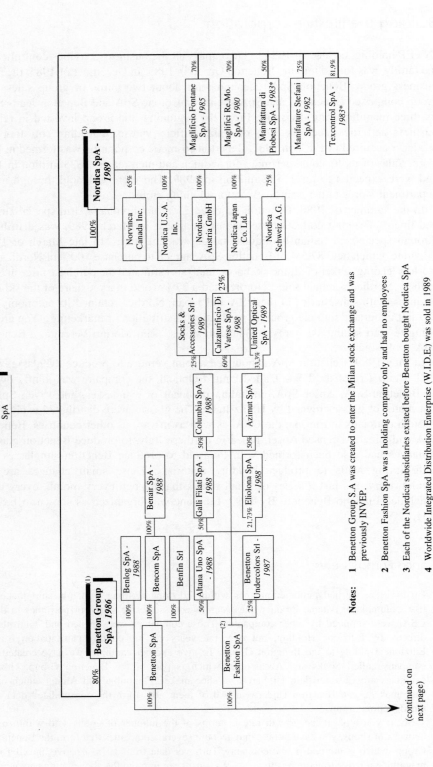

Notes:

1. Benetton Group S.A was created to enter the Milan stock exchange and was previously INVEP.

2. Benetton Fashion SpA was a holding company only and had no employees

3. Each of the Nordica subsidiaries existed before Benetton bought Nordica SpA

4. Worldwide Integrated Distribution Enterprise (W.I.D.E.) was sold in 1989

(continued on
next page)

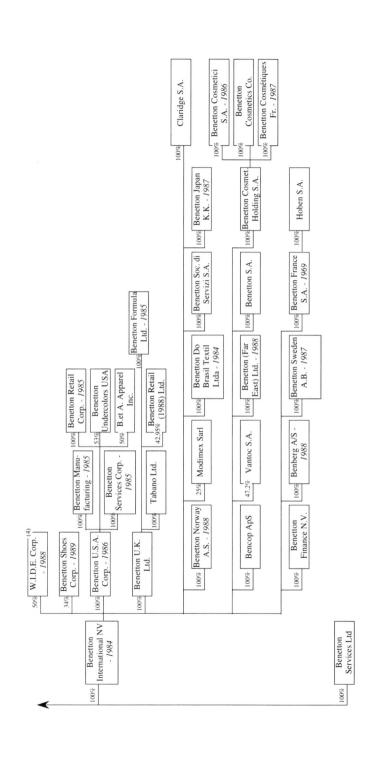

Exhibit 6.31 *Edizione Holding: industrial sector*

comparing. It's not really a comparable figure because of slight differences in accounting . . . Really, every year we have experienced several changes in terms of the social structures of the company: acquisitions, mergers, etc. Declining profits for the group are misleading. Consolidating a number of smaller, less profitable operations into the Benetton Group has brought the figure down. Turnover has increased but net profit has decreased slightly, and 1989 is estimated to be the same as 1988.

Aldo Palmeri selected a certain number of business functions and put them under the control of Cantagalli. All the money was controlled by Palmeri, everything else by Cantagalli. Aldo's reorganization in 1986 thus applies not only to the organigrams but to the consolidated financial data from 1986 on.

The companies were already there, but they were not consolidated into the Benetton Group data because the majority of them were directly owned by Edizione the way Altana used to be owned by Edizione. In a way, Edizione sold its own companies to the Benetton Group – of course, to companies that were an integral part of the apparel industry. Actually, it's rather like introducing another layer of management. A further possible change would be to sell these companies to Benetton SpA because they all belong to the same Benetton network. All these companies, such as Benberg, or Benetton Japan, or Benetton Retail are companies that own and directly manage a certain number of shops. So, these are companies on the commercial side.

There is another family of companies that manufactures finished products – Columbia, Altana, Di Varese, United Optical, etc. and a third family of companies representing the external manufacturing capacity. Now, sooner or later, I think the strategy of Edizione would be to put them together. To give you an example, the American institutional investors were very curious about our transfer prices. And that is a further reason why I think that eventually big subcontractors will belong directly to the Benetton Group and will be part of the consolidation. Although they will still own their facilities and act as managers–operators, they are not independent at all because it is the Benetton Group which fixes transfer prices. From the accounting point of view, it will add another twist to the financial statements. This is why in the last three to five years we have increased the turnover enormously, while slightly decreasing the profitability on percentage. The majority of people see these figures as an indicator of saturation. If you pull the Financial Statements apart, you will still see growth of + 10%.

What will be the future evolution? Are ski boots considered apparel? Or are they something related to a certain lifestyle? I always say that the three biggest changes in terms of product policy that happened to our group was that in the 1970s we manufactured sweaters; in the 1980s our product became apparel no matter whether it was sweaters, socks or something else; and probably in the 1990s we will be a lifestyle corporation. If you design around a lifestyle, you can introduce several products like cosmetics, a travel agency and related products. So Benetton is becoming a way of living, a way of presenting yourself. And to do that you need apparel, glasses, watches, and so on.

Globalizing the corporation

In conjunction with the reorganization begun in 1983, Aldo Palmeri began working towards the goal of a global Benetton, characterized by a distribution of sales, finance and manufacturing among the world's core economic regions. (Exhibits 6.32 and 6.33 give information on each of these regions: Europe, North America and the Far East.) With the exception of manufacturing, the company had made substantial progress toward realizing these goals by January 1990.

EEC	Population (millions)	Population growth (% pa)
Belgium/Luxembourg	10.3	0.10
Denmark	5.1	0.03
France	55.9	0.42
Greece	10.0	0.37
Ireland	3.5	0.29
Italy	57.4	0.23
Netherlands	14.8	0.52
Portugal	10.4	0.79
Spain	39.0	0.46
UK	57.1	0.22
FRG	61.2	−0.12
EFTA		
Austria	7.6	0.07
Finland	5.0	0.44
Iceland	0.25	0.01
Norway	4.2	0.36
Sweden	8.4	0.22
Switzerland	6.5	0.10
North America		
Canada	26.0	0.87
USA	246.3	0.97
Far East		
Australia	16.5	1.43
Hong Kong	5.7	1.29
Japan	122.6	0.58
New Zealand	3.3	0.67
Singapore	2.6	1.18
South Korea	42.0	1.09
Taiwan	19.7	1.26

Notes:
1. With the exception of data on Iceland, all of the above information is contained in *The World Competitive Report*, published annually by IMD International and the World Economic Forum. Unless otherwise noted, the figures for Iceland are contained in *Yearbook of Nordic Statistics 1989/90*, published by the Nordic Council of Ministers and the Nordic Statistical Secretariat.
2. Population figures are estimates for mid-1988. Population growth rates are annual compound percentage changes for the period 1982–1988. The figure for Iceland corresponds to the 1980–1988 period.

Exhibit 6.32   *The world's core economic regions: demographics*

Sales

Although Benetton's first non-Italian shop was opened in Paris in 1969, adding more foreign shops did not receive much attention until 1973. By 1979, however, the number of foreign shops had reached 100 and, in the same year, Benetton International Holding was founded to incorporate their activities. All the same, the most substantial international growth in sales and outlets occurred in the 10 years following 1979. By 1989, the Benetton network included 1600 shops in Italy, 2389 in the rest of Western

EEC	GDP (billions)	GDP growth (% pa)	GDP ($) per capita	Savings rate (%)	Inflation (annual %)	Unemployment (annual %)
Belgium/Luxembourg	160.4	4.3	15,590	21.6	4.4	9.7
Denmark	107.5	2.2	20,952	20.3	5.7	8.6
France	949.2	1.9	16,990	21.1	6.1	10.0
Greece	52.5	1.8	5,244	10.9	18.8	7.7
Ireland	32.6	2.4	9,194	25.4	7.1	16.7
Italy	828.9	2.7	14,430	21.6	9.5	12.2
Netherlands	228.3	2.1	15,467	24.8	2.0	8.3
Portugal	41.7	2.05	4,006	18.8	17.9	5.8
Spain	340.1	3.3	8,709	22.7	9.3	19.5
UK	822.8	3.3	14,415	16.6	5.3	8.2
FRG	1,201.8	2.5	19,637	25.7	2.1	7.9
EFTA						
Austria	127.2	1.9	16,737	25.9	3.2	3.6
Finland	105.2	3.2	21,248	26.3	6.1	4.6
Iceland	5.9	1.8	16,600	19.1	35.2	0.9
Norway	91.2	3.6	21,710	27.4	7.8	3.2
Sweden	178.9	2.3	21,195	21.0	6.7	1.6
Switzerland	183.7	2.4	28,217	28.5	2.7	0.7
North America						
Canada	486.5	4.3	18,747	23.3	5.3	7.8
USA	4,847.3	4.1	19,678	15.2	3.8	5.5
Far East						
Australia	247.0	3.8	14,942	26.0	8.1	6.7
Hong Kong	54.5	8.1	9,600	31.0	6.9	1.4
Japan	2,843.4	4.3	23,191	33.3	1.4	2.5
New Zealand	41.8	1.7	12,693	23.4	11.4	7.6
Singapore	23.9	6.0	9,009	40.0	1.2	3.4
South Korea	171.3	10.6	4,082	38.0	4.0	2.5
Taiwan	116.7	8.6	5,913	37.0	0.8	2.0

Notes:

1. Gross Domestic Product and per capita Gross Domestic Product figures are for 1988, calculated at 1988 prices and exchange rates. Gross Domestic Product Growth rates are annual compound percentage changes, computed on a local currency basis at 1985 prices for the 1982–1988 period. For Iceland 1980 was the base year.

2. Savings rate is measured by Gross Domestic Savings of residents and non-residents as a percentage of 1988. GDP inflation figures are averages for the 1982–1988 period. Unemployment figures are total unemployment as a percentage of the 1988 labour force.

Exhibit 6.33 *The world's core economic regions: economics*

Europe, 830 in the Americas and 127 in the Far East. According to one executive, growth in the number of shops and garments sold had succeeded largely due to Benetton's strategy of moulding young entrepreneurs within its selling culture. In volume terms, this strategy succeeded in increasing exports from 2% of the company's 1977 sales to over half, or $200 million of the company's $370 million turnover by

1983. Then, too, by 1988, exports represented 62% or $702 million out of Benetton Group SpA's $1133 million in sales.

In addition to the 'traditional' markets mentioned above, from 1985 on, Benetton began to open shops in Eastern Europe and the Soviet Union. In March 1985, the first East European store was opened in the Skala Metro department store in Budapest. By the end of 1988, Benetton had established 20 shops throughout Eastern Europe. Also in 1988, Palmeri announced a joint venture to restructure two factories in the USSR – one in Armenia and one near Leningrad – to play a key role in supplying the 50 shops Benetton planned to open throughout the USSR before the end of 1989.

Despite the magnitude and distribution of Benetton's sales at the end of the 1980s, some members of management believed that the revenues earned in Europe were disproportionately large. Gilberto Benetton expressed his views on this topic at a shareholders' meeting in the spring of 1989. 'We believe that the sales we are making in Europe could easily be repeated in North America and the Far East.' To this end, the company planned to set up joint ventures with local manufacturers in Japan where, by the end of 1990, they expected to have 200 shops, with plans to expand to 400 during the 1990s. 'Our sales in Japan tripled in the last three years, and we expect them to double to $133 million in 1989,' said Palmeri. To strengthen its position in the Far East, Benetton set up a trading company in Hong Kong which bought raw materials directly from local manufacturers.

Finance

Although Benetton began expanding its sales outside Italy as early as 1969, globalization of the finance function did not begin until several years later. Specifically, in June 1986, the Benetton Group SpA floated 15.6 million shares in the European capital markets. Of these shares, 11 million were issued outright on the Milan and Venice bourses, 4.48 million shares were attached to warrants and sold in the Euromarkets, out of which a small number were set aside for Benetton's European agents. Simultaneously, Sige of Italy's IMI Group arranged a domestic bond issue with warrants convertible into 7.8 million shares. In total, the operation represented approximately 20% of the company's equity and raised an estimated $200 million.

Outside Europe, Benetton Group SpA began trading on the New York Stock Exchange in June 1989, and the company capitalized at $1.2 billion. Then, in January 1990, Aldo Palmeri completed negotiations for a joint venture in Japan which he intended to list on the Tokyo stock exchange the following year. By the end of 1990, Aldo planned to list 25% of Benetton's shares throughout world markets. He explained:

> If Benetton is to operate on a truly global scale, it is indispensable to have a presence on the major international stock markets. That's my idea. To globalize our presence in the most important stock exchange markets in the world in order to have the most flexible instrument to support my problem of development everywhere.

Although his plans to globalize Benetton stock fitted into the expansion of manufacturing and commercial activities in the USA and East Asia, listing much more than 25% of the company's shares was not likely, given the comment made by Gilberto Benetton in October 1988. 'I don't think the family will ever sell more than 30% of its shares.' Indeed, those who failed to interpret that signal received a clearer message when Gilberto responded to a question about how much control the Benetton family wanted to retain over the company: *'moltissimo'* ('very much' in Italian).

Manufacturing

In contrast to the company's success at globalizing both sales and finance throughout the 1980s, manufacturing remained concentrated in Italy. In fact, even though Benetton Group SpA owned manufacturing facilities in France, the USA, the UK and Spain, as well as manufacturing licences in 13 other countries, non-Italian production represented only 15% of the group's 1988 sales. In Aldo's opinion, this was a serious weakness of the company and needed to be corrected. 'We have to spread production worldwide if we want to maintain the profitability of the company.' For the 1990s, Aldo believed that a global redistribution of Benetton's manufacturing would be his most important challenge.

Exporting Benetton's culture

'The original Benetton formula was based on a brilliant intuition, but now we are applying it scientifically to a sophisticated industrial model,' said Palmeri in 1987. He described the Benetton model as a nucleus surrounded by independent businesses. On the production side, contractors and subcontractors (the *indotto*) had been organized to cover all labour-intensive phases of production. There were 350 such units accounting for 80% of production; the capital-intensive parts, including cutting and dyeing, however, were handled by the company's three remaining factories at Castrete, Villorba, and Cusignana, which together employed about 650 workers.

Benetton's entry strategy to new markets was to first open a shop in the most prestigious shopping centre, a flag store, and then ask the agents to spearhead the search for new stores. After that, some form of joint venture was set up for manufacturing and, if the market developed successfully, some manufacturing was finally installed. 'Even when we opened in Spain, West Germany and France, we sent Italians out to do the job – the sort of people who run the shops in Italy. We did the same in the USA,' said Palmeri in February 1989. Pricing policies differed in the various countries.

The Benetton culture was exported through the agents, especially the old agents, who were used as *senior-inter-pares* in each of the existing markets, and as spearheads to open up new markets. However, in May of 1989, one dissatisfied shopowner accused Benetton of engaging in fraud, extortion and financial misrepresentation in a US Federal court. A handful of US shopowners also sued Benetton for unfair trade practices and alleged violations of franchise statutes. These suits were dismissed in October by a district court judge, but the plaintiffs then filed an amended complaint. Benetton presented a counterclaim for defamation, claiming that its outlets did not qualify as franchises because no royalties were paid by shopowners; there was no minimum quota for purchases, prices were not fixed but suggested, and there was no geographical guaranty. There had been a few civil court cases in Italy and France, too. 'With some 5000 shops around the world, we have only three or four lawsuits. I think that's an excellent performance,' said Palmeri in an 1989 interview. 'If a North European shopowner loses money, he probably would kill himself; a South European would slip away at night; but an American would go to a lawyer and sue somebody,' commented a Benetton executive.

In 1989, Benetton's strategy was still to manufacture as much as possible in Italy and to install manufacturing only to go around protective barriers. In Spain, for example, it might not be necessary to manufacture after 1992. When Benetton set up a plant, they really tried to set up an organization around it, a scheme based on subcontractors. The difficult thing was to recreate a series of small subcontractors outside Italy. As production shifted to lower-wage Asian countries, Benetton needed to duplicate its subcontractor system. Asian factory owners tended to fill foreign brand name orders and then sell overruns under some other brand name.

'Why should an American pay $80 for a Benetton sweater if an identical Korean-made garment is at a discount store for $30?' asked an analyst. As a result, prices were 40% higher in the USA than in Europe; Benetton had to pay one-quarter of the price in tariffs and 8% in transportation to the USA.

The final cost of each item in the USA was higher than in Italy because it had to be sent there; the problem was how to be efficient, not in shipping costs, where there is no leverage, but in labour costs. In the USA, a competitor called Esprit manufactured in the Far East. In the EEC, import quotas were a defensive barrier based on imports from previous years. With 1992, the EEC market would probably be even more difficult to enter from low-wage countries; otherwise, Benetton's inability to move up-market would leave the company caught in a crowded market segment, where branding would be the only way to differentiate.

Since 1982, and even more so in the late 1980s, lookalike competitors like Stephanel, were also building an international network of shops and squeezing Benetton's margins. The saturation of Benetton's markets by these competitors could slow down the company's growth. Stephanel used a black and red colour theme and sought to present a better quality image. Poco Loco of Norway, Absenderodo of Spain, Cacharel, Rodier, Chipie, and Hermes of France, Shyam Ahuya of Bombay, India, recent entrants to the global market, were all chasing the same Benetton consumer.

Some observers believed that Benetton had the capability to grow 15% per year in the foreseeable future. Palmeri said, 'We will give the overall strategy and guidelines on fashion; otherwise, the subsidiaries will be totally autonomous. They will have their own communications system; they will be in charge of their own distribution networks; they will be the main source of analysis of their market areas.' Luciano once commented, 'We have simply evolved. Our world is different and the world outside has changed, so we are merely adjusting to a different kind of life and developing products for a new adventure.' With the USA and Japan still to be conquered, there was a family belief that growth would continue at the same rate as in the recent past.

R. Howard: I find it curious that back in the early 1980s when the family realized that growth opportunities in Italy were limited, they went into the rest of Europe and then the United States. But now, it seems that the number of stores being opened around the world is declining, implying that Benetton has more or less started to reach the point of saturating the entire world.

F. Furno: Well, in a way, I believe that this could be true for certain countries in Europe, particularly Italy. But if you look at the figures on the number of shops in Europe, you see that in the late 1980s we've found an opportunity for further growth. Saturation in terms of the number of shops could be true for Italy, maybe the USA, but certainly not for other European countries, or particularly for the Far East. I believe that the family is thinking of a big expansion program in the Far East where, up to now, they have been involved through licence agreements with local entrepreneurs. But after 5–6 years of experience, they have decided to change this strategy to have a more direct involvement, moving from a licence agreement to a more serious joint venture. The most significant example is represented by what we have done in Japan where, after five years of licensing, we have created a joint venture. So up to now we have earned money just with the payment of a royalty from our licensee, but from now on we will receive both royalties from the joint venture and, on top of that, profits as well. As you can see, it's a deeper involvement of the company in that part of the world. And we believe there is plenty of room to grow.

R. Howard: Can the Benetton culture really be exported? Can you transfer the culture that you developed in Italy to foreign clothing industries?

G. Cantagalli: I think that if this company wants to be successful, it must export its culture. The secret of our success is mainly in the culture, in the values, in the philosophy of this company. Of course, you must not be so arrogant as to think that you can export your culture without any consideration for the country you move into. You need, of course, to adjust and adapt the model that you export to the country, to the situation, to the culture in which you are going to be integrated. But, you must also pay a lot of attention so as not to lose the main factors of your company culture.

We made this experiment in many countries – also in the Far East. We set up a trading company three years ago in Hong Kong and, at that time, it was necessary to hire a man to run that company. The alternatives were to hire a Chinese who would be very aware of the Chinese culture, the Far East culture, the environmental context, but who didn't know anything about the Benetton system; or to send a man from here that knew the Benetton system very well but didn't know anything about the country where he was going to work. We decided to hire a Chinese who knew everything about that country but nothing about Benetton. And it was a failure. Later we sent an Italian. Of course, he knew the Benetton system very well. He didn't know anything about China, about Hong Kong, about South Korea, about those countries. And, I must say that it has been a big success. That's why I think we must export our culture and make the necessary adjustment to the local situation. And I think that we have to do the same thing in the Soviet Union, in the USA. This model will work if we follow our own philosophy – do everything with the Benetton spirit.

Financial performance

In 1988, two-thirds of Benetton's 17% rise in revenues came from the acquisition of shoe, yarn and shirt businesses that were previously owned by Edizione. Net earnings in 1988 remained at $93.8 million on sales of $1063 million; Benetton SpA paid high dividends, 70% of earnings. Net profits were unchanged despite a 17% growth in sales. Debts also doubled for Benetton SpA, which was forced to raise profit margins to retailers at the expense of its own margins; sales and margins were squeezed by strong competition and price-cutting by other retailers. To increase margins, the company planned to close down some outlets and enlarge others.

Case 6.4 Edizione Holding SpA (B)

This case was written by Research Associate Robert Howard, under the supervision of Professor Werner Ketelhöhn, as a basis for class discussion rather than to illustrate either effective or ineffective handling of a business situation.

Diversification into financial services

IN Factor SpA

From the company's founding, Benetton had been sensitive to the needs of its partners at each point in its business system. To illustrate, Aldo explained that Benetton's subcontractors could not handle the burden of extended credit inherent in the company's production cycle. To help subcontractors survive the financial constraints of this cycle, Benetton created its own factoring service:[1] IN Factor SpA. With the growth of the organization, the volume of factoring offered to Benetton's 'captive' market also grew. In 1983, for example, the leasing and factoring business accounted for only $2.5 million. Yet, by 1986, sales of these services to its subcontractors and shops had reached $400 million.

By the mid-1980s, services originally created to support Benetton's own business had reached a position that even outside competitors such as Stephanel and Gruppo Finanziaro Tessile (GFT) were using them. 'At that point,' explained Aldo, 'we could just stay where we were, or we could seek to grow the business. And, given the demand our services had generated on the outside, we decided to develop it.' In other words, the move into financial services resulted from a series of decisions taken to seize financial opportunities and not, as some observers believed, from a casual drift into a new business by some of Palmeri's financial experts.

---

[1] Factoring companies paid cash for bills owed to others in return for a fee. The same factoring company then accepted the risk of collecting the debt.

In fact, in the opinion of one analyst, the Benettons were really after Italy's $875 billion in personal savings – most of which was in low-interest earning accounts and high yielding government debt. Comments by Luciano Benetton tended to support this opinion; specifically, he stated that the move into financial services was not the result of sudden inspiration, but made a lot of sense in Italy where financial services had been underdeveloped. One manager added that it was the poor level of service in Italy's financial sector which drew Benetton's competitors to their offerings in the first place. Quantifying the opportunity in factoring alone, the manager mentioned that, by 1989, Italy had become the largest factoring market in the world – with $51.2 billion in bills factored by 80 companies. By comparison, he pointed out that, in the same year, the United States factored $46.7 billion through 17 companies; Britain, approximately $20 billion through 32 companies; and Japan, $13.5 billion through 43 companies.

IN Holding SpA

To begin its diversification, IN Holding SpA was created in July 1987 – as a subsidiary of the family-controlled Edizione SpA – with $100 million of the Benettons' money. Although Gilberto Benetton supervised the family's own financial services in IN Holding, Giovanni Franzi, former head of Merrill Lynch in London, acted as Managing Director.

One important feature of IN Holding, emphasized Palmeri, was that its services were separate from Benetton's clothing business and had no connection whatsoever with the Benetton trademark. In fact, as president of IN Holding and Managing Director of the Benetton Group SpA, Aldo Palmeri was the only link between the two operations. 'They will be financially and legally separate. The industrial companies will not be obliged to buy IN Holding's services. We want the public to see it that way as well. If we buy a bank, we want it to be said 'IN Holding bought it', not "Benetton bought it",' stated Palmeri.

Giovanni Franzi also went to great lengths to stress that apparel and financial services were independent businesses. 'In no way do we rely on our store owners or shops for distribution – nor on its customer base for clients. It's true that Benetton's agents, who are invariably store owners too, have prospered; and we'd love to tap this supply of potential clients for our portfolio management. But, although we manage some of these agents' money on a discretionary basis, it has not been easy to capture.'

Shortly after Franzi's appointment, the management of IN Holding put together a portfolio of services that included corporate finance, leasing, factoring, mutual funds, insurance, securities underwriting, interest rates and currency swaps. To market these services in Italy, Franzi planned to create a retail network modelled after Benetton's apparel system. Likewise, the network was to be based on independent agents, rather than employees earning a commission. Giancarlo Cassol, previously with the large Italian insurer Riunione Adriatica di Sicurita and known as one of Italy's most successful financial salesmen, was in charge of setting up the network. By the end of 1988, IN Holding's 70 area managers had set up 120 sales outlets and 400 financial consultants or sub-agents throughout Italy. Anticipating strong growth for financial services into the future, Cassol planned to have 750 agents in place by the end of 1989, 1000 agents by 1991, and 2000 by 1993. Palmeri shared Cassol's enthusiasm. Reflecting on the success of Benetton's apparel business, Palmeri said, 'Our sales force is based on a culture of personal risk, commitment and entrepreneurship. It has worked in our industrial business, and it should work in financial services. We're essentially customer led, both in fashion and financial services. We expect the area managers and financial consultants at IN Holding to come up with the ideas for what their clients want and what they can sell.'

In addition to building its network of agents, by the end of 1987, IN Holding had entered into a joint venture with Merrill Lynch in venture capital called Credito Industriale Sammarinese, purchased a 50% share in the Italian subsidiary of Prudential Insurance Company, formed a joint venture – Finalter SpA – with GFT to provide financial services to the Italian textile industry, and added IN Capital Investments SpA – a retail distribution network for financial products – to its list of companies. Moreover, by the end of 1988, IN Holding had further expanded to include IN Broker, an insurance brokerage, a 50% interest in Leasing SpA and Finleasing Italia SpA, a 20% stake in Banco di Trento e Bolzano, and a 10% interest in leasing companies in France and West Germany run by Banca Nazionale del Lavoro, Italy's largest bank. With the exception of IN Broker, the 1988 additions were included in Sipi SpA.

Given that IN Holding was less than two years old at the beginning of 1989, companies within Benetton Group SpA still accounted for a large part of its revenues. As Franzi explained at that time, 'Our factoring business, IN Factor, still relies on a large number of companies related to Benetton, like suppliers and subcontractors, for 70% of its business. Our recently set-up IN Broker also acts as insurance broker for the Benetton Group and related companies. But, it will increasingly generate business from outside.'

By mid-1989, the number of IN Holding's subsidiaries had increased to include IN Capital SpA, IN Capital Fiduciaria which handled portfolio management, IN Capital Gestione SpA which managed mutual funds, mergers and acquisitions, and IN System, a software house with Bruno Zucarro as President, owned in part by System Management – Italy's largest software company (Exhibit 6.34).

Commenting on the future, Franzi added, 'At the operating level, we rely on alliances with major specialists – like Prudential in the insurance field – which can help us put together the right products fast. We'll forge more of these equity links so that, come 1992, we'll have a powerful distribution network to rival Italian banking groups and insurance companies like Fideuram (IMI Group), Interbancaria (BNL Group), Prime (Fiat, Monte dei Paschi), or investment banks like Mediobanca, Sige (IMI) or Euromobiliare.'

Indeed, Benetton's diversification into financial services appeared well timed to meet the growing demands of a market where such services were either non-existent or poorly developed. Ultimately, the management of Benetton Group SpA believed that by moving into new activities, clothing operations would account for only half of the total business by the end of the 1990s.

Annex I: Transferring the Benetton system to another industry

Asked his opinion about this issue, Franco Furno declared:

> Edizione Holding SpA has certain minor participations in several businesses such as banks and other organizations – portfolio participations. Italjolly owns a chain of hotels; ISA is a sort of subholding company that controls banks, again minor banks. Saes is a holding

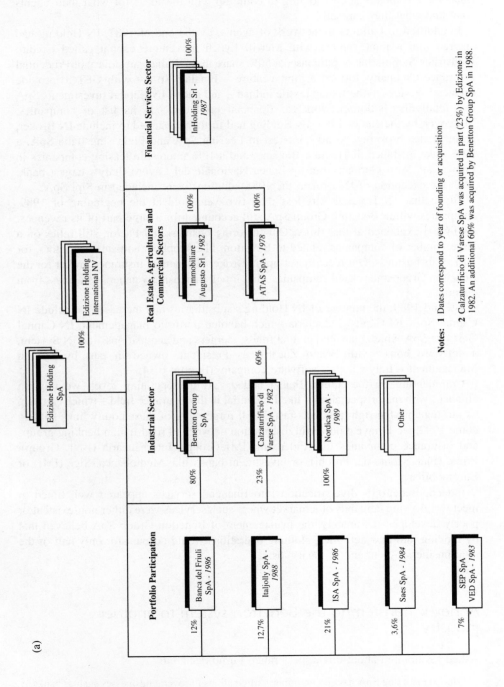

(a)

Portfolio Participation

Banca del Friuli SpA - *1986*	12%
Italjolly SpA - *1988*	12,7%
ISA SpA - *1986*	21%
Saes SpA - *1984*	3,6%
SEP SpA VED SpA - *1983*	7%

Industrial Sector

Benetton Group SpA	80%
Calzaturificio di Varese SpA - *1982*	23%
Nordica SpA - *1989*	100%
Other	

Real Estate, Agricultural and Commercial Sectors

| Immobiliare Augusto Srl - *1982* | 100% |
| ATAS SpA - *1978* | 100% |

Financial Services Sector

| InHolding Srl - *1987* | 100% |

Edizione Holding SpA

Edizione Holding International NV — 100%

Notes: **1** Dates correspond to year of founding or acquisition

2 Calzaturificio di Varese SpA was acquired in part (23%) by Edizione in 1982. An additional 60% was acquired by Benetton Group SpA in 1988.

(b)

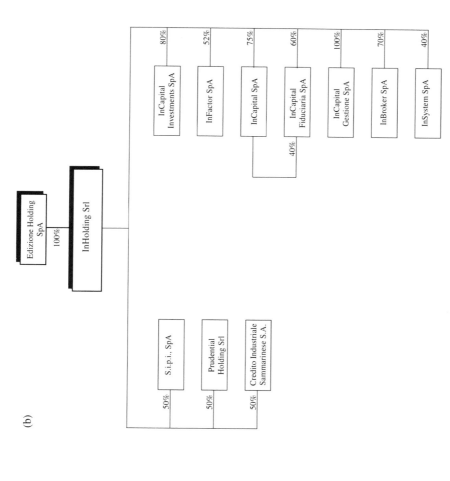

Exhibit 6.34 (a) The Edizione Holding Group; (b) Financial Services Sectors

company that has several businesses, mainly in commercial distribution, such as Bloomingdale's.

I don't think the idea to enter financial services was just to diversify into new opportunities for growth. Palmeri saw the coherence and the possibility to create a network of financial services that could initially work for the network of Benetton companies. Just to give you an example, in leasing there are 700 subcontractors that have an incredible need to lease their machinery. So why should they go and ask another leasing company when we have our own, and that's also true for factoring. All our suppliers, both subcontractors and raw material producers, need factoring services; so we created a company to serve that need. Prior to that they just bought their services on the market. This is where the awareness came from.

Case 6.5 Edizione Holding SpA (C)

This case was written by Research Associate Robert Howard and revised by Research Associate Juliet Taylor Burdet under the supervision of Professor Werner Ketelhöhn as a basis for class discussion rather than to illustrate either effective or ineffective handling of a business situation.

Surprise

Late in 1989, Luciano Benetton froze the growth of the financial companies. In spite of Aldo's ambitious goals and carefully laid plans, as well as the proven results of the venture, in February 1990, the Benettons announced that they would sell 50% of their participation in a joint venture with Britain's Prudential Insurance Company. This sale, to Abeille, a subsidiary of France's Victoire Group, was estimated by Edizione's Managing Director, Gianni Mion, to be worth between $56 and $80 million. According to Mion, the Benettons planned to raise another $300 million by the end of 1990 by selling other financial subsidiaries such as IN Capital, the branch of IN Holding that specialized in securities trading, underwriting and corporate finance. Mion explained, 'We don't believe that we have the capacity to play a role in finance on an international level.'

The financial services operation was reputedly in need of more capital before additional development could take place. By April 1990, the Benettons had decided to retain the leasing and factoring business, but fund management and banking were still under review.

The Benetton family preferred to concentrate on the industrial side of the business, manufacturing and marketing apparel, which they emphasized was their core activity. The divestiture decisions had contradicted the ideas of Aldo Palmeri, Managing Director of the Benetton Group and President of IN Holding, who had masterminded financial services precisely to offer support to the development of the core business. With a new acquisition and diversification plan, the Benettons preferred to use the additional money for direct investment in their primary sector and not in the financial services operation.

Benetton planned to spend the majority of its revenues from the financial services divestitures on Nordica, for which it had paid $150 million. Nordica, the biggest ski-boot maker in the world with sales of $241 million, had roughly one-third of the world market. But, the company only made ski boots, and Luciano's first concern was to extend the product line into ski-wear and other sports clothes, creating a holding company able to manufacture and distribute a whole range of products in the sporting goods segment.

On the subject of 'control' at Benetton, Vice President of Operations Giovanni Cantagalli said, 'The problem at Benetton is not to have control but rather to find the right balance between who controls what. When should one of the family take over and when should a management member take responsibility for this or that problem? Each side needs a recognized role and Benetton's growth in its core business activity, its diversification and acquisitions, will mean that these roles need clearer delineation.' This problem might soon be amplified by the arrival of the next generation of a dozen or so young Benettons, one of whom was already in the company.

Commenting on the break-up of the financial services network, Cantagalli felt that the energy, human resources, and finances needed for diversification outside the apparel segment far outweighed the benefits derived from the financial business. Cantagalli said, 'Let a bank do these jobs; they can do them better than we can. But many people thought that they could take the Benetton industrial culture and move it into a different industry. To repeat the same organizational model as Benetton's in another industry with success is, I think, a utopian idea.' Cantagalli also commented on Palmeri's role during his eight years with Benetton:

> Aldo put these financial companies together over the past few years. Some would say they were not too successful and others that it was too soon to tell. Some people feel that if we had stayed in the business, we would have been successful in a few years' time. Anyway, the decision has been taken now. Benetton's return on the sales of these financial services companies will certainly exceed what they paid for them. So, to a certain extent this investment was successful. Palmeri was involved in listing this company on the stock exchange both in Italy and in the US. As long as he was in finance, he did a very good job. He was personally, professionally rewarded for his work and he did not suffer much as Managing Director of Benetton, since he mainly concentrated on these other activities. One could not say that he followed the business operations of the Benetton group.

Reflecting on what Aldo Palmeri was likely to do without the main financial services companies, Cantagalli stated, 'Now that the family has decided to give up and sell these services, there will be an internal readjustment of responsibilities. Unless there is something else that can be created to satisfy Palmeri's aspirations, he has to concentrate on something he neglected for several years.'

Case 6.6 Jeanneau 1986

This case was originally prepared by Michael Birchard, Research Associate, and then revised by James Henderson, Research Associate, under the supervision of Professor Jan Kubes, as a basis for class discussion rather than to illustrate effective or ineffective handling of an administrative situation.

One day in June 1986, Mr Harold Ehrenström, President of Lear Siegler Overseas, sat in his Geneva office, perusing the financial results of one of his operations, Jeanneau S.A., a world leading leisure boat manufacturer, located near Nantes, France. 'The results for 1986 are below expectations,' he thought. Although sales of FF516 million were 9% above 1985, net profits had fallen to only 2% of sales (Exhibits 6.35–6.37).

Mr Ehrenström reflected on the past 17 years of tremendous sales growth at Jeanneau. In 1969, when he took over as President, sales were FF20 million. By 1986, Jeanneau had experienced a 21% per annum sales growth, had produced over 50,000 boats, and had become the undisputed market leader in France for its three product lines: sailboats, motorboats and microcars. However, in 1985, Jeanneau's sales lead was usurped by its rival, Bénéteau, located only a few kilometres away. While Jeanneau had focused on the French market and had diversified into microcars in 1981, Bénéteau had concentrated on one product line, sailboats, for the domestic and export markets. It was clear to Mr Ehrenstöm that some strategic decisions regarding product lines and markets had to be made in order to reach headquarters' financial targets of 5% return on sales and 10% return on assets.

European leisure boat industry overview (1970–1986)

Product

Leisure boats were classified as either 'power' or 'sail' boats. Powerboats included dinghies (or runabouts),

	1980	1982	1984	1986
Sales	172.4	289.5	424.1	515.8
Cost of Sales				
Material	78.9	152.6	208.2	218.4
Labour and overhead	47.8	85.6	117.2	185.2
Gross margin	45.7	51.3	98.7	112.2
Advertising and selling	6.4	16.1	27.2	40.4
Administration	10.1	16.1	27.2	33.1
Operating profit	29.2	17.8	41.6	38.7
Financing costs	2.9	6.6	10.1	14.5
Provisions	n/a	0.7	1.2	n/a
Profit before tax	26.3	10.5	30.3	24.2
Taxes	13.2	5.6	15.8	12.1
Net profit	13.1	4.9	14.5	12.1
Employees	855	1,040	1,231	1,258
Investments	10.0	8.6	18.7	16.2

Exhibit 6.35 *Jeanneau S.A.: income statement (millions of FF)*

inflatables and cabin cruisers. Sailboats were sub-classified as sailing dinghies and yachts (equipped with an auxiliary motor) (Exhibit 6.38).

Manufacturers continually introduced new models of leisure boats. Sometimes a new design or product could rejuvenate the whole product line. For example, the sailboard, representing the highest growth product for 1977–1986, brought new life to the sailing dinghy category. Other times, manufacturers incorporated new materials and designs. For example, Mylar sails and Kevlar hulls were new materials recently incorporated in many models. Manufacturers also followed the buyers' trend to trade-up by introducing larger boats. For example, the average sailboat size had increased from 16 to 24 feet in 1970 to 30 to 46 feet in 1986. For power boats, sizes ranged from 12-foot dinghies or runabouts to 50-foot cruisers. In general, the average product life of a leisure boat (before a redesign or an upgrade) was three to five years.

Boat prices varied considerably. Expensive models tended to be custom built with special interior/exterior designs and with a wide variety of accessories. Lower-priced models were mass produced with standard materials and designs. However, the buyer would typically have to spend 20–40% of the purchase price equipping this lower-priced boat to his needs. On average, though, a 30- to 32-foot sailboat would cost FF300,000. A top model of 48 feet would cost approximately FF1.4 million. The average price for a 21-foot power boat was approximately FF184,000.

Market

In 1986, the world-wide market for leisure boats amounted to FF20.7 billion (Exhibit 6.39).

	1980	1982	1984	1986
Assets				
Current assets				
Cash	n/a	0.8	0.9	6.0
Accounts receivable	25.1	47.2	118.8	144.1
Inventories	64.2	82.9	138.7	136.7
Other current assets	6.4	4.1	6.9	6.7
Total current assets	95.7	135.0	265.3	293.5
Fixed assets				
Plant, property and equipment	48.3	64.2	93.7	125.6
Accumulated depreciation	16.5	27.5	46.7	55.6
Net fixed assets	31.8	36.7	47.0	70.0
Intangible assets	0.1	0.5	0.1	–
Other assets	0.3	1.8	1.4	1.4
Total assets	127.9	174.0	313.8	364.9
Liabilities and shareholder's equity				
Current liabilities				
Short-term debt	–	5.0	34.6	48.5
Long-term debt due	–	–	–	3.2
Accounts payable	12.6	31.6	59.8	59.8
Accrued liabilities	15.4	27.1	45.4	43.3
Accrued income tax	–	5.6	5.1	10.3
Other current liabilities	14.1	2.9	13.3	16.6
Total current liabilities	42.1	72.2	158.2	181.7
Long-term debt due	–	9.2	31.1	26.9
Deferred interco. charges	–	–	3.3	5.1
Deferred income tax	3.6	5.8	–	17.5
Reserves	2.5	2.2	7.5	5.6
Shareholder's equity	79.7	84.6	13.7	128.1
Total liabilities and shareholder's equity	127.9	174.0	313.8	364.9

Exhibit 6.36 *Jeanneau S.A.: balance sheet (millions of FF)*

The buyers in this market could be classified into the following segments:

1 *The enthusiasts or professionals* spent most of their free time on a boat, belonged to a sailing club and participated in races. The enthusiasts were well informed about market offerings and purchased selectively, changing boats every two or three years. Performance (mainly speed) was the major buying criterion. The boats had to incorporate the latest technology and design such as Kevlar hulls or Mylar sails. Price was of little importance. This group accounted for approximately 20% of leisure boat purchases in 1986.

Percentage

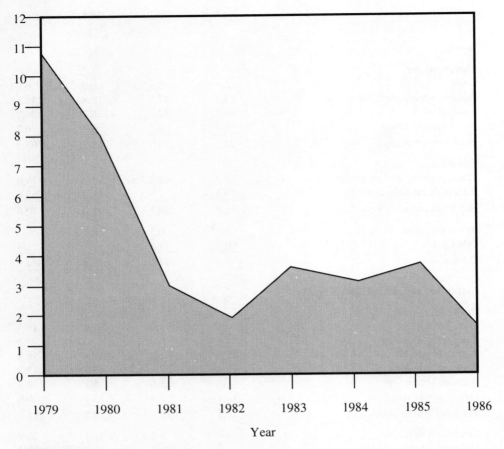

Exhibit 6.37   *Return on sales*

2 *Pleasure buyers* purchased a leisure boat for limited use during the year. The manufacturer's image, price and service availability were very important. Therefore, these buyers typically shopped around visiting many dealers or boat shows before making a final purchase decision. The boats were then used for four to five years before being replaced. This group accounted for approximately 55% of boat sales in 1986.

3 *Charter companies* purchased fleets of boats (usually over 30 feet long) and located them in popular cruising areas. Price was the major buying criterion, closely followed by durability and the boat's functional features such as ease of handling and the number of berths. Most charter companies owned their own service facilities and required the manufacturer's direct assistance only for major breakdowns. They used a boat an average of five years. As boat owners found financing and maintenance of a new boat increasingly difficult, as well as opportunities to use a boat limited, chartering became a popular alternative. As a result, this group grew from approximately 10% in 1980 to 20% of total sales in 1986.

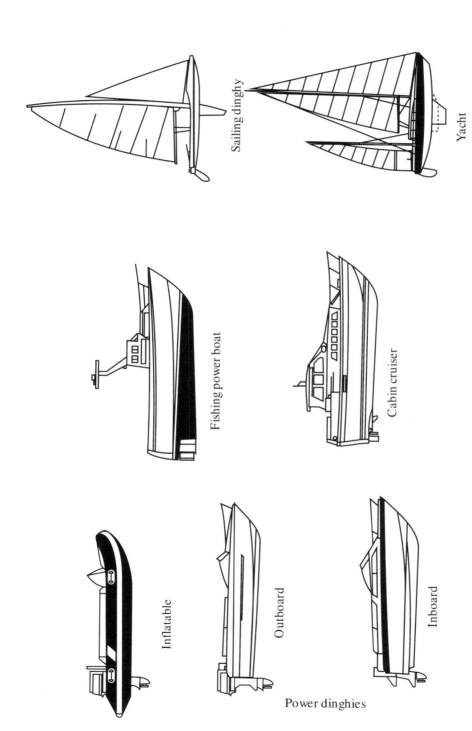

Sailing dinghy

Yacht

Fishing power boat

Cabin cruiser

Inflatable

Outboard

Inboard

Power dinghies

Exhibit 6.38 *Product categories (drawn to differing scales)*

Segment	US/Canada	Europe	Rest of world	Total
Motorboats	14,000	1,400	700	16,100
Sailboats	2,450	1,850	300	4,600

Source: Company estimates.

Exhibit 6.39   *World pleasure boat market, 1986 (millions of FF)*

4 *Institutions* included sailing schools and clubs as well as hotels in yachting areas. They purchased sailboards, small sailing boats (up to five metres long) and small powerboats for water skiing. Price and the boat's durability were the major buying criteria. This group represented approximately 5% of sales in 1986.

With higher purchase prices and maintenance costs, leisure boat users were increasingly choosing arrangements other than ownership – chartering, time-sharing and multiple ownerships. Time-sharing was similar to chartering: the organizing companies would finance their boat purchases by selling limited cruising times in advance for a specific time period. Multiple ownership was usually arranged privately with several users buying a boat together and sharing the time for its use.

Evolution of the leisure boat market

Market growth was influenced by several factors including economics, logistics, the second-hand market and geography. Product requirements differed in each country. For example, in Germany and Italy there was a higher demand for powerboats, for fancier boats with teak decks and luxury interiors. Growth rates differed among countries as well. North America and the Northern European countries experienced declines in leisure boat demand throughout the 1980s. For example, in France, boat registrations

	1980	*1982*	*1984*	*1986*
Sailboats				
< 16 feet	3,407	1,944	1,301	1,006
16–33 feet	6,407	4,133	2,641	2,241
> 33 feet	862	773	763	1,024
Total	10,739	6,850	4,705	4,271
Powerboats				
< 16 feet	18,999	17,540	13,817	13,729
16–33 feet	3,915	2,977	2,871	3,358
> 33 feet	289	147	184	265
Total	23,563	20,644	16,872	17,352

Source: Fédération des Industries Nautiques (FIN).

Exhibit 6.40   *Leisure boat registrations in France*

increased 15% per annum from 1971–1980; however, registrations had since declined 8–12% per year (Exhibit 6.40). In other countries such as Germany, England, Italy, Scandinavia and the United States, similar declines occurred but at different times and rates. In the United States in 1986, for example, the drop in the dollar's strength, coupled with President Reagan's scheduled elimination of interest charge deductions for tax purposes on boats, caused a one-time sales reduction of 20% (Exhibit 6.41). On the other hand, growth was expected to continue in the Caribbean and Mediterranean countries such as Spain and Greece.

Economic trends greatly influenced the growth of the leisure boat industry as a whole, as well as each of its product categories. During the post-war prosperity years, the industry expanded rapidly, especially in the United States. In Europe, rapid growth did not occur until the end of the 1950s but continued from then until 1974 at 10% per year. During the recession years of 1975 and 1980, growth had stopped. Between 1980 and 1986, it had reversed. Economic trends also affected the buying behaviour and the evolution of sales of the two different product segments: sailboats and powerboats. After the 1973 oil crisis, steeply rising fuel costs depressed sales of powerboats, mainly small outboard dinghies and medium-sized (16 to 30 feet) power cruisers. Buyers began preferring sailboats, to save fuel and also to follow the 'back-to-nature' trend. In some Swiss and German lakes, powerboats were prohibited due to pressure from ecologists. However, by 1986, the price of oil had declined, and powerboating became more affordable and popular.

Limited mooring facilities inhibited expansion of the boat industry in Europe. In 1986, potential leisure boat buyers were faced with congested marinas where a mooring space could cost up to 19% of the price of a medium-sized boat.

The second-hand market was growing rapidly each year. For example, in France in 1970 used boats represented only 15% of the total leisure boat sales; by 1986, they represented 63% of total sales. In 1986, a fully-equipped 3-year-old sailboat would still sell for 70% and a 10-year-old sailboat for 40–50% of the original purchase price. Prices of powerboats tended to depreciate faster; the price of a 3-year-old second-hand boat was 65% of a new one.

	1982 Prod.	Sales	1984 Prod.	Sales	1986 Prod.	Sales
England	64,200	1,048	19,970	3,316[2]	10,170	1,672
Italy	16,477	n/a	8,947	n/a	15,378	n/a
West Germany	17,770	659	17,198	797	23,498	960
Sweden	10,905	540	8,000	591	11,500	760
United States	453,725	77,424[2]	584,030	87,189[2]	569,400	87,171[2]
Japan	16,437	n/a	8,833	n/a	6,965	n/a

Source: ICOMIA, 1987.

[1]All production figures include exports. They are not representative of country demands.

[2]Included in this sales figure are motor, accessories and equipment manufactures and maintenance services.

Exhibit 6.41 *Production[1] and sales development for selected countries (millions of FF)*

The leisure boat business system – 1986

The suppliers

The suppliers to the leisure boat manufacturers could be separated into three groups:

1 The large chemical and glass companies such as BASF, SPRA and Saint Gobain, supplying the polyester resin, gelcoat, and fibreglass used to make hulls. While the boat industry represented a small portion of their output, overcapacity contributed to keen price competition. For large boat builders, price and consistent quality were key purchase criteria.

2 The large inboard/outboard motor manufacturers such as Volvo, Renault and Yanmar. For the large leisure boat producers, quality, image and price were the key purchase criteria. The motor manufacturers actively promoted their brands to the sailor/powerboater. Therefore, brand names of the motors were easily recognizable.

3 The hundreds of small firms supplying components such as masts, winches, sails, woodwork, metal fittings and upholstery. Competition was fierce as many manufacturers offered similar components all of equal quality. Discounts ranged from 20% for small to medium-sized manufacturers to 35% for larger manufacturers. In general, these firms were not always well managed.

The relative weight of primary materials, engines and components in the cost structure of the different product categories varied significantly (Exhibit 6.42). Purchases represented up to 70% of the ex-factory price for a medium-sized powerboat and 50% for a medium-sized yacht. On average, purchases represented 53% of French manufacturers' sales in 1986.

	Sailboat 25 feet	Sailboat 37 feet	Powerboat 21 feet
Engine	28	17	58
Fibreglass	18·	18	13
Components			
Interior	16	17	11
Mast/sail	17	23	n/a
Windows	3	2	9
Wood	8	8	6
Deck fittings	5	11	3
Ballast (keel)	5	4	n/a
Total	100	100	100

Exhibit 6.42 *Percentage primary materials and components in different product types (GRP boats)*

Product development

The leisure boat industry underwent an evolution in production process and materials development. Efforts were made to maintain or improve the strength, stiffness and weight of the hull without dramatically increasing the cost of production.

In the 1950s and 1960s, most boats were made of wood, but then gelcoat/reinforced polyester (GRP) began to be increasingly used. In the 1970s, aluminium was also introduced as a construction material, but the manufacturing process was expensive (Exhibit 6.43). In the 1980s, new materials such as Kevlar and carbon fibre were introduced to increase strength and stiffness and to reduce weight. However, these materials were also costly to use. Often hybrid fibres were developed, for example Kevlar/glass or carbon/glass.

	1965			1985		
	Wood	Alum.	GRP	Wood	Alum.	GRP
Sailboat < 30 ft	54	46	0.2	n/a	1.8	98
Sailboat > 30 ft	55	n/a	35	0.1	3.9	96
Power dinghies	60	n/a	38	n/a	2.0	98
Power cruisers	85	n/a	7	1.0	5.0	94

Source: FIN.

Exhibit 6.43 *Use of materials for boat construction: percentage of total number of boats constructed*

Introducing or redesigning models was critical as product life cycles declined. In 1980, the major boat manufacturers each introduced two or three new models of leisure boats; by 1986, they were introducing seven to ten new/updated designs. Each new model involved significant investments in research and development, tooling and assembly training. As a promotional tool, manufacturers often contracted well-known racers or designers to either develop or endorse new product designs.

Production

The production of a leisure boat started with the 'lay-up' process. In the 'lay-up' area, a large environmentally controlled room, the mould for the hull and deck was first covered with a gelcoat, for a smooth outside finish. Over the gelcoat, the glass, Kevlar or glass/Kevlar hybrid fibre in a polyester resin matrix was sprayed or rolled on. For the deck, in order to increase the strength and rigidity against the constant weight of the sailors or powerboaters, a balsa wood 'sandwich' construction was applied. Small square blocks of the light balsa wood were placed in between layers of the glass fibre. When dry the hull and deck were removed from the mould; the hull was then reinforced where the keel was placed. The interior of the boat would then be ready for reservoirs, the engine, electricity and the woodwork modules before the deck was attached via a crane. Finally, fine carpentry work, interior fixtures and exterior equipment were attached.

With the introduction of GRP moulds, the manufacturing time for each unit declined – long production runs resulted. One mould, which cost about the price of a finished boat, could be used to make up to 100 boats, Production per year of one model ranged on average from 30 to as much as 500 units.

Larger manufacturers were attempting to cut costs by standardizing manufacturing processes, by consolidating designs of models within a product line and across product lines, and by introducing information systems such as CAD/CAM and MRP. In this way, they hoped to reduce waste, raw materials and work-in-process inventory levels. A large boat had approximately 1500 different parts.

Marketing

Advertising and promotion budgets had increased over the past several years. An average of 2% of sales were spent in France. Promotional efforts focused on advertising in specialized boating periodicals, exhibitions and boat shows, providing sales aids to dealers, and participating in competitions. Manufacturers used trade magazines to report results of boat tests, to introduce new models and to describe the company's product line. As most boat users read at least one trade magazine per month, these reports were highly influential. Boat shows were considered a particularly effective marketing tool, but the cost ranged from FF50,000 to FF5 million per show. Manufacturers also participated in boat races using their current models or prototypes. Winning regattas was excellent publicity which could also be used in the company's advertising.

Distribution

The channels of distribution used depended on the size of the leisure boat manufacturer and the markets, as shown in Table 1.

Table 1 Distribution channels for leisure boat manufacturers

For the domestic market, most manufacturers sold their products through dealers. Some manufacturers – mainly the small ones – sold their products directly from the factory rather than, or in addition to, using dealers. For the export markets, a leisure boat manufacturer would use an importer/distributor or its own sales distribution network overseas before the boats would go through the dealers.

Dealers

Dealers tended to be concentrated in the main marine recreational areas. In France, for example, most of the 350 (down from 500 in 1981) dealers in 1986 were situated on the Mediterranean and the Atlantic.

Most dealers had been initiated by boat enthusiasts who had decided to combine business with pleasure. They typically began by trading in used boats, then selling accessories and marine equipment such as inboard/outboard engines, boat trailers and, finally, sometimes offering repair services and rentals. In France, the average dealer in 1986 would typically employ three to four people, carry two 23- to 35-foot boats in inventory and sell around FF2 million. Of that FF2 million, new boat sales represented 50%; second-hand boats represented 25%; and accessories and maintenance services accounted for the remaining 25%. However, margins were highest (up to 50%) on accessories and maintenance. New boats carried a 15% margin and little profit was made on used boats. Some dealers were more than ten times larger than the average; in 1986, approximately 10% of the dealers accounted for more than 50% of sales.

Dealers seldom carried more than one or two lines of directly competing products. However, in order to have a broad range of sizes and types of boats available, they liked to carry several complementary boat lines. Thus, only the few manufacturers with a full product line could have exclusive representation.

Manufacturers offered dealers few incentives beyond margins and credit terms. Margins usually ranged between 10% and 20% of the manufacturer's list price with credit terms at 60 days after delivery.

Dealers often faced financial difficulties. Competitive pricing forced them to increase discounts (usually 5–10%) and to offer trade-in arrangements. Having used boats in inventory tied up capital for a long period, as much as four months to a year. Without capital, they could not purchase new boats for inventory and exhibitions. Seasonality also created financial difficulties. Dealers would begin purchasing around February, complete most buying by April, sell by mid-summer but often not receive the boats until late autumn. In order to assist the dealers, manufacturers were forced to extend the terms of payment from 60 days to as many as 120 days. Allowance for bad debts was as high as 2% of a manufacturer's sales.

Jeanneau S.A.

Background

In the early 1950s, Henri Jeanneau, a keen powerboat racer, began designing and constructing his own wooden boats. They were so popular that he gave up his hardware business and focused solely on building boats. As one of the first manufacturers to use plastics, in 1959 Henri Jeanneau offered polyester hulls with wooden decks. By 1960, his boats were made entirely of polyester.

In 1964, the company was incorporated under the name, Société Jeanneau S.A. However, by September 1969, Mr. Jeanneau had sold off 75%, of his company to Bangor Punta Corporation, a diversified Eastern American multinational, which already owned three successful yacht and powerboat manufacturing, companies (O'Day, Jensen-Marine and Starcraft). Mr. Harold Ehrenström, President of Bangor Punta Overseas, located in Geneva, added Jeanneau to the portfolio of companies already under his responsibility. Henri Jeanneau remained at the company as general

	1984	1985
Sales	1,941.7	2,370.7
Cost of goods sold	1,480.6	1,805.3
Gross margin	461.0	565.4
Selling, general admin.	276.1	339.8
Interest	33.0	54.6
Other expenses	–6.3	–12.1
Income before tax	158.3	183.1
Income tax	73.2	82.3
Net income	85.1	100.7

Assets

Current assets
Cash		32.0
Short-term investments		11.6
Accounts receivable		346.9
Inventories		447.1
Other current assets		34.6
Total current assets		872.2
Net property, plant and equipment		382.7
Goodwill		122.4
Investment		114.9
Total assets		1,492.2

Liabilities and shareholder's equity

Current liabilities
Notes payable		10.1
Current portion of long-term debt		4.4
Accounts payable		201.6
Income taxes		12.8
Accrued liabilities		227.5
Total current liabilities		456.4
Deferred liabilities		109.7
Long-term obligations		283.9
Shareholder's equity		642.2
Total liabilities and shareholder's equity		1,492.2

Source: Annual Reports.

Exhibit 6.44 *Financial highlights of Lear Siegler (millions of US$)*

manager until 1972, when Michel Richard, who had been with the company since 1968, took over.

Bangor Punta was a decentralized conglomerate. Strategic and operating decisions were left to the individual companies. For Jeanneau, the focus was on increasing market share and introducing new products. By 1983, its sales had reached over FF350 million, and it had become the largest European boat manufacturer with an annual production of over 4000 units.

However, in February 1984, Lear Siegler Inc. (LSI) acquired Bangor Punta (Exhibit 6.44). LSI was a diversified holding company in California with more than 200 product lines in three major segments: aerospace/technology, automotive and commercial/industrial. The company's focus was financial, as shown in some of its objectives:

1 To identify and pursue acquisitions in high growth markets.
2 To maximize profitability and return on investment under any economic conditions through better utilization of resources, a constant surveillance of operations and strict financial controls.
3 To recognize changing economic conditions and to redeploy affected assets.
4 To achieve annual productivity improvements in all divisions.

LSI followed a formal annual strategic planning process. The process included a review of each product's competitive standing, and the market and economic conditions affecting its performance. During its review, a written marketing plan and goals for the coming fiscal year were developed.

Via its annual planning process, LSI exercised a much tighter control than Bangor Punta over the specific objectives of Jeanneau's three product lines. Therefore, management focus shifted from increasing market share and introducing new models to improving the firm's operating results such as return on assets, return on sales and productivity.

Organization

Jeanneau's original organization structure developed along two lines of responsibility: marketing and finance, and production and purchasing (Exhibit 6.45). However, the company's rapid growth during the years of expansion had created communication problems between these two functions. For instance, production managers wanted longer runs and fewer schedule changes. The marketing people, on the other hand, had had difficulty predicting market requirements and would give sales estimates which often had to be changed. The purchasing department demanded low inventories, but production pressed for higher inventories to facilitate the frequent changes in production schedules.

Changes were made in the structure of the organization. Firstly, the company was reorganized along three areas of responsibility: marketing, technical and administrative. Secondly, some new departments were added: spare parts, production methods and management information systems. Finally, some departments were split up: sales into the different product areas and regions; and purchasing and procurement into separate departments (Exhibit 6.45).

Mr Ehrenström reported to the LSI Industrial/Recreational Group Vice President on the long-range strategic and operational plans. Mr Richard, the General Manager, apart

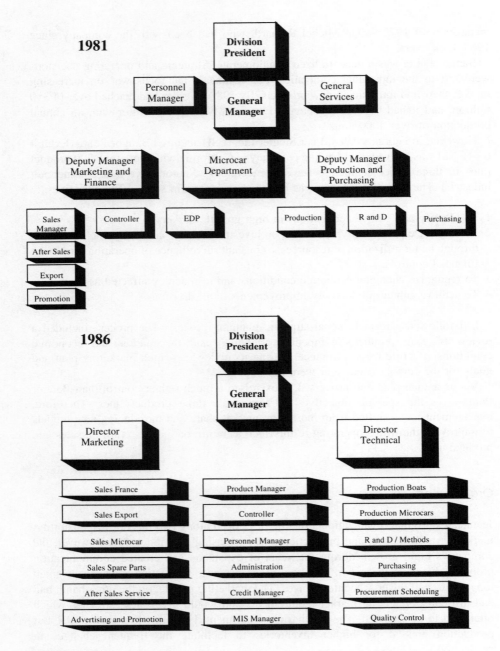

Exhibit 6.45 *Jeanneau's organization structures, 1981 and 1986*

from general management activities, had the operating responsibility for the administrative group and also made the final product decisions.

In 1986, the management group at Jeanneau had been with the company an average of 12 years while the average for the workforce, which had grown from 845 people in 1981 to 1124 in 1986, was 6 years.

Products

Jeanneau's 70 models and variations of leisure boats covered three ranges (Exhibit 6.46):

1 Sailboats from 10 feet to 48 feet.
2 Powerboats (dinghies, outboards and cabin cruisers) from 8 to 33 feet.
3 Fishing/leisure craft from 12 feet to 33 feet.

The company had originally focused on building simple, sturdy cruising boats for the pleasure buyer segment. However, certain more recent models (Espace, Trinidad, Selection, Sun-Rise 34), were larger, as sophisticated and as highly finished as competitor models. The plan for 1987 was to replace or update old models with 17 new models.

Model	Year of introduction	Length (ft)
Sailboats		
Bahia	1984	22
Fun	1982	23
Tonic	1985	23
Eolia	1984	25
Fantasia	1982	27
Attalia	1983	32
Sun Rise	1985	34
Selection	1984	37
Sun Shine	1983	38
Espace	1985	34–41
Sun Légende	1986	41
Sun Kiss	1983	45
Trinidad	1982	48
Powerboats		
Noisette	1981	8
Bourlingue	1975	12
Aqua Peche	1971–82	11–13
New Matic	1973	12
Trimatic	1978	12
Djerba	1977–86	12–17
Cap Camarat	1982–86	17–21
Skanes	1977–79	15–21
Leader	1986	19–28
DB Series	1985	19–33
Almeria	1978–79	28–32
Cap	1985	12–18
Esteou	1980–83	16–24
Eau Claire	1985	31–46

Exhibit 6.46 *Jeanneau's product line*

Gross margin and price competitiveness were not equal along the product lines, as shown in Table 2.

Table 2 Cost of structures of each product line

	Sailboats	Powerboats
Sales	100%	100%
Cost of sales		
Materials	39.7%	43.3%
Labour	27.1%	26.5%
Overhead	11.1%	10.9%
Total COGS	78.0%	80.8%
Asset turnover	1.33	1.31
Return on assets	4.76	3.29
Price	FF270,000	FF230.00
	(Attalia)	(Skanes 6.50)

Unit sales of all product lines had steadily increased from 1972 to 1980, but levelled off soon afterward (Exhibit 6.47). Three models within the sailboat line, Attalia 32, Sun Rise 34 and Sun Légende 41, accounted for over half the sailboat sales in 1986. The situation was not the same in the powerboat line due to the diversity of models and versions available.

	1976	1978	1980	1982	1984	1986
Unit sales						
Sailboats	934	1,425	1,393	1,268	1,458	1,448
Powerboats	1,482	1,656	1,578	1,603	1,677	1,517
Fishing boats	595	674	982	768	581	461
Houseboats	n/a	n/a	n/a	n/a	56	57
Dinghies	1,252	1,040	3,775[1]	2,367	900	747
Microcars	n/a	n/a	n/a	3,327	2,751	2,965
Total	4,263	4,795	7,733	9,333	7,423	7,195
Sales (FF million)						
Sailboats	n/a	n/a	120.9	152.1	271.4	334.8
Powerboats	n/a	n/a	25.7	27.2	35.1	42.1
Fishing boats	n/a	n/a	17.2	23.8	30.6	31.8
Houseboats	n/a	n/a	n/a	n/a	9.3	11.8
Others	n/a	n/a	8.6	10.7	10.3	10.0
Microcars	n/a	n/a	n/a	75.7	67.4	85.3
Total	n/a	n/a	172.4	289.5	424.1	515.8

[1]Includes windsurfers.
Source: Company.

Exhibit 6.47 *Product line sales and units*

Product development

Constant developments in new products and new product materials occurred at Jeanneau: Kevlar, CAD/CAM and prototypes. Jeanneau was one of the first leisure boat companies to introduce Kevlar material. Not only was it lighter and more sturdy than fibreglass, it was used as a promotional tool. In 1985, Jeanneau introduced a CAD/CAM system (Computer Aided Design/Manufacturing), unique in the French leisure boat industry. The CAD system could provide optimal layouts for new models and could integrate the different requirements in foreign markets. The CAM system consisted of numerically controlled machines in the woodwork shop. The CAD system would transfer the specification to the machines to cut out patterns. Much tighter tolerances allowed for better fitting and pre-assembly of the modules for the interiors of the boats. Also in 1985, the company set up its Advanced Technology Workshop, a separate prototype department. This group developed and sold one-off racing yachts and motorboats to competitors in such prestigious races as the Tour de France (88) la Voile, One Ton Cup, Route du Rhum (1986 winner), and the Formula 3000 (speedboats). Participation in races was used not only to demonstrate the speed and technical aspects of a new boat but also to gain further media attention.

Procurement and purchasing

The procurement department, consisting of 9 people, scheduled purchasing according to forecasted sales and inventory levels. The purchasing department, consisting of 8 people, was responsible for finding the suppliers and negotiating contract terms. In 1986, the total number of suppliers was 1000, providing Jeanneau with approximately 3500 different supplies. In general, Jeanneau's purchasing policy was to spread orders among several suppliers and to shop around for the best prices. Jeanneau's size enabled it to get higher discounts than most of its competitors. These discounts amounted to 5–10% for commodity purchases, such as resin and motor supplies, and 20–35% for components. This advantage was reflected in Jeanneau's purchasing costs as a percentage of sales, 42% in 1986, below the industry average of 53%.

Most purchases came from only a few suppliers: fibreglass, engine, resin and wood. These companies were contracted on a yearly basis according to projected sales. The smaller suppliers were contracted on an ad hoc basis.

In the early 1980s, Jeanneau had started in-house manufacturing of some components such as wood work, stainless steel parts and upholstery. With overcapacity among suppliers, management did not feel it was worthwhile to manufacture items such as masts and sails in-house.

During 1981, a computerized system was introduced to coordinate purchases and inventory. In 1984, the company employed stricter materials management with the introduction of cycle counting and stock reduction. The computer system was further updated in 1986, with a larger computer mainframe and new software.

Production

Jeanneau's production facilities, in 1986, covered 68,000 square metres of floor space in Les Herbiers and in three other close locations – Chataigneraie, Mouchamps, and Rochetrejoux. The production facilities included three moulding centres, five assembly and finishing halls, carpentry, upholstery and stainless steel workshops. The assembly and finishing facilities were divided by product line: powerboats, dinghies, small sailboats, large sailboats and the Microcars. The approximately 940 production workers were of average skill, except in higher skill areas such as carpentry and tooling.

Seasonality and incorrect sales forecasts often caused difficulties in production scheduling. Typically, annual production schedules were started in September at the end of the selling season. They were subsequently revised on a monthly basis to take into account the results of boat shows and other marketing developments. However, more frequent changes were not unusual, causing congestion and, therefore, loss of labour hours. Some production people believed that these frequent changes were due to poor sales planning by the marketing department. The marketing people, however, claimed that long-range forecasting was impossible and that their short-term forecasts were sufficient to revise schedules in a controlled manner. In 1985, the problem of seasonality was partially solved. Jeanneau's management and the unions came to an innovative arrangement on staffing levels which more closely aligned production to demand. A flexible work week was introduced where employees worked 42 hours in spring and summer and 35 hours in autumn and winter.

Production followed a mix of build-to-order and build-to-stock depending on the model. Boats in the 8- to 12-foot range were mass produced in a 'rotational moulding' process developed by Jeanneau. Boats above 12 feet started in the 'lay-up area' where the gelcoat, glass/Kevlar mix was laid, by hand, into the hull and deck moulds. The finished hulls were then transferred to work bays where pre-assembled kits were fitted into the interior and on the deck. Workers were organized into dedicated teams of 1 to 6 responsible for wood, electrical and other assemblies. The teams would then move from boat to boat or were periodically re-assigned to different functions as requirements changed.

The company started to subcontract work to improve production flexibility. In 1986 only 5% was subcontracted, and the target was 10%.

In an effort to control costs, Jeanneau management created a Methods Department, which was responsible for applying every technique possible to diminish production costs in each shop.

Jeanneau management felt that it had achieved a significant improvement in the quality of its boats by increasing emphasis on detailed finishing. With continual monitoring at each stage, from the gelcoat application in the workshops where the temperature and hygrometer were regulated, to the final tests for buoyancy carried out in the pool, quality was ensured.

Marketing and distribution – France

Jeanneau's share of the French sailboat market increased from 18% in 1981 to 24% in 1986. Its share in the French powerboat market was 18%. The Sales and Marketing department, consisting of one director, 2 area sales managers and 9 other employees, were responsible for national advertising and promotions, and support for the 130 French dealers and the used boat centre, Base Alpha.

Jeanneau promoted its products nationwide through a variety of methods:

• advertising in most trade magazines
• participating in all boat shows (such as La Rochelle, Cannes etc.)
• participating in boat races with prototypes of existing models

- promoting special projects such as a cooperative promotion campaign with a car manufacturer.

The advertising and promotion budget had grown from FF3.5 million in 1981 to FF20.0 million in 1986. The split among the different components had evolved as follows:

Table 3 National advertising budget, Jeanneau

	1981	1986
Advertising and promotion material	50%	60%
Boat shows	24%	28%
General promotion (special projects)	26%	12%

Advertisements were divided into three categories: corporate, featuring their wide product lines and dealer network; special services such as the financing programme and the used boats data centre; and specific models.

An advertising campaign was launched in 1986 featuring a new corporate logo. A market study confirmed the lack of awareness of the Jeanneau name. The low company profile was considered a weakness in the marketing programme, as there was no carryover among the different models. Therefore, the new logo now took a prominent place beside the name of each specific boat and was used in all advertising and promotion material.

Jeanneau had a good relationship with its dealers but turnover was low. They were visited irregularly by Jeanneau's sales managers or other company executives – usually only on a dealer's request. However, dealers often visited the company's premises in Les Herbiers. Jeanneau sent its dealers in France price lists quoting the maximum prices that buyers could pay. The dealers were invoiced for these amounts less 15%. Most dealers, however, gave the usual industry discounts to buyers (5–10%).

Jeanneau promised a two to four week delivery time for boats in stock. For larger boats, construction and delivery could take up to 6 months. The terms of payment were usually 60 days, but longer terms were given between September and February, the off-season months. Financial difficulties facing the dealers forced Jeanneau to increase its terms of payment to 90 days and even 120 days in the off-season. Most dealers carried some boats in inventory; however, Jeanneau did not supply boats on consignment.

Because the dealers were often not professionally managed, Jeanneau provided training programmes covering selling techniques, servicing problems, materials and product knowledge, and simple business management.

Through the dealers, Jeanneau offered a number of special services to prospective buyers. The company had reached an agreement with a French finance company to offer a financing package for the purchase of a new boat. Jeanneau also offered a one-year 'all risk' insurance coverage. All boats had a one-year full guarantee for the hull and parts.

Dealers were furnished with Jeanneau's promotional material, but the company did not pay for any local advertising.

A used-boat information service for the dealers and public was supplied by Jeanneau. All used boat inventory held by Jeanneau's dealers was compiled on a computerized database at the National Centre in Paris: Base Alpha, on the Seine river. This database was then redistributed among all the dealers. New boats were on permanent display at the centre in Paris so that dealers, who did not or could not hold certain boats in inventory, could send prospective buyers to see the boats there.

Marketing and distribution – export markets

Jeanneau's export sales grew from less than 20% to over 40% of total leisure boat sales. The company exported mainly sailboats (51% of sailboat sales in exports) to more than ten countries, but the majority of sales came from England, Germany, Greece and North America (Exhibit 6.48). Despite the increase in total sales abroad, in 1985 over 90% of Jeanneau's powerboat line was still sold in France. In a move to increase foreign sales, several powerboat lines were introduced in Germany, Switzerland and Italy. Also in 1985, a new powerboat line, with models such as the DB33, was designed specifically with export markets in mind.

Jeanneau's Sales–Exports Department consisted of one director and two sales managers. They did not sell directly to dealers in the export markets but, instead,

	1980	1982	1984	1986
France	149.6	161.9	250.5	254.9
EEC				
Holland and Belgium	5.3	5.0	4.0	7.3
Germany	2.9	4.1	20.2	28.5
UK	2.6	14.2	16.1	20.9
Denmark	0.8	0.3	1.6	5.5
Greece	0.4	7.3	7.7	14.4
Spain	1.6	1.5	2.7	9.1
Other EEC	1.3	7.5	4.0	1.3
Other Europe				
Sweden	0.8	0.1	n/a	2.3
Switzerland	5.4	6.3	11.5	12.9
Norway	n/a	1.0	3.1	10.2
Finland	n/a	0.5	1.3	11.0
Other Europe/Africa	0.4	2.6	2.0	0.1
Caribbean	1.1	0.4	1.4	4.9
Pacific and Australia	0.8	0.9	0.5	0.6
North America				
USA	0.2	0.8	10.1	21.5
Canada	n/a	n/a	13.3	21.4
South America	n/a	n/a	0.6	1.8
Asia	n/a	0.3	6.1	1.9
Total	22.8	51.9	106.2	175.6

Exhibit 6.48 *Jeanneau: French and foreign sales (millions of FF)*

contracted with an importer/distributor in each country who handled the complete product line, or the power boats and sailboats separately. Boats were never modified to suit local needs unless it was required by the import authorities.

Jeanneau charged the importers in French francs on the same basis as the French dealers. Marketing policy in each country, including appointment of dealers, promotion, and even pricing, was generally left up to the importer. Thus, Jeanneau's sales in any of the export markets depended substantially on the local importer's competence. For example, in Germany before 1981, Jeanneau had used a single person as an importer for the boats. His office was in his home; he did not have a showroom or service facilities, and he sold directly to local buyers. The result was a low market share in Germany. Since then, the company replaced the importer, and sales increased fivefold.

Starting in 1980, Jeanneau increased its activities in the USA and Canada. North America, however was expensive to service as freight alone added 15–20% to the cost of the leisure boat. By 1986, the continent accounted for 24% of export sales. As early as 1983–84, Jeanneau decided not to push further into dollar-based markets for fear that the dollar would deteriorate.

Diversification moves

In 1979, Jeanneau's management decided to pursue dealer recommendations to market a sailboard. The production was subcontracted to a manufacturer using fibreglass technology. Since this technology was more expensive than the injection moulding or thermoforming technology used by other manufacturers, Jeanneau's windsurfers were not price competitive. Dufour, for example, with its injection moulding technology, introduced the Dufour Wing sailboard for only FF2500 compared with Jeanneau's model at FF3500. While Dufour was able to sell over 50,000 units in 1980, Jeanneau's sales were less than 3000. The project was dropped after two years.

In 1980, management decided to begin manufacturing the Microcar, a 49 cc fibreglass body, two-seater product, for the market of vehicles not requiring a driver's permit. To date, the French Transport Ministry had supported a no-licence policy for the smaller gas and diesel engine Microcars. This diversification fitted with the company's existing resources in two ways:

1 The production of the body used the same technology as boat building (i.e. fibreglass moulding)
2 The labour force could be employed throughout the year, filling slack production periods caused by the seasonal nature of the boat business (Exhibit 6.49). Of the 140 people assigned to Microcar production, two-thirds could be shifted to boat production.

Sales of the Microcar started in early 1981; by September 1,340 units had been sold, generating 8% of that year's sales and 3.6% of the profits. By 1986, Jeanneau had achieved a 22% market share of the 13,500 unit market. Sales were FF86.3 million, 16.5% of total sales, and accounted for 22% of total profit. Purchased components accounted for 72% of cost, while direct labour was only 20% with an 8.8% return on assets. Between 1983 and 1985, Jeanneau introduced three models: a 4 kW diesel engine (the industry standard) and specially designed 50 cc and 125 cc gasoline engines. Microcar prices for a top of the line model moved from FF17,000 in 1981 to FF48,000 in 1986 (more than for a Fiat Panda).

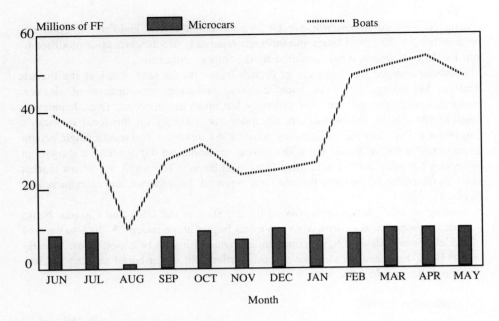

Exhibit 6.49 *Monthly sales, 1985–1986*

A sales manager with a staff of four sold the cars to the 170 French dealers (typically moped, and home and garden outlets in rural locations). Terms of sale to the dealers were 30 days.

The average user was 50 years old, lived in a rural area and travelled a short distance. A 1983 study estimated that 40% of the French population over 18 did not have a driver's licence.

The other competitors were small in comparison with Jeanneau. Ligier (17% market share), one of the early market entrants in 1982, had seen its market share decline quite rapidly with the entrance of other competitors. Aixam, with a 13% market share focused totally on microcars, enjoyed a better product design but its quality was questionable. The rest of the sales were spread among 10 other competitors.

The competition

Leisure boat manufacturers differed in what they produced:

1 Manufacturers specializing in one product line only (sailboats or powerboats).
2 Manufacturers producing both product lines.
3 Manufacturers who produced other products in addition to leisure boats.

The boat manufacturing industry in Europe in 1986 had contracted substantially since the general decline in demand in 1980. For example, in France in 1980, 55% of the sales came from 5 manufacturers, while in 1986, only two companies, Jeanneau and Bénéteau, accounted for 53% of total sales (Exhibit 6.50).

Profitability tended to be low (less than 3%) for boat manufacturers. After-tax profits were less than 3% due to seasonality, pressure to invest in new plants and equipment,

Company	1981	1985
Bénéteau	195	504
Jeanneau	192	480
Yachting France	102	Restructured
Dufour	95	Out of business
Wauquiez	45	Receivership
Gibert Marine	40	95
Kelt	36	40
Amel	32	56
Kirie	n/a	60
Other	(276) 475	(146) 569
Total	1,237	1,872

Exhibit 6.50 *Sales of French leisure boat manufacturers*

and the need to increase promotion and introduce new models in order to remain competitive. Other companies went into receivership as demand declined. Substantial interim financing was also required. In France, for instance, most manufacturers had an equity level of about 20%, long-term debt of 30% and short-term debt of 50% of the firm's total liabilities.

Bénéteau

Bénéteau had a well-known history in France. The firm, started by Benjamin Bénéteau in 1884, spent the years after World War II renewing the traditional 50 ton trawlers of the Bénéteau fishing fleet. As the average life of a trawler was 15–20 years, there were not many new boats to build. Moreover, wood was gradually being replaced by steel, which Bénéteau was not able to handle.

	1980	1982	1984	1986
Sales	220.3	250.4	419.5	559.5
Cost of goods sold				
Materials	108.3	110.6	195.6	264.2
Labour and overhead	67.6	74.2	124.8	180.1
Gross margin	44.3	65.6	99.1	115.2
Selling, general and administration	15.9	37.0	53.3	73.8
Interest charges	10.4	15.5	19.9	23.2
Profit before tax	18.0	14.2	25.9	18.2
Gains and losses	n/a	n/a	–2.3	–5.5
Taxes	–7.3	–6.4	–10.8	–4.2
Net income	10.6	7.8	12.8	8.5

Source: Translation into American accounting from Annual Report.

Exhibit 6.51 *Bénéteau income statement (millions of FF)*

	1980	1982	1984	1986
Assets				
Current assets				
Cash	0.8	6.9	14.2	n/a
Accounts receivable	20.6	42.7	88.1	108.1
Inventories	55.0	73.7	100.3	152.9
Tax refund	2.8	4.2	3.9	14.6
Other current assets	5.4	4.7	4.1	33.1
Total current assets	84.6	132.2	210.6	308.6
Fixed assets				
Plant, property and equipment	54.8	64.4	93.0	114.3
Depreciation	19.6	32.0	45.0	45.2
Net fixed assets	35.2	36.4	48.0	69.1
Intangible assets	0.4	n/a	0.3	4.2
Other assets	n/a	1.0	1.8	28.3
Participation in and loans to subsidiaries	n/a	n/a	n/a	22.5
Total assets	120.2	169.6	260.7	432.7
Liabilities and shareholder's equity				
Current liabilities				
Short-term debt	9.2	40.5	55.6	96.6
Accounts payable	32.3	29.0	36.7	53.8
Accrued liabilities	2.4	2.2	5.5	16.2
Accrued income tax	0.6	6.1	4.5	21.9
Profit sharing	1.4	0.3	0.9	n/a
Other current liabilities	13.4	17.9	52.1	11.5
Total current liabilities	59.3	96.0	155.3	200.0
Deferred income taxes	5.7	n/a	n/a	n/a
Long-term debt	25.7	26.8	32.8	84.7
Shareholder's equity	4.8	4.8	13.3	31.0
Provisions for charges	n/a	7.2	6.6	13.4
Investment credits	n/a	7.2	6.6	13.4
Reserves	24.7	29.9	48.1	96.4
Total liabilities and shareholder's equity	120.2	169.6	260.7	432.7

Source: Annual Reports.

Exhibit 6.52   *Bénéteau balance sheet*

Mrs Annette Roux, Bénéteau's granddaughter, decided to continue the family boat-building tradition. In 1964, she took over the business, a tiny, ailing boat yard with 17 employees, and introduced a small polyester boat, designed by her father, to the growing leisure boat market. By 1986, the company had become the largest leisure boat manufacturer in France with 1,100 employees and sales of FF558 million (Exhibits 6.51 and 6.52). In France, Bénéteau had the second largest market share with 22% of the sailboat market and 14% of the motorboat segment.

Mrs Roux had followed a consistent strategy over the years: expanding and focusing on one product line, improving manufacturing techniques, building up a wide dealership network, exporting and using heavy promotion.

Product line

In 1986, sailboats accounted for almost 90% of Bénéteau's sales. Approximately 3000 units were sold in 1986, primarily from two sailboat lines. The 'First' line of racing sailboats, introduced in 1977, accounted for 85% of units sold. The second line consisted of more recently introduced cruising boats, Idylle and Oceanis. Every year since 1981, Bénéteau renewed or expanded a quarter of its product range, which now encompassed 40 designs. The price of their First 29 (29 foot boat) was approximately FF242,000. Bénéteau pricing was competitive in all product lines and, while the quality of the boat was standard, buyers considered it good value for the money.

Improving manufacturing

In the period 1981–1986, Bénéteau had invested a total of FF199.1 million in new plant and production improvements. Over FF115 million of this investment was spent in 1985 and 1986 on the construction of another French plant in Challans and a plant in South Carolina, USA. Four of Bénéteau's six plants had been built since 1980. At the new Challans plant, assembly-line techniques were used after the hulls were formed, to complete up to two Oceanis boats per day. The American plant installed kits of materials and fittings sent from France into locally produced hulls.

Wide dealership network

Mrs Roux realized the importance of a large and strong dealer network for a high growth strategy. Thus, her policy was to aggressively persuade existing dealers to switch to Bénéteau. One or two models would be introduced to a dealer to 'complement' their products. Then the dealer would be 'followed up' with regular visits from Bénéteau people. In this way, the company was able to acquire many of its competitors' dealers, so that by 1986 it had a network of 110 dealers in France, second only to Jeanneau's 130.

Export markets

Bénéteau was aggressive in export markets with almost 60% of sales outside France. The firm had its own sales organizations in the USA, the UK, Spain and Italy, as well as 40 international dealers, 27 of whom were in the USA. Exports had been only 29% of sales in 1981. By 1986, 26% of sales were in other European countries, 22% in the USA, and 9% in other regions.

Heavy promotions

Bénéteau spent heavily on promotions (in 1986, FF19.8 million). Mrs Roux, through constant media exposure, built up a consistent image of Bénéteau as a dynamic, successful and fast-growing company. Each new model was publicly introduced with a news conference and then followed up in various magazines. Bénéteau advertised heavily in all trade magazines, with the theme 'an experienced boat builder who builds reliable and excellent performing boats', using colourful advertisements that spread over six to ten pages.

The company initiated a computerized data centre for used boats and a service for its customers where it would arrange for their own boats (bought from Bénéteau) to be chartered. Bénéteau claimed this programme could save its customers up to 50% of the boat's purchase price. Some market participants felt that this plan was not really practical and that it was merely a marketing gimmick.

Like Jeanneau, the company also participated in all major boat shows, entered races with prototype models (such as in the Admiral's Cup), and sponsored races. In 1985, it started a three year sponsorship of a Bénéteau 'First' class race held in New York.

Two problems, or potential problems, however, faced Bénéteau: its high debt structure and its lack of profitability in the USA. Bénéteau was highly leveraged in comparison with Jeanneau despite the increased capital base in 1984 and 1985, via the sale of shares on the secondary share market in Paris. (The Bénéteau family maintained control of 72% of the stock.) Competitors wondered about its financial capabilities; however, profits were above the industry average. In 1986, Bénéteau lost FF2.4 million on FF4.9 million in sales for its US business, Bénéteau Inc. Apart from the start-up costs, the management attributed the loss to the decline in the US market.

Other sailboat and powerboat competitors in Europe

In 1986, Gibert Marine (Gib'Sea) was the third largest manufacturer in the French market with sales of FF100 million in 1985. The 280-employee company specialized in large well-appointed sailboats which accounted for 75% of its sales. Although the company had indicated its sales objective as: 33% France, 33% Europe and 33% North America, approximately 60% of sales were, at the time, within the French market, giving Gibert an 8% market share. The company had a range of 20 sailboats of which the 52-foot Gib'Sea was their newest model. The company had also recently opened a new plant.

In 1986, Kirie bought out Kelt, another sailboat manufacturer, thus creating the combined company, Groupe MCP. The company, with combined sales of FF72 million in 1985, had a total of 14 models of the Kirie 'Feeling' line of sailboats, two Kelt sailboats and a line of American motorboats produced under licence. The 'Feeling' line accounted for 95% of production, 55% of which was sold in France, the rest to Scandinavia, Germany and the United States. In the States, Kirie contracted with Custom Yachts to build under licence the Feeling 346 (under the name Elite). New introductions of models included 32- and 34-foot boats.

Wauquiez's sales were FF65 million in 1985 on unit sales of 70 sailboats. Eighty per cent of the company's line of prestigious boats (with such well-known brand names as Hood, Pretorien, and Centurion) were exported, mainly to the USA. However, the 180-employee company had experienced several unprofitable years.

In the French powerboat market, Guy Couch was the largest producer, followed by Jeanneau and Bénéteau. Its sales of FF100 million, in 1985, came mainly from the sale of larger ocean fishing boats. Three new models were introduced in 1986: 31-foot, 42-foot and 46-foot sport boats.

Exhibit 6.53 lists the leisure boat competitors in France.

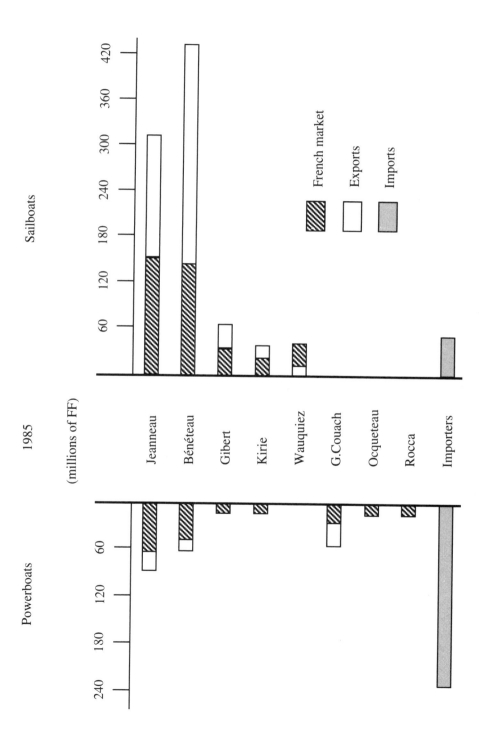

Exhibit 6.53 *French leisure boat competitors*

In the export markets, the major competition came from the Italians, British, and Scandinavian companies (Exhibit 6.54).

In the UK, the largest leisure boat manufacturer was Marine Projects, with standard quality boats carrying brand names such as Sigma and Moody sailboats, and Princess powerboats.

In Scandinavia, Nautor was the most well known with its 'Rolls Royce' sailboat of the industry, the 'Swan' line. These boats, of excellent quality with a luxurious design and finish, were also very highly priced. The company enjoyed sales of FF70 million from a production of 44 boats. Nautor exported most of its production, selling through agents around Europe, the United States and the Far East.

The larger Italian companies specialized in powerboats. They were considered at the forefront of design and style.

	Sales
Sailboats	
Germany	
Dehler	100
Bavaria	60
England	
Westerly	90
Sigma Moody	50
Scandinavia	
Nautor	70
Powerboats	
Italy	
Riva	70
Mochi	100
Granchi	110
Ferretti	70
England	
Princess	270
Fairline	133
Sunseeker International	79
Birchwood	40
United States	
Bayliner (Brunswick)	3,133
Sea Ray (Brunswick)	2,275
OMC (several brands)	1,300

Source: Company.

Exhibit 6.54   *Other leisure boat manufacturers' sales (millions of FF)*

The future

Harold Ehrenström considered the following questions as he prepared his next long-range planning report for LSI Industrial/Recreational Group:

1 How to increase sales, profitability, return on assets and sales per employee?
2 How to compete against Bénéteau?
3 What role should each product line (sailboat, motorboat and microcar) play in the next five years?
4 On which markets should management focus its efforts?

Part Three
Adjusting to Environmental Pressures

Introduction

7 Global corporate policies
Case 7.1 Olivetti
Case 7.2 Canon

These cases were selected for discussion of the following concepts: adapting a strategic posture to market needs; seeking central coordination; and seeking local adaptation

8 A framework for environmental analysis
Case 8.1 Country note on Indonesia

This case was selected for discussion of the following concepts: country environment; environmental monitoring; identification of events, trends and pressures; specification of events, trends and pressures; and setting priorities

9 The macroeconomic environment
Case 9.1 Introductory note on Czechoslovakia

This case was selected for discussion of the following concepts: assessing foreign investments; economic scenarios; and assessing country risk

10 The political environment
Case 10.1 Central and Eastern European automobile industry

This case was selected for discussion of the following concepts: the political environment; leaders and support groups; and understanding a political system

Introduction

Overview

There are four important dimensions on which the international manager has to build knowledge and develop skills:

1 Understanding the country's environment.
2 Understanding the industry's environment.
3 Understanding the business unit and corporation.
4 Developing management skills.

We have found that one of the most important tasks of management development programmes within big corporations is to spread a common framework for the understanding of the corporation and its competitive environment. These efforts essentially create a common language within and across the corporation's units. In Parts One and Two of this book we provided cases to discuss useful frameworks that facilitate a common understanding of both an industry and the corporation. In this part we provide useful cases to discuss the understanding of political and economic trends and events.

Normally, management development programmes also include the building of management skills under headings such as: communication skills, listening skills, negotiation skills, influencing skills, leadership skills, etc. We believe that such training efforts, which are usually coordinated to cultivate a common strategic perspective throughout the corporation, still lack a common framework for assessing country environments which would complete the corporation's strategic perspective.

To illustrate our argument further we have drawn an executive's profile, shown in the figure on page 242. On a scale from zero to 100 (think about it as percentages), we drew an executive's possible mastery of each one of the four dimensions needed for strategic international management. What we are illustrating is the potential impact of neglecting one dimension in the shaping of a shared corporate perspective. Consider a corporation that leaves the understanding of the country's environment to chance and does nothing to build a shared perspective: our graph tells us that 50% of the corporation's shared perspective of strategic management is left to randomness. Clearly we assume that the four dimensions are equally important, a common assumption in all the frameworks presented in this book.

Following on from this reasoning, we could argue that corporations doing nothing about some of the other dimensions are leaving more and more of their shared, strategic management perspective to chance. For instance, they reduce it to 25 per cent if they ignore two dimensions, and leave everything to chance if they work on only one dimension and ignore the other three.

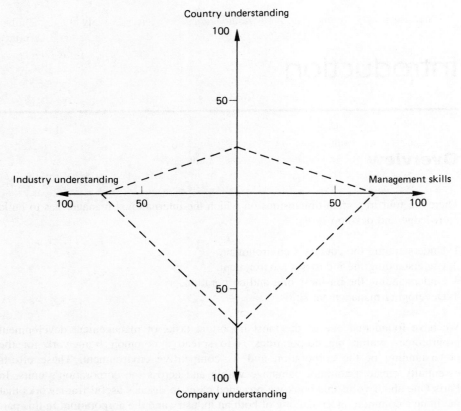

Strategic management profile

Consider the executive's strategic management profile shown in the figure. Several things should be noted:

1 No one dominates all dimensions fully: this executive has 25 per cent dominance of the country's environment and 70 per cent of the other three dimensions. Hence the importance of management teams.
2 This means that every executive can improve his abilities in some of the four dimensions.
3 Corporations should choose common frameworks for the shaping of shared perspectives in all four dimensions.

Normally, corporations worry more about building management skills and developing the understanding of the company and corporation as a whole. Since the early 1980s, however, corporations have worked more and more towards achieving a shared perspective of the competitive environment. But even now, the whole field of environmental country analysis in management development awaits formalization because the advent of industry analysis, which was introduced by microeconomists in the 1980s, positioned the work of environmentalists relatively low. In a way, this was due to the rock-like stability of Western European, Far Eastern and North American economies.

When European, Japanese and American economies were relatively stable, scholars and practitioners of strategic management did not worry about understanding certainty, i.e. static and known rules of the game. The environment was safely assumed away and people worried about competing against Japanese, Germans and the like. But in the 1990s, this stability has gone; and markets and opportunities are disappearing and appearing. Western Europe may turn into the greatest market in history; the Soviet Union has ceased to exist; Germans and Japanese may struggle for Eastern European markets; and the decade has begun with a big recession. As a result of all this activity, understanding the country environments where the corporation competes, is becoming an increasingly important area for strategic management. Therefore, to increase the robustness of their management development programmes during the 1990s, corporations should put into place the processes that create a shared perspective for all four dimensions.

About the Cases

Part Three: *Adjusting to Environmental Pressures*, presents cases dealing with the understanding of a country's environment and the management of strategic dilemmas. We don't pretend to present cases for specialists on either macroeconomics or political science. We just want to illustrate how, from our own practical experience, frameworks originating in those disciplines can be applied by country managers in order to understand the environment in which they operate. Before we present them, we would like to recognize the contributions of Professors George Taucher and Dominique Turpin towards their Canon and Olivetti cases, and research associates James Henderson, Robert Howard, Joyce Miller and Srinivasa Rangan to different cases. Undoubtedly, we are indebted to many staff members at IMD for their enthusiastic support during the different phases of our research.

These real life business situations – cases – demonstrate how to understand the economic and political forces in a country. Insights can be gained from these cases into the identification of environmental events, trends and pressures – with their significance to the strategic posture of a company. From our discussions we have found that for Nestlé, Tetrapak and other corporations, there was more to the world than Western Europe, Japan and the USA; and many more environments than the competitive one. For corporations with major operations in Russia, Ukraine, India, mainland China, Brazil, Mexico, Indonesia, Philippines, Nigeria and the like, we recommend looking at a few of the alternative environments before deciding on a global strategic posture.

In adapting a corporation's strategic posture to the different country environments, dilemmas over technological adaptation; new product introduction; political and economic situations; and operational policies, appear for each country – as illustrated by the Canon and Olivetti cases. In all of these situations the basic dilemma between central coordination and local adaptation holds, but the solutions adopted are not always the same; instead, they are country-specific.

For example, a technology is appropriate to a country only if it is economically more productive than the challenging technology. So, how much of the technology used in each country should be decided at headquarters? Products marketed in countries with young populations are usually different from those marketed in countries with aging populations; which products should have a global standard? The political processes of certain countries demand different strategic postures from developed western countries; what should be the global ethical posture? And obviously, financial policies and accounting practices in high inflation countries should differ from those used by the same corporations in low inflation countries.

The process of policy adaptation is essentially a synthetic proposition: the management team identifies key events, trends and pressures in its environment so that it can examine their impact on the strategic posture and operations of its business unit. It is a bottom-up process in which all executives in a market participate in the adaptation of the strategic posture of the corporation to specific environmental pressures in that market. The philosophy of this approach is to push strategic decision-making closer to the people with market knowledge; closer to the country/customer.

By specifying the events, trends and pressures we can evaluate whether or not these phenomena have a positive or negative impact on the strategic posture of the corporation. Once all events, trends and pressures have been specified, a strategic agenda for the participants in the industrial sector has been created. Then, business people can act either as an association or as individuals in their efforts to influence changes in the environment through lobbying. Each industrial sector builds its own strategic agenda, as the events, trends and pressures affect them differently. A corporation's strategic agenda is a simple list of events, trends and pressures and their impact on the corporations' operations in the country. This agenda must generate action plans for different scenarios constructed by the agenda. If the pressures are too strong, the strategic posture of the corporation may be modified.

The strategic agenda defines the events, trends and pressures occurring in the environment, whose impact on the strategic posture of a corporation must be evaluated.

Experienced business people try to understand the country's culture, politics and economy by appealing to frameworks originating in these disciplines. They ask: why oversimplify a country's complexity when we have disciplines offering useful frameworks to understand it? This fundamentalist approach to country analysis starts with macroeconomics.

In our experience, country managers have a rudimentary understanding of how economies work – they are doers, not economists – and use their views to raise questions with experienced economic consultants. We strongly recommend using such expert advice. Furthermore, country specialists should and must be recruited to construct a fundamental understanding of an economy.

Thus, instead of representing country risks with a single number – measuring country risk – our fundamentalist approach, which can be discussed with our two country notes, provides a broader understanding of what is happening in the environment of the host country. We propose to first understand the political and economical actors, their objectives, resources and alliances in a country. Next, we propose to understand the economic decisions and public policy formulation, so that likely country scenarios are identified. Then, we believe that, with our understanding of the pressures applied to the decision-makers we can guess what the major policy decisions will be. In this way, inflation, devaluations, economic incentives, social pressures and so on, can be monitored close enough to the real events, so that we can guide the business unit through that environmental ocean.

7

Global corporate policies

Case 7.1 Olivetti

This case was prepared by Research Associate Joyce Miller, under the supervision of Professors George Taucher and Dominique Turpin, as a basis for class discussion rather than to illustrate either effective or ineffective handling of a business situation.

In late 1986, Elserino Piol, Executive Vice President Strategies and Development in the Olivetti Group, one of the world's foremost information technology companies and the second largest indigenous personal computer manufacturer in Europe, was concerned about the company's photocopier business. Their Agliè plant located near Olivetti's headquarters in Ivrea was producing about 20,000 units annually, most of which were sold in Italy. This operation was expected to be an important component for Olivetti in creating the 'integrated office', where several pieces of standalone equipment would be linked up in a multi-functional, automated system.

But the window of opportunity was closing. With the fast pace of development in the telecommunications technology that provided the networks and links between formerly disparate pieces, several new contenders were poised to enter the office-of-the-future market. A few months earlier, Mr Piol had travelled to Tokyo to meet with senior management in Canon Inc., a major Japanese copier manufacturer, to sound out the possibilities for co-operation. At this point in time, Mr Piol wondered whether it might make sense to form a basic technology alliance with a leader in the copier field.

Ing. C. Olivetti & Co., SpA

Ing. C. Olivetti & Co., SpA was the parent company of the Olivetti Group, whose product line included distributed data processing and office automation equipment, typewriters, calculators, cash registers, and photocopiers (Exhibit 7.1).

In 1986, the Olivetti Group obtained a net income of L565.5 billion on sales of L7,317 billion, up 12.3% from the previous year[1]. At this time, Olivetti had manufacturing activities in 27 plants in seven countries.

	1986	1985
Distributed data processing and office automation		
Electronic professional typewriters, videotyping systems	14.0	13.2
Personal computers	28.5	29.5
Minicomputers and terminals	28.0	32.2
Printers	7.0	7.2
Telecommunications equipment	2.8	2.7
Total	80.3	84.8
Office products		
Portable and office manual and electric typewriters	8.2	5.9
Calculators, cash registers	6.7	5.7
Copiers	3.6	2.3
Office furniture	1.2	1.3
Total	19.7	15.2
Overall total	100.0	100.0

Source: Annual Report.

Exhibit 7.1 *Olivetti Group revenue breakdown, by market sector in 1986 and 1985 (%)*

Founded in 1908 and headquartered in the foothills of the Italian Alps, just over the border from Switzerland, Olivetti was known for many years as the family-owned company that turned out elegantly designed typewriters. By the mid-1960s, Olivetti was the sixth largest industrial organization in Italy, and 80% of its revenues from the sale of manual and electronic typewriters, calculators, accounting machines and office furniture were generated outside Italy.

In the following decade, as a result of its ambitious growth strategy, Olivetti became seriously undercapitalized, and it appeared that the company would either go bankrupt or fall into the hands of the Italian government. In April 1978, a dynamic leader from outside the family was brought in to turn the company around. Carlo de Benedetti, an Italian industrialist who had previously spent several months as Managing Director of Fiat, took over as Vice Chairman and CEO. De Benedetti invested over $17 million of his own personal fortune in the company (and thereby became the majority shareholder) and launched a programme to revitalize Olivetti.

[1] In 1986, US$1 = L 1490.

Olivetti becomes a strong force in office automation[2]

By the mid-1980s, De Benedetti had established Olivetti as the strongest European competitor to IBM in office automation by upgrading the company's electronic typewriters, and introducing a line of microcomputers and minicomputers. An industry analyst commented:

> De Benedetti immediately slapped a 10% price increase on products, laid off 20,000 workers, and gave priority to developing the company's pioneering electronic typewriter. He subsequently replaced Olivetti's mechanical models with a new line of electronic machines, and he did this in record time. He accelerated the development process and beat IBM to the market by several months. In the process, de Benedetti incurred debts of over $1 billion to pay for retooling Olivetti's plants and boosting the output of electronic-based equipment. In three years, R&D costs – which had been less than $30 million when de Benedetti took over – soared to more than $100 million.

To support these outlays, de Benedetti undertook a series of venture capital moves in the USA, spending $60 million to assume interests in 22 small high-tech companies, a strategy that de Benedetti hoped would give Olivetti early access to new developments and keep the company abreast of emerging trends. During the 1970s, Olivetti had often been too late into the market with new products, which had weakened its position in the office equipment market. De Benedetti believed that tracking progress in the American market would provide insights to enhance Olivetti's position in Europe and ensure that the company anticipated customer demands. As well, de Benedetti searched relentlessly for ways to improve performance, cut costs and reduce debt while maintaining Olivetti's forward momentum towards the integrated office market. New accounting systems were introduced, control was tightened, low-profit products were discontinued, and plants were closed or revamped.

Competition in office automation from IBM, DEC and Xerox was the greatest threat to a small contender like Olivetti. These giants had significant financial resources and had spent heavily on R&D in the early 1980s. De Benedetti was also concerned about emerging competitors in the office automation field, namely, the Japanese. De Benedetti was convinced that Olivetti needed a more global thrust.

Increasingly, computer-based office information systems were replacing conventional office machines, although the typewriter was still the core of Olivetti's business. In 1982, de Benedetti launched Olivetti's first personal computer – the M20 – which generated sales of $56 million worldwide within one year. According to a senior marketing executive:

> We put our personal computer lab in Cupertino, California, in order to be right there in Silicon Valley, where you literally breathe the state of the art.

At this time, Apple Computer, the market leader, had total sales of $850 million and IBM obtained revenues of $630 million in this sector. Olivetti subsequently launched the M24, an IBM-compatible desktop PC, which laid the foundation for Olivetti to become the second largest personal computer manufacturer in Europe. An Olivetti salesman remarked:

---

[2] Parts of this section are paraphrased from IMD Case GM 352, Building Alliances (B): Ing. C. Olivetti & Co., SpA.

The M24 was the most successful PC we ever had. When PCs came out in the USA, there were only a few outlets able to sell them. This led to the birth of PC dealers, and each manufacturer had to create this infrastructure.

In Europe, Olivetti helped shape this market because we had an established network of dealers, or *concessionaires*, who were selling our typewriters and other office products. In some countries, like Spain, we'd had these dealers in place since before World War I. No one in the USA had a network like ours, or was this far along. These were exclusive outlets, and most got on the bandwagon to sell PCs as well. We also had a tier of independent dealers. We couldn't manufacture enough M24s to keep up with the demand.

A strategic alliance with AT&T

In December 1983, Olivetti entered into an agreement with American Telephone & Telegraph Co. (AT&T), which had dominated the American telecommunications industry for years. The AT&T monopoly was deregulated in early 1983, and the company launched its first digital private branch exchange (PBX) system soon afterward. Such a system enabled an office to become its own in-house phone company. PBX systems could be connected to other digital equipment such as terminals, PCs, and even large mainframe computers. Voice and data were transmitted over a single telephone line, which combined to make the PBX the 'hub of the automated office-of-the-future and the target of every equipment manufacturer wishing to stay in the race.'

AT&T spent $260 million to acquire a 25% stake in Olivetti. The 1983 agreement was described as an industrial, commercial and financial alliance in the office automation field, and it granted Olivetti exclusive European distribution rights for all AT&T office automation products. AT&T received reciprocal distribution rights for Olivetti products in the American market. The idea was that the Olivetti dealers would sell AT&T's private automatic branch exchanges in Europe in addition to their existing line of office products. By July 1984, one out of every three microcomputers moving off the assembly line in Olivetti's modern Scarmagno plant, near the company's headquarters in Ivrea, carried the AT&T logo and went into a box marked for shipment to the US. The PC6300 and PC6300 Plus, both supplied by Olivetti, were AT&T's most successful personal computers on the market. An Olivetti executive commented:

> By mid-1986, the bloom was coming off the alliance. We were just too different. We were each part of the other's product line, but we each continued to manufacture products in competition when we should have been sourcing them from the partner. This was only one of the things that put stress on the relationship. It was also becoming clear that AT&T was rethinking its computer strategy and planned to emphasize its local area networks and data communications equipment in order to go after the larger network business – between office locations or between big computers in different places.
>
> 1984 to 1986 were very successful years for us, and the alliance with AT&T certainly helped Olivetti build its reputation in Europe and the USA. No one had any trouble making their budgets. Around this time, people began thinking that maybe the copier was an interesting product to get serious about.

Olivetti's copier business

Olivetti entered the copier business in 1962 through a licensing agreement with Old Town Corporation, an American firm based in New York. By the mid-1960s, Olivetti had come up with its own design for a low-end machine that used a liquid toner, an approach employed by many copier manufacturers at the time. Olivetti had arrangements to buy both the toner and the specially coated zinc-oxide paper that served as a photoconductive surface as well as the final copy. The company had some commercial success with this machine, primarily with vendors in Italy, France and Spain. Giovanni Ravera, who joined Olivetti around this time, recounted:

> Initially, we concentrated on developing our processes. It wasn't long before we realized that the electrofax technology we were using was becoming obsolete, and we began developing plain paper copiers (PPCs). Everyone was doing this. In 1968, a design group was formed in New Jersey, and much of their effort was focused on a high-speed, high copy volume machine invented by one of the American technicians.
>
> There was some commercial development but not a lot of success. These machines were sold through Olivetti's sales organization for general office products. It was difficult for this group to sell these more sophisticated high-end products, these rather delicate machines. At the time, Xerox was building a specially dedicated sales and service organization, which eventually became its key success factor in the industry, and we had no equivalent effort.

Olivetti began active development work on manufacturing PPCs following the US Federal Trade Commission's 1975 decree that required Xerox to offer unrestricted licensing of all of its copier patents and related know-how. Throughout the development phase, Olivetti purchased low-volume copiers (under 20 copies per minute, or cpm) from Sharp Corporation on an original equipment manufacturer (OEM) basis. These units were sold under the Olivetti label with some minor customization. Olivetti's intention was to replace these machines with its own production of low-end copiers at a later stage. Beginning in 1978, Olivetti produced and marketed a mid-volume copier.

Expanding OEM relationships

In 1976, Olivetti began buying in high-end machines on an OEM basis from Sharp as well. This relationship lasted for close to seven years, at which time Olivetti renewed the arrangement with Konishiroku Photo Industry (now called Konica), another Japanese copier manufacturer. Typically, OEMs were companies that produced their own copiers and/or manufactured products in the office electronics or reprographics sectors. OEM machines generally had a different design and different technical specifications from those sold under the manufacturer's own badge.

Olivetti, like many of its competitors, completed its product line by purchasing machines on an OEM basis. This was seen as a way to protect the existing customer base against competition from other suppliers able to offer the full range of models. The argument was made that these OEM sales were subsidiary to and aimed at facilitating the placement of the company's own-manufactured machines. In general, Olivetti resold these machines at a higher price than the level at which they were offered in the European Community by the original suppliers.

Olivetti introduces its own low-end machine

In 1981, Olivetti began producing low-volume copiers (10–20 cpm) in a newly refurbished plant in Agliè, 25 km north-west of Torino. At this time, Olivetti was one of the few companies in Europe still designing and manufacturing copiers. Kodak and

Xerox each had a significant market position in Europe, but the designs came primarily from Japan and the USA, respectively. UK-based Gestetner was also in the market, and Océ, a Dutch firm, was manufacturing mid-volume machines in Europe for the European market. Both of these companies imported OEM machines to fill out their product lines. In the mid-1970s, Océ had carried out basic research aimed at developing a low-volume model to replace OEM imports. However, the project was later abandoned when the company saw that it could not earn an adequate return while such low market prices prevailed.

In the early 1980s, Olivetti was able to reduce its reliance on OEM imports to one model with technical features between those of its own low- and mid-volume products. However, Olivetti's dependence on Japanese imports subsequently increased, as the company was unable to develop a successor product to its mid-volume machine. Market prices were depressed at the time of the investment decision. An economic evaluation of the project showed a negative return, and production was never begun. In late 1985, Olivetti concluded an arrangement to import personal copiers from Canon Inc., the inventor of this technology and the only producer of these machines worldwide. Mauro Achiluzzi, in Olivetti's Office Products Marketing area, elaborated:

> We wanted to sell Canon's personal copier in Italy under the Olivetti badge. Canon had a good product, and we had a good commercial network that we needed to feed with products. We're strong in Italy and have a presence in Spain, France, the Netherlands, the UK, as well as some activity in Scandinavia. Initially, Canon Tokyo wasn't prepared to do OEM business with what was theoretically a competitor, but eventually we convinced Canon Europe to go ahead. The arrangement didn't create too much turbulence in the marketplace. Canon was selling in its own channel and we were selling these products in ours, and there wasn't too much competition between the sales organizations.

Olivetti's sales and marketing organization

In 1986, the company was set up in four independent business units: office products, personal computers, systems, and software. Olivetti had 33 marketing subsidiaries that

Country	Branches	Dealers
Italy	150	1,250
Germany	30	610
France	45	500
Spain	35	275
UK	25	380
Other	15	685

Source: 'Olivetti's Worldwide Copier Strategy', presentation delivered at Dataquest's Copying and Duplicating Industry European Conference, June 24–26, 1987.

Exhibit 7.2 Olivetti's 1986 sales network in Western Europe (the 'domestic market')

operated in conjunction with a dealer organization to cover more than 100 countries (Exhibit 7.2). Mr Achiluzzi explained:

Each of our marketing subsidiaries has a specific geographic responsibility, and within these organizations we have division managers responsible for each of the product lines. Annual budgets or targets – in terms of quantity, product mix, cost, bottom line – are prepared and submitted to Ivrea, and this is the commitment of the subsidiary to the headquarters. A local stock is kept to feed customer orders locally.

We have a strong franchise in Italy, with 1250 dealers. Close to half of them are exclusive. We have *concessionaires* in Spain as well, but fewer than in Italy. Olivetti gives these more exclusive dealers a territory that is not covered by our existing branches, and they give us a commitment about what they will sell, within a limited category of products.

Most observers concluded that Olivetti's marketing and distribution organization was the key factor in its success, particularly in Italy. A salesman in Olivetti Nederland, one of Olivetti's smaller European subsidiaries, remarked:

Beginning in the mid-1980s, there was an opening up of new technology. Quality was coming out as a buzzword, and people were prepared to make the necessary investments. Everyone was trying to come out with quality products, from cars to copiers.

In the early years, we burned our fingers on coated paper technology where we used a ball of ink and created copies from that. We've always been in the office equipment business, and at a certain stage, the copier became an indispensable part of this. We had to get into this business. Olivetti had carefully built its image as a total office supplier. We were even making office furniture.

Historically, we haven't done very well because we were so bloody awful at copiers. There was a general reluctance in many of the sales arms to handle copiers. This was not the best job to have. We had no specific know-how and we didn't have the best copier. This was not our core business. We were in typewriters – office products – and, more recently, in computers. At the moment, we're producing copiers at a limited level, and most of these go into Italy where we have a strong dealer network. In the marketplace, Olivetti is not really perceived as having a decent product range. We have tended to follow with me-too products rather than come in with something highly innovative.

The reason we didn't do very well in copiers was also a result of the management focus at the time. In the mid-1980s, we had made a substantial investment in the M24, and we needed to understand the technology and the software, as well as whether or not we had to work with partners or could do it alone. We were also thinking about how to build up the sales channel to support this activity. The PC business was a big money generator per unit, for the organization and for the individual salesman.

In late 1986, Olivetti held a 5% share of the PPC market in Western Europe, with an 85% share in Italy, 10% in France, and 3.5% in Spain (Exhibit 7.3). Filippo Demonte, the head of Olivetti's Office Products business, commented:

The Office Products group is an industrial division handling calculators, cash registers, typewriters, printers, copiers and hard disk drives. Historically, Olivetti has held a strong position in many of these sectors, but it is becoming clear that the hard disk drive and copier operations will not be able to survive on their own. The market that Olivetti has access to is too small, and we can't finance the necessary R&D efforts to sustain these activities. In the copier division, in particular, the production volume doesn't justify the overhead required to produce these relatively high-tech products. Copiers are a key part of Olivetti's overall strategy; otherwise, we could continue simply on an OEM basis. We need to look for an opportunity to transform this liability into an asset.

	1984	1985	1986 (estimated)
Personal copiers	2,830	10,620	14,600
	2.8%	6.2%	7.0%
Category 1	16,880	16,920	16,220
(up to 19 cpm)	4.4%	4.4%	3.9%
Category 2	4,830	4,350	4,370
(20–39 cpm)	2.6%	2.3%	2.0%
Category 3	2,010	0	0
(40–59 cpm)	3.3%	0	0
Own production total	23,720	21,270	20,590
	3.7%	3.4%	3.0%
Grand total	26,550	31,890	35,190
	3.6%	4.0%	3.9%

Source: InfoSource S.A.

Exhibit 7.3   Olivetti brand: sales quantity and market share in Europe, 1984–1986

The copier operation in Agliè

In 1955, Olivetti had acquired the land and buildings of what had formerly been a large-scale textile operation in the small town of Agliè, near Olivetti's headquarters in Ivrea. Olivetti transformed this property into a factory to assemble typewriters initially, and, beginning in 1970, low-end copiers. Over the years, Olivetti had built up a network of local suppliers for fine mechanical parts (metal, plate and plastic) to facilitate its production of office machines in numerous factories located around Ivrea. These firms also supplied other Italian companies, like IBM and Honeywell-Bull.

From the beginning, the Agliè operation benefited from the existing supplier infrastructure. This operation was expected to become a key component for Olivetti in creating the 'automated office'. One of Olivetti's major strategic objectives was the integration of different technologies to develop the office-of-the-future. Mr Demonte elaborated recently:

> On its own, the copier is a self-standing machine; a huge black and white instant camera. The copier becomes interesting in the automated office – the application of information technology to the office – when there is not only a power cord connected to a wall outlet, but there is also a second cord connected to an office computer; in effect, when the copier becomes a computer peripheral. For the copier to be a true peripheral, it must be possible to cut in between the object page to be copied and to thus separate the image-generation function from the image-reproduction function. Digital technology makes this possible, for the most part. The digital copier is the building block for integrating the copier into the automated office. In principle, the digital copier is made from a scanner and a laser beam printer. Once you have this, it's not necessary to have the scanner unit and printer unit in the same electrophotographic box.
>
> At present, there is competition among several technologies to enable the copier to become a computer peripheral. A decade ago, everybody was using a thermal transfer approach, which required a special ribbon where the ink was melted by the printer heads.

Today, the ink-jet technology used in bubble jet printers is a much better approach, offering a standard of reproduction that was once thought impossible to achieve. Many companies, including Olivetti, are working to further develop ink-jet technology. Currently, Canon is using a lightweight printer head to spray ink through nozzles that are one-third the diameter of a human hair. The biggest obstacle to increasing the speed is finding a way to dry the ink fast enough. There is no solution yet, but many are working on it.

Olivetti's ink-jet area is expected to develop into a growing and profitable business over the next decade. Until this point, we've developed a technology that is similar to Hewlett-Packard's technology to make bubble jet printers, and we've gained a strong position with our dry-ink-jet non-impact printing calculator. Our bubble jet printers are very sophisticated electromechanical printers, and we're now the largest producer of printers in Europe. For Olivetti, this was a natural transition from the typewriter. We have a research lab of 70 people in Ivrea working on ink-jet physics, chemistry and application, and in addition, we have about 60 people in an R&D group in Yverdon, Switzerland, looking at how this technology could be implemented in new products.

Olivetti had put together a group of close to 70 engineers in Agliè who were involved in designing low-end copiers. These machines were fully developed by this group, and there was ongoing R&D concentrated on photoconductors and toners.

By late 1986, the Agliè operation was turning out about 20,000 units annually. However, several assembly line problems were occurring, and the source of these difficulties could often be traced back to external parts. The high reject rate was resulting in additional costs for Olivetti as well as its suppliers. Mr Demonte remarked:

> We're losing money in the copier business. But, closing up the operation entirely would certainly lead to additional expenses. We have a large infrastructure built up to support this business. We have a strong market position in Italy, and we can't just pull out of that. There would also be a question of what to do with the dealer channel and after-sales service organization. It isn't part of Olivetti's culture to just switch off something like this. Moreover, there are strong employment laws in Italy.
>
> We have tried several times to enter a partnership in the copier business. Sometimes, the companies we contacted wanted to buy our operation outright. At one point, we approached one of our Japanese OEM suppliers, but they didn't want to be in a joint venture with an industrial operation. We always asked for R&D, management and production to be put into such a venture, and the Japanese counter-proposal was always to have the management and R&D in the venture and then subcontract out the production to a Japanese company. They were concerned about the quality of the end product as well as the level of production know-how.

Exploring the possibilities for cooperation

In late 1986, Elserino Piol, Executive Vice President, Strategies and Development, travelled to Tokyo and approached senior Canon management with the idea of cooperating in some way in the copier business. Mr. Piol was intrigued by Canon's replaceable cartridge technology, which was introduced in 1982 in the world's first personal copiers, and he believed that great potential benefits for both parties could be derived if the two companies could work together. Mr Piol elaborated:

> I strongly felt that we could mutually benefit from this kind of cooperation. In our initial meetings, I found Canon's top management to be quite open and willing to talk about cooperating with a foreign company. Before going to Tokyo, I had also initiated discussions with another large copier manufacturer that was not Japanese but had a large European

Company name	Registered office	Activity sector	Curr.	Share capital as of Dec. 31, 1986	% own Group 1986	1985
Parent company						
Ing. C. Olivetti & C°., SpA	Ivrea	CO.	Lit	547,378,877,000		
Italian subsidiaries and their controlled companies						
Alitec, SpA	Marcianise	CO.	Lit	4,000,000,000	100.00	100.00
Alladium Image Products, SpA	Ivrea	I.T.	Lit	200,000,000	50.00	–
Baltea, SpA (ex Olivetti Accessori, SpA)	Ivrea	I.T.	Lit	70,000,000,000	100.00	100.00
Balteadisk	Arnad	I.T.	Lit	3,000,000,000	65.00	100.00
Diaspronsud, SpA	Pozzuoli	I.T.	Lit	2,000,000,000	100.00	100.00
F.lli Franchini, Srl	Sassuolo	I.T.	Lit	300,000,000	66.66	–
Ciesse Control System, Srl	Mestre	I.T.	Lit	50,000,000	80.00	–
Ciesse Italia, SpA°	Padova	I.T.	Lit	200,000,000	96.00	–
Ciesse Emilia, Srl	Bologna	I.T.	Lit	20,000,000	88.00	–
Ciesse Lombardia, Srl°	Milano	I.T.	Lit	50,000,000	70.00	–
Ciesse Roma, Srl°	Roma	I.T.	Lit	50,000,000	61.00	–
Ciesse Toscana, Srl°	Firenze	I.T.	Lit	50,000,000	75.00	–
Elea, SpA	Ivrea	E.S.	Lit	12,000,000,000	100.00	100.00
Eurofly Serivce, SpA	Toriono	E.S.	Lit	1,000,000,000	62.00	62.00
Hermes Italia, SpA	Roma	I.T.	Lit	5,000,000,000	100.00	51.00
Fotorex, SpA	Sesto S. Giovanni	I.T.	Lit	1,000,000,000	100.00	99.98
Immobiliare Ivrea An Giovanni, SpA	Ivrea	E.S.	Lit	18,500,000,000	100.00	100.00
Ivrea San Giovanni Leasing, SpA	Ivrea	E.S.	Lit	10,000,000,000	100.00	100.00
Indesit Elettronica, SpA	Teverola	I.T.	Lit	2,000,000,000	100.00	65.00
Lexikon, SpA	Ivrea	I.T.	Lit	200,000,000	100.00	–
Modinform, SpA	Marcianise	CO.	Lit	4,000,000,000	100.00	100.00
OCN.PPL. SpA (ex (EPP.PPL. SpA)	Marcianise	I.A.	Lit	12,000,000,000	100.00	100.00
Olivetti NC-Systeme GmbH	Frankfurt	I.A.	DM	2,000,000	100.00	100.00
OCN Sistemi, SpA	Ivrea	I.A.	Lit	2,000,000,000	100.00	100.00
Olinet, SpA	Ivrea	I.T.	Lit	1,000,000,000	100.00	–

Name	Location	Currency	Category	Capital	%	%
Olivetti Peripheral Equipment, SpA	Ivrea	Lit	I.T.	13,000,000,000	100.00	100.00
Olivetti Prodest, SpA	Ivrea	Lit	I.T.	2,000,000,000	80.00	–
Olivetti Synthesis, SpA	Ivrea	Lit	I.T.	8,000,000,000	100.00	100.00
Olivetti Value Services, SpA	Ivrea	Lit	E.S.	200,000,000	70.00	–
Olteco-Olivetti Telecommunicazioni, SpA	Ivrea	Lit	I.T.	8,000,000,000	100.00	100.00
Sixcom, SpA °°	Milano	Lit	S.E.	2,000,000,000	60.00	60.00
O.S.E. – Olivetti System Engineering, SpA	Ivrea	Lit	S.E.	300,000,000	51.00	51.00
Radiocor, Srl	Milano	Lit	E.S.	500,000,000	76.00	–
Servizi e Sisstemi Telematici, SpA	Milano	Lit	S.E.	240,000,000	100.00	100.00
Sistemi e Impianti Industriali, SpA	Ivrea	Lit	E.S.	200,000,000	100.00	100.00
SOAB – Sistemi per l'Automazione Bancaria, SpA (ex OCN, SpA)	Ivrea	Lit	I.T.	27,000,000,000	100.00	100.00
Software Sistemi, SpA	Bari	Lit	S.E.	3,000,000,000	100.00	100.00
PBS. SpA	Bari	Lit	S.E.	2,000,000,000	100.00	100.00
Syntax, SpA	Ivrea	Lit	S.E.	2,000,000,000	100.00	100.00
Tecnost, SpA	Ivrea	Lit	S.E.	30,000,000,000	69.22	100.00
Mael Computer, SpA °	Carsoli	Lit	I.T.	2,500,000,000	70.00	70.00
Mael, Srl °	Roma	Lit	I.T.	20,000,000	100.00	100.00
Mael Sistemi, SpA °°	Carsoli	Lit	I.T.	700,000,000	69.38	99.14
OSAI A-B, SpA °	Ivrea	Lit	I.A.	2,613,636,000	68.00	68.00
OSAI A-B GmbH	Wuppertal	DM	I.A.	750,000	100.00	100.00
OSAI A-B Ltd. °	Poole	£	I.A.	715,357	100.00	100.00
Tecnosafe, SpA °	Ivrea	Lit	S.E.	3,000,000,000	100.00	100.00
B.T.R. Elettronica, SpA °	Milano	Lit	S.E.	305,000,000	70.49	24.59
CIS. SpA °°	Ivrea	Lit	S.E.	370,000,000	50.18	–
LART, SpA °	Ivrea	Lit	S.E.	827,000,000	70.01	–
Tecnost Systemelektronic GmbH °	München	DM	I.A.	500,000	100.00	100.00
Tecnotime, SpA ° (ex Ages Italia, SpA)	Ivrea	Lit	I.T.	4,000,000,000	100.00	100.00
Dating Impianti, Srl°	Milano	Lit	S.E.	20,000,000	100.00	–
Dating SpA°	Milano	Lit	S.E	300,000,000	100.00	–
Tecnotour, SpA° . (ex Italcontrolli, SpA)	Zola Predosa	Lit	I.T.	600,000,000	71.00	51.00

Exhibit 7.4 Olivetti's consolidated subsidiaries (as of December 31, 1986) (Continued overleaf)

Company name	Registered office	Activity sector	Curr.	Share capital as of Dec. 31, 1986	% own Group 1986	% own Group 1985
Teknecomp, SpA	Ivrea	CO.	Lit	60,000,000,000	32.77	50.30
Circuiti Stampati Italia, SpA°	Venaria Reale	CO.	Lit	2,000,000,000	100.00	100.00
Di. W.S. Plastic, Srl°	Abbiategrasso	CO.	Lit	800,000,000	100.00	–
Eleprint, SpA°	Ivrea	CO.	Lit	7,600,000,000	100.00	100.00
Manifattura Valle dell'Orco, SpA°	Ivrea	CO.	Lit	2,500,000,000	100.00	100.00
Nord Elettronica, SpA°	Altare	CO.	Lit	900,000,000	100.00	100.00
Societa Generale Elastomeri – S.G.E., SpA	S. Olcese	I.T.	Lit	685,700,000	56.25	–
Tecsisnter, SpA°	Ivrea	CO.	Lit	2,500,000,000	100.00	100.00
Tekne Finanziaria, SpA	Ivrea	F.A.	Lit	6,000,000,000	100.00	100.00
Tesis, SpA	Milano	S.E.	Lit	450,000,000	51.11	51.11
Unit, SpA	Ivrea	S.E.	Lit	470,000,000	51.06	51.06

Foreign subsidiaries and their controlled companies

Company name	Registered office	Activity sector	Curr.	Share capital as of Dec. 31, 1986	% own Group 1986	% own Group 1985
Olivetti Management of America Inc.	Dover	E.S.	US$	1,000	100.00	100.00
Olivetti USA. Inc.	Irving	I.T.	US$	–	100.00	100.00
Bunker Ramo Corporation	Dover	I.T.	US$	100	100.00	–
OPE Printers Inc.	Tarrytown	I.T.	US$	10	100.00	100.00
Société Informatique pour l'Automation Bancaire S.A.B. S.A.	Paris	I.T.	F.Fr.	83,000,000	51.00	–
S.I.A.B. Italia, SpA	Ivrea	I.T.	Lit	220,000,000	100.00	–
TA Triumph-Adler AG	Nürnberg	I.T.	DM	80,500,000	98.40	–
Adler Business Machines Pty. Ltd.°	North Ryde	I.T	Aus.$	8,700,000	100.00	–
TA Triumph-Adler (N.Z.) Ltd.°	Wellington	I.T.	NZS	79,800	100.00	–
The Office Appliance Company Ltd.°	Wellington	I.T.	NZS	20,000	100.00	–
Adlerwerke vorm. Heinrich Kleyer AG°	Frankfurt	I.T.	DM	20,000,000	97.47	–
Imperial Typewriter Sales Pty. Ltd.	North Ryde	I.T.	Aus.$	24,000	100.00	–

	Location	Category	Currency	Amount	%	%
Kommanditgesellschaft TA Triumph-Adler Centrum für Bürokommunikation Hamburg GmbH & Co.°	Hamburg	I.T.	DM	2,000,000	80.00	–
TA Roytype (U.K.) Ltd.	London	I.T.	£	100	100.00	–
TA Triumph-Adler Centrum für Bürokommunikation Düsseldorf GmbH°	Ratingen	I.T.	DM	1,000,000	100.00	–
TA Triumph-Adler Centrum für GmbH° Bürokommunikation Frankfurt GmbH°	Frankfurt	I.T.	DM	600,000	100.00	–
TA Triumph-Adler Centrum für Bürokommunikation Hamburg GmbH°	Hamburg	I.T.	DM	50,000	80.00	–
TA Triumph-Adler Centrum für Bürokommunikation Nürnberg GmbH°	Nürnberg	I.T.	DM	600,000	100.00	–
TA Triumph-Adler Centrum für Bürokommunikation Stuttgart GmbH°	Stuttgart	I.T.	DM	500,000	100.00	–
TA Triumph-Adler Centrum für Bürokommunikation München GmbH°	München	I.T.	DM	100,000	100.00	–
Triumph-Adler Royal Inc.°	Mountainside	I.T.	US$	1,000	100.00	–
Triumph-Adler (U.K) Ltd.°	London	I.T.	£	2,270,712	100.00	–
Triumph-Adler France S.A.	Rueil-Malmaison	I.T.	F.Fr.	34,000,000	100.00	–
Triumph-Adler Wohnungsbaugesellschaft GmbH°	Nürnberg	I.T.	DM	35,000	95.00	–
Olivetti International S.A.	Luxembourg	F.A.	Ecu	500,000,000	100.00	100.00
Acorn Computer Group Plc.	Cambridge	I.T.	£	6,639,090	79.83	79.83
Acorn Computer Group Ltd.	Cambridge	I.T.	£	10,000	100.00	100.00
Acorn Computer (Far East) Ltd.°	Hong Kong	I.T.	HK$	100	100.00	100.00
Acorn Computer Corporation°	Woburn	I.T.	US$	1,000,000	100.00	100.00
Acorn Leasing Ltd.°	Cambridge	E.S.	£	100	100.00	100.00
Acorn Research Centre U.S.A. Inc.°	Palo Alto	E.S.		–	100.00	100.00
Acorn Soft Ltd.°	Cambridge	S.E.	£	100	100.00	100.00
Acorn Video Ltd.°°	Maidenhead	I.T.	£	100	100.00	100.00
Laserdrive Ltd.°	Santa Clara	S.E.	US$	3,946,000	54.72	–
Vector Marketing Ltd.°	Cambridge	S.E.	£	90	100.00	100.00

Exhibit 7.4   continued

Company name	Registered office	Activity sector	Curr.	Share capital as of Dec. 31, 1986	% own Group 1986	1985
Austro Olivetti GmbH	Wien	I.T.	Sch.	38,800,000	100.00	100.00
British Olivetti Ltd.	London	L.T.	£	12,000,000	100.00	100.00
Deutsche Olivetti GmbH	Frankfurt	I.T.	DM	50,100,000	100.00	100.00
Deutsche Underwood GmbH	Frankfurt	I.T.	DM	50,000	100.00	100.00
Gnosis GmbH	Seeheim	S.E.	DM	50,000	100.00	100.00
Mercedes Büromaschinen Werke GmbH	Frankfurt	E.S.	DM	150,000	100.00	100.00
Hermes Precisa S.A.	Salo Paulo	L.T.	Cruz.	31,362,000	100.00	100.00
Hispano Olivetti S.A.	Barcelona	I.T.	Pta	983,125,300	100.00	100.00
Olivetti Computers S.A.	Madrid	I.T.	Pta.	50,000,000	99.90	99.90
Syntax Iberica S.A.	Barcelona	S.E.	Pta	10,000,000	99.00	99.00
MicroAge Europe S.A.°°	Luxembourg	F.A.	Ecu	12,000,000	93.78	100.00
MicroAge (U.K.) Ltd.°	Salisbury	I.T.	£	1,500,100	100.00	–
MicroAge Europe, SpA°°	Ivrea	I.T.	Lit	200,000,000	100.00	–
MicroAge France S.A.°	Paris	I.T.	F.Fr.	1,000,000	100.00	100.00
Olivetti (Hong Kong) Ltd.	Hong Kong	I.T.	HK$	5,500,000	100.00	100.00
Olivetti (Malaysia) Sdn. Bhd.	Kuala Lumpur	I.T.	Ringgit	1,000,000	100.00	100.00
Olivetti (Singapore) Pte. Ltd.	Singapore	I.T.	S$	7,000,000	100.00	100.00
Olivetti (Suomi) O.Y.	Helsinki	I.T.	Fmk	3,600,000	100.00	100.00
Olivetti-Logabax	Paris	I.T.	F.Fr.	130,019,000	87.59	100.00
Assistance Maintenance et Technique Informatiques S.A.°	Aubervillers	E.S.	F.Fr.	250,000	100.00	100.00
Gestion et Techniques Informatiques S.S.°	Ecully	S.E.	F.Fr.	1,000,000	69.91	49.98
Imprimerie Ruf Sarl	Paris	I.T.	F.Fr.	150,000	100.00	100.00
O.L.I. S.A. Olivetti Lorraine Informatique°	Vandoeuvre	I.T.	F.Fr.	1,000,000	66.66	66.66
Olivetti Formation Conseil S.A.°	Saint-Ouen	E.S.	F.Fr.	250,000	85.00	85.00
Olivetti A/S	Kobenhavn	I.T.	Dkr.	79,400,000	100.00	100.00
Ambrasoft A/S	Holte	S.E.	Dkr.	5,100,000	66.67	66.67

Company	Location		Currency	Amount		
Olivetti Africa (Pty) Ltd.	Johannesburg	I.T.	Rand	2,100,000	100.00	100.00
Lole (Pty) Ltd.	Johannesburg	E.S.	Rand	3,600	100.00	100.00
Quintus (Pty) Ltd.	Johannesburg	E.S.	Rand	200	100.00	100.00
Underwood Africa (Pty) Ltd.	Johannesburg	E.S.	Rand	200	100.00	100.00
Olivetti Argentina S.A. C.e.I.	Buenos Aires	I.T.	Aus.	10,802	100.00	100.00
Olivetti Australia Pty. Ltd.	Sydney	I.T.	Aus.$	14,450,000	100.00	100.00
Olivetti Canada Ltd.	Markham	I.T.	CS	7,134,000	100.00	100.00
Olivetti China Ltd.	Hong Kong	I.T.	HKS	100,000	100.00	100.00
Olivetti Colombiana S.A.	Bogota	I.T.	C.Pes	15,000,000	100.00	–
Olivetti de Chile S.A.	Santiago	I.T.	Cil. Pes.	415,640,350	100.00	100.00
Olivetti de Venezuela C.A.	Caracas	I.T.	Bol.	5,000,000	100.00	100.00
Olivetti do Brasil S.A.	Sao Paulo	I.T.	Cruz.	311,400,000	100.00	100.00
Hileia S.A.	Manaus	CO.	Cruz.	6,571,000	60.00	60.00
Oliund Comercia e Representaçoes Ltda	Sao Paulo	E.S.	Cruz.	15,488,280	100.00	100.00
Olivetti Hellas A.E.	Athens	I.T.	Dr	86,200,000	100.00	100.00
Olivetti International (Service) S.A.	Lugano	E.S.	S.Fr.	50,000	100.00	100.00
Olivetti Investments N.V.	Curaçao	E.S.	US$	10,000	100.00	100.00
Olivetti Management S.A.	Lugano	E.S.	S.Fr.	50,000	100.00	100.00
Olivetti Mexicana, S.A.	Ciudad de Mexico	I.T.	M.Pes.	1,238,625,000	100.00	100.00
Olivetti New Properties N.V.	Curaçao	E.S.	US$	10,000	100.00	100.00
Olivetti Norge A/S	Oslo	I.T.	Nkr	25,610,000	100.00	100.00
Olivetti Pacific Distributors Ltd.	Hong Kong	I.T.	HK$	100,000	100.00	100.00
Olivetti Peruana S.A.	Lima	I.T.	Soles	9,002,612,000	100.00	100.00
Olivetti Portuguesa Sarl	Lisboa	I.T.	Esc.	19,000,000	100.00	100.00
Inforimport Lda	Lisboa	I.T.	Esc.	1,000,000	99.00	99.00
Olicom Lda	Lisboa	I.T.	Esc.	1,000,000	99.00	99.00
Olivetti Properties of Japan	Tokyo	E.S.	Yen	100,000,000	100.00	100.00
Olivetti Research Ltd.	Cambridge	I.T.	£	100,000	100.00	100.00
Olivetti Uruguaya S.A.	Montevideo	I.T.	U.Pes	103,362,500	100.00	–
Rapida S.A.	Barcelona	E.S.	Pta	154,560,000	73.45	73.45
Risk Management S.A. (ex Risk Insurance Corp. S.A.)	Panama	E.S.	US$	100,000	100.00	100.00

Exhibit 7.4 *continued*

Company name	Registered office	Activity sector	Curr.	Share capital as of Dec. 31, 1986	% own Group 1986	% own Group 1985
Olivetti Realty N.V.	Curaçao	F.A.	US$	50,000	100.00	100.00
Olivetti Nederland B.V.	Ed Leiden	I.T.	Fl	10,278,000	100.00	100.00
Demaret B.V.	Den Haag	F.A.	Fl	10,000	100.00	100.00
Het Handelswapen B.V.	Ed Leiden	F.A.	Fl	100,000	100.00	100.00
Olivetti Supplies, Inc.	Middletown	I.T.	US$	1,000	100.00	100.00
Olivetti Holding B.V.	Amsterdam	F.A.	Fl	30,401,000	100.00	100.00
Decision Data Computer S.A.	Bagnolet	I.T.	F.Fr.	2,500,000	51.00	–
Decision Data Computer (Belgium) S.A./NV	Bruxelles	I.T.	B.Fr.	1,250,000	51.00	–
Decision Data Computer (G.B.) Ltd.	London	I.T.	£	8,700	51.15	–
Decision Data Computer GmbH	Düsseldorf	I.T.	DM	750,000	51.00	–
Hermes Precisa International S.A.	Yverdon-les-Bains	I.T.	S.Fr.	46,000,000	47.17	47.17
Cyber°	Yverdon-les-Bains	I.T.	S.Fr.	50,000	100.00	100.00
Hermes AG°	Zürich	I.T.	Sfr.	3,000,000	100.00	100.00
Japy Hermes Precisa Francs S.A.°	Paris	I.T.	F.Fr.	26,518,800	100.00	100.00
Olivetti-Hermes (Svizzera) S.A.°	Zürich	I.T.	S.Fr.	8,000,000	100.00	100.00
Hermes Vendita – S.A.°	Zürich	I.T.	S.Fr.	50,000	100.00	100.00
Inco Service S.A.°	Zürich	E.S.	S.Fr.	50,000	96.00	–
Olivetti Vendita – S.A.°	Zürich	I.T.	S.Fr.	50,000	100.00	100.00
Paillard S.A.°	Yverdon-les-Bains	I.T.	S.Fr.	50,000	100.00	100.00
Precisa S.A.°	Yverdon-les-Bains	I.T.	S.Fr.	500,000	100.00	100.00
SAMECA – Société Africaine de Mécanographie S.A.°	Alger	I.T.	Dinar	1,300,000	100.00	100.00
Olivetti A/B	Upplands Vasby	I.T.	S.Kr.	10,000,000	100.00	100.00
Olivetti Advanced Technology Center Inc.	Cupertino	I.T.	US$	1,000	100.00	100.00
Olivetti Corporation of Japan	Tokyo	I.T.	Yen	2,437,500,000	80.00	80.00
Olivetti de Puerto Rico, Inc.	San Juan	I.T.	US$	1,000	100.00	100.00
Olivetti S.A. Belge	Bruxelles	I.T.	B.Fr.	50,000,000	100.00	100.00
Olimark S.A.	Bruxelles	I.T.	B.Fr.	20,003,000	51.00	51.00

Notes: The activity sectors are as follows:

I.T.   Information technology (data processing, office automation, office products)
S.E.   Software & Engineering
CO.   Componenets
IA.   Industrial automation and tooling
F.A.   Financial activity
E.S.   Education and support; other.

°   Ownership percentage refers to that held by the subsidiary to which these companies belong.
°°   Shareholding owned by several companies; ownership percentage refers to Group share.
*   The close of financial year of all subsidiaries in December 31, with the exception of: MicroAge. Inc. (September 30), Transaction Management, Inc. (T.M.I.) September 30, Sphinx Ltd. (July 31), TABS Ltd. (March 31), Butel Technology Ltd. (September 30), Start Computer Center GmbH (January 31), MicroAge U.K. (March 31).
**   Companies for which the Group's share determined on the basis of voting rights is different from that calculated on the basis of equity.

Source: The Olivetti Group, 1986 Consolidated Financial Statements.

Exhibit 7.4   *Olivetti's consolidated subsidiaries (as of December 31, 1986)*

presence. Olivetti needs a partner to share R&D with, one whom we could acquire technology from and would give us access to an additional market in the copier business.

Olivetti was one of the first firms with a strategy to acquire technology not strictly by in-house development but also through joint ventures, alliances, venture capital companies, and so on. At present, we have close to 200 joint ventures in operation (Exhibit 7.4). Olivetti has a lot of experience with this kind of arrangement.

In 1986, Canon was the dominant player in Europe, placing an average of 17,000 units each month, which represented a 22.7% share of the European copier market. For years, Canon had used an OEM strategy in Europe, while all other sales were handled by its Amsterdam-based regional headquarters, Canon Europe. This arrangement had enabled Canon to concentrate on cementing its position in the highly competitive domestic market. Over time, the larger of Canon's European sales subsidiaries that were subsequently put in place began to operate more independently. As of late 1986, Canon had only a small position in southern Europe and believed that it would be expensive and time-consuming to develop its own distribution channels there.

Filippo Demonte, who as head of the Office Products Group was directly responsible for Olivetti's copier business, remarked:

> For whatever arrangement we might enter into, it is important that Olivetti be the majority shareholder. Any venture has to be 100% under Olivetti management so that we can guarantee to the government and to the company that we would not be selling Italian technology to a foreign company. In these things, it is important not only to show but also to *be*. Moreover, succeeding in Italy is more likely if you are a successful Italian company than if you are a successful foreign company; the same principle that exists everywhere. It is important to the policy makers, the opinion makers, the unions and other national bodies. Having majority ownership would also ensure that we could participate in Italian government, inter-government programmes, and Europe-wide programmes.

Mr Piol believed that much could be learned from being in a partnership with a company like Canon, particularly with regard to production process, supplier relationships and basic copier technology. He explained:

> If we were to put together some kind of joint venture with Canon – and I'm not sure just what that would look like in terms of ownership, structure, and the kind of assets and staff each partner would put into it – there could be some significant benefits on both sides.
>
> This could be an opportunity for Canon to strengthen its presence in Europe, and we could learn about Japanese techniques. The Japanese have more exacting goals for quality and better control over development time. Right now, we're working with an inventory level of 45 days, and in Canon, it's five. We've used value engineering techniques many times in the past to improve this level, but not with the same success as the Japanese. They apply these techniques in a strict and methodical way, with a determination not to stop until good results – results which may seem impossible to obtain – are achieved. On the other side, it's hard to know how strongly Canon would ask us to adopt the Japanese way.
>
> In the early stages of such a venture, I imagine that we would manufacture an Olivetti machine, which would be received by the Canon and Olivetti sales organizations, as well as their dealers in Europe. Over time, we would license the basic technology from Canon Japan and refine it for European needs. Perhaps we would also buy the photographic drums and mirror mechanisms from Canon factories in Japan and/or France, and Canon would presumably make a profit on these sales. One of the essential negotiating issues would be to determine the kind of R&D that would be done in Agliè and its scale, as well as whether we could eventually compete with other Canon design centres.

Mr Demonte added:

It would be interesting to have Canon as a partner because then we would have a parent that is both a shareholder and a customer. When we're speaking with the shareholder, we'll be talking about profit and loss, net equity, and so on. When we're speaking with the customer, we'll be talking about the level of logistical and quality improvement. As well, we'll be trying to anticipate what the customer wants, which should help us with the product design specifications and in the production level we attain.

On the one hand, we would be an Olivetti company. On the other side, we would become part of Canon's copier machine division and part of the Canon family of copiers. One of the inherent challenges with any venture where two partners are involved is to manage the identity question. There will always be some people on both sides who will have difficulty making the distinction. Big companies are not made in such a way as to understand that they don't own a whole organization.

Case 7.2 Canon

This case was prepared by Research Associate Joyce Miller, under the supervision of Professors George Taucher and Dominique Turpin, as a basis for class discussion rather than to illustrate either effective or ineffective handling of a business situation.

We are grateful for the assistance of Professor Gene Gregory in the preparation of this case study.

From its humble beginnings in a small workshop in Tokyo's Roppongi district, Canon Inc. had become, by 1986, one of the world's leading manufacturers of cameras, business machines, and precision optical equipment. In the following year, Canon would celebrate its 50th anniversary, and President Ryuzaburo Kaku planned to use the occasion both to review the company's past achievements and carefully plan for the future. Mr Kaku's aim was to make Canon into a premier global corporation:

> Well before the yen entered the steepest arc of its upward curve, Canon had seen the necessity of moving manufacturing into its markets, of putting production close to the place of consumption. The new phase of 'internationalization' was initially prompted by the trade imbalance (and trade friction) between Japan and the chief countries where Canon sells . . . Canon has advanced quite briskly towards becoming truly global – and the intention is to take the global process further by establishing R&D centres in its markets as its national companies develop into free-standing businesses within the global corporation.
>
> The imperatives of global rationalization – especially in copier operations – require Canon ownership and finely-tuned management of R&D, production and marketing. As with all strategic alliances, the fine line between compelling necessity and expediency is not always readily apparent.

In the mid-1980s, Olivetti, a long-time player in the office equipment market with particular strength in Italy, was looking for a way to bolster its presence in the European copier market. Canon, at the time, was eager to expand its market share in Italy and to strengthen its European manufacturing base.

Canon Inc.

A young company by Japanese standards, Canon traced its history back to November 1933 when a small group of camera enthusiasts led by Mr Goro Yoshida founded Precision Optical Research Instruments Laboratory in Roppongi, then a suburb of Tokyo, to conduct research into quality compact cameras. Two years later, the Hansa Canon, Japan's first 35 mm focal plane shutter camera, remarkably resembling the German-made Leica, was introduced in Tokyo. In 1937, Precision Optical Industry Co., Ltd was established to manufacture the Hansa Canon, with Mr. Saburo Uchida as its first Executive Managing Director. When Mr. Uchida was drafted for service in the army in the late 1930s, Dr. Takeshi Mitarai, a practising physician who had invested in the new company and become its auditor, took over the company's management and became its president in September 1942.

During the war, Precision Optical was forced to abandon 35 mm camera production to become a supplier to the Japanese military. In this capacity, the company developed an indirect X-ray camera for mass-screening to detect tuberculosis infection. In 1944, the company diversified into binocular production with the acquisition of Yamato Kogaku Seisakusho. After rapid reconversion to camera production, with the war's end, the company changed its name to Canon Camera Co., Ltd in 1947. Over the next two decades, the company grew into the world's leading camera manufacturer.

Canon's international operations began modestly in 1951 with the appointment of Hong Kong-based Jardine Matheson as its sole worldwide agent. Responding to the growing US market for quality cameras, Canon established its first overseas branch office in New York in 1955, and two years later formed Canon Europa in Geneva as an exclusive distributor in Europe.

Vertical integration and product diversification

Early in the decade, Canon began the dual processes of vertical integration and product diversification that accounted for much of its strength in the domestic and world markets. Subsidiaries were established to produce micromotors and metal parts, and a supplier of precision components was acquired. Then, in 1956, the first major expansion of the product line was made with the addition of personal cine-cameras.

An overly ambitious diversification strategy led to Canon's first and, thus far, only major product failure. Introduced in 1958, the Synchroreader, designed to record voice messages on paper for educational use, proved to be technologically far ahead of its time. Within a year of its introduction, the product had to be withdrawn from the market, leaving the company with a division staffed with electronic engineers who could not be dismissed simply because management had made a serious strategic error in product planning and marketing.

Determined to transform adversity into advantage, Canon harnessed the skills of these people to make a major move into business machines with microfilm equipment for banking use in 1959 and, in a major new departure, with the development of the Canola 130 electronic calculator introduced to the market in May 1964. Success in the calculator market set the stage for venturing into the copier market in 1968, with a 'New Process' plain paper system that challenged and eventually broke the tight hold of Xerox.

Competitive pressures intensify

In 1974, Canon found itself in serious trouble. Malfunctioning calculators, with faulty light emitting diode displays, had to be recalled in large numbers, a mishap that could not have come at a more inauspicious time. Ferocious competition, led by Casio and Sharp, had driven prices to the ground, forcing many calculator makers to withdraw from the market. Those that remained were operating at the margin, with little or no profit. At the same time, the growth of camera sales slowed as markets became increasingly saturated. Exports of camera and other products decreased under the pressure of a higher yen, and production costs were rising as a result of higher petroleum prices. In the first half of 1975, Canon was forced to suspend dividends for the first time in its history, an experience still regarded in the company with some horror almost 20 years later. The combination of forces battering the company exposed the company's structural and managerial weaknesses. Ryuzaburo Kaku, then in charge of Finance, recalled:

> Canon's technical strength – demonstrated in a stream of pioneering that began with Japan's first 35 mm precision cameras – had not been backed by a coherent management strategy. Marketing was weak. Competitors were copying [our] products before [we] could fully exploit [our] sales potential. Canon was like a ship that constantly changed course and got nowhere . . . Components were being manufactured in too many scattered locations . . . As in many old Japanese companies, our people were so afraid of making mistakes that they did nothing. We've had to teach them not to fear being creative – or even failing.

Introduction of the premier company plan

Mr Takeo Maeda, the new president who had assumed office just before the gale of misfortune swept over the company, responded with a 6-year premier company plan. Launched in 1976, the plan called for a restructuring and internationalization of the company, and the introduction of new efficient production systems, to avoid the pressures of yen appreciation, protectionism and energy shortages in the future. The objectives of the plan were clear and ambitious. Canon was to become a leading corporation in Japan within three years, and a world leader in the subsequent three years. The new plan began by reducing operations, curtailing costs and undertaking efforts to strengthen camera, calculator and copier sales. An operating profit rate of 15%, with no debt, became the principal tenets of financial management. Sales were targeted to increase 15% annually – considered to be a reasonable growth rate – with the goal of substantially increasing market share in all product lines. All this was to be achieved through more rapid and higher quality product development, improved production, and total marketing management.

A new matrix organization linked the three major product divisions – camera, business machines and optical products – with functional committees for new product development, production and marketing. The Canon Development System (CDS) was established to improve the efficiency of R&D, shortening the time to market for new products. The task of the Canon Production System (CPS) was to resolve quality problems, eliminate waste, and activate employees within the new rationalized organizational structure. The objective of the Canon Marketing System (CMS) was to relate the company's products and services to customer satisfaction in all of Canon's worldwide markets. Pushing responsibility down the line, the three product divisions were to operate as autonomous vertical profit centres. Division chiefs were appointed and delegated the authority to act fairly independently.

The new plan was only just put into action when Mr Maeda suddenly passed away. Mr Kaku, who as Managing Director had been largely responsible for shaping the new direction of the company, was elevated to the presidency and charged with the task of completing the reforms underway.

The Canon way

From the outset, Canon had been endowed with a strong corporate sense of purpose. Self-motivation, self-awareness and self-management were the three pillars on which the company had been created. Mr Kaku continued to give these philosophical principles primary importance, adapting and embellishing the company purposes for the task ahead (Exhibit 7.5). In his words:

[When I took over, Canon was] 'sluggish' and 'full of bureaucratic attitudes' which drained the organisation of its ability to respond to changes in the operating environment . . . .

[My basic philosophy was] to build a company which further upholds human rights and dignity, while striving to develop better technology and products through innovation.

Our corporate philosophy
• To be a global corporation providing
kyosei 'living and working together for the common good'
in all countries where we operate

Our mission	*Our objectives*	*Our business development goals*	*Our values*
• To make a positive contribution through continued growth and reinvestment in the world's communities	• To be a responsible global citizen • To have unique and quality products • To build an ideal company for continuing prosperity	• To combine our traditional hardware strength with software systems development • To create information systems and networks which integrate hardware, software and services • To operate on a global scale	• Respect cultural differences • Encourage self-motivation, self-awareness and self-management • Respect dignity, value initiative and recognize merit • Work together in harmony • Sustain our physical and emotional health

Exhibit 7.5 *The Canon way*

A decade later, in 1985, Canon was well on the way to becoming a premier company by world standards. Significant increases in investment and R&D had resulted in a spate of new products, many of them 'firsts' in the marketplace. Canon's product line ranged from 35 mm and video cameras to copiers, electronic typewriters, laser printers, facsimile machines, and microlithographic equipment for producing semiconductors and medical equipment. At this time, Canon's manufacturing and marketing organisation spanned over 100 countries and employed 34,100 people (Exhibit 7.6). In 1985, profits rose to ¥37 billion on net sales of close to ¥956 billion. Business machines accounted for 71% of sales, with cameras and optical equipment generating 21% and 8%, respectively.

The response to *endaka*

But new problems were on the horizon. Unlike most other Japanese companies, Canon relied heavily on overseas markets for the bulk of its business, with North America and Europe each accounting for 30% of sales. Although the process of globalizing manufacturing was well underway, a high percentage of overseas sales were still generated by exports, making Canon particularly vulnerable to *endaka* (yen appreciation), which followed the Plaza Accords in 1986.[1]

Canon's response to the rising yen was guided by past experience. R&D expenditures were increased, cost reduction efforts were broadened and intensified, and capital outlays for overseas production facilities were boosted. After posting record profits for the previous ten years, Canon's income dropped 70% in 1986 to ¥10.7 million, threatening a cut in dividends. Shinji Tatewaki, who had just returned to Canon's copier division in Tokyo after heading up the company's Chicago sales office for several years, recalled:

> The US government devalued the dollar and, within the space of virtually a day, the yen was worth significantly more against other currencies. In 1984, the yen was strong at ¥251 to one US dollar. Then the level dropped down to ¥150. Production costs increased dramatically, and there was no way that we could recover the loss. We had to reconstruct our entire operations. We launched a large-scale cost reduction activity and a campaign to avoid waste. In Canon Tokyo, people soon began pinning '¥150 badges' on their shirts. We were all focused on what we had to do to live in a ¥150 world.

Because of the strength of the yen, Canon products made in Japan had become more expensive overseas. Further expansion of overseas production was essential. In addition, as a *Forbes* reporter commented:[2]

> Canon's strongest defence against a rising yen is innovation. With innovative products, price is less important than in commodity-type products . . . .
> This means heavy spending on research and development, of course. Canon's R&D amounts to some 11% of parent company sales, one of the highest ratios among Japanese companies outside the chemical and pharmaceutical industries.

Given the increasing trade friction in the US and European markets, Canon had further cause to reposition itself to maintain future growth. Three-quarters of the

---

[1] In 1985, the lowest rate was US$1 = ¥263.65; the highest rate was US$1 = ¥199.80. In 1986, the lowest rate was US$1 = ¥203.30; the highest rate was US$1 = ¥152.55 in Tokyo.
[2] From Fuji to Everest, *Forbes*, May 2, 1988.

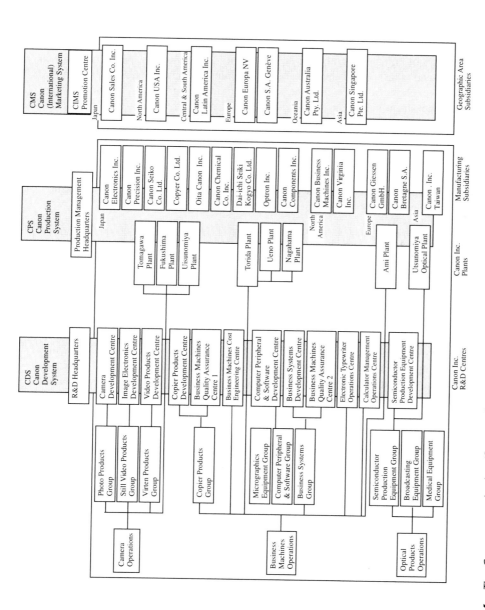

Exhibit 7.6 *The Canon organization (Source: Canon Handbook)*

company's sales were in office equipment, including both standalone machines, such as copiers, and the systems that would combine them in the 'office-of-the-future'. It was in this sector that globalization became increasingly imperative.

Canon's copier business

Canon first entered the copier market in 1965 with a coated paper copier, based on technology licensed from RCA. Realizing the limitations of this technology, Canon formed a team of engineers led by Dr Keizo Yamaji, to develop a copier drum with an insulating layer that would be suitable for plain paper copying using a more photosensitive chemical than the one then used in xerography. This new design prolonged the drum's life and reduced the risk of discharging toxic chemicals. Introduced in Japan in April 1968, Canon's 'New Process' (NP) plain paper copying system was completely free of Xerox patents. Hiroshi Tanaka, who was part of this effort, commented:[3]

> Engineers working on the plain paper copying project thoroughly investigated the patents held by Xerox. In the process, we learned how not to violate patents and how to obtain patents to protect our own technology. The NP technology was completely free of Xerox's airtight patent network.

In 1972, the company launched a second generation 'liquid dry' NP system, which used plain paper and liquid toner and turned out dry copies. This new technology reduced machine breakdowns by eliminating the complex heat-fusing mechanism and simplifying the developing and cleaning process. These machines had lower production costs, were more compact and more reliable than anything available at the time, and they matched Xerox on copy quality. Canon subsequently licensed out this technology to 20 manufacturers in Japan and three in the United States.

NP copiers were manufactured at the Toride factory on the outskirts of Tokyo, which had been set up a decade earlier to make synchroreaders and later, cameras. Toride used a flexible manufacturing system that could accommodate differences in models and electrical specifications. The four assembly lines could handle any NP model after a 2-day changeover. Each line had the capacity to turn out between 3000 and 8000 units monthly. About 2000 parts were required to produce the range of NP copiers.

Initially, copiers were sold in Japan through Canon Business Machines Sales Inc., set up in 1968 to market calculators. In 1971, this subsidiary was merged with Canon Camera Sales Inc. to form Canon Sales Inc., whose shares were listed on the first Tokyo Stock Exchange a decade later. Beginning with 200 people dedicated to the sale and service of copiers, the new company sold Canon copiers outright and offered customers a Total Guarantee System.

In the early 1970s, Canon established a dealer network throughout Japan. Dealers received extensive training and, within a few years, had completely taken over the task of servicing copiers. Canon did not begin selling its NP systems in the US until 1972, when a dealer sales network was established. However, these copiers were being distributed in Europe through Canon's marketing unit in the Netherlands as early as 1972, although sales were modest.

---

[3] Harvard Business School case study, *Canon Inc., World-wide Copier Strategy*, 1983, page 2.

The personal copier breakthrough

Canon's copier strategy was formed largely by its camera strategy. 'A camera for everyone' was translated into 'a copier for everyone'.

Canon's copier line initially was aimed at small and medium-scale users, a market that had been largely ignored by Xerox, the Xerox strategy focused on large users in government, business, and universities. Following Canon's strategy, Dr Keizo Yamaji, who had become the General Manager of Canon's Reprographic Products Division, wanted to open up an entirely new market for the PPC. Dr Yamaji had market data showing that there were over 4 million offices in Japan with fewer than five employees that were not being addressed by the conventional copier business. The lowest-priced unit available was ¥500,000, about US$2300, which was too expensive for a small business. As well, professional service engineers needed to come in regularly to maintain these machines. Again, this cost limited their use to larger offices. The 'dream' was to come up with a compact, maintenance-free copier that would cost about $1000 and could be sold to small offices, for home use, or as a personal desk-side copier. This idea was totally different from the Xerox system which, until this point, had dominated the world copier business.

Introduced in late 1982, Canon's personal copier (PC) represented a revolution in reprographic technology. The PC used a replaceable cartridge that eliminated the need to maintain the machine regularly. After making 2000 copies, the user simply replaced the cartridge, which contained a photoreceptive drum, toner assembly, cleaner, and charging device. Cartridges were available with four toner colours.

In time, copier manufacturers around the world began purchasing Canon's personal copier on an OEM basis. For example, Olivetti began importing Canon personal copiers in late 1984. Increasingly, large firms operating internationally were completing their product line by buying certain models from other producers.

Canon in Europe

In 1957, Canon Europa was established in Geneva as Canon's sole distributor for Europe. Over the following decade, a network of national distributors was developed to market, distribute and service Canon cameras and calculators. To better manage the increasing volume of European business, especially in EC countries, the European headquarters functions were transferred to Canon Amsterdam NV in 1968, leaving Canon Geneva as a finance company.

With the introduction of the Premier Company Plan and the Canon Marketing System, the first task was to reorganize the complex system of multiple national distributorships that had evolved over the first two post-war decades. Given the rapid diversification of product lines and the increasing importance of global rationalization of marketing, total control over the marketing and distribution system became imperative to respond to customer needs. In 1975, Canon gradually began the process of replacing distributors with integrated Canon marketing subsidiaries in each country. Over the following years, Canon Europa NV was established, with 19 subsidiaries, including Canon Amsterdam NV, to manage the intricate European organization. A senior manager in Canon described the process:

> In some countries, we had to start from scratch; in others, we already had relationships with distributors. In France, for instance, Canon's camera importer wanted to get into the copier

business, and we quickly had the 200 people in this organization selling copiers directly. In the UK, we were using Marubeni, a *sogo shosha* or general trading house, which then sold products through several companies. This arrangement lasted only 2–3 years. Then we had to build something up ourselves. We put cameras and copiers together and distributed through dealers. In Germany, Canon's camera distributor was not so interested in selling copiers. Eventually, we were able to put together an arrangement, but it was strictly a sales and marketing venture. In Italy, our camera importer was also not interested in copiers. Cash recovery was a real problem. For copiers, Canon couldn't expect to get payment for up to ten months after the sale. In the camera business, payment was available within 30 days. We had a good business in Italy with calculators, but it was clear that we needed more sophisticated salespeople to market copiers.

In many cases, Canon ended up buying out the distributors because of their limited financial strength and cashflow problems. This put a major strain on Canon's own financial resources.

Over the next several years, Canon's marketing capabilities in Europe grew substantially. Over time, the various national subsidiaries that were established began to operate more independently and purchase products directly from Japan.

Canon begins producing copiers in Europe

In 1972, Canon acquired the assets of ECE GmbH, a small German R&D house specializing in advanced electrostatic technology in Giessen, near Frankfurt. ECE had contributed significantly to perfecting Canon's 'liquid dry' copy technology, and Canon had been helping the firm financially since 1969. By mid-1973, the ECE facility had been converted into a factory with the capacity to turn out 1500 low-volume PPCs monthly, to be sold throughout Europe as well as in some Middle East and African markets.[4]

ECE's original management team had remained in place after the acquisition, and Canon Giessen was staffed almost entirely by Germans. Tsukasa Kuge, one of the few dispatched from Tokyo, arrived in 1973 and remained in the operation until 1975, returning for an additional five months in 1977. Mr Kuge recalled:

By acquiring a well-organized high technology company with considerable experience and know-how in copier development, we were able to start up a new production unit rather quickly. Much of the time usually spent on the details of technology and transferring know-how was saved, which reduced the drain on managerial and technical resources in Tokyo. After a time, R&D activity was to be dedicated entirely to the development of Canon's product, and the R&D activities both in Giessen and in Tokyo had to be performed in conformity with each other, so I was sent over.

In the early 1970s, the copier market was not so segmented as it is today. We began making what we felt would sell the best, and we planned to move up in quality. In the beginning, more than 30 people were doing research and development, and they were creating many ideas that were also implemented back in Japan. Over time, Giessen's R&D capability was made smaller as production became more important.

---

[4] InfoSource's classification scheme was generally used as a way to segment the market, as follows: Category 1 – less than 20 copies per minute (cpm); Category 2 – 20–39 cpm; Category 3 – 40–59 cpm; Category 4 – 60–89 cpm; Category 5 – 90 + cpm. The Personal Copier category was subsequently added for copiers generating less than 10 cpm.

After two years in operation, a team of 130 people were manufacturing 500 NP machines (20 cpm) each month under a rigid quality control programme. Production was slated to increase at a level of 20–35% annually. Giessen's assembly process was similar to Toride's, but on a much smaller scale. In 1975, the production capacity at Giessen was doubled, and new lines were added to produce copier drums and toner.

A second plant in Europe

In August 1983, Canon responded to an invitation from the French government to establish a personal copier factory in Liffre, in Bretagne. At this time, Canon was also looking at the feasibility of establishing a PPC assembly plant in Virginia, USA.

By the end of 1984, the Liffre plant was turning out about 3000 copiers per month, and lines were subsequently added to produce electronic typewriters and facsimile transceivers.

Canon's European presence in 1986

By 1986, Canon had become a leading player in the European market, placing more than 200,000 units out of an estimated total market of 897,780 (Exhibit 7.7). Canon's aim was to become the world's leading PPC manufacturer. To achieve this, the company's goal was to obtain at least a 30% unit share in the three major copier markets: Japan, Europe, and the US (Exhibits 7.8 and 7.9).

Canon offered the full range of copiers, from its innovative personal copier to its NP-8000 series (up to 70 cpm), which competed head-on with Xerox and Kodak machines. In the near future, Canon planned to introduce a digital colour copier that many believed would not only transform the office environment, but also

	1984	1985	1986 (estimated)
Personal copiers	82,640	111,350	110,050
	81.7%	65.2%	52.8%
Category 1	57,880	49,110	54,020
(up to 19 cpm)	15.0%	12.6%	13.0%
Category 2	30,370	28,500	31,410
(20–39 cpm)	16.2%	15.2%	14.6%
Category 3	11,960	10,050	7,330
(40–59 cpm)	19.9%	19.1%	14.2%
Category 4	0	0	640
(60–89 cpm)	0	0	· 8.5%
Total	182,850	199,010	203,450
	24.7%	24.7%	22.7%

Source: InfoSource S.A.

Exhibit 7.7 *Canon brand: sales quantity and market share in Europe, 1984–1986*

Company	1985	1986
Canon	125	138
Fuji Xerox	97	111
Konishiroku	35	35
Matsushita	6	7
Minolta	34	33
Mita	28	27
Ricoh	168	162
Sharp	33	38
Toshiba	32	36
Total	558	587

Source: Dataquest Incorporated

Exhibit 7.8   *Estimated PPC placements in Japan, 1985 and 1986, by brand (thousands of units)*

revolutionize the whole industry. It was rumoured that newly-emerging domestic competitors were also developing colour copiers based on a different product concept.

Currently, Canon had sales subsidiaries in virtually every European country (Exhibit 7.10), as well as independent business machine distributors that dealt with a network of retailers. Many of Canon's European distributors sold only Canon products. In the camera business, they relied mostly on the retailers. In calculators, they used another channel. Business equipment needed more support, and it was becoming apparent that more sales channels were needed to sell copiers. At the same time, Canon's machines were becoming more expensive because of the 15.8% duty that the European Commission had placed on most copiers imported from Japan. This temporary rate was set in 1986, but there was an expectation that the rate would be officially set at 20% in 1987.

In the low end, Canon was also finding that its copiers were not competitive enough. Other Japanese copier manufacturers were very price conscious. Moreover, customers were getting more sophisticated. In the past, they would accept lower copy quality but, increasingly, they wanted superior reproduction, easy-to-use machines with low maintenance requirements, and customers were becoming more concerned about environmental factors. Canon needed to get a new product in this category, or new technology.

Canon's Giessen facility was one of the largest and most integrated copier plants in Europe, employing 400 people and turning out 4000 PPCs each month. Giessen manufactured NP systems in Category 2 and Category 3, together with components like photosensitive drums, the heart of the plain paper copier. About 80 suppliers were contracted locally to provide services and parts, including moulded casings, lids, platen glass, print boards, paper supply cassettes, fixing rollers, solenoids, DC controllers, halogen lamps and low voltage electric sources. Likewise, Canon's Bretagne operation employed about 430 people and used numerous local suppliers. Little R&D was being carried out in either of these operations, aside from modifying designs sent from Tokyo to meet local manufacturing and local market needs. In principle, the R&D laboratories

	Personal copiers	Segment 1	Segment 2	Segment 3	Segment 4	Segment 5	Segment 6	Total
Adler-Royal	–	16.0	3.2	–	0.4	–	–	19.6
Canon	165.0	52.0	48.3	4.5	13.5	1.4	–	284.7
A.B. Dick	–	3.2	0.8	0.5	0.3	–	–	4.8
Gestetner	–	8.1	2.5	0.3	0.4	–	–	11.3
Harris/3M	–	34.0	13.5	5.2	–	–	–	52.7
Kodak	–	–	–	–	7.2	3.4	1.1	11.7
Konica	–	26.0	7.5	4.1	5.0	0.1	–	42.7
Minolta	5.4	26.1	25.8	1.7	0.6	–	–	59.6
Mita	–	53.0	20.4	–	4.5	–	–	77.9
Monroe	–	11.5	5.0	–	0.6	–	–	17.1
Océ	–	–	–	–	2.6	–	–	2.6
Panasonic	–	19.2	12.1	0.8	–	–	–	32.1
Pitney Bowes	–	7.4	11.8	1.8	2.0	–	–	23.0
Ricoh	5.0	26.0	7.9	3.6	4.0	–	–	46.5
Sanyo	3.6	3.1	–	0.9	–	–	–	7.6
Savin	–	17.6	2.0	12.1	5.4	–	–	37.1
Sharp	28.0	64.3	8.2	10.1	10.0	–	–	120.6
Toshiba	–	43.2	13.0	7.0	–	–	–	63.2
Xerox	–	59.0	18.0	26.3	9.1	0.8	9.2	122.4
Others	7.0	4.9	2.4	–	–	0.6	–	14.9
TOTALS	214.0	474.6	202.4	78.9	68.4	12.5	10.3	1,061.1

This segmentation is based on the following criteria:

Segment	Speed (copies per minute)	Typical monthly volume range
PC	under 20	N/A
1	0–20	0–10,000
2	21–30	5,000–20,000
3	31–45	5,000–30,000
4	40–75	10,000–75,000
5	70–90	25,000–125,000
6	91+	100,000+

Source: Dataquest Incorporated.

Exhibit 7.9 *Estimated PPC placements in the US, 1986, by brand (thousands of units)*

that Canon set up abroad were linked with R&D in Japan and part of the global rationalization of Canon's R&D effort. These laboratories were intended to serve Canon's global operations, not local production. Currently the General Manager of Canon's 145-person Peripheral Development division in Tokyo, Tsukasa Kuge had also

Country	Canon subsidiaries	Canon affiliated companies
France*	1,868	–
UK	1.071	–
Germany	812	–
Spain	–	387
The Netherlands	384	–
Finland	380	–
Sweden	332	–
Austria	193	–
Italy	187	–
Belgium	105	–
Switzerland	51	–
Luxembourg	9	–
Total	5,392	387
	Combined total	5,779

* Canon Bretagne is included in the French subsidiaries
Source: Canon Handbook.

Exhibit 7.10   *Canon's European distribution capabilities (number of employees as of December 1985)*

been directly involved and was familiar with Canon's European operations. Kuge remarked:

> The idea was for Giessen to concentrate on mid-range copiers. We had personal copiers being produced in Liffre and Categories 1, 4 and 5 in Toride. We had significantly fewer people working in R&D in Giessen than in the beginning. Over time, production became much more important, and it was more effective to do the R&D in Japan.
>
> In developing products, Canon follows a policy of *mochi wa mochi-ya*. The idea is to have the proper development in the proper place. *Mochi* is the sticky rice cake that is traditionally cooked for New Year's celebrations. The raw material is popular and the cooking process is simple. Anyone can make rice cakes, but *mochi*-making is a hard and time-consuming task. The job of making rice cakes should belong to the most skilful rice cake maker; namely, *mochi-ya*.
>
> Ultimately, Canon needs to have a greater R&D capability in Europe if we are to become an insider. We could develop this capability with some incremental investment based on Giessen's original potential or, alternatively, we could set up a new, greenfield site in Germany or Switzerland, for instance. As well, we need to further investigate options for locally-produced parts.

Mr Kaku commented:

> When we first began production in Europe . . . there were no compelling economic reasons to transfer this original technology. But it is our established policy, in keeping with our basic corporate purposes, to participate to the fullest in the development of the societies which we serve through our products.

A possibility for co-operation

In late 1986, Elserino Piol, Executive Vice President Strategies and Development in the Olivetti Group, travelled to Tokyo to speak with senior Canon management about joining forces in the copier business. Olivetti had a firm hold on 85% of the copier market in Italy – which represented about 5% of the total market in Europe – and Olivetti was looking for a way to double its share. Canon had had some difficulty serving the southern part of Europe, and it was possible to conclude that combining the sales effort with Olivetti could expand the total sales for both companies. However, it was also possible that such an alliance would lead to conflicts between the two salesforces.

Currently, Canon had the highest installed base in all of Europe. However, the market was still relatively undeveloped. There was a huge potential for growth with the coming developments in digital technology and colour copying, and the further integration of the copier into the office environment. At this point, the question for Canon was whether it made sense to enter a venture with a company that was ostensibly a competitor in the copier business. Olivetti was a leading player in the office products market with a long history in the business, and this was an area that Canon wanted to enter more strongly in the future. For both partners, such a venture would be a way to learn the way of thinking, history, technology and philosophy of the other.

In the past, Japanese manufacturers had tended to manufacture products in Japan and then export them to Europe and North America. Early on, Canon realized that this tendency could not continue. Canon's philosophy was to produce products in the market where they were used. In fact, Canon was the first Japanese company to set up a factory for copiers in Europe, which was done to have some insurance for the future. Over the years, Canon had set up many ventures, but they had always been built up from ground zero. The transfer of technology was much easier this way, and it was more secure. This would be the only major joint venture for Canon in copiers that involved manufacturing and R&D, and it would be only the second joint venture that Canon had entered into outside Japan. The first one, Lotte Canon, was established in 1985.

Canon's technology was ahead of Olivetti's, so its patents, know-how and projects would probably be put into the joint venture. Canon had just started production of a new Category 1 copier in Toride. In looking at Olivetti's R&D and manufacturing capability and its sales channels, there was also the possibility of transferring this production into such an operation. The question of Olivetti's relationships with other OEM suppliers would still have to be resolved. Furthermore, Olivetti's suppliers were quite different from Canon's standards on quality, and significant improvements would probably have to be sought on the product cost side. More than 20 years earlier, Canon had launched programmes to study the potential of its suppliers. Although studies could be expensive, the result often saved time and costs in terms of quality assurance. As well, Canon came to understand the level of quality support it needed to provide to its suppliers. As a result, Canon's suppliers had become involved in developing Canon machines, and they operated on a just-in-time basis. This collaboration was natural and ongoing. Moreover, through this arrangement, Canon had gathered a lot of cost data and continually looked for ways to improve. Typically, Canon's inventory level in Japan was less than five days. In Giessen it was seven days, although work was ongoing to bring this level down further.

In Tokyo, Canon had a very different system from the one used by Olivetti and most other European and North American manufacturers. Canon used a mass production system, and the underlying driver was how to improve production volume within a certain time frame. This was based on minutes and seconds, and the idea was to look continually for ways to shorten the work cycle. Canon used conveyor belts, and most people in the copier area worked on a 20–30 second cycle. In contrast, in Olivetti, one person typically worked 25–30 minutes at a station and assembled a lot of parts. The whole unit was manually pushed on a cart to the next station, and there was usually some waiting time for the next step.

There were also differences in the development system. Traditionally, Canon's R&D people concentrated on perfecting the design. There were no major modifications once the drawing was completed and moved into production. Canon looked continually for ways to improve the quality in each step, to make cost reductions, and to develop products faster. In Canon, the objective was for production costs to be reduced every year, which could be achieved by changing the design to use cheaper parts, negotiating with suppliers for price discounts, changing the production process in the factory to work more effectively, and so on. This was the kind of thinking that Canon would need to transfer into a joint venture.

Canon had never entered into this kind of alliance before. The challenge for both parties would be how to adapt and how to implement changes. The key would be how to structure such a venture, how to leave the good parts of each partner's culture and build on a common basis. Canon had always had a philosophy of coexistence.

8

A framework for environmental analysis

Case 8.1 Country note on Indonesia

This case was prepared by Research Associate U. Srinivasa Rangan, under the supervision of Professors Jan Kubes and George Taucher, as a basis for class discussion rather than to illustrate either effective or ineffective handling of a business situation.

Indonesia lies along the equator between the southern tip of the Asian mainland and Australia. Its western and southern coastlines abut the Indian Ocean. In the north are the straits of Malacca and the South China Sea and, in the west, the Pacific Ocean. The total land surface of Indonesia is about 1.9 million square kilometres divided into more the 13,000 islands of varied size and character, nearly 12,000 of which are uninhabited. The five major islands are: Java, Sumatra, Kalimantan, Sulawesi and Irian Jaya. The country, which is comparable to Mexico in land area, stretches over 5100 km east to west and 1900 km north to south (Exhibit 8.1).

In 1979, Indonesia was the fifth most populous nation in the world, with about 140 million people. Of that number, 55% were below the age of 20. Population grew at an average rate of 2.5% per annum from 1970 to 1975. Population distribution throughout Indonesia was very uneven, so that the country as a whole suffered not so much from overpopulation as from extremely uneven distribution of its population. Thus, whereas the average density for Indonesia as a whole was 58 inhabitants per square kilometre, the corresponding figure for Java was about 600 and for the rest of Indonesia 22. The population on Java was

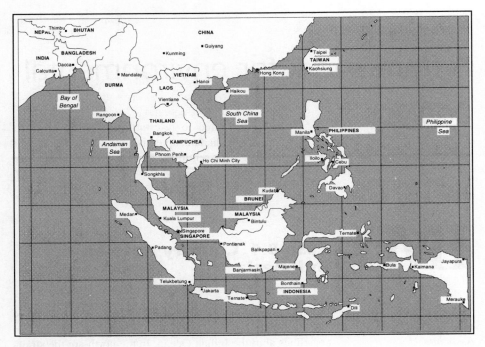

Exhibit 8.1   *Indonesia*

also by no means evenly distributed – due to a large amount of mountainous and forested land – and, in some regions, the population density exceeded one thousand per square kilometre. With a view to alleviating the population pressures in Java, the Indonesian government encouraged internal migration under which families from overpopulated areas of Java were settled in less populated parts of the country–such as Sumatra and Kalimantan. About 20% of the country's population lived in urban areas and the rest in rural areas.

Historical background

The people of Indonesia, basically of Malay origin, are divided into approximately 300 ethnic groups speaking about 365 languages and dialects. The Indonesian motto – unity in diversity – signifies the concern of the government to preserve the unity of the people in spite of diverse ethnic and cultural origins.

The location of the Indonesian islands, in an area through which important trade routes ran, ensured that the country was affected by influences from outside. The three major external influences were: Indian (Hindu and Buddhist) over a period of about ten centuries up to 1000 AD; Islamic starting from the 14th century; and European (Dutch) since the 17th century. The successive waves of external influences led to a mosaic of cultural diversity since the common people adopted part of each new religion as an additional layer to their basic traditional beliefs. Thus, although Islam is currently the dominant religion (90% of the population), it includes elements of all past beliefs. For instance, the women in Indonesia do not wear veils as is customary in many other Moslem societies.

Despite the diversity of ethnic groups and languages, the country has linguistic unity, since a national language which has evolved from a Malay dialect has been accepted and is widely used in Indonesia. Its adoption has been facilitated because it was not associated with one of the dominant ethnic groups, and the script used is roman.

A Dutch colony since the middle of the 19th century, Indonesia gained its independence in 1945. Although the Dutch tried to re-establish their hold on the country after the surrender of the Japanese who had occupied islands during the Second World War, a spontaneous outburst of nationalist sentiment throughout the country and the effective international intervention led to a confirmation of Indonesian independence in December 1949.

The first 15 years after independence were essentially a period of national consolidation. Although there was a rapid succession of governments which attempted to come to grips with major problems like the maintenance of internal security, economic development, civil service retrenchment, etc., the main figure during this period was President Sukarno who gave the fledgling nation a sense of direction. Drawing strength from his revolutionary standing and from the widespread public feeling that he alone could hold the nation together, Sukarno was the architect of the unity of Indonesia. He was committed to secularism and social justice. By choosing to align Indonesia with the non-aligned movement, Sukarno paved the way for his successors to steer the ship of foreign policy along a neutralist stance. But, Sukarno failed to come to grips with the economic problems facing the nation. By 1965, the Indonesian economy was in a shambles. Every group from farmers to businessmen was ranged against Sukarno. That year Sukarno compounded his domestic isolation by his violent reaction to the Malaysian Federation.

Towards the end of 1965, the army seized power. The ostensible reason was a planned conspiracy by the Communists to overthrow the regime. The following month saw massive anti-Communist struggles in Java, with estimates of those killed ranging to many hundreds of thousands. Sukarno was forced to delegate extensive powers to General Suharto, the army chief of staff. In 1967 Sukarno resigned and Suharto assumed the presidency.

The coming to power of Suharto, according to most observers, did not essentially alter the situation in which the middle class élite continued to rule the country. There was a change from a moderately left of centre authoritarian type of civilian government to a military-led authoritarian regime, but there was not, in fact, a switch from a really left-wing to a right-wing regime. The new order represented a counter-revolution only in the sense that some of the social forces like land reform movements and trade unions were effectively weakened; the land reform movements of 1960 were discontinued, and professional associations and trade unions were banned. The urban consumers benefited by the artificially low price levels of rice and other necessities. This was achieved at the expense of the Javanese peasants who have been forced to sell their crops at low prices and, in turn, led to a scarcity of food. For instance, the countrywide scarcity of food which occurred in 1973 was not only in the month immediately preceding the harvest but also after it.

Democracy was restored when, in July 1971 when general elections were held. The government strongly supported the so-called Sekber Golkar which subsequently won a handsome victory. In addition to the seats allotted to the armed forces, the member of Sekber Golkar guaranteed the regime a comfortable parliamentary majority, and in

1972 Suharto was re-elected as president. In spite of increases in the number of civilian cabinet ministers, the government remains predominantly military: the majority of local officials at all levels are military officers. Golkar remains the dominant political voice but is closely linked with the military.

Economic survey

Indonesia, often called Asia's slumbering giant, because of its great resources – oil, coal, minerals, timber, rubber, palm oil, coffee, tea and fertile plantations. However, it is proving difficult to wake the country up to realize the full potential of its rich resources. For instance, although impressive gains have been made in increasing the gross national product since independence, the structure of the economy has remained basically the same as in the pre-1949 Dutch colonial days. In the primary product export sector, labour intensive emphasis on spices, sugar and coffee has given way to land and capital intensive extraction of oil, minerals and timber, while the traditional agrarian economy, despite impressive gains in productivity, remains backward and comparatively neglected. The new and post-independence manufacturing sector remains below 10% of total output. Although the average per capita income is tabulated at around US$360, over two-thirds of Indonesians live in conditions more like those of Bangladesh, with a figure of US$90. Thus, the primary challenge for the economic planners in Indonesia is to keep the economy growing faster than the population, while at the same time trying to spread the benefits of economic development more evenly.

Indonesia's present economic strategy is based on the use of unprecedented financial resources (from oil revenue and international aid) to develop the infrastructure and establish a heavy industry, both through direct government intervention and through encouraging the expansion of the private sector. The main constraints that seem to affect Indonesian development plans are the entrenched social mores of the population and the lack of trained/skilled manpower. In this context, the role of Indonesia's Chinese community is noteworthy. The Chinese community is small, probably no more than 4 million, but its economic significance is immense. Concentrated in Indonesia's main cities, the Chinese had, until recently, dominated trading and manufacturing sectors in the country. Even today they manage a large share of the business of Indonesia's ruling élite. The government of President Suharto has introduced numerous economic changes aimed at improving the role of Pribumis (indigenous people) in business. There are increasing pressures on the government to improve the country's non-oil export performance by boosting the domestic private sector manufacturing industry. But, the government is aware that such an improvement is possible only if the economic straitjacket on the country's Chinese entrepreneurs is loosened. Risk of increased communal tensions versus sub-optimal growth seems to be a quandary facing the government.

Labour force – present and future

The Indonesian labour force was estimated at 49 million in 1975. Of this, 56% depended on agriculture, 12% on industry and 22% on the services sector. The country's literacy rate was about 70%. Although some 24 million students were enrolled in the various educational levels in 1975, only about 158,000 students were in the tertiary stage. The primary and secondary school enrolment ratios are 70% and 22% respectively.

Economic planning

Since 1969, economic activity has been guided by a series of five-year plans that have sought to bring about controlled expansion. The plans are not in any way intended as absolute directives, but they have tended to be implemented rigidly. As one British businessman with long experience of Indonesia is reported to have said: 'Their macroeconomic planning tends to be very good. A small number of highly competent, well-trained economists know what can be done and what has to be done, but incompetence and dishonesty at lower levels often defeat their efforts. Economic plans are interpreted with inflexibility and it is impossible to get speedy reaction to change in circumstances.'

With this background, the first five-year plan, Repelita I (1969 to 1974) can be considered a qualified success. This involved expenditures of 2 billion dollars (US) aimed at a 4.7% annual growth in gross national product. It concentrated on agriculture, particularly food production, and the infrastructure. Spending on industry was to be limited to sectors supporting agriculture, such as fertilisers, cement and machinery for cultivation or the processing of agricultural products. The emphasis was to be laid on the improvement of the tax structure and the curtailment of current expenditure. The plan encouraged foreign investment. Regulations were frequently changed in order to attract and regulate foreign private investment. Most of the targets set for the plan were

	1960	1965	1971	1972	1973	1974	1975
Current prices							
Agriculture	54.0	58.6	44.8	40.2	40.2	32.4	31.6
Mining	3.6	2.5	8.0	10.8	12.3	22.0	20.0
Manufacturing	8.4	7.6	8.4	9.8	9.6	8.2	8.8
Electricity/gas/water/construction	2.3	1.7	4.0	4.3	4.3	4.3	5.2
Transport and communications	3.7	2.1	4.4	4.0	3.8	4.2	4.1
Other	28.0	27.5	30.4	30.9	29.8	28.9	30.3
Total	100.0	100.0	100.0	100.0	100.0	100.0	100.0
Constant prices							
Agriculture	45.2	43.7	38.3	35.3	34.6	33.5	31.9
Mining	11.6	11.7	16.3	18.2	19.9	19.2	17.7
Manufacturing	7.5	7.4	7.4	7.7	7.9	8.6	9.2
Construction etc.	2.9	2.6	4.0	4.6	4.8	5.5	6.0
Trans/Comm.	4.2	3.9	3.9	3.9	3.9	4.1	4.1
Other	28.6	30.7	30.1	30.3	28.9	29.1	31.1
Total	100.0	100.0	100.0	100.0	100.0	100.0	100.0

Exhibit 8.2 *Percentage sectoral distribution of Gross Domestic Product (GDP)*

achieved, but rice output rose by 25% instead of the planned 47%, and production of fertilizer and cement also fell short of the targets. Thus, agriculture contributed about 30% of the gross domestic product. (The breakdown of gross domestic product by sectors is given in Exhibit 8.2.)

Agriculture

Agriculture is the dominant sector in the Indonesian economy. Independent peasant farmers account for the larger part of the production, notably rice and food crops, but there is an important estate sector that produces mainly for export. Indonesia is a major supplier of rubber and a less significant producer of a wide range of other commodities such as coffee, tea, tobacco, copra and oil palm products.

Before the second world war, Indonesia was self-sufficient in basic foodstuffs, although some low quality rice was imported to release some high quality rice for export. Since 1945, however, production has failed to keep pace with demand and grain (mainly rice) has been imported. Rice is the major staple food of Indonesians. From the simplest villager to the highest Javanese official, a meal without rice is almost unthinkable. By 1973, Indonesia was the world's largest rice importer, accounting for around one-third of the international trade.

The government had sought to improve rice production by provision of credit from the State Bank, extension of services, provision for needs like fertilizers and seeds at fixed prices and self-processing equipment to allow farmers to process their own grain and earn higher prices. But by suppressing on-farm prices (government purchase price of rice), the government has dampened rural development and penalized the indebted farmer who had to sell at low selling prices and buy his needs at high buying prices. The tenants' or sharecroppers' burden was aggravated by landowners and creditors passing down losses to the farmers. Thus, subsidies, official loans and extension of technology usually bypass the small holder and accrue to the wealthy and large landholders. The Indonesian government is seriously concerned about the falling and inadequate rice production.

Though food for domestic consumption remains Indonesia's top agricultural priority, the government's desire to increase the country's non-oil export earnings has been instrumental in focusing attention more sharply on the country's traditional export crop sector. There is also a growing realization that a major expansion of the country's estate and small holder plantation sector could play a sizeable role in solving two of the country's most pressing problems – creating jobs and reducing poverty.

When considering the cash crops, one has to distinguish between two types of agriculture business: estates and smallholders. For instance, in 1969, over 70% of rubber output came from smallholdings; smallholdings also accounted for 45% of tea output, 80% of tobacco and almost all pepper, copra, coffee and spices. Oil palm and sugar are predominantly estate crops. Since 1969, the marked production increases were in sugar and oil palm. During the first five-year plan, the smallholders were completely neglected, leading to very slow increases in production from these holdings. Furthermore, replanting, which was essential for rubber and coconut, was completely neglected. Over half of all rubber trees are well past maturity, and some 50% of coconut trees are over 40 years old in the smallholder sector.

The present government plans call for massive investments over the next decade to expand the plantation area for rubber, palm oil, coffee, sugar, coconut and cocoa, and to rehabilitate around a third of the area currently under these crops. The government's massive transmigration programme, aimed at moving 2.5 million people from overpopulated Java to the outer islands, is expected to go hand in hand with the expansion of the country's cash crop sector, but many of these workers have spent most of their productive life engaged in rice production and have little or no experience in raising other crops. The Department of Agriculture is expected to play a leading role in helping to open up new areas and raise and train these workers. However, recently, World Bank sources expressed doubts as to whether Indonesia can produce enough skilled agricultural experts and extension workers[1] over the next decade.

Petroleum and mining

Indonesia is the only Asian member of OPEC and is the second largest producer of crude petroleum east of the Gulf, after China. It is also believed to have three-quarters of the total reserves in South East Asia. Major deposits of natural gas have also been found in Indonesia. Though prospecting has so far covered only a small part of the country's total area, it is felt that it is rich in a number of other mineral resources. Since 1967, foreign investment in prospecting and production has also been welcomed. (The production of major minerals over the last few years is given in Exhibit 8.3.)

	1972	1973	1974	1975
Crude petroleum ('000 tons)	36,950.0	45,615.0	46,850.0	45,392.0
Tin concentrates ('000 tons)	21.9	22.5	25.6	25.3
Bauxite ('000 tons)	1,276.0	1,229.0	1,290.0	993.0
Coal ('000 tons)	180.0	149.0	156.0	206.0
Nickel ('000 tons)	14.1	15.8	16.0	14.6
Silver (tons)	8.6	9.6	6.6	4.6
Gold (kilograms)	330.0	351.0	256.0	321.0
Natural gas (mil.cub.ft.)	150,800.0	186,100.0	202,300.0	222,200.0
Iron sands ('000 tons)	300.0	281.0	365.0	343.0

Source: *U.N. Statistical Yearbook; U.N. Monthly Bulletin of Statistics;* International Tin Council

Exhibit 8.3 *Production of major minerals*

[1] Extension workers were semi-skilled technicians who were employed by government agricultural agencies to offer practical advice to the farmers on various agricultural techniques.

Since 1973, the crude oil exports have had a major impact on the Indonesian economy. The increased earning from oil is being used to expedite development, which in turn is increasing consumption. Energy consumption has more than tripled in a decade. This consumption is extremely expensive because of Indonesia's lack of refining capacity and the subsequent needs to import, particularly the middle distillates. The country, however, also has other fuel resources, good prospects for long-term development of geothermal energy, and extensive scope for the development of hydroelectricity.

Manufacturing

The contribution of the new, post-independence manufacturing sector in Indonesia remains low. At the end of 1974, it was about 10% of the gross domestic product. The industry gets a small share of the government's development budget, but a relatively high share of the inflow of foreign capital. Much of the foreign investment has gone into the refining of basic metals and into textiles and leather products. Since 1969, a number of major manufacturing projects were initiated or completed by Pertamina, the state oil corporation in charge of petroleum production.

The government's manufacturing strategy seems to be largely dependent on attracting foreign investment. Since the foreign investment law of 1967, more than 400 manufacturing investment projects have been approved. The law also requires a degree of Indonesianization of personnel. It also requires that new foreign investments take the form of joint ventures between foreign and Indonesian companies. These requirements seem to have had a deterrent effect on potential investors.

The official policy on the manufacturing sector, as gleaned from the ministerial pronouncements, seems to be as follows: more industries which process indigenous raw materials will be developed in the manufacturing sector; special attention will be given to industries which support the agricultural sector, i.e., those producing agricultural equipment and fertilizers, and those which process agricultural products. While an effort will be directed toward causing a growth of medium and large-scale industries complementary to the growth of small-scale ones, the primary consideration will be given to labour-intensive industries. Crucial to the manufacturing sector development is the policy on regional dispersal of industry. The strategy is to encourage industries to settle outside Java.

An important feature of the industrial scene is that most large-scale industry is state owned. Much small-scale industry is privately owned by the Chinese community. The present government has introduced numerous economic changes aimed at improving the role of Pribumis in business. Positive discrimination in favour of the Pribumis has led to many more indigenous Indonesians taking advantage of the country's universities and technical colleges. While Pribumis are now given preference in the areas of manufacturing and processing, the government has had to expand the state sector in industry acting as a proxy for the Pribumis, who, unlike the Chinese, rarely have sufficient capital to invest in new industrial ventures.

The relatively small size and narrow base of Indonesia's manufacturing sector means that it is still very much a series of modern enclaves in the midst of a predominantly traditional agricultural and cottage industry economy. The government believes that its role is to step in at the top end of the scale in a bid to help create the basis for a much deeper and broader self-sustaining structure. However, it is believed that it would have

		1971/72	1972/73	1973/74	1974/75
Timber	Value	170	275	720	615
	Volume	8,840	12,701	15,704	12,434
	Price	19	22	46	49
Rubber	Value	215	211	483	425
	Volume	809	826	902	842
	Price	266	255	535	505
Palm oil	Value	45	42	89	184
	Volume	212	245	279	303
	Price	212	171	319	607
Coffee	Value	54	83	79	92
	Volume	72	111	96	105
	Price	750	748	823	876
Tea	Value	31	31	31	50
	Volume	46	46	46	51
	Price	674	674	674	980
Tobacco	Value	20	32	46	36
	Volume	19	27	35	26
	Price	1,053	1,185	1,314	1,385
Pepper	Value	21	21	31	22
	Volume	24	24	25	14
	Price	875	875	1,240	1,571
Palm kernel	Value	5	4	6	8
	Volume	59	51	37	30
	Price	85	78	162	267
Copra	Value	8	6	3	–
	Volume	67	61	21	–
	Price	119	98	143	–
Copra cake	Value	12	14	19	22
	Volume	236	303	224	236
	Price	51	46	85	93
Tapioca	Value	14	12	7	30
	Volume	434	304	117	455
	Price	32	39	60	66
Other food stuffs	Value	28	26	49	47
Animal and product	Value	23	42	90	92
Tin	Value	64	70	98	166
	Volume	20	21	22	24
	Price	3,200	3,333	4,455	6,917
Copper	Value	–	13	56	102
	Volume	–	28	126	222
	Price	–	464	444	459
Other minerals	Value	18	19	21	28
Miscellaneous	Value	18	76	77	114
Total value		784	977	1,905	2,033

Source: Bank Indonesia

Exhibit 8.4 *Non-oil exports, 1971/72 – 1974/75 (value: millions of US$; volume thousands of tons; price: US$/ton)*

to give much more attention to creating the right incentives, infrastructure and business climate for private and foreign investors to set up light engineering and downstream plants before industrial development became self-generating on the scale that the government would like to see.

International trade

Indonesia's international trade pattern is similar to that of many other developing countries which are agrarian and resource-based economies. Crude petroleum, forestry products, coffee, rubber, tin, palm oil, tea and fishery products account for nearly the entire exports of the country. On the import side, capital goods (machinery, electrical equipment and parts), iron and steel, chemicals, rice and transport equipment account for the bulk of the imports. The rise of petroleum prices in 1973 meant that the import of refined petroleum products has gone up in value and is now a substantial chunk of imports.

In the external trade sphere, the country has been exceedingly fortunate. In addition to higher prices for petroleum products, the traditional commodity products like coffee and rubber have also experienced steep price increases in the international markets. (Exhibit 8.4 indicates the trend in volume, value and prices of non-oil exports in the recent years.)

Indonesia's economy has, in recent years, become increasingly dualistic, with a strong oil sector and less healthy non-oil sector. The country's balance of trade clearly indicates this situation. The overall balance of trade would not have been favourable in recent years if it were not for the higher oil price rise – in spite of the very favourable commodity prices for non-oil exports. The need to import rice to feed the growing population is an important factor to reckon with in the future.

The balance of payments of the country benefited from the windfall effect of the rise in oil revenues in two ways: first, the rise in export receipts, and second, improved credit standing in the international capital markets enabling the country to borrow in the international markets. Further, the Tokyo club which brings together a consortium of governments willing to extend foreign aid to Indonesia has pledged substantial

	1971	1972	1973	1974	1975
Merchandise: exports	1,311	1,793	3,215	7,265	6,888
Merchandise: imports	1,230	1,445	2,663	4,634	5,469
Trade balance	81	348	552	2,631	1,419
Other goods, services and income – net	–500	–732	–1,082	–2,083	–2,555
Unrequited transfers – Net	46	51	55	49	27
Current account balance	–373	–333	–475	597	–1,109
Capital inflow – net	437	654	737	405	354
Errors and omissions	–93	57	78	–312	–97
Change in reserves	–29	378	340	690	–852

Source: IMF; World Bank

Exhibit 8.5 *Balance of payments (millions of US$)*

	1971 Amount	%	1972 Amount	%	1973 Amount	%	1974 Amount	%	1975 Amount	%
GNP	3,605		4,404		6,507		10,260		12,086	
Factor payments to abroad (net)	-66		-159		-245		-507		-555	
GDP	3,671		4,563		6,752		10,768		12,641	
Imports	611		862		1,316		2,293		2,778	
Exports	529		754		1,354		3,105		2,850	
Total resources	3,753	100.0	4,671	100.0	6,714	100.0	9,956	100.0	12,569	100.0
Consumption: private	2,832	75.5	3,400	72.8	4,790	71.3	7,012	70.4	8,744	69.6
Consumption: public	341	9.1	414	8.9	716	10.7	1,147	11.5	1,253	10.0
Gross domestic investment	580	15.4	857	18.3	1,208	18.0	1,797	18.1	2,572	20.4

Source: World Bank

Exhibit 8.6 Resources and expenditures (at current prices in billions of Rupiahs)

amounts of aid to Indonesia. In 1974, the aid pledged amounted to about $1.5 billion. (The balance of payments details are shown in Exhibit 8.5.) The higher level of foreign borrowing, either in the form of aid or in hard loans from international capital markets, implies that, in future, the debt servicing will rise in value and as a percentage of exports. This raises questions as to the ability to increase exports to meet the debt service requirements.

Domestic resource management policies

In the first half of the 1970s, gross investment grew very rapidly, expanding in real terms by about 18% a year. (Exhibit 8.6 gives details about the consumption and investment patterns from 1971 to 1975.) The rapid growth in investment reflects the impetus given to the economy by the boost in oil prices and commodity prices.

9

The macroeconomic environment

Case 9.1 Introductory note on Czechoslovakia

This note was prepared by Research Associates, Robert Howard and James Henderson, under the supervision of Professor Jan Kubes as a basis for class discussion.

The 'velvet revolution' of November 1989 led by Czech and Slovak artists and writers freed the country after 40 years of totalitarian oppression. Czechoslovakia was not the first country in Central and Eastern Europe to go through such drastic changes. Having witnessed the revolutions in Poland, Hungary and East Germany, the Czech citizens were ready to move. On November 17, eight days after the fall of the Berlin Wall, 50,000 Czech citizens took to the streets of Prague in the largest demonstration against the Communists in over 20 years. The police intervened with brutal beatings. Yet 100,000 students continued the demonstrations which spilled over into other cities such as Bratislava and Brno. Five days later, under the newly formed Civic Forum, led by banned playwright Vaclav Havel, 200,000 students, artists and liberal Christians demonstrated. On the next day, there were 300,000. By November 27, the people – calm, fearless, and excited – knew that their day had finally come. There was no reaction from the police. It was now only a matter of time before the Communist government would step down. One month later, on December 29, 1989, Vaclav Havel became President.

But the immense challenge of rebuilding what was once a European industrial powerhouse had barely begun. Indeed, political changes had taken place – elections were held in May 1990 and the Civic Forum under the leadership of Vaclav Havel won. Yet, even in June 1990, the economic and social changes required to revamp a country of uncompetitive, worn-out, state-run industries were still on the agenda. Where would the newly elected Civic Forum start?

- How should property and industries be privatized?
- When should the Czech koruna, the country's currency unit, be convertible?
- How would the country increase its export sales?
- How would the country avoid hyperinflation?
- How would mass unemployment, an almost inevitable consequence of the restructuring, be avoided?
- What should the sequence of economic measures be?
- At what speed should the economic measures be taken?

This note provides a brief description of the country and the situation in Czechoslovakia up to October 1990.

History

The Slavic people in the regions comprising modern-day Czechoslovakia – Bohemia, Moravia, Slovakia, and parts of Silesia – had for centuries been incorporated into one or more European empires.

Before World War I

The eastern part of the country, Slovakia, was ruled by the Hungarian Magyars, of Mongolian descent, from the 11th century to the early 20th century. Despite the Hungarians' attempt to suppress the Slovak culture, the people resisted. For example, they created their own language out of several local dialects (though the language was still similar to Czech). Many Slovaks emigrated to the USA to escape the poor living conditions. However, after the collapse of the Austro-Hungarian empire in 1918, Slovakia joined its neighbouring Czech province to form Czechoslovakia.

The Czech lands of Bohemia and Moravia expanded and contracted according to the aspirations of their rulers, then under the auspices of the Holy Roman Empire. Bohemia and Moravia, populated by Germans and Czechs, suffered under hundreds of years of religious conflict between the Catholics and Ultraquists (who later became Lutheran.) From 1526 onwards, the two provinces were absorbed into the Hapsburg empire, where only strict Roman Catholicism was accepted. By the mid-1800s, after the emancipation of the serfs, through further education and with the threat of doom under the Austrians, the Czechs of both Bohemia and Moravia turned to their Slavic roots. Czech literature, music and art blossomed. As the Hapsburg and later the dual Austro-Hungarian empire declined, the Czechs gained confidence in creating their own state. Not until the collapse of the Austro-Hungarian empire in 1918 did the state of Czechoslovakia finally come into being.

Interwar years and WWII

Czechoslovakia accounting for 70% of the Austro-Hungarian industrial capacity was in a position to prosper. Consequently, during the interwar period, the country was one of

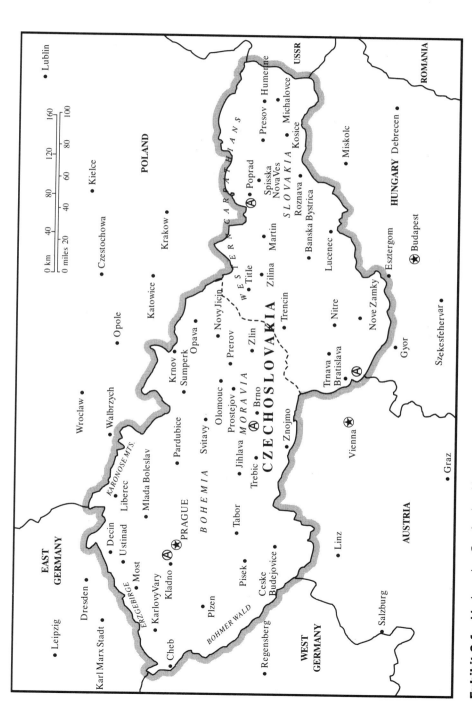

Exhibit 9.1 *Modern-day Czechoslovakia*

the most industrialized and economically advanced democracies in Europe. Czechoslovakia had a well-established manufacturing tradition, especially in metallurgy, machines, cars, arms and light industry (shoes and textiles). And, these were but a few of the high quality industrial products made in the country during the 1920s and 1930s.

However, in September 1938, the French, English, Italian and German governments agreed that Czechoslovakia should relinquish those parts of the country inhabited by a majority of ethnic Germans to the Nazis. Then, Nazi Germany increased its control of all Czech lands, namely Bohemia and Moravia, and it became a German protectorate during World War II. Meanwhile, border territories were also ceded to Hungary and Poland, while a separate Slovak state was established under Nazi guidance. At the end of 1945, Czechoslovakia was liberated by the Russians and was restored as an independent state (Exhibit 9.1).

Communist Czechoslovakia

The Communist Party of Czechoslovakia (CPCS) won 38% of the vote in the 1946 elections because of the country's growing socialist spirit and appreciation of the USSR for liberating the country from the Nazis. Democracy was short-lived. The CPCS, under the influence of Stalin, strengthened its position and suppressed all opposition. The party brought the economy increasingly under central control as it stressed investment in heavy industry, and focused on the needs of the USSR and other East European countries. As the most advanced economy in Comecon,[1] Czechoslovakia was the largest supplier of sophisticated machinery to its Central and Eastern European neighbours. However, many of Czechoslovakia's trading partners began to develop their own basic industries. As demand from these countries subsided, China became an important new customer, eager to purchase equipment from Czechoslovakia until their break in trading relations.

The road to democracy

Economic hardship proved to be the impetus for political change. Soon after the break with China and the worsening of economic conditions, the CPCS began to make concessions, including more freedom of the press, and a revival of arts and literature. By the middle of 1967, the CPCS buckled under the pressure for reform, which led to the formation of a coalition government under the leadership of Alexander Dubcek, a non-Communist. Under Dubcek's 'socialism with a human face', many reforms, including freedom of the press and tolerance of other political parties, were made within the small span of a couple of months. By August 1968, the Soviet Union, fearful that this revolution would spill over into other countries, decided to send in Warsaw Pact troops. Dubcek was replaced by Gustav Husak, who oversaw the return to the old way of life. Under Husak, roughly 500,000 of the country's 1.65 million party members were expelled or forced to resign. Economic reforms were reversed and popular

---

[1] The Council of Mutual Economic Assistance (CMEA or COMECON) was formed in 1949 by the Soviet Union and the Communist states in Eastern and Central Europe to divert trade away from Western nations and achieve a greater degree of self-sufficiency among Communist nations. At that time, COMECON included the USSR, Bulgaria, Czechoslovakia, East Germany, Hungary, Poland, and Romania.

resistance to the government faded. The Czech people lost confidence, purpose and became apathetic. Productivity stagnated. Only the intelligentsia and expelled Communists kept the spirit of freedom alive through their statement of democratic rights called Charter 77. This movement continued until the Velvet Revolution in November 1989.

The political situation in 1990

By April 1990, 23 political parties and movements had been founded in Czechoslovakia. The most important ones were Civic Forum in the Czech Province, and the Public Against Violence in Slovakia which were the political movements that led to the original democratic revolution. On June 8 and 9, 1990, voters in Czechoslovakia elected representatives to the Federal Assembly (the Czechoslovak national parliament, divided into two equal chambers) and the National Councils in the Czech and Slovak federal republics (the parliaments of the respective republics, modelled on the federal government) for the first time in 40 years. Civic Forum had a clear majority in the Czech province and Public Against Violence in Slovakia. The main assets of these two parties were its immensely popular leader, Vaclav Havel, and its initiation of the Velvet Revolution. However, as the party had not clearly defined its political stance, it started to split into several factions. The Communists, or the remnants of the traditional one-rule party, were the runners up with 16% of the popular vote. The rest of the vote was shared amongst the Christian Democrats, who based their policies on Christian values, and the Hungarian, Moravian and Slovak regional parties (Exhibit 9.2).

	% of vote		Number of seats House of Nations		House of the people
	Czech	Slovak	Czech	Slovak	
Civic Forum	51.6	–	50	–	87
Public Against Violence	–	34.9	–	33	
Communist Party	13.7	13.6	12	12	23
Christian Democrats	8.7	17.8	6	14	20
Slovak National Party	–	11.2	–	9	6
Hungarian Christian Democrats	–	8.5	–	7	5
Regional Parties from Moravia and Silesia	8.5	–	7	–	9
Others	17.5	14.0	–	–	–

Exhibit 9.2 *Results of the General Election, June 1990*

Growth of separatism

Although the Czechs and Slovaks shared virtually the same language, their affiliation with different states prior to 1918 had left significant differences in their views of each other. The Slovaks often mistrusted the dominant Czech people. Having the capital, Prague, and more industry situated in the Czech province, and the term 'slovakia' at the

	A	B	C	D	E	F	G	H	I	J	K	L	M	Total
Austria	8	9	9	10	5	6	5	6	6	6	6	6	6	88
Czechoslovakia	6	5	6	10	5	5	5	5	4	6	5	4	4	70
Hungary	5	4	5	10	5	5	5	5	5	6	6	4	4	69
Poland	4	4	5	10	5	5	3	4	5	5	5	3	4	62

Notes:

		Points			Points
A:	Economic expectations versus realities	12	H: Law and order tradition		6
B:	Economic planning failures	12	I: Racial and nationality tradition		6
C:	Political leadership	12	J: Political terrorism		6
D:	External conflict risk	10	K: Civil war risks		6
E:	Corruption in government	6	L: Political party developments		6
F:	Military in politics	6	M: Quality of the bureaucracy		6
G:	Organized religion in politics	6			

Source: International Country Risk Guide, 1990

Exhibit 9.3 *Comparative political factors in Czechoslovakia, Poland, Hungary and Austria*

end of the name Czechoslovakia, often made the Slovaks feel forgotten. By June 1990, under strong pressure from the Slovaks, the country's name was changed to the 'Czech and Slovak Federated Republic' (CSFR) in order to emphasize the two separate nations. To keep the federation together, Vaclav Havel would eventually have to act on the demand for less central control, away from a federal to a confederal structure. For example, the federal government would have jurisdiction over foreign policy, financial affairs, defence and long-term economic policy (fiscal and monetary policy), and the Czech and Slovak Republics would be given control over industrial matters (privatization), education, cultural, health and social policies (Exhibit 9.3).

The social situation in 1990

In 1990, approximately 9.8 million of the 15.6 million Czechoslovak citizens lived in Moravia and Bohemia, while 5.8 lived in Slovakia. In addition to the Czechs (62% of the population) and the Slovaks (28% of the population), several other ethnic groups resided in the country.

The Hungarian minority, concentrated in Slovakia, was by far the largest of these groups (with 5%), followed by the Poles in Moravia, Ukrainians and Russians in Eastern Slovakia and finally a few hundred thousand Sudetenland Germans. The Communist government attempted to strip the Czechoslovak people of their religious beliefs but were successful with only 20% of the population. The majority (66%) still practised Roman Catholicism. A low rate of population growth concerned the people of Czechoslovakia. Families were having fewer children, and the population was slowly ageing.

The country was heavily urbanized, with approximately 65% of the population living in towns over 2000 people and half in cities over 10,000. The agricultural workforce had declined rapidly over the last 20 years. In 1970, 17% of the workforce (7.6 million) was in agriculture which declined to an estimated 10% in 1989. Of the other 90%, the majority of labour was in industry: metallurgy, electrotechnical, metal working, fuel and textiles. Services and small business were the fastest growing sectors for employment (Exhibit 9.4).

The income distribution in Czechoslovakia was fairly even with approximately 15% of the workforce earning Kcs 1–2000 per month, 65% earning Kcs 2–4000 and the top 20% earning greater than Kcs 4000. With the general deterioration of incomes over

	1975	%	1985	%	1989	%
Agriculture and forestry	1,120	16.3	1,040	14.0	950	12.5
Industry	2,712	39.4	2,845	38.4	2,910	38.1
Construction	622	9.0	630	8.5	696	9.1
Transport and communications	469	6.8	501	6.8	512	6.7
Trade, supplies	707	10.2	832	11.2	832	10.9
Science and research	158	2.3	175	2.4	182	2.4
Social services:						
Housing	91	1.3	140	1.9	160	2.1
Education	354	5.1	435	5.9	480	6.3
Culture	82	1.2	126	1.7	128	1.7
Health	266	3.9	326	4.4	350	4.6
Other non-productive	216	3.1	263	3.5	295	3.9
Other	84	1.2	96	1.3	124	1.6
Total	6,881	100.0	7,409	100.0	7,619	100.0
Total socialized employed		99.9		99.7		99.3
Total private employed		0.1		0.3		0.7

Source: Federal Statistics Office.

	Poland 1989	%	Hungary 1989	%	Austria 1989	%
Agriculture and forestry	4,494	26.0	863	16.3	288	9.2
Industry	4,053	23.4	1,434	27.0	813	26.0
Construction	962	5.6	331	6.3	221	7.1
Transport and communications	930	5.3	412	7.8	215	6.8
Trade	1,190	6.9	518	9.8	396	12.6
Other (includes private sector)	5,671	32.7	1,637	30.9	1,188	38.1
Total	17,300	100.0	5,295	100.0	3,121	100.0
Total socialized employed	11,472	66.3	4,795	90.6	461	16.1
Total private employed	6,000	33.7	400	9.4	2,661	83.9

Source: Federal Statistics Offices

Exhibit 9.4 *Structure of labour force in Czechoslovakia, Poland, Hungary and Austria*

	Czechoslovakia	Poland	Hungary	Austria
Population				
65 and over	11.6%	10.0%	13.4%	15.0%
15–64	65.1%	64.8%	66.7%	67.4%
1–14	23.3%	25.2%	19.9%	17.6%
Current population	15,640	37,769	10,589	7,635
Population growth rate to year 2010	0.3%	0.5%	0.0%	−0.1%
Urbanization rate	66%	61%	57%	56%
Unemployment rate	0%	6%	1%	5.4%
Percentage with university education	9.3%	6.5%	7.0%	14.0%
Religion	Roman Catholic	Roman Catholic	Roman Catholic	Roman Catholic
Standard of living (GDP per capita)	$2,737 to 7,900	$1,719 to 4,600	$2,784 to 6.100	$16,675

Exhibit 9.5 *Comparative social statistics for Czechoslovakia, Poland, Hungary and Austria*

time (only a 3.4% increase from 1978 to 1988), most families had two income earners and more than one job per person.

Virtually no unemployment existed in Czechoslovakia before the Velvet Revolution. A high percentage of women and people over the age of retirement chose to work. Yet labour productivity was low in comparison to the West. Factories had traditionally been overstaffed because of the tendency for central planning to favour output targets over the efficient use of labour. As a result, any restructuring would result in a rapid increase in unemployment. Already the government expected about 70,000 to be out of work by year end. And any large increases in unemployment could cause a backlash in a population that took job security for granted.

The Czechoslovak people were considered highly educated. The education system was similar to Germany's with an apprentice programme, general or technical secondary schools and universities. Technical skills were particularly advanced based on the country's strong industrial tradition. Most Czechoslovaks learned German as their second language, and English or French as their third. The quality of education was considered so good that the graduates were often overqualified for their jobs (Exhibit 9.5).

The economic situation in 1990

In June 1990, the Czech government was faced with an inordinate number of issues regarding the economic reform of its country. Industrial output was rapidly declining; traditional foreign markets in Eastern and Central Europe were collapsing; the industry structure was skewed; and the country had few financial resources to

	Czechoslovakia	Poland	Hungary	Austria
Currency unit	koruna	zloty	forint	schilling
Dollar (1989)	17.00	1439	59.07	13.23
Deutschmark	11.10	765	31.42	7.03
Franc	3.39	234	9.3	8.08
Parallel market	156%	0	22%	0
(% Black market > Official)				
GDP:				
GDP: (1989) in $ billions	43	70	29	126
GDP growth:				
1986–1988	1.5%	1.0%	1.5%	2.0%
1989	1.0%	−0.2%	−0.2%	4.0%
1990 Forecast	−3.0%	−15.0%	−5.0%	4.5%
Inflation: (1989)				
Inflation	3.0%	580%	20%	3.5%
Discount rate	8.5%	104%	20%	6.5%
External accounts (in $) (1989)				
Foreign trade balance (millions)	420	−425	425	−7,075
Current account balance (millions)	454	−1,586	−1,439	59
Exports/GDP	34%	12%	21%	24%
Exports to CMEA countries	53%	35%	40%	9%
Foreign debt	8	40	19	10
Debt service as % of GDP	18%	57%	66%	8%
Industry structure:				
Industrial output per capita (1988)	1,932	1,044	1,247	6,653
Major industries	Heavy industry	Agrifood	Agrifood	Paper
	Glass	Coal	Oil	Engines
	Machinery	Automobiles	Chemicals	Iron/steel
	Automobiles	Electrical	Machinery	Plastics
	Trucks	Machinery	Buses	Elec. app.
	China	Chemicals	Auto comp.	Yarns
	Plastics	Iron/Steel	Leather	Machinery
	Iron/Steel	Footwear		Tourism

Exhibit 9.6 *Comparative economic statistics for Czechoslovakia, Poland, Hungary and Austria*

improve the situation. Unlike other Central and Eastern European countries, however, Czechoslovakia lacked a large foreign debt (Exhibit 9.6).

Macroeconomic overview

Net material product

In the old Communist system, five-year plans ruled. During the 1970s net material product grew at approximately 5% per year, but this growth hid the declining competitiveness of Czechoslovak industries. Exports to the West started to decline.

During 1981 and 1982, the country experienced negative growth due to the worldwide recession and the government restrictions on hard currency imports to reduce its indebtedness. Although the country recovered during the rest of the 1980s, few of the five-year plan targets were met. And because inflation was hidden, most of the growth could be considered an illusion. With the decline in demand from the USSR and other CMEA countries, the government expected to see its NMP decline by 3% in 1990.

Inflation

Under Communist rule most prices were fixed, with the exception of 1982 and 1985 when they were increased as part of a domestic austerity programme. Full-scale price liberalization was set for January 1991. During those first few months, short-term inflation was expected to soar from 7% in 1990 to 50%. Already the discount rate was set at 8.5% and was likely to increase. Banks were allowed a maximum of 14% differential; thus they could charge up to 22.5% on loans.

External accounts

The Czech currency was called the koruna. As of October 1990, it was still not convertible. However, the new government had stabilized what was an unmanageable system of four official exchange rates and the black market rate. As of January 1990, the government adjusted the koruna weekly against a basket of five other currencies. Internal convertibility was expected in January 1991.

Foreign debt was still low relative to other Eastern European countries. At the end of 1989, it was $7.9 billion, but was expected to increase to $9 billion by the end of 1990. Most foreign banks saw Czechoslovakia as a good credit risk and were, therefore, willing to support the country further.

An estimated 55% of Czechoslovakia's exports – predominantly machinery goods and automobiles – went to the Soviet Union and other East European countries. A declining portion over time went to the Western nations, with the developing countries picking up the slack. With the collapse of the Soviet Union and the re-unification of Germany, the Czechoslovak industries lost two major markets for their products. And, access to Western markets was limited due to the low quality of the goods produced.

Industry structure

Czechoslovakia was a leading industrial power at the beginning of WWII with well-established manufacturing industries. When the Communists took over, they steered the industrial base towards heavy industry – arms, military aircraft, iron and steel, and chemical products – at the expense of other industries – food processing, shoes, glass and textiles. Between 1948 and 1988, the share of heavy industry grew from 45% to 53% of GNP (excluding arms), whereas consumer products dropped from 50% to 25% over the same time period. However, in 1989–1990, heavy industries suffered the most. Petrochemical facilities were working at low capacities, and heavy engineering was having difficulties selling products. In addition, the suspension of the arms exports severely affected the country's exports.

The central plan set targets for both the inputs and outputs of a particular sector. The enterprise was therefore considered the mechanism to reach the target of outputs. Price played a subordinate role. As a result of this highly complicated and unmanageable system, several economic abnormalities occurred. First, output targets and inputs were mismatched, often resulting in chronic shortages of inputs. With the absence of hard currency, imports were restricted, which often forced the enterprises (often monopolies) to integrate backwards. Secondly, because price and profit were not the motivating factors for enterprises, there was little incentive to produce goods of high quality. Thirdly, managers of the enterprises were motivated to overstate their input needs in order to ensure that their production targets would be met. Any excess was warehoused. Fourthly, both direct and indirect costs were disregarded – for example, environmental damage. Fifthly, with the central planners deciding on investment priorities, managers did not have to concern themselves with financial implications of new investments. These non-market actions characterized the framework of the industrial sector of Czechoslovakia and would be difficult to change overnight.

With the removal of the central planning system, the state-owned companies would have to fend for themselves for the short term. But, access to financing was practically non-existent, based on the lack of liquidity in the emerging banking system whose assets accounted for only 1% of total capital. Credit limits were already overdrawn. As a result, the enterprises had no choice but to look to foreign investors to ensure their survival.

Managing change in Czechoslovakia

Changing the country from a centrally planned economy to one based on market forces was not an easy task. The implications from the economic policies would be severe both politically and socially. Yet, most analysts felt that the country had a great ability to absorb the wrenching changes required, as well as the luxury of being able to wait and see how its neighbouring countries would fare.

Poland had freed prices and moved towards partial convertibility of its currency (the zloty) in January 1990 despite hyperinflation of 580% per year. Strict monetary and fiscal restraints followed, along with such microeconomic liberalization as the freeing of external trade and more privatization. Development of a banking system was also underway. By June, the hyperinflation had dropped to a manageable amount. Yet, the consequences were severe. GDP dropped an estimated 6% in the first half of the year. State sectors were suffering badly, with production down by one-third. The private sector, however, had started to boom.

Hungary also liberalized prices in 1990, leading to an increase in inflation from 20% in 1989 to an average of 30% in 1990. The country, unlike Poland, had experienced several years of reform. The government had maintained a high interest rate and had limited government borrowing to curb inflation. An embryonic financial system had taken hold, thus making privatisation simpler. Partial convertibility of the Hungarian currency (the forint) took place in 1990, with full convertibility scheduled for 1993. The results of the economic programme had not been so severe in Hungary. Official statistics predicted that the GDP would fall 9% in 1990; however, with the strength of the small business sector, most felt that the figure would fall an estimated 5%. The re-orientation of trade from the East to the West had been dramatic. Exports were up 9.2% for the first half of 1990.

Having witnessed the progression of its two neighbouring countries, the Czech government was faced with similar problems:

- What should the economic model for the country be in the end?
- What were the means to this end: what policies were required to enable the country to have a free market economy?
- How fast should these policies be implemented?
- What should be the sequencing of these policies?

Economic model for Czechoslovakia

Most Western economists agreed that the economic model could wait. They argued that discussions over whether to be a free market economy based on the US model, or a social democracy based on the Swedish model, were futile. Both countries already had private ownership, private financial markets and full convertibility. What was more important was to get the countries back on their feet economically.

Within the Civic Forum and Public Against Violence, discussions about Czechoslovakia's future direction had already started. Factions in the party, originally a political movement, had already formed. Mr Vaclav Klaus, the President, led a band of free marketeers who believed in economic shock therapy. Others, including the Prime Minister, Vaclav Havel and Mr Valtr Komarek, the Economic Policy Coordinator, believed more in left-of-centre policies with government intervention.

The means of economic transformation

Most of Central and Eastern Europe had been advised about ways to revitalize the region. For example, the World Bank had set out a table of economic reforms necessary for each Communist state, as follows:

1 Macroeconomic stabilization and control
   Implementation of stabilization programmes:
   Government and enterprises: Fiscal tightening
                               Tight credit policies
                               Addressing existing problems (money overhang,
                                 bank losses)
                               Expenditure-switching measures for external
                                 balance
2 Price and market reform
   Goods and Services: Domestic price reform
                       International trade liberalization
                       Distribution systems (transport and marketing services)
                       Housing services
   Labour: Liberalizing wages and labour market
   Finance: Banking system reform
                       Other financial markets
                       Interest rate reform

3 Private sector development, privatization, and enterprise restructuring
   Facilitating entry and exit of firms
   Enterprise governance
   Establishing private property rights
   Clarifying and allocating property rights: Agricultural land
                                               Industrial capital
                                               Housing stock
                                               Commercial real estate
   Sectoral and enterprise restructuring, including break-up of monopolies
4 Redefining the role of the state
   Legal reforms: Constitutional, property, contract, banking, competition
                  Reform of legal institutions
                  Regulatory framework for natural monopolies
   Information systems (accounting, auditing)
   Tools and institutions for indirect economic management:
                  Tax system and administration
                  Budgeting and expenditure control
                  Institutions of indirect monetary control
   Social areas: Unemployment insurance
                  Pension, disability
                  Social services: health, education

Speed of reform

Most economists agreed that attempts to gradually reform centrally planned economies failed. In fact, the Czechs could witness what the Communist governments of Poland, Hungary and Yugoslavia had done in the late 1980s to create such economic instability in their countries. Despite 'freeing' prices, much of the original state infrastructure remained. International trade was still controlled by quotas and foreign exchange rationing. Most of the state-owned companies, monopolies protected from outside competition, realized that the government would always support them either through higher wages, or through more loan guarantees. As a result, the governments started to borrow heavily and print more money to cover the 'investments' and wage increases in their state-owned firms. Hyperinflation ensued; huge government debts piled up.

'You don't try to cross a chasm in two jumps,'[2] said a Polish economist about the country's economic shock treatment in 1990. Rapid transformation to a market economy was of utmost importance to the Polish; less so for the Hungarians after their failed first attempts.

The Czechoslovak government, however, was at odds. Mr Klaus, the Finance Minister, and his team laid down their aims for the economy starting January 1, 1991 as follows:

- Elimination of excess demand by increasing prices of consumer goods and moving towards complete price freedom;
- Elimination of subsidies to industries and consumers;
- A distribution of shares in nationalized enterprises to the population;
- A restrictive monetary and fiscal policy to curb inflation.

[2] *The Economist*, January 13, 1990

Critics of Mr Klaus' strategy, namely Mr Valtr Komarek, warned about the consequences of high unemployment, consumer revolt, inflation and the sell-off of state industries to foreigners for very low sums. Mr Komarek proposed that the economy should first be restructured to improve its competitiveness before being opened to market forces.

Sequencing of reform policies

One of the biggest issues facing the Czech government was the sequencing of the policies for reform. For example, should privatization take place before or after price liberalization and convertibility? Should privatization take place without a full financial system in place? These were only two of many questions the Czech government had to ask. The answers were not so simple, since little experience in such widespread transformations had taken place. Yet, there were some helpful clues from the economists. For example, economists agreed that convertibility was important, that is, making foreign exchange freely available for trade, but that capital flows had to remain controlled. Similarly, microeconomic reforms – such as privatization and price liberalization – had to be countered with macroeconomic stability of strict monetary policy and cuts in government borrowing.

By the end of June 1990, the Czechoslovak government was expected to come up with its stabilization plan for the country. But the sequencing, speed and determinants of reform were still up in the air.

10

The political environment

Case 10.1 Central and Eastern European automobile industry

This note was prepared by Research Associates James Henderson and Robert C. Howard, under the direction of Professor Jan Kubes, as a basis for class discussion rather than to illustrate either effective or ineffective handling of a business situation.

At the start of the 1990s, it looked as if the decade would be a challenging one for the Western European car manufacturers. Faced with the prospects of a Japanese onslaught, tough environmental protection laws, and no competitive advantage, Western European car manufacturers seemed to have only one ray of hope still glimmering: the Central and Eastern European (CEE) car market.

As one expert from Volkswagen explained, if the number of persons/car decreased to 4 in CEE (in the USA it was at 2), a demand for an extra 11 million units would be created (excluding the USSR and East Germany). If that demand could materialize over the next decade, scrappage replacements alone could generate a sustained demand for 5 million cars per year. For Western producers – GM, Ford, Renault, Fiat, Peugeot, Volkswagen and others, the opportunities were enormous. Yet, so were the difficulties of transforming the worn-out state-run car companies, component suppliers, and dealers of Eastern Europe.

This note briefly describes the automobile industry in both Western and Eastern Europe, from the position of the Western car manufacturer interested in investing in Eastern European automobile operations.

Country	1986	1987	1988	1989	1990
Austria	262,200	243,200	253,100	276,000	288,600
Belgium	395,000	406,300	427,200	461,000	473,500
Denmark	169,400	129,400	88,600	78,000	80,900
Finland	143,200	152,300	173,500	177,000	139,100
France	1,911,500	2,105,200	2,217,100	2,274,000	2,309,100
Ireland	59,800	55,700	60,800	78,000	83,100
Italy	1,825,400	1,976,500	2,184,300	2,362,400	2,348,200
Netherlands	560,100	555,700	482,600	495,600	502,700
Norway	167,400	115,100	67,800	55,000	61,900
Portugal	114,200	129,200	227,100	193,000	212,700
Spain	689,100	796,000	998,000	1,095,700	982,300
Sweden	271,100	316,000	344,000	307,100	229,900
Switzerland	300,200	303,300	319,400	320,000	323,000
UK	1,882,500	2,013,700	2,215,600	2,301,000	2,008,900
Germany	2,829,400	2,915,700	2,807,900	2,832,000	3,040,800
Total W. Europe	12,275,000	12,925,000	13,282,000	13,075,000	12,996,200
USA	11,139,800	10,277,700	10,479,900	9,852,600	9,104,000
Japan	3,146,000	3,274,800	3,717,400	4,404,700	5,070,000
Bulgaria	76,000	75,000	67,000	65,000	55,000
Czechoslovakia	118,700	110,200	135,300	133,900	135,000
Hungary	118,000	139,600	128,200	127,900	165,000
Poland	247,100	237,500	234,100	229,300	205,000
Romania	91,000	84,000	54,000	56,000	48,000
USSR	1,020,000	979,000	907,000	840,000	840,000
Yugoslavia	138,900	159,500	186,400	309,100	250,000
Total E. Europe	1,809,700	1,784,800	1,712,000	1,761,200	1,698,000

Sources: Economist Intelligence Unit, *World Car Forecast*, February 1991, SMMT: *World Automotive Statistics*, 1991 and Casewriter's estimates

Country	Pop	Persons per car	1987	1988	1989
Austria	7,586	2.7	2,609,390	2,684,780	2,784,792
Belgium	10,254	2.7	3,522,794	3,625,902	3,735,844
Denmark	5,130	3.2	1,558,096	1,587,641	1,596,116
Finland	4,964	2.8	1,619,848	1,698,671	1,795,908
France	55,994	2.5	21,575,000	21,950,000	22,520,000
Ireland	3,550	4.7	711,087	736,595	749,459
Italy	57,558	2.4	22,000,000	22,800,000	23,500,000
Netherlands	14,790	2.8	4,950,000	5,117,748	5,250,647
Norway	4,202	2.6	1,592,195	1,623,137	1,621,955
Portugal	10,460	7.3	1,236,000	1,290,000	1,427,000
Spain	39,417	3.7	9,643,448	10,218,526	10,787,424
Sweden	8,401	2.4	3,253,601	3,366,571	3,482,656
Switzerland	6,611	2.4	2,678,909	2,732,720	2,745,491
UK	57,028	2.7	19,929,294	20,605,514	21,347,739
Germany	60,977	2.1	27,223,810	28,304,184	29,190,322
Total W. Europe	357,612	2.7	124,103,472	128,341,989	132,535,353
USA	248,231	1.8	135,431,112	137,323,632	140,655,000
Japan	123,220	4.0	28,653,669	29,478,342	30,776,243
Bulgaria	8,973	7.9	1,083,126	1,138,433	1,138,000
Czechoslovakia	15,658	5.2	2,615,303	2,724,442	2,999,987
East Germany	16,586	4.8	3,462,184	3,462,000	3,462,000
Hungary	10,567	5.9	1,538,877	1,660,258	1,789,562
Poland	38,170	8.4	3,961,953	4,231,700	4,519,094
Romania	23,153	75.4	260,000	284,000	307,000
Soviet Union	288,742	22.8	11,970,369	12,581,000	12,688,000
Yugoslavia	23,725	7.7	2,837,670	3,040,362	3,089,605
Total E. Eur.	425,574	14.0	27,729,482	29,554,367	30,406,008

Source: The World Automotive Market, 1990

Exhibit 10.1 World-wide sales/registration of new cars, 1986–1990; total car registrations and population, 1988–1990

Company		Micro	Small	Small sport	Middle			Luxury			Speciality
					Lower	Upper	Sport	Lower	Middle	Upper	
Volkswagen Group	Volkswagen	Polo (F)	Golf (N)	Cabriolet (NC)	Jetta (NC)	Passat (N)	Corrado (N)	Audi 90 (NC)	Audi 100 (NC)	Audi 200 (NC)	Quattro (NC)
	Audi										
	Seat	Marbella (NC)	Ibiza (NC)		Malaga (NC)						
Fiat Group	Fiat	Panda (NC)	Tipo (N) Uno (F)	Uno Turbo (F)	Regata (R)	Tempra (D)		Croma (NC)			
	Lancia Alfa Romeo	Y10 (NC)	Delta (NC)	Delta Turbo (NC) Spider (F)	Prisma (D) Alfa 33 (F) Sprint (NC)	Dedra (N) Alfa 75 (F)		Thema (N)	Alfa 164 (NC)		
	Innocenti Ferrari Maserati	Various (NC)								Maserati	Ferrari
PSA Group	Peugeot	105 (N)	205 (F)	205 Rallye	309 (F)	405 (F)		505 (D) 605 (N)			
	Citroën	2CV (D) AX (N)	ZX (N) Visa (NC)		BX (F)	CX (R)		XM (N)	XM (N)		
General Motors	GM-Opel	Corsa (NC)	Kadett/Astra (F)		Ascona (D) Rekord (D) Kadett/Astra (F)	Vectra (N)	Manta (D) Calibra (N)	Omega (NC)	Senator (NC)		
	Saab							Saab 900 (F)	Saab 9000 (F)		
Ford	Ford	Fiesta (N)	Escort (N)	Fiesta CRX	Orion (N)	Sierra (F)	Scorpio (F)	Scorpio (F)			
	Jaguar								Jaguar XJ (F)	Jaguar XJS (F)	
Renault	Renault	R4 (NC)	Clio (N) R5 (R)	Fuego (D)	R18 (D) R19 (N)	R21 (F)	Alpine (NC)	R25 (F)			

Notes: NC = No change; N = New; R = To be replaced; F = Facelift; D = Dropped.

Exhibit 10.2 *Western European car manufacturers' models under each segment*

An overview of the Western European automobile industry

In 1989, worldwide vehicle sales reached approximately $850 billion, corresponding to a total volume of 50.3 million cars, trucks and buses. The Western European car market accounted for approximately 29% of the total value and volume sales (Exhibit 10.1).

Products/markets

In unit terms, passenger cars accounted for roughly 75% of sales and were usually classified by size, price and marketing intent in the following categories: micro, small, small sport, middle (lower, upper, sport), and luxury (lower, middle, upper, speciality). Typically, Western European car companies concentrated on selected categories, rather than the whole range (Exhibits 10.2 and 10.3). A number of smaller European

Company	1987	1988	1989	1990
Volkswagen	*1,855,271*	*1,937,383*	*2,108,779*	*2,045,628*
VW	1,259,782	1,292,924	1,355,295	1,377,740
Audi	352,217	371,277	361,125	360,043
Seat	243,272	273,182	302,359	307,845
Fiat	*1,759,139*	*1,929,260*	*2,001,068*	*1,884,023*
Fiat	1,317,389	1,446,644	1,477,082	1,368,521
Lancia	255,682	267,978	294,561	281,819
Alfa Romeo	186,068	214,638	217,761	222,217
Innocenti	–	–	11,664	7,843
Ferrari	–	–	–	1,839
Maserati	–	–	–	1,784
PSA Group	*1,503,081*	*1,677,713*	*1,702,545*	*1,712,257*
Peugeot	922,802	1,057,024	1,056,843	1,081,040
Citroen	580,279	620,689	645,702	631,217
GM total	*1,383,419*	*1,424,712*	*1,544,832*	*1,569,932*
GM Opel	1,313,871	1,358,617	1,478,599	1,512,397
Saab	69,548	66,095	66,233	57,535
Ford total	*1,493,638*	*1,486,977*	*1,584,916*	*1,532,930*
Ford	1,476,274	1,465,121	1,562,811	1,514,573
Jaguar	17,364	21,856	22,105	18,357
Renault	1,313,894	1,313,474	1,395,961	1,307,317
Mercedes Benz	435,430	441,823	434,603	435,878
Austin Rover	416,144	446,268	411,198	389,178
BMW	295,829	354,446	382,514	366,457
Volvo	267,367	267,332	266,009	233,257
Porsche	14,377	15,550	18,200	18,089
Japanese	1,413,204	1,466,588	1,455,316	1,540,525
East European	161,239	151,361	163,453	131,259
Others	80,641	81,892	79,550	90,006
Total	12,392,673	13,003,866	13,467,428	13,251,132

Source: Ward's Automotive Yearbook, 1991

Exhibit 10.3 *Total unit sales of each European volume car manufacturer*

companies – such as Porsche and Rolls Royce – catered for niche segments of the market.

The various markets (countries) ranged in their level of development. Often the number of persons/car helped companies estimate the amount of growth left in that market. For example, for the past couple of years, the USA had seen car sales decline as the number of persons/car remained stable, at around 2. In developing countries, however, the potential was enormous. In countries like Malaysia, Mexico and Romania, where the level of development differed significantly from the USA, there were 14.3, 16 and 75.4 persons/car respectively. Prospects did not bode well for Europe which, on average, had reached levels similar to the USA. The growth in sales during the 1980s, therefore, was not expected to continue into the 1990s (Exhibit 10.4).

Industry pressures

The last half of the 1980s were successful years for Europe's car makers, with mostly stronger sales and positive net margins to repair the damage from the previous downturn. But, as they entered the 1990s, the Western European car manufacturers faced a number of pressing issues: an uncompetitive business system, net margin squeezes, markets opening up in 1992, tougher environmental laws and, finally, the onslaught of the Japanese.

Country	1991	1992	1993
Austria	290,000	263,000	288,000
Belgium	465,000	470,000	503,000
Denmark	93,000	125,000	140,000
Finland	100,000	130,000	150,000
France	2,090,000	2,100,000	2,300,000
Germany	4,000,000	3,350,000	3,700,000
Ireland	70,000	84,000	88,000
Italy	2,250,000	2,300,000	2,350,000
Netherlands	480,000	490,000	510,000
Norway	55,000	80,000	110,000
Portugal	230,000	250,000	290,000
Spain	860,000	1,000,000	1,150,000
Sweden	180,000	230,000	280,000
Switzerland	300,000	280,000	330,000
UK	1,550,000	1,800,000	2,160,000
Total	13,013,000	12,982,000	14,314,000

Source: Economist Intelligence Unit, 1991 (includes East Germany).

Exhibit 10.4 *A market forecast of the demand for passenger cars in Europe to 1995*

An uncompetitive business system

The European car manufacturers were continuously compared with their Japanese and American counterparts along the business system – from component supply to distribution. The conclusions were not positive.

Component supply

The relationship of European suppliers and car manufacturers was not usually based on mutual trust and cooperation but, rather, on win–lose confrontations. The European system was adversarial, reflected in competitive bidding and profitability differentials between suppliers and OEMs. The Japanese manufacturers, on the other hand, shared costs and benefits with their suppliers. European producers used many more direct suppliers than Japan. For example, on average, Europeans would have 800–2000 direct suppliers, while the Japanese would have only 160–300 (according to a study conducted by the Boston Consulting Group in 1990). In addition, the European car makers had a larger degree of vertical integration than their Japanese counterparts. Value added/sales for European companies averaged around 47% (without component divisions) and 56% (with component divisions) in comparison with 37% for the Japanese manufacturers.

Product development

European producers were considered strong technological innovators but slow in developing new products, which was critical to remaining competitive with both the Japanese and Americans (Exhibit 10.5).

Performance criteria	Japanese	American	European
Average engineering hours per new car (millions)	1.7	3.1	2.9
Average development time per new car (in months)	46.2	60.4	57.3
Number of employees in project team	486	903	904
Number of body types per new car	2.3	1.7	2.7
Average ratio of shared parts	18%	38%	28%
Supplier share of engineering	51%	17%	37%
Engineering change costs as share of total die costs	10–20%	30–50%	10–30%
Ratio of delayed products	1 in 6	1 in 2	1 in 3
Die development time (months)	13.8	25.0	28.0
Prototype lead time (months)	6.2	12.4	10.9
Time from production start to first sale (months)	1	4	2
Return to normal productivity after new model (months)	4	5	12
Return to normal quality after new model (months)	1.4	11	12

Source: Kim B. Clark, Takahiro Fujimoto and W. Bruce Chew, 'Product Development in the World Auto Industry,' *Brookings Papers on Economic Activity,* 1987.

Exhibit 10.5 *Product development performance by regional auto industries, mid-1980s*

Country	1979	1989
Japan	25	18
Europe	41	36
USA	35	27

Source: Boston Consulting Group, 1990.

Exhibit 10.6 *Final body and assembly productivity in Japan, Europe and USA (hours)*

The average age of new models in Europe was 4.6 years versus 2.1 years in Japan. At the same time, the number of models in Europe was 47 compared with 73 in Japan (for a smaller market).

Operations

According to the Boston Consulting Group study, the relatively poor performance of the European car manufacturers was not due to a low level of capital, investment, technology or cost factors; rather, the cause was lower operating efficiencies in both manufacturing and product development. Instead of using a team environment like the Japanese, Europeans divided their tasks into different functions such as engineering, manufacturing and purchasing (Exhibit 10.6).

Distribution

The European distribution system was 30 years behind that of the United States. In many countries, there was a two-tier dealer structure consisting of 36,200 main dealers and 42,500 subdealers. (The two-tier system disappeared in the US during the 1930s.) Most of the small repair shops were supplied by the main dealer who acted as a wholesaler. In a comparison of averages, USA dealers sold 393 cars per dealer, while European dealers (including the subdealers) sold only 280 cars a year. Not only did the structure differ from the USA, but so did the legalities. Car manufacturers still enforced exclusive dealerships. By having this clause in their franchise, it was difficult for new imports to gain market access. The European Commission would not be deciding on the future of the car distribution structure until 1995. However, until that time, if car manufacturers started to lose market share (as Fiat had in Italy), dealerships would be the first to go, thus creating more room for importers.

Margin squeeze

When the cyclical industry took a downward turn at the beginning of 1990, car manufacturers started to feel the pressures of the early 1980s again. Apart from Volkswagen and General Motors' Opel Division, which were gearing up for the immense demand from East Germany, other car companies – Renault, Peugeot, Fiat and Ford – were beginning to feel the pressure. Renault's turnover was expected to fall

Manufacturers' sales		100
Cost of sales		
Materials	52	
Labour	15	
Overhead	4	
Depreciation	8	79
Gross profit		21
Selling general and administration	15	
Operating profit		6
Dealer mark-ups		10–20

Source: Annual Reports.

Exhibit 10.7 *Industry average income statement, 1989 (%)*

6.2% in 1990, which would hurt the bottom line severely. Volvo, Renault's alliance partner, was also not expected to be profitable in 1990. Ford was suffering in the UK, its largest market, as a recession took hold. As well, the company had to contend with the rising losses of its acquisition, the UK luxury car maker, Jaguar. Fiat was the first company to lay off tens of thousands of workers, while its share in the Italian market tumbled to 47.4% from 58.9% in 1988. Peugeot was also expected to have idle assembly plants. Volkswagen and General Motors were working at full capacity to meet the new demand surge in Germany (Exhibit 10.7).

1992

Traditionally, the European car industry consisted of national players who dominated their home market – Fiat in Italy, Renault and Peugeot in France, Volkswagen in Germany and Rover in the UK. Because of the large number of persons employed in a nation's auto industry, car makers were often at the forefront of both domestic politics and international trade disputes. To enhance the success of their national car companies, it was not uncommon for governments to enact a variety of legislative measures. Favourable tax benefits to local producers, restricted import levels – either through tariffs or voluntary export restraints – to foreign producers, protection from foreign acquisition and, finally, technical and physical barriers were some of the more common practices. As a result of these actions, car manufacturers were motivated to continue selling in their home market and make little effort to look outside.

In 1990, the Memorandum on the Single Market for Cars was signed by the European Commission. It indicated the need to provide the European car industry with a pan-European regulatory environment to control state aid and to establish an open external economic environment. Some of the highlights of the Memorandum were:

- speeding up technical harmonization and EC type approval programmes (such as having yellow headlights in France and clear ones in the rest of Europe, emission standards, roadworthiness tests, etc.)

- aligning the different national indirect taxes
- determining the level of 'local' content in each car
- lifting restrictions on foreign cars manufactured or assembled in another member state.

These actions were expected to create enormous savings in manufacturing, marketing and distribution, but the final effect would not be positive for all manufacturers. The less competitive companies would be likely to ask for more time to adjust and restructure their operations, whereas the more competitive companies would probably want to steam ahead.

Tough environmental laws

The US Environmental Protection Agency estimated that 50% of the world's smog and ozone depletion could be traced directly to motor vehicles. In the 1970s, the US government issued its Clean Air Bill, which forced car manufacturers to cut their emissions. The catalytic converter was the result, cutting emissions of carbon dioxides, hydrocarbons and nitrogen oxides by up to 96%. Catalytic converters had just started to catch on in Europe. They were not mandatory on cars until 1992, thus giving many of the European countries time to introduce the unleaded fuel necessary for these devices.

Further discussions were taking place on recyclability of cars as well. As more cars were sold, over time more cars ended up in the scrap heap, with many items non-recyclable. It was, therefore, expected that the European Commission would introduce some form of recycling legislation.

In the meantime, car companies responded by spending research and development funds in upgrading fuel economy, lowering emissions and improving the car's recyclability. Some of the research areas were: better engine electronics; low friction drive trains; raised gearings; lighter materials; electric and hybrid electric cars; and, finally, disassembly plants for recycling.

The Japanese onslaught

Japanese car manufacturers seemed to be following a calculated strategy: focus on the American market and then a decade later turn toward Europe. Already in the non-protected markets of Switzerland, Finland, Norway and Ireland, their combined market share was 25–45%. In other countries – such as Italy, Spain, France and the UK, quotas had been instituted to curb any expansion plans. (For example, in Italy the quotas virtually kept the Japanese out of the market, in France and Spain, it was held at 3% market share.) But, by 1993 these large protected markets would become open to the Japanese competitors, allowing them an estimated 13–17% market share through voluntary export restraint agreements.

Some countries that were hungry for job creation, such as the UK, saw the Japanese car producers as their friends. Nissan, Toyota and others were wooed to set up transplant factories through tax subsidies. Nissan was already producing 100,000 cars in the UK with plans to increase to 200,000. Toyota and Honda were also building plants in the UK. Mitsubishi had an assembly deal in the Netherlands (Exhibit 10.8).

UK	Capacity
Rover/Honda	360K
Nissan	300K
Toyota	250K
Honda	60K
Suzuki	20K
Belgium	
Mitsubishi	80K
Portugal	
Daihatsu	50K
Germany	
Toyota/VW	30K
Mazda/Ford	120K
Spain	
Nissan	155K
Suzuki	40K
Toyota	200K
Mitsubishi	200K

Source: Ward's Research from Industry Sources, 1991.

Exhibit 10.8 *Japanese assembly plants in Europe, 1995*

Analysts estimated that another 2 million units of new capacity were expected from Japanese transplant factories. (The European car manufacturers were already about 2 million cars *below* full capacity.)

The Central and Eastern European automobile market

One ray of hope remained for the European car manufacturers beleaguered by an uncertain future: the Central and Eastern European car market. After 40 years of restricted supply, pent-up demand for new and used cars was bursting at the seams.

The Eastern European people were fed up with the constant short supply of low quality cars. However, because cars were so scarce, people tended to hold on to whatever they had. In Hungary, for example, 50% of the vehicles continued to be in use for 24 years, whereas in the West practically all those cars would have been scrapped. Scrappage rates in Eastern Europe was a mere 1–2% versus an estimated 5–6% in the West. Therefore, by taking the extra scrappage up to the year 2005, demand forecasts ranged from as low as 2.1 million cars per year to a high of 7.3 million (Exhibit 10.9).

Yet, the alternatives to supply this unmet demand lay in the hands of the Central and Eastern European governments, their large worn-out automobile industries and their policies towards investment.

Countries	1989	Scenario 1	2005 Scenario 2	Scenario 3
USSR	22.80	16.60	10.00	6.25
Hungary	5.90	4.34	3.57	2.86
Czechoslovakia	5.20	3.84	3.23	2.70
Poland	8.40	6.25	5.00	4.17
Romania	75.40	12.50	8.33	5.55
Bulgaria	7.90	5.55	5.00	4.00
Yugoslavia	7.70	5.88	5.00	3.85

Scrappage rates calculation: (Old car park + New sales – New car park)/Old car park
Source: Economist Intelligence Unit, 1991, The Motor Industry of Eastern Europe, Prospects to 2000 and Beyond.

Exhibit 10.9 Demand scenarios for the Eastern European car market (persons per car)

The Central and Eastern European automobile industry

Background to the present situation

The first signs of an automobile industry in Central and Eastern Europe began in the early 20th century in Czechoslovakia, the 'industrial powerhouse' of the Austro-Hungarian empire. Indeed, it was a famous Czech named Porsche who designed the rear-mounted air-cooled engine used in Volkswagens and Porsche 911s. He started his career at a small company called Tatra, located in Koprivnice, which in 1990 was still manufacturing 800 limousines a year based on the same rear-mounted air-cooled engine design. No other country in Central and Eastern Europe had an automobile industry like the one in Czechoslovakia.

The CEE automobile industry suffered heavy setbacks during World War II and had to be completely rebuilt under the Communist regimes. The period between 1950 and 1965, the height of the Cold War, saw a slow, gradual reconstruction of the industry based on war reparations. During the 1970s, some CEE governments such as Yugoslavia, Poland and Romania turned to Western help to jump start their automobile industries (Fiat in Poland and Russia for the FSO, FSM and VAZ plants; Renault in Romania for the Dacia model.) The help consisted of technology licences, and the construction of large, turnkey body pressing and assembly plants. The technologies were already outdated by the time the plants were running. However, vehicle production in CEE eventually experienced rapid growth.

By the 1980s this growth had virtually stopped as a result of inadequate reinvestment and poor planning. Car models had remained the same since the 1960s and 70s, and the region had not been able to build its own strengths from the licensed technologies. As Western car companies were developing new technologies, the Eastern European industries languished under severe state control, limited development incentives, a lack of hard currency, a heavily protected domestic market and a constant shortage of basic materials and components supply.

Some companies responded by developing new models for the Western markets, such as the Skoda Favorit and the Lada Samara. Others tried to integrate vertically into components manufacturing in order to remove the shortage problem. (Outsourcing for CEE car companies was approximately 15–20% compared with 60% in the West.)

However, by the end of the 1980s, CEE governments began to realize the seriousness of the problems with their car industries. Prior to the political changes occurring in 1989, major discussions had taken place, i.e. Fiat had been considering doing business in Poland and Volkswagen in Czechoslovakia. It was not until the events of 1989 that the poor situation in these countries became really clear. The newly-formed governments had a range of policy decisions to make.

Government policy alternatives

The transformation of the car industry was inevitable, but how that was to take place was still not resolved. A range of alternatives faced government policymakers:

1 Government protection of domestic markets versus market liberalization.
2 Maintenance of production subsidies versus reducing or terminating them.
3 Rapid versus slow closure of companies with losses.
4 Privatization versus state ownership.
5 Breaking up versus retaining large organizations.
6 Liberalizing direct investment versus encouraging agreements with Western manufacturers.

Both the CEE governments and Western car manufacturers had to create scenarios to 'see' what were the implications of each policy alternative.

Spanish option

Eastern European governments were enamoured by the way that SEAT, the former Spanish state-owned car company, was sold to foreign interests. Volkswagen, its new owner, put a massive capital injection into the company to turn it around. SEAT kept its brand name and became a manufacturer of cheap, less sophisticated models, mainly for the Spanish and Portuguese markets.

Company descriptions

Western car manufacturers had a large range of companies to research when deciding to invest. They also had to consider how they could integrate these firms into their own range of cars. Would they become satellite operations of Western car manufacturers? Would they keep their brand name and be sold to Western markets? The following list provides a description of the major car operators in Eastern Europe including their models, their production and sales over the last five years, and finally, their reputation. Exhibit 10.10 shows the production figures for the last five years.

Company	1986	1987	1988	1989	1990
Soviet Union					
ALZK	181,000	182,032	115,322	145,000	n/a
GAZ	130,000	125,000	130,000	135,000	n/a
VAZ (Lada)	738,000	724,740	731,455	725,000	n/a
ZAZ	150,000	168,400	155,036	150,000	n/a
Czechoslovakia					
Skoda	183,000	170,500	162,000	186,500	187,000
Tatra	n/a	352	400	490	450
East Germany					
Veb (Trabant)	141,000	140,000	145,600	146,000	n/a
Veb (Wartburg)	76,931	78,600	73,120	73,840	n/a
Poland					
FSO	95,119	98,006	100,000	99,000	n/a
FSM	200,140	204,510	205,000	206,000	n/a
Romania					
Dacia	72,000	75,000	80,000	80,000	n/a
Oltcit	23,000	30,000	30,000	30,000	n/a
Yugoslavia					
IMV	42,033	47,556	54,309	51,465	n/a
IDA	2,262	3,094	1,887	4,709	n/a
Cimos	1,902	2,377	3,086	4,781	n/a
Unis-Tas	17,689	20,670	17,452	26,153	n/a
ZJA (Yugo)	175,462	211,202	217,207	220,174	n/a

Source: Economist Intelligence Unit, 1991, *The Motor Industry of Eastern Europe, Prospects to 2000 and Beyond.*

Exhibit 10.10 *Production figures for the leading Central Eastern European car manufacturers*

USSR

1 *AZLK (The Lenin Komsomol Automobile Factory)*
   Product range: 1500–1600 cc front-wheel drive passenger cars (Moskvich 2141). (Middle lower segment)
   Production capacity: 170,000–180,000 units
2 *Gaz (Gorky Automobile Factory)*
   Product range: 2500 cc large category Volga passenger cars and executive limousines. (Luxury lower segment)
   Production capacity: 130,000 units
3 *UAZ (Ulianovsk Automobile Factory)*
   Product range: petrol and diesel driven four-wheel drive off-road vehicles. (Speciality segment)
   Production capacity: 140,000 units

4 **Vaz (Volzhsky Automobile Factory)**

Product range: 1200–1600 cc, 4-door, rear-wheel drive Ladas based on a Fiat licence, 3- and 4-door front-wheel drive Lada Samaras. (Middle lower segment)

Production capacity: 750,000 units

5 **Zaz (Zaporozhetz Automobile Factory)**

Product range: 1100 cc front wheel drive Tavria cars and small off-road vehicles

Production capacity: 150,000–160,000 units.

Czechoslovakia

1 **AKMB (Automobilnovy Koncern Mlada Boleslav-Skoda)**

Product range: 1289 cc, front-wheel drive Skoda Favorit passenger cars. Before 1990, it produced the old rear-wheel drive Skoda 105 and 120 models. (Middle lower segment)

Production capacity: 180,000 units

2 **Tatra Kombinat**

Product range: 3500 cc Tatra executive limousines based on air-cooled rear-mounted engines. (Luxury lower segment)

Production capacity: 2000 units

East Germany

1 **Veb Sachsenring Automobile Werk**

Product range: Trabant passenger cars with plastic body fitted with a 1100 cc engine manufactured under a Volkswagen licence. (Before the beginning of 1990, the old 2-stroke engines were still produced for the Trabants.) (Micro segment)

Production capacity: 145,000 units

2 **Veb Automobile Werk**

Product range: 1300 cc Wartburg passenger cars fitted with engines manufactured under a Volkswagen licence; until October 1989, the old 2-stroke cars were manufactured. (Small segment)

Production capacity: 80,000 units

Poland

1 **FSO (Fabryka Samochodow Osobowych)**

Product range: 1300 cc and 1500 cc, 5-seater 125p cars (based on the 20-year-old Fiat 125 licence), 1500 cc and 2000 cc Polonez cars and assembly of some Fiat models. (Middle lower segment)

Production capacity: 95,000 units

2 **FSM (Fabryka Samochadow Malolitrazowych)**

Product range: 650 cc, 4-seater Polski 126E mini cars (based on the 20-year-old Fiat 126 licence.) (Micro segment)

Production capacity: 210,000 units

Romania

1 *Dacia, Uzina de Autoturisme*
   Product range: 1200–1400 cc Dacia passenger cars based on the 20-year-old
   Renault 12 licence. (Middle lower segment)
   Production capacity: 85,000 units
2 *Oltcit SA*
   Product range: 1100 cc Oltcit passenger cars, based on the 15-year-old Citroën Visa
   licence. (Small segment)
   Production capacity: 50,000 units
3 *Motor Car Enterprise*
   Product range: 2500–2600 cc petrol and diesel engine four-wheel drive ARO
   passenger cars and small trucks.
   Production capacity: 20,000 units

Yugoslavia

1 *IMV (Industria motornih vozil)*
   Product range: Assembly of mainly 20-year-old Renault 4, and 18. (Micro and
   middle lower segments) Plans for the Renault 5, 9, 19, 21, 25 cars and production
   of parts. Cooperation with Renault started in 1971.
   Production capacity: 54,000 units.
2 *IDA (Industrija delova automobila, Livnica zeljeza i tempera)*
   Product range: Assembly of Opel Corsa, Kadett, Vectra, Omega, and Senator
   passenger cars, production of certain parts. Cooperation with GM since 1981.
   Production assembly: 5,000 units.
3 *Cimos (Tovarna Automobilov)*
   Product range: Assembly of Citroën AX11, AX14, BX15, BX16, CX, XM V6 and
   XM 2L passenger cars, and production of certain parts.
   Production capacity: 5,000 units
4 *Unis-Tas (Tvornica automobila)*
   Product range: Assembly of Volkswagen Golf, Jetta, Passat, and Audi 80, 100, 200
   passenger cars, and production of parts. Cooperation with Volkswagen since
   1973.
   Production capacity: 30,000 units.
5 *ZJA (Zastava Jugo Automobili)*
   Product range: production of Yugo 45, Yugo 55 Yugo 60, Yugo 65, Yugo Florida,
   Yugo Uno, Skala passenger cars, assembly of FSM 126, FSO 125, Lada, and Fiat
   Croma passenger cars. Yugos were originally based on the 20-year-old Fiat 126
   design. (Micro and small segments)
   Production capacity: 220,000 units.
6 *Investmetali*
   Product range: Assembly of Peugeot 205, 309, 405 and 505 passenger cars.
   Production capacity: 900 units.

Part Four
Doing Business in Turbulent Environments[1]

Introduction

11 Crisis management
    Case 11.1 Delipan
    Case 11.2 Indunic
    Case 11.3 Sevysa

These cases were selected for discussion of the following concepts: crises under social revolts; crisis management, people crises: company crises; and perceived importance of crises

12 Turnaround management is not Rambo management
    Case 12.1 *Berlingske Tidende*
    Case 12.2 Taking charge at Inter Drinks Company

These cases were selected for discussion of the following concepts: innovating; doing things differently; efficiency improvements; starting the turnaround; selling the vision; 'Rambo-like' measures that may need to be taken

13 Managing in turbulent environments
    Case 13.1 PACCASA-LOMBARD (A)
    Case 13.2 PACCASA-LOMBARD (B)
    Case 13.3 Skoda–Volkswagen–Renault negotiations

These cases were selected for discussion of the following concepts: typical management issues; adapting strategic decisions; adapting business policies; and the CEO and corporate culture

14 Inflation's impact on financial policies
    Case 14.1 An ethical problem?

This case was selected for discussion of the following concepts: impact on financial statements and ratios; revaluing assets and depreciation expenses; impact on investment decision; and reviewing other policies

15 Devaluation's impact on the strategic posture
    Case 15.1 Aluminum S.A.

This case was selected for discussion of the following concepts: origin of devaluations; exposure to devaluation risk; and impact on an exporting firm

---

[1] Based on Ketelhöhn, Werner, 'Doing the business in turbulent environments', *IMEDE Perspectives for Managers*, No. 4, June 1989.

Introduction

'This Palace's congress, comrades, has never heard such discussions as ours; and we are not far from the truth, I think, when we say that, in the last sixty years, nothing like this has occurred in this country,' said Mikhail Gorbachov, General Secretary of the Soviet communist party, on July 1, 1988, in his closing speech of the XIX Federal Conference where he had proclaimed 'there is no alternative to perestroika' (UPI, AP, AFP, EFE, Moscow).

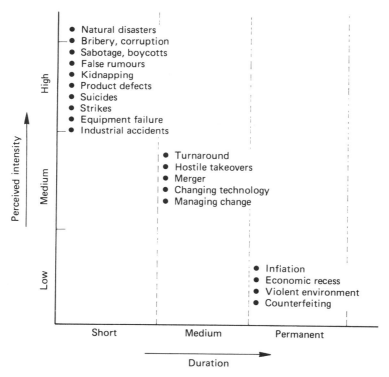

Environmental disruptions

Overview

The collapse of the Soviet Union at the beginning of the 1990s, and other internationally famous disruptions like the Arab oil embargo in 1973, the Iranian and Central American revolutions, the Yugoslavian civil war, nuclear plant accidents,

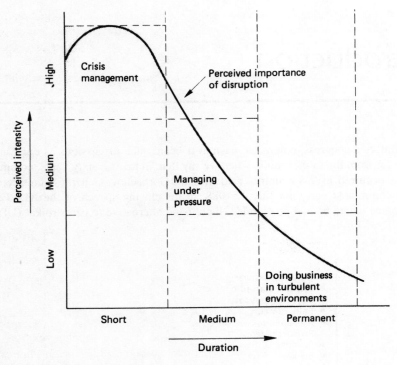

Generic management approaches

natural disasters; and many other turbulent situations like corporate theft, hostile takeovers, boycotts, strikes and inflation make up a wide range of unusual disruptions to the 'normal' ways of doing business. These environmental disruptions which are classified in Figure C using two empirical dimensions, must and can be managed, but how does one do business under these conditions?

To manage in turbulent environments, corporations have to change from 'business as usual' to managing extraordinary events. Rather than improvise organizational responses, both corporations and government must proactively identify management processes with which to respond to extraordinary disruptions of the 'normal' ways of doing business. This can be done using frameworks that first classify turbulent situations into families of problems, as in Figure C, which submit management teams to similar pressures; and then, create generic management processes with which executives can respond to situations belonging to a family of disruptions, as illustrated in Figure D.

Turbulence varies in duration and intensity

First we recognize that the duration of the abnormality calls for different management responses. Short intense disruptions, like the February 3, 1975 suicide of Eli Black,

CEO of United Brands, are best handled by crisis management teams.[1] Permanent turbulence, on the other extreme, like the Soviet democratic revolution or the Yugoslavian civil war, demands longer lasting changes in a corporation's operating policies in those markets.

A second distinction is to recognize that disruptions vary in the intensity with which managers perceive their impact on the corporation. For example, the Bhopal industrial accident in India provoked a short and intense disruption of the normal ways of doing business at Union Carbide; it also triggered a more sustained change process in the company. Mastering emergent technologies, managing change, launching a turnaround, facing a hostile takeover and implementing a merger, are medium duration disruptions which last between one and three years; they are recognized as special forms of managing under pressure. Thus a second genre of management processes are those concerned with medium duration and medium intensity disruptions of the 'normal' ways of doing business. These disruptions may also originate in the competitive environment of the firm, such as the 1988 hostile takeover attempt made by Ticino financier Tito Tettamanti on Sulzer Brothers Ltd.

Corrupt public administration, counterfeiting, inflation, devaluations, civil war and revolutionary governments create long-term disruptions to the 'normal' ways of doing business. We call managing under sustained environmental turbulence, *doing business in turbulent environments*.

The main theme of the cases selected for this fourth and last part is concerned with the processes that adapt a corporation's strategic posture to cope with ongoing disruptions of the social, political and economic environment. Managing in turbulent environments is the third genre of management processes that needs to be studied to be able to respond to ongoing disruptions in the business environment.

In summary, the intensity with which a disruption is perceived by management depends upon the duration of the turbulence. Since managers eventually learn to cope with sustained long-run turbulence, its perceived intensity tends to decline over time. Thus perceived intensity and duration correlate as illustrated in the generic management approaches diagram.

The Central American experience

We asked a sample of 87 Nicaraguan, 44 Salvadorean and 18 Guatemalan managers, to report on their perception of the most important problems during five years of the Central American social revolt (1977–1982). Their answers reveal three major findings:

1 Disruptions originating in social revolts belong to one of three generic management problems: short duration with high intensity; medium duration with medium intensity; and sustained duration with lower intensity.
2 As illustrated in the generic management approaches diagram, executives respond with different management approaches to each family of disruptions: crisis

---

[1] Eli Black jumped out of a window of the 44th floor in the PanAm building in New York, when it was uncovered that United Brands supposedly bribed Economics minister Abraham Bennaton Ramos and President Oswaldo Lopez Arellano, in exchange for lower export taxes on bananas from Honduras.

management for short intense disruptions; management under pressure for disruptions with medium intensity and duration; and managing in turbulent environments for disruptions with long duration.

3 Managing in turbulent environments also includes short-term crises and medium-term turbulent disruptions.

Doing business in turbulent environments requires flexible management and adaptable business policies. Headquarters must include local managers' perceptions in its strategic decision process. Likewise, country managers' knowledge of local economic and political conditions must be tapped if the corporation decides to compete in a turbulent business environment. The global implications of changing corporate business policies in response to local conditions, i.e. the message that this sends to other countries, must be evaluated at headquarters in a logical and objective manner; put in place, it forms a part of the market-to-market learning processes.

About the Cases

In Part Four: *Doing Business in Turbulent Environments*, we provide the opportunity to discuss cases dealing with the adaptation of a strategic posture to countries subjected to violent social revolts. Before we present them, however, we would like to recognize the contributions of Professor James C. Ellert and research associates Juliet Burdet Taylor, Pablo Duran, James Henderson, Roger Quant Pallavicini, Barbara Robins, Amy W. Webster and Srinivasa Rangan, to different cases. Undoubtedly, we are indebted with many staff members at IMD and INCAE for their enthusiastic support during the different phases of our research.

These case studies are useful for discussing frameworks for understanding how to do business in turbulent environments. We call this managing in turbulent environments. We provide case studies from several Central American and East European countries. Useful generalizations can be drawn from these discussions for use in other markets subjected to the same generic disruptions. These crises may also occur in developed countries like the USA (Los Angeles in 1992), Russia (Moscow in 1993) and Germany (Berlin in 1992), not permanently subjected to violent social revolts. The Central American experience suggests that, since there is no time to learn in crisis situations, crisis management teams must not only understand the enterprise system in a specific market, but also be trained to handle crises.

However, since no one knows enough to forecast all environmental pressures in advance, excellent European companies tend to adapt their business practice to specific country conditions in a series of small steps rather than relying on centrally conceived sweeping strategies. As expressed by Mr Helmuth Maucher's address on management practice to an attentive audience of IMEDE professors in spring 1988, his efforts to simplify corporate reporting practices included reducing country reports to one page of reliable figures; he added, 'this forces country managers to think about what is really important and eliminates the need for further analysis at headquarters.'

The role of the CEO is to transmit his or her perspective about the business across the corporation, so that this perspective influences the way in which far away country managers handle difficult situations. Responsibility and authority for these decisions must be articulated by top management so that country managers, who are in touch with local realities, can react with flexibility, while keeping HQ informed. They should also open communication channels with economic and political authorities to maintain the flows of information.

Contradiction between local and global policies reflects differences in the perspective of a subsidiary's mission; but this is also a pleasant reality: no matter how centralized a CEO wants to make his business, local management, if of any value, will act according to local needs, whether or not it violates global policies. The job of local management is to defend the best interests of their subsidiary; and the job of the CEO is to provide a guiding business perspective.

Finally we provide the opportunity to discuss the revision of important financial policies when the environment presents permanent inflations below 25% per year. For higher inflations, we don't believe that traditional financial approaches are helpful. The details of these analyses can be found in consultation with financial specialists.

When the value of goods and services changes on a daily basis, say by to 10% per day, the distortions imposed on the economy are of such magnitude that any analysis of end-of-year financial statements sheds little light on the business' productive capability, working capital needs and other policies. Under such bizarre conditions we have seen two complementary approaches in use: first, some business people simply work in dollars, a currency relatively stable to theirs; but when the economy's distortions are also reflected in the country's dollar prices of goods and services, they switch to a barter business, which is a difficult trade to learn.

What we have learned from the experiences presented in our cases is that country managers operating in inflationary markets have to adjust their policies to permanent disruptions of the economic environment. Specifically, long-term financing has to be examined for its exposure to inflationary and devaluation risks. But on the other hand, there may be some benefits and planned financial profits if long-term debt is acquired in local currency at pre-inflation fixed interest rates. A whole new game of monetary caution and speculation may open new opportunities and risks and distract the management team from its fundamental business.

11

Crisis management

Case 11.1 Delipan

This case was prepared by Mr Pablo Duran and revised by Research Associate Barbara Robins, under the supervision of Professor Werner Ketelhöhn, as a basis for class discussion rather than to illustrate either effective or ineffective handling of a business situation.

At 8.00 am on February 12, 1980, Pablo Blandon, President and General Manager of Delipan, was in his office preparing a report for the board of directors about the state of the company. His concentration was broken by the telephone ringing. When he lifted the receiver, he immediately recognized the same threatening voice: 'We are warning you for the second time. If you do not resign, you will be killed by the popular forces.' Pablo put the phone down; he wiped his forehead and lit a cigarette. Nervously, he began to think about who it could be that was threatening him, what was the objective, and was it really necessary to think about resigning. He wondered what decisions he would have to take in order to prevent someone from murdering him.

History of the company

Delipan was founded in 1958 by Pablo's mother, Mrs. Gloria de Blandon, with the purpose of producing baked goods such as sweet breads and French bread. After many years of hard work, Mrs. Blandon had built up a small business which consisted of one production centre and one sales branch. Although the enterprise was slow to grow, its revenues always managed to cover the expenses of Mrs Blandon's family.

In 1978, Mrs Blandon decided to retire and transfer the company to her four sons so that they could develop it further. Carlos Blandon (Pablo's elder brother) was named

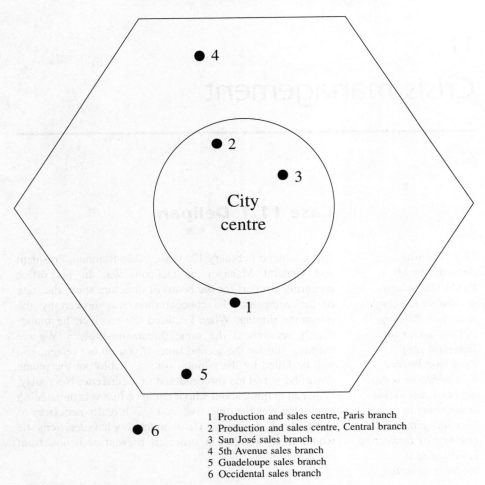

1 Production and sales centre, Paris branch
2 Production and sales centre, Central branch
3 San José sales branch
4 5th Avenue sales branch
5 Guadeloupe sales branch
6 Occidental sales branch

Exhibit 11.1   *Production centres and sales branches, end 1979*

President and General Manager. Carlos worked with great enthusiasm. He quickly opened one more production centre and an additional sales branch to serve another geographical district of San Salvador, capital of El Salvador. By the end of the year, sales had increased.

In the middle of 1979, Pablo's services were contracted to manage the administration of the company and its expansion plans. He was appointed Development Manager. By the end of 1979, the two brothers had established two production centres and six sales branches located in strategic locations within the capital (Exhibit 11.1). Opening up these sales branches, combined with a strategy of offering high quality products at moderate prices, produced a sales growth of 55% over the sales for June to December of the previous year (Exhibit 11.2).

The financial results obtained in December 1979 were very encouraging, since profits had increased from ¢53,100 in 1978 to ¢137,600 in 1979 (Exhibits 11.3 and 11.4). Pablo thought that a great deal of this growth was due to the opening of the new sales branches. This method of selling bakery products had a certain advantage over the competition, which sold their products only through supermarkets and various neighbourhood stores

	1978	1979
January	–	86.2
February	–	76.4
March	–	81.9
April	–	75.8
May	–	79.9
June	12.5	88.0
July	76.3	102.7[2]
August	73.4	109.6
September	77.2	112.3
October	81.4	118.1
November	75.0	107.8
December	86.6	108.5[3]
Total	482.4	1,147.2

[1]One Salvadoran colon equals US$4.

[2]In July, the 5th Avenue and San Jose branches were opened.

[3]The Occidental branch was inaugurated.

Exhibit 11.2   *Monthly sales record, 1978/1979 (thousands of colones)*[1]

	1978	1979
Sales	482.4	1,147.2
Cost of sales		
Raw materials	168.8	416.3
Direct labour	48.2	104.9
Indirect costs	33.7	96.9
Gross profit	231.7	529.1
Less:		
General expenses		
Cost of sales	96.5	202.0
Administrative expenses	72.3	182.3
Financial expenses	4.8	3.2
Other expenses	5.0	4.0
Profit before tax/debts	53.1	137.6

Exhibit 11.3   *Statement of earnings and losses, 1978/79 (thousands of colones)*

ASSETS

AVAILABLE		30,600.00
Cash	14,000.00	
Banks	16,600.00	
ACCESSIBLE		70,500.00
Loans to shareholders and employees	37,600.00	
Deposits	2,100.00	
Inventory	30,800.00	
– raw material 19,700		
– other material 11,100		
FIXED		265,460.00
Buildings and office equipment	10,560.00	
Machinery and industrial equipment	160,000.00	
Transport equipment	72,800.00	
Buildings and equipment in branches	63,750.00	
	307,110.00	
Minus: Accumulated depreciation	41,650.00	
DEFERRED AND TRANSITORY		11,100.00
Insurance	3,500.00	
Anticipated expenses	3,300.00	
Installations	4,300.00	
TOTAL ASSETS		**377,660.00**

LIABILITIES

SHORT-TERM DEBTS		47,478.00
Suppliers	9,700.00	
Accounts payable	25,600.00	
	12,178.00	
LONG-TERM DEBTS		72,220.00
Other financing	31,420.00	
Bank loans	40,800.00	
CONTINGENCIES		5,600.00
Provision for labour benefits	5,600.00	
Contribution for future capital increases	34,100.00	34,100.00
TOTAL LIABILITIES		159,398.00
CAPITAL AND RESERVES		218,262.00
Share capital	50,000.00	
Legal reserves	14,400.00	
Retained earnings	153,962.00	
in 78 43,390.00		
In 79 110,472.01		
TOTAL LIABILITIES & CAPITAL		**377,660.00**

Exhibit 11.4 *General balance as of December 31, 1979*

Memorandum

To: Board of Directors

From: Pablo Blandon

Subject: Distribution Strategy

Date: August 1979

In accordance with your request for information regarding the distribution strategy that the enterprise should follow, I wish to inform you of the advantages and disadvantages of distributing our bread through supermarkets and other stores versus through our own branches.

SUPERMARKETS AND STORES

Advantages

1 It is not necessary to make investments in buildings and equipment.
2 No rent to be paid.
3 Greater penetration of the market can be achieved, covering all areas of the capital.
4 All social classes can be served.
5 Fewer sales personnel needed.

Disadvantages

1 Additional transport personnel required.

2 No direct client contact.
3 Additional transport trucks are required.

4 Other brand names are sold within the same sales centre.
5 Constantly requesting replacement of old or damaged bread.
6 Demanding 20% sales margin.
7 Investment in packaging required.

OWN SALES BRANCHES

1 A better image of the company is projected.
2 Direct service to the client is maintained.
3 The sales at one branch equals dealing with 25 distributors.
4 Sales effort is controlled.

1 Necessary to invest $10,000 in buildings for each sales branch.
2 Rent of 800.00 colones for locales.
3 The number of employees increases by at least 3 persons per branch.
4 A large part of the market remains uncovered.

Exhibit 11.5 *Memorandum to staff*

(Exhibit 11.5). The brothers predicted that, by using the same policies, a profit of ¢185,500 could be attained in 1980 and ¢224,800 in 1981 (Exhibit 11.6).

In 1980 Carlos decided to retire from the business for personal reasons. The other family members and shareholders then named Pablo as President and General Manager.

After taking over, Pablo decided to employ an assistant manager. A reliable assistant would give him more time to control the operations of the various sales branches and production centres. In January 1980, he appointed an auditor, known to the family, who had strong preferences for administration, principally in Market and Operational Control. It was the first time that someone other than a family member, with the exception of the accountant, would be working in the administration area.

	1980	1981
Net sales	1,376.6	1,652.0
Cost of sales		
Raw materials	495.5	594.7
Direct labour	123.9	148.7
Indirect costs	110.1	132.1
Gross profit	647.1	776.5
Less:		
General expenses		
Cost of sales	234.0	280.8
Administrative expenses	220.2	264.3
Financial expenses	3.0	3.3
Other expenses	4.1	3.3
Profit before tax	185.5	224.8

Exhibit 11.6 *Statement of projected earnings and losses, 1980/81 (thousands of colones)*

In addition to hiring an assistant, Pablo held a meeting with the employees[1] in order to initiate a rapport and to explain the company's current situation. At the meeting, he gave a brief history of the company from its founding through to when it became a limited company owned by his family members. He reminded the employees of the cooperation that had always existed between the workers and the administrative staff. He made it clear that such a relationship needed to be maintained more than ever as 1980 would be a difficult year due to the political–social situation in El Salvador.

Socio-political conditions in El Salvador

The prevailing situation in El Salvador was characterized by terrorism, kidnappings, political repression, peaceful and violent street demonstrations, workers' strikes, work stoppages, sabotage and attempted uprisings by armed Marxist groups.

The principal characteristic of the situation was political polarization and the growth of extremist groups from both the left and the right; the two prominent forces were Marxism and the ultra right.

Problems facing management

Pablo considered that, since the company was going through some very tough times, especially regarding security, the expansion strategy that had been planned should not be implemented, in spite of the excellent financial results of the previous year.

[1] The personnel totalled 75 persons, with the majority having one to two years of primary school education.

However, he did not entirely give up the idea of implementing an alternative growth strategy because he saw that the current socio-political destabilization in the country was creating some great opportunities. The large bakeries were suffering continuous labour conflicts, strikes and shutdowns; these problems were impeding them from adequately supplying the market with their products, thereby creating a continuous demand. 'A turbulent river is an opportunity for the fishermen,' thought Pablo.

On December 15, 1979, the Board of Directors of Delipan had asked Pablo to write a report on the effects that the socio-political events in the country were having on the company's operations. Pablo described each of these factions in terms of their influence on Delipan and on business in general:

Terrorism

In the last three months of the year, most acts of terrorism have involved placing bombs in different enterprises and public buildings within the capital. These acts have produced great fear amongst company owners. The potential losses for our company could be substantial, not only in material, but also in loss of sales and profits. In addition, serious cash flow problems could occur due to the low level of liquidity that the company has at this moment because of the expansion policy which was financed with company funds.

The objective of these terrorist acts is to destabilize the country and to destroy enterprises with a certain image of financial stability. Our six sales branches, distributed throughout the capital, represent an image of a solid and growing enterprise, for which Delipan could be a possible target.

Kidnappings and assassinations

Since 1970, kidnappings of wealthy individuals and assassinations of political figures have taken place. These acts are generally attributed to guerrilla groups. However, during 1978/79, middle-class individuals were being kidnapped by groups of delinquents that were taking advantage of the turmoil to commit their offences. This personal danger, which could affect our staff members, has prompted people to start taking security measures.

Street demonstrations

Since October 1979, street demonstrations by political and labour union groups have increased. Through them, the coup d'état that recently occurred in the country was being condemned. Street demonstrations generally involve the burning of vehicles, attacks on commercial and industrial installations, setting fire to premises, and confrontations with security personnel. Due to these events, we were obligated to install protective devises in the sales branches.

Generally, the demonstrations take place in the city centre where Delipan has two branches, and in most cases the date and hour of such activities can be anticipated because they are organized publicly. Sales in the city centre have decreased because of the constant danger which has discouraged and demotivated the staff.

Strikes and work stoppages

The process of social–political unrest has enabled the unions, led by leftist political groups, to gain more power and to intensify demands for better social conditions. Generally, the unions resort to calling indefinite strikes which paralyse operations and cause great losses.

The political groups and the unions have intensified their search for new followers as a way of promoting their campaign. These activities increase the possibility that people from outside Delipan could try to form an activist union within the company. Information was recently received that the Food and Drink Industry Union was holding talks with our personnel about forming a union in Delipan. This union could be under the jurisdiction of a Central Union that is characterized by political interests. If this should take place, an immediate deterioration of the worker–management relationship would occur, as it could end in strikes and eventual financial losses that could not be sustained by the company. It has been calculated that, in the event of a strike, the company has only 15 days worth of cash to cover obligations such as administrative salaries, rents, service and suppliers' payments, bank interests, etc.

Political repression

In response to the social unrest, the military security corps have intensified their operations against the political organizations and the unions. The number of disappearances, deaths and torture in the country has increased dramatically during the last part of 1979.

The leftist groups responded to the repression with more violence; violence has generated more violence and hate has generated more hate. At present, there is a climate of great anxiety and danger for the entire population.

Pablo's decision

Pablo wondered how to remain untouched by this situation and what steps he should take in this respect. He thought about the death threat.

Without warning, the external auditor of the company, Pedro Molina, stormed into his office and said: 'Pablo, it is no longer possible to continue working in this country! This morning I have been threatened with death if I do not resign. What's happening, man? Never in 40 years of exercising my profession has this happened to me!'

'Pedro,' answered Pablo, 'take a seat and try to calm down. I am in the same situation and have even thought of emigrating.'

'However, what we have to do is analyse the situation wisely. These problems can have a snowball effect that can carry everyone away. Where do you think we should start?'

Case 11.2 INDUNIC

This case was prepared by Professor Werner Ketelhöhn, and revised by Research Associate Barbara Robins, as a basis for class discussion rather than to illustrate either effective or ineffective handling of a business situation.

In April 1978, Rolf Beck, General Manager of INDUNIC, sat down to plan his operating budget for 1978/1979. He realized that his assessment of future demand, planning of inventory policies and selling strategies should somehow include consideration of Nicaragua's latest political and economic troubles. Guerrilla war in the last part of 1977, and the assassination of Pedro Joaquin Chamorro[1] in January 1978, had created an uncertain marketplace and destabilized Nicaragua's economy. The rest of Central America was relatively stable and prosperous, but the Nicaraguan market, centre of INDUNIC's operations, was weak. A more careful assessment of future demand, inventory and selling strategies for the coming years was of utmost importance if INDUNIC were to maintain its growth rate of the past five years.

Rolf was especially interested in determining optimum inventories both for raw materials and finished products. He knew that one way to lower the risk and monetary investment in inventory was to use smaller production runs, but he felt unsure about making such calculations.

Rolf decided to hire a consultant to help him solve the problems; the consultant was asked to make proposals for the following:

- What strategy should INDUNIC use to maintain its rate of growth?
- What production plan should INDUNIC follow, and why?

Rolf gave the consultant the relevant background information so that work on the assignment could be started immediately.

---

[1] Pedro Joaquin Chamorro was a journalist and the undisputed leader of the legal political opposition groups.

Some political background

The legal opposition movements had not succeeded in loosening Somoza's[2] grip on the Nicaraguan government nor in toppling his corrupt dictatorship. Somoza and his collaborators maintained that Nicaraguans had only two choices: Somoza or communism.

In 1961, a group of young idealists founded the guerrilla group, Frente Sandinista de Liberacion Nacional (FSLN). They were committed to the idea of violence as the only way to reduce Somoza's power. They worked consistently toward their goal, but in the early years experienced problems with strategy, unity and resources. By 1977, the opposition to Somoza's dictatorship had reached a peak. The business community, and the population in general, had concluded that a violent social revolt was the only way to throw out the ruling party and the military. The FSLN had grown significantly in size as well as in experience with guerrilla warfare. International support had also increased; financing, arms and training camps were provided by the International Socialist Movement and political foundations in Venezuela, Costa Rica and West Germany. A climate of confrontation developed between the Nicaraguan government and its traditional political parties, the workers, students, businessmen and the Catholic Church.

In January 1978, Pedro Joaquin Chamorro was assassinated by a repression gang connected with Somoza. This paramilitary act of violence shocked the Latin American political and business community, and served as a catalyst for opposition forces inside and outside Nicaragua. In an immediate reaction, leaders of the Nicaraguan business community threatened to paralyse the economy of Nicaragua until Somoza agreed to resign. They organized a nationwide business strike which was followed by guerrilla actions and urban riots. For 15 days (the second and third weeks of January) the country's economy stopped.

Businessmen paid salaries for the two weeks in which no work was done. Contacts with the FSLN leaders brought consensus for coordinating a second business strike in conjunction with attacks by the FSLN guerrilla forces. As a result, Nicaragua's economy deteriorated quickly.

INDUNIC's background

In the early 1970s, Central America had experienced a high and growing demand for household electrical equipment. At that time, the market was being served by firms based in industrial countries which shipped their products to all the Central American markets. Because of the growing demand, and the possibility of business protections provided by the Central American Common Market laws, an aggressive group of businessmen asked Rolf Beck to research specific product lines, raw material suppliers and specialized labour requirements.

Rolf's study identified a feasible project. He recommended that investments be made in a company which would manufacture six product lines. In each product line, different models would be manufactured, some more expensive than others, but with common production processes; they would compete in the same market and have identical percentage contribution margins.

---

[2] The Nicaraguan dictator whose family had been in power for over 40 years.

	72/73	73/74	74/75	75/76	76/77	77/78
Total	430	649	885	1,298	2,063	2,886
Δ %	–	51%	36%	47%	59%	40%
Nicaragua	430	649	814	865	1,107	1,200
Δ %	–	51%	25%	6%	28%	8%
Exports	–	–	71	433	956	1,689
Δ %	–	–	–	510%	121%	77%

Exhibit 11.7 *Total annual sales (thousands of $)*

The business group accepted Rolf's recommendations and named Rolf as project manager of INDUNIC, which started operations in mid-1971. In time, Rolf became the General Manager.

INDUNIC's first two years were difficult. A new start was necessary in 1973 after all the facilities were destroyed in a December 1972 earthquake. In time, however, sales jumped from $430,000 in 1973 to $2,886,000 in 1977/1978 – an average rate of growth in sales of 43%. This success was primarily due to Rolf's managerial capabilities and hard work (Exhibit 11.7) and was achieved with no new capital injection. A policy of reinvesting all profits had been religiously followed up to 1977/1978, and the plan was to continue in the foreseeable future.

Exports to Central America had started in 1974/1975 with 4% of sales (Exhibit 11.7) and, in only three years, they had reached 58%. In these three years, exports grew from $430,000 in 1975/1976 to about $1,689,000 in 1977/1978. Rolf wondered how long this rate of growth could be maintained in Central America; with a population of about 17 million, and an agriculturally based economy, there were obvious limits to INDUNIC's growth rate. However, INDUNIC was exporting to only two of the five Central American countries.

The first half of INDUNIC's 1978 business year in Nicaragua was very successful because political events had not yet developed. Total sales were expected to grow by 8% because of this strong first half and the performance of product line No.1 in the local market. Moreover, INDUNIC's sales were seasonal (Exhibit 11.8), with 62% of sales occurring in the six months before December 31. A first peak in sales normally occurred in November and December of each year, and a second peak in April and May. Low sales occurred in July and August and again in February and March. Rolf was not sure if the seasonality of each of the product lines was the same, but he knew that if the problems in Nicaragua stabilized in May, some growth in local sales was feasible.

July	Aug.	Sept.	Oct.	Nov.	Dec.	Jan.	Feb.	Mar.	Apr.	May	June
5.9	5.7	7.3	10.3	15.9	17	4.1	4.5	5.1	6.8	11.4	5.9

Exhibit 11.8 *Sales seasonality (%): $ monthly sales/$ yearly sales*

Rolf thought that INDUNIC's sales in Nicaragua for 1977/1978 would be reduced to the sales level for 1975/1976. His assessment was strongly influenced by economists' predictions that Nicaragua's economy would grow by only 4%. An original 8% growth rate had been halved because of the violent acts of social revolt in early 1978. Furthermore, a weakened economy would impose restrictions on Rolf's ability to grant credits to Nicaraguan wholesalers and retailers.

Production

INDUNIC's factory was basically an assembly line with some sophisticated quality control equipment. Assembly of electrical household products was conceived as a series of projects. The work force, mainly women, was divided into eight teams with a forewoman as the team leader. Assembly teams varied between 15 to 30 members, depending on the product they were assembling. Each assembly team worked a production batch until completion, which typically took 30–45 days (Exhibit 11.9). Typical lot sizes were 500–1 000 units, with a total value as high as $300,000 per lot. This represented an enormous financial responsibility for each team and its leader.

	Product line					
	1	*2*	*3*	*4*	*5*	*6*
Assembly time	45 days	45 days	30 days	30 days	30 days	30 days
Raw material lead time	6 months	4 months	4 months	6 months	7 months	4 months
Minimum order	500 units	500	10	1000	250	3000
Increments	100 units	500	5	500	50	500

Exhibit 11.9   *Assembly time and raw material orders*

Rolf's inventory policy was to shift inventories from raw materials to finished products as soon as possible. On average, one week was devoted to evaluating missing materials and reordering for each production lot. The lead time between when purchase orders for raw materials were sent and their receipt at the warehouse fluctuated, but it was generally 4–7 months. Suppliers required a minimum order for each product line. These minimum order sizes determined the production run lot size, because INDUNIC's orders were always minimal, given Central America's relative low demand in world markets. Furthermore, financially, it was better to store finished products than raw materials because of the low cost of labour in relation to raw materials (Exhibit 11.10).

Indirect assembly costs were divided into one-third for variable costs, and two-thirds for fixed costs. That is, one-third of the indirect costs depended on volume and was considered variable. Set-up costs for each assembly run were calculated to be 20% of the total labour cost for that run. Inventory cost, i.e. the cost of carrying inventories of raw materials or finished products was estimated to be 2% per month of all inventory investments. Rolf had estimated that 8% of his sales dollars were spent on other financial expenses related to working capital needs, exports and financing wholesalers. Exhibit 11.11 shows Rolf's sales projections and Exhibit 11.12 shows each year's results for all product lines; Exhibits 11.13–11.17 show the monthly sales for 1973/74–1977/78.

Product line	Direct cost		Indirect cost		Stand cost	Variable (% of S.P.)		Sales price
	Mat.	Labour	Fixed	Var.		Sales	Fin.	
1	98	5	7	3	113	7%	8%	170
2	190	6	8	4	208	7%	8%	277
3	1,799	36	74	35	1,944	5%	8%	2,699
4	93	3	4	2	102	7%	8%	135
5	299	7	9	4	319	6%	8%	400
6	14	1	2	1	18	7%	8%	22

*Unaudited figures

Exhibit 11.10 Costs, margins and sales price ($)*

Year	1	2	3	4	5	6
74/75	1,000	900	58	1,415	–	7,400
75/76	1,200	1,404	46	5,345	350	9,785
76/77	800	3,920	55	6,500	590	7,350
77/78	2,612	3,912	100	7,902	756	8,500
78/79	3,840	4,577	90	8,567	416	22,383

*By Rolf Beck

Exhibit 11.11 Sales projection per product line (units)*

Year		1	2	3	4	5	6
74/75	Nicar.	604	630	69	1,290	–	7,625
	Export	172	44	–	355	–	1,005
75/76	Nicar.	539	1,136	9	2,295	169	4,683
	Export	263	410	13	1,580	69	3,408
76/77	Nicar.	443	1,698	38	2,652	219	1,603
	Export	743	1,874	44	2,574	157	–
77/78	Nicar.	1,151	1,788	41	2,085	234	5,761
	Export	1,568	2,855	21	4,944	153	1,852

*Unaudited figures

Exhibit 11.12 Sales per product line (units)*

Product line	July	Aug.	Sept.	Oct.	Nov.	Dec.	Jan.	Feb.	Mar.	Apr.	May	June
1	–	–	–	–	–	–	–	–	–	–	–	–
2	16	29	32	92	54	244	52	9	18	73	78	8
3	–	–	–	–	–	–	–	–	–	–	–	12
4	28	51	31	97	81	192	115	64	40	32	237	62
5	–	–	–	–	–	–	–	–	–	–	–	–
6	53	267	530	804	1,132	1,410	395	2,024	357	255	67	49

Exhibit 11.13 *Monthly sales (units), 1973/74 (unaudited figures)*

Product line	July	Aug.	Sept.	Oct.	Nov.	Dec.	Jan.	Feb.	Mar.	Apr.	May	June
1	–	–	–	–	183	37	29	142	13	81	147	16
2	30	14	18	20	181	114	31	28	11	31	125	13
3	6	0	9	14	12	0	0	0	13	2	0	4
4	115	24	47	83	302	45	41	62	130	209	250	18
5	–	–	–	–	–	–	–	–	–	–	–	–
6	44	1,356	1,021	1,105	1,737	242	151	448	22	682	829	258

Exhibit 11.14 *Monthly sales (units), 1974/75 (unaudited figures)*

Product line	July	Aug.	Sept.	Oct.	Nov.	Dec.	Jan.	Feb.	Mar.	Apr.	May	June
1	44	59	38	117	51	189	28	42	65	70	161	278
2	44	31	301	52	112	470	22	7	19	17	370	31
3	0	3	2	0	5	3	0	0	6	4	0	0
4	129	263	187	329	713	777	351	288	213	247	274	256
5	0	0	18	39	38	41	2	3	4	38	15	10
6	213	316	1463	1718	729	430	252	398	738	557	473	1,154

Exhibit 11.15 *Monthly sales (units), 1975/76 (unaudited figures)*

Product line	July	Aug.	Sept.	Oct.	Nov.	Dec.	Jan.	Feb.	Mar.	Apr.	May	June
1	3	30	15	220	12	197	2	38	116	156	287	27
2	193	103	193	557	371	811	168	110	279	180	567	70
3	14	0	8	0	9	5	6	9	7	5	3	16
4	470	294	581	390	1,511	971	212	19	1	432	328	82
5	4	67	69	13	0	107	1	1	25	44	26	17
6	30	284	901	38	215	129	0	3	0	3	0	0

Exhibit 11.16 *Monthly sales (units), 1976/77 (unaudited figures)*

Product line	July	Aug.	Sept.	Oct.	Nov.	Dec.	Jan.	Feb.	Mar.	Apr.	May	June
1	216	163	279	252	621	281	25	91	180	195	229	189
2	271	318	246	657	780	887	73	288	142	471	383	129
3	–	8	2	14	–	17	–	4	–	1	11	5
4	239	914	333	830	1354	735	78	199	164	664	1,066	489
5	12	67	22	68	67	25	15	–	18	–	28	18
6	–	750	1,030	979	237	–	–	1,061	706	761	1255	834

Exhibit 11.17 *Monthly sales (units), 1977/78 (unaudited figures)*

Developing a strategy

Rolf was eagerly waiting for the consultant's proposed solutions for an overall strategy which would maintain INDUNIC's rate of growth. He wondered if the accuracy of his own forecasting would correspond to the recommendations made by the consultant.

That same afternoon Rolf left for an urgent meeting with his colleagues in the Chamber of Industry. There, industrialists were assessing the economic consequences of January's countrywide business strike and planning the next political move in their fight against Somoza.

Case 11.3 Sevysa

This case was prepared by Research Associate Juliet Burdet, under the supervision of Professor Jan Kubes, as a basis for class discussion rather than to illustrate either effective or ineffective handling of a business situation.

Another one of those days . . .

Fax from Nike Europe, Amsterdam, to Yves Steinmann, General Manager, Sevysa, Aclens, Lausanne, Switzerland, January 1992:

> Confirm need for intensive promotional campaign to sustain impetus of Nike Airpower launch in Switzerland. Please confirm and submit your plan by February 15, 1992.

Yves Steinmann, General Manager of Sevysa, Nike's official importer for Switzerland, threw the fax onto the desk and answered his telephone. 'Mr Steinmann, Amman Sports, here, Alain Dubois. We have a problem. I've spoken to your salesman, Monsieur Clerc, and he referred me to you. Our order has not arrived and a lot of customers are disappointed. We wanted an additional 200 pairs of Nike Air 180 shoes. Can you be sure they are available by the end of the month, please, and send the existing order today?'

Steinmann placated the retailer, promising delivery as soon as he had news from the warehouse. He wrote 'Advertising' on his pad and dialled the number of his Marketing Manager, Jöelle Rossier. There was no reply. He looked at his watch and saw that it was not yet 8 am. Leaving his office, Steinmann walked over to the warehouse, passing a display of fluorescent biking shorts, of running shoes going back over several decades and an impressive mountain bike, dismantled and suspended from the ceiling. Sevysa's warehouse manager, Paolo de Paoli, looked up as Steinmann entered his office.

'Bonjour, Paolo,' said Steinmann. 'We have another problem with deliveries. The people at Amman Sports have not received their Nike Air 180 order. Can you find it on the computer for me? They want it today.' 'I'm sorry, Yves,' said the warehouse manager, 'I don't have to look in the computer; the stock has not arrived from Nike. This is not the first complaint. Everyone who ordered them has been on the phone. Guess we advertised too soon this time.' 'Paolo, please try and find out what's going on,' said Steinmann, 'and by the way,' he continued, pointing to the rows and rows of boxes stacked up along one side of the warehouse, 'I thought we were going to liquidate those shoes; they must be a year old.'

Sevysa had been founded by Yves Steinmann in 1978. Its headquarters were located on a small industrial site in Aclens, outside Lausanne. A light modern building housed the main administration and functional departments, and provided storage space for the range of sports equipment distributed by the company. Nike sports shoes made up almost 80% of Steinmann's total business, but by 1992 he had become exclusive distributor for a number of up-market sports products including Oakley sunglasses, Dynastar skis, Lange ski boots, Kestrel bicycles and Conformable inner soles. Consolidated sales for the year ending May 1992 were SF30 million.

Returning to his office, Steinmann looked at his watch. It was 8.25 am. Leafing through the mail on his desk, Steinmann read a note from Sevysa's finance director, Claude Mellana, telling him that Nike was setting up an independent distribution company in Belgium, probably bypassing the exclusive distributor. Two more sports shops had left messages. Steinmann crossed the hall to a meeting room and made himself the strongest ristretto he could squeeze out of the machine. Between fielding requests from Nike or complaints on delayed orders from retailers, Steinmann knew it was going to be another one of those days.

How it all began

A job offer

Steinmann's affair with Nike had started almost 14 years earlier during his three year stay in the United States where Nike, founded in 1964 by two ex-track and field champions, Bill Bowerman and Phil Knight, was quickly growing into a multi-million dollar company on the strength of its successful hi-tech running shoes, manufactured in the Far East.

Steinmann, 26 years old, had returned to his parents' house in Bienne, Switzerland, in the summer of 1978 wearing Nike running shoes, a Nike emblazoned jacket and carrying an assortment of Nike duffel bags. During dinner, Yves Steinmann brought his parents up-to-date on his plans. 'Yes. What's all this Nike?' asked Monsieur Steinmann, a sales director for a machinery company. 'You look as though you're advertising the stuff.' 'Let me tell you the full story,' replied his son. 'Nike was the Greek goddess of victory. I *am* advertising it, Dad. I am the official Nike sports shoe representative for Switzerland.' Yves extended a foot. 'Look at these shoes. Aren't they fantastic?'

The Steinmanns accepted their son's announcement calmly and urged him to continue his story. 'What made you pick Nike specifically?' Yves' father asked. 'Well, I guess you could say that Nike picked me,' Yves replied. 'Remember, I left the building site job in Denver and began to give ski lessons on Mount Hood, Oregon? Well, one day the man riding up in the chairlift next to me started to chat. He was the man I told you about, Dan Hanna, a very successful entrepreneur. We started to ski together and he asked if I was interested in doing some wild skiing at the top of the mountain. Next day, he turned up in a helicopter to pick me up. We continued to ski together and towards the end of the season, he asked me what I planned to do. When he heard that I had trained as an architectural draughtsman and had left Switzerland because of the depressed building business, he just said, "You're working for me. I need someone to help design my car-wash facilities." It turned out that he was the biggest car-wash manufacturer in the US.'

'After I'd been working for Mr Hanna for about two years, he came to me and said, "Yves, I have a new job for you. You're leaving car-wash design and going into sports equipment." He had bought a sporting goods store in Portland, Oregon, that had been completely run down by the previous manager. He wanted me to manage it for him until his son was ready to take over. I refused and told him I had zero knowledge of the retail business, or any business at all. But, he just said, "No problem, I'll get a consultant to teach you and help run the shop until you can do it yourself." So he did. That's how I got interested in sports equipment.'

'We had some very funny moments. For instance, the previous manager had ordered 50,000 pairs of socks, which of course we had to liquidate. I organized sock clearance sales – tennis socks, ski socks, every kind of sock. I would put little ads in the paper and people came flocking in. Some would come for the socks and then buy a pair of skis or ski boots or a tennis racket. Anyway, in less than a year, we had turned the place round. I learned a lot from the consultant.'

Yves continued his story. 'Earlier this year, in the spring, a woman came into the shop and gave me her card. She was a Nike sales rep. We started discussing Nike, she detected my foreign accent and asked where I came from. When I told her Switzerland, she said, "How interesting . . . Nike doesn't sell in Switzerland." The next thing I knew, I was meeting Jim Moody, Nike's international director . . . and here I am, exclusive distributor. It turned out well. I was ready to come back and I'm very excited about the idea. Last year Nike sold $28 million worth of shoes and they'll double that amount this year. It's difficult to start on your own, but I know I can sell this stuff even without any capital. I'll do it like a grocer, buying a few cases of bananas at a time, then buying the next batch when I've sold them. After all, I have no goals and nothing to lose.'

Starting up

With no money in his pocket, but full of enthusiasm, Yves Steinmann became Nike's exclusive distributor in Switzerland. Using his bedroom as a warehouse/office, Yves set to work. In the summer of 1978, he started going around to retailers and pushing Nike shoes at trade shows. Steinmann succeeded in selling about 300 pairs of shoes in the first six months of business and another 1700 pairs by the end of his first year. The Nike shoes impressed Swiss Olympic long-distance runner, Markus Ryffel, but a promotion contract was not possible because it would have cost Steinmann SF6000, which of course he could not raise. When not on the road, Yves spent his time packing, insuring and mailing out orders. All stock was paid to Nike up front, but as retailers traditionally paid within 30–60 days, Steinmann quickly learned the basic principles of liquidity.

The Swiss market was dominated by the world leader, Adidas, followed by Puma and a handful of lesser known brands. Nevertheless, after 18 months of operation, Steinmann had signed up 150 retailers and moved his warehouse to his cousin's furniture store. Any hesitation by sports shops to sell these funny new shoes was quickly dispelled when the industry heard about Nike's popularity with serious American runners. It was Nike's policy to support its sales and distribution with substantial promotions, and the running and athletic press acclaimed Nike products with enthusiasm. The company's image continued to glow with the successes of more and more US athletes and Olympic gold medalists.

By the end of 1979, Steinmann realized that he could not continue as a one-man show. He needed additional space and, above all, help. But, when the time came to hire a secretary and some sales reps, Yves found he had almost no money to pay their salaries. He managed to find a mother who, having raised her family, wanted to return to work. Steinmann took her on as a half-time secretary at a modest salary. A couple of runners from the Swiss national team had just finished their university studies and were looking for work. One of them, André Nicol – who was also a former Olympic bobsled champion, had contacted Nike earlier to ask for the exclusive distributorship of the company's products in Switzerland. The other, Pierre Martin, was looking for anything to do with running or sports equipment. Steinmann managed to convince these two men to work for him as sales reps for commission only. Another rep was hired under the same conditions. Each man received 10% of sales.

All told, with his three employees, a new warehouse barn in the tiny village of Boussens, and first-year sales of SF650,000, Steinmann's new company got underway. He called it *Sevysa*, based on his own name, written backwards.

Quick success

In 1980, sales started exploding and had more than doubled by the beginning of 1981. However, Sevysa soon began to experience the typical growing pains of a company that had increased sales fast but was plagued by cashflow problems.

Leading up to the first crisis

A revolutionary new shoe

When Nike produced a revolutionary new shoe that had taken US athletes by storm, and would certainly do the same in Europe, Steinmann saw a chance to improve his market share and make a profit. The shoe's extreme lightness, its waffle sole for improved traction and waistline shape for better fit would certainly appeal to the top end of the Swiss running fraternity. A moccasin cut that replaced the usual rigid last gave the shoe maximum front foot flexibility, and an EVA (ethyl vinyl acetelyne) mid-sole ensured comfortable cushioning.

Steinmann pushed the moccasin model to the full with his retailers, and sales took off as hoped; orders flooded in and deliveries were made to stores. Runners were happy and retailers were delighted with the immediate success of the new model, which started selling like hot-cakes. Could Steinmann finally breathe a sigh of relief after his fight to keep the company in business in the face of its critical cash situation?

A huge pile of defective running shoes

Not long after the first deliveries were made, the phone rang in Steinmann's office. It was the chief buyer for Pierre Sport, Lausanne's largest sporting goods shop and mecca for the serious runners of the area. 'Steinmann, what's this junk you've sent us?' asked the irate buyer. 'These new Nikes are useless; half of them are split down the sides. Don't expect any payment for this order. We can't sell them.' Another store called to say, 'Steinmann, we've waited so long for these moccasins and the damn things are full of holes before they're even worn. I can tell you this is going to be a field day for Adidas. What else can I sell to my runners?'

The complaints continued; day after day shoes were returned to Steinmann, who immediately contacted Nike in the USA to explain his problem. But Nike, trying to manage its own fast-moving domestic business, was incredulous. No one seemed to believe Steinmann's story or acknowledge the fact that his large stock of potentially unsaleable shoes would probably break as well.

'Nike Air'

Steinmann's problems resulting from the splitting moccasin shoes persisted, but they were partly alleviated by the arrival of another revolutionary new product from Nike, its 'Air' model. This shoe used a unique patented gas process – an outer membrane smaller than the molecules of air it contained would compress these molecules to form a comfortable cushion which supported the foot. Nike claimed that this cushioned sole would retain its elasticity throughout the whole life of the shoe. This technology was to become an all-time hit for Nike.

For Sevysa's dealers who had ordered 'Nike-Airs', it was not difficult to substitute this new shoe for the previous defective moccasin model. However, many of the dealers that had not ordered the 'Air' shoe dropped Steinmann, saying: 'Forget American gear. We'll stick to Adidas and Puma.'

The demand for the original moccasin had been high, and Steinmann continued to sell the shoe to people who really wanted it under any circumstances. Business had to go on, and an embarrassed Steinmann was telling dealers, athletes and coaches, 'Don't pull the shoelaces too tight or you will break the shoes!'

When everything goes wrong at the same time . . .

Very soon, Steinmann's cash situation deteriorated to the point where he knew the company could not continue much longer without new funds. Suddenly, everything started to escalate. The Nike disaster had compromised Steinmann's credibility with many retailers. A large part of his inventory was unsaleable. The straight 10% commission on sales he had promised to his reps when the business started (or approximately SF70,000 in 1981) had been too generous, too idealistic, and was unsustainable at Sevysa's rapid growth rate. In spite of good sales results overall, liquidity was non-existent. On top of everything else, Steinmann realized that if he did not take on some professional management help, particularly in the accounting area, he could lose control of the business completely, and that it would probably collapse very quickly.

Clearly a visit to the bank was the next item on the agenda.

'It's the cash . . .'

As Monsieur de Benestrale, manager of the local branch of the SVB Bank, lit a pipe and called his secretary to ask for coffee, Steinmann sat down and placed a Nike duffel bag and a large attaché case on the floor beside his chair. 'How's business, Monsieur Steinmann?' de Benestrale asked.

'Business itself is good in a way,' replied Steinmann reflectively as he accepted a cup of coffee. 'Business is good, I mean the potential is huge. . . but cash is not good at all.' 'Aha,' said de Benestrale, who had been helping Yves Steinmann with his cashflow crises since he had first started selling Nike. 'I thought business was about making cash.'

Not appearing to hear the bank manager's last statement, Steinmann unzipped his duffel bag and placed an impressive looking moccasin-style running shoe on the desk in front of de Benestrale. The older man, a modest jogger himself, picked up the shoe with a certain reverence. 'Very nice,' he said, turning the shoe over to admire the waffle sole. Steinmann placed another in front of him, then another and a fourth one.

'They are brilliant,' said Steinmann. 'Everyone wants a pair. But, look at the side of the laces; can you see the split? Every one of these shoes is split or is about to split. I have a huge stock that is unsaleable. These shoes were my great hope, but they're defective and Nike is not acknowledging its fault. All my cash is tied up in inventory. Here is a statement of the situation. If I can't solve this problem quickly, it's the end of Sevysa. The stores are furious and want the shoes replaced at once. I'm losing my credibility every day. I simply cannot afford to put another order through to Nike. It's absurd.'

De Benestral waved his hand in the air as though about to hold forth to the younger man on the inadvisability of increasing his debt.

'But look, Monsieur de Benestrale,' said Steinmann quickly, sweeping the shoes off the table and producing two files from his outsized attaché case. 'Look, here are my future orders up to September, and here are my accounts receivable. It's really only a question of time before we sort this out. And look at this,' Steinmann continued, placing yet another shoe on de Benestrale's desk. 'This is the new Nike "Air" that is going to sell as never before. The whole foot is cushioned by bubbles of air, can you imagine, sir, bubbles of air?'

Driving back to his office, Yves Steinmann breathed a sigh of relief. The bank had saved him again. De Benestrale had extended his credit line by SF200,000, but how many more of these last minute salvaging operations could the company stand? One thing Steinmann had learned quickly was that if you open your own business, you had better know how to deal with banks, time and time again.

SAM Sport S.A.

Although his inexperience had sometimes hindered Steinmann in solving complicated internal problems, early in 1981 he had hit upon an idea that he thought would alleviate one of his most pressing problems, the high commission he was paying sales staff. He separated the sales part of his business from the rest and created a new 'company,' SAM Sport S.A. He convinced his two sales reps, Martin and Nicol, to invest SF25,000 each in this new company. Steinmann, pressed for cash at the time, had nothing to put in. He then redesigned the salesmen's compensation package, by putting them on salary without commission. Instead, SAM Sport as a whole was to receive the 10% commission on sales, which would then be divided up among the three partners. In this way, Steinmann received a third of the commission on sales himself.

Keep talking to Nike

Steinmann's negotiations with Nike continued, although the US company – preoccupied with its rapid domestic growth – took a long time to admit its fault. Only after Steinmann had himself photographed sitting on a huge pile of defective shoes did Nike slowly begin to react.

Finally, some Nike experts came from the USA to Switzerland to inspect the defective stock, which involved five or six different models, and the lengthy inquiry dragged to an end. The experts made their report to the US headquarters, and Nike admitted that the fault lay with their new Far Eastern manufacturers, which seemingly had used a lower denier nylon than had been specified by Nike for the shoes. However, the US company was still unwilling to compensate Steinmann with cash. A solution still had to be found.

First loss

In spite of Steinmann's efforts to save the situation by a second visit to the bank – to increase his credit line up to SF500,000, the cumulative effect of the broken shoe disaster caused Sevysa to make its first loss. In October 1982, with sales of SF2.9 million, Sevysa's books showed a deficit of approximately SF256,000. The company was soon so heavily leveraged that bankruptcy seemed imminent. Steinmann thought that he might just be able to save the situation if he could create a new company with additional capital. But, where was he going to find that kind of money?

At this point, Nike intervened and proposed a scheme that would compensate Steinmann for the losses he had incurred because of the defective moccasins. Nike wanted Steinmann to prove his seriousness as a Nike distributor by forming an incorporated company. In exchange for this gesture, Nike would give him a bank guarantee of SF2 million.

Leading up to the second crisis, 1986

Sevysa S.A.

SAM Sport was dissolved at the end of 1982 and, in February 1983, Sevysa S.A. was founded. Steinmann had managed to find 15 people to invest a total of SF500,000 in the new company. Yves Steinmann, the major shareholder, held 24% of the shares. His father, Willy Steinmann, Pierre Yves Rossel (his brother-in-law), and André Nicol held the major part of the balance. The official gathering to register the company with the lawyers was animated. Several of the shareholders claimed the right to control the company, since they believed they were saving it with their investments. In the end, Yves Steinmann's father was named Chairman of the Board, but there was no formal nomination of a CEO. Thus, the question of control remained unclear.

In the new organization, Pierre Martin took over promotion, while André Nicol handled marketing and sales. Steinmann himself was responsible for finance, and

Pierre-Yves Rossel headed up administration. Two years earlier, Steinmann had convinced his brother-in-law to leave his secure job as draughtsman for the town council and join Sevysa. Rossel believed that the new little company had a future, and agreed to start with Sevysa in accounting and accounts receivable. Rossel soon felt ill-at-ease in his administrative job, so Steinmann changed his area of responsibility so that Rossel reported directly to him. It soon became apparent that the former salesman, Martin, had little imagination as a manager as well as an aversion to hard work. He was quickly pushed out by Nicol, who took over Martin's responsibilities. The company was therefore led by Steinmann and Nicol.

Nike US – managing growth

The Nike Company, more successful than ever, was enjoying a period of substantial growth. From 1982 to 1986, Nike's sales had increased from $700 million to over $1 billion. One of the ways Nike coped with this period was to revolutionize the standard industry practice for ordering and inventory management. Nike redefined its Forward Purchasing Programme so that distributors were forced to plan their stock requirements and place orders six months before delivery. This affected brandholders and distributors alike. The programme gave Nike more flexibility in scheduling the manufacturing operations with its fast-growing network of Far Eastern subcontractors. In addition, it allowed Nike to test product acceptability and make rapid adjustments if needed. However, this programme change created dramatic organizational and logistic problems for distributors such as Sevysa and its retailers.

Sevysa – trying to manage growth

With the Nike name fast becoming a passport to success, Sevysa's business also boomed. Retailers which had previously given prominence to Adidas and Puma, while displaying Nike shoes with 'others', started to change their tune. 'Nike makes the best shoes and they sell!' claimed the dealers, and Nike display racks were given the prime spot in the shops. Sevysa's sales rose higher than Steinmann could believe. Between 1982 and 1986, turnover increased from SF3 million to SF12 million. Yet, still the threat of bankruptcy remained.

It was normal for a company like Sevysa to need financing for inventory during the 40- to 60-day time lapse between paying suppliers and receiving payment from retailers (Exhibits 11.18 and 11.19). Steinmann had invested in more inventory and new lines, including Nike apparel, but Sevysa's ordering remained more often guided by instinct than by following a systematic forecasting method. Inability to master inventory requirements had resulted in overstocking, frequent price discounting and liquidation, which prevented the company from making a profit.

The faster sales grew, the less efficient the business became. Steinmann's time was spent trying to keep his head above water and satisfy demands made on him by the company and clients alike. In an attempt to cope with the pressure, Nicol and Steinmann had continued to hire more staff; the original staff of 15 had more than doubled. But, since they were usually too busy to train new people, the extra staff simply increased overhead with little improvement in performance or output. The goal at the time was: 'supply and ensure that capacity continues to grow with demand.'

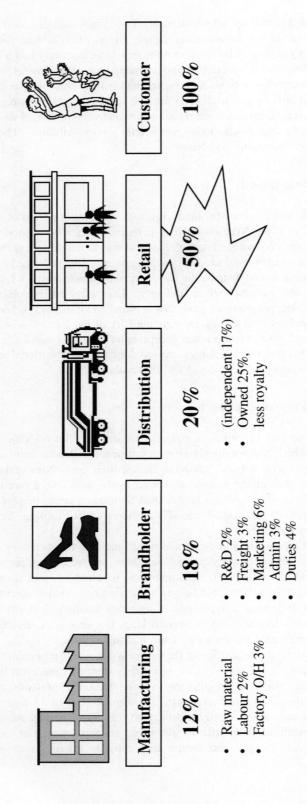

Manufacturing	Brandholder	Distribution	Retail	Customer
12%	18%	20%	50%	100%

- Raw material
- Labour 2%
- Factory O/H 3%

- R&D 2%
- Freight 3%
- Marketing 6%
- Admin 3%
- Duties 4%

- (independent 17%)
- Owned 25%, less royalty

Exhibit 11.18 The retailer represents the highest value added in the business system, giving him bargaining power

Task and time involved

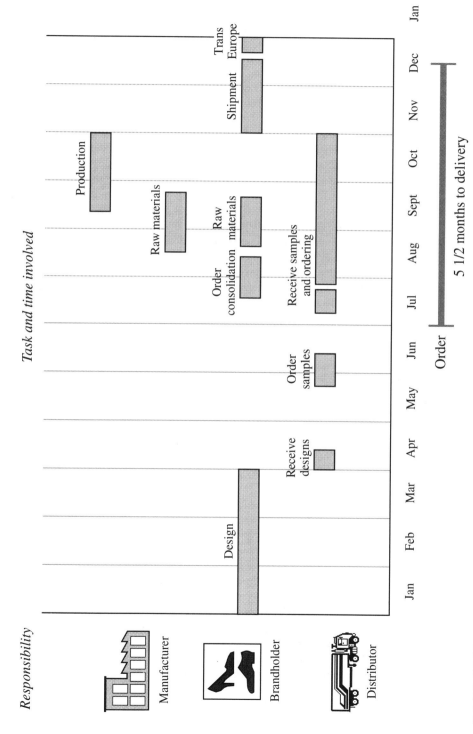

Exhibit 11.19 Long lead times from manufacture to retail characterize the business system causing varying inventory risk

Steinmann knew that the difference between making a profit and a constantly strained financial situation was strict inventory control, and the ability to collect receivables on time. He knew he needed systems, better planning and effective training for his staff. And, Steinmann knew fear – the fear of watching it all disappear in front of his eyes . . . for mastering the situation continued to elude him.

Yet, no matter how stressful it was going to be and how inadequate he sometimes felt, Steinmann was determined to keep the company going and make it profitable.

Repositioning Nike . . . and another crisis

Statistics and market share information on the Swiss running shoe industry tended to be inadequate and unreliable, and segment boundaries were rather fuzzy. Steinmann did not rely on official data as he claimed to have developed an 'instinctive feel' for competitive performance and results over his years in the business. One thing was clear to him in 1986. Sevysa had to broaden Nike's hold on the Swiss market if it wanted to survive.

Sevysa had always concentrated on the upper end of the running shoe market. Retailers had tended to force Nike into this top 'professional' segment because of the company's image as a supplier of hi-tech shoes. So far, it had been an easy segment to sell in, and Nicol attributed the successful growth from 1982 to 1986 largely to his own talents. By the end of the decade, Sevysa expected to have 40% of this segment, which was forecast to reach 100,000 pairs by 1990, in front of Adidas with 30% and Reebok with 10%.

However, the top segment was limited in volume, and brand loyalty was almost non-existent. High research and development costs, and constant updating of technology, made hi-tech shoes very expensive. Furthermore, the ageing of the population in Switzerland was more pronounced than in other western societies. Demographic research showed that there would be fewer 18 to 29-year-olds around in the 1990s to buy professional-level running shoes.

Steinmann wanted to put more emphasis on the second and third levels of the market, where the real volume was to be found and where continued growth was expected. The generation of older buyers that was emerging was expected to force the top shoe producers down into a much wider and more diverse market segment, forecast to reach sales of about two million pairs by 1990. With this huge middle segment dominated by Adidas and Puma, both of which had a brand awareness of over 95%, gaining a significant presence would require investing in substantial press and TV advertising, billboards and a revised promotional plan for Sevysa. The bottom end of the market was also in a state of constant transition, as many cheap new entrants were beginning to arrive and sell alongside the private label shoes found in such outlets as Switzerland's mega-market, Migros, and the international shoe chains such as Bata or Bally (Exhibit 11.20).

When Steinmann tried to convince Nicol that the company should be planning its marketing and promotional activities to correspond with consolidation of the second segment, he met with a strong rebuttal. Nicol insisted that Sevysa should push for an even greater market share in the top segment, where 80% of Nicol's total promotion budget was allocated for image building – mainly through sponsorship at track races and long-distance running events. Steinmann wanted to reach the amateur runners and joggers who did not respond to the same promotional approaches as Nicol's élite semi-professional runners.

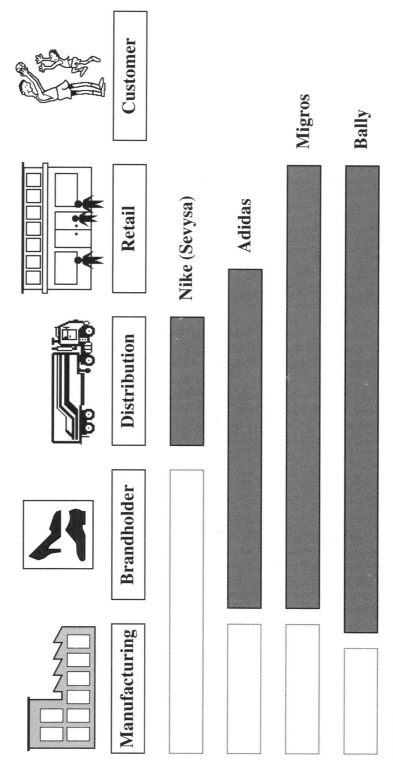

Exhibit 11.20 The extent of integration among players in Switzerland differs . . . .

As Nicol became increasingly hostile, Steinmann realized how wide the gulf was becoming between them. Confronted with his partner's growing indifference to marketing priorities, a frustrated Steinmann felt forced to start taking on more and more responsibility. A new cash crisis loomed ominously ahead. Steinmann desperately wanted an increase in volume sales and the budget to pay for it. Yet, during the year 1986, sales growth slowed down. Things were coming to a head again, and Steinmann was worried about his partner's apparent lack of concern.

Is it my lack of business experience?

Yves Steinmann decided to talk things over with his father.

> Things are going so fast, Dad, I can barely keep up. I should have talked to you sooner. Our sales are excellent, so I suppose it's my lack of experience that is keeping us from making a profit. We cannot seem to get a grasp on costs. One problem is that we are overspending in the wrong area now, and I can't seem to get André Nicol to understand. He's out on the circuits with the promotion team almost every day in the season, while I am trying to grow our share of the second segment of the market. There are five of them giving away our money in the name of our 'image'. We need that money to advertise. It's big sales we need now, and awareness . . . not image.
>
> We don't seem to have a clear market focus and André seems to have lost control. I'm also at fault, I know. I'm responsible for hiring too many people. But, at least I have my feet on the ground. The overhead is going to kill us. I've tried to explain that we can't make a profit in the top segment because our selling costs are astronomical. The market is shifting, and we have to shift with it or we'll be shut out. I blame myself for not being emphatic enough with André. I have tried to talk to him, but he comes back with all those fancy theories . . . I'm the first to admit my ignorance in many areas, but at least we've come this far and we're still in business. He cannot admit his weaknesses. Do you think he cares about market research, client feedback, forecasting, trends and competition? Reebok, one of the largest sports shoe producers in the world, has got a nice hold on the Swiss market. It's our fault. We helped them in.

Monsieur Steinmann listened to his son:

> Yves, I understand what you're saying and I know you are for fair play. But, this situation has gone on too long. Nicol has been feeding off you. You have always been the doer while he just continued talking and achieving very little. I remember quite early on I told him that I thought his sales approach was weak. I gave him a structure, remember? But he never used it. Becoming a shareholder must have gone to his head. I wonder sometimes if he actually wanted to destroy us and take over the company himself . . . Anyway, as you say, Sevysa is treading on very thin ice financially. You must get him to understand this. We could go bankrupt.

Bankruptcy and liquidation?

When the books were closed in 1986, the company was technically bankrupt. On sales of just under SF12 million, Sevysa made a loss of SF451,000. The company had one year's inventory in stock and 15 employees too many; marketing and sales techniques were weak and administration disorganized.

Shortly after Steinmann's conversation with his father, four out of five members of the board voted for the liquidation of the company. However, realizing that his inexperience had contributed to the downfall, Steinmann fought to keep the company alive. He convinced the others that he would take full responsibility for running Sevysa. Steinmann was still not nominated as General Manager, but he committed himself to turning the company around.

12

Turnaround management is not Rambo management

Case 12.1 Berlingske Tidende

This case was written by Research Associate Amy Webster, under the supervision of Professor Werner Ketelhöhn, as a basis for class discussion rather than to illustrate either effective or ineffective handling of an administrative situation.

'Agreed!' Chresten Reves said one morning in January 1983. As he shook hands with the Chairman of the Board of Directors of the Berlingske, the oldest and largest publishing house in Denmark, he added, 'I am confident that we will turn this company around in no time and that your trust in my personal abilities will be rewarded.' These were his farewell comments after the intense meeting that had just taken place. He then arranged to meet with his key managers the next morning to address the major issues.

Chresten Reves had been appointed President of the Berlingske Group in the summer of 1982, after it had been taken over by a Danish business consortium. Six months later, he was ready to make some major strategic decisions, two particularly significant: how to lead the company through a difficult but inevitable technological transition, and how to turn his major publication into a market-driven product.

Company history

The Berlingske publishing house originated as a book printing business in Copenhagen, founded in 1733 by Ernst

1836	First high-speed press
1854	Use of new telegraph communication
1859	Marinoni flat-bed press
1881	First rotary printing press (web press)
1882	First telephone
1900	First typesetting machine
1903	From Gothic black-letters to Roman types
1914	First photograph
1953	Modern copper plate press for printing magazines
1983	New electronic technology

Exhibit 12.1 *Technological developments*

Henrich Berling. In 1749, the first edition of its newspaper, *Berlingske Tidende*, was published; in the 1980s it was one of the oldest still existing newspapers in the world. In 1765, the original premises of the publishing house were moved to a stately town house on Pilestraede, in the heart of old Copenhagen. In 1983, the publishing company was still there in a completely renovated house. From its origin as a book printing business, a large modern printing house had been established, the chief business of which was publishing newspapers. In 1983, the Berlingske House published two of Denmark's largest dailies, the *Berlingske Tidende* and *B.T.*.

Until 1901, the public authorities made their announcements through the Berlingske newspapers, making them an important factor in community life. The publishing house maintained a conservative policy throughout the years, never allowing itself to become a party organ. During leftist regimes, the papers belonged to the opposition press, maintaining a vigilant criticism.

Management was based on the firmly established tradition of using sound journalistic and business principles, editorial independence, and freedom of speech and the printed word.

During its 230 years of development, the company went through periods of growth and expansion, as well as stagnation and decline. Due to the efforts of managers and editors and to technological developments (Exhibit 12.1), both circulation and the number of publications continued to increase over the years (Exhibit 12.2). In 1983

1749	*Kjobenhavnske Danske Post-Tidender* (Berlingske)
1833	*Berlingske Tidende* (weekdays)
1913	*Berlingske Tidende* (Sundays)
1916	*B.T.* (weekdays)
1921	*Søndags-B.T.* (weekly magazine)
1929	*Jydske Tidende* (weekdays, established in Jutland)
1938	*Billed Bladet* (weekly magazine)
1971	*Weekendavisen* changed from evening daily to weekly newspaper

Source: The story of an old newspaper, dedicated to friends and guests, and Resume of the History of Berlingske, both published by Berlingske Tidende.

Exhibit 12.2 *History of Berlingske Publications*

they included 4 dailies, 2 weeklies and 2 magazines as well as a larger number of free sheets. Of the six newspapers, three were Copenhagen morning papers and the rest were provincial and regional papers.

Ever since its foundation, the Berlingske business also included magazine publication. The weekly magazine, *Søndags-B.T.*, started in 1921, achieved considerable popularity in just a few years (circulation, 177,000 in 1982). Having installed Denmark's first rotogravure plant, the company then launched the illustrated magazine, *Billed-Bladet* (circulation 292,000 in 1982). Book printing activities were also developed over the years, building upon the original book printing business of 1733.

The Berlingske Group was owned by 17 private individuals related to the Berling family. 'Det Berlingske Officin A/S' handled the technical production of the newspapers at its printing operations in Pilestraede and in Husumtryk. The Berlingske weekly magazines were also produced there. In addition to the newspapers, the group owned the book printing establishment and the publishing house.

The 1977 strike

In the late 1960s, the Danish press[1] was burdened by heavy production costs. The situation worsened in 1973 when the price of paper suddenly rose, while wages were on a continuous increase. At the same time, advertising revenues were slumping and it became more difficult to raise newspaper prices. Growing costs coincided with declining earnings.

The cost problem was greatest for Copenhagen's two largest publishing houses, Berlingske and Politiken, which had difficulty controlling the expenses of the intensive production techniques. Wages and working conditions of the technical personnel had been set through special agreements with powerful unions. Permanent negotiations, marred by threats of strikes or delays, were continually altering these agreements. As a result of pressure from the unions, a framework agreement had been signed in 1960 which gave typographers the highest wages in the trade and the maximum safety advantages. They also had the right of participation in any rationalizing or automation of the technical production.

In 1974, Berlingske's profits began decreasing dangerously. Advertising revenues declined by 30% between 1971 and 1975. By 1977, it had become imperative to reduce the technical staff and modernize the production process. The typographers did not realize the gravity of the company's financial problems and opposed management's policies. Following fruitless negotiations, management specified teams and their working hours, but the typographers refused to accept them. Management had no other choice but to send the workers home. They were protesting vehemently about becoming redundant with the new technology.

This situation eventually resulted in a bitter labour conflict, the worst one to occur in Denmark for decades. In 1976, management proposed various schemes for gradual reduction and early retirement. The union rejected all these proposals, along with the proposed budget for 1977. Workers refused to work overtime, which caused delays and reduced circulation. By the end of January 1977, production had decreased by 10%.

---

[1] See Exhibit 12.3 for a background note on the Danish newspaper industry.

At the turn of the century, Denmark counted about 200 newspapers. In 1980, only 47 dailies and 10 Sunday papers were still left. Most of these were private and had severed their former political ties in an effort to ensure editorial independence. Of the 47 dailies, 10 were national papers published in Copenhagen (mostly morning papers), while the remaining 37 were considered regional or local papers (mostly afternoon papers).

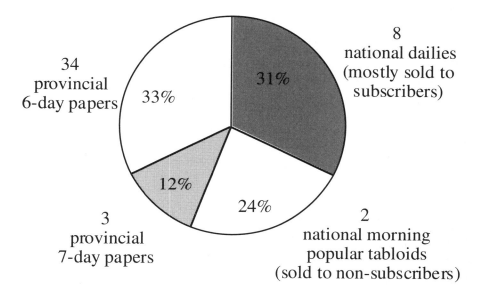

Readership in Denmark was one of the highest in Europe: in 1987, 373 newspapers were sold per 1000 inhabitants; 83% of the Danish adult population read newspapers. The Sunday papers were read by 66% of the population. 70% of the Danish readers only read one paper per day, 20% read two dailies, while 10% read more than two. The Danish people were consistent readers: 60% of newspapers were sold through subscriptions.

The Danish newspaper industry was characterized by a constant or slightly decreasing weekday market and a more rapidly decreasing Sunday market, in spite of the growing number of households. The purchase price of Danish papers was one of the world's highest (DKr5 or $0.70). Dailies held about 30% of the total national advertising budget. There was no major competition because of the absence of advertising on radio and television. Distribution was handled through local agents or postal services. Papers were sold directly to sales outlets, not through agents. The retailer's commission was about 20–30% of the final price.

In the 1970s, the traditional Danish big city morning papers, which were also the main outlets for political information and debate, were outdistanced in sales both in and out of town by sensationalist noon tabloids mostly sold at newsstands. Two Copenhagen noon papers reached about 250,000 in circulation by 1975, apparently hurting the morning papers. Modern tabloids aspired to be full-fledged papers, adding quite a lot of political discussion to their main stock of human stories and city gossip. Most tabloids, however, were launched by the owners of big morning papers. As a result, the market shares controlled by big ownership groups increased and the local press became even more concentrated. The biggest chains or group in Denmark (such as Berlingske and Politiken) controlled 63% of the circulation.

Sources: The Press in Denmark, in *The Press in Europe* published by the Associación de editores de diarios españoles, 1987; *The Danish Newspaper Trade*, report by Det Berlingske officin A/S, 1988.

Exhibit 12.3 *Background note on the Danish newspaper industry in the 1980s*

	Berlingske		Politiken		Other newspapers		Total growth (%)	
	1976	1977	1976	1977	1976	1977	1976	1977
Daily circulation	42	37	42	45	16	18		+ 1
Sunday circulation	48	44	32	34	20	21		+ 2
Total circulation	43	38	41	44	17	18		+ 1
Advertising	42	37	30	30	28	33		+ 9
Classified advertisements	60	54	25	29	15	17		+ 7
Total advertising volume	53	47	27	30	20	23		+ 8

Source: *The Battle of the House of Berlingske*, a description of problems, parties and events, Schedule 2, Det Berlingske Officin A/S.

Exhibit 12.4 *Percentage market shares in the Metropolitan Press 1976–1977 (2nd half-year)*

On January 30, 1977, publication of the three Copenhagen newspapers was suspended. The printing house was closed and 1100 workers were out of work. While the workers were supported by left-wing groups and trade unions, the House of Berlingske received backing from the trade associations.

Over four months later, the typographers resumed negotiations when it became clear that they were losing the support of the trade union association. An agreement was reached to terminate 2500 workers who would receive a settlement of DKr25 million[2] over a 5-year period. After 141 days of conflict, *Berlingske Tidendell* and *B.T.* were published again, but it was clear that the union would continue its fight to prove that everyone was needed for production. During the following summer, production was often delayed. Major issues, such as the implementation of new technology, had still not been resolved.

Economic losses during the strike exceeded DKr20 millions.[3] In addition, management had seriously worried about the potential loss of market share. The main competitors, *Politiken* and *Ekstra Bladet*, had honoured a gentlemen's agreement not to increase production during the conflict. However, their production was sold out every day, and *Berlingske* subscribers who had previously bought *Politiken* as a supplement gradually became *Politiken* subscribers (Exhibit 12.4).

The 1982 take-over

After the 1977 conflict, Berlingske's market position was greatly weakened. The *Berlingske Tidende* was particularly affected. Its circulation decreased by about 4000 copies,[4] to the benefit of its major competitor, *Politiken*, which also gained in

[2] Cheques equivalent to one year's salary were given to each worker.

[3] In 1977, DKr5.89 = US$1.00.

[4] The Sunday *Berlingske Tidende* was the hardest hit; its circulation decreased by 20,000 copies. When referring to the *Berlingske Tidende* in this Case, the Sunday issue is not included unless specifically mentioned.

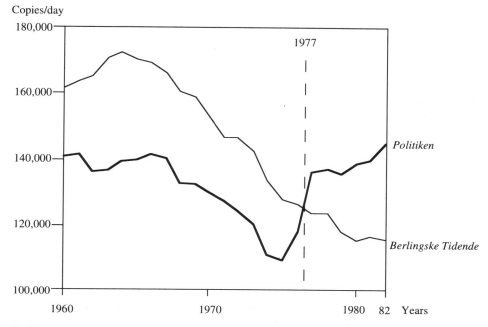

Exhibit 12.5 *Comparative circulation: Berlingske Tidende versus Politiken (weekdays), 1960–1982). (Source: Circulation figures of major newspapers 1870–1987, Det Berlingske Officin A/S)*

advertising revenues (Exhibit 12.5). Increasingly heavy expenses had exceeded Berlingske's income from the time of the bitter labour conflict until 1982 (Exhibit 12.6). Heavy debts had to be taken over. The Berling family was obliged to leave the publishing group, ending the family's 233-year ownership. Almost 100 Danish

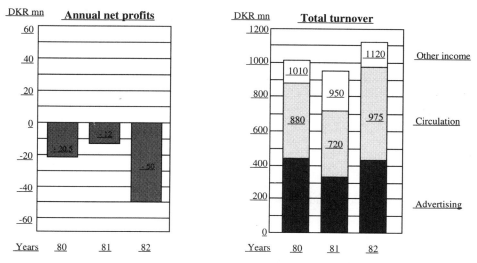

Exhibit 12.6 *Financial review of the Berlingske Group, 1980–1982. (Source: Det Berlingske Officin A/S Annual Report 1984)*

companies and private individuals set up a foundation to invest DKrl63.8 million[5] in a new company. This foundation was named 'The Berlingske Association of 1982'.

The foundation took over the bankrupt company. Five individuals[6] were appointed by the investors to sit on the board of directors of the new concern. Except for one person, who had already been on the board before the takeover, none of the other members had any link to the newspaper industry. Their main purpose was to guarantee the Berlingske's position in Denmark and save what had been a traditional Danish institution for more than two centuries. *Berlingske Tidende* stood for democratic and capitalistic values.

The newspaper had been published throughout the takeover, but the company was in bad shape. The board's first task was to carry out the economic plan which had been developed for the reconstruction. This plan aimed to restore the company's financial health within five to ten years. If the plan for recovery were unsuccessful, it was agreed that the foundation could utilize the 'Berlingske' name elsewhere.

Chresten Reves

The board of directors of the new concern looked for a professional, competent and dynamic man to manage and implement the company's turnaround. They found Chresten Reves, who had a promising personality as well as a positive track record in newspaper management (Exhibit 12.7).

Before accepting the job, Reves took a close look at the company (see Exhibits 12.8–12.10 for the profit and loss statements, the balance sheet, and Exhibits 12.11–12.15 for market data). Then he gave the Chairman of the Board his opinion of the company's main problems; Reves' views were quite different from those of the other candidates. Chresten Reves was convinced that the product was the major problem:

> *Berlingske Tidende* has to be changed, because circulation has dropped dramatically over the years. We must start by reversing the negative evolution of both circulation and advertising. In addition, technological conversion from lead print to photo composition is long overdue. This can only be accomplished through successful negotiations with the labour unions.

The board agreed to the priorities set by Reves. He was not given *carte blanche*, however, and was under pressure to show results rapidly. He was to report to the board on a monthly basis.

When Chresten Reves took over, one of his first tasks was to appoint a new management team. The organizational structure of De Berlingske Dagblade A/S[7] needed to be rebuilt and the staff renewed. Soon, there were agreements with 10, later 20, managers to leave the company. Chresten Reves looked for a qualified new advertising manager. Sales and editorial positions were also changed. In 1981, Berlingske management had been decentralized, and the three newspapers of

---

[5] DKr114.7 million of this amount was share capital. In 1982, DKR8.36 = US$1.00.

[6] The Director of the United Breweries, a lawyer, a Member of the Supreme Court, the Director. of the Scandinavian Tobacco Company and the Director of the Danish Distillers.

[7] 'De Berlingske Dagblade A/S' was the main operation in the group; it consisted of the three Copenhagen dailies: *Berlingske Tidende*; *B.T.* and *Weekendavisen*.

Chresten Reves was 47 years of age when he was appointed President of the Berlingske Group. His work experience, although mostly in the newspaper industry, also included other sectors, such as banking and the food and beverage businesses.

After 15 years with the press association, Reves served for four years as General Manager of the *Aalborg Stiftstidende*, a regional newspaper in North Jutland. It was a small newspaper, although the largest and best established in its market. The owner of the company, which was family-owned, died three years after Mr Reves joined. A newly constructed factory and plant also created several problems. However, Chresten Reves managed to bring major improvements to the newspaper and produce some excellent results.

At the Berlingske, Reves was considered by his colleagues as open-minded and liberal. He had managed to establish a team spirit among young and well-educated managers. According to him. good working relationships were particularly essential in the newspaper business:

> It is crucial in this business to be on good speaking terms with the editors, to communicate with them, let them know what you think, formulate the policies with them. A dialogue has to be established through formal meetings as well as informal ones during which the editors can submit their problems.

Chresten Reves often walked around the company to meet the staff and let them know what he stood for:

> Journalists need appraisal and feedback. They are writers who express their opinions to the world and must be respected as such.

Chresten Reves used a follow-up system as a management tool. First thing each morning, he made a recording of thoughts from the previous day for his secretary to type up for his calendar. Thus, every day he had a detailed list on his agenda of problems to solve. Routine and impromptu meetings with the rest of his staff and with board members took much of his day. The rest of the day was spent following up on reports and problems pending, and having special meetings with outside people.

Exhibit 12.7   *Background note on Chresten William Reves*

	1982	1981
Sales income	1,109.9	945.8
Materials and provision	366.9	290.0
Wages, salaries and social costs	584.2	476.6
Retirement expenses	16.3	3.8
Other operation expenses	182.9	164.7
Depreciation	6.6	13.8
Profit of main operations	(47.0)	(3.1)
Interest received	12.9	8.6
Interest paid	14.5	16.3
Operational profit	(48.6)	(10.8)
Other income	0.1	0.1
Profit before taxes	(48.5)	(10.7)
Taxes	1.6	1.3
Consolidated profit	(50.1)	(12.0)
Minority share	1.1	0.9
Annual net profit	(51.2)	(12.9)

Source: Det Berlingske Officin A/S Annual Report 1982.

Exhibit 12.8   *Profit and loss statement 1982 (millions of Dkr)*

	1982	1981
Current assets		
Liquid assets	23.0	21.6
Accounts receivables	138.4	118.3
Pre-paid expenses	13.4	3.6
Inventory	23.3	24.0
Total current assets	198.1	167.5
Fixed assets		
Reserves	4.3	4.4
Holdings	20.8	20.2
Equipment	11.1	27.4
Property	8.1	73.7
Goodwill	1.5	8.8
Other fixed assets	3.6	4.0
Total fixed assets	49.4	138.5
Total assets	247.5	306.0

Source: Det Berlingske Officin A/S Annual Report 1982.

Exhibit 12.9   *Assets on 31 December 1982 (millions of Dkr)*

	1982	1981
Short-term debt		
Dividends to minority shareholders	0.2	0.3
Bank debts	27.0	93.4
Other creditors	84.9	90.5
Tax owed	1.4	1.2
Salaries and social expenses owed	120.7	94.5
	234.2	279.9
Long-term debts		
Creditors	1.2	0.8
Mortgage loans	0.9	14.5
Foreign debt	0	1.0
Pension	2.1	0
Deferred tax	0.6	0.5
	4.8	16.8
Provision for taxes		
Allocation to Investment Fund	0.9	1.0
Participating securities*	30.0	0
Equity capital		
Share capital	60.0	60.0
Reserves	10.1	10.1
Revaluation Fund	0	6.2
	70.1	76.3
Loss carried forward	(96.2)	(72.4)
Det Berlingske Officin A/S equity capital	(26.1)	3.9
Minority share of group equity	3.7	4.4
Total group equity	(22.4)	8.3
Total equity and participating, securities*	7.6	8.3
Total liabilities	247.5	306.0

*An interest-bearing investment which the shareholders paid to the company when its equity capital was negative.

Source: Det Berlingske officin annual report 1982.

Exhibit 12.10   *Liabilities on December 31, 1982 (millions of Dkr)*

	1970	1971	1972	1973	1974	1975	1976	1977	1978	1979	1980	1981	1982
Berlingske Tidende	15.6	13.4	13.1	12.9	11.2	9.4	9.8	6.2	8.9	8.4	8.2	8.2	10.2
Politiken	12.3	10.3	9.8	10.2	8.2	6.4	7.6	9.2	8.8	8.4	7.9	6.3	7.9
Atuekt	4.2	3.3	3.5	4.4	3.7	2.8	2.6	4.4	3.7	3.8	3.6	4.8	3.0
Børsen	–	–	–	–	–	–	6.6	9.0	9.5	9.4	9.1	9.5	8.6
Morning papers	**32.1**	**27.0**	**26.4**	**27.5**	**23.1**	**18.6**	**26.6**	**28.8**	**30.9**	**30.0**	**28.8**	**28.8**	**29.7**
B.T.	9.7	9.8	10.8	11.8	11.6	8.5	9.4	5.8	9.2	8.8	9.0	6.5	10.4
Ekstra Bladet	8.3	8.6	9.4	9.6	9.4	6.7	7.2	10.2	8.7	8.2	8.0	7.2	9.8
Noon papers	**18.0**	**18.4**	**20.2**	**21.3**	**21.0**	**15.2**	**16.6**	**16.0**	**17.9**	**17.0**	**17.0**	**13.7**	**20.2**
Berlingske Sø	3.3	3.3	3.8	4.0	3.8	3.5	4.0	2.3	3.6	2.9	2.7	2.3	3.1
Politiken Sø	2.2	2.0	2.1	2.3	2.3	2.3	2.8	2.7	2.7	2.3	2.5	1.8	2.5
Aktuelt Sø	1.4	1.5	1.5	1.9	2.0	1.6	1.7	2.4	2.0	2.2	1.8	2.6	1.8
Sunday papers	**6.9**	**6.8**	**7.4**	**8.2**	**8.1**	**7.4**	**8.5**	**7.4**	**8.3**	**7.4**	**7.0**	**6.7**	**7.4**
Weekendavisen	1.9	1.3	0.9	1.1	1.1	1.1	1.2	0.6	1.1	1.0	0.7	0.7	0.8
Berlingske total	30.5	27.8	28.6	29.7	27.7	22.52	24.4	14.9	22.8	21.1	20.6	17.7	24.5
Politiken total	22.8	20.9	21.3	22.1	19.9	15.4	17.6	22.1	20.2	18.9	18.4	15.3	20.2
Aktuelt total	5.6	4.8	5.0	6.3	5.7	4.4	4.3	6.8	5.7	6.0	5.4	7.4	4.8
Børsen	–	–	–	–	–	–	6.6	9.0	9.5	9.4	9.1	9.5	8.6
Total market	**58.9**	**53.5**	**54.9**	**58.1**	**53.3**	**42.3**	**52.9**	**52.8**	**58.2**	**55.4**	**53.5**	**49.9**	**58.1**

*For example, in 1970, Berlingske Tidende sold 15,600 columns of 535 millimetres each of display advertising space.

Source: In-house statistics 1970–1982, Det Berlingske Officin A/S.

Exhibit 12.11 *Market development: display advertisements, including consolidated advertisements (1000 columns @ 535 millimetres*)*

	1970	1971	1972	1973	1974	1975	1976	1977	1978	1979	1980	1981	1982
Berlingske Tidende	26.5	25.1	23.9	22.2	21.0	22.2	18.5	11.7	15.3	15.2	15.3	16.5	17.5
Politiken	20.9	19.2	17.8	17.5	15.4	15.1	14.4	17.4	15.1	15.2	14.8	12.6	13.6
Aktuelt	7.1	6.2	6.4	7.6	6.9	6.6	4.9	8.3	6.4	6.9	6.7	9.6	5.2
Børsen	–	–	–	–	–	–	12.5	17.1	16.3	17.0	17.0	19.0	14.8
Morning papers	**54.5**	**50.5**	**48.1**	**47.3**	**43.3**	**43.9**	**50.3**	**54.5**	**53.1**	**54.2**	**53.8**	**57.7**	**51.1**
B.T.	16.5	18.3	19.7	20.1	21.8	20.1	17.8	11.0	15.8	15.9	16.8	13.0	17.9
Ekstra Bladet	14.1	16.1	17.1	16.5	17.6	15.8	13.6	19.3	14.9	14.8	15.0	14.5	16.9
Noon papers	**30.6**	**34.4**	**36.8**	**36.6**	**39.4**	**35.9**	**31.4**	**30.3**	**30.7**	**30.7**	**31.8**	**27.5**	**34.8**
Berlingske Sø	5.6	6.2	6.9	6.9	7.1	8.3	7.6	4.4	6.2	5.2	5.0	4.6	5.3
Politiken Sø	3.7	3.7	3.8	3.9	4.3	5.4	5.3	5.1	4.7	4.2	4.7	3.6	4.3
Aktuelt Sø	2.7	2.8	2.7	3.3	3.8	3.8	3.2	4.5	3.4	4.0	3.4	5.2	3.1
Sunday papers	**11.7**	**12.7**	**13.5**	**14.1**	**15.2**	**17.5**	**16.1**	**14.0**	**14.3**	**13.4**	**13.1**	**13.4**	**12.7**
Weekendavisen	3.2	2.4	1.6	1.9	2.1	2.6	2.3	1.1	1.9	1.9	1.3	1.4	1.4
Berlingske total	51.8	52.0	52.1	51.1	52.0	53.2	46.1	28.2	39.2	38.1	38.4	35.5	42.1
Politiken total	38.7	39.1	38.8	38.0	37.3	36.4	33.3	41.9	34.7	34.1	34.5	30.7	34.8
Aktuelt total	9.5	8.9	9.1	10.9	10.7	10.4	8.1	12.9	9.8	10.8	10.1	14.8	8.3
Børsen	–	–	–	–	–	–	12.5	17.0	16.3	17.0	17.0	19.0	14.8
Total market	**100**	**100**	**100**	**100**	**100**	**100**	**100**	**100**	**100**	**100**	**100**	**100**	**100**

Source: In-house statistics 1970–1982, Det Berlingske Officin A/S.

Exhibit 12.12 *Display advertisements: market shares (%)*

	1970	1971	1972	1973	1974	1975	1976	1977	1978	1979	1980	1981	1982
Berlingske Tidende	34.6	32.0	32.2	34.0	29.7	21.7	21.3	13.8	23.0	23.7	21.3	12.6	14.3
Politiken	11.5	10.5	9.6	10.1	10.3	9.2	10.0	16.8	12.6	14.0	14.2	7.9	10.5
Aktuelt	2.9	2.6	3.6	5.4	5.0	3.9	3.1	6.5	5.9	6.5	5.4	8.8	4.4
Børsen	–	–	–	–	–	–	5.0	7.4	6.3	6.1	6.4	7.7	5.8
Morning papers	**49.0**	**45.1**	**45.4**	**49.5**	**45.0**	**34.8**	**39.4**	**44.5**	**47.8**	**50.3**	**47.3**	**37.0**	**35.0**
B.T.	2.8	2.7	3.0	3.1	3.6	3.1	3.6	3.0	4.2	3.2	3.5	2.2	3.8
Ekstra Bladet	4.5	4.1	3.9	4.6	5.6	5.5	5.3	5.2	7.5	5.1	5.3	3.9	4.7
Noon papers	**7.3**	**6.8**	**6.9**	**7.7**	**9.2**	**8.6**	**8.9**	**7.2**	**11.7**	**8.3**	**8.8**	**6.1**	**8.5**
Berlingske Sø	25.6	24.3	26.3	29.6	27.1	22.9	26.3	14.1	25.2	27.4	26.0	16.0	18.2
Politiken Sø	8.0	6.8	6.2	7.1	7.7	6.3	7.2	9.0	9.5	9.8	9.3	5.3	8.0
Aktuelt Sø	1.1	1.0	1.3	1.7	1.4	1.1	1.3	2.6	2.0	2.5	3.2	4.8	2.5
Sunday papers	**34.7**	**32.1**	**33.8**	**38.4**	**36.2**	**30.3**	**34.8**	**25.7**	**36.7**	**39.7**	**38.5**	**26.1**	**28.7**
Weekendavisen	1.4	0.4	0.3	0.3	0.3	0.4	0.3	0.2	0.2	0.6	0.3	0.1	–
Berlingske total	64.4	59.4	61.8	67.0	60.7	48.1	51.5	30.1	52.6	54.9	51.1	30.9	36.3
Politiken total	24.0	21.4	19.7	21.8	23.6	21.0	22.5	31.0	29.6	28.9	28.8	17.1	23.2
Aktuelt total	4.0	3.6	4.9	7.1	6.4	5.0	4.4	9.1	7.9	9.0	8.6	13.6	6.9
Børsen	–	–	–	–	–	–	5.0	7.4	6.3	6.1	6.4	7.7	5.8
Total market	**92.4**	**84.4**	**86.4**	**95.9**	**90.7**	**74.1**	**83.4**	**77.6**	**96.4**	**98.9**	**94.9**	**69.3**	**72.2**

Source: In-house statistics 1970–1982, Det Berlingske Officin A/S.

Exhibit 12.13   *Market development: classified advertisements (1000 columns @ 535 millimetres*)*

	1970	1971	1972	1973	1974	1975	1976	1977	1978	1979	1980	1981	1982
Berlingske Tidende	37.5	37.9	37.3	35.5	32.7	29.3	25.5	17.8	23.9	24.0	22.4	18.2	19.8
Politiken	12.4	12.4	11.1	10.5	11.4	12.4	12.0	21.6	13.1	14.2	15.0	11.4	14.5
Aktuelt	3.1	3.1	4.2	5.6	5.5	5.3	3.7	8.4	6.1	6.6	5.7	12.7	6.1
Børsen	–	–	–	–	–	–	6.0	9.5	6.5	6.2	6.7	11.1	8.0
Morning papers	**53.0**	**53.4**	**52.6**	**51.6**	**49.6**	**47.0**	**47.2**	**57.3**	**49.6**	**50.9**	**49.8**	**53.4**	**48.4**
B.T.	3.0	3.2	3.5	3.2	4.0	4.2	4.3	2.6	4.4	3.2	3.7	3.2	5.3
Ekstra Bladet	4.9	4.9	4.5	4.8	6.2	7.4	6.4	6.7	7.8	5.2	5.6	5.6	6.5
Noon papers	**7.9**	**8.1**	**8.0**	**8.0**	**10.2**	**11.6**	**10.7**	**9.3**	**12.2**	**8.4**	**9.3**	**8.8**	**11.8**
Berlingske Sø	27.7	28.8	30.4	30.9	29.9	30.9	31.5	18.2	26.1	27.7	27.4	23.1	25.2
Politiken Sø	8.7	8.1	7.2	7.4	8.5	8.5	8.6	11.6	9.9	9.9	9.8	7.7	11.1
Aktuelt Sø	1.2	1.2	1.5	1.8	1.5	1.5	1.6	3.4	2.1	2.5	3.4	6.9	3.5
Sunday papers	**37.6**	**38.1**	**39.1**	**41.1**	**39.9**	**40.9**	**41.7**	**33.2**	**38.1**	**40.1**	**40.6**	**37.7**	**39.8**
Weekendavisen	1.5	0.5	0.3	0.3	0.3	0.5	0.3	0.2	0.2	0.6	0.3	0.1	–
Berlingske total	69.7	70.4	71.5	69.9	66.9	64.9	61.8	38.8	54.6	55.5	53.8	44.6	50.3
Politiken total	26.0	25.4	22.8	22.7	26.0	28.3	27.0	40.0	30.7	29.2	30.4	24.7	32.1
Aktuelt total	4.3	4.2	5.7	7.4	7.1	6.8	5.3	11.7	8.2	9.1	9.1	19.6	9.6
Børsen	–	–	–	–	–	–	5.9	9.5	6.5	6.2	6.7	11.1	8.0
Total market	**100**	**100**	**100**	**100**	**100**	**100**	**100**	**100**	**100**	**100**	**100**	**100**	**100**

Source: In-house statistics 1970–1982, Det Berlingske Officin A/S.

Exhibit 12.14 *Classified advertisements: market shares (%)*

	1970	1971	1972	1973	1974	1975	1976	1977	1978	1979	1980	1981	1982
Morning papers	**43.0**	**40.2**	**37.2**	**36.4**	**36.1**	**35.9**	**35.8**	**37.6**	**38.9**	**37.7**	**37.6**	**38.8**	**38.6**
Noon papers	**44.2**	**47.5**	**50.9**	**52.3**	**52.5**	**52.7**	**53.0**	**51.2**	**50.2**	**51.7**	**51.9**	**50.4**	**50.5**
Sunday papers	**12.1**	**11.6**	**11.2**	**10.6**	**10.7**	**10.6**	**10.4**	**10.3**	**10.0**	**9.7**	**9.6**	**9.9**	**9.8**
Weekendavisen	0.7	0.7	0.7	0.7	0.7	0.8	0.8	0.9	0.9	0.9	0.9	0.9	0.8
Berlingske total	45.0	45.8	46.7	46.8	47.0	46.9	46.1	43.1	41.4	42.2	42.0	41.1	40.7
Politiken total	41.0	42.1	43.2	43.2	42.6	42.6	43.3	45.2	46.4	45.9	45.9	46.3	46.8
Aktuelt total	12.8	10.7	8.5	8.1	8.3	8.0	7.9	8.6	9.0	8.7	8.6	8.9	8.6
Børsen	1.2	1.4	1.6	1.9	2.1	2.5	2.7	3.1	3.2	3.2	3.5	3.7	3.9
Total market	**100**	**100**	**100**	**100**	**100**	**100**	**100**	**100**	**100**	**100**	**100**	**100**	**100**
Jyllands-Posten	12.2	12.2	12.0	11.7	11.4	12.0	11.9	12.6	13.0	13.2	13.2	14.5	15.1

Source: In-house statistics 1970–1982, Det Berlingske Officin A/S.

Exhibit 12.15 *Market shares for circulation (%)*

'Berlingske Dagblade' had been organized as profit centres. Each newspaper was a separate operation and had to produce regular product reports.

Reves knew that changing the organization (Exhibit 12.16) and eliminating the confusion inside the company was part of Berlingske's turnaround. The new team's first task was to manage the turnaround, while simultaneously facing severe pressure to cut costs. Reves brought a younger man with him from his previous job, who later became Circulation Director. Most of the managers, however, were chosen from the Berlingske staff. Reves believed that personal contacts were essential and he made careful choices based on competence and personality. After many meetings and discussions, he focused on the most promising individuals for promotion to new jobs.

Chresten Reves chose three co-directors to assist him: Aage Deleuran as Editing Director; Hans Gundesen as Marketing and Sales Director; and Erik Jensen as

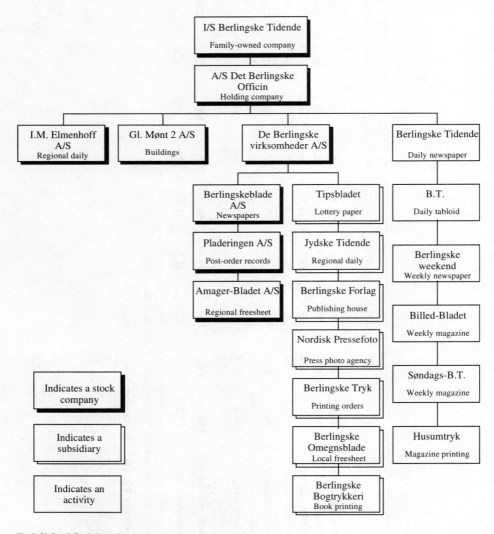

Exhibit 12.16   *Organizational chart, 1981*

Technology and Personnel Director. Mr. Deleuran had been with the company almost 40 years and was completely devoted to the Berlingske newspapers. He had been through the good days as well as the hardships. His experience and expertise in editorial matters would be invaluable. Mr Gundesen had been with the company for 10 years in the advertising and circulation departments. Mr Jensen was the President's right-hand man. He had been heavily involved in the negotiations with the typographers' unions in the 1970s and was still in charge of personnel and technology. If anyone could find common ground with the unions, thereby enabling the company to recover, he would be the one.

Berlingske publications

The Berlingske publications (Exhibit 12.17) benefited fully from numerable sources and technical aids for accessing comprehensive information rapidly: they subscribed to the world's largest news agencies; they also had the largest press files and the most up-to-date telephoto plant in Scandinavia. Their staff comprised correspondents in most international news centres as well as a large number of outside contributors. However, circulation of all the Berlingske publications had suffered badly from the labour conflicts and, in 1983, had not yet regained their lost market share (Exhibit 12.18).

The most successful publication was the *Berlingske Tidende*, the oldest Danish newspaper to be still operating in 1983. This paper, considered the backbone of the Berlingske concern, had priority over the other newspaper operations. Circulation

Exhibit 12.17 *The Berlingske pubications*

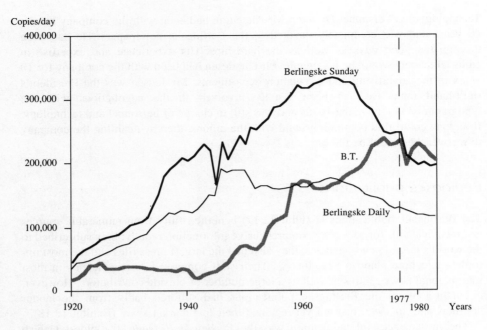

Exhibit 12.18 *Circulation of Berlingske main publications, 1920–1982. (Source: Circulation figures of major newspapers 1870–1987, Det Berlingske Officin A/S)*

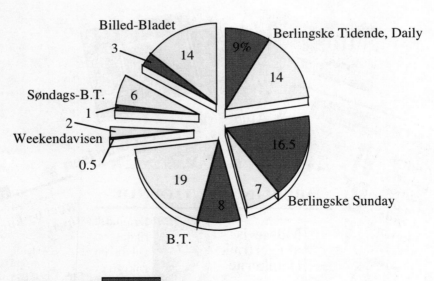

Exhibit 12.19 *Market data: advertising and circulation income per publication. (Source: Det Berlingske Officin A/S Annual Report 1983)*

income was mostly generated by *B.T.* and advertising income by *Berlingske Tidende* (Exhibit 12.19).

The *Berlingske Tidendel* was a serious and conservative broadsheet which provided foreign as well as national and local news. Since the 1960s, its circulation had been on the decline (Exhibit 12.20), which was attributed to various events: the advent of television, competition from sensationalist tabloids, the appearance of free sheets, quality problems, conflicts with unions, delays in introducing new technology, etc. *B.T.*, also published by the Berlingske group, was a close competitor; every fourth reader of the *Berlingske Tidende* also read *B.T.*

For many years, the *Berlingske Tidende* had been known in the Copenhagen community as *Aunt Berlingske*. This nickname indicated the importance of tradition in the newspaper house and the stiff bureaucratic ways that still prevailed. Some interpreted this term as one of endearment for an old newspaper that was an intrinsic part of Danish history. But in 1983, the paper badly needed a fresh new look. The

Year	Circulation figures	Readers in 1000	Average number of readers per issue	Total advertising volume (mm*)	Display advertising (mm*)	Classified advertisements (mm*)
1960	161,498	379	2.3	21,263,455	7,198,065	14,065,390
1961	163,611	378	2.3	21,447,085	7,128,590	14,318,495
1962	165,056	383	2.3	23,611,845	7,947,015	15,664,830
1963	170,845	458	2.7	24,102,100	8,492,200	15,609,900
1964	172,471	419	2.4	25,740,615	8,738,770	17,001,845
1965	170,165	388	2.3	26,397,050	8,571,990	17,825,060
1966	169,276	387	2.3	26,192,935	8,586,615	17,606,320
1967	166,108	376	2.3	24,863,195	8,523,725	16,339,470
1968	160,382	–	–	22,852,815	8,139,500	14,713,315
1969	158,898	385	2.4	24,484,960	8,083,495	16,401,465
1970	153,158	353	2.3	26,880,660	8,347,285	18,533,375
1971	146,665	348	2.4	24,253,425	7,158,365	17,095,060
1972	146,886	369	2.5	24,202,590	6,981,615	17,220,975
1973	142,373	389	2.7	25,088,560	6,912,510	18,176,050
1974	133,724	360	2.7	21,839,155	5,974,030	15,865,125
1975	127,714	351	2.7	16,642,410	5,021,840	11,620,570
1976	126,189	318	2.5	16,645,555	5,254,105	11,391,450
1977	123,362	180	1.5	10,697,955	3,336,080	7,361,875
1978	123,457	–	–	17,382,160	4,820,680	12,561,480
1979	118,132	344	2.9	17,303,050	4,606,045	12,697,005
1980	115,351	323	2.8	15,773,310	4,384,410	11,388,900
1981	116,673	331	2.8	11,155,360	4,407,340	6,748,020
1982	115,676	334	2.9	13,108,160	5,454,585	7,653,575

*Advertising volume is measured in millimetres.

Sources: Circulation figures and market figures, 2nd half-year figures. Danish Media Subscript, the whole year, 1969–1986 Gallup Marketing Subscript, the whole year, 1960–1968. Advertisement statistics of Berlingske Tidende.

Exhibit 12.20   *Berlingske Tidende: circulation and advertising*

editorial department had lacked the time and resources to focus on quality and modern techniques. Articles were rather long and the layout was unclear with no specific sections. Advertisements were placed randomly. In addition, there were still delays in production and distribution.

The second Copenhagen morning paper published by Berlingske was *B.T.*, Denmark's most widely read newspaper. This paper was a popular sensationalist tabloid, targeted at low and middle income readers. It was a 'boulevard' publication. *B.T.* was published 6 days a week, and was ready for sale at 9 am. Except for some photographers and the newspaper archives, *B.T.* and *Berlingske Tidende* shared no staff.

The third national paper published by the Berlingske House was the *Weekendavisen*. This was an up-market weekly paper, published every Friday. The editorial quality was higher than in the other publications; it included thorough intellectual, political, cultural and scientific articles and debates. The majority of its readers had a higher education. Longer articles and the absence of pictures gave the paper a serious look. This élite paper was, however, less profitable than the others. It attracted less advertising and, with a smaller target group, had a smaller circulation (46,000 in 1982). A break-even product, it was nonetheless a source of pride to management, providing the Berlingske House with a respectable image and a good reputation.

The Berlingske House also published two newspapers in the province of Jutland: *Jydske Tidende* in Kolding, and *Amtsavisen* in Randers. The positioning of these publications was clear; both papers were local and catered to the residents of the town and its surroundings. Local staff reported on local matters. Most advertisements were also local and the papers were printed in their home market. Competition with other local papers, three of which controlled the three major cities, was difficult.

Berlingske's competitors

In 1983, there were three major quality newspapers in Denmark – all politically independent. *Politiken* was a social-democratic/liberal newspaper covering general news, published 7 days a week with an average of 24–40 pages per issue. It reached a circulation of 145,000 in 1982. *Jyllands-Posten*, the leading provincial paper, followed with 102,000 and *Berlingske Tidende* with 116,000. Finally, *Borsen* was a national financial and general newspaper directed toward private trade. It was published 5 days a week with about 32–112 pages per issue and its circulation in 1982 was 34,000.

Politiken was a broadsheet paper, divided into two main sections, which was excellent on cultural issues and society features. It often counteracted the Berlingske initiatives and provided aggressive competition.

Berlingske Tidende's major competitor in the provinces was *Jyllands-Posten*. This paper had poor economic coverage but was the unquestionable leader in the provinces. The newspaper's Editor-in-Chief was also Managing Director, which was considered a good way to avoid many conflicts. At *Jyllands-Posten*, there were more journalists, fewer technicians and sales people, and higher salaries than at the Berlingske – 'Every dollar earned was invested in quality.'[8]

---

[8] Said by an editorial staff member of the *Berlingske Tidende*.

Copies/day

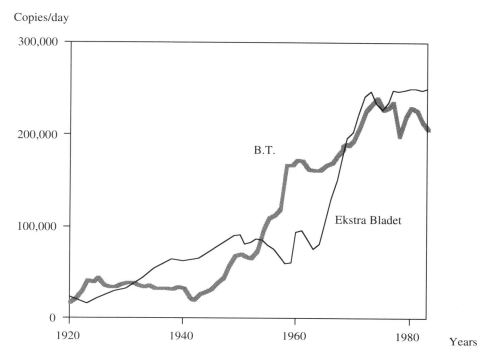

Exhibit 12.21 *Comparative circulation of sensationalistic tabloids, 1920–1982 (Source: Circulation figures of major newspapers 1870–1987, Det Berlingske Officin A/S)*

Two major popular papers shared the sensationalist news market, focusing on scandals and using photographs extensively. *B.T.* began publication in 1916; a similar paper, *Ekstra Bladet*, had already been started in 1904 by the competitor, *Politiken*. In 1983, the latter had a circulation of 250,000, while *B.T.* followed with 213,000 (see Exhibit 12.21). Both newspapers watched each other carefully and imitated each other's competitive moves. They were both politically independent, were published 6 days a week and averaged 48 pages per issue. *Ekstra Bladet* registered higher circulation figures, but *B.T.* was nonetheless Denmark's most widely read newspaper.

During Berlingske's difficult years, its competitors inevitably gained in market shares. *Politiken* was not as badly hurt by the labour struggles and its circulation kept increasing (Exhibit 12.22). *Borsen* managed to attract most of the business advertising and experienced the most positive development of all Zealand papers during the 1960–1983 period. *Jyllands-Posten* grew steadily in the provinces and *Berlingske Tidende*'s countrywide coverage disappeared.

Technology

The introduction of desktop publishing technology had been long delayed by the typographers' conflict. When it finally became a reality after the takeover in 1983, the Berlingske House was still operating with 70-year-old equipment based on the Gutenberg technique. The introduction of phototypesetting would gradually develop

Year	Circulation figures	Readers in 1000	Average number of readers per issue	Total advertising volume (mm*)	Display advertising (mm*)	Classified advertisements (mm*)
1960	140,695	319	2.3	13,572,915	7,128,890	6,444,025
1961	141,623	324	2.3	13,481,330	6,922,250	6,559,080
1962	135,959	331	2.4	14,053,630	7,364,775	6,688,855
1963	136,531	372	2.7	13,987,375	7,641,700	6,345,675
1964	139,155	325	2.3	14,057,685	7,560,015	6,497,670
1965	139,917	347	2.5	14,047,455	7,356,880	6,690,575
1966	141,482	340	2.4	13,937,205	7,181,765	6,755,440
1967	140,432	329	2.3	13,507,815	7,187,625	6,320,190
1968	132,851	–	–	12,678,535	7,013,615	5,664,920
1969	132,193	320	2.4	12,586,270	6,716,080	5,870,190
1970	130,265	308	2.4	12,697,240	6,558,905	6,138,335
1971	127,127	310	2.4	11,136,995	5,528,555	5,608,440
1972	124,513	320	2.6	10,385,125	5,238,835	5,146,290
1973	120,331	291	2.4	10,881,060	5,481,050	5,400,010
1974	110,904	304	2.7	9,891,765	4,395,720	5,496,045
1975	109,459	306	2.8	8,337,675	3,422,545	4,915,130
1976	118,077	306	2.6	9,399,920	4,071,805	5,328,115
1977	136,163	365	2.7	13,937,595	4,935,020	9,002,575
1978	137,187	–	–	11,461,660	4,719,560	6,742,100
1979	135,727	410	3.0	11,981,845	4,494,595	7,487,250
1980	138,856	382	2.8	11,834,620	4,239,815	7,594,805
1981	139,736	407	2.9	7,591,445	3,382,715	4,208,730
1982	144,782	438	3.0	9,801,885	4,160,860	5,641,025

*Advertising volume is measured in millimetres.

Sources: Circulation figures and market figures, 2nd half-year figures. Danish Media Subscript, the whole year, 1969–1986. Gallup Marketing Subscript, the whole year, 1960–1968. Advertisement statistics of *Berlingske Tidende*.

Exhibit 12.22   *Politiken: circulation and advertising*

Year	Weekly paid	Administrative staff	Editorial staff	Total
1965	1,660	1,093	364	3,117
1969	1,710	1,137	381	3,228
1970	1,160	1,160	382	3,297
1974	1,808	1,001	361	3,170
1978	1,309	702	316	2,327
1981	1,598	801	413	2,812
1982	1,561	845	400	2,806

Source: Det Berlingske Officin A/S.

Exhibit 12.23   *Number of employees in the House of Berlingske*

	1978	1979	1980	1981*	1982
Sales income	766	950	1000	946	1110
Profit of main operations	(2)	(11)	(16)	(3)	(47)
Operational profit	(6)	(15)	(22)	(11)	(49)
Annual net profit	(7)	(20)	(21)	(13)	(51)
Total assets	286	293	307	306	247
Owner's capital	63	42	21	8	8
Number of employees (full time)	3,022	3,091	2,974	2,763	2,718

*11-week labour conflict over negotiation of union's agreement.

Source: Det Berlingske Officin A/S Annual Report 1982.

Exhibit 12.24   *The Berlingske Group – five-year overview (millions of DKr)*

into the extremely efficient process of the future, namely computer-to-plate publishing.

The process began in 1983 with the introduction of the Atex system – the most advanced available system on the market for publishers. It provided a direct on-line connection from the journalist's workplace to the photo composition department for advertisement display, placing and pagination, editorial, advertising and graphic word processing. Other parts of the production system to be added later included: automatic full-page set-up, electronic pictures (making film obsolete) and direct on-line communication with advertisers.

This was only the beginning in a long process of technological transition. Chresten Reves knew it would not be easy. Vivid images of the 1977 strike were still haunting people's memories. Delicate negotiations would have to be handled. In case of a positive outcome, a long and painful process would begin; the technical staff would have to adapt, be convinced and trained. In addition, Reves wanted to review the product strategies thoroughly.

Case 12.2 Taking charge at Inter Drinks Company

This case was prepared by Research Associate U. Srinivasa Rangan under the direction of Professors James Ellert and Jan Kubes as a basis for class discussion rather than to illustrate either effective or ineffective handling of an administrative situation.

It was January 14, 1982, only three weeks since Helmut Fehring, Managing Director of Inter Drinks Company (IDC), had returned from a year spent in an intensive executive training programme. The old bottling company and its problems no longer looked the same to him as before. He was now more aware of the difficulties this small regional company had to face in an increasingly competitive environment, and he had started to identify priority areas for management attention. This afternoon he was determined to develop an action plan.

His three key functional managers had already brought several important issues to his attention which needed early decisions. Stefan Wiener, the Production Manager, was recommending that the company invest in a new bottling line to replace one of the old slower bottling lines. As Stefan explained with some urgency to Helmut, 'At five million Swiss francs, it's a big decision, but we have to order the line this month to have it installed before the summer season. The problem has become acute and time is running out.' Earlier that day, the Marketing Manager, Karl Muller, had urged that the marketing strategy and measures to improve sales force effectiveness be given priority attention. The Finance Manager, Hans-Vogel Schmidt, had been pressing for a decision on his recommendation to use more computer facilities. Helmut Fehring realized he would have to act soon or be overwhelmed by too many disjointed functional decisions.

Company background

IDC (Inter Drinks Company), founded in 1933 by Ludwig Wiener, was located in Zug in the German-speaking part of Switzerland. During a trip to Berg, a nearby mountain resort, Mr Wiener had noticed the number of influential Europeans and Americans who came to this resort for the therapeutic value of the local springs. The resort hotel supplied 10,000 bottles of mineral water every year to its guests. This gave Mr. Wiener the idea of producing and marketing this mineral water systematically.

In 1935, Mr Wiener followed up on the idea, establishing IDC as a limited company with a share capital of SF57,600 (Swiss francs).[1] The objectives of the company were: 'To exploit the mineral water sources by distributing bottled mineral water under the company's brand name, producing and distributing various non-alcoholic drinks, and providing work opportunities in the industrially undeveloped area around Berg.'

After its inception as a limited company, IDC grew rapidly. The first products marketed under the company's brand name, Berg, were carbonated mineral water, curative water, and lemon and orange drinks made from concentrates. In 1937, the company introduced drinks based on fruit juice, such as orangeade and grapefruit, into Switzerland. These products were produced under a licence from a Dutch company. Later, soft drinks made from various other fruit juices were introduced in quick succession.

In 1954, the company began bottling soft drinks produced by Schweppes, a well-known British extracts company. Schweppes had been looking for a bottler in Switzerland and had asked manufacturers for samples of mineral water. Schweppes found the water supplied by IDC to be best-suited for use in its Indian tonic water and thus IDC was awarded the licence.

Pepsi-Cola, a US-based supplier of concentrates, also found IDC's mineral water well suited for its soft drinks. The company had been searching for a bottler to compete against Coca-Cola, which had been in the Swiss market since 1947. In 1962, IDC obtained the franchise to bottle Pepsi-Cola in Switzerland (Exhibit 12.25).

Product	Flavours	Bottle sizes (litres)	
Soft drinks			
Schweppes	Tonic Water	0.18	
	Bitter Orange	0.18	
	Bitter Lemon	0.18	
	Ginger Ale	0.18	
	Soda Water	0.18	
Pepsi-Cola	Cola	0.3	1.0
Berg Brand	Citron	0.3	1.0
	Orange	0.3	1.0
	Grapefruit	0.3	1.0
	Himbo	0.3	1.0
	Simbo	0.3	1.0
Private label	(same as for Berg Brand)		1.0
Mineral water			
Berg Brand	–	0.3	1.0
Private label	–		1.0

Source: Company Records.

Exhibit 12.25 *IDC's product line*

[1] SF2.00 = $1.00 in 1983.

Over the years, IDC's manufacturing facilities were expanded to keep pace with the projected increases in demand for its products. Soft drink consumption followed a seasonal pattern, with June to September accounting for nearly 40% of IDC's sales. In 1980 the company sold 57.9 million bottles of soft drinks and mineral water from its modern plant near Berg. However, the facilities were capable of producing 120 million bottles annually, working two shifts.

In 1959, the company acquired a subsidiary, Aditya, located in Lausanne in the western part of Switzerland; Aditya was run as a separate company (see *Relationship between Aditya And IDC*).[2]

Recent trends

When IDC was established in 1935, Hans Fehring had joined the company as a major shareholder. As the company grew over the years, the shareholding pattern changed; in 1981, the Fehring family controlled 44% of the voting stock, the Wiener family 11%, Schweppes company 12% and about 180 small shareholders held the balance. The small shareholders were mostly distributors and retailers.

In recent years, the geographic area covered by IDC had become smaller and the company marketed its own Berg brands only in central Switzerland.[3] Schweppes and Pepsi were also being bottled by IDC for sale in only the central and western parts of Switzerland, whereas the company had previously supplied all of Switzerland. IDC attributed the loss of territory to the franchisers' rationalization plans. However, as the company still received sublicensing fees from the bottlers in these areas, it claimed that the loss was a minor problem.

Helmut Fehring attributed the company's poor financial performance to shrinking profit margins. He explained, 'In recent years, the pressures on profitability in this industry have been tremendous. We have seen our margins continuously eroded by cut-throat competition.' Fehring was pleased, however, that use of IDC's capacity had improved substantially over the past three years. 'Better capacity utilization should help us improve our profit picture,' he said. Provisional results indicated that IDC should make an after tax profit of SF200,000 in 1981 (Exhibits 12.26 and 12.27).

The Swiss soft drink and mineral water industry

Switzerland

In 1981, Switzerland was the richest country in Europe, with the second highest per capita income (SF26,000) in the world after Kuwait. Its population and economy, however, had remained unchanged throughout the 1970s due to a low birth rate, ageing population and low immigration levels. This situation was not expected to vary much within the next decade.

---

[2] Data in text and exhibits refer to IDC unless specifically indicated.
[3] In 1983 population of Switzerland = 6.3 million, with about 70% in the central (German-speaking) part.

	1976	1977	1978	1979	1980
Net sales[1]	16,085	14,813	14,936	16,163	17,410
Manufacturing costs					
Sugar	2,448	1,926	1,676	1,712	2,122
Other raw materials	1,555	1,280	1,674	1,853	2,151
Packaging (one way)					
Caps and labels	1,224	1,122	1,566	1,517	1,595
Production personnel – wages and benefits	882	968	973	1,168	1,463
Depreciation[2]	2,089	1,274	1,242	1,3980	1,470
Power and fuel	102	96	112	360	399
Other production overhead	495	672	761	777	787
Total manufacturing costs	8,795	7,337	8,004	8,777	9,987
Gross profit from operations	7,290	7,476	6,932	7,386	7,423
Add: gross profit from merchandising[3]	449	435	1,636	2,430	1,890
Gross profit	7,739	7,911	8,568	9,816	9,313
Other expenses					
Salaries and employee benefits	2,660	2,876	3,105	3,316	3,698
Rents	171	147	149	157	164
Interest payments	1,049	810	675	595	560
General admin.	637	394	620	1,146	948
Selling expenses	1,922	1,939	2,163	2,436	2,436
Advertising and promotion	1,818	1,961	1,937	1,809	2,142
Misc. income	585	742	571	540	636
Investment write-off	–	(1,984)	–	–	–
Net profit	67	(1,458)	490	897	1

[1] After discounts and year-end rebates.

[2] For investment analysis, IDC treated major capital investments as if they were written off over 8 years with the exception of bottles and crates which were written off over 3 years.

[3] The company had a trading operation unrelated to its bottling activities and products. The contribution made on sales to Aditya is also included under this head.

Notes: This income statement does not include Aditya.

Under Swiss law, the company was subject to 30% tax rate and was allowed to carry forward   losses up to four years for tax purposes.

IDC, like other Swiss companies, enjoyed wide discretion in reporting depreciation charge.

Source: Company Records.

Exhibit 12.26 *Income statement (thousands of SF)*

Two important factors were Switzerland's cultural diversity (German 65%, French 15% and Italian 12%) and the role of tourism in the economy. In recent years, tourism had stagnated as the Swiss franc had appreciated in relation to other major currencies except the German mark. Germany had always been Switzerland's major trading partner, however, and German tourists considered it a favourite holiday destination.

	1976	1977	1978	1979	1980
Assets					
Current					
Cash	95	112	72	392	529
Accounts receivables	2,303	1,970	2,069	1,600	1,826
Inventory and goods in transit	1,254	1,246	1,537	1,417	1,617
Miscellaneous	54	40	27	734	408
Subtotal	3,706	3,368	3,705	4,143	4,380
Fixed					
Plant, etc.	10,568	9,984	9,404	9,016	9,297
Automatic vending machines, etc.	1,166	851	584	477	450
Bottles and crates	1,287	1,080	1,062	1,233	2,115
Subtotal	13,021	11,915	11,050	10,726	11,862
Misc. (non-current)					
Securities and participations	4,685	4,320	4,246	3,479	3,168
Overdue customer receivables	1,653	989	932	689	608
Subtotal	6,338	5,309	5,178	4,168	3,776
Total assets	23,065	20,592	19,933	10,037	20,018
Liabilities					
Current					
Banks	1,362	1,294	1,376	–	450
Customer deposits	–	66	15	870	2,047
Accounts payable	1,762	2,334	1,940	1,706	1,856
Sugar reserve	428	428	698	699	698
Accrued expenses	164	183	327	244	239
Subtotal	3,716	4,305	4,356	3,519	5,290
Long-term					
Mortgage loan	11,943	10,564	9.624	8,898	8,246
Pension fund	1,350	1,125	865	635	496
Subtotal	13,293	11,689	10,489	9,533	8,742
Net worth					
Capital plus legal reserves	5,985	5,985	5,985	5,985	5,985
Retained earnings	71	(1,387)	(897)	–	1
Subtotal	6,056	4,598	5,088	5,985	5,986
Total liabilities	23,065	20,592	19,933	19,037	20,018

Note: This balance sheet does not include Aditya.
Source: Company Records.

Exhibit 12.27 *Balance sheet (thousands of SF)*

Industry

Historical growth rates indicated relatively mature and stagnant markets for both soft drinks and mineral water. However, some analysts felt that, based on comparisons with neighbouring European countries, there was substantial growth potential for per capita consumption in Switzerland (Exhibit 12.28).

	1976	1977	1978	1979	1980
Soft drinks					
Switzerland	47.5	47.0	48.8	51.3	52.5
Germany	67.6	65.2	65.8	67.9	68.0
France	NA[1]	NA	NA	NA	24.0
Italy	NA	NA	NA	NA	20.0
Austria	NA	NA	NA	NA	34.0
Mineral water					
Switzerland	36.2	34.5	34.4	36.4	37.9
Germany	30.4	33.9	36.6	39.3	40.8
France	NA	NA	NA	NA	48.8
Italy	NA	NA	NA	NA	29.0
Austria	NA	NA	NA	NA	4.0

[1] NA = not available.
Source: Industry Sources, EIU Reports.

Exhibit 12.28   *Per capita consumption levels in Europe (litres per year)*

	Soft drinks	*Mineral water*
1972	290	178
1973	323	200
1974	305	198
1975	285	211
1976	300	230
1977	281	218
1978	302	218
1979	318	231
1980	321	241

Source: Industry Sources.

Exhibit 12.29   *Swiss soft drink and mineral water consumption (millions of litres)*

In 1980, an estimated 321 million litres of bottled soft drinks (worth SF195 million in ex-factory prices) and 241 million litres of mineral water (worth SF75 million) were consumed in Switzerland (Exhibit 12.29).

Bottlers

In total, 63 bottlers served the Swiss soft drink and mineral water industry.[4] Some bottlers operated several plants, located near major cities and other centres with high consumption, usually serving the entire Swiss market with nationally known brands.

[4] Includes mineral water and carbonated ordinary water.

385

Others, operating one or two bottling plants each, served limited geographic areas with their own regional brands. The high cost of transportation generally prevented the regional bottlers from serving distant markets. Even international brands such as Schweppes, Pepsi-Cola and Coca-Cola were bottled by regional bottlers, with each franchised bottler serving a specific exclusive geographic territory.

In 1980, the four largest national soft drink bottling companies together accounted for 45% of Swiss production, up from 36% in 1975. The concentration was higher in mineral water, where the top four accounted for 66% of the market, up from 55% five years earlier (Exhibit 12.30).[5]

	Estimated market share in 1980
Soft drinks bottler[1]	
Refresca (CocaCola brands)	12.0
Rivella	11.5
Unifontes	11.0
Migros	10.0
Henniez	7.0
Sibra	5.0
I.D.C. (Berg brand)	5.0
Others	38.5
Total	100.0
Mineral water bottler	
Henniez	26.0
Valser	20.0
Migros (Aproz brand)	11.0
Passuger	9.0
Unifontes (Fontessa brand)	4.0
Others	30.0
Total	100.0

[1] International, national and regional brands.
Source: Industry Sources.

Exhibit 12.30 *National market shares (in litre volume) of top bottling companies*

During the late 1970s and early 1980s, it was estimated that the Swiss soft drink and mineral water industry had an excess capacity of 35%. Anticipating a growth in consumption, bottling plants had been expanded, but the increase had failed to materialize. This excess capacity, in turn, had led to intensified competition in both price and promotion.

[5] Most bottlers produced both soft drinks and mineral water.

Brands

Regional brands tended to compete on price alone. National and international brands, on the other hand, carried premium prices but were advertised heavily to compete for consumer awareness and brand loyalty. These companies could spend proportionately more on brand promotion because the national bottling companies were financially stronger and because the local franchises also received financial assistance from their international suppliers.

A relatively recent industry development was the use of private labels. Major food chains began introducing soft drink and mineral water products under their own 'house' brands. Private labels, produced either by a chain's own bottling facilities or under contract by an independent bottler, put even more pressure on prices. Typically, such a contract would be an oral agreement between the chain and the bottler. Though the latter usually preferred a written contract, the excess capacity in the industry gave the bargaining power to the chains and enabled them to avoid binding written agreements (Exhibit 12.31).

Over time, the national, international and private brands accounted for an increasingly larger share of soft drink and mineral water sales in Switzerland. In 1980, four brands (Sinalco, Rivella, Coca-Cola and Aproz)[6] accounted for 64% of all soft

	Container size (litre)	Shops	Horeca	Chains
Soft drinks				
Schweppes	0.18	0.65	1.95	0.48
Queens	0.18	0.55	1.95	0.40
Pepsi-Cola	0.3	0.55	3.00	–
	1.0	1.15	–	0.85
Coca-Cola	0.3	0.75	3.00	–
	1.0	1.35	–	1.05
Berg/Aditya	0.3	–	1.85	–
	1.0	1.15	–	–
Coop/Denner Private label	1.0	–	–	0.60
Mineral water				
Passuger	0.3	–	1.20	–
	1.0	0.90	–	–
Henniez	0.3	–	1.20	–
	1.0	0.70	–	–
Berg/Aditya	0.3	–	1.20	–
	1.0	0.45	–	–
Coop/Denner Private Label	1.0	–	–	0.25

Source: Industry Sources.

Exhibit 12.31 *Representative consumer retail prices, 1980 (SF)*

[6] Sinalco and Coca-Cola were international brands; Rivella was a national brand; and Aproz was the house brand of Migros, Switzerland's largest food chain.

drink sales. Similarly, four national brands (Aproz, Valser, Henniez and Passuger) accounted for 78% of mineral water sales.

The various colas (Coca-Cola, Pepsi-Cola and others) had increased their combined market share from 15% in 1973 to 25% in 1980, at the expense of fruit flavoured drinks whose combined share had declined from 55% to 45% during this period.

New entrants

Another recent development was the entry of large breweries into the soft drink and mineral water industry. Stagnant consumption of beer during the 1970s had resulted in excess bottling capacity in that industry. As of 1980, it was estimated that the country's five largest breweries could account for nearly 25% of both soft drink and mineral water production.

Consumers

Soft drinks and mineral water were consumed at home or in HORECA (hotels, restaurants and canteens). In 1977, 230 million litres of soft drinks and 188 million litres of mineral water were consumed in homes, while 51 million litres of soft drinks and 30 million litres of mineral water were consumed in HORECA. Industry observers believed that the ratio of home to HORECA in total consumption had not changed significantly in recent years. Statistics showed that around 60% of soft drinks and nearly 100% of mineral water consumed 'on the premises' in HORECA were premium priced brands. In the home, on the other hand, premium priced brands accounted for only 30% of soft drinks and 63% of mineral water.

Distribution

Soft drinks and mineral water were distributed in Switzerland through small local stores and retail chain outlets. The small neighbourhood store, the typical traditional Swiss retailer, stocked most of the daily food requirements of its nearby customers. It was estimated that mineral water and soft drinks accounted for 3–8% of the turnover in neighbourhood stores, with margins ranging from 20–50%. These small retailers generally would carry an inventory of about one week of sales. They typically stocked the more popular brands, receiving their supply from one or more beverage wholesalers in the area.

Between 1970 and 1980, as major food chain stores began to dominate, the need for small food retailers decreased and their number declined from 20,000 to about 8000. By the late 1970s Switzerland's four largest chains accounted for 83% of all food and 60% of all non-alcoholic beverage sales (Exhibit 12.32).

Mineral water and soft drinks represented 1–2% of the chains' total turnover. Their margins on branded products ranged from 25–50%. Margins on their own private labels were lower, from 20–25%. Chain stores normally carried an inventory of three days of sales at the outlets and another three days of sales at their warehouses.

Migros, the dominant food chain store with about 480 outlets throughout Switzerland, carried only Aproz, its own private label, soft drinks and mineral water. Other chains, however, such as Coop, Denner and Usego, did not follow this policy and would carry branded products as well as their own private labels, bottled under agreement by independent bottlers. These chains would either receive delivery directly

	Food	Beverages[1]
Migros	48	24[2]
Coop	24	24
Denner	6	6
Usego	5	5
	83	59

[1] All categories.

[2] Migros does not sell any alcoholic beverages – including beer.

Sources: Company Statistics.

Exhibit 12.32 *Shares of food chains in total consumer purchases*

from the bottler or through each outlet's local beverage wholesaler. Migros, on the other hand, operated its own bottling and distribution facilities.

In 1980, there were approximately 27,000 HORECA establishments in Switzerland, with 74% having fewer than five employees. These small outlets accounted for 44% of all HORECA mineral water and soft drink sales, while non-alcoholic beverages accounted for 20–40% of total sales in these small HORECA. In larger outlets, the corresponding ratio was 10–20%. In HORECA, mark-ups would be as much as 300% on mineral water and soft drinks and 100% on food. Each establishment would typically be served by one or two local beverage wholesalers who restocked inventories on a weekly or bi-weekly basis.

In recent years, Swiss brewers had begun to diversify into restaurant ownership. It was estimated that nearly 10% of all HORECA soft drink and mineral water consumption was in these brewery-owned restaurants.

Wholesalers (also called distributors) were an important link in the distribution chain from the bottler to the consumer. They stocked various alcoholic and non-alcoholic beverages and delivered them to their customers, the retailers and HORECA outlets located within a given geographical area. Many distributors would also make door-to-door deliveries directly to a consumer's home if the purchase were large enough. Bottlers would either deliver to distributors' warehouses or the distributors would collect the merchandise at the bottling plants.

Generally, distributors would carry a bottler's full line, as well as competing brands, with a typical inventory of 20–30 days of sales; most of this inventory would be financed through the bottler's trade credits. Mineral water and soft drinks represented 40–50% of a distributor's turnover, with margins averaging around 30%.

Over the years, beverage wholesaling in Switzerland had changed. The industry was becoming more concentrated as small family-owned wholesalers were gradually merging and being acquired by larger operations. As a result, between 1965 and 1980, the number of beverage distributors in Switzerland decreased from around 1100 to around 800. In 1980, 10% of the beverage wholesalers accounted for nearly 80% of distribution sales, with one or two large distributors dominating each major geographic market. Within each market, distributors tended to avoid competitive price cutting and respected the others' customer lists.

Mainly through acquisitions, breweries began entering the wholesaling industry; as of 1980, it was estimated that about 40% of beverage distribution was through brewery-owned wholesalers, compared with only 10% in 1975.

Competition

In central Switzerland, where IDC marketed its products, the main bottlers of soft drinks and mineral water were: Coca-Cola, Unifontes, Eptinger and Henniez. Coca-Cola supplied soft drinks only, Eptinger and Unifontes bottled both mineral water and soft drinks; Henniez supplied only mineral water in IDC's region.

Coca-Cola, Unifontes and Henniez were national bottlers; Eptinger, like IDC, was a regional bottler. Coca-Cola, which was a fully-owned subsidiary of the international parent company, bottled its three house brands (Coca-Cola, lemon-based Sprite and orange flavoured Fanta). Unifontes, which was owned by a beer company, bottled and marketed a lemon-based drink (Elmer), an orange-based drink (Orangina) and a bitter lemon drink (Queen's). Henniez mainly sold its house brand. The regional bottler Eptinger sold both mineral water (Eptinger) and soft drinks (Pepita). IDC management was unable to determine the relative size and market shares of its competitors. (The marketing manager's 'rough guesses' are given in Exhibit 12.33.)

Industry-wide pricing policies were controlled annually by the Swiss Soft Drink and Mineral Water Bottlers' Association. The association, a cartel of all the producers, set wholesale and retail prices for all products produced in Switzerland. Wholesale and retail margins were comparable for all soft drink and mineral water bottling companies. The official wholesale margins for soft drinks ranged from 25–40% and retail margins from 25–35%.

This price-fixing practice did not preclude price competition. Regional brands especially would augment the trade margins indirectly by offering volume discounts and year-end cash rebates on total purchases. According to the IDC's marketing manager, the secret nature of such arrangements made it extremely difficult to estimate their impact on margins.

Estimates of amounts spent on media advertising by IDC's competitors were not available. Coca-Cola followed its international strategy, advertising in cinemas, on television and billboards; Unifontes and Eptinger used only television, billboards and news magazines. IDC's sales and marketing managers believed that Coca-Cola was spending proportionately more on media advertising than IDC or its competitors.

	Bottles (millions)	*Swiss Francs* (millions)
Coca-Cola	200	100
Unifontes	80	35
Eptinger	60	24
Henniez	100	35

Source: Marketing Manager, IDC.

Exhibit 12.33 *Estimated sales of competitors within IDC's market region in central Switzerland*

Coca-Cola did not use trade or consumer promotions, whereas Unifontes, Henniez and Eptinger followed the same promotion practices as IDC (see *Marketing*).

Coca-Cola, with six bottling plants in IDC's region, had been distributing directly but, after some pressure from wholesalers, Coca-Cola began selling through wholesalers as well. Unifontes, Eptinger and Henniez followed the usual industry practice of selling through wholesalers. For the direct distribution, Coca-Cola company used its own salesmen/drivers (around 55 in IDC region) to deliver at retail and HORECA outlets. IDC's sales manager estimated that Unifontes employed 20–30 salesmen and Eptinger employed about 20 to cover IDC's region. Henniez had no salesmen in the region, but its three regional sales managers called on distributors regularly. Henniez seemed to rely on media advertising to generate demand at the retail level.

IDC's sales manager described the sales activities as being comparable among all the companies. He believed that all sales personnel were paid fixed salaries, but that Coca-Cola paid less than IDC, whereas Unifontes and Eptinger paid more. He had also heard that Coca-Cola used an incentive bonus system, but he did not know how it worked nor whether Eptinger and Unifontes had a bonus system linked to sales performance.

Relationship between Aditya and IDC

Helmut Fehring explained, 'The relationship between Aditya and IDC is important to understanding this company.' Aditya, also a bottling operation, was the only subsidiary of IDC and its marketing activities were confined to the French part of Switzerland.

	1976	1977	1978	1979	1980
Net sales	8,502	7,675	7,803	9,271	9,119
Less:					
Bought materials	3,635	3,131	3,342	4,402	4,189
Production personnel – wages and benefits	600	600	504	613	725
Depreciation	612	1,656	957	1,189	1,120
Other manufacturing – related expenses	764	690	584	741	779
Gross profit	2,891	1,598	2,416	2,326	2,306
Less:					
Salaries and benefits	979	1,092	817	770	828
Interest	923	806	670	479	475
General admin.	133	182	176	167	167
Selling expenses	376	383	368	431	473
Advt. and promotion	894	983	708	818	962
Add:					
Misc. income	212	196	324	343	601
Net income	(202)	(1,652)	1	4	2

Source: Company Records.

Exhibit 12.34   *Income statement for Aditya S.A. (thousands of SF)*

The Aditya mineral water bottling plant, originally owned by an American expatriate, had been in existence since 1920. In 1959, when IDC wanted to expand its bottling capacity, this plant had been for sale and Managing Director Hans Fehring, Helmut's father, decided to purchase it. IDC took a controlling interest (70% of voting stock) in Aditya that same year. In 1966 Helmut Fehring, then 25 years old, took over as the General Manager after spending one year at IDC as assistant to the Managing Director. He generally operated the company on an independent basis. In 1969 Stefan Wiener, the founder's son, joined Aditya as its Production Manager. In 1968, the Aditya plant had been completely rebuilt with new bottling lines installed. In 1971 when both Fehring and Wiener left Aditya to return to IDC, a new manager was hired who invested even more in additional bottling lines. Then the company, which had been profitable until 1971, started experiencing heavy losses. Thus, in 1974, IDC management decided to replace the general manager with a 46-year-old French-speaking Swiss, Mr Languetin, who had been the sales manager for a consumer products company. Although sales then improved (20% of sales were to the Coop chain), the company continued to experience a loss (Exhibits 12.34–12.36).

	1976	1977	1978	1979	1980
Assets					
Current					
Cash	51	23	27	511	361
Accounts receivable	1,487	2,132	1,605	1,211	1,227
Inventory	637	799	934	726	694
Miscellaneous	46	31	23	165	23
Fixed	14,342	12,942	10,500	10,743	10,150
Non-current	11	11	73	66	47
Total assets	16,574	15,938	13,162	13,422	12,502
Liabilities					
Current					
Banks	3,933	5,701	1,505	–	–
Customer deposits	–	–	–	1,056	1,206
Accounts payable	916	1,176	413	352	529
Accrued expenses	93	107	112	189	238
Long-term					
Mortgage loan	7,822	6,776	8,975	9,621	8,500
Pension fund	357	377	355	398	221
Net worth					
Capital plus legal					
Reserves	1,800	1,800	1,800	1,800	1,800
Retained earnings	1,653	1	2	6	8
Total liabilities	16,574	15,938	13,162	13,422	12,502

Source: Company Records.

Exhibit 12.35 *Balance sheet for Aditya S.A. (thousands of SF)*

Soft drinks	Shops	Horeca	Chain	Total
Schweppes	4,020	5,900	2,010	11,930
Pepsi-Cola	2,188[1]	412	750	3,350
Aditya	2,000	450	–	2,450
Private label	–	–	3,450	3,420
Mineral water				
Aditya	2,000	1,200	–	3,200
Private label	–	–	3,400	3,400
Total	10,208	7,962	9,580	27,750

[1] The split between 0.3 litre and 1.0 litre containers was 1:4.
Source: Company Records.

Exhibit 12.36   *Aditya sales by outlet, 1980 (SF)*

Mr Languetin was a confident man who took pride in his achievements and felt he had the loyalty of his subordinates. He freely expressed his opinions on the various issues facing IDC and Aditya, 'The mentality in IDC is too much on giving instruction. I have no time for bureaucracy and form filling. My job is to sell, not answer memos on cost control.'

The Aditya subsidiary only bottled its own brand of mineral water and soft drinks for sale in the French part of Switzerland. However, it also marketed Pepsi-Cola and Schweppes which was bottled at the IDC plant in Berg and then transported by road to Aditya for distribution.[7] In 1980, IDC spent around SF150,000 on transporting these products. Languetin admitted that he would prefer that his region's Schweppes and Pepsi-Cola requirements be bottled by Aditya instead of IDC. He felt that it could be done with SF50,000 in additional expenditures for labour during the peak season. But Wiener, the Production Manager in Berg, would have none of it. 'It was a strategic decision,' he said.

Fehring described his position, 'My main concern is to fit Aditya into our overall plans. We are basically running two entirely different companies in two different cultures, one in the French area and the other in the German part of the country. The mental attitudes, work habits and personal interactions differ considerably between these two companies, which essentially prevents us from being a centralized company. In my opinion, this affects the efficiency of our operations.'

IDC functions

Production

Soft drink production began with the formulation of each batch, mixing the concentrate, sugar and carbon dioxide. The standard bottling process was as follows: empty bottles, which had been cleaned, sterilized and dried, moved along an automated

[7] IDC's average selling prices (ex-factory) to Aditya in 1980 were: Schweppes 18 cl (SF 0.21/ bottle); Pepsi-Cola 30 cl (SF 0.16/bottle); Pepsi-Cola 1 litre (SF 0.35/bottle).

line to be filled at successive stages with the flavour mixture from a huge tank and carbon dioxide under high pressure. After the capping and labelling operations, the bottles were automatically removed from the line and put into crates which were mounted on pallets for storage.

Small bottling runs, such as low volume flavours and promotion items, required that the labelling be done manually, frequently by temporary workers. Fehring admitted that even the automated bottling lines always required a team of seven to eight people to ensure that the bottling operation functioned smoothly. Moving the crates and pallets to the storage area, as well as loading them into trucks for delivery, also had to be done manually.

The Production Manager, Stefan Wiener, had a degree in food technology; he was 39 years old and had been with IDC since 1969. He ran a tight ship at the plants and commanded the respect of his subordinates and peers alike. He was thorough and methodical and his knowledge of production operations was extensive. Helmut Fehring said, 'There has never been any occasion when I disagreed with Stefan's decisions.'

Stefan Wiener had definite ideas as to how the production area should be improved. He said, 'There is too much waste. Each time we shift from one flavour to another we lose about 250 litres. We usually have three or four set-ups every day for both lines I and II at the Berg plant. That seems to be inevitable and so we have to look for economies elsewhere. What we need is a new faster machine at Berg to replace the old 18 cl bottling line. We could then eliminate the second shift for one team of eight workers which should save us about SF280,000 annually. Also, we might be able to save some on the overtime payments we now pay to meet rush orders, about SF50,000 a year. If we invest in a new line, there would probably be other intangible benefits also.'

IDC had three bottling lines at the Berg plant and two at Aditya (capacity of the various bottling lines is given in Exhibit 12.37). Fehring claimed that the actual capacity of the bottling lines was only 80% of the rated capacity when installed. All the bottling lines, except the litre bottling line at Berg and the ones at Aditya, were old. Therefore, frequent breakdowns occurred, and the maintenance men were needed constantly, which resulted in maintenance costs (SF315,000 in 1980). Although the

Plant	Line	Bottle size (litre)	Effective speed[1] (bottles/hour)	Capacity per week[2] (bottles/week)	Capacity per year[3] (million bottles)
IDC (Berg)	I	1.00	21,540	711,900	31.32
	II	0.30	7,400	244,600	10.76
	III	0.18	12,555	414,950	18.26
Aditya	I	1.00	19,200	634,600	27.90
	II	0.30	10,000	330,500	14.54
		0.18	15,000	496,000	21.80

[1] Effective speed = 80% of rated capacity.

[2] 1 week = 33.05 hours production. The weekly working hours were 45 hours for the workers: the extra time was set aside for tea and lunch breaks and cleaning and preparation of machines for filling.

[3] 1 year = 44 weeks; single shift basis.

Exhibit 12.37 *Bottling line capacities*

Plant	Bottle size (litre)	Pepsi	Schweppes	Own brand (mineral water and soft drinks)	Private label (mineral water and soft drinks)	Total
IDC (Berg)	1.00	4,430	–	10.008	9,075	23,513
	0.30	5,200	–	2,970	–	8,170
	0.18	–	26,200	–	–	26,200
Aditya	1.00	–	–	4,200	6,900	11,100
	0.30	–	–	1,700	–	1,700
	0.18	–	5,900	–	–	5,900

Source: Company Records.

Exhibit 12.38 *Production at IDC and Aditya plants (thousands of bottles)*

economic life of a bottling line and its accessories could be as long as 15 years, the company's capital investments policy was to reassess investments over an eight year horizon with the capital investment being written off during this period.

IDC followed the 'chase strategy', which was traditional in the bottling industry. The company would produce orders as they were received. Wiener felt that this strategy, compared with the 'level production strategy' which led to unsold inventories, had served the company well over the years (Exhibit 12.38). Wiener felt that the current high interest rates (7–8% per annum) made inventory costs prohibitive and that if level production were used, such costs could be around SF15,000 a year. He claimed that changing the production strategy would also mean investing half a million francs in bottles and crates, which he felt was unnecessary (Exhibit 12.39).

Wiener summed up the problem areas in the production function as the following: loss of labour time due to frequent flavour changes and short runs; lack of adequate

Product	Bottle size		
	18 cl	0.3 litre	1 litre
Schweppes	0.11	–	–
Pepsi-Cola	–	0.06	0.18
Soft drinks			
Berg/Aditya brand	–	0.06	0.16
Private label	–	–	0.27
Mineral water			
Berg/Aditya brand	–	0.02	0.03
Private label	–	–	0.06

[1] Includes sugar, the raw materials, and packaging (non-returnable bottles and caps and labels, etc.)

Exhibit 12.39 *Variable manufacturing costs, 1980 (SF)[1]*

warehousing capacity: and the constraint imposed by the well's water capacity during summer. He felt that additional warehousing capacity (requiring about SF120,000) might not be needed if a new bottling line were installed.

Marketing

IDC's marketing department was headed by Karl Muller; he was 36 years old and had been with the company since 1979. Earlier he had been responsible for marketing strategy in a large Swiss-German consumer products company. Muller was shy and quiet, but he had an aptitude for systematic analysis and organizing data and was well-liked by his subordinates. For marketing purposes, IDC's products could be divided into four distinct categories: two international brands (Schweppes and Pepsi-Cola); flavoured soft drinks; and mineral water. The last two categories were broken down further into IDC's own brand (Berg) and private labels.

	Shops	Horeca	Chain	Total
Soft drinks				
Schweppes	2,084	3,370	980	6,434
Pepsi-Cola	1,239	1,084	294	2,617
Berg Brand	4,235	584	–	4,819
Private label	–	–	2,150	2,150
Mineral water				
Berg Brand	362	211	–	573
Private label	–	–	817	817
Total	7,920	5,249	4,241	17,410

Exhibit 12.40   *Sales by outlet, 1980 (thousands of SF)*

	Shops	Horeca	Chain	Total
Soft drinks				
Schweppes	6,949	9,912	2,269	20,130
Pepsi-Cola	13,607[1]	2,084	566	6,257
Berg Brand	8,142	1,824	–	9,966
Private label	–	–	4,575	4,575
Mineral water				
Berg Brand	1,811	1,004	–	2,815
Private label	–	–	4,300	4,300
Total	20,509	14,824	12,710	48,043

[1] The split between 0.3 litre and 1 litre containers was 5:3.

Source: Company Records.

Exhibit 12.41   *Sales by outlet, 1980 (thousands of bottles)*

In 1980, nearly three-quarters of IDC's sales volume comprised branded products being distributed by wholesalers to central Switzerland; 60% to retail stores and the rest to HORECA outlets. The private labels, which IDC began producing in 1979 for the Coop and Denner food chains (1345 stores nationwide), were distributed directly[8] (Exhibits 12.40 and 12.41).

There were about 650 distributors, 4000 shops and 18,000 HORECA outlets (excluding chains) in the Swiss-German area served by IDC. 'The 400-or-so distributors we work with are an indispensable link to the outlets,' explained Fehring. 'How else could we reach 22,000 potential outlets?' In recent years, the 50 largest wholesalers had accounted for approximately 60% of IDC's sales of branded products.

IDC's prices and profit margins varied by brand and container size. The international brands were premium priced and enjoyed higher unit contribution margins than the other brands. The private labels, on the other hand, were priced competitively and were the least profitable. The small single serving bottles produced exclusively for the HORECA outlets were generally more profitable than the larger bottles (Exhibit 12.42).

	Container size (litre)	Shops	Horeca	Chains
Soft drinks				
Schweppes	0.18	0.30	0.34	0.30
Pepsi-Cola	0.30	0.25	0.52	–
	1.00	0.52	–	0.52
Berg/Aditya	0.30	–	0.32	–
	1.00	0.52	–	–
Private labels	1.00	–	–	0.47
Mineral water				
Berg/Aditya	0.30	–	0.21	–
	1.00	0.20	–	–
Private	1.00	–	–	0.19

[1] After discounts and year-end rebates; applicable to IDC as well as Aditya.

[2] The company could distinguish between bottles of similar sizes for different outlets as the containers were dissimilar in shape.

Exhibit 12.42 *Average ex-factory prices[1] by outlet[2], 1980 (SF)*

In recent years, IDC had spent nearly 14% of its branded products sales on advertising and promotion. The total expenditure was shared between IDC and the international franchisers for Schweppes (50%) and Pepsi-Cola (30%). For its own Berg brand, however, IDC had to carry the entire costs (Exhibit 12.43).

IDC's advertising themes varied by brand. Schweppes was advertised as a product used by 'sophisticated' people for 'intimate' occasions. Pepsi-Cola, whose advertising

[8] Private labels displayed the chain's name prominently and identified IDC as the bottler in smaller print.

	1979		1980	
	A	P	A	P
Schweppes	186	144	110	126
Pepsi-Cola	225	180	234	234
Soft drinks	581	394	791	515
Mineral water	–	99	–	128
Total	992	817	1,139	1,003

Exhibit 12.43 *Advertising and promotion expenditures (thousands of SF)*

was coordinated by Pepsico International, followed Coca-Cola with a 'me too' position. Fruit flavoured drinks were aimed at mothers with emphasis on the 'health promoting' benefits of soft drinks with a mineral water base.

The prices of IDC's Berg products were determined by the prices set by the bottlers' association. The prices of international brands followed the recommendations of the concentrate companies. IDC published a suggested price list for distributors and retailers, although the company had no direct control over the final prices charged to the consumer. The company also followed the industry practice of giving unofficial trade discounts and year-end cash bonuses.

Fehring himself handled the annual negotiations regarding the private labels sold to the chains. The national sales manager and the marketing manager also called on each chain's headquarters once or twice a year to resolve operating problems.

IDC used both trade and consumer promotions as a more open way to compete. With trade promotions, the customer's final price was maintained and increased margins were given to the wholesalers, HORECA and stores. With consumer promotions, IDC absorbed the cost, reimbursing the wholesalers and retailers for their lost margins. In most cases, promotional material was also paid for by IDC.

The salesforce was the primary link between the company and its distributors and retailers. Marketing Manager Muller commented, 'To succeed in this business, a good salesforce is essential. They have to deal effectively with the retail and HORECA outlets and maintain good relations with the distributors. We have enough people to handle the job, but their performance could be improved considerably.'

Helmut Fehring commented on some recent industry developments and their implications for independent regional bottlers. 'We are feeling seriously threatened by the brewers. They have a lot of money and have been able to acquire bottlers and distributors. They can introduce new products, advertise heavily and, for a while, even sustain substantial losses. Distributors are getting larger and more demanding, expecting increasingly higher margins. And all the retail chains want to copy the Migros chain; they want to buy from us at lower prices so they can charge less. Times are changing fast and we may have to totally revise our marketing strategies.

Salesforce

IDC's marketing area was organized into three regions, each headed by a regional manager who reported to Mr Jeanneau, the national sales manager. He, in turn, was responsible for setting sales and expense budgets as well as coordinating sales with the other functions in the company. Jeanneau, 35 years old, was a French-speaking Swiss but had mostly lived in the Swiss-German area. After joining the company in 1973, he was promoted to his present position in 1976. He enjoyed his work as well as having a good rapport with his salesforce.

In 1980, IDC's salesforce dealt with approximately 400 distributors who in turn sold to around 12,000 outlets (9000 HORECA, 3000 small stores) incurring selling expenses of SF2.44 million (Exhibit 12.44).

The budget was determined jointly by the marketing and sales managers, who used past trends to project the next year's sales for each product. The regional sales managers were also consulted so that the national budgets could be converted into regional sales quotas, which would then be allocated to the individual salesmen. Mr Jeanneau and the regional managers were paid by salary, but they also would receive a prize (such as a free holiday within Europe) for reaching budget goals.

The regional sales managers would travel with the salesmen some of the time to observe the salesmen's activities. In addition, each salesman made weekly reports citing the outlets visited, the amount of time spent per outlet, details on orders received as well as his expenses. Monthly statistics were kept on this information. Jeanneau described the system as one in which good wages and trust played a major role. He believed IDC's sales management practices were more or less in line with industry norms.

An IDC salesman would handle 500–1,000 accounts, including both retail outlets and distributors. He would typically see two distributors and 10–14 retailers every day, and visit the major accounts every three weeks. The salesman could determine his own schedule, but would keep his manager informed. Each salesman travelled about 26,000 km a year by company car, spending a quarter of his time on the road.

Each salesman was expected to seek new accounts and was given quotas to meet. When the target was not met, the regional sales manager would accompany him to determine the reasons. No guidelines existed regarding the amount of sales expected from new accounts.

Jeanneau believed that the salesmen were satisfied with the existing system of compensation and supervision, citing the low (compared with industry norms) turnover of people in his salesforce. Most would work eight years for the company. The IDC salesforce ranged in age from 25–60, the average being 45. The salesmen agreed with Jeanneau's assessment that they were satisfied with the company. One commented,

	1978		1980	
	Actual	*%*	*Actual*	*%*
Salesmen compensation	995	46	1,169	48
Car expenses	584	27	633	26
Travel expenses	346	16	390	16
Social expenses	238	11	244	10
Total	2,163	100	2,436	100

Source: Company Records.

Exhibit 12.44 *Breakdown of selling expenses (thousands of SF)*

'This company is run by humane people who treat you right so long as you do your work.'

Jeanneau claimed it would be difficult to implement a performance-related bonus scheme for salesmen because 'the distributors did not have clearly defined territories, thus there was no accurate record for individual salesmen.' He also felt that the salesforce would not welcome such a change. On recruitment and training, Jeanneau mentioned the problem of finding suitable candidates in Switzerland's tight labour market.

Fehring's concern about the effectiveness of the salesforce was not shared by Mr Jeanneau. He explained, 'I am convinced our salesforce is the right size. We have 31 salesmen in the field, most with previous experience, continuously calling on distributors and retail outlets. Their performance is systematically monitored; they have to make regular reports to the regional sales manager, and they attend briefing sessions at headquarters once a month. I think they are highly motivated and are trying to maintain our customers' goodwill. Our salesmen are thinking of the company's interests and they average nine hours of extra work per week. Of course, there is always room for improvement. For instance, they are poor in organizing their work and sticking to planned call schedules. They prefer easy-to-sell products over ones that are profitable for the company.' As Jeanneau pointed out, however, the salesforce could be appraised by the fact that the plant almost never had any surplus stock.

Purchasing

Purchasing the major components of variable cost (sugar, concentrates, caps, labels and carbon dioxide) was the purchasing manager's responsibility. However, Fehring himself had always been aware of minimizing costs in purchasing. In 1975, when the rise in sugar prices brought substantial losses to the company, Fehring personally took over the sugar purchasing.

Despite IDC's objective to minimize costs, room for manoeuvring was limited in most cases. For example, the price of concentrates was not under the company's control; international brands were dictated by the suppliers; and purchases of caps and labels were on long-term contracts with little flexibility in the short-term.

Sugar represented about 50% of raw material costs. Since the company's sugar requirements were well determined, IDC contracted for its requirements one and a half years before the date the sugar would actually be used. The company did not have to pay until the stock was delivered and, except for the minimum stock of sugar required by Swiss law, IDC did not carry much stock at the bottling plant.

However, as sugar prices fluctuated widely, the actual date that the contract was signed could greatly affect the company's profitability. For example, in 1981, the decision to buy sugar had been postponed. Fortunately, during the interval, the price of sugar dropped from SF180/100 kg to SF108/100 kg. Fehring found the main problem was to forecast the price as accurately as possible. He also felt satisfied with his decisions on sugar purchasing, considering that they were based merely on subjective price assessments.

Finance

Fehring felt that financial issues were not of major concern. Capital investments had mostly been financed from operations and bank loans. The company was gradually repaying these loans and was attempting to reduce its debt. Fehring explained this approach, 'It has to do with the Swiss attitude toward financial prudence; IDC's Board of Directors disapproves of large debt financing. Our present debt–equity ratio stands at 2:1, but the board wants to reduce it to 1:1. I know that there are circumstances when we should increase the leverage to benefit with increased return on equity, but try telling that to our board!' However, Fehring felt confident that future company expansion could be financed by reinvesting profits. At this point, he was planning to cooperate with the board's aim to reduce the debt on the balance sheet.

The head of Accounting and Finance was Mr Schmidt; he was 36 years old and had been with IDC since 1975. The Cost Accounting Department and the EDP (Electronic Data Processing) Department reported to him. Schmidt was considered competent and conscientious. He had spent a lot of time devising an extremely accurate cost accounting system for the company as well as cost control forms for the Berg and Aditya plants. More recently, he had been working on a system to produce bi-monthly proforma financial statements for top management's use.

Personnel

IDC was a medium-sized company, employing 131 people in 1981 (25 in administration at the Zug headquarters, 66 at the Berg plant in production; the rest of the personnel were either in sales or technical jobs such as telephone and computer operators). In recent years, staff changes had been negligible (2 in administration, 8 at Berg plant).

Fehring admitted having some concern about the his staff's productivity, but he was not really certain how to measure productivity over the years. He was also not sure he wanted to reduce the workforce either at headquarters or at the plant. He said: 'All the people in administration have been with us a long time. They have been loyal staff and there has been practically no turnover. Even if they have not been very productive, I'm not sure I could ask any of them to go.'

According to Production Manager Wiener, there was a lot of turnover and absenteeism at the plant level, which he felt affected the efficiency of bottling operations. 'Unfortunately, our plant manager is not greatly respected, and so there is always some tension between the old workers and the new guys. However, he is well liked by the workforce and he does get the work done.'

Fehring added, 'We also have to remember the different cultures in this organization, not only between IDC and Aditya but also the cultural division between Zug and Berg. You know, white collar versus blue collar, city versus country and so on. Naturally, a lot of conflict resolution problems from the shop-floor reach Stefan and he gets caught up in these "fire-fighting" jobs.'

Organization structure

IDC was organized along functional lines. The general manager of Aditya reported directly to the managing director of IDC. But there was a dotted line relationship between the marketing and production functions of Aditya and those at IDC (Exhibit 12.45).

Fehring expressed satisfaction with present company structure, 'This system inevitably tends to promote thinking along functional lines among the staff. The

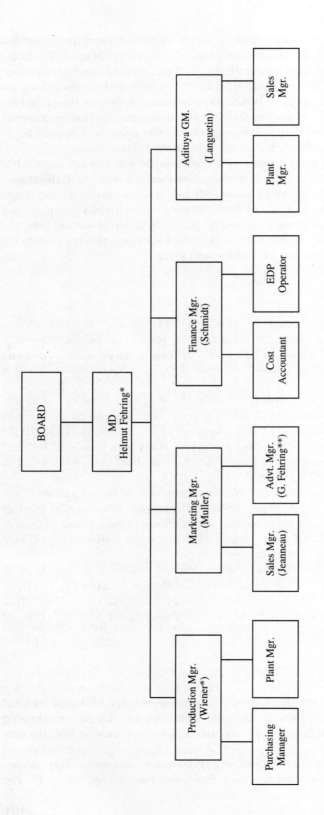

* Member of the Board of Directors
** Gunter Fehring: younger brother of Helmut Fehring who had been with the company since 1968

Exhibit 12.45 Company structure. [Source: Company records]

reporting relationships also create some illogical situations such as Aditya's general manager overseeing the marketing function. However, he is an excellent marketing man, whereas Karl Muller, our marketing manager at IDC to whom Mr Languetin reports on marketing issues, is more of an analyst and staff person.

Fehring continued, 'Frankly, I am more concerned about the civil servant mentality of our people. They are not trained to solve problems and they tend to work on assumptions rather than facts. Perhaps they have difficulty quantifying issues. On the positive side, however, people are mostly amiable and get along well together. There are no cliques or informal groups impeding the work of the company.'

Fehring stressed the important role of the Board of Directors in his decision making. He mentioned three people as being particularly influential: Mr Genscher, IDC's President, who had been the general manager of one of Switzerland's largest food processing companies, was strong in business acumen; Bernhard Fehring, Helmut's cousin, who had his own restaurant business, had a good eye for details; Mr Leutweiler, a prominent businessman in the Zug canton, was an entrepreneur always looking for new opportunities. Helmut Fehring said, 'When I was gone a year for the training programme, the board, and particularly Mr Genscher, worked closely with the operating managers. Consequently, the directors continue to take a close interest in the company's affairs. This can sometimes be a challenge for me, but it is also an asset.' Fehring also mentioned pressures coming from some of the shareholders who wanted reasonable dividends as a return on their investments.

Fehring discussed the problems changing from a family-owned business to a professionally managed company. He said, 'When Stefan and I took over from our parents in 1971, my brother and Stefan's brother-in-law became the advertising and marketing managers respectively. We four were to be the operating management on an equal basis, but of course it didn't work. One person must exercise authority and we had no leader, so I was frustrated. In 1976, when the company was not doing well, I went to the board and asked for the full authority of a Managing Director enabling me to run the company as I saw fit. The board agreed and, of course, there were some hard feelings. Stefan's brother-in-law and a few people in the Sales Department left, but that difficult time is behind us now.'

Management control systems

Fehring went on to say, 'For its size, I think IDC's management control system is a good one; it's simple and decentralized and operates well.'

Fehring described each functional area as a responsibility centre where each manager was responsible for the activities designated to him. Fehring felt that this system was quite flexible and worked efficiently for the most part. But it was also true that he frequently had to intervene in decisions requiring interface between different functions.

Production Manager Stefan Wiener felt that the Marketing Department did not understand production problems. The Sales Department had given short notice for several small runs in order to fulfil some customers' orders. This meant disruptions in production scheduling and losing considerable working time making changeovers. Meanwhile, Marketing Manager Karl Muller believed that the company had occasionally lost sales because production had been late. Both the production and marketing managers claimed that the Finance Department did not provide enough information to enable them to take necessary follow-up action.

The formal management control process at IDC revolved around the annual marketing plans, which were used by the Finance Department to project the next year's budget. After the functional managers and the MD agreed on the annual budget, the related sales budget would be given to the Sales Department. Management would then receive monthly operating statements which compared projected sales with actual sales and projected costs with actual costs. The functional managers would be informed within three weeks about any variances.

In 1978 the company installed a modern computer system (IBM 34) to assist in the administrative and managerial work. The computer department was under the control of the finance manager. According to Fehring, the hardware was up-to-date and allowed for ample expansion. The software handled many functions: payroll, invoicing, maintenance of debtors' and creditors' records and preparation of monthly accounting statements, as well as issuing statistical monthly statements on bottle sales and monthly inventory statements. Finance Manager Hans-Vogel Schmidt was eager to expand the use of the computer. He felt that adding several new software programs would enable him to provide the other departments with all the information they required. He had recently urged Fehring to decide quickly so that the new system, estimated to cost about SF600,000, could be implemented before the summer season.

Fehring's concerns

Fehring realized that he must think about the longer-term issues relating to his company, but he was also aware that several short-term issues which would affect the long range needed his immediate concern. 'Where do we want to go and how do we achieve it? Strategic direction has been missing in this company and some important decisions must be made now. What should my priorities be?'

'If indeed our productivity has been gradually declining, should I first look for ways to improve productivity? Or should I focus on a new marketing strategy? Do I seek out innovative marketing ideas, try to improve the performance of the salesforce or perhaps address both issues simultaneously?'

Fehring admitted that IDC salesmen had never received any real direction about which products to push or which outlets to emphasize. 'I feel that our longer-term marketing plan should be clear on both dimensions: products and channels. If specific products are directed into specific channels, the organizational structure of our salesforce will have to be readjusted accordingly. I see three alternatives: product-based, channel-based and regional, the one we have now.'

Fehring went on to express concern about the quality of the selling effort at IDC. 'I don't see any fire in our salesforce. They need more motivation.' At the same time, he wondered about the effect of his decisions on the people involved. 'What will be the costs of my decisions, not only in money but in people? Can I make changes using the existing personnel? For me, the people in this company matter most of all.' Helmut Fehring knew that these decisions had to be made now and that it was up to him to make them.

13

Managing in turbulent environments

Case 13.1 PACCASA-LOMBARD (A)

This case was written by Dr Roger Quant Pallavicini and revised by Research Associate Barbara Robins, both under the supervision of Professor Werner Ketelhöhn, as a basis for class discussion rather than to illustrate either effective or ineffective handling of a business situation.

Enno Roman was the Regional Executive Vice President of PACCASA-LOMBARD. On February 1, 1979, he left his office in Dominica and boarded the regular flight for Amaranda,[1] where he would meet Gabriel Targa, General Manager of PACCASA-LOMBARD in Amaranda. He knew that PACCASA's operation in Amaranda was facing one of the most difficult periods it had ever confronted. Nevertheless, he looked forward to the challenge of clarifying the issues and formulating options for the company which could be presented to the board of directors. However, most of all, he wanted to ensure that his final recommendations would be accepted.

The meeting between the two men started briskly; Gabriel Targa got straight to the point:

> Enno, you already know from our monthly reports that, since the board of directors' decision to support Loretti's[2] overthrow, our production and sales have declined dramatically. In fact, we have now entered a situation where we are eroding the capital of the company in order to survive! (Exhibit 13.1.) There are many reasons which have led to this situation: the forced shutdown during the armed struggle; the occupation of our facilities by Loretti's army which led to the destruction of our offices and warehouses; and the occupation of the factory by the workers for the first few months following the revolutionary triumph.

---

[1] To encourage a careful analysis of the case, the true location has been replaced by a fictional country.

[2] Loretti – the Amarandean dictator who had been in power for over 40 years.

	1978	1977	1976	1975	1974	1973
A S S E T S						
Current assets:						
Cash on hand and in the banks	321,568	1,147,955	458,960	2,081,622	2,116,540	1,114,646
Securities and Accounts receivable						
Commercial	369,006	593,496	7,848,844	8,421,988	7,409,233	5,924,325
Employees	11,226	46,095	12,469	10,067	176,598	9,608
Claims	101,989	571,786	112,975	245,368	67,835	66,983
Accounts receivable – Affiliates	2,445,340	–	–	–	–	174,989
Shares receivable – Executives	296,791	479,025	568,405	–	52,989	–
Other	27,702	65,247	30,203	21,302		35,139
Minus: Provision for doubtful accounts	5,000	55,824	75,054	44,384	100,685	133,452
Net securities and Accounts receivable	3,247,054	1,699,825	8,497,842	8,654,341	7,605,970	6,077,592
Inventories:						
Finished goods	1,800,677	946,466	659,157	623,564	753,268	488,355
Parts and accessories	1,735,937	3,436,721	3,728,533	1,980,357	1,464,465	1,706,281
Work in process	525,886	539,537	488,379	306,684	379,391	218,128
Raw materials	1,244,820	1,268,440	1,568,713	1,084,461	867,480	796,285
Materials and supplies	675,395	745,821	768,759	737,127	709,436	781,951
Materials and accessories-in-transit	–	287,575	32,568	1,526,610	492,013	458,194
Total inventories	5,982,715	7,224,560	7,246,109	6,258,803	4,666,053	4,449,194
Prepaid expenses and deposits	116,689	71,793	253,625	107,380	126,677	96,497
Total current assets	9,668,026	10,144,133	16,456,536	17,102,146	14,515,240	11,737,929
Investments, at cost	112,275	158,935	252,480	2,786,640	2,802,040	3,302,182
Long-term Accounts receivable	–	–	172,783	202,739	–	–
Accounts Receivable – Affiliates	10,831,504	11,277,256	6,865,750	3,088,591	1,319,868	–
Property, plant and equipment, net	4,791,644	6,191,336	3,953,824	4,345,901	4,627,967	4,603,183
Deferred assets			129,902	147,570	463,101	435,199
	25,403,449	27,771,660	27,831,275	27,673,587	23,728,216	20,078,493

Current liabilities:						
Loans payable	2,242,857	4,510,857	4,040,000	2,000,000	2,000,000	2,500,000
Long-term bond fee	–	92,000	184,000	184,000	184,000	184,000
Commercial accounts payable	561,020	659,148	693,381	1,851,353	612,039	645,939
Inter-company accounts payable	5,007,614	5,157,801	1,026,925	–	79,021	113,925
Dividends payable	1,680,000	1,680,000	–	–	–	–
Other accounts payable	259,163	–	–	–	–	–
Accumulated expenses payable:						
Commissions	–	–	498,046	707,259	610,057	233,857
Vacations, allowances and payroll	83,873	20,385	212,754	212,395	141,300	54,241
Other	–	–	52,145	–	28,255	–
Interest	557,057	397,061	115,507	89,504	106,743	90,337
Deductions payable:						
Taxes payable for benefits	36,331	–	41,156	61,156	72,000	116,643
Social insurance and other	167,939	93,020	22,352	22,022	41,996	14,998
Bonuses payable	541,785	443,190	319,521	123,216	131,589	85,592
Provision for contingencies	–	104,712	–	21,337	1,190,201	1,220,201
Income tax	–	–	629,946	–	–	–
Patriotic tax on capital	304,048	304,048	–	–	–	–
Total current liabilities	11,441,687	13,462,222	7,835,733	5,272,242	5,197,201	5,259,733
Long-term debts, minus:						
Maturity within one year A$184,000	2,572,048	608,095	92,000	276,000	460,000	644,000
Total liabilities	14,013,735	14,070,317	7,927,733	5,548,242	5,657,201	5,903,733
Shareholders' equity						
9,000 common shares authorized and issued with a nominal value of A$1,000 each	9,000,000	9,000,000	9,000,000	9,000,000	9,000,000	9,000,000
Retained earnings:						
Legal Reserves	900,000	900,000	900,000	900,000	900,000	900,000
Reserve for revaluation	2,941,972	2,941,972	–	–	–	–
Available	(1,452,258)	859,371	10,003,542	12,225,345	8,171,015	4,274,760
Total retained earnings	2,389,714	4,701,343	10,903,542	13,125,345	9,071,015	5,174,760
Total shareholders' equity	11,389,714	13,701,343	19,903,542	22,125,345	18,071,015	14,174,760
	25,403,449	27,771,660	27,831,275	27,673,587	23,728,216	20,078,493

Exhibit 13.1 *Balance sheet, 1973–1978, as of December 31 (A$)*

	1978	1977	1976	1975	1974	1973
Net sales	18,872,621	16,421,593	26,916,704	32,971,033	25,470,665	18,462,792
Cost of sales	18,618,990	14,691,360	18,134,233	20,946,994	16,153,786	12,988,852
Gross profit on sales	253,631	1,730,233	8,782,471	12,024,039	9,316,879	5,473,940
Operating costs:						
Sales	561,912	1,127,980	1,425,697	1,866,405	1,556,218	1,108,485
Administration	2,146,494	2,838,734	1,740,443	1,387,745	1,194,922	1,158,043
Publicity and sales promotion	12,525	5,817	52,830	31,108	85,316*	53,513**
	2,720,931	3,972,531	3,218,970	3,285,258	2,836,456	2,320,041
Operating income	—	—	5,563,501	8,738,781	6,480,423	3,153,899
Operating loss	(2,467,300)	(2,242,298)	—	—	—	—
Other income:						
Exchange adjustments due to devaluation	—	555,217	—	—	—	—
Interest income	50,427	57,821	16,434	19,111	185,636	118,321
Other	1,014,630	3,515	486,142	367,280	345,551	248,840
	1,065,057	616,553	502,576	386,391	531,187	367,161
Other expenses:						
Financial Expenses	736,484	753,709	509,888	291,769	382,273	428,384
Bonuses	145,112	307,394	622,428	819,073	633,082	459,634
Other	27,790	—	—	—	—	1,421
	909,386	1,061,103	1,132,316	1,110,842	1,015,355	889,439
Earnings before extraordinary expenses and income taxes	—	(2,686,848)	4,933,761	8,014,330	5,996,255	2,631,621
Income taxes	—	—	629,946	—	—	—
	—	(2,686,848)	4,303,815	8,014,330	—	—
Extraordinary expenses	—	(3,097,323)	1,136,221	—	—	—
Net earnings	—	—	3,167,594	8,104,330	5,996,255	2,631,621
Net loss	(2,311,629)	(5,784,171)	—	—	—	—
Net earnings per common share: (9,000 shares)						
Before extraordinary expenses	—	—	478	890	566	292
Extraordinary expenses	—	—	126	—	—	—
Net earnings	—	—	352	890	—	—
Net loss per common share: (9,000 shares)						
Before extraordinary expenses	—	(338)	—	—	—	—
Extraordinary expenses	—	(304)	—	—	—	—
Net loss	(257)	(642)	—	—	—	—

Exhibit 13.2 Statement of earnings, 1973–1978, as of December 31 (A$)

Roman thought for a few moments before he responded:

What troubles me is that all of this has happened during a period when conditions are so unfavourable internationally. I realize that the policies adopted at the shareholders' meeting in April 1978, which aspired to maintain full employment for our workers, can no longer be maintained. I would like to hear your ideas as to what we should do. I believe there are many options, and they could all represent life or death for this company.

Targa handed Roman the complete report (Exhibits 13.3 and 13.4) and proceeded to give a short explanation:

Costs are rising, especially for the energy and transportation that is vital to our industry. The national market is very depressed; we can satisfy it using only one-third of our production capacity. The markets in our partner countries in the Caribbean Community are not so depressed as the local market; however, due to the political and economic instability in the whole archipelago, our sister companies cannot continue to absorb our production – they have enough with the factories in San Andres and Dominica. Our only hope now is with the extra regional markets, although I know you are pessimistic about them. I asked you to come so that we could discuss some options which could be presented to the board of directors.

Exhibit 13.3 *Memorandum: report on the status of PACCASA-LOMBARD*

TO:	Enno Roman, Executive Vice President
FROM:	Gabriel Targa, General Manager
SUBJECT:	Report on the status of PACCASA-LOMBARD (Amaranda)
DATE:	February 1, 1979

Sales

The sales for the year to distributors and specific projects reached a total of 35,097 units with a value FOB Factory of A$9,670,678 (or an average of A$275.74 per unit) versus 211,945 units or A$32,762,921 in 1975, which was the last year of normal operations (Table A).

In 1978, the associated companies of Dominica and San Andres purchased a total of 32,380 units from Amaranda so as to alleviate its distressing situation. The units were purchased at normal prices and had a total value FOB Amaranda of A$9,231,943 (or A$285.11 per unit).

In this manner, we were able to achieve total sales of 67,477 units with a value of A$18,902,621 (or an average of A$280.13 per unit) versus sales in 1975 of 212,089 units at A$32,971,033 (or an average of A$155.46 per unit).

Production

The production volume was limited by the sales levels attained in the second half, and by the necessity to take into account the physical and economic capacity of the company to accumulate inventories of the finished product in its warehouses.

With a capacity to produce approximately 210,000 large units, the production actually reached 75,050 large units and 53,351 small units (small frames, which are equivalent to 2,667 large units). In other words, the total production was of 77,717 units or 37% of the total capacity.

However, the above-mentioned average of 37% capacity does not totally reflect the gravity of the situation. If one looks at the production month by month (as seen in Table B), total production in the last six months was 20,949 units, or 20% of total capacity.

Employment level

In spite of the meagre sales and production volumes, the first mandate of the last General Assembly of Shareholders of April 25, 1978 – to maintain normal employment and salary levels – was adhered to so as not to cause social problems and massive lay-offs. As observed in Table

A, at the beginning of 1978 there were 112 employees. That level was maintained throughout the year, ending with 106 employees, the difference due to normal fluctuation levels.

The second mandate of the Assembly of April 25 was that the same level of employment had to be maintained as long as the company was in a break-even situation.

For the reasons noted above, and because structural and technological errors were found in accessories that were to be shipped to the United States (shipments which we hoped would keep us at a break-even level), we have experienced ever-increasing losses.

Notwithstanding labour problems, difficulties in acquiring foreign exchange and exportation permits, etc., it was estimated in the Emergency Plan approved by the Assembly that in order to reach the break-even point without reducing personnel, it would be necessary to produce and sell 5000 major units and 17,000 sets (58,000 small units) of accessories per month. The monthly sales deficit to the clients of 2,075 major units per month was covered, in an artificial manner, through sales or transfers to the affiliated companies of Dominica and San Andres, but, due to the inappropriateness of the existing facilities, only an average sales and production of 4446 small units was reached, as opposed to the goal of 68,000 per month.

As a result, the deficit for the year, as stated in the Audited Financial Statements, was of A$2,311,629.12.

Gains and losses

The loss suffered for 1980 was A$2,311,629. It would have been more than double that figure had it not been for the backing of the associated companies in Dominica and San Andres, which curtailed their own production so as to be able to purchase from our factory a total of 32,380 major units at normal sales prices (an average of A$280.13 per unit), or 42% of the total production and 49% of the total sales of Amaranda.

In order to maintain the production of large units at the level of 75,050 units per year, the cooperation of our Dominican associate was necessary. It ensured the flow of raw materials and accessories imported from outside the area. It served to overcome the difficulties of obtaining sufficient foreign exchange so as to secure a regular flow of direct imports to Amaranda. This collaboration meant that the company did not have to freeze funds, nor utilize dollars, but was able to use Amarandean pesos to pay for a lot of its essential imports of raw materials and accessories originating from outside the area.

Because of the accumulated losses in 1977 and 1978, the capital of the company decreased in those two years from A$19,908,542 to A$11,389,714. From this last figure, one would have to subtract A$2,941,972, the amount corresponding to a revaluation of the fixed assets accounted for in 1977 and based on the official devaluation of the peso for that year.

Given that such a revaluation does not correspond to a real gain but is simply a bookkeeping adjustment, the real capital as of December 31, 1978 has been reduced to A$8,447,742, which implies that, by the end of the past year, the erosion of the social capital of the company increased by A$9,000,000.

Prospects for 1979 – external factors

1 New hikes in energy prices with devastating effects on the economies of non-oil producing countries.
2 Rising costs of production materials.
3 Rising transportation costs of raw materials and finished products.
4 Sustained interest rates for the financing of construction.
5 Continued political, economic and social turbulence in the Caribbean archipelago.
6 Decreased competitiveness due to:
   a High freight costs of imported raw materials and accessories because the tariffs of inter-Caribbean land freight recently increased by 40%.
   b High costs of sea freight of the finished product. (Because of the susceptibility of cracking, the finished product has to be packed in wagons or containers, and as there is no direct service in the Caribbean or South American zones, a transfer in Miami is necessary.)

c An increase in the protectionist tariffs in the countries outside of the Caribbean Common Market (CCM) where similar factories exist. For each unit (the average unit being 40 kilos with a production cost of $41.04), the approximate CIF cost would be (including administrative, financial and sales costs) for example: Panama $56.00, Dominican Republic $58.00 and Venezuela $60.00. The corresponding costs to the distributors (after the duties and interning costs) would be $144.02, $105.00, and $230.00. These costs eliminate all possibilities of competition with the factories inside these countries.

d In the few countries of the hemisphere where our type of product is not produced, and in some – like in the Dominican Republic– where the industry is relatively new, we are faced with strong 'dumping' competition, principally from the conglomerate CEFESA of Colombia. With state subsidies and preferential freight tariffs from the Gran Colombian freight line, CEFESA is offering a panel similar to the one we have been utilizing as an example, at the price of $21.93 C&F St. Domingo. As a result of the low tariffs in force in the CCM, and the reduced prices that CEFESA is offering, its penetration in the CCM can already be felt, especially in San Andres, Kitts and Dominica, and its intensification is imminent.

7 Because of the critical economic and fiscal situation that confronts Dominica and San Andres, and the corresponding depression in their local markets forcing them to reduce production, the associated companies in those countries are not able to continue importing panels from Amaranda without risking their own economic stability and without attracting serious complaints by the authorities for the unjustified consumption of foreign exchange.

8 For the same reasons, as well as the lack of foreign exchange, it is also not permissible for the Dominican associate to keep importing, with dollars generated by Dominica, raw materials and accessories for re-exportation to Amaranda, and then be paid with compensated pesos.

Prospects for 1979 – internal factors

1 As depicted in Tables A and B, the company is in a precarious economic situation which does not permit it to properly attend to the essential maintenance of its installations, much less make any improvements.

2 The labour situation inside the plant has worsened rapidly, perhaps, because of the insecurity and low morale that results from idleness – e.g. five or six operators doing the work of two, the discontentment in the factory has turned into chaos. Some acts can be qualified as sabotage to our already meagre production, such as losing pieces by leaving them scattered all over the floor after not removing them from the mould within the signalled time.

An example of such a situation was when the labour union seized the factory in September 1978 and denied entry to the supervisors and administration staff for ten days. According to the local labour inspectorate, the sole explanation for this action was that management refused to utilize unorthodox methods, judged as humiliating, to punish a worker for a quarrel that he had with a co-worker.

Notwithstanding the very low level of production, and in spite of the economic sacrifice that the company has made by keeping all the personnel at a full salary, (not to mention all the other benefits that have always been rendered, such as subsidizing meals, the daily consumption of milk, subsidized transport, etc.), a petitioned document was sent at the end of last year to the Ministry of Labour demanding an endless number of costly improvements, including investments in the factory, which the company could not fulfil in its present economic condition.

It was the Ministry of Labour itself, by request from our management, that judged it convenient to suspend negotiations until the results of the operations for the year were completed. Recently, the management was summoned to reopen discussions of the petition, but this time it was the Ministry of Industry that urged the Ministry of Labour to postpone discussions while its staff, together with those of the Ministry of Foreign Trade, verified the situation of the company.

Dividends

Based on the results of the preceding exercise, the Ordinary General Assembly of Shareholders met on March 23, 1977 and declared a cash dividend of A$3,360,000 – 50% to be paid in May and 50% in August 1977. The May payment was made, but due to the economic and political situation that presented itself in the middle of the year, the members of the board judged that it would be irresponsible to debilitate the company in a moment when the future appeared to be difficult, as well as to contribute to the worsening crisis in the country left by the overthrown dictator. The board members assumed responsibility for not complying with the payment of the second part of the declared dividend already accounted for in favour of the shareholders, until the next assembly to be held in 1978 ratified the decision.

The next assembly, held on April 25, 1978, ratified the decision taken by the board members and further resolved to suspend indefinitely the second payment of the dividend of A$1,680,000 until such time as the board would judge it prudent to pay. Since that time, it has not been possible for the board to even consider payment of the dividend. Rather, it will propose to the Assembly to renounce all payments of any dividends so as to strengthen the economic situation of the company and help it meet its commitments.

It has been my duty to report to you the labour problems that the company has had to face. In spite of the indifferent attitudes that some factory workers exhibit, one has to take into account the tensions, the insecurity, and the demoralization that competent workers, accustomed to working with interest and diligence, have experienced when faced with the idleness that results from a production volume that barely reaches 20% of its normal level. Also, accustomed to producing complicated pieces, they have become impatient with having to dedicate their efforts to the production of small and simple units such as accessories.

	1975	1976	1977[a]	1978
1 Units produced	189,242	133,167	100,034	77,717
2 Total salaried employees	120	124	112	109.25
3 Productivity (Units/man/month)	131.4	89.5	74.4	59.3
4 Sales to clients (A$)	32,762,921	25,711,817	12,587,933	9,670,678
5 Transfers to associated companies (A$)	208,112	1,204,887	3,833,660	9,231,943
6 Total sales (A$)	32,971,033	26,916,704	16,421,593	18,902,621
7 Sales to clients (Units)	211,945	141,290	63,468	35,097
8 Transfers to associated companies (Units)	144	2,659	31,658	32,380
9 Total sales (Units)	212,089	143,949	95,126	67,477
10 Net profit (loss (A$)	8,014,330	3,167,594	(5,784,170)	(2,311,629)
11 Dividends declared (with previous year as base) (A$)	3,960,000	2,430,000	3,360,000[b]	0
12 Dividends paid (April) (A$)	3,960,000	2,430,000	1,680,000[b]	0
13 Retained profit (A$)	13,125,345	10,903,542	4,701,343[c]	2,701,343[c]
14 Capital (A$)	22,125,345	19,903,542	13,701,343[c]	11,389,714[c]

Notes:
[a]In 1977 there were three months during which nothing was produced due to labour stoppages, civil war and the time utilized to repair the installations.
[b]Only half of the declared dividends were paid in April 1977 as recorded in the Balance Sheet as of December 31, 1976.
[c]These figures were recovered in A$2,941,272 of Unrealized Profit corresponding to the revaluation of fixed assets accounted for in 1977 by recommendation of the external auditors based on the devaluation of the peso.

Exhibit 13.3 *Table A*

	First trimester 1978	Second trimester 1978	Third trimester 1978	Fourth trimester 1978
1 *Production*				
Large Units, Grade 'A'	33,458	17,349	10,942	10,007
Accessories Type 'A'				
Equivalent in Large Units 'A'	–	–	1,244	1,423
Total Units 'A'	33,458	17,349	12,186	11,430
Total Units 'B'	783	847	860	804
Total Units 'A' and 'B'	34,241	18,196	13,046	12,234
Percentage Units 'A'	97.7%	95.3%	93.4%	93.4%
Percentage Units 'B'	2.3%	4.7%	6.6%	6.6%
2 *Productivity*				
Total personnel employed	112	110	109	106
Units/man/month	101.9	55.1	39.9	38.5
3 *Fuel*				
No. of gallons of diesel utilized	97,713	59,435	61,451	39,133
Gallons/Units	2.85	2.27	4.71	3.2
4 *Hours lost*[a]				
Total hours lost	2,281	3,521	4,127	2,703
Hours lost/man/month	6.8	10.8	12.6	10.2
5 *Net profit*				
Net profit (loss) in A$	453,882	(878,497)	(729,982)	(1,157,032)

Note: [a]'Hours lost' are the labour hours during which the plant personnel is absent from the factory, though still drawing a salary and taking part in social security while attending to labour union or personal matters reported as urgent.

Exhibit 13.3 *Table B*

Background

Roman, a man of 60, was educated in the best universities in England and the United States. He had lived and travelled in many countries; however, his personality reflected various native idiosyncrasies. He was born in Amaranda and had lived there until his mid-thirties. During his youth, he and his family had fought against the Loretti dictatorship, for which he had had to serve a jail term and exile. At that point he had decided to settle in Dominica.

Targa, on the other hand, was a provincial man in his early forties. He had graduated with a degree in law from the National Autonomous University of Amaranda and immediately had joined PACCASA as Head of Personnel. Targa had worked at PACCASA for over 20 years.

PACCASA – (Panels of the Caribbean Community, S.A.)

PACCASA was founded as a limited company dedicated to the production of prefabricated panels for walls and dividers for all types of construction. It had started operating in Dominica as a local enterprise, with its raw materials – agglutinants,

Memorandum

To   : Mr. Enno Roman
From   : Gabriel Targa
Subject : Sales Statistics – Amaranda
Date   : February 1, 1979

Sales to	1975		1976		1977		1978	
	Units	A$ Pesos	Units	A$ Pesos	Units	A$ Pesos	Units	A$ Pesos
Clients – Amaranda	55,154	8,389,049	23,622	4,156,785	10,858	2,113,642	35,097	9,670,678
Clients – San Lucia	27,246	4,208,538	29,026	4,812,836	18,098	3,530,427	–	–
Clients – Kits	69,966	10,243,758	69,229	11,645,277	29,458	5,787,473	–	–
Clients – San Andres	59,579	9,921,576	19,413	5,096,919	5,054	1,156,391	–	–
Total clients	211,945	32,762,921	141,290	25,711,817	63,468	12,587,933	35,097	9,679,678
Affiliated companies (San Andres and Dominicana)	144	208,112	2,659	1,204,887	31,658	3,833,660	32,380	9,231,943
Total	212,089	32,971,033	143,949	26,916,704	95,126	16,421,593	67,477	18,902,621

Exhibit 13.4 *Memorandum: sales statistics – Amaranda*

kaolin and special plasters – imported, at high prices, from England, Germany and the United States. The first factory was founded in Dominica in 1955, the second in Amaranda in 1966 and the third in San Andres in 1973. Each of these factories had developed similar production capacities, and they supplied most of the Caribbean Communities' consumption.[3]

Although it was legally independent, PACCASA Amaranda[4] was associated with the Dominican and San Andrean companies through common majority shareholders. The corporation also included a small Creole multinational, which permitted them to benefit from the sharing of human and technical resources, which would have been unaffordable to any of the three companies individually.

It quickly became clear that there was an urgent need to acquire the technology necessary to locate, exploit and process indigenous raw materials without incurring a high risk of lost production (percentage-wise), and without sacrificing the quality of the finished product. Thus the association with LOMBARD INC. originated in 1966.

LOMBARD INC., a North American multinational company, was one of the largest manufacturers of diverse aggregate elements in the world. It supplied PACCASA with geologists and technical assistance to discover and extract the raw material deposits – agglutinants in Dominica, kaolin and gypsum in San Andres. In 1978, 80% of the raw materials used in the corporation's three factories originated from its own archipelago in the Caribbean Community.

The authorized paid capital of PACCASA-LOMBARD in Amaranda at the 1966 start date of operations was A$2,250,000[5]. Various additions had increased the capital to its 1979 level of A$9,000,000, represented by 9000 common shares. These shares were distributed as follows:

Amarandean shareholders	24%
Shareholders from the Caribbean Community	24%
US shareholders	50%
Shareholders from other countries	2%
Total	100%

PACCASA-LOMBARD's board in Amaranda comprised the same people as those on the boards of the companies in San Andres and Dominica, with the addition of the Amarandean representatives. Generally it could be said that the board always looked after 'the one and the whole'.

The members of the PACCASA-LOMBARD board of directors in Amaranda were:

1 *Amarandean shareholders*

Wilfredo ('Wil') Marzipan: President of the Board. 60 years of age, Doctor of Medicine. A shy, sensible and humanitarian man. Not much of a head for business. In addition to his residence in the city and his house by the seaside, his only capital was invested in his PACCASA-LOMBARD shares. He was currently thinking of moving his residence to the United States.

---

[3] An archipelago of six islands, each an independent country. San Andres, with 3.5 million inhabitants; Kitts with 2.0 million; Santa Lucia with 1.5 million; Amaranda and Dominica, each with 1.0 million; and finally Tabora, with 0.9 million inhabitants. In 1958, the six countries united to form the Caribbean Common Market (CCM).

[4] In 1978, PACCASA Amaranda constituted 20% of the net consolidated value of the total corporation.

[5] A$5 (Amarandean pesos) equalled US$1.

Rafael Tulone: 50 years of age, a successful and wealthy man. He was a shareholder in the three archipelago companies and many of the other enterprises in Amaranda.

2 **Shareholders from the Caribbean Community**
Stefan Ferreiro 60 years of age, from San Andres. Very traditional, conservative and somewhat mistrustful with a 'know-it-all' attitude.

3 **North American shareholders**
Roy Pecanthrope: Representative for the North Americans. 36 years of age, Harvard MBA. Very analytical and argumentative – loved to play 'the devil's advocate'. Pulled a lot of weight on the Board, but he respected the opinion of those who were closer to the political and economic situation in Amaranda and the Archipelago. He was sharp, with a long-range view on matters.

4 **Shareholders from other countries**
Paolo Mentori: 28 years of age. Son-in-law of Rafael Tulone.

Finally, Gabriel Targa, General Manager of PACCASA-LOMBARD, was a member of the board of directors ex-officio. Enno Roman was also a member as vice president and shareholder, though he never considered himself as the spokesman for any group.

Everyone had a vote, though they almost always proceeded by consensus rather than by voting. According to the statutes, the resolutions of the Executive Board were taken by an affirmative vote by four out of its six members.

Political background

Forty years of power had led to a corrupt and oppressive Loretti dictatorship. The civil struggle had not been successful in attaining freedom, and the Amarandean people had come to believe that such a goal could only be attained by force. In 1961, a group of young idealists founded a guerrilla group – the Amarandean Liberation Front (FAL) – whose mission was to reduce Loretti's power through the use of violence. Over the years the group grew in size; it gained experience in guerrilla warfare and developed international recognition.

At the beginning of 1976, Fermin Landazuri, leader of the opposition party, was assassinated by a paramilitary group obviously connected with the Loretti dictatorship. Almost immediately, the forces of the country joined together in the 'rebellion for liberation'. At the same time, the Association of Private Enterprises of Amaranda (APEA), the umbrella organization of the various private enterprise institutions, called for a national strike to demand the dictator's resignation. The strike lasted for 15 days, during which time all the supporting companies voluntarily paid their workers' wages.

The political uprising continued, until the dictatorship was overthrown on May 28, 1977.

Economic conditions

During 1975, economic conditions in the country began to decline sharply, and consequently international reserves were substantially diminished. Due to the scarcity of foreign currency, and as a means of having more control over the private enterprises, the government fixed the exchange rate in October 1976. The official rate was 3.00 Amarandean pesos per US$1. The government then established lists of priority goods to be imported, fixing different rates – according to priority – of A$3.00, A$4.00 and

A$5.00 Amarandean pesos for every US dollar. In the black market, the dollar was fetching A$5.50 Amarandean pesos, though this rate was increasing day by day. At the beginning of 1977, the government officially devalued the currency, establishing an exchange rate of about A$5.00 for US$1.

The new leaders

After the revolutionary triumph, a system of government was installed in the country in which all the political parties participated; however, political and military control was in the hands of the former guerrillas of the FAL, who did not hide their leftist tendencies nor their intimate friendship with Fidel Castro of Cuba.

The leaders of the revolution proclaimed that power was now in the hands of the farmers and workers and that, in the new society, there would be no place for the bourgeoisie. The revolutionary government promptly initiated relations with all the socialist governments. In addition to confiscating all personal property of the overthrown dictator and his supporters, it nationalized the banks, all the private financial institutions, all insurance companies and the mines. This meant that 40% of the country's gross domestic product was under state control. No major steps were taken to nationalize the manufacturing sector; however, plans existed for the State to assume control of transportation and the exploitation of all natural resources. At the end of 1978, the continued confiscations and nationalizations had reached a point where an accusation by the unions that a company was 'disinvesting' was motive enough for the Ministry of Justice to intervene and eventually have it confiscated.

In June 1977, the revolutionary government decreed an obligatory payment of wages lost during the months of April and May to all workers drawing a salary of 5000 pesos or less, and up to that amount for those drawing a higher salary. A few days later the new government introduced a reconstruction tax payment of 8% of the capital[6] of companies and individuals as of June 30, 1977, to be paid in four equal parts of 2% for the duration of three consecutive years.

A few months after the revolutionary triumph, the FAL installed the Supreme Council of the Revolutionary Government (SCRG) at the head of its administration. The SCRG was made up of 4 members: Commander Pedro Chacon, who presided over it, the economist Dr Alberto Fuentes, the writer Silverio Maza and the contractor Maximo Schomberg. In addition, there was a decision in the Cabinet to replace centrist Ministers with FAL staff members. The ministers replaced were the Ministry of Defence, the Ministry of Economic Planning and the Ministry of Agriculture. However, within a short period of time, the political differences between the FAL and private enterprises ended in Schomberg's resignation from the SCRG.

Major problems facing the revolutionary government

After two years of rebellion, the country was destroyed. The flight of capital had been enormous. Cotton, coffee and sugar crops, the principal export commodities of the country, were reduced by at least 20% in 1977 and 1978. A good number of contractors and professionals abandoned the country, and the uncertainty paralysed the initiative of many others. Credit was very limited and new private investments suffered a total paralysis due to the mistrust that investors had of the new economic system.

---

[6] 'Capital' was defined as the difference between the assets and the liabilities of each taxpayer. A deduction was made for the amounts lost due to destruction during the revolution.

The only significant investor was the State; international aid was used in a desperate struggle to 'increase production' for the recovery of the country. By March 1978, the government had received $490 million in international emergency loans, $42 million in food and nearly $155 million in donations and credits. However, $90 million of aid in credit and donations from West Germany had been frozen, due to ideological disputes between the two governments.

At the beginning of 1978, unemployment was estimated to be around 30%, and the inflation rate at 60%. The external debt of Amaranda was $1800 million, of which $800 million was to be paid in 1978. The international reserves of the country, which the FAL found amounted to the ridiculous sum of $3.5 million, were enough to pay 3 days' worth of wages.

Mixed results

A decline in the Gross Domestic Product (GDP) of nearly 24% in 1977 was followed by a growth of 10.7% in 1978. For 1979, the government planned to increase the GDP by 18.5%, a goal which both internal and external observers considered unrealistic. A recovery was not expected before 1980 (Exhibit 13.5).

Exhibit 13.5 *Economic outlook: Amaranda*

The outlook for Amaranda improved after the economic reactivation programme was introduced in 1977. Progress was made in all areas of the economy; however, it was forecast that a total recovery would not be achieved until 1980. The problematic areas were a weak balance of payments, scarce credit and poor confidence in the Falinist regime (the FAL) by investors.

Gross domestic product

According to official estimates, real growth would rise by 18.5% in 1979 after an increase of 10.7% in 1978, and a marked decline in 1977. However, the goal for 1979 seemed to be unrealistic, and it was likely that the expansion would be considerably less.

Agriculture

Commercial harvests improved in 1978 because of favourable international prices, a larger cultivated area, and a better overall harvest.

Agriculture was marked as the sector of highest priority in the government plan for 1979. It was hoped that overall production for 1979 would rise by 22%; this growth was to be achieved through the expansion of cultivated areas, and by increasing the minimum wage of field workers, thereby reducing the problem of scarce manual labour during the key periods of planting and harvesting.

In addition, the government planned to support small land-owners through a $65 million loan from the Inter-American Development Bank (IDB) in order to finance purchases of insecticides, fertilizers and other goods.

Industrial production

Industrial production was improving, although it still had a long way to go before reaching former levels. In 1978 the manufacturing sector grew by 7.3% but failed to meet the official goals. Obstructions in the supply of raw materials reduced overall production, and lack of financing caused many factories to be under-utilized.

Certain industries were earmarked to grow in 1979: food processing by 12% after a decrease of 3.5% in 1978; the textile industry by 70%, to be obtained through the reactivation of the textile company La Mariposa; the chemical industry by 25%; and the paper industry by 16%.

Investments

Regaining the confidence of investors depended more on politics than on economic conditions. Even though the economy was still largely in the hands of private farmers and industry, the government had not given any positive signs to the private sector. It was expected that the government would seek greater cooperation during 1979.

The government was preparing a code of laws for foreign investment and, until details were made known, it was improbable that any important commitments would be made. During 1979, investments would be mostly in the hands of the government.

It was projected that investments of gross fixed capital would rise to 20% of GDP, an increase of 16% over the previous year, i.e. $340 million. The plan for 1979 anticipated a public investment programme of $405 million, with 48% of its total disbursements channelled towards the development of the infrastructure.

Financing for the investments was to come, for the most part, from foreign sources (75%), largely from loans already obtained though not yet disbursed, as well as donations and long-term loans registered with international financial institutions.

In the area of private investment, the government forecast an increase of 25% over 1978, though this figure seemed to be overly optimistic.

Budget

The central government's budget of A$8.79 thousand millions for 1979 (A$5:$1), represented a real increase of 25% over the budget for 1978. A deficit of A$2,748 million, equal to 9.7% of the GDP, was included, which was an increase of A$862 million over the deficit of 1978. The deficit would be financed with foreign loans. Nevertheless, the government still hoped to subtract A$300 million from the expenses.

Money and credit

Credit was scarce in 1978, and most was channelled to the state industries, although private-sector enterprises in priority areas had access to some funds. The interest rate for high-priority industries was 14% per annum; medium-priority at 15% per annum; and low-priority (producers of luxury goods) at 17% per annum.

To control credit even further, the government was to establish credit limits by industry; small producers, non-traditional producers, exporters and programmes of importance would have first choice. Credit was to be authorized for specific purposes and not for general use.

External commerce

During 1979 the government hoped to restrict imports to a 10% increase ($950 million), and increase exports by 45% ($680 million). This would narrow the deficit to $270 million, in comparison to $400 million for 1978. However, the goal was considered to be unrealistic.

The deficit for 1978 (in contrast to the surplus of $200 million in 1977), was principally due to an accelerated economic activity, which required a considerable increase in imports, particularly petroleum and petrochemicals. In order to keep the import levels in line with the government's goals, controls were imposed for 1979. The official exchange rate A$5:$1 was to be granted only for authorized goods such as foodstuffs, medicines and raw materials.

The greater part of the exports from Amaranda would continue to go to the Caribbean Common Market and the United States. However, both Western and Eastern Europe were projected as growth markets for Amarandean products.

Foreign currency

In 1979, international reserves, though rising, were still at dangerously low levels, and for that reason exchange controls were imposed. Servicing the debt continued to decrease the reserves even though the flight of capital which took place in the months following the Falinist victory has been halted. For an external debt estimated at $1.7 thousand million, the 1978 payments were $185 million, and in 1979 payments were expected to be $190 million.

Although reserves were weak, the peso, fixed at A$5:$1, was not under great pressure, and a devaluation was not foreseen within the next twelve months.

By the end of 1979, the government had reduced the inflation rate from 60% to 30% and was hoping to control it at 20% in 1979. The reduction was based on the control of basic commodity prices, and it was rumoured that the government would freeze wages and prohibit strikes and shutdowns.

Public investment had been channelled primarily to the industrial sector. The Minister of Industry said in January 1979 that, in order to survive, the industrial sector needed $280 million because no industry in Amaranda could survive without the importation of raw materials and energy from abroad.

Private investment continued to be paralysed and, according to an external analyst, 'regaining the confidence of the investor depended more on the political rather than the economic conditions'. The government had given no indication that any priority would be given to the private sector.

The creation of 100,000 jobs reduced the level of unemployment from 30% to 17% in 1978; the goal for 1979 was 61,000 more jobs, which would reduce the figure to 13%.

Back to the meeting

Targa continued the dialogue with his boss and friend:

> I think, Enno, that we should try our luck. This country has to recover, and the door of opportunity knocks! The government has great plans for the construction of dwellings which promises a brighter future. But, for the moment, we should look for opportunities to export to other countries: to the USA, to Canada, to Cuba and other socialist countries, wherever!

Roman spoke quickly and forcefully:

> Don't forget that there is no foreign currency available to buy raw materials. Also, I have confidential information that, for next year, only 8000 dwellings will be constructed; we could complete that order within 15 days. It is true that there are big plans and possibly credit, but will that credit come? And even if the government guarantees the foreign currency, how are we going to fulfil our obligations with new markets? The USA and Canada do not trust our promises. On the other hand, you have to keep in mind that each country has an industry like ours, and that there are import tariffs that we would not be able to overcome with our higher transportation costs. Furthermore, our competitors in Mexico and Colombia are selling at a lower price than in 1975 – a price lower than production costs.

Targa knew that if the government found out that they were formulating options for the company, it would confiscate the business. He also worried enormously that the personnel would be out in the streets if the plant should shut down – he did not want to consider that possibility.

Meanwhile, Roman had decided that his recommendation would favour 'hibernation' until the political situation had settled. This could be done by obtaining authorization to close the firm temporarily and by compensating the dismissed workers. According to the Labour Code of Amaranda, in cases where the Minister of Labour authorized the temporary closing of a company, due for example to a shortage in raw materials, the company was obliged to pay 15 days of salary to the workers. But, he thought that this amount was unfair, and he preferred to recommend that they pay the greatest number of months that would be financially viable for the company – perhaps six months' salary.

Roman could think of six possible options which he could present to the board of directors. He wanted to present them fairly and honestly, yet in a way that would ensure that his choice was successful.

Roman's assessment

The North American board members would look very thoroughly into the whole idea of continuing operations, but in the final analysis they would probably be sceptical about the possibility of continuing because of the confusing international news coverage about the revolution.

The Amarandean board members – Tulone and Marzipan – would be thinking along the same lines as Targa, although Rafael Tulone would probably be indecisive. In recent meetings he had said that the situation merited a serious analysis. There was also the possibility that Dr Marzipan would be an ally to the North Americans for personal reasons.

The other Caribbean shareholder – Ferreiro – would probably be looking for ways to continue operations.

As for Gabriel Targa, Roman thought that, with a bit of psychological encouragement, Targa would side with him.

But the key question was – what strategy should Roman employ to get the board to agree to his option?

Case 13.2 PACCASA-LOMBARD (B)

This case was written by Dr Roger Quant Pallavicini and revised by Barbara Robins, both under the supervision of Professor Werner Ketelhöhn, as a basis for class discussion rather than to illustrate either effective or ineffective handling of a business situation.

The board of directors met on February 15, 1979 in the beautiful city of Acahualpa, capital of Amaranda. In the course of the meeting, Enno Roman's proposal to continue operating, but to close the company temporarily, was accepted.

Before the meeting took place, Roman had made an analysis of each member of the board to anticipate how they would vote. From his analysis, he perceived two possible alternatives – each with different scenarios:

1 *Close the operation*
  a Simply close and liquidate the enterprise.
  b Liquidate the enterprise by selling it:
    (i) to an individual;
    (ii) to the government.
  c Close the enterprise, thereby provoking its confiscation with or without compensation.
2 *Continue operating*
  a Continue operating in the same manner, actively searching new markets while waiting for the local market to recover.
  b Close temporarily and continue operations at a later date.

In his analysis, Roman anticipated that Wil Marzipan would be in favour of a temporary closure. His shares in PACCASA-LOMBARD were one of his few possessions. He thought that it would take a long time to resolve his move to the United States; at 60 years of age, such things are not decided quickly. Therefore, he could discount the fact that he would press for the liquidation of the company.

As for Rafael Tulone, at first Roman thought that he would be in favour of a closure because such a loss would not gravely affect him. However, a more important consideration was that a closure could attract the government's criticism of Tulone's other interests in Amaranda.

Paolo Mentori would follow his father-in-law, Rafael Tulone.

The most difficult to convince would be Ferreiro and Pecanthrope. Roman thought that his own vote, together with Marzipan, Tulone and Mentori, could win the majority; however, if at all possible, he did not want to impose a solution on two of the strongest members with whom he had to keep on dealing in San Andres and Dominica. He therefore decided to use the time he had before the meeting to informally convince Ferreiro and Pecanthrope. If there were time, he would also approach the others.

He spoke first with Pecanthrope, who was of the firm opinion that the enterprise had to be closed. The argument he used was that there was little hope for a multinational company, such as the one he represented, to operate properly in a socialist and anti-imperialist economy. In principle, he was willing to take the chance of a total loss if the government decided to confiscate the enterprise without any indemnity. The arguments that Roman used emphasized that LOMBARD INC. owed some loyalty to the country that had hosted it. In addition, he argued that any opposition to the company from the government of Amaranda could have serious repercussions for the interests of the company in other countries, at least in San Andres, where the guerrilla friends of FAL could take reprisals. He ended by telling Pecanthrope that, if he were willing to lose everything now, he may as well wait a while longer to see if such a possibility could be avoided after all. Things could only get better. It would be difficult for them to get worse.

Pecanthrope agreed that Roman had a very good feeling for the situation and that he had strong arguments for continuing the operation. He said he would give it serious thought before the meeting. He also wanted to talk with his superiors before giving Roman a final answer.

Roman did not speak to Ferreiro, who was in Europe, but he was sure that he had made an impression on Pecanthrope. If Pecanthrope voted in favour of his plan, Ferreiro would be likely to do the same.

The proposal

Roman's plan was accepted and it was therefore agreed to propose the following to the government.

1 Temporary suspension of the operating activities of PACCASA-LOMBARD until such time as there was a reasonable expectation that it could be operated without incurring any losses.
2 Maintaining, during this period, a commercial operation to attend to the needs of the government's construction programmes and the construction industry of Amaranda in general.
3 Retention of the necessary personnel for the commercial operation, including the warehouse.
4 Maintenance of the equipment and installations so that they would not suffer any deterioration during the non-operative period.
5 Exportation of raw materials and other products that could deteriorate (due to humidity, for example) or otherwise be lost, due to non-use in the short term, to the associated companies in Dominica and San Andres at current prices.
6 Full payment of any outstanding loans, plus an economic compensation (the amount to be decided by the board of directors), so that the company could exist without any risk of being unable to meet its loans and commercial obligations, as well as the costs

of maintaining its commercial operations. Payment to those employees who would opt for a termination of employment.

7 The ultimate approval of the General Assembly of Shareholders. The next Assembly was scheduled for the middle of March 1979.

The strategy

The board of directors debated for several hours on the strategy of how to communicate these decisions to the revolutionary government of Amaranda. The board of directors discussed:

- who to approach and in what order
- the best way to make the approach.

They discussed the possibility that the proposal be taken to the Ministry of Labour, which, according to the law, would be the one to authorize a temporary lay-off of labourers. The Labour Minister was a politician who was not a member of the FAL, but of one of the former parties that opposed the dictator. He was classified as moderate and, although he zealously guarded his independence and the legal order, he abided by the general political orientation directed by Amaranda's revolutionary junta.

The possibility of going to the Ministry of Industry was also discussed. This Ministry was the best informed about the economic situation of the country with regard to foreign exchange, and it understood the conditions of the CCM.[1]

Other members of the board suggested going directly to the top – to Commander Chacon himself. Those against this proposal argued that Commander Chacon had the political power, but understood little of economic and industrial matters.

The question was raised as to whether it was better to fully expose the real situation of the company or present solely those aspects that would not lend themselves to misinterpretations. There were certain points that could be considered sensitive if they were interpreted in the wrong way, such as the transactions between companies of the PACCASA group.

Finally, it was decided to let Enno Roman formulate his own strategy. It would be his responsibility to obtain the result he sought...as long as it was supported by the board of directors.

How to tell the employees

Before closing the meeting, they debated as to how and when to break the news to the workers of PACCASA-LOMBARD.

The Workers' Syndicate of PACCASA-LOMBARD was affiliated with the Federation of Workers of Amaranda (FWA), an independent syndicated federation. It did not follow the political regulations of the recently created Falinist Federation of Workers (FFW), which was considered by the FAL as one of the people's organizations that should build the central axis for the political mobilization of the country.

[1] Caribbean Common Market.

424

The FFW supported the government in its objective to put an end to labour disorder and the political discredit caused by company takeovers, strikes and the petitions for salary raises, and to stimulate a rise in production and labour discipline. The FWA, on the other hand, took the phrases created by the revolution seriously: e.g. 'workers to power', 'better living conditions', 'out with the bourgeoisie'....

The board of directors discussed when the process should begin, the way it should proceed and how to negotiate with the Labour Union about the amount of compensation that the employees who would be dismissed should receive.

As in the former decision, it was left up to Enno Roman to use his own discretion. After all, it was his strategy and he knew the country and the company better than the others.

Roman's responsibilities

Enno Roman left the session brooding over the responsibilities that had been placed on his shoulders and the steps that he would need to take to fulfil his promise.

Having always organized the important tasks ahead of him, he decided in the tranquillity of his private study that evening to write down, step by step, the actions to be taken.

In addition to communicating with the government and the workers, he took upon himself another important responsibility: communication to the news media. The news media of Amaranda was, for the most part, sensationalist, a sickness that had been aggravated during the revolutionary period. When reporting was involved with a North American company, especially a joint venture, the risk of the news media reporting antagonistic comments was high. Nobody could foresee the consequences that such propaganda could bring on the company.

---

1 Accounts receivable – inter-company

TO: PACCASA DOMINICANA (Panels)	A$ 3,750,477.40
TO: PACCASA SAN ANDRES (Panels)	1,414,593.10
TO: INTERCARIBE , S.A. (Georgia)	8,111,803.10
TOTAL Accounts receivable (Inter-company)	A$ 13,276,843.60

Note: (a) The amounts owed by Dominica and San Andres correspond almost exclusively to panels that these affiliates have purchased from Amaranda. They have done so to alleviate the situation of the latter, even when it implied a reduction in their own production.

    (b) In the same manner that the original enterprise in Dominica largely financed the installation and start-up costs of Amaranda, the latter and Dominica incurred loans to finance the installation and start-up costs of San Andres. The loans of PACCASA to San Andres amounted to A$7,336,019.20.

        Due to the evident disapproval of Amaranda by the authorities in San Andres since the fall of the dictatorship, it was judged that PACCASA – Amaranda would be more secure if San Andres were not the primary debtor. The debt was therefore transferred to a Georgian affiliate, INTERCARIBE S.A., though always leaving PACCASA – San Andres as sole guarantor.

INTERCARIBE S.A. was organized as a trading company with the intention that it would serve for the commercialization of the products of the Group in markets outside the Caribbean area.

The INTERCARIBE S.A. accounts receivable of A$ 8,111,803.10 is broken down in the following manner:

Balance on Dec. 31, 1977				**7,336,019.18**
Interest January	1978 – 1%	73,360.80		7,409,379,38
Interest February	" "	74,093.82		7,483,473.20
Interest March	" "	74,834.70		7,558,307.90
Interest April	" "	75,583.10		7,633,891,00
Interest May	" "	76,338.90		7,710,229.90
Interest June	" "	77,102.30		7,787,332.20
Interest July	" "	77,873.30		7,865,205.50
Interest August	" "	78,652.10		7,943,857.60
Interest September	" "	79,438.60		8,023,296.20
Interest October	" "	80,233.00		8,103,529.20
Interest November		81,035.30		8,184,564.50
Interest Credit Nov. 1978			462,500.00	
Invoice No. 0784 Accs. Nov./78		312,518,00		
Interest Dec. 31,1978		77,220.60		8,111,803.10

Payment obligation of the loan principal of: A$7,336,019.18 is as follows:

(a) Monthly interest of 1% over the balance is capitalized on a monthly basis.
(b) The principal of $7,336,019.18 is payable: A$2,445,339.70
   December 31, 1979
   December 31, 1980   2,445,339.70
   December 31, 1981   2,445,339.70
                               A$7,336,019.18

2. Inter-company accounts payable

To: DOMINICA (Raw materials and accessories)	A$3,264,203.70
To: SAN ANDRES (Raw materials and accessories)	A$1,277,778.10
To: ASISA (Accessory)	A$ 58,820,00
Total	A$4,600,801.80

Note: There exists a reasonable balance between what PACCASA/Amaranda owes to Dominica and San Andres, and what these two companies owe PACCASA.

Exhibit 13.6 *Inter-company accounts, as of December 31, 1979*

Balance owing from 1977 invoices for accessories	US\$ 40,681.18
Balance owing for 'royalties'	\$ 54,178.45
Total balance owing as of December 31, 1978	US\$ 94,859,63
	A\$948,596.32

Note: Until December 31, 1977, the 'Royalties and Trademarks contract' between PACCASA–Amaranda and LOMBARD INC. specified that for technical assistance, the licence to fabricate models of Lombard, as well as the use of its logotype and its registered trademark 'LOMBARD', PACCASA–Amaranda would pay LOMBARD INC. a royalty of 2.5% of its net sales to clients. Considering however, that technical assistance required in the fabrication of panels has considerably diminished, once the contract came due at the end of 1977, a reduction of the rate of the 'royalty' to 1.75% was negotiated.

The figure of US\$54,178.45 as of December 31, 1978 corresponds to the accumulated 'royalties' pending payment as of October 1, 1976.

In the middle of 1977, a moratorium on the payment of the total debt of US\$94,859.63 was negotiated until further notice.

Exhibit 13.7 *Accounts payable – LOMBARD INC., as of December 31, 1978*

BANK OF THE CARIBBEAN   *PRINCIPAL*

1 Loan renegotiated on July 10, 1978. Payable in 20 equal quarterly fees with an interest of 12% p.a. on the balance, after 1 year of grace.
2 Loan renegotiated on July 10, 1980. Interest of 18.5% on balances. Term and method of payment suspended while the renegotiation of the external debt is being concluded.

Note: The accounts payable to Georgia for the loan of \$7,336,019.18 made to San Andres, constitutes the reserve with which PACCASA-Amaranda could meet its obligations with the Bank of the Caribbean (\$4,510,817.30), LOMBARD INC. (\$948,596.32) and other miscellaneous obligations. This is possible even though the manufacturing operations would, as proposed, be suspended until they can be reinstated with a level of production reaching at least the break-even point.

Exhibit 13.8 *Banking obligations, as of December 31, 1978*

INTERNATIONAL

Case 13.3
Skoda–Volkswagen–Renault negotiations – the Renault–Volvo proposal

This case was prepared by Research Associate James Henderson, under the supervision of Professor Jan Kubes, as a basis of class discussion rather than to illustrate either effective or ineffective handling of a management situation.

'So it is all set. October 15, one week from today. We will arrive the night before in Prague so that we can be at the Ministry early in the morning ... Great. Good-bye Mr Bakala.' Mr Serge Chaput put down the phone after speaking to Mr Zdenek Bakala, Vice President of Corporate Finance of Credit Suisse First Boston, the financial advisor to Skoda Automobilovy Koncern. It was not always easy to get through to Czechoslovakia. Finally succeeding after the usual three tries, he had made sure that the conversation was worthwhile. Chaput flipped through his agenda to October 15–16 and wrote: 'Presentation of final proposal to the Czech ministry, CSFB, and Skoda management.' Serge Chaput then looked at his watch; it was 8:45. 'Just enough time,' he said to himself, 'to review today's agenda before the team meeting at 9:00.' As the Director of Department of International Projects for Renault, Mr Serge Chaput was responsible for coordinating Renault's proposed takeover of Eastern Europe's most prized automobile company, Skoda Automobilovy Koncern. After four long months of laying the ground work, Chaput and his team were ready to put the Renault's final proposal together.

As he was reviewing the agenda, Chaput imagined one possible scenario if Renault did successfully acquire the Czech automobile company. 'Volvo, our new partner, could fill the top end of the car range, Renault could be positioned as the middle-of-the-road car and Skoda could be positioned at the lower end. It could fit together quite nicely.'

Background to Renault

History

In 1899, Louis Renault and his two brothers, Fernand and Marcel, founded what was to become France's largest automobile company. By 1914 Renault Frères was already

Balance Sheet	1985	1986	1987	1988	1989	1990E
Assets						
Cash	3,950	3,815	4,359	3,554	4,238	
Prepaid expenses	1,585	1,999	1,957	2,034	2,472	
Accounts receivable	8,882	11,381	10,978	12,216	14,208	
Other receivable	4,096	3,694	3,184	3,994	3,387	
Inventory	23,490	25,099	23,011	24,850	26,168	
Current assets	42,003	45,988	43,489	46,648	50,473	48,400
Financial	21,882	22,342	17,894	24,166	31,052	
Intangibles	28	34	24	32	232	
Property and equip.	38,962	39,067	38,304	39,175	40,323	
Total fixed assets	60,872	61,442	56,222	63,373	71,607	71,000
Deferred charges	2,492	2,049	1,826	182	–	
Total assets	105,367	109,479	101,537	110,203	122,080	119,400
Liabilities and shareholder's equity						
Accounts payable	16,944	21,328	21,611	24,435	27,111	25,000
Debt	73,832	68,835	56,048	37,993	37,998	43,500
Other payables	8,885	9,897	10,070	11,976	12,551	14,500
Others	1,694	2,565	2,711	2,807	1,883	1,000
Total	101,355	102,625	90,440	77,211	79,543	84,000
Investment subsidies	320	313	293	262	197	
Reserves	9,966	12,356	12,961	12,364	14,120	14,000
Shareholder's equity	(9,450)	(11,433)	(7,811)	14,012	22,466	17,900
Minorities	3,176	5,618	5,654	6,354	5,242	3,500
Total liabilities and equity	105,367	109,479	101,537	110,230	122,080	119,400
Income statement						
Sales	111,382	134,935	147,510	161,438	174,477	164,000
Cost of goods sold	98,036	110,998	118,567	125,269	134,664	129,500
Gross profit	13,346	23,937	28,943	36,169	39,813	34,500
Other operating income	887	712	491	502	538	300
Selling and administration	18,622	21,100	20,230	22,286	27,407	28,000
Operating income	(4,389)	3,549	9,204	14,385	12,944	6,200
Interest cost	5,402	5,524	4,185	3,460	2,166	2,000
Financial income	(64)	87	128	162	115	150
Extraordinary items	(2,654)	(4,139)	(3,083)	(2,816)	(1,445)	(4,000)
Other expenses	–	–	–	1,611	1,869	–
Equity earnings	254	817	1,498	2,315	2,146	1,100
Earnings before tax	(12,255)	(5,210)	3,562	8,975	9,725	1,150
Tax	1,330	(648)	127	(62)	(909)	(500)
Minorities	(28)	(176)	(433)	(79)	473	300
Net income loss	(10,953)	(6,034)	3,256	8,834	9,289	950
Other financial information						
Cash flow	(6,031)	626	9,811	16,856	15,050	n/a
Capital expenditures	8,269	5,551	7,021	7,295	10,361	13,200
Depreciation	4,894	6,484	6,122	7,943	6,607	7,100
Number of employees	190,277	190,849	182,827	178,213	174,573	157,400
Vehicles sold (units)	1,962	1,816	1,901	1,913	2,003	1,850

Exhibit 13.9 *Renault's Financial Statements, 1985–1989 (millions of FF)*

on its way to building a strong international presence with 31 dealers outside France. After World War II, the De Gaulle government nationalized Renault Frères. The company was then designed as a showpiece for other French companies, and as a pioneer of social and union progress for the French working class. By the end of 1959, Renault was estimated to be the sixth largest automobile maker in the world. With the introduction of new models, such as the best-selling R5, Renault continued its rapid expansion in the 1960s and 1970s. In order to enter the American market, Renault first sold its cars through American Motors Corporation. The company later acquired a minority stake in AMC in 1980. However, the investment soon turned sour as the North American market went into a deep recession in 1981–1982.

The early 1980s were disastrous for Renault; without government backing the company would have been technically insolvent by 1986. In 1980, Renault, the sixth largest producer worldwide, assembled 2.05 million vehicles. By 1985, with a drop in product quality and an ageing product line, output had declined to 1.67 million units, relegating the company to number eight worldwide. The combination of a decline in sales, a high cost structure and an ambitious capital expenditure brought disastrous financial results. In 1985, the company's worst year, Renault lost FF 12.7 billion.[1] Only a cash injection of FF9.3 billion from the French government kept the company alive. From 1985 on, Renault, under the leadership of Georges Besse and then Raymond Lévy, began to turn the organization around despite its huge debt burden of FF57 billion. Assets and investments were sold off; the workforce was reduced by 20% between 1984 and 1989; debt was slashed; and new products, such as the R25, R21 and R19 were launched. By 1989, a revitalized and leaner Renault, with FF174 billion in sales, appeared from the wreckage with a substantially healthier financial situation. The company's aim for the 1990s was to retain its 10% market share in Europe and remain profitable through the downturns in the economy (Exhibit 13.9).

Organization

In 1990, Renault and Volvo, the Swedish luxury car manufacturer, signed a far-reaching alliance agreement. Under this agreement, Volvo was to take a 45% stake in Renault Vehicules Industriels, its commercial vehicle division. In exchange, Renault was to take 45% stake in Volvo Truck Corporation and a 20% stake in Volvo Car Corporation. The rest of the Renault Group, was controlled by the French government (Exhibit 13.10). Apart from this strategic alliance, Renault was organized into four divisions comprising Automobiles, Commercial Vehicles, Other Industrial Companies (robots, farm equipment and components), and Finance and Services. The Board of Directors comprised six members of the French government; the Chairman, Raymond Lévy; two members from Volvo; three from outside; and six employee representatives.

Product/markets

Renault had the widest product line of all the car manufacturers in Europe, covering both the major market segments – sub-compact, compact, mid-sized and full sized – as well as the speciality segments – sport and minivan. Renault originally pursued a brand

---

[1] In 1990, Kcs3.1 = FF1; Kcs17 = $1; Kcs10.5 = DM1; Kcs2.9 = Skr1.

Balance Sheet	1985	1986	1987	1988	1989	1990E
Assets						
Cash	4,202	4,537	5,138	4,368	5,374	
Investments	10,192	13,240	17,359	11,264	13,096	
Accounts receivable	11,244	12,346	12,724	13,945	15,837	
Inventories	16,044	18,235	16,561	19,401	19,411	
Current assets	41,682	48,358	51,782	48,978	53,718	53,000
Financial assets	10,926	11,157	11,601	18,102	21,200	26,500
Intangible assets	620	593	350	297	429	300
Property plant and equip.	9,565	12,074	13,373	15,610	18,868	18,300
Other assets	–	–	956	3,964	3,928	3,800
Total assets	62,793	72,182	78,062	86,951	98,143	101,900
Liabilities and shareholder's equity						
Accounts payable	7,364	7,731	8,288	9,129	9,844	7,100
Short-term loans	10,269	10,977	9,829	11,610	19,898	26,700
Other	9,223	12,840	13,251	13,761	13,104	14,900
Current liabilities	26,856	31,548	31,368	34,500	42,846	48,700
Long-term debt	7,419	6,401	6,169	6,758	5,006	6,500
Pension provisions	1,866	2,346	2,580	2,830	3,137	3,800
Other	–	651	1,003	1,017	1,115	–
Untaxed reserves	17,738	20,980	24,338	26,528	26,044	25,400
Shareholder's equity	8,798	10,124	12,264	14,834	19,581	17,200
Minority interests	116	132	340	484	414	300
Total liabilities and equity	62,793	72,182	78,062	86,951	98,143	101,900
Income statement						
Sales	86,196	84,090	92,520	96,639	90,972	83,000
Cost of sales	77,996	75,534	74,463	77,110	72,328	68,700
Selling and administration	–	–	9,122	10,028	11,292	11,200
Depreciation	1,725	2,062	2,213	2,293	2,535	2,600
Operating income	6,475	6,494	6,462	7,028	4,817	500
Restructuring costs	–	–	–	–	–	2,400
Interest expense	n/a	n/a	1,937	1,961	2,723	3,700
Financial income	7,765	7,502	10,948	10,028	9,377	5,300
Extraordinary items	–	193	–	176	413	–
Others	(163)	(165)	–	–	–	
Earnings before tax	7,602	7,530	9,011	8,243	7,011	(300)
Tax	1,713	2,249	2,220	2,500	2,248	700
Untaxed reserves	(3,330)	(2,694)	(3,426)	(2,311)	365	–
Minorities	(13)	(36)	(74)	(103)	–	
Net income	2,546	2,551	3,291	3,329	5,129	(1,000)
Other financial information						
Cash flow	5,457	5,017	5,991	7,069	7,523	n/a
Capital expenditures	3,506	3,425	3,864	3,948	6,281	4,000
Sales of vehicles (000s)	n/a	461	474	467	480	420
Number of employees	67,850	73,150	75,350	78,600	78,690	68,800

Exhibit 13.10 *Volvo's Financial Statements, 1985–1989 (millions of sKr)*

Product class	Models	Planned replacement
Micro-class	R4	X06 (date uncertain)
Sub-compact	R5, Clio	Clio in 1990
Compact	R9, R11, R18, R19	R19 in 1989
Mid-size	R21	New R21 in 1993–4
Full-size/luxury	R25	New R25 in 1992
Minivan	Espace	Revamp in 1992
Sport	Alpine	Revamp in 1992
	Fuego	Dropped
	R5 Turbo	Dropped
Break	R21 Nevada	

Country	1985	1986	1987	1988	1989	Position
Europe	10.7%	10.6%	10.6%	10.1%	10.4%	#6
France	30.8%	26.5%	28.6%	29.0%	29.1%	#2
Germany	2.7%	3.2%	3.1%	2.8%	3.5%	#9
UK	3.9%	3.7%	3.9%	3.9%	3.8%	#7
Italy	n/a	n/a	7.9%	7.1%	7.2%	#4
Spain	n/a	n/a	22.9%	20.9%	19.0%	#1
USA	2.4%	2.0%	0.2%	0	0	n/a
Argentina	36%	34%	34%	32%	32%	#1

Exhibit 13.11   *Renault's product portfolio and position in selective markets*

name strategy using numbers – such as the R5, R19, R21 and R25; but, more recently, it had decided to switch to names for its next line of models, commencing with the Chamade and Clio.

In the French market, Renault was second behind the Peugeot/Citroën Group. In 1980, the company commanded the market with a 40% share, only to see it decline to 29% by 1989. The domestic market, accounting for 43% of Renault sales, was followed by Spain, Italy, UK and West Germany, each representing more than 100,000 per year. Renault had maintained a presence in some of the Eastern European markets. In Yugoslavia, Renault had a production arrangement with IMV to assemble 54,000 cars per year. Renault had also worked with Dacia, the Romanian car manufacturer, which produced the R12 under licence in the early seventies. In East Germany, where the company expected to sell 8,000 cars in 1990, it had already recruited 200 dealers. Exhibit 13.11 lists the models represented under each product class and the company's position in each market.

Product development

Renault was in the process of completely revamping its product line, starting in 1990 with the R5 replacement called the Clio. The total Clio project cost FF6.5 billion and took longer than expected (54 months) to complete due to the introduction of a new product development process using teams. However, subsequent projects were expected to take a far shorter period of time. Among Renault's other new product development projects were the R25 replacement (due in 1992) and the R21 replacement (due in 1993). Renault also planned to launch a micro sub-compact car (code-named X06) in 1994–1995 and was currently seeking a suitable country, with low labour costs, for its production. The company expected to replace its product line every six years.

Production

Through improved production methods, reduction of the workforce, and better component sourcing, the break-even volumes had been reduced from 2 million vehicles per year during the early 1980s to 1.5 million in 1989. Management's goal was to reduce this figure to 1.2 million in order to remain profitable through the economic downturns.

In the early 1980s, Renault had approximately 2000 component suppliers, but after 1986 the amount was reduced to 800, one of the lowest by European standards. Generally, no more than two sources per component were used. Renault management kept a keen eye on in-house component manufacturing units. If they were not profitable, management preferred to sell them off. However, the company's level of integration was still rather high at 60% value added to sales.

Renault management succeeded in reducing the workforce by 20% from 1984 to 1989. Improved assembly methods and just-in-time inventory management were instituted. Production capacity was increased by 24-hour work schedules rather than by constructing new assembly plants. As a result of these actions, the annual output of cars per worker increased from 10.9 in 1984 to 16.4 cars in 1989.

Of Renault's 44 plants, 23 were located in France; other production locations were in Spain, Belgium, Portugal, Yugoslavia, Turkey, several countries in South America and Southeast Asia.

Investment programme

Renault's investment programme was not entirely clear, mainly due to the company's significant debt load. In addition to the Skoda project, the French company set its sights on increasing capacity in Yugoslavia, Turkey and Iran. With new models launched on a six-year product replacement cycle, total product development and capital expenditures were expected to run about FF12–20 billion per year (excluding the Skoda project) or about 11% of sales (7% for capital expenditures and 3–4% for research and development). Its expenditure programme was likely to consume all of Renault's cash flow, leaving little opportunity for the company to reduce its still heavy debt load.

Renault's labour relations

Renault traditionally had been one of the French industry models of management and labour relations. The basic goal of the company was to maximize employment. As bankruptcy threatened in 1986, Renault management and the French government had to radically reform the company's objective from employment maximization to profit improvement. The six unions, including the largest, Communist-run CGT, played a non-interventionist role during the massive lay-offs, as they realized that the survival of the firm was at stake. However, once Renault had turned itself around, the unions, especially the CGT, became more vocal as more layoffs and plant closings were expected.

Skoda–Renault discussions before October 1990

Renault had had relatively little contact with the Czechoslovak automobile industry before 1989. Most of its efforts had been concentrated in Yugoslavia and Romania. In the spring of 1989, Renault was contacted by BAZ, a rear axle manufacturer located in Slovakia, in order to discuss the possibility of manufacturing light commercial vehicles. But once the Communist government fell and privatization legislation came into effect, any advantages Renault might have had fell apart. In May 1990, the CSFR government announced its plans to privatize both BAZ and Skoda. As a result, Renault sent a delegation both to the CSFR government and to Skoda. However, the delegation soon realized that they were not the only interested party. It turned out that Volkswagen had been there for several months already.

The Skoda project was led by Mr Serge Chaput of Renault's Department of International Projects. Joining Mr Chaput on the project team were Mr Jean Marc Lepeu, his supervisor, Mr Dominique Druart, his assistant, Mr Antoine Rousselin from finance, and Mr Rémy Hursault from engineering. Meetings with Skoda and the Czechoslovak government were scheduled to determine the feasibility of the project. Meanwhile, the same team was also looking at the feasibility of manufacturing vans in the BAZ plant despite the federal government's preference for car assembly.

During the negotiations, the Renault delegation was constantly frustrated by the number of government officials they had to deal with regarding both privatisations. Who were the actual owners of these companies? In May, they dealt with the officials of the Czechoslovak Federal Government; however, after the bipolarization of the country into the regional governments and the dissolution of the Federal Ministry of Industry, the Renault team had to start the discussions over again with the Czech Republic Ministries for Skoda and the Slovak Republic Ministries for BAZ. And, not all the ministries agreed with each other.

The Slovak officials reiterated the Federal Government's position – wanting BAZ to be a car assembly facility. After long internal discussions, the Renault team agreed that a small market such as Czechoslovakia would not be able to support two car makers. They dropped the BAZ deal and concentrated solely on Skoda.

After a rather complicated start, Serge Chaput and his team had learned who their negotiating partners would be. The Skoda management comprised Mr Petr Dedek, the General Director, Mr Ivan Bures, the Deputy General Director, Mr Zdenek Patocka, Director of Development, Mr Zdenek Beran, the Director of Finance and Mr Pavel Novacek, the Director of Personnel. The Czech government members involved in the process included Mr Frantisek Vlasak, the Deputy Prime Minister and Chairman of the Czech Economic Council, Mr Miroslav Gregr, the Minister of Industry, Mr Karel Dyba, Minister of Economic Development and Mr Tomas Jezek, Minister of Privatization, all with their various political leanings and personal agendas.

Renault's first proposal came out in July after a preliminary feasibility study of the Czech car plant and its suppliers. The proposal suggested that Skoda would be an excellent production site for the new mini sub-compact model – the X06 which Renault was developing. The X06 that the Renault team proposed would be an excellent vehicle for the East European market because it would be affordable. Only rough financial figures had been drawn up at the time.

After discussions with eight different car manufacturers, Skoda chose Renault and Volkswagen as the two final contenders. Larger delegations of Renault management were sent to Skoda and to the Czech government. For example, in September, Raymond Lévy, Renault's President, and Pehr Gyllenhammer, the President of Volvo, joined President François Mitterand and the Minister of Industry, Roger Fauroux, on a visit to Czechoslovakia. In his address to the Czech Federal Parliament, Mitterand hinted that he would support French industry, and he made repeated warnings about the potential dangers of German hegemony due to its reunification.

Both Skoda's management and its union officials were invited to Paris for discussions and plant tours. But, the Skoda union members did not always receive a very good reception. The first time the union representatives were invited to Paris, they were not allowed to see their French counterparts, CGT, CFDT and others. Since Renault was still going through some restructuring and had idle capacity in France, the Renault team realized the labour situation would not favour the Renault-Skoda partnership. The CGT would probably argue, as it had for many other cases, that any plant of a French firm outside the country meant fewer jobs in France and French workers had to be employed before foreign workers.

Renault's view of Skoda

At 9 am on October 8, 1990, Serge Chaput led the five-member Skoda project team into the conference room at the Renault headquarters in Boulogne-Billancourt. Joining the five-man team were members from personnel, marketing and corporate counsel.

Chaput started off the discussions. 'I just spoke with Zdenek Bakala of CSFB, and we are expected to be in Prague and Mlada Boleslav (home of Skoda) next week to present our final proposal. We are here today to review what we have and what we still need to do. By the end of the week, we will have to send the documents to Skoda and the Czech government.'

Lepeu added, 'I think we still have a very good chance to get the company, if we play our cards right. We have already encountered some resistance from CGT (the Communist-led union), and there have been some negative press reports which are simply unfounded. Most of the outside world believes we spent all our time in the halls of the Czech government, while Volkswagen spent all of its time in the company. We have to change this bias.'

Chaput said, 'First, I think we should review our company report on Skoda to see if everything is totally clear or if we have missed something.' Each member picked up his copy and turned to the front page.

The next section briefly describes the contents of that report.

Skoda Automobilovy Koncern

Skoda, originally a heavy machinery manufacturer, acquired Czechoslovakia's original car manufacturer, Laurin and Klement, at the end of World War I. Laurin, a mechanic, and Klement, a bookseller, started their company as a bicycle and later motorcycle manufacturer. In 1905, they introduced their first car, the Voituretta. Under the Skoda umbrella, the car manufacturer flourished; assembly line production methods were installed, and new models were introduced, some of which were to become internationally renowned. After World War II, under the Communist regime, Skoda was nationalized and split into two separate groups: ANZP (Automobile Plant State Enterprise, Mlada Boleslav), and the bigger heavy machinery operation.

Under state ownership, the car company continued to fare well and remained technologically competitive with Western car manufacturers despite its continuous lack of financial resources. Excellent engineering skills enabled the company to launch new models once every 8–9 years. In fact, in the early 1970s, Skoda was supposed to purchase a car design concept from Ital Design, but was blocked by the Soviets who feared that the new model would represent too much competition for their car, the Lada. The design was later purchased by Volkswagen and was used as the basis for Western Europe's best selling car, the Golf.

By 1989, it became clear to the Skoda management that their survival was on the line. Despite the company's introduction of the Skoda Favorit, which generally received good reviews in the West, the firm needed a constant injection of funds to modernize its facilities. The government reaped all gains from its export sales and taxed the company heavily on its profit. In return, the government gave investment capital back to Skoda according to its capital expenditure plan, but it was never enough. With the collapse of the central planning system, prospects did not look very promising. Joining a Western partner seemed like the only viable alternative. Skoda commissioned Price Waterhouse, the accounting firm, to help them in their search.[2]

Product development

Its newest (and only) model, the Favorit, was introduced in 1988 as a replacement for the Skoda 120/Coupé Rapid 136 which had been in production since 1976. The Favorit development programme was started in 1983 and took three and a half years until completion. Designed by the famous Italian firm, Bertone, equipped with front-wheel drive and MacPherson strut suspension, the Favorit is considered competitive with Western European models, receiving favourable product reviews. However, the engine – based on a 25-year old blueprint – badly needs to be upgraded, especially since it fails to meet the strict European emission standards without a severe loss in power and a large increase in cost. Any increase in price will jeopardize the company's low-cost competitive advantage.

More projects are underway in the 620-person research and development department at Mlada Boleslav, including a new engine range and a saloon, coupé, station wagon and pickup based on the Favorit design. However, lack of financial resources once more overshadows the projects.

As the discussion turned to Skoda's product development, Mr Hursault asked, 'What are we going to do with their research and development department if we still decide to go ahead with the X06? All the product development has taken place here. I feel that our first proposal was not acceptable to the Skoda management, despite the fact that they kept us in the running. We will have to come up with a better solution. This company has some strengths, and research and development is one of them. Maybe we should keep the Skoda brand name. At least it has a consumer franchise in Eastern Europe.'

Chaput, keenly aware of this issue, decided to note it down as a point for further discussion. But, time was running out, so a decision had to be made soon. After a few minutes of arguments for and against, the team went on . . .

---

[2] Refer to Exhibit 13.12 for Skoda's financial statements over the last five years.

Balance sheet	1985	1986	1987	1988	1989	1990E
Assets						
Cash	75	144	160	−316	205	290
Accounts receivable	1,417	1,617	1,829	3,013	3,249	4,100
Inventory	1,119	1,304	2,173	1,817	1,461	1,700
Current assets	2,611	3,065	4,162	4,514	4,915	6,100
Financial assets	68	229	1,176	934	325	250
Property plant and equip.	4,078	4,178	5,400	6,810	7,702	8,350
Total fixed assets	4,146	4,407	6,576	7,744	8,028	8,600
Total assets	6,757	7,472	10,738	12,258	12,943	14,700
Liabilities and capital						
Liabilities with foreign creditors/suppliers						
Credits	1,811	2,092	3,946	5,186	6,567	6,400
Accounts payable	501	767	1,158	2,074	1,420	2,600
Total foreign liabilties	2,312	2,859	5,104	7,260	7,987	9,000
Settlement with State budget	−903	−509	−196	−656	−516	−900
Capital						
Profits	926	523	31	−380	−727	0
Capital	4,422	4,599	5,799	6,034	6,199	6,600
Total liabilities and capital	6,757	7,472	10,738	12,258	12,943	14,700
Income statement						
Sales	8,083	8,047	7,705	7,825	9,921	12,800
Operating expenses:						
Material expenses	5,170	5,314	5,220	4,335	6,770	*9,500
Production costs	483	606	681	1,710	1,027	1,000
Depreciation	265	261	266	332	480	500
Wages and salaries	706	717	721	756	760	800
General and admin. costs	152	182	192	257	352	300
Total operating expenses	6,776	7,080	7,080	7,390	9,389	2,100
Operating income	1,307	967	625	435	534	700
Financial costs	260	332	488	691	901	900
Other income	23	35	39	10	6	600
Income before tax	1,070	670	176	−246	−363	400
Tax	144	147	145	134	364	400
Net income	926	523	31	−380	−727	0
Other financial information						
Capital expenditures	186	441	2,482	1,787	747	900
Number of employees	20,069	20,053	19,835	20,242	20,698	19,800
Unit sales	176,070	177,802	168,059	158,150	183,139	186,700

* Note: Material expenses had been subsidized by about 100%. However, removing all the tax burdens on component supply, Skoda management estimated 38% of the material costs were due to inefficiencies, and unnecessary value added taxes.

Exhibit 13.12 *Skoda's Financial Statements, 1985–1990 (millions of Kcs)*

Component supply

The Skoda Favorit consists of 2000 components, of which 970 are manufactured in-house. The other 1000 components are furnished by approximately 200 suppliers. Of the 200, twenty come from the West and the rest from the state-owned component suppliers.

The typical state-owned component supplier is a monopoly. But, in the central planning economy, it could not abuse its powers; the government dictated its selling price and its quantity of supply. Because the prices were often artificially low, the supplier had to use lower quality raw materials. In this type of planned system, Skoda was virtually powerless to improve the quality and/or quantity of its components. As a result, the company resorted to manufacturing its own components, which explains its current high level of vertical integration of just under 50%.

It is only a matter of time before a liberalized pricing system will be introduced. As a result, Skoda will probably see its component supply prices double. In addition, many of the suppliers' statutes already have been changed; thus, they have to operate as independent concerns facing the same problem as Skoda – lack of funds for modernization.

Mr Chaput reported on the supplier situation, 'Well, there will have to be a drastic increase in the quality offered if all the suppliers are going to remain. But, given the Czech people's willingness to work and their engineering skills, I think they can do it. Our suppliers were reasonably impressed, especially with the weapons plants that want to become automotive suppliers. How easy it will be to retool their plants is another question . . . .'

Production

Skoda's operations, centred in Mlada Boleslav, have another four smaller plants in Czechoslovakia. The Mlada Boleslav operations, the largest of the Skoda facilities, includes its main assembly plant, the engine plant, an aluminium and cast iron foundry, a forge, a tool shop for spare parts, and a research and development centre. The two smaller operations, Vrchlabi and Kvasiny, concentrate on the assembly of special Favorit (i.e. those which meet emission standards for Western markets.) The fourth plant is a repair centre and a components facility. Each factory site has a great deal of excess land for expansion in the future.

The production process starts with Skoda's cast iron foundry (18,000 tons/year) for the production of the engine blocks and an aluminium foundry for the production of components (6600 tons/year). All car body panels are produced in the press shop which is equipped with antiquated 20-year-old machinery. These parts are then welded together by 104 newly installed Kuka robots before the finished car bodies enter the 20-year-old paint shop. In the past, Skoda used low-paid prisoners to work in its paint and press shops. However, when Vaclav Havel decreed that prisoners be liberated, Skoda was forced first to find new workers and eventually to modernize its press and paint shops. If both the press and paint shop bottlenecks were replaced by new processes (at an estimated cost of FF5.1 billion) the capacity of the plant would jump from 180,000 cars to 230,000–250,000. From the paint shop, cars move to the assembly line where the various components (electronics, steering, engines, columns, brakes, axles, seats and so on) are mounted. Once completed, the cars are put through a testing procedure. More than 70% of the cars have a small defect of some sort. A large repair centre full of cars is at the end of the assembly line where these defects are fixed.

Many of the members started to chat during Skoda's summary of the production facilities. Shaking his head Mr Hursault remarked, 'What a mix of new and old. Just behind the Kuka robots are these loud old stamping machines. The working conditions

Export Sales in Convertible Currency

Legend:
- Others (9,000)
- Netherlands (900)
- Malta (1000)
- Yugoslavia (1,200)
- France (1,200)
- Italy (1,800)
- Denmark (1,900)
- Belgium (2,100)
- Greece (2,100)
- Poland (3,700)
- Turkey (4,100)
- England (9,400)
- Germany (12,300)

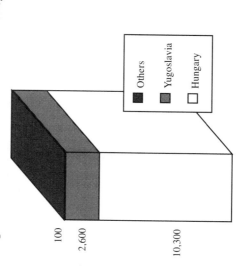

Distribution of Skoda's Sales

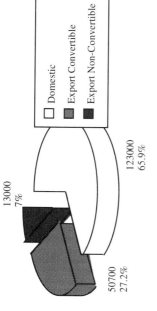

Legend:
- Domestic
- Export Convertible
- Export Non-Convertible

13000
7%

123000
65.9%

50700
27.2%

Export Sales in Non-Convertible Currency

Legend:
- Others
- Yugoslavia
- Hungary

100

2,600

10,300

Exhibit 13.13 *Skoda's sales, 1989–1990*

are appalling. The foundries and the spare parts factory are the same. Do you remember the oil on the ground? All these things would have to be cleaned up . . . .'

Skoda is heavily overmanned by West European standards. Its annual output of 8.73 cars per employee is much lower than the average 13 cars per employee in Western Europe. However, the labour costs are estimated at Kcs4500 per car (10% of cost price versus 25% for Western car manufacturers). Two thousand of the production employees, Cuban and Vietnamese guest workers, are expected to leave for political reasons by the end of 1992. The rest of the 11,600 production workers are expected to be kept, given the company's plans to increase output over the next five years from its present 180,000 per year to 400,000.

'There's no way we can guarantee employment of all 21,000 workers,' said the Director of Personnel. 'Just no way. Given that their component supply prices could increase by 100%, Skoda's prices will have to increase radically. And, there is no assurance that demand will continue in Czechoslovakia. With any large price increase, demand could plummet. Then, what do we do with the employees?'

The total cost of increasing the capacity to 400,000 from the 250,000 (after the improvement of the paint and press shops) is estimated at FF7.1 billion.

Sales and distribution

Skoda, unlike many other European car manufacturers, has very little control over the marketing and distribution of its cars. For both the domestic and export markets, the company sells most of its cars at a 'wholesale' price of Kcs49,855 to state-run distribution agencies. A few cars are also sold through Skoda's 12 retail outlets in Czechoslovakia.[3]

Domestic sales

For the mass market, Skoda sells its cars to the state-run distribution company, Mototechna, which has a network of 'sales' offices around the country. Skoda Favorits are sold for Kcs85,000 and the profit on each sale is shared between the government and Mototechna. Since demand consistently exceeds supply, customers wait as much as two years for their cars. No market research, product positioning, advertising and promotions are carried out, as Skodas are simply produced to fill these waiting lists.[4] Skoda's other clients comprised government agencies, the police force, education, health and defence departments. But, once again, demand outstripped supply.

Skoda's management is expecting the domestic distribution situation to change dramatically. They would like to see a new sales network consisting of private agents be established and prices freely set (within a certain limit agreed on by Skoda). Management foresees a gradual increase in annual sales in Czechoslovakia from 120,000 to 150–180,000 cars.

Mr. Lepeu provided his views. 'We have to create a whole new mentality, which will require training. We need to teach them the basics of sales and marketing, and this is not going to happen overnight . . . .' He continued on another topic. 'The Czechs seem to be less enthusiastic about our proposal than Volkswagen's. It may be because of the models. I think Volkswagen wants to use Skoda to produce a modified version of its

---

[3] For a breakdown of Skoda's sales in 1989 and 1990, refer to Exhibit 13.13.
[4] Refer to Exhibit 13.14 for a breakdown of sales of different car models in Czechoslovakia from 1985.

	1985	1986	1987	1988	1989
Total new registrations	133,384	137,270	143,186	144,535	162,983
Skoda	110,107	107,220	93,751	96,859	114,261
Tatra Limousines	235	346	352	400	470
BAZ	738	554	53	–	–
Imports	22,304	29,150	49,030	47,276	48,252
Poland	n/a	2,400	n/a	3,191	3,031
USSR	13,347	15,588	12,461	10,733	14,410
Romania	4,371	5,060	9,023	15,220	17,646
East Germany	1,976	–	–	–	–
Italy	1,906	599	652	405	631
France	8	351	674	704	478
Germany	n/a	n/a	127	345	244
Korea	–	–	–	–	3,000
Others	696	5,152	26,080	16,668	8,798

Source: Czechoslovakia Automotive Industry Statistics.

Exhibit 13.14 *Evolution of car sales in Czechoslovakia*

Golf in 1995 or 1996, which is larger than our X06 model. But, I still believe in the X06 proposal. Eastern Europe is in the same development stage that Europe was in during the 1950s and 1960s. Small, affordable cars – like the Fiat 127, VW Beetle, the R4 and the 2CV – were the most popular cars in those days. Although today this segment is small in Europe (at 4% market share), it will probably account for the largest segment in Eastern Europe.'

Export sales

Skoda's management has very little control over the sales of its cars outside Czechoslovakia, which are sold to the trade organization, Motokov. (Skoda cars represent approximately 15% of Motokov's $2 billion in sales.) All the Skoda overseas offices are part of this trade organization. The Skoda Favorit, positioned as a 'small, economical family car', has enjoyed its greatest success in Western European markets such as the UK, Germany and Scandinavia. Proceeds from exports of Skoda Favorits, sold for Kcs131,590 each, are kept by Motokov and the government.

Jean Marc Lepeu continued, 'If we carry the Skoda name, I think we should build up a separate sales and distribution network. Otherwise, the image of the car may water down the image of Renault . . . .'

Organisation

Of Skoda's 21,000 employees, 11,600 are production workers; 4100 are technical and administrative staff, and 5300 are considered as 'overhead'. Like many state-run organizations in Czechoslovakia, Skoda's organization is top heavy with its seven levels of decision-making. The new Skoda company will probably go through a severe internal restructuring to improve organizational efficiency.[5]

[5] Refer to Exhibit 13.15 for the organization chart of Skoda.

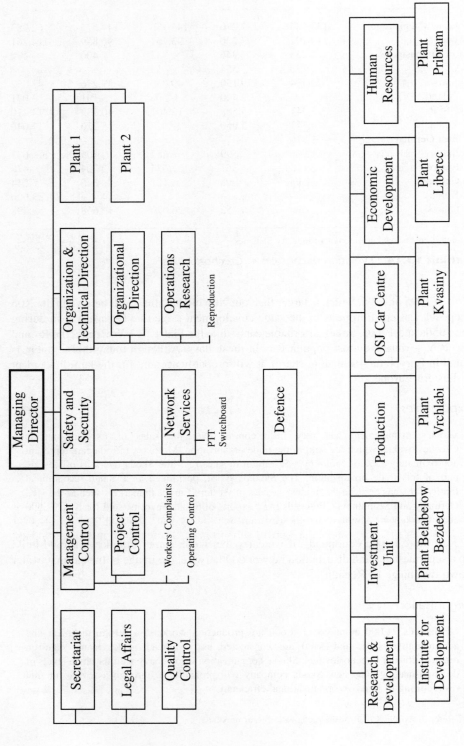

Exhibit 13.15 *Skoda organization chart*

Social burden

A decreasing portion – from 14% in 1985 to 7% in 1990 – of the company's fixed assets are allocated to the social care of its employees. In comparison to its Western European counterparts, this amount is simply too high. Skoda offers its workers such social benefits and facilities as restaurants, housing and accommodation, recreation and sports centres, schools, day care and health care possibilities. Skoda's management is expected to eliminate some of its costly social programmes in order to be more in line with the Western car manufacturers.

The environment problem

Although the Skoda management is concerned about the company environmental effects, financial shortages prevented them from doing anything about it. No study has yet been conducted to assess the company's total damage to the environment; thus, the management is unsure how much it would cost. However, as a first step, plans are underway to reduce both the water and air pollution from the plants in Mlada Boleslav, Vrchlabi, and Kvasiny.

Serge Chaput commented on the environmental problem, 'I don't think I want to know how much oil has seeped from the plant floor into the ground. The clean-up will cost a great deal.'

Valuation

How much is Skoda actually worth? Both a book value estimate or a discounted cash flow calculation are among the methods available to value Skoda. However, book value is simply a restatement of assets and a discounted cash flow depends largely on the assumptions. Price Waterhouse estimated that constructing a greenfield plant capable of producing 300,000 cars per year would cost approximately FF19 billion. Using this figure as a benchmark, we tallied up Skoda's useful assets and came to a figure close to FF4725 million.

At this point, Antoine Rosselin spoke up, 'I have also provided a discounted cash flow analysis of Skoda. But, as you can see, I have assumed a great deal, and my team had a rather difficult time trying to arrive at a discount rate for a country that does not have a convertible currency. As you can also see, we came up with a preliminary value based on Skoda's assets. I think our best approach would be to determine how much we are willing to pay above this FF4725 billion. It depends on how much top management wants to have this deal. It's clear that Dr Carl Hahn is backing the deal for Volkswagen. Have we got that kind of support here? There is no doubt this company is and could be very profitable.'

Skoda's negotiating position

1 Investments to increase production of the Favorit in the Mlada Boleslav plant from 180,000 in 1990 to 350,000–400,000 per year by the year 2000.
2 Immediate access to engine production know-how to upgrade the current series used in the Favorit model (particularly with respect to the emission standards set in Western Europe). In the longer term, Skoda management wants the joint venture partner to construct a new engine plant with an annual capacity of 500,000 units. Some of this output would then supply the partner's other models. The costs of a new engine plant run around FF8.4 billion.
3 Retention of the Skoda brand name for new models.

4 Retention of the in-house research and development for the design of new Skoda models.
5 Access to the partner's marketing and sales network outside of Czechoslovakia.
6 Czech government majority ownership (subject to change).
7 Job security for Skoda's 21,000 employees (subject to change).
8 Total investments are expected to be around FF20.6 billion or KCs59 billion.

The Skoda debt is expected to be retired by the government in order to sweeten the deal. Some other issues remain unclear: the environmental liability, the percentage ownership in the joint venture, the management of the joint venture, the tax treatment, and the final purchase price.

The members of the Renault team felt that the Skoda team was trying to be as objective as possible with both teams, despite some of the difficulties Skoda had had with Renault so far.

Renault's view of the Czech government position

After discussing Skoda's position, the group moved to the position of the government. The Czech government was more interested in the health of the overall automobile industry and region's economic situation than in the company *per se*. The Renault team, therefore, had to consider the members' political leanings, the instability of the privatization programme and their desire to minimize unemployment.

The government continued to argue about the speed of the privatization programme. Some argued that privatization should only take place after introducing realistic prices and a clear tax and accounting system so that assets could be properly valued. If these assets were sold off quickly, then only the government bureaucrats or the foreigners making purchases would benefit. Despite the reluctance of these party members, Mr Klaus, Minister of Finance, had stormed ahead in May 1990 with preliminary privatization legislation – such as the Joint Venture and Joint Stock Company Acts. Although the acts spelled out many of the issues concerning foreign partners such as tax treatment, repatriation of funds, management, and legal forms, certain items remained ambiguous (see Annex). Other economic measures, such as small-scale privatization, price liberalization and internal convertibility, were planned for the following January.

Fortunately for the Renault team, each member in the government negotiating team supported the privatization of Skoda. Mr Vlasak, the Deputy Prime Minister, advised Prime Minister Petr Pitthard on the economic issues. It was understood that he was one of the developers of the privatization programme. He was considered slightly right of centre and believed in the use of foreign capital. He was considered the most influential on the team and probably wanted a deal since he was about to retire. Mr Jezek had been recently appointed to lead the newly formed Ministry of Privatization, and he was considered slightly right of centre. Mr Dyba, the Minister of Economic Development and a disciple of Mr Klaus, the radical Czechoslovak Finance Minister, was probably the farthest right in his political leanings. Before entering the political arena, Mr Gregr, the Minister of Industry, had been a director of a forklift company, where he tried to manage the company in a Western fashion. He was considered conservative right but was not a great friend of foreign capital.

Czechoslovakia's unemployment had increased rapidly after the government's recent decision to ban the export of arms, which had led to the closing of several weapons plants. In an attempt to keep future unemployment as low as possible, the Czech and Slovak governments had started to promote the automobile industry as a possible solution. By increasing automobile and truck production, the governments reasoned, many jobs would be kept and possibly even created, not only in the automobile companies but also in the component supply network. Then, many of the weapons manufacturers, searching for ways to survive, could produce automotive components. It seemed to the French team that the government was looking for an answer to all its problems at once.

One statement by Serge Chaput summed up the issues. 'From my talks with Mr Vlasak, the political situation will be less important than we thought. Mr Vlasak repeated that the company was in control of the discussions and that they, along with CSFB, would consult the government about the prospective partner. The government will step in and intervene only if the two proposals are similar . . ..'

Renault's view of Volkswagen

The meeting closed so that everyone could resume their daily schedules. They were expected to return on the following morning. Serge Chaput, after having lunch with some of the team members, went back to his office. The documents on Volkswagen that he had requested on the previous day lay on his desk. The Manager of Competitive Intelligence had put together numerous press articles and background information on Volkswagen for Chaput's perusal. Chaput, in an effort to anticipate the contents of Volkswagen's proposal, also wanted to find weaknesses that he could show Skoda and the Czech government.

The following section provides some excerpts from the document on Volkswagen.

Volkswagen

Volkswagen was founded in 1937 by Ferdinand Porsche at the request of the German government. Backed by the National Socialist government, Porsche, a Czech, designed an odd-looking little car around his air-cooled rear mounted engine which would be affordable to the average German worker . . . .

Chaput, noting the point that Ferdinand Porsche was a Czech, thought to himself, 'The historical links are deep. Even Dr. Carl Hahn's grandfather was a Czech.' He decided to read on, skimming over the first part.

... In 1990, Volkswagen is clearly the winner in the long race for leadership of the European market. However, the gap between VW and the next company, Fiat, is widening as demand in unified Germany, Volkswagen's largest market, begins to soar. The company's next aim is to surpass Ford and Toyota and become the second largest car company worldwide.[6]

Organization

Volkswagen is governed in accordance with the 1976 co-determination law – by a Managing Board and a Supervisory Board. The Managing Board, which sets the corporate strategy, is comprised of the managing director and the heads of nine departments. The Supervisory Board, consisting of an equal number of shareholders and labour representatives, allocates the company's finances (approves acquisitions and divestitures) and determines overall employment levels.

---

[6] Refer to Exhibit 13.16 for the financial statements of the Volkswagen for the past five years.

Balance Sheet	1985	1986	1987	1988	1989	1990E
Assets						
Cash	3,960	8,553	8,153	10,809	9,929	
Investments	4,326	364	426	488	2,360	
Accounts receivable	7,157	8,675	9,403	11,848	14,472	
Inventories	6,348	6,802	6,618	6,506	7,301	
Current assets	21,971	24,394	24,600	29,651	34,062	38,000
Leasing and rental	3,717	4,106	4,919	5,427	5,561	
Financial	574	1,099	1,125	1,304	1,621	
Intangible	–	2	29	76	134	
Property, plant and equip.	8,740	12,111	13,406	13,836	15,493	
Fixed assets	13,031	17,318	19,479	20,643	22,809	25,000
Total assets	34,822	41,712	44,061	50,294	56,871	63,000
Liabilities and shareholder's equity						
Current liabilities	10,569	12,451	13,043	15,398	17,605	21,000
Long-term liabilities						
Payable 1–5 years	1,291	1,456	1,999	2,121	3,289	3,500
Payable > 5 years	947	1,344	1,217	1,929	1,934	1,800
Other liabilities	14,372	14,514	14,864	17,090	19,107	20,000
of which taxes	n/a	992	925	1,358	2,001	
of which pensions	5,029	5,294	5,889	6,314	6,652	
Shareholder's equity	7,395	11,947	12,938	13,756	14,936	16,700
Total liabilities and equity	34,822	41,712	44,061	50,294	56,871	63,000
Income Statement						
Sales	52,709	52,794	54,635	59,221	65,352	68,000
Cost of sales	n/a	46,746	48,526	51,314	56,196	62,000
Gross profit	n/a	6,048	6,109	7,907	9,156	6,000
Selling and distribution	n/a	3,905	3,980	4,662	5,203	5,300
General and administrative	n/a	1,475	1,518	1,659	1,949	2,000
Other costs	n/a	1,930	2,232	2,780	3,524	2,500
Other operating income	n/a	2,562	3,163	2,817	3,733	5,000
Operating earnings	n/a	1,300	1,542	1,623	2,213	1,200
Interest expense	1,449	1,130	1,446	841	1,608	1,400
Financial income	1,654	1,398	1,657	1,456	2,607	2,600
Other Profit/Loss	n/a	(446)	(586)	(102)	(225)	
Earnings before tax	2,720	1,122	1,167	2,136	2,987	2,400
Tax	1,993	542	569	1,356	1,949	
Net earnings	596	580	598	780	1,038	
Other financial information						
Cost of materials	26,623	28,655	31,331	32,888	32,533	40,000
Labour cost	13,913	14,747	15,192	15,144	16,107	17,000
Depreciation	4,631	2,950	4,558	4,751	5,234	
Cash flow	5,227	3,530	5,156	5,530	6,273	
Number of employees	259,000	276,000	260,000	252,000	251,000	260,000
Capital investments	3,388	6,371	4,592	4,251	5,606	5,400
Vehicle sales (000 units)	2,398	2,758	2,774	2,854	2,941	3,000

* Note that Volkswagen's income is, on average, 77% of income reported in US accounting standards (due to the differences in depreciation.)

Exhibit 13.16 *Volkswagen's Financial Statements, 1985–1989 (millions of DM)*

Product/market strategy

Volkswagen manufactures a full range of automobiles, from mini sub-compacts to full-sized luxury cars, under three marques – Volkswagen, Audi and SEAT. Its main range, manufactured under the Volkswagen label, consists of: the Polo, its smallest and most economical car; the Golf, its best seller; the Jetta; the Passat, its full-sized model; and the Corrado, its sports car. The luxury range of vehicles are covered by the subsidiary, Audi. VW's Spanish subsidiary, SEAT, acquired in 1986, also produces a range of lower-end cars under its own name.

Volkswagen dominates the German market and leads in Spain, Mexico, Brazil and China. In France, Italy, Japan and Scandinavia, the company enjoys a leading importer position. The USA has proven to be a disappointment for the company, whose status has declined from being the leading importer in 1980 to an 'also ran' with a modest 1.5% market share.

In Eastern Europe, Volkswagen has been slowly building up its presence with car production in Yugoslavia and engine production in East Germany. After the fall of the Berlin Wall, Volkswagen quickly moved into East Germany, taking over the old Zwickau plant which produces the Trabant.[7]

Product class	Volkswagen	Audi	SEAT
Sub-Compact	Polo	n/a	Marbella
Compact	Golf	n/a	Ibiza
Mid-Size	Jetta	n/a	Malaga/Toledo
Full-Size	Passat	Audi 80	n/a
Luxury	n/a	Audi 90, 100, 200	n/a
Breaks	Passat	Audi Quattro	n/a
Minivans	Vanagon	n/a	n/a
Sports	Golf GTI	Audi Quattro	n/a
	Corrado	n/a	n/a
	Scirocco	n/a	n/a

Country	1985	1986	1987	1988	1989	Position in 1989
Europe	14.5%	14.7%	15.0%	14.9%	15.0%	#1
Germany	28.8%	28.8%	29.5%	28.9%	27.5%	#1
France	4.9%	4.8%	8.6%	9.2%	10.3%	#3
UK	5.7%	6.1%	5.8%	6.0%	6.2%	#5
Italy	7.2%	7.5%	12.3%	12.5%	12.9%	#2
Spain	n/a	20.1%	20.2%	19.9%	20.3%	#2
USA	2.5%	2.3%	2.2%	1.8%	1.5%	#11
Canada	n/a	n/a	3.9%	3.4%	2.9%	#6
Brazil	n/a	41.5%	36.8%	39.1%	37.4%	#1
Argentina	n/a	16.0%	11.9%	11.5%	10.2%	#5
Mexico	31.5%	34.1%	32.8%	23.7%	27.9%	#1
Japan	n/a	n/a	0.9%	1.1%	1.1%	#1 imp.

Exhibit 13.17 *Volkswagen's product portfolio and position in selective markets*

[7] Refer to Exhibit 13.17 for a list of the models represented under each product class and the company's position in each market.

Product development

Developing products (including engines) has become a delicate balance between obtaining economies of scale on the one hand and retaining the individual marques' characteristics on the other. For example, in 1990, both Volkswagen and Audi launched 6-cylinder engines for their separate car models. In an attempt to obtain economies of scale, however, the new SEAT Toledo has used the same underbody as the Volkswagen Jetta.

New models are coming on stream in 1991, including a revamped Polo, the third generation Golf, and Jetta, all of which are critical to the VW Group. A sporty version of the Golf is expected for 1993 and a new Passat is scheduled for 1996. Supermini cars are also due from a SEAT–Volkswagen–Ford cooperation project.

Production

Volkswagen relies on a large number of direct suppliers (both in-house and externally). A consulting study conducted in January 1990 revealed that Volkswagen turned to 1760 suppliers, while the average number used in Europe was about 1400. In addition, Volkswagen's level of vertical integration is one of the highest in the industry, with value added/sales at an estimated 60%.

Volkswagen is a high-cost manufacturer in comparison to its European rivals. Annual output of 11.6 cars per employee falls short of the European average of 13. Material and labour costs are too high and cause concern not only to management but also to the investment community. Material costs/sales are approximately 5% more than the European average, and labour costs/sales are higher because of the country's elevated wage rates. VW management has responded to these high-cost problems by increasing automation, reducing its workforce through attrition rather than by lay-offs, and increasing production outside its high-cost German base. In spite of objections from Germany's strong IG Metall union, capacity expansions are being planned for lower wage countries such as Spain, Mexico, China, East Germany, Portugal and Yugoslavia.

'If there were a downturn in Germany, Volkswagen would suffer – especially with its union,' Chaput thought. 'They are such a high-cost producer, but they somehow still manage to create demand for their products.'

Investment programme

Volkswagen is about to embark on a DM37 billion (FF125 billion) product development, plant modernization and capacity expansion plan over the next five years which is causing concern in the investment community. This programme will be financed by cash flow, a DM2.5 billion (FF8.5 billion) line of credit from worldwide banks, and by investment grants from the European Community. Investors are concerned that Volkswagen will become overextended because of this ambitious expansion. Any increase in debt, they feel, will severely affect the already meagre bottom line.[8]

'We must point this out to the Czechs,' thought Chaput. 'How will they manage to pay for all this capacity expansion?'

Volkswagen's acquisition of SEAT

In 1986, Volkswagen was asked by the Spanish government to take a majority stake in SEAT. The Spanish car manufacturer, which had already produced Volkswagen cars under licence, was suffering from heavy losses that the government could no longer afford to

---

[8] Refer to Exhibit 13.18 for the 5-year investment plan.

	1991E	1992E	1993E	1994E	1995E	Total
VW Germany	3,470	3,600	3,200	2,830	2,860	15,960
of which						
VW Golf/Jetta						1,000
VW Polo						1,500
People Carrier						3,500
Others						2,000
SEAT	2,807	2,622	1,772	846	415	8,462
Audi	1,233	1,008	1,147	996	783	5,167
Mosel Plant (E. Germany)	160	1,479	1,628	335	10	3,612
Autolatina	304	304	222	219	259	1,308
VW Brussels	253	206	158	147	89	853
VW de Mexico	342	336	230	181	177	1,266
VW of South Africa	199	145	81	71	51	547
Total	8,768	9,700	8,438	5,625	4,644	37,175

Source: Ward's Automotive International, 1992.

Exhibit 13.18 *Volkswagen's investment plan, 1990–1994 (millions of DM)*

cover. Volkswagen, interested in the deal, saw SEAT as an excellent production site for its sub-compact, the Polo. However, by moving the model production to Spain, the company was likely to face opposition from its union at home.

Volkswagen agreed to take a 50% stake in SEAT, which was later increased to 100% in 1990 for a total of FF4.3 billion. In turn, the Spanish government agreed to retire the company's debt and to provide a cash infusion of FF817 million. SEAT increased production capacity of its own marque within the Volkswagen Group, reduced its workforce, purchased components from the group to save on costs and started new development programmes. By 1988, after 11 years of losses, SEAT became profitable, much to the delight of its owners.

'This will be Volkswagen's big drawing card,' Chaput realized. 'Renault cannot relate the same type of success story. We will have to build on our Volvo alliance instead.'

Volkswagen's relationship with labour

The German co-determination system attempts to promote cooperation rather than confrontation between management/shareholders and the workforce who are both equally represented on the Supervisory Board. In the case of Volkswagen, non-confrontation is so important that often divisive issues are avoided rather than resolved. When reduction of the workforce is necessary, the management practises only non-coercive methods such as early retirement and increased automation, rather than the plant shutdowns and forced lay-offs frequently used in other companies. When VW proposes to increase its production abroad, IG Metall agrees only if its local levels of employment are maintained.

The potential deal with Skoda does not pose a substantial problem for the powerful German union, IG Metall. German plants are at full capacity struggling to meet the surge in demand resulting from the recent unification of East and West Germany.

Skoda–Volkswagen discussions before October 1990

Volkswagen's initial contacts with Skoda began in 1986 when the Czech company was looking for a Western partner to co-develop its new engine range. Although no partnership agreement was ever concluded, the Volkswagen management got to know their Skoda counterparts. Discussions with Volkswagen were not resumed until 1989 when talks of the new engine began again. From then on, consultations with Volkswagen intensified. Dr Carl Hahn, who is also part Czech, visited the company shortly after the Velvet Revolution. By the time our team arrived, it was apparent that the Volkswagen team had been at Skoda for some time.

Chaput reflected, 'We have spent about as much time at Skoda as Volkswagen has, but the general feeling is that Volkswagen was at the company much more and that we spent more time in the government halls. We have to change this bias.'

Implications for Renault

Volkswagen is likely to treat Skoda as another brand alongside Volkswagen, Audi and Seat. The company already has the advantage of having successfully restructured SEAT, a company which was in similar circumstances in 1986. Under the VW proposal, the production of a slightly modified car would continue with a new jointly developed model to be introduced later.

If Volkswagen were to acquire Skoda, the company could reduce its cost base significantly and increase its already widening lead in Europe. With its Skoda base, Volkswagen could bid for leadership in the Central and Eastern European automobile markets.

Renault's negotiating position

After reading the Volkswagen document, Chaput jotted down a few notes. There was still a lot to go over before the team could consolidate its position, answering several difficult questions concerning the joint venture:

1 What will Renault's highest offer price be?
2 What will be the percentage of ownership?
3 What management positions should be held by the French?
4 Which model should be produced?
5 Should the Skoda brand name be kept?
6 What should the investment plan be and how will it be financed?
7 Job security?
8 Should there be separate marketing and sales networks?
9 Should there be a separate R&D department?
10 What should be done about the environmental liability?
11 How could the funds be repatriated?

For the financial aspects of the joint venture, the Renault team had to determine a range that they could accept in the negotiations.

Annex: Elements of the Czechoslovakia Joint Venture Act

Who can participate: Any organization in Czechoslovakia and on the western side, legal entities and organizations.

Authorization: should be addressed to the Federal Ministry of Finance which will act in agreement with the Ministry of Finance, Prices and Wages from the Republics. (Authorization had since changed to the Republican Ministry of Industry.)

Participation in the Joint Venture: Western companies can own up to 100% of the company established in Czechoslovakia.

Autonomy: Joint ventures will not be subject to any production targets.

Reserve Fund: No less than 5% of the profit from the joint venture, after payment of all taxes, could be allocated to the reserve fund until the minimum amount is reached: 10% of the equity.

Taxes: Income tax amounts to approximately 40%.
　　　　Wages tax amounts to 50% of the total wages paid.
　　　　Tax on dividends is at 25%.
The Federal Ministry of Finance is authorized to grant tax holidays which could not exceed two years.

Foreign Exchange: Accounts with a foreign bank may be opened only when authorized by the State Bank of Czechoslovakia. Loans from foreign banks also require authorization from the State Bank. Thirty per cent of the hard currency earnings must be held at a Czechoslovak bank.

Profit Transfer: Any foreign shareholder may transfer their hard currency income to other countries as long as the joint venture has the necessary hard currency reserves. It is not clear for the repatriation of domestic currency income.

Management Structure: There are no restrictions on the nationality or structure of the directors of the joint venture.

14

Inflation's impact on financial policies

Case 14.1 An ethical problem?

This exercise was prepared by Professor Werner Ketelhöhn and revised by Research Associate Barbara Robins, as a basis for class discussion rather than to illustrate either effective of ineffective handling of a business situation.

Gary Forsyth was the department head for a multinational company in charge of the investment staff in Latin America. He had just received another memo from David Anderson, analyst in charge of Nicaragua, asking for a meeting to discuss the situation in Nicaragua.

For some time David had been informing him on the irregularities of several accounts which the Nicaraguan branch had with its Central American distributors (Exhibits 14.1 and 14.2). On previous occasions, Gary's boss had said that he would personally attend to the problem, and that patience was called for because the state of war in Nicaragua made it a special case.

Gary was sure that David was going to ask for authorization to go to Nicaragua to clarify the situation with the local associate and manager, and he wasn't sure how to respond to the request.

	1976	%	1977	%	1978	%	1979	%
Assets								
Cash and banks	1,399,559	5.9	1,452,077	4.9	133,374	0.3	1,335,604	2.6
Cash	5							
Petty cash	18,290		98,163		113,172		275,284	
Local banks	218,787		27,400		30,130		30,575	
Foreign banks	1,162,173		91,604		36,776		571,819	
Other national deposits	304		1,234,282		(121,534)		367,968	
			629		74,831		89,958	
Accounts receivable	3,784,842	16.1	4,526,647	15.2	10,671,639	27.7	21,555,093	41.65
Local clients	1,591,035		2,013,175		2,222,016		3,478,456	
Foreign clients**	2,076,239		2,430,470		5,869,250		12,394,860	
Other debtors	118,164		99,664		1,838,061		5,172,523	
Advance payment to emp. and func.	2,300		2,137		2,950		70,670	
Loan to emp. and func.	183,134		131,201		1,182,934		1,856,465	
Retained taxes	–				188,306		102,603	
Cheques protested					–		2,500	
	3,970,872		4,676,647		11,303,517		23,078,078	
Reserve for bad accounts	(186,030)		(150,000)		(631,878)		(1,522,985)	
Inventories	4,180,054	17.7	8,638,842	29.1	8,399,276	21.8	4,609,985	8.9
Raw material	929,720		3,729,057		1,851,729		1,030,785	
Work in process	173,923		193,499		597,561		311,297	
Finished goods	1,992,853		2,760,656		3,863,662		1,255,779	
Other merchandise	3,805		3,240		–		–	
Rework and accessories	1,032,048		1,025,437		1,613,719		2,632,661	
Imports in transit	100,705		979,953		1,076,348		240,373	
	4,233,054		8,691,842		9,003,020		5,470,895	
Estimate of obsolete inventory	(53,000)		(53,000)		(603,743)		(890,910)	
Prepaid expenses	136,001	0.6	46,041	0.2	159,857	0.4	2,286,915	4.4
Insurance (property, machinery and equipment)	127,883		25,744		64,027		269,651	
Others	8,178		20,297		95,830		2,017,264	
Total assets	9,500,455	40.3	14,663,607	49.4	19,230,772	49.9	29,974,978	57.9

	1976	%	1977	%	1978	%	1979	%
Investments	—	—	427,566	1.4	1,960,854	5.0	1,573,584	3.0
Goodwill	—		—		—		—	
Shares	—		10,000		400,000		400,000	
Affiliated companies**	—		417,566		1,560,854		1,173,584	
Reserve for devaluation of investments	—	—	—	—	—	—	—	—
Property, machinery and equipment	13,075,083	55.5	13,882,023	46.8	15,938,220	41.3	15,989,240	30.9
Land	670,375		749,710		749,710		749,710	
Buildings	2,698,911		4,184,586		4,185,032		4,975,034	
Machinery and production equipment	10,199,171		10,592,629		13,067,902		14,450,800	
Furnishings and office equipment	418,230		941,167		1,091,558		937,050	
Other goods	201,712		234,715		295,186		306,773	
Moving equipment	488,006		639,371		1,074,204		1,018,256	
Construction-in-process	352,838		—		561,280		173,063	
Fixed assets-in-transit	618,493		290,591		—		3,147	
	15,647,737		17,632,770		21,024,872		22,613,833	
Accumulated depreciation	(2,572,654)		(3,750,747)		(5,086,652)		(6,624,593)	
Deferred Assets	880,435	3.7	639,827	2.2	417,251	1.1	—	—
Organizational expenses	39,141		34,432		17,457		—	
Other	11,822		—		—		—	
Installation expenses	—		—		—		—	
Research and projects	—		10,450		10,450		—	
Application expenses	829,472		594,945		389,344		—	
Other assets	126,558	0.5	61,650	0.2	883,742	2.3	4,400,270	8.5
Machinery and equipment not in use	—		24.690		30,115		20,319	
Advertising	29,335		27,534		67,228		421,138	
Guaranteed deposits	5,991		9,426		46,887		50,388	
Anticipated dividends	91,232		—		739,512		3,908,426	
Total assets	23,582,531	100	29,674,672	100	36,564,214	100	51,750,691	100

Liabilities							
Short-term liabilities	11,095,694	47.0	16,034,206	54.0	16,387,586	42.5	29,871,960	57.7
Bank loans	4,662,834		4,117,627		1,761,158		4,057,500	
Other loans	628,961		405,189		893,212		649,135	
Credits on raw material	3,795,225		9,422,332		10,506,887		18,867,018	
Other creditor accounts	1,068,153		1,198,614		1,777,677		2,798,270	
Accumulated liabilities	940,470		661,159		1,195,741		3,285,188	
Accounts payable partners	–		229,285		262,910		214,848	
Long term liabilities	5,045,472	21.4	3,975,263	13.4	8,399,110	21.8	9,168,243	17.7
Bank loans	3,165,033		2,515,125		7,228,967		8,247,500	
Other loans	1,787,195		1,460,138		1,170,144		920,743	
Other creditor accounts	93,245		–		–		–	
Deferred liabilities	43,892	0.2	21,110	0.1	4,923		10,777	
Advance payment on sales	43,892		21,110		4,923		10,777	
Differential exchange	–		–		–		–	
Total liabilities	**16,185,057**	**68.6**	**20,030,579**	**67.5**	**24,791,619**	**64.3**	**39,050,981**	**75.5**
Share capital	7,397,473	31.4	9,644,093	32.5	13,772,595	35.7	12,099,711	24.5
Capital authorized in shares	5,500,000		5,500,000		11,000,000		11,000,000	
Accumulated profit (Loss)	(67,367)		1,348,077		–		2,222,595	
Period profit (Loss)	1,645,571		2,246,016		2,222,595		(1,072,884)	
Accumulated profit to be distributed	–		–		–		–	
Legal reserve	319,269		550,000		550,000		550,000	
Total profit and capital	**23,582,531**	**100**	**29,674,672**	**100**	**38,564,214**	**100**	**51,750,691**	**100**

Exhibit 14.1 *Balance sheet*

	1976	1977	1978	1979
Gross sales	24,804,027	34,696,079	41,994,927	54,090,532
Rebates and discounts	212,282	366,260	882,288	281,314
Net sales	24,591,745	34,329,819	41,112,639	53,809,218
Less cost of sales	18,220,409	25,557,024	30,598,062	44,024,790
Gross profit	6,371,336	8,772,795	10,514,558	9,784,428
Sales expenses	2,792,840	3,866,513	4,742,957	3,112,313
Contribution	3,578,496	4,906,282	5,771,601	6,672,115
Administrative expenses	1,575,579	1,888,606	2,767,569	2,843,822
Financial expenses	723,588	834,749	1,246,349	1,971,913
Other (expenses) income	366,242	63,089	464,913	(2,929,263)
Net profit (loss)	1,645,571	2,246,016	2,222,595	(1,072,884)

Exhibit 14.2   *Statement of earning and losses*

15

Devaluation's impact on the strategic posture

Case 15.1 Aluminum S.A.

This case was prepared by Professor Werner Ketelhöhn and revised by Research Associate Barbara Robins, as a basis for class discussion rather than to illustrate either effective or ineffective handling of a business situation.

In March 1979, Rodrigo Gutierrez, General Manager of Aluminum S.A., was considering how the Nicaraguan civil war had affected the economic performance of his company. The company was a subsidiary of a well-known multinational operating in all Central American countries. The company was founded in 1960 to take advantage of the newly-created Central American Common Market (CACM) and had been successful in an economically prosperous region.

Aluminum S.A. was a Nicaraguan manufacturer of aluminium pots and pans with standard operating profits of C423,000 (Cordobas) per month (US$60,429). Approximately half of Aluminum's sales were exported to other Central American countries with payments made in US dollars.

Central America

Central America, located in the middle of the American continent, was a narrow strip of land (called the Central American Isthmus) joining North and South America (Exhibit 15.1).

Exhibit 15.1   *Central America*

Six republics formed Central America: Costa Rica, Nicaragua, Honduras, El Salvador, Guatemala and Panama. The first five were former Spanish colonies, so they shared a common history before becoming republics. Panama, however, because of its canal, had an economy and a culture which was heavily influenced by the United States.

The Central American region has had a turbulent history of foreign power struggles. For example: Mexico's Emperor Iturbide annexed the Central American republic shortly after its independence from Spain in 1821; William Walker, a 31-year-old American adventurer, proclaimed himself President of Nicaragua until he was ousted by a combined force of Central American armies in 1857; the old English Victorian empire faced the rising American empire on the Atlantic coast of Nicaragua in a bid for control of the inter-oceanic canal through the isthmus; finally, in 1979 the expanding Russian empire was trying to gain a beach-head on the American continent with its bid to control Nicaragua.

After World War II, five cash crops formed the backbone (roughly 65% of the total) of Central American exports: coffee, sugar, bananas, beef and cotton. Of these, only cotton and coffee were competitively traded outside the USA. The Americans offered much better prices for the others; hence the importance of US quotas.

The following paragraph outlines the relationship between the USA and the Central American region:

Immediately after World War II, the United States welcomed the democratizing changes underway in Central America; it even put pressure on Nicaragua's dictator, Anastasio Somoza Garcia. But US policy shifted again with the beginning of the cold war. By the early 1950s, the United States supported the region's right-wing authoritarian regimes. It considered them a force for stability. When the politics of any Central American country moved to the left of centre, the United States intervened. For example, through the covert action of the Central Intelligence Agency (CIA), in 1954 the United States supported armed actions to help overthrow the regime of Jacobo Arbenz Guzman in Guatemala, which it believed was supported by the Soviet Union and which had purchased weapons from Czechoslovakia. The United States continued to provide resources to the Somoza regime in Nicaragua. The one exception was Costa Rica. When violence erupted in Costa Rica in 1948 over disputed election returns, the United States remained neutral. In subsequent years, Costa Rica–in contrast to the rest of Central America–maintained its democratic traditions with US support. It abolished the army, expropriated the banks, and developed strong health and social security systems.[1]

The Central American economy

Central America's economic growth strategy in the 1960s and 1970s called for investing in infrastructure and in social sectors such as health, nutrition and education; increasing and diversifying agricultural exports; developing import-substitution industries (of which Aluminum S.A. was a part), and creating the Central American Common Market (CACM). In terms of economic growth, the strategy was highly successful: gross domestic product (GDP) grew at an average rate of 6% a year between 1965 and 1977. This growth percentage was a bit more than 6% in the 1960s, about 5% in the early 1970s, and around 3.5% in the late 1970s. Most of the growth came from expanding exports of existing crops and some improvement in productivity, particularly in medium-sized and large farms. Industry expanded and inter-regional trade increased as a result of the CACM (established by a treaty effective in 1961). In general, however, the import substitution strategy not only seemed to be making the rich richer, but failed to produce significant savings in foreign exchange, so the benefits of growth were unequally shared. Central America's poor remained largely outside the development process during the 1960s and 1970s (see Annex 1).

The five Central American countries were poor because they lacked both human and natural resources; their per capita GNP was barely $1000 per year. Guatemala had some proven oil reserves, whereas the others had to find other ways to solve their energy problems. Considering the level of technology in the region, a slow struggle to achieve a modest level of prosperity was the most they could hope for. None of the countries had iron or coal fields on which to develop heavy industry; a Japanese-like development model was not likely either considering the poverty of their human resources. Their economies had been based on agricultural exports and would continue to be so in the near future.

The Central American development model was seriously jeopardized by the increase of oil prices in the mid-1970s. Changes in the international economy plunged Central America into a severe crisis; trade deficits grew and foreign indebtedness climbed sharply while the population continued to grow at the rate of 3%. Since Central America mainly exported agricultural commodities, it would have to bear the greatest impact of the oil problem; its development strategies were designed for cheap oil and, with its price increase and Central America's commodity price decrease, the trade deficit (the difference between the value of imports and exports) increased considerably.

---

[1] Dominguez, Jorge and Lindenberg, Marc, *Central America: Current Crisis and Future Prospects.* Headline Series No. 271, Foreign Policy Association, November/December 1984.

Central America's short-term solution to financing its trade deficit was to borrow (Table 1).

Table 1 Service of external public debt in Central America as a percentage of all exports[2]

	1977	1978	1979
Guatemala	2.3	2.9	3.3
El Salvador	3.8	6.2	9.0
Honduras	7.6	9.4	11.6
Nicaragua	14.4	23.6	25.6
Costa Rica	12.2	15.8	17.6

Given the problems of negative commercial balances and high debt service payments, the Central American countries began to deplete their foreign exchange reserves and to experience shortages of hard currency.

The Nicaraguan social revolt

In Nicaragua, the centralization of power in the hands of the Somoza family had eliminated most channels for peaceful social change and eroded the regime's political base. A broad revolutionary coalition had emerged by 1978 which included members of all social classes. Although the country continued to achieve a high rate of economic growth in the 1970s, most benefits went to the traditional upper income classes and, in particular, the Somozas and their associates. Despite a reconstruction boom following the 1972 earthquake in Managua, the capital city, real wages for workers declined (see Annex 1) and corruption exploded.

Economic deterioration in Nicaragua had begun slowly during the second half of 1977, triggered by an unfavourable political climate. Somoza's family had been ruling Nicaragua for nearly 40 years, and legal civic opposition movements had not succeeded in loosening Somoza's grip on the Nicaraguan government. Decades of power had gradually led to a corrupt governing party and unfair use of political power. The business community and general population had gradually concluded that only through a violent social revolt could the ruling party and military class be thrown out of power. Somoza and his collaborators were convinced that Nicaraguans had only two choices: Somoza or communism.

In 1961, a group of young idealists founded the Frente Sandinista de Liberacion Nacional (FSLN), a small guerrilla group that saw only one way to reduce the power of Somoza: violence. They had worked consistently toward their goal and had experienced ups and downs in membership, resources, unity and strategy. However, by 1977, resistance and opposition to Somoza's dictatorship were reaching a peak in Nicaragua, especially among professional and business people. The FSLN had grown

[2] Belli, Martinez and Mayorga, *Nicaragua: Implicaciones Economicas de los Sucesos de Septiembre*, INCAE, January 1979.

in the number of militants, sympathizers and collaborators, as well as in experience with guerrilla warfare. Some FSLN leaders and cadres were trained in Cuba, and rebels operated from neighbouring countries with their governments' tacit agreement.

International support had also reached a peak. Financing, arms and training camps were being provided by the international socialist movement, Venezuela, Costa Rica and some West German political foundations. The international community supported change in Nicaragua which contributed to the revolutionary climate. The opponents of Anastasio Somoza Debayle, son of the founder of the Somoza dynasty – including businessmen, political parties and the directorate of the FSLN – had supporters in Europe, Costa Rica, Panama, Venezuela, Mexico and Cuba. Even the United States, a supporter of the Somozas in the past, curtailed its support during President Jimmy Carter's administration because of his emphasis on promoting human rights; the United States even indicated that it might work with the revolutionaries if they came to power.

Corruption and repression of Somoza's dictatorship had created a climate of internal confrontation between Nicaragua's government and its traditional political parties, organized workers, students, business groups and organizations and the Catholic Church. In January 1978, Pedro Joaquin Chamorro Cardenal, journalist and undisputed leader of the legal political opposition, was assassinated. This paramilitary act of violence shocked the Latin American political and business community and served as a catalyst for all opposition forces inside and outside Nicaragua. As an immediate reaction to this assassination, leaders of the Nicaraguan business community provoked a nationwide business strike and asked for Somoza's resignation while threatening to paralyse the economy of Nicaragua. For 15 days (second and third weeks of January 1978), the country's economy stopped while urban and rural guerrilla actions followed urban decomposition and riots. Businessmen paid all salaries for the two weeks when nobody worked, and a series of contacts with guerrilla leaders was made for a second business strike, this time coordinated with guerrilla attacks to different cities. Five cities suffered guerrilla attacks and were subsequently destroyed by Somoza's army; for a month in September 1978, the economy was paralysed. The country suffered great human and economic losses.

Nicaragua's economy was severely affected by the socio-political turmoil of late 1977 and 1978. INCAE economists predicted a growth rate of only 4% for the 1978–1979 fiscal year, down from an original forecast 8%. The violent social revolt was accelerating Nicaragua's structural economic problems and precipitating the intensity of trade deficits. Moreover, this political crisis accelerated the capital flight that started in late 1977 and peaked at $275.1 million in 1978.

Nicaragua's economy

Nicaragua, with 139,000 square kilometres and 2,500,000 inhabitants, had had a GNP of C15,026 million in 1978. Like the other Central American countries, cash crops accounted for 65% of all exports. Industry, however, had been growing at a faster pace (12.2%) than the economy and made up about 30% of GNP.

The cash crops were planted in May and June of every year so that the GNP and its yearly growth was rather easy to forecast. Starting in 1976, however, the government's fiscal deficits were rapidly increasing (Table 2).

Table 2 Nicaragua: financial indicators[3] (millions of dollars)

	1976	1977	1978	1979*
Fiscal deficit	70.8	149.2	169.1	9.3
Financing	70.8	149.2	169.1	9.3
External	52.7	139.9	9.9	8.3
Internal	18.1	9.3	159.2	1.0
Capital movements	–	(67.1)	(275.1)	
Reserves	158.5	164.8	80.9	
Net reserves	55.9	(1.1)	(225.4)	

*From January to March of 1979.

Somoza's government was unable to finance these deficits with external resources because it had lost the traditional support of friendly foreign sectors. This loss of support had forced the Central Bank to finance 95% of the government's deficit in 1978. At the same time, the net international reserves had dropped to $225.4 million because of both government deficits and the flight of private capital.

As the economic activity decreased, the government's deficit continued to increase and, by March of 1979, it was already bigger than the previous year's equivalent deficit. Economic consultants had estimated a deficit of C800 million for 1979 ($114.3 million). This estimate resulted from the difference between government income and expenses. In summary, the economic picture was:

- Nicaragua had no international reserves with which to finance government deficits. Obviously, the country could not influence international prices of its cash crops.
- The violent social revolt had triggered the flight of private capital because of the perceived high political risk; any increment of internal credit would cause further capital drain.
- The economy was in a strong recession, and GNP had dropped about 7% in 1978; somehow the economy had to be reactivated.
- 1979's projected deficit was C800 million and the year's exports were estimated to be $650 million; in March of 1979, $280 million had already been exported.

The company

Aluminum S.A. was selling around $6,500,000 per year, with before-tax profits of $700,000. The company remitted about $300,000 each year to headquarters in dividends in a mature industry with few technological innovations; Aluminum S.A. was considered to be a cash cow at headquarters.

---

[3] Ramirez, Noel, Las Causas de la Inflacion en Economias Pequenas en vias de Desarrollo con Tasas Fijas de Cambio: Un Analisis Comparativo de Costa Rica y Nicaragua, PhD dissertation, Yale University, 1982.

		Inflation indexes		Index
Standard sales	40,000 units	Export price	(f1)	0.0%
Nicaragua (50%)	20,000 units	Domestic price	(f2)	0.0%
Exports (50%)	20,000 units	Raw materials	(h1)	0.0%
		Labour	(h2)	0.0%
Pricing policy	Cordobas per unit	Supplies	(h3)	0.0%
Nicaragua	C105/unit	Energy	(h4)	0.0%
Exports	C90/unit	Salaries	(h5)	0.0%
		Other inputs	(h6)	0.0%
Accounts receivables				
Nicaragua	60 days after delivery	Variable cost		(hv)
Exports	15 days after delivery	Inflation		0.0%
Discounts				
Nicaragua	10% for cash payment			
Exports	None			

Exhibit 15.2   *Basic sales information*

Company operations ran smoothly with few technical or financial complications and, being considered a strong employer, the company had a workforce of about 400 well-paid people. It was company policy to maintain their wages 30% above industry average, which made Aluminum's labour the best paid in Nicaragua.

Aluminum's workers and executives had a good working relationship, and the company was considered to be a model for Nicaraguan industry. Relations with the community were also smooth; involvement in the violent social revolt that raged through Nicaragua in 1978 was avoided.

Raw materials were imported (100%) and then processed locally to produce a wide collection of pots and pans. Sales were roughly divided between 50% for exports and 50% for the local marketplace (Exhibits 15.2 and 15.3).

	Factory*	Nicaragua**	Exports**
Commissions		3%	4%
Labour	5%		
Raw materials	44%		
Supplies	4%		
Financial		8%	6%
Other inputs		2%	3%
Energy and oil	2%		
Contribution	0.45	0.87	0.87

*Percentage of average sales price.
**Percentage of country sales price.
Monthly fixed costs in Cordobas

Salaries	C580,000
Other inputs	C90,000
Depreciation	C80,000
Rent	C75,000

Exhibit 15.3   *Variable costs as percentage of sales price*

	Nicaragua	Exports
Sales price	105.00	90.00
Variable sales costs	13.65	11.70
Contribution to standard costs	91.35	78.30
Variable costs	53.63	53.63
Contribution to fixed costs	37.72	24.68
Unitary fixed costs	20.63	20.63
Standard cost	74.25	74.25
Profit or loss	17.10	4.05

Exhibit 15.4   *Monthly unitary profit and loss statement (Cordobas)*

	Total	Nicaragua	Exports
Sales price	3,900,000	2,100,000	1,800,000
Variable sales costs	507,000	273,000	234,000
Contribution to standard cost	3,393,000	1,827,000	1,566,000
Variable costs	2,145,000	1,072,500	1,072,500
Contribution to fixed costs	1,248,000	754,500	493,500
Fixed costs	825,000		
Total standard cost	2,970,000		
Profit or loss	423,000		

Exhibit 15.5   *Monthly profit and loss statement (Cordobas)*

		Inflation indexes		Index
Standard sales	40,000 units	Export price	(f1)	43.0%
Nicaragua (50%)	20,000 units	Domestic price	(f2)	16.0%
Exports (50%)	20,000 units	Raw materials	(h1)	43.0%
		Labour	(h2)	25.0%
Pricing policy	Cordobas per unit	Supplies	(h3)	30.0%
Nicaragua	C122/unit	Energy	(h4)	30.0%
Exports	C129/unit	Salaries	(h5)	15.0%
		Other inputs	(h6)	30.0%
Accounts receivable				
Nicaragua	60 days after delivery	Variable cost	(hv)	
Exports	15 days after delivery	Inflation		39.9%
Discounts				
Nicaragua	10% for cash payment			
Exports	None			

Exhibit 15.6   *Basic sales information*

	Factory*	Nicaragua**	Exports**
Commissions		3%	4%
Labour	5%		
Raw materials	44%		
Supplies	4%		
Financial		8%	6%
Other inputs		2%	3%
Energy and oil	2%		
Contribution	0.45	0.87	0.87

*Percentage of average sales price.
**Percentage of country sales price.
Monthly fixed costs in Cordobas
   Salaries   C667,000
   Other inputs   C117,000
   Depreciation   C80,000
   Rent   C75,000

Exhibit 15.7 *Variable costs as percentage of sale price*

	Nicaragua	Exports
Sales price	121.80	128.70
Variable sales costs	15.83	16.73
Contribution to standard cost	105.97	111.97
Variable costs	75.05	75.05
Contribution to fixed costs	30.92	36.92
Unitary fixed costs	23.48	23.48
Standard cost	98.52	98.52
Profit or loss	7.45	13.45

Exhibit 15.8 *Monthly unitary profit and loss statement (Cordobas)*

	Total	Nicaragua	Exports
Sales price	5,010,000	2,436,000	2,574,000
Variable sales costs	651,300	316,680	334,620
Contribution to standard cost	4,358,700	2,119,320	2,239,380
Variable costs	3,001,830	1,500,915	1,500,915
Contribution to fixed costs	1,356,870	618,405	738,465
Fixed costs	939,000		
Total standard cost	3,940,830		
Profit or loss	417,870		

Exhibit 15.9 *Monthly profit and loss statement (Cordobas)*

In 1977, double digit inflation prompted Rodrigo to maintain a simple but effective decision support system (Exhibits 15.2–15.5). This quick decision support system allowed Rodrigo to estimate inflation's impact on a standard monthly profit and loss statement (Exhibits 15.6–15.9).

Rodrigo's thoughts

In order to collect his thoughts and gain a clearer understanding of the political situation in Nicaragua, Rodrigo made a written assessment of the Nicaraguan political actors involved in the violent social revolt (see Annex 2).

Rodrigo also wondered what Roberto Incer (see Annex 3), President of the Central Bank, would do. How would Incer finance the government's deficit? What other measures could be taken to raise the scarce foreign exchange? What effects would these measures have on the operations of Aluminum S.A.?

In an effort to understand Roberto Incer's economic thinking and possible advice to Anastasio Somoza, President of Nicaragua, Rodrigo outlined what he considered to be Incer's alternatives:

- Incer could refuse to finance the fiscal deficit and reduce domestic credit, which would reduce public expenditures and hence economic activity. What would happen to private expenditures? Unemployment?
- Incer could propose an increase of taxes to finance the deficit. However, agricultural exporters were near or below their breakeven points, and it was not clear whether they could bear an additional export tax and remain profitable. Would this depress the economy even further?
- Incer could propose to finance the economy with additional credit from the Central Bank. This would surely create an inflationary process because the lack of imports (no international reserves) would increase local prices. What would be the effect on the exporters' competitiveness? What would be the effect on real economic activity?

Considering these alternatives, Rodrigo wondered what other possibilities were available to Roberto Incer. The already depressed economy was a constraint to any economic decision; also, the crop exporters' competitiveness (65% of exports) was another constraint; finally, unemployment – which was nearing 30% of the workforce – was extremely important in light of the violent social revolt. Roberto Incer had to somehow re-activate the economy, contain unemployment, increase agricultural exporters' competitiveness and, at the same time, finance the government's projected deficit.

Annex 1: Nicaragua's economic facts

Nicaragua exported $600 million per year in 1977–1978 despite the violent social revolt of 1978. Although the economy was growing during the 1970s, the following statistics[4] show how wealth was being distributed.

Social deal

Year	Consumer price index	GNP growth index	Deflated labour salaries
1972	100.0	100.0	100.0
1973	118.1	105.1	91.7
1974	132.6	118.4	86.3
1975	135.1	121.0	76.5
1976	138.9	127.0	89.5
1977	154.7	136.6	80.1
1978	161.7	127.0	76.7

It is clear from this table that the violent social revolt had a negative impact on Nicaragua's economic growth and that the benefits of growth were not going to the working class and campesinos.

From 1960 to September 1978, Nicaragua had maintained a fixed (seven Cordobas per dollar) exchange rate with respect to the dollar. Until 1977, capital movements had been used as a source of foreign exchange and had helped finance part of the import bill.

In September 1978, the Central Bank started a foreign exchange control system designed to stop the flight of private capital. For practical reasons, about 10% of total exports were not included in the control system and were left to be traded in a parallel market. However, in November 1978, a list of priority imports had to be established to control the flight of private capital even further; goods on the list could be imported at the official exchange rate; all other goods had to be imported at the parallel market rate.

As shown in the table, the flight of capital ($275.1 million in 1978) was enough to cause a drop of $224.7 million in international reserves, despite a positive trade balance of $99.2 million. The net effect was a reduction in real economic activity and increased unemployment.

These measures were, however, too late, and by January 1979 the Central Bank was demanding a deposit two months in advance for all imports except raw materials and CACM imports.

---

[4] Ramirez, Noel, Las Causas de la Inflacion en Economias Pequenas en vias de Desarrollo con Tasas Fijas de Cambio: Un Analisis Comparativo de Costa Rica y Nicaragua, PhD dissertation, Yale University, 1982.

Annex 2: Nicaragua's political support sectors

Rodrigo jotted down his impressions about the different political actors in the Nicaraguan violent social revolt. The following brief inventory of political actors was the result of Rodrigo's exercise. He realized that, in any such assessment, there was ample room for personal bias and heated disagreement among otherwise cool-headed analysts. He also knew that the nature of political analysis was emotive, so he was careful to exercise great restraint in the search for a clear picture of what was going on.

Rodrigo grouped the political actors as follows (Exhibit 15.10):

The regime

Somoza, his ministers and a few government employees. Their objectives were to maintain power and make money. Their resources were weapons, information, organization, government money, status, but they lacked legitimacy.

The social sectors

The campesinos   The poorest among the poor, whose sole purpose in life was to survive. Traditionally, they had supported two political parties: the Conservative party and the Liberal party, but had remained largely untapped until the FSLN and MDN began campesino organizations with a small degree of success. The majority of campesinos supported the Liberal and Conservative parties by tradition, and were considered to be largely an unmobilized sector.

The workers   Also poor, they were, however, organized in several trade unions which were considered effective pressure organizations. Survival and political power were their main objectives and, although money was a scarce resource, they had gained legitimacy through their work capacity, violence and organized mass demonstrations in their struggle against Somoza.

The middle class   Nicaragua's middle class was generally in disagreement with Somoza's government and was a source of strong support for FSLN-MDN organizations. Their objectives were political power, increased income and a better quality of life. Their resources were information, organization and violence.

The agro-exporters   These people had prospered under Somoza's government by working great expanses of land with export crops. Some were Conservatives and others Liberals, and a few supported the revolution. Clearly, they were pursuing political power and money; they were ready to use their money, administrative experience and technology in this endeavour.

The political parties

The FSLN-MDN   This was a coalition of a Marxist-Leninist armed group with a middle-class agro-exporters association of revolutionary businessmen. They wanted to

Actor	Violent opposition	Legal opposition	Support sectors	Central combination	Support sectors	Legal opposition	Violent opposition
Regime							
Social sectors							
Political parties							
Pressure groups							
Foreign sectors							

Exhibit 15.10 *The sectors are viewed as a continuum based on their degree of support versus benefit from the political regime in a position of authority*

rule Nicaragua and were using all the resources at their disposal: weapons, information, organization, violence, technology, money, status, legitimacy and so on, to eliminate Somoza's government.

The Liberals   This was Somoza's official party, split into several factions because of the dictatorship. They had been slowly displaced from power and wanted to regain it. Their resources were legitimacy, status and some money.

The Conservatives   An aristocratically-oriented club, they had lost power to the Liberals in the late 1920s. They had some status, legitimacy and money, but had no organizations of importance.

The pressure groups

The Church   The Catholic Church wanted to increase its influence over the Nicaraguan people; its resources were legitimacy and status, with which they supported the FSLN-MDN.

The Press   The local and international press were pursuing influence and money (ratings). Their main resource was information which they used to attack Somoza and his government.

The National Guards   Their need for power and money transformed them into Somoza's Praetorian guard. They controlled weapons and violence.

The Business Associations   Like many other players, they were mainly interested in money and power. They supported FSLN-MDN with technology, organizations and money.

The foreign sector

Latin America   These governments were seeking to increase their legitimacy, status and influence over their populations. They supported FSLN-MDN with money, weapons, status, legitimacy and training bases.

Europe   Europeans were willing to demonstrate their support for socialism in Central America (although not in Africa) with direct intervention in the internal affairs of Nicaragua; they were seeking to increase their status, legitimacy and influence in the third world. Europeans supported FSLN-MDN with money, weapons, status, legitimacy and information.

The United States   Carter's administration was seeking to increase US status by cutting its support to Somoza's government; it refused to finance trade deficits, weapons, ammunition, troops, goods or help with information. The USA became suddenly neutral which, by default, was sinking Somoza's administration.

The USSR-Cuba   A Castro-inspired social revolt; they were seeking power, influence and a communist beach-head in the American continent. Castro was using Cuba's resources to support the FSLN-MDN with money, weapons, troops, training goods, information and so on.

Annex 3: Roberto Incer Barquero

Roberto Incer, President of the Central Bank of Nicaragua, was a 47-year-old economist, who had been in his position for approximately ten years. Roberto was born and raised in Boaco, a province of Nicaragua, in a hard-working middle-class farming family. A brilliant student and avid reader, he studied law at the National University of Nicaragua and after graduation received a Master's degree in Economics from Yale.

He started his professional career in the National Bank of Nicaragua and, in the early 1960s, became head of the department of economic studies at the Central Bank of Nicaragua. Under his leadership, the Central Bank of Nicaragua promoted a tax-free industrial zone in order to take advantage of Nicaragua's comparatively cheap labour, introduced export incentives, and redesigned Nicaragua's coffee export effort. During his 10-year tenure as President of the Nicaraguan Central Bank, the country enjoyed an average growth rate of about 7% per year.

A man of vision, Roberto was an honest public servant whose goal in life was to work for the development of Nicaragua through a basic strategy of strengthening cash crops and industrial exports. He had always been a strong believer in Nicaragua's agricultural potential as the backbone for development, and was constantly worried about the international competitiveness of Nicaraguan cash crops.

Roberto Incer was a strong promoter of people and of institutions. He had financed Master's degrees for about 450 Nicaraguans, independent of political beliefs and based solely on the person's abilities and academic records. Several cultural projects were financed by him, as well as small national parks and scientific studies. In short, Roberto was an honest caretaker of Nicaragua's development and its people's well-being.

In August 1978, after negotiations with the IMF, the following new tax package was approved:

1 10% tax retention was to be for export sales taxes.
2 Some sales tax exonerations were suspended for industry.
3 Presumptive sales were to be used in the calculations of sales taxes.
4 Sales taxes were increased from 6% to 8%.
5 Other taxes were increased from 10% to 50%.

Roberto and his staff thought that these measures would increase government income by 3% of GNP. However, because of Nicaragua's civil war, the existing tax base had been considerably eroded. A 7% drop in GNP and a weakened economy were not producing the desired tax income; the central government still had to finance a projected C800 million deficit.

Index